Modern Theories of Justice

Modern Theories of Justice

Serge-Christophe Kolm

The MIT Press
Cambridge, Massachusetts
London, England

This book was set in Times Roman by Asco Trade Typesetting Ltd., Hong Kong. Printed and bound in the United States of America.

Library of Congress Cataloging-in-Publication Data

Kolm, Serge-Christophe.
  Modern theories of justice / Serge-Christope Kolm.
    p. cm.
  Includes bibliographical references and index.
  ISBN 0-262-11208-6 (hc : alk. paper)
  1. Justice. I. Title
JC578.K68   1996
320'.01'1—dc20   96-2509
                                              CIP

10 9 8 7 6 5 4 3

Contents

I INTRODUCTION: JUSTICE AS JUSTIFICATION

1 Justice as Reason in Society: An Overview

1.1 Presentation

What should be done when different people's desires or interests oppose one another and cannot all be fully satisfied? *Justice* is the *justified* answer to this question and its science is the *theory of justice*.

The topic of justice, more exactly, is the very large part of *social ethics* (the science of the final answers to the question "What should be done in society?") and of the definition of the *social optimum* and of what is *right* or *good* in society, that focuses on the conditions of humans as individuals or in groups.

The modern theory of justice, however, is at least as much *economics* as it is philosophy (which includes ethics), and it should logically occupy a very large part of economics. Economics, indeed, is the science of the allocation of scarce resources, where "scarce" refers to human wants. It is concerned with both how this allocation is performed and how it *should* be performed. The second half of the topic is therefore a priori and logically half the discipline. This is *normative economics*. Since the reference is to agents' desires or needs, the foundation and certainly the challenging part of normative economics is *economic justice*. Given the functions of politics and of the state, normative economics and economic justice have a large common ground with *public economics*, the economics of the public sector.[1] Moreover economic justice is not only a very large part of justice in society, it can also be seen as all of it, since desires, interests, conditions, and rivalries between them can be expressed in economic terms. Finally, the specific tools, concepts, methods, and analyses elaborated by economics have a prominent place in the modern theory of justice.[2]

Indeed the modern theory of justice is the product of the necessary new alliance between economics and philosophy. It can be thought of as a philosophical mind in an economic body—and a bodyless mind is

---

1. See notably my books of 1964 (where the term "public economics" is coined), 1968b, 1969b, 1969c, 1970a, and 1970b.

2. The expression *political philosophy* is practically used for social ethics in modern English, although, strictly speaking, this domain should also include the nonethical philosophy of politics. The term *welfare economics* refers to a particular theory within normative economics, yet one that is replete with conceptual mistakes when it comes to distribution and justice (see chapters 14 and 15).

as unreal, or at least powerless, as a mindless body can be out of place and dangerous.[3]

Note, however, that this book defines and explains, simply and sufficiently, all the necessary concepts, in emphasizing their meaning and their important properties.

Of course, outside the two "normative sciences" of economics and philosophy, justice is the very subject of *law*, a central concern of *politics*, an essential topic in *sociology* and *psychology*.

More important, justice is a central question of all life in society. Note that it is by nature "social" and "distributive." Facing the question of justice is in fact a condition for the very existence of a society. Hence in all societies the most elaborate thinking is notably applied to solving, dissolving or displacing the question of justice. The modern world is too advanced to accept displacement into the hands of an autocrat or into the exclusive obedience to a tradition. But it is not advanced enough to trust sufficiently the dissolution of the justice problem into the self-mastery of one's desires[4] or into their extention to others' wants or needs in altruism or charity.[5] Therefore it has to rely on solution, and hence on rationality, since justice should be justified—that is, supported by valid reasons. Justice theory thus is a problem of utmost importance, which normally mobilizes the best advances in our understanding of society.

This book presents two things:

1. **The complete introduction to the theory of justice and the solution of its main problem (macrojustice).**

2. **The rational presentation and evaluation of the various particular theories, principles, or criteria of justice** that have been proposed in the second half of the twentieth century.

This book intends to show *the essentials* of these topics, all the essentials, and only the essentials. It thus constitutes an introduction to my

---

3. This also refers to Pascal's emphasis on the necessary association between *l'esprit de finesse* and *l'esprit de géométrie*. The hermeneuts' dictum that "science does not think" is also a case in point.

4. As proposed by Hellenistic philosophies or Buddhist psychology (see *Happiness-Freedom*, Kolm 1982a).

5. This possibility is analyzed exhaustively in the book *The Good Economy, General Reciprocity* (Kolm 1984a).

other books on this subject, which develop, complement and apply its points.[6]

The theory of justice, on the one hand, is but rationality applied to the question of justice, and justice is the necessary result of this application. The most basic, general, and operational of these consequences are presented here; they concern notably liberties, equalities, and the general structure of justice.

On the other hand, the second half of the twentieth century has been exceptionally fertile in proposals of particular theories, principles, or criteria of justice. No other period in history can match it on this ground, except perhaps the end of the eighteenth century. The present state of minds and of information makes it useful to consider these views in themselves and specifically. According to the general principle of this book, we focus on what is *essential* in each of these "modern theories of justice." In addition these theories often came as the products of the history of thought, as reactions against previous theories, rather than as the pure, direct, and simple application of reason to the social problem. As a result their rationales and natures are varied, antagonistic to one another, and often surprising, although they are also, by the same token, always interesting and challenging. This applies, notably, to utilitarianisms, liberalisms, "Original Positions," "Social Choice," "Public Choice," various Social Contracts, egalitarianisms, libertarianisms, and so on. Therefore, the presentation of these theories is useful only if accompanied by their rational evaluation, and this requires the joint presentation of the bases of justice rationality.

The presentation of these "modern theories" along with an introduction to the bases of the theory of justice has several advantages. This presentation can be organized according to the deepest logic of the topic, omitting no essential distinction. The various specific theories appear as particular cases of the general theory, and hence the crucial differences between them stand out naturally and conspicuously. The basic concepts and problems of these theories can be the object of a general discussion, which these theories serve in turn to illustrate. These theories are then rather easily evaluated according to their meaningfulness, justification or arbitrariness, consistency on various

---

6. They are presently published in French, with a few essays in English.

grounds, comprehensiveness or omissions, logic, relevance, interest, importance, operationality and ethicity (that is, are they really moral theories). This also shows how to remedy the various possible imperfections of these theories, and the degree to which these repairs affect their whole intent and conclusions. In the end, certain of these theories are complemented, others are rescued, others turn out not to be possible but have raised major issues, until all the valid elements find their place in the general theory of justice.

The bases of this theory presented here include notably the reason for equality, the types and values of liberties, the allocation of the usufruct of human capacities, the dimensions of needs ("welfare" is an ambiguous concept), the logic of accountability and responsibility, the comparison of inequalities, the general structure of the question and the possible options, the associations of principles and second-best justice, the ways and motivations of the implementation of justice, and applications to public economics (income justice, freedom justice, etc.).

Thus each particular modern theory of justice is presented here by its essential points and problems, its comparison with other theories, the solutions to its problems when they exist, and its main consequences. If a theory turned out not to be a possible theory of justice, I will sufficiently show why, and present the rest only insofar as it can have some other use for the present purpose, since to do otherwise would be a waste of time. However, in all cases, for the elaboration of the specifics of the theory, or of a number of more particular sub-theories, I refer the reader to its original presentation and, if necessary, to later good accounts. Of course, mere assertions of solutions cannot count as justifications or theories. It should also be kept in mind that each chapter of this book is backed by one or several of my books on this topic noted earlier, which it summarizes (although the present book is fully self-contained).[7]

---

7. A few other recent books aim at presenting the contemporary theories of justice, with coverages varied in scope and in intended scope, and which relate to either philosophy or economics. The first thing to point out is that they are very different from the present book. This difference is prima facie surprising, since these works deal with a smaller or larger part of the material of the present book, and the difference does not stem from a priori very different political outlooks. Less surprising (unfortunately), these other works are quite different from one another according as they originate in

The organization of this book results from a combination of the three relevant criteria of importance, proximity of topics, and history. The present part I constitutes an introduction, which presents the general method and structure of justice, the rationality of equalities of liberties or means (and of ends as a borderline case), the values of freedom, the organization of distributive justice, and general distinctions and the resulting classifications of theories of justice and of their properties. The other six parts consist mostly of developments of the general principle of "prima facie (ideal) equalities of various liberties or means, plus the consideration of other approaches.

1.2 The Reason of Justice

By its very definition, *justice is justification*, and hence *rationality in the normal sense of the term: for a valid reason, or "justified."* This

---

philosophy or in economics. I strongly recommend all these other works, which I see as complementing the present one. In particular, I present most theories in emphasizing their essential points, contribution, and possibly weaknesses, and the reader who wants a presentation closer to the original is referred to either the original or a synthetic presentation in one of these other books. When the present work proposes an assessment that differs from that of the others, the reader will have sufficient material to decide for himself very easily. Finally, all these authors present particularly well their own contributions to social ethics, which is of major importance in all cases and will be more or less discussed or noted in the present work. Philosophy offered Brian Barry's outstanding *Theories of Justice* (1989) (noncontemporary Hume is added). Marc Fleurbaey's *Economic Theories of Justice* (1996, in French) provides the most complete presentation of contemporary economic models of justice, in a particularly clear and didactic way. Thomson (1996), Moulin (1988, 1995), Young (1994), and Peters (1992) present principles of fairness and of cooperative choices in books whose excellence permits the present one to dispense with most of this presentation. John Roemer's *Theories of distributive Justice* (1996), apart from an unfortunate confusion of "fundamental preferences" for "extended sympathy" (see chapter 7 below), offers good formal presentations of a number of economic criteria of optimality or of just distribution, and an elaborate discussion of a recent debate that revives the age old ethic of responsibility and of equal opportunity with new applications, analyses, and meanings. A forthcoming work by Hausman and MacPherson will doubtlessly be very important. Other excellent and recommended general books are more focussed in intention, because they focus on the authors' own contributions as is the case with Gaertner and Klemisch-Ahlert (1992) and Broome (1991a), or because they survey a subfield such as strict "Social Choice" for Feldman (1980) or Kelly (1978), or because they focus on the abstract conceptual level of social ethics and justice, which is the case of many philosophers' contributions among which the deep and subtle works of Cohen, Nagel, Raz, Lukes, Raphael, Pettit, Baker, and others mentioned in the references. There doubtlessly are still other broad surveys of the field, notably in lecture notes of the many courses on this topic in the world.

apparently inocuous remark turns out to be highly discriminating for certain essential topics. It shows both that a number of very well-known proposals cannot be retained, and that the necessary general form of justice is the *ideal equalities of liberties or means* adjusted within a structured *moral polyarchy*.

The reference to reason mobilizes both strong rationalities and weaker ones, and it invalidates both logically superficial and logically elaborate views of justice. The strong rationalities used in justice theory are deductions, and rationalities of the type of negative reasons (or reasons *in absentia*) such as that which imposes equality, described below (and in chapter 2). Yet there still remains a place for weaker rationalities, such as systematic dialectics,[8] informed and educated "sense of justice," justness of judgment or "wisdom." Rationality thoroughly rules out, however, moral intuitionism, emotivism, and aestheticism, that is, opinions based on a priori views of the solution, on emotions such as indignation, and on the satisfaction of beauty, although these may all signal the existence of a problem. The ethical progress in justice consists in replacing irrational views by rational ones and weak rationalities by strong ones, and notably prejudice by judgment, justness by justification, and emotion and intuition by reason.[9]

Among the various elaborate proposals that are at odds with the strong rationality of social ethics, *for reasons and with qualifications and remedies that will be presented in the text*, one can find, for instance, cardinal utility (except for uncertainty), and therefore *strict* utilitarianism and certain other solutions, theories of the Original Position (their main conclusions may however be *directly* justified for limited application), an a priori necessary social ordering for the definition of the general social optimum, an absent or minimal public sector, unqualified threat advantage as ethics, a multidimensional maximin (this "maximize the lowest" is a priori undefined, yet several solutions are possible), various requirements of providing solutions for non-existing situations, and so on. It should however be empha-

---

8. In the sense of Plato's *Republic* (Rawls's "reflective equilibrium" is a subcase).

9. Note also that this common use of the term "intuition" is particular, since in its usual meaning intuition is a type of knowledge about facts rather than about values (about what is true rather than about what is good, right or just).

sized that the discussions that accompanied such proposals have often been major steps in the evolution of collective ideas and of the micro-sociology of the discipline's paradigms.

Reason, by contrast, implies the following structure. People's competing claims are mostly for means to pursue their ends (the ends themselves constitute the extreme, borderline case). These means are liberties in the large sense of rights, powers, opportunities, avail-abilities, capacities, or possibilities. Furthermore, choosing an un-equal allocation that is not relevantly distinguishable from its opposite (permutation) implies the lack of a reason—or arbitrariness—which equality alone avoids.[10] This explains Aristotle's dictum that "justice is equality, as everybody thinks it is, apart from any other conside-ration."[11] Hence "Men are free and equal in rights" can summarize *the general principle of justice as reason in society*. This is indeed the basic modern principle of justice, dating back two centuries.

Equal liberty applies, however, to many possible kinds of liberty in the broad sense. It can apply to freedom to act, to means of action, to opportunities, and at the limit to agents' ends (this is the case where *all* means are relevant, including capacities to appreciate, enjoy and be satisfied).[12] Rationality then shows two basic structures of justice: One cannot apply the same specific principle or set of principles to all cases; and several such principles must often be applied together—this requires rules of adjustment such as compromises, priorities, second-best egalitarianisms or application of one principle from the outcome of another ("superimposition").[13] Second-best egalitarianism will often be of the type "maximize the smallest," or "maximin."

Indeed any theory that claims to answer *all* questions of justice by application of the same specific principle or set of principles is easily proven to be mistaken, by counterexamples, and to be insufficient for practical application. Simplistic and reductionist universal claims are

---

10. Details of this justification of equality are suggested in chapter 2 and presented in full in *The General Theory of Justice* and *Equal Liberty* (Kolm 1990b, 1993e). Note that an individual's just allocation can depend on others' allocations and characteristics.

11. *Nichomachean Ethics*.

12. See chapters 3, 6, 7, 8, and 9.

13. The theory of the combination of principles is presented in *The General Theory of Justice* (Kolm 1990b).

unwarranted and impossible dogmatism. Sometimes work and sometimes need determine what each person should receive (in the case of
work, the reason is sometimes moral and not only for incentive). The
ideal equality is sometimes of freedom to exchange, sometimes of
qualified incomes, and sometimes of satisfaction. Justice therefore necessarily is *rational circumscribed moral polyarchy*. Only the method of
justice as justness and justification is universal.

However, it turns out to be crucial to distinguish *macrojustice*, which
concerns the most general principles of justice in a society notably as
concerns the overall distributive justice of the allocation of resources,
from *microjustice* concerned with the multifarious issues of specific
or local justice, and from *mesojustice* which refers to issues that are
specific but sufficiently important to have a global impact (for instance, concerning education and social policies). The basic point is
that the problem of macrojustice will turn out to be roughly solved in
theory, as a mix between process-freedom, income justice and the
satisfaction of basic needs, in proportions that depend on the state of
the society considered, and after the respect of basic human rights.

Furthermore the consideration of particular theories of justice may
be legitimate both as a heuristic device and for their relevance in more
or less extended domains. Such a theory a priori consists of a set of
valued items and of rules of adjustment when the ideal equalizations
are not all consistent.

1.3   The Essential Equalities of Liberties

Rational justice depends primarily on the properties and types of
liberty. These properties are the related *natures* of the concept of
freedom, of the agent, of the domain of freedom, of the constraints,
of the reasons for valuing freedom or for disliking it, of the situation
in the process of action, of the use of this liberty, of the conditions of
its existence, as well as the extent of this freedom.

In particular, the many possible reasons for valuing liberty[14] can be
summarized by the contrast between liberty for having and liberty

---

14. See chapter 2 and *Happiness-Freedom* (Kolm 1982a).

for being, or liberty that has a price and liberty that has a dignity (in Kant's terms), or liberty as an asset and liberty as a condition (of existence or action), or instrumental freedom and existential-ontological freedom. The former is valued for the value of the chosen item. The latter value of liberty results from its providing its holder with existence as agent, chooser and creator, and with activity, self-respect, responsibility, and social existence.

Furthermore the domain of free choice may depend on other persons' acts, or it may not: This is "dependence" and "independence."

Protection against the core existential unfreedoms is necessary for the very *existence* of persons as social agents and is thus a *condition* for justice rather than one of its solutions. It therefore has to have priority. The *basic Rights of Man and of the Citizen*[15] and the satisfaction of *basic needs* constitute this protection for dependent and independent unfreedoms, respectively.[16] The priority of these *rights* implies that they should be *limitless*, because they are essentially *nonrival* among themselves—since rivalries in their use can be attributed to the allocation of means with which they are used.[17] Their existential necessity implies that they should be *inalienable*. Basic needs include the essential basic cultural needs necessary to social existence, which are defined by the very aspect of culture that creates them.[18] These basic existential liberties and needs satisfaction are not only means but also conditions of dignity ("He who values freedom for anything but itself does not deserve it and will soon loose it," Tocqueville claimed): They thus have "no price" in Kant's sense, that is, no possible substitute, and so they have absolute priority. This general priority is furthermore often desired by everyone and indeed it is in everyone's well-considered interest. In fact respecting the basic Rights of Man and of the Citizen has constitutional priority in all liberal-democratic states.

---

15. They are the rights of the 1789 Declaration except the last, seventeenth article (see chapter 4).

16. This enlightening but shorthand taxonomy requires the definition and delineation of basic rights (see chapter 4), possibly a delineation between these rights and needs (since a priori one may need a right and have a right to the satisfaction of a need), and a qualifying discussion about the social dimension of basic needs (see chapter 11).

17. See chapter 4.

18. See chapter 11.

Table 1.1
Needs, rights, and liberty

Dependence / Value	Independent	Dependent
Instrumental	Equity	(Symmetrical possibilities)
Existential	Basic needs	Basic rights

The *instrumental value*, by contrast, of *independent liberty*, is shown to coincide with the principle that no person prefers what another has to what she herself has, for which the term *Equity* has been specified (for *equ*al *i*ndependent *i*nstrumental liber*ty*).[19] When this principle precludes efficiency (see below), it extends into an efficient maximin in liberty.[20] Equal instrumental nonindependent liberty is also similarly characterized.[21] Table 1.1 classifies these essential cases of equality of liberty.[22]

An important conclusion is that the theoretical problem of defining equality and maximality in liberty is solved for the most important cases, notably by the principle of Equity and its extensions for instrumental freedom, and by limitlessness for the existential basic rights (and for the right to unhampered property and exchange).[23] This, however, is the form of several possible theories of justice.

1.4   Global Distributive Justice

Global distributive justice then has to allocate society's resources. The shortest outline of the main issues this raises is as follows. The most important of these resources are, by far, the *human resources*. This is true in production, but human capacities are also used in consump-

---

19. See chapter 7. This liberty can have, *in addition*, a value in itself, under a certain condition (see chapter 7).

20. See chapter 9.

21. See Kolm 1993e.

22. The cultural part of basic needs may suscitate a "consumption externality" (rather than one on the possibility of choices); see chapter 11.

23. This is the right leading to full process liberalism, considered below, that is, the "right to properties" of article 17 of the 1789 Declaration.

tion. Note that capital is accumulated past resources, and that the allocation of nonhuman natural resources is commonly derived from other resources by a number of possible devices, such as general agreement, first occupancy, allocation according to needs or to capacities, etc.

The allocation of the human resource mobilizes two opposite moral criteria whose conflict sets an ethic of liberty against an ethic of solidarity. One principle is *process-freedom*, that is, the liberty to benefit from the results of one's acts, which entails usufruct of oneself (possibly "self-ownership"). The other principle sees this "natural" allocation as no valid reason for the corresponding allocation of its benefits, and it thus ideally *shares equally* the benefit of this resource (equality resulting from rationality as noted earlier). Hence there are two extreme, polar cases in which only one of these principles is respectively followed.

One of these cases is full process-freedom, "to each according to his work," unfettered free exchanges, and the resulting acquisitive legitimacy of rights and properties. This *full process liberalism* is the historically central, liberty-based, and deontic justification of the free market. Yet it in fact also logically requires notable public sectors, taxes, and transfers that vicariously implement free exchanges and agreements impaired by "market failures" (the Liberal Social Contract).[24]

The opposite extreme case ideally equalizes the effects of *all resources*, used in production *and* consumption and in life in general. This is full or complete redistributive (or eudemonistic) Justice, approximated by *first helping the most miserable* when equality is impossible or inefficient ("Practical Justice").[25] This latter criterion—"the last shall be the first"—is an obligation when basic needs are not all satisfied.

---

24. See chapter 5 and *The Liberal Social Contract* (Kolm 1985a). The *purely private* part is the theory of Locke (1689), of the 1789 Declaration of Rights or of Nozick's recent elaboration (1974). This is also what was called "political" economy in the nineteenth century, Marx's "critique" of which basically consists of denying that the supply of labor is actually free (see chapter 9).

25. See chapter 7, section 7.2, and *Justice and Equity* (Kolm 1971).

A notable *intermediate* case consists in letting each individual receive the uncompensated benefit of his capacities when he uses them in consumption, while ideally equalizing the outcome of the capacities used in *production*. This is the basic rationale behind opinions that favor a reduction in income inequalities. This view, however, raises two conceptual problems:

First, to take consumptive capacities, which determine tastes, preferences, and the like, off the economic process leaves us with the bundles of consumption goods rather than with incomes. Incomes may additionally be computed with prices that are unjust. Moreover, in spending their incomes the individuals use their unequal skills for exchange, bargaining, and dealing on markets, which are not consumptive uses of capacities (the "natural" allocation of which is endorsed by assumption). However, equating the bundles of consumption goods is a multidimensional equality that is generally inefficient in the sense that other allocations are unanimously preferred.[26] A corresponding second-best efficient multidimensional maximin can, however, be defined, and it turns out to require specific limits to income discrepancies (and, in particular cases of local justice, equalities of incomes in the end).[27] A similar conflict with unanimous efficiency may arise when various topics of justice are considered incommensurable and the relevant equalities are demanded in each of the corresponding "spheres" (as emphasized by Weber and Walzer).

The second problem is that possible injustice in benefiting from different productive capacities is manifested through the consumption goods or incomes that one obtains with these capacities. Therefore, as concerns productive capacities, the target of the equalization is actually earned income. Yet the resulting disincentive effects on the labor supply creates a situation where everybody prefers certain unjust situations, which leads one to resort to various possible types of second-best justice. The reason for this fact is commonly misunderstood by scholars. The choice of earned income as the basis for redistribution is a conceptual and moral one (rather than being the choice of a second-

---

26. This equality is however proposed by Tobin (1970).

27. This is "efficient super-equity"; see Kolm 1973a, 1987f, 1993d, g, 1995a, c, f, 1996b, and chapter 4 below.

best proxy for unobservable capacities—which are in fact revealed by wage rates, for given effort). The point is that an individual is not seen as benefiting from his capacities for production which he does not actually use in production (and hence to obtain an income and consumption goods). The use of one's mind and body not for production is, by definition, for "consumption," and this is seen as a private matter not amenable to redistributive compensation by this conception of justice.[28]

By contrast, the more general and very common ideals in between the latter one and full process liberalism, in various possible degrees, can be efficiently implemented by the equal sharing of the incomes earned during a given duration (such as the first n hours of the week), while other labor earnings are untaxed. This is "fixed-duration income equalization".

The noted polar cases (and other cases) are not opposed and incompatible dogmatic alternatives but rather complementary viewpoints and building blocks. If, in particular, people are convinced by one of the two latter redistributive ethics, then full process-freedom guarantees its voluntary implementation, possibly with lower disincentive effects or through the vicarious (and apparently forced) public implementation made necessary by the public good aspects of "collective gift-giving" (several persons giving to the same individuals).[29]

When, more generally, an ideal equality is impaired by impossibilities of any type, or by the joint relevance of other criteria, then the issue becomes the *comparison of the injustice of the inequalities*. This question has become, since 1966, by far the most elaborate use of logic by ethics.[30]

Yet the most important question of distributive justice may in the end be the close analysis and consideration of *needs*, and its most urgent policy certainly is the *alleviation of misery* as both a source of suffering and shackles to human existence and dignity.[31]

---

28. This question is considered in detail in chapter 6.

29. See chapters 5 and 8, and Kolm 1984b, 1985a.

30. See chapter 10. The essay *The Optimal Production of Social Justice* (Kolm 1966a), which introduced all the essential elaborate concepts and results of this topic, was followed by an abundant literature.

31. See chapter 11.

Finally, the *implementation* of justice requires the relevant *motivations, power* and *information*. These *motivations* have three possible sources, which are often more or less present together. (1) *Directly moral motivations*, which rest on a sense of justice or on sentiments of respect, fairness, equity, solidarity, community, reciprocity, benevolence, or duty. (2) *Individuals' concern about other persons' opinions* of them; these other people can in this way induce or require, at no cost to themselves, moral behavior of the judged actors; these others' views express a moral judgment, whether or not these people themselves benefit from the action. (3) *Self-interest*, either through a coincidence with a moral view, or by an equilibrium of the recurrent social game. These ways of implementation and motivation may be present in the public at large, or more concentrated in the political-public process (voters, activitists, statesmen and politicians, public officials), or again they may be absent and the rules of society are only the terms of a truce.[32]

1.5 Reason and Classical Solutions

Strong rationality does not only provide the general structure and method of justice, it also questions a number of famous concepts, arguments and conclusions.

The most bizarre case is that of utilitarianism, which seeks to maximize the sum of pleasures minus pains, or of utilities.[33] Bentham, drawing on previous ideas, made it a dominant view in English philosophy for the exclusively political purpose of opposing the ethic of equal rights of the American and French Revolutions. He himself did

---

32. See chapters 12 and 13. This moral implementation originates in society at large for classical Libertarianism ("left-anarchists")—see the theory of *General Reciprocity* (Kolm 1984b)—in government for the extreme and widespread "state-moralism" (the assumption that the state can implement any ethics) and for certain more realistic considerations, and it does not exist for Buchanan's constitutional Social Contract (1975) and for the original and classical Public Choice school. A domain of application of game theory studies rules that emerge from various social interactions, and Gauthier (1986) argues that there emerges respects of rights and a particular rule of fair sharing —in an analysis that needs to be perfected in specifics but constitutes an important research program.

33. See chapter 14 and Kolm 1992b, 1993c.

not believe that adding pleasures of different people makes sense. Yet utilitarianism became a dominant outlook in English-language philosophy and, later, in academic economics. It was never considered beyond these two particular scholarly circles. This is why the view sometimes held that "there was utilitarianism, then came the egalitarian Rawls and then the libertarian-liberal Nozick," is very odd and utterly parochial. In the actual world there was private full-process liberalism, whose domination started two centuries ago (it had been expressed by Locke and was elaborated by early nineteenth century "political economy"), and it was progressively fought and partially repelled by egalitarians who imposed public redistribution; utilitarianism just does not exist. Yet a number of influential contemporary political philosophies came as reactions against aspects of utilitarianism. These aspects concern logic, ethics, or implementation.[34] The logical flaw supersedes the others (since it is strange to accuse a proposal of being immoral or unimplementable when it does not make sense in the first place).

Indeed utilitarianism, as well as a few other proposals such as the bargaining solutions of Gauthier (Raiffa-Kalai-Smorodinski) and of Nash (whose derivation is furthermore based on two logical insufficiencies),[35] requires a concept of a "cardinal utility" in the precise technical sense that there is meaning in *ratios of differences in levels* of a utility function, or at least, practically, in *comparing such differences*.[36] It thus suffices that there is *no reason* to translate the expression "I prefer *a* to *b* more than I prefer *c* to *d*" by a comparison of the *differences in utility levels* within each pair. Other criticisms are superfluous. For instance, there should also be meaning in "I prefer *a* to *b* 3.8 times more than I prefer *c* to *d*," and, for standard utilitarianisms, in such comparisons where "I prefer *a* to *b*" is replaced by "I am happier with *a* than I am with *b*," which may provide incomprehensible expressions. Utilitarianism furthermore needs to compare different individuals' comparisons expressed as differences in utility levels, but this interpersonal aspect need not even be considered since the very

34. For instance, logic for Arrow, ethics for Rawls, implementability for Buchanan.
35. See chapter 12, appendixes A, B, and C.
36. See chapter 12.

writing of an individual's comparison as a difference is per se devoid
of reason. It is thus also superfluous (and possibly nonsensical) to
accuse utilitarianism of not protecting individuals, or of not being able
to justify the selection of the rules it considers (for "rule utilitarianism"), or to point out that nobody will want to implement its precept.
There, however, exist a number of interesting "utilitaromorphisms,"
each requiring a specific discussion and some leading indeed to a
utilitarian form but with limited validity (see chapter 14).

For example, Bentham, in opposition to all strict utilitarians,
admits at one point that for lack of a better measure, he would add
money units.[37] His position then becomes economists' "surplus theory" (Dupuit 1844) as a second best because of difficulties (indeed,
lack of meaning) in measurement. But the maximization of the surplus
(the sum of the willingnesses to pay) cannot define the optimal distribution among self-interested individuals, since the surplus for transfers
is always zero. Surplus theory is only a partial theory of efficiency,
which should be complemented by distributional criteria and policy
(possibly in complementing its criterion of "compensability"—of the
losers by the beneficiaries—by an actual "compensation") and which
is not always well defined (Scitovsky 1941).[38]

In another case a utilitarian form results from the a priori definition
of the optimum as a maximum, and from a hypothesis of independence of the evaluation within subsocieties with respect to the situations of other individuals. Yet none of these two assumptions can
be taken as a general one and the meaning of what is added is
problematic.[39]

The most utilitarian in spirit are cases where state a is chosen rather
than state b because "an individual prefers state a to state b more than
another prefers state b to state a" (for instance, an individual will
enjoy a certain good more than the other individual would, or a
certain job will be less painful for him than it would be for the other).
But, first, these reasons are restricted to occasional choices of local
justice, usually for choices that are not very important (note that this

---

37. See Bentham (1973) and chapter 14.
38. See chapter 14.
39. See chapters 10, 14, and 15.

reason differs from helping out the most unhappy in absolute level). Second, these comparisons do not lead to an additive form for the reason noted above. However, they do lead to such a form if the preferences are *weak*, that is, close to indifference (then, cardinal utility is meaningful).[40] Hence utilitarian choices exist, but for cases of *microjustice*, for issues that are restricted in importance, in intensity, and in scope of population. This is far from the universal and in particular global validity usually claimed by utilitarians.

Finally, cardinal utility can be a valid concept for choices in uncertainty (the von Neumann–Morgenstern concept), and this has been used by Harsanyi to propose two brilliant reasons for utilitarianism. By the first reason, utilitarianism is the most valid form of a theory which, however, cannot be a moral theory (as it will be explained in the next paragraph). The second reason merely acknowledges that holding the individuals accountable for the effects of the occurrence of a risk on themselves amounts to moral indifference about the dispersion of the individuals' welfares resulting from the risk. However, a comprehensive view of justice does not hold individuals accountable for the occurrence of a risk if they are not responsible for it, and it seeks to limit its unjust effects on welfare, which rules out utilitarianism.[41] This theory also assumes a priori that the optimum is defined as a maximum (see below). However, this framework constitutes the basis of the theory of social insurance and of the "welfare state," which constitute a major field of social policy.[42]

The first of these "proofs" of utilitarianism rests paradoxically on (about) the very concept that Rawls was to elaborate specifically in order to displace utilitarianism that he criticized on moral ground as sacrificing individuals to some "collective interest." The concept that provides these two contrary conclusions is an "original position": either the allocation or the rules of society should be those that the individuals would have chosen before they knew what actual individuals they were going to become. This guarantees impartiality. Yet such an individual *would take the risk to sacrifice an actual individual if this*

---

40. See chapter 12, appendix A, and chapter 14.
41. See chapter 14.
42. See Kolm 1995g, 1996d.

permitted sufficiently many others to have sufficiently more, since all the actual individuals are his possible alternative future embodiments. Such a construct thus *cannot prima facie yield a theory of justice for actual individuals*. Of course, if each actual individual could be held "responsible" for the choice of the "original" individuals, this conclusion might have to be reversed. But the basic issue is the distribution among the opposed interests of the actual individuals, and the hypothetical "original" individuals are by definition devoid of any characteristic that would relate them to any specific actual individuals rather than to others—they have no differentiating "selves" while the issue is the effect of the differences. This "original" choice might in particular lead to violations of the basic rights of individuals and of the interests of the poorest, which Rawls seeks to defend (the fact that one can imagine, choose and define a hypothetical structure of ignorance and information in the original position that would lead to the choice of these principles cannot support them, contrary to assertion, since there also exist other structures that lead to other principles—such as utilitarianism). In relation to the previous remark, it also turns out that the phenomenology of choosing justly among divergent interests, which rests on impartiality and objectivity, cannot be described by the self-interested ignorance of an "original position": justice is not blind-folded egoism, but open-eyed and informed objectivity.[43] Hence, finally, not being derivable from a theory of the Original Position can constitute a test of validity of principles of justice.

More important, the principles of justice proposed by Rawls, which tend to pass this test, are roughly among those that can be justified by the direct rationality of justice described above (and more precisely in chapter 2). They are indeed standard ("I must disclaim any originality for the views I put forward. The leading ideas are classical and well-known")[44]: the priority of "basic liberties" which should be "equal for all and maximal" (a classical view, and these basic liberties are the basic Rights of Man and of the Citizen), nondiscrimination, an ideal equality in incomes and other "primary goods" (wealth, power, posi-

---

43   The individuals "in the original position" are explicitly assumed to be egoistic. A late suggestion that they could be endowed with a "sense of justice" hardly helps since one cannot define "justice" from a "sense of justice" without either tautology if the considered "sense" is what it should be or opposition to facts if it refers to the actual moral sentiment (in assuming that people all want the "difference principle").

44.   Rawls (1971), preface p. viii.

tion and self-respect), and a retreat to first helping the most deprived people because of the disincentive effect of "taxing the rich" on their production (the "difference principle"). Thus by his whole theory Rawls has in part rescued a community of scholars misled by utilitarianism back to the standard modern ethics of "liberty, equality, fraternity" (he emphasizes voluntary adhesion to the rules of justice and peaceful coexistence of communities), and has produced inspiring analyses. Yet these "principles" need the following few precisions, qualifications, and perfectings: (1) The maximization of the lowest disposable income leads to roughly equal and rather high incomes, achieved by very high (unequal) lump-sum taxes. Hence the de facto limit is set not by disincentive to work but by basic liberty which may be violated by this taxation requiring excessive work, and by politics since democracy would reject this fiscal policy. These constraints, the value of leisure and of leisurely work, and the modalities of redistributive policy should be introduced. (2) In the measure in which the "primary goods" are not independent, "maximize the minimum" jointly in *several* "primary goods" requires that one define these multidimensional minimum and, particularly, maximum. (3) To begin with, the concepts of "more" or "less" for these primary goods should be defined, since, apart from measurable "income" and "wealth," these entities are "power," "positions," "self-respect," and sometimes "opportunities." (4) The inequalities in individuals' social and market skills in using these goods should be considered. (5) Through these social and market interactions, an individual's possibilities depend on others' endowments in primary goods, a fact that the theory should include. (6) With any redistribution scheme, the most productive individuals may work more, rather than less, as a result of redistributive taxation in order to make up for this loss of income (thus the "difference principle" vanishes). (7) Even if they tended to work less, they may not do so because they are assumed to be convinced by the ideal of equality in "primary goods." Notice, by the way, that all these problems happen to be solved by the concept of "Practical Justice" or "maximin in fundamental preferences" proposed at the same time in my book *Justice and Equity* (see chapter 7).[45] (8)

---

45. It was more precisely a "leximin" (see below). A crucial point is the definition and justification of the interpersonally comparable and ordinal "fundamental preferences," which are very different from Arrow (1977) and other's "extended sympathy," despite a formal similarity (see chapter 7).

This set of principles cannot have exclusive validity in any large society (this limit was explicit for Practical Justice). (9) The presentation of the logic of the "basic liberties" (basic rights) should be improved (see chapter 4).

Rawls's proposal resulted from the ethical criticism of utilitarianism. Merely logical criticism, by contrast, led to another field. The minimal departure from utilitarianism that retains all its properties except the logically meaningless sum and the psychologically meaningless cardinal utility consists of the maximization of a "social welfare function," an increasing function of the levels of individuals' utilities. If we want to define such a function for many hypothetical utility functions of each individual, in a way that satisfies a number of conditions that might be a priori worthy of consideration, we obtain the problem that Arrow proved to be without solution (see chapter 15). Since these conditions are satisfied by the utilitarian sum (were it meaningful), this result can be interpreted as the proof that even "ordinal utilitaranism" is impossible (that is, with utilities representing only preference orderings, and hence defined only up to an arbitrary increasing function), and thus as the final logical blow to utilitarianism (which, however, did not think of considering nonexisting utility functions, although it can). This topic then developed into the interesting mathematical study of the limits to the aggregation of orderings. It also inspired remarkable side-fields concerning voting procedures and the informational difficulties of implementation when individuals hide their true preferences.

Yet what does this "impossibility" of "social choice" actually mean for social ethics? First, there is no reason to define the optimum as a maximum. I have even shown that this can violate standard sense of justice and rationality (which means: "for a reason").[46] To define "rational" as such a maximization is an eccentric and rather irrational use of the word (economists came to this use for individuals' choices in order to shun the discussion of the hypothesis of a maximizing behavior). Utilitarianism derived its maximization from its special (but specious) theory rather than assuming it in abstracto. Furthermore maximization is usually defended by equivalent technical conditions that relate choices on several possibility sets (or is replaced by

---

46. Chapter 15 explains all the remarks of this paragraph and provides the references.

weaker properties which also raise the difficulty mentioned). Therefore the central problem of this Social Choice Theory is actually posed in the following way. A situation of social choice consists of one set of possible alternative social states (states of society) of which one must be chosen and of one structure of preferences (or utility function) for each individual. A number of "conditions" about these various choices, most of which relate several of them, are assumed. The theory then proves that it is not possible that a number of these choice situations all have a solution. However, it so happens that the *actual* sets of possibilities and of individuals' preferences are not among the situations used in the proof. Furthermore the imaginary situations considered are very numerous; they are extraordinary by the smallness of their possibility set (two or three states only) and by the similarities among individuals' preferences, and certain have to assume non-sensical individual preferences. At any rate, given their use by the theory, these pluralities cannot mean different dates, issues, circumstances or populations, or uncertainty, or a "constitution." Even when there are certain reasons to consider several sets of preferences and of possibilities, this could not justify the set of social choice situations used by the theory. In addition most of the "conditions" can be at odds with justice and reason. Furthermore the social status of these "conditions," and the fact that ethics is about influencing individuals' values rather than only taking them as given, raise further difficulties of meaning for this theory.

Finally, this theory does not even contain explicit items with which so basic ethical concepts as impartiality, equality of treatment, or equal treatment of equals can be defined (by contrast, it can trivially consider rights, liberties, powers or means in incorporating them within the definition of each alternative social state). Now, when individuals' well-being or fulfillment of their ends are end values of justice, their manifest inequality in any large society leads to the second-best justice of first taking care of the most miserable, notably when not all basic needs are satisfied, that is, to Practical Justice (as, however, a nonuniversal borderline case).

More generally, the conclusion from all the difficulties of this "Social Choice" approach should have been the end of the aggregative utilitarian outlook, the closure of this fortuitous mishap, and the necessary return of its handful of followers (in the world) to the rational principle of justice, the political opposition to which was the reason why utilitarianism was launched in the first place: "free and equal in rights" as the necessary form of impartial individualistic social ethics, which *most of the world's thinking and thinkers never left*, and which is variously applied in basic rights, basic needs and the relief of misery, process-freedoms, real liberties, and solidarities.

Among these other theories, we have already noted that *private* full process liberalism (that is, the free exchange views of Locke, of the full 1789 Declaration, mineteenth century "political economy," recently revived by Nozick) should be complemented by serious consideration of market failures, and hence by a much enlarged liberal public sector implementing full process-freedom ("liberal social contracts").[47] We have also remarked that the ideal equalities in separate "spheres of justice" (Weber, Walzer) should completely work out the consequences of the fact that such allocations are generally dominated by others that everyone prefers, and how a similar dilemma transforms a possible irrelevance of individuals' preferences for distributive justice, and hence an ideal of equal consumptions, into income justice and its problems.[48]

General liberty, however, can be seen in two ways. Either one considers only the actor's freedom or one considers also that his actions can affect and in particular restrict the freedom of others. In the first case, the "free fox in the free poultry yard" constitutes a paragon of a free society. In the second case, "your freedom ends where the other persons' freedom begins." Enslaving one's neighbor is (extreme) freedom in one case and not in the other. These two views constitute the bases of two very different brands of liberalisms (that is, liberty-based conceptions). Only the second view is moral (although the first is valued by Nietzsche, Spencer and the authors to be considered). Yet the first conception may be used as the foundation of explanatory theories that aim to explain how interactions can lead to institutions, constitutions, or rules of behavior. Then these entities may have a moral *form*, even if the individuals have no intrinsic moral *motivations*, if the underlying balance of power is not too uneven (you respect your neighbor because he makes himself respected directly or in-

---

47. See chapter 5.
48. See the detailed analysis in chapter 6.

directly, for example in exchange for his respecting you and under the threat of retaliation or the control of agreed-upon institutions).

Indeed all the views so far considered are impugned by the cynical but possibly realistic conceptions that present society as only a battlefield for people mainly devoid of moral concern; rules and principles as only terms of a truce that everyone prefers to the harms, costs, and losses of open fighting; politics as only the prolongation of war by the means of the market; and morality as only a possible fortunate form of such explicit or tacit agreements (Buchanan, the original school of Public Choice, Gauthier, and, for a part, neo-"libertarians").[49] These conceptions are not moral in the strict sense that "to each according to his unbridled threat advantage" could hardly stand as an ethical principle, although they propose to explain actual rules of morals as well as politics. They indeed deny that moral sentiments can sufficiently motivate people for having a significant influence on their behavior, and therefore that a priori moral principles can be implemented. They are explanatory, positive sociological theories that set out and work out an important research program, and their frequent moral-sounding stances can only in fact amount to technical advice on how to foster interests (possibly of everybody). However, real people often express moral concern, they often are very sensitive to others' opinions (these others can thus have their moral views implemented at no cost for them), and politics is not all explicable by egoistic interest.[50] There nevertheless remains the fact that the possibilities of motivations limit the implementability of moral principles. Now, useful ethics should advocate only implementable principles, that is, those for which the required motivation, power, and information exist or can be obtained, and each of the three implementabilities—motivational, informational, and power—is necessary for a possible ethics.

Indeed other analyses focus on the possibilities of individuals' moral motivations, including altruisms of various types and intensities and senses of duty and of justice.[51] These possibilities concern both the

---

49. See chapters 12 and 13.

50. See chapter 13.

51. See *The Good Economy, General Reciprocity* (Kolm 1984b) and the references provided in this book.

motivations that the individuals can have, and the consequences that these motivations can lead to in the economy and in society. This topic is justice in the pre-modern sense of the term, that is, the personal virtue of behaving justly toward others. The possibilities are analyzed according to the origin, development, reinforcement and destruction of these motivations, including the roles of education, imitation, and others' opinion. One topic of central importance is that of *reciprocity*, a widespread behavior in between pure exchange and gift-giving. Another concerns the question of *collective gift-giving*, whereby a number of people not sufficiently altruistic to give by themselves have the small amount of altruism that makes them prefer that all give rather than none: Then they want to be forced to give and agree with this "forced free transfer" (not only "they must be forced to be free," as Rousseau said, but they want to be forced to be free). In crucial instances where certain equalities and liberties conflict, altruism is their conciliator and makes liberty the instrument of just equality. Furthermore these sentiments, attitudes, and relations are at least as important in themselves: The good society is made of good people, not only of satisfied ones.

It should be emphasized here that distributive justice is indeed the central problem of individualistic social ethics; that is, the relevant choices are among states such that certain persons prefer one and other persons prefer the other. In other words, individualism a priori rules out states dominated by others that everybody prefers (with possible indifference for some persons but not for all); that is, states that are not Pareto-efficient (or, for short, efficient). This principle has a number of reasons and, also, of qualifications. Certain reasons are moral.[52] It will be argued that implementing unanimous preference (hence Pareto-efficiency) manifests collective liberty. Unanimity is also an equality of power. Criteria of "welfare" would lead to the same advice. Furthermore it so happens that, practically, any public measure is bound to displease someone, which implies that the choices are among Pareto-efficient alternatives. This may be due to a lack of the information that would permit the required compensatory transfers, but this ignorance is an actual constraint on public policy. In any case

---

52. Another one is epistemic; see chapter 6.

competitive electoral politics guarantees Pareto-efficiency, since a non-efficient program can be defeated by the unanimity of votes by some other one, by definition. Indeed the sheer sequentiality and repeated-ness of the social game tends to implement Pareto-efficient states. At any rate, it should be emphasized that *inefficiencies caused by strategic behavior* (either simultaneous—such as the celebrated *prisoner's dilemma* game—or with sequential actions) are *eliminated* by the setting of *an institution that can enforce promises and promises conditional on enforceable promises.*[53] Therefore the setting of such institutions is desired by unanimity, and the inefficiency resides in fact in their possible absence. However, of course, certain preferences are not morally "respectable" (malevolence, malicious envy, etc.) and should not be followed for the ethical choice.[54]

Last, we should not forget that the nonindividualistic part of social ethics is both very important and delicate. For instance, the respect and safeguard of cultures has to have priority just after the respect and safety of individuals, or the legacies of civilizations or natural sites should be respected even if all present and future individuals prefer benefits that would require their destruction. Such duties transcend personal views and their possible oppositions. They are beyond the question of justice although they have consequences for justice.

---

53. For example, *a situation of the "prisoner's dilemma" type does not lead to inefficiency if there is an institution for enforcing promises and promises conditional on enforceable promises.* Indeed consider the classical setting of this game. Two individuals can respectively choose actions a and b for one, and a' and b' for the other. Acting separately leads them to choose b and b'. Yet, both prefer that the choices be a and a'. Assume now that the institution mentioned exists. Then, for promises that demand to be enforced, any participant benefits from issuing singlehandedly the promise which is, for the first participant: *"I promise to do a if the other promises to do a',* or just *"does a'"* if the actions can be in a sequence, and to do b if he does not" (or the equivalent for the second participant). The other participant, knowing this promise of the first one, *benefits from promising to do a',* or from just *doing a'* if sequences are admitted (or a if the roles are reversed). They can thus reach the state that is better for both than the equilibrium reached otherwise. Similar proofs can be presented for the other cases where strategic behavior induces inefficiency (the simple enforceability of promises suffices for asymmetrical situations where only the player on one side needs the guarantee). These conclusions also extend to cases of any number of individuals.

54. Preferences should then be "cleaned," "laundered," or "ironed" to suppress their unethical features (see Goodin 1986; and Kolm 1991c, 1993f, 1995a, and chapter 9 for the discussion of the case of envy and the indication of how to perform this operation in this case).

1.6   Organization of Content

Importance, relevance, proximity, and history have guided the organization of this book, with the following result:

Of the seven parts and sixteen chapters, part I, in three chapters, constitutes an *introduction* which presents the *basic concepts, properties*, and *distinctions*, and part VII, in a final chapter, provides *concluding considerations* concerned with the *structure* and *method* of justice.

Part VI analyzes *the theory of Social Choice* (chapter 15) and *utilitarianisms* (chapter 14). Both simply derive justice from the maximum of a function of individuals' ends (with mathematical refinements).

Full liberties of acts and processes are the topic of both part II and part V, with two chapters each. Part II is concerned with liberties *a priori morally bound* by other persons' liberties. Part V introduces that there may not be such a priori moral bounds (yet respect for others may, but need not, result from social interaction or agreement). This aspect (introduced with the theory of *Public Choice, neo-"libertarians"* and *"morals by agreement"*) makes part V not strictly ethical as the rest of the book is. This part (chapters 12 and 13) compares the various views of *freedom* and the consequences as regards the respective roles of the *market* and of the *state*. In part II, chapter 4 analyzes the *basic human rights*, their reason, and their structure, and chapter 5 is concerned with the basic theory of *full process-freedom* which adds unconstrained free exchange but needs an essentially publicly implemented *Liberal Social Contract* for dealing with the "failures" of markets and agreements.

The derivation of the just allocation from equalities (often of liberties) is the topic of parts III and IV. Part IV (chapters 10 and 11) is set apart because of the logical specificity of its topics: It is concerned with the comparisons and measures of *inequalities* (from Kolm 1966a) and *poverty*, and, from the latter, with the questions of *misery* and *basic needs*, and with the fundamental question of *needs* in general. Part III includes two chapters (7 and 8) that deal respectively with two specific contemporaneous works, both based on *equality of liberty* and *maximin* in allocation (though they differ much in other respects): *Justice and Equity* and *Justice as Fairness* and Rawls's work. These chapters are preceded by chapter 6 which prepares the ground in analyzing two essential and related topics: the possible reasons for the *inefficiency of equality*, among which the multidimensionality of the equalizand (that which should be equalized) and the resulting theory of *efficient super-equity* which justifies basing distributive justice on incomes; and the question of capacities, or human resources, of various types. Finally, chapter 9 presents a series of theories which are "egalitarian" in various respect: equality of resources, "fundamental insurance," modern theories of exploitation, responsibility, equality of opportunity, genuine envy (a consumption externality), and maximin in liberty.

The reader interested in a particular topic can and should go directly to it (there are sufficient references to the other relevant parts of the text). This can notably be the case for comparing and measuring inequalities, utilitarianism, Social Choice, Rawls's "justice as fairness," Public Choice, interpersonal comparisons (chapter 7), Equity and equal liberty (id.), needs, and exploitation, for example.

1.7 A Note on References

Each crucial topic of the general theory of justice outlined above, and hence each particular possible and relevant theory of justice and its main foundations and applications, is analyzed in greater depth and detail in one or several of the books and essays I have published over the last few decades. These works provide the developments of concepts, arguments, and proofs, whose presentation here, though self-sufficient, it often only by sketches, briefs summaries, or allusions. These works will thus have to be mentioned (most will be in footnotes). For this I offer both apologies and the excuse that most of these works are not yet available in English (as is notably the case for all that are in book form, which is most of them). The topics covered by these studies include the general logic and the method of justice, the general form of equality of liberty ("Equity" and its properties and related concepts), full process-freedom and the Liberal Social Contract ("liberal" means liberty-based), public economics with its various criteria, the comparison and measure of inequalities (in English), reciprocity and possible altruism, "first helping the most distressed" with the Practical Justice of leximin with fundamental utility, efficient multidimensional maximin, basic rights and basic needs, the use and limits of electoral democracy, the analysis of justice-motivated global social change, applications in all domains of economics, analyses of liberalisms, socialisms, anarchisms, utilitarianisms, Social and Public Choices, etc., and last, but not least, the relevant psychology of happiness and of liberty.

It should finally be recalled that all important social or human problems involve more or less all the dimensions of man and of society, and anyone who tries to understand them separately is bound to misunderstand them all. Distributive justice, notably, is economics, and it is also philosophy, politics, sociology, psychology, anthropology, and history. Man and society are one, with different facets, and therefore the social science is either one, or neither social nor science.

2 Justice, Liberty, and Equality

2.1 The Nature and Operation of Distributive Justice

Justice is simple, but the world is complicated, so the application of justice in the world contains a few intricacies. Understanding the field of the existing, possible, and necessary conceptions of justice and social ethics is much helped by first *minimally* investing in the consideration of its necessary basic structures. This is the aim of this chapter.[1]

Definition

Justice is the ethical judgment about the situation of social entities, with respect to the value of its situation *for* each of these social entities (possibly as evaluated by the entity itself but not necessarily so a priori), and notably as these situations result from the effects of society.

Such a social entity is called a "justiciable" (that is, amenable to considerations of justice). The considered justiciables are often individuals, but there is also justice for more or less constituted groups such as nations, families, firms, cities, classes, regions, and so on, or perhaps even for cultures, which may or may not be conceptually or informationally "reducible" to individuals (and should or should not be considered in this way). The term "situation" denotes here any object of this judgment.

Justice is *respectful* when it values a justiciable's situation because the justiciable values it. The "situation" then consists of items that serve the justiciable's purpose or preference, such as, for instance, goods, rights, freedoms, powers, treatments, or "satisfaction." Claims of justice or complaints concerning injustice, from the justiciables on their own behalf, concern respectful justice. They constitute the *direct demand* for justice. This book will mostly focus on this most important category of justice.[2]

---

1. A complete analysis of the logic of the judgments of justice can be found in *The General Theory of Justice* (Kolm 1990b; see also 1994e).

2. In other cases, what is deemed to be good for a justiciable may not coincide with the justiciable's own view. The case of *vicarious needs* will be briefly considered in chapter 11. Respectful justice concerns justiciables' preferences and not their information about facts: it is violated by applications of the idea that justiciables "do not know

When "more" for a justiciable implies "less" for another, the problem of justice is one of *distributive justice*. This is in particular the case of respectful justice that arbitrates between the opposed desires of various justiciables. Distributive justice requires that there be several justiciables. A central application of distributive justice is the allocation of the goods, resources, services, or commodities that are scarce and raise rival desires directly or indirectly, that is, *economic justice*.[3]

The Variables of Justice

A question of justice has to consider several types of variables.[4]

The problem is defined by the variables that describe the considered situation of the justiciables (and therefore also define the justiciables themselves): These are the *situational variables*.

The ethical judgment of justice may bear *directly* on these variables; it then belongs to *direct justice*. Yet this judgment on these variables may alternatively be derived from more fundamental ethical judgments generally concerning other variables; it then belongs to *indirect* or *derived justice*.

Therefore, for a judgment of justice, there is a set of variables that incur directly the ethical evaluation. They are the *directly ethically relevant variables* (or the social ethical *end values* for justice). They are related to the situational variables, with which they coincide for direct justice but not for derived justice. The directly ethically relevant variables may refer to justice, for these justiciables or for others, but they may also be other values for social ethics (referring, for instance, to the respect, defense, or promotion of group, culture, nature, or various transcendences).

Finally, there may be *instrumental variables* for implementing justice. These may coincide with the situational variables (and hence also with the directly ethically relevant variables).

---

what is good for them" if this goodness refers to their final preferences but not if it only refers to means to satisfy them. Note also that the justiciables' situations considered need not be *end values* for the justiciable nor for the social ethic: They may derive their values from those of other items that are related to them.

3. Another distinction is that between *comparative justice* and *noncomparative justice*. It is analyzed in detail in *The General Theory of Justice* (op. cit.).

4. A "variable" here is not a symbolic representation but the item, fact, etc., itself.

Theories of Justice, and the Operation of Distributive Justice

A theory of justice is a set of considerations whose conclusion is the judgment of justice in a category of problems of justice.

Such a theory consists in providing *a reason* for this judgment. The activity of *providing a reason* defines *rationality*. Hence a theory of justice is an exercise in rationality. We will see that this is the reason for the important place of equality (of whatever it may be) in justice. A theory of justice is the more successful the less it rests on "intuitions," sentiments, and a priori judgments, and the more it rests on reason, proofs, and clear and explicit statements about the underlying conception of man and of society.[5]

Theories of justice can be either *pure* or *mixed* theories. Pure theories of justice consider only one kind of directly ethically relevant variables (they are also called *univalued* theories of justice). By contrast, mixed theories of justice consider several kinds of such variables (they are *plurivalued* theories, and the number of these types may be smaller or larger). *Simple* theories of justice are mixed theories with only a few types of directly ethically relevant variables (often only two or three). Scholars' and ideologists' theories of justice tend to be either pure or simple. By contrast, the "theories" revealed by all the choices concerning an overall, complex society are always of the mixed kind. Indeed it cannot be otherwise: For any theory of justice—or more generally of social ethics—that is pure or simple or indeed with any pre-established list of criteria, one can find counterexamples of actual or realistic cases where these criteria must not be applied and others have to be chosen, an opinion that everybody shares. Furthermore any practical application of a general criterion requires other particular specifying criteria, if only for providing an operational definition of the terms (we would, for instance, have to define sufficiently terms such as income, action, liberty, need, utility, preference, possibility, and person, and for an ethical application this choice of definition has actual consequences and is also an ethical choice). Thus an actual possible theory of justice (or of social ethics) for a complex society as a whole is always an *open-ended moral polyarchy*, where *open-ended* means that one cannot

---

5. "Where mystery begins, justice ends" (E. Burke).

hope to be able to provide a priori a sufficient, closed, and exhaustive list of criteria. However, a simple theory may intend to propose only a best approximation, with a few principles that constitute the general rules, or even merely provide the tone or a dominant outlook, whereas other concerns may bring in qualifications, specifications, limitations, or exceptions. In fact, the solution of the problem of overall and general macrojustice (see chapter 1), and notably of the corresponding essential principles of the just distribution and of the just allocation of resources, constitutes a simple construction, resting as it does on a combination of the three polar cases of the allocation of the human resource (process-freedom, income or consumption justice, and non-suffering and needs), as will be explained in further chapters.

Pure theories of justice are often completely determined by the very nature of their directly ethically relevant variables, and they do this by one of two devices: the directly ethically relevant variables are either *nonrival* or ideally *equal*, with nonrivalry being either for variables directly related to justiciables or for a single global aim. This will be shown shortly. The possibilities intervene directly either for limiting a global aim or equal items relative to the justiciables, or when they forbid the relevant equality. For mixed theories of justice the various pure criteria may also conflict among themselves, in particular given the possibilities (for instance, conflicts among various equalities, or among equalities and overall social concerns). The theory must then provide the required principles of adjustment, such as, for example, various possible types of compromise, priorities, "second-best" solutions or successive application ("superimposition").[6]

2.2   Reduction to Nonrivalry

Nonrivalry can take one of two forms.

In the one case, the items are attributed to the various justiciables, who value them positively, but there is no direct rivalry among these variables and they can be attributed at *satiety* to all. This is the case of the general Rights of Man and of the Citizen or basic liberties—like

---

6. The detailed logical analysis of the various types of combination of criteria is presented in Kolm 1990b.

the right to worship, to speak freely, to apply for positions, to hold property, to compete, to exchange, to vote, not to be arrested arbitrarily, to be judged fairly according to the due process of law, and so on. One person (or social entity, more generally) having more of one of these rights does not imply that any other of these rights is reduced—this holds whether the rights be of the same type or of different types in this category, and whether the rights be of different persons (justiciable) or of the same person (a particular qualification will be noted below). However, this change may affect the person's uses of his rights, and it may affect other persons in other ways. These other ways of influence include in particular the various effects of the *uses* of these rights, the cases of "nosy" direct preferences over others' actions, and the scarce resources needed to use or to enforce these rights. (This important structure will be further discussed in chapter 4.)

In the second case, the variables that are *directly* ethically relevant are not even assigned in themselves to the justiciables, although they are related more or less directly to the situational variables and possibly to other variables related to the justiciables and that concern them. Examples include cases where the variable deemed to be directly ethically relevant is a *global social aim* such as national power, "social welfare," or culture or nature per se, or when it is some quality of society.

2.3   Why Equality? Equality as Minimal Irrationality

Equality can be of many types of items, which can also have various forms—for instance, there can be various equal facts or equal rules (expressed as functions). The nature of these variables crucially differentiates the various theories, and hence it will be discussed below. It is, however, essential to first see the basic reason for equality. Equality is not an arbitrary ethical stance. On the contrary, its essence is nonarbitrariness, and it is not an ethical position but a logical requirement of rationality in the normal sense of "for a reason."[7]

Indeed justice refers to *practical reason* (in Kant's sense): It is intended for choice. When the alternatives of a choice are defined as

---

7. The question of the pure rationality of equality is discussed in detail in Kolm 1993e. This is not the only possible reason for equality, however. An exhaustive analysis of the

mutually exclusive—a representation that is always possible—only one of them can exist by definition. Hence a fully rational (or rationally complete) choice requires a reason for this *unique* outcome. In particular, justice must select the relevant "situations" of various justiciables. The *other relevant* aspects of the justiciables are called their "characteristics."[8] Permuting both their situations and their characteristics between two justiciables produces an ethically indistinguishable state (since all that can relevantly distinguish the two justiciables is then permuted—it amounts to a mere "relabeling"). Hence, if one situation is just, so is the other. If, furthermore, these justiciables have the same relevant characteristics, this permutation amounts to permuting only the "situations." But since these two permuted states are indistinguishable from the point of view of justice, one can provide no reason for choosing one rather than the other. Now, if these two individual situations are different, so are these two permuted states. Then choosing one rather than the other is *irrational* by the very definition of rationality. (Note that a lottery with equal probabilities cannot provide an answer since this equality of probabilities would have to be justified, which constitutes exactly the same problem— leading to an infinite regress; furthermore a lottery does not a priori constitute a reason, as its outcome rests on a process that is irrelevant to the question considered).[9] This irrationality is avoided only if these two justiciables have identical (that is, equal) situations. This is *equal*

---

possible reasons for equality is proposed in Kolm 1990b. For example, equality may result from nondependency, a particular case of liberty. Or it may be justified by a desire to avoid envy or jealousy (see Kolm 1991b, 1993f, 1995a, and chapter 9 below). Of course it is not moral to yield to such immoral sentiments as these may be. However, such sentiments are commonly detrimental to the quality of society, to social peace and cooperation among its members (and to their happiness and serenity). Then, if one cannot eradicate the propensity to experience these sentiments, it may be legitimate to avoid them by the adequate allocation. Equality then is a possibility, although not the only one in general (see chapter 9 below). Finally, let us recall that the intuition that justice necessarily is equality of something is explicitly expressed by Aristotle: "Justice is equality, as everybody believes it is, quite apart from any other consideration" (*Nichomachean Ethics*).

8. This includes relevant aspects of relations, positions and relative positions, etc., and not only the more strictly intrinsic aspects.

9. For instance, the outcome of flipping a coin rests on the dynamics of falling bodies. However, lotteries may be second-best processes when the considered direct equality is ruled out for some reason (impossibility or conflict with another criterion that has precedence).

treatment of equals in the relevant characteristics. It is mere *equality* when no differentiating characteristic is deemed to be relevant. Other solutions are irrational, and they elicit sentiments and resentments that attach to what is arbitrary and unjustified.

What a justiciable should have (her "situation") may a priori have to depend on the given characteristics of all justiciables and on what the others have. But in particular cases and views it is deemed to depend only on this justiciable's characteristics ("decomposability"). Then the irrationality of inequality is seen directly. The reason for a justiciable's allocation (situation) is based on her characteristics, and identical characteristics leads to identical justified allocations. For example, if I give you one bread for the only reason that you lack three hundred calories, and I refuse to give one bread (which I have) to another person who also lacks three hundred calories, this appears as arbitrary, irrational, and unjust. I propose that it is unjust because it is irrational in the field of justice. Justice is bound by this rationality as much as it is by arithmetic when I have to give you back due change.

Note that the above described reason for equality is not a "principle of nonsufficient reason" saying that "if there is no reason for inequality, then we should choose equality." This kind of age-old argument[10] indeed fails to be a purely logical one, since if a priori there is sufficient reason neither for equality nor for any inequality, this could be taken as a reason for selecting any specific inequality as well as equality (either equivalence of permutations and uniqueness of the social choice should be added as above,[11] or this "principle" is an ultimately moral stance that can be deemed arbitrary).[12]

---

10. This argument is to be found in Aristotle (*Nichomachean Ethics*), Hobbes (*Leviathan*), Locke (*Second Treatise on Government*), Condorcet (project for a Declaration of Rights), and, in modern times, in Isaiah Berlin and following on from him in many other contemporary writers (such as Benn and Peters, S. Lukes, and A. Atkinson).

11. Notice that uniqueness suffices if and only if an individual's situation is a priori deemed to depend only on this individual's (relevant) characteristics and not on other individuals' characteristics and situations, since then the "reason" applied on identical characteristics provides identical situations.

12. For the same reason, the reason for equality presented above provides the foundation in rationality of the theory of probability. In changing the names of the variables, it shows the rational necessity of the "Laplace principle" (Bayes, Condorcet) classically stated as an axiomatic but arbitrary "principle of insufficient reason" (the basis then reduces to rationality and to the hypothesis of uniqueness: an event has only one probability).

The necessary equality can be that of individualized (relative to justiciables) directly ethically relevant items, when the justiciables' relevant characteristics are identical. This latter identity is in particular the case when no characteristic is mentioned in the complete setting of the question, since this implies that the actual differences in justiciables' characteristics are considered irrelevant. For individualized variables that are not directly ethically relevant, the relevant characteristics include their relations with the directly ethically relevant variables, either individualized ones or others. Then equality requires in fact certain identities of these relations.[13]

The above reasoning thus shows that there is a prima facie reason in favor of equality and against inequality, which results from the very requirement of rationality.[14] Of course, for a given type of items, other reasons may also be present and relevant, and they may in the end lead to another choice. These possible impediments consist of the actual possibilities, and of the consideration of other valued aspects of the situation that may either not refer to justice for these justiciables or imply ideal equalities in other items.

2.4 Liberties

Action and the Definition of Freedom

Respectful justice usually concerns justiciable *agents*, and therefore its theory rests on a theory of action. An *agent* can perform *actions* and is endowed with a *will*. A will has *intention* and can influence—determine in part, be a cause of—certain *acts* of this agent. An *action* of an agent is a *set of wilful or voluntary acts of this agent that aim at the same objective*. An agent's *action* is more *free* when it is more *caused by his will*. The other causes of an action constitute the *constraints* on it and determine the corresponding *domain of liberty*, or *of possibles*, or *of choice*.[15]

---

13. The general logic of equality is discussed in more detail in Kolm 1990b, 1993e.

14. Prima facie means in the absence of other reasons that imply another conclusion and overpower this one (the use of *prima facie* reasons in ethics has, for instance, been emphasized by Ross 1930).

15. The question of the definition of freedom is analyzed in depth in Kolm 1982a. The definition could a priori be extended to acts (including those of the reflex, impulsive, or

A *right* is a socially defined possibility to determine an aspect of the world (or a feature, a property, a characteristic of the world) or the socially defined guarantee that this aspect exist. It has a right-holder (a person, an individual, a group, an institution, and possibly others notably for respect, protective and immunity rights). A right is a right to act, to have others act or abstain, or it does not specify its means (as with a simple right to have something). An agent's right can generally be seen as a socially defined liberty in a broad sense of the term, since it implies directly or indirectly the possibility of a choice by this agent. More specifically, however, a right can be a liberty, a power, a respect or an immunity, a claim, or a privilege. A property right over an object is a bundle of more specific rights about the use of this object. The definition of a right can be moral, legal, conventional, or otherwise institutional.[16]

---

even compulsive kinds) and not restricted to actions. On the contrary, a deeper and more restricted definition of liberty would define more free as more caused by *reason*. Notice that reason needs the will in order to influence acts or actions. Then freedom requires *autonomy* (in Kant's sense, or Rousseau's principle that "to be free is to obey a rule chosen by oneself"). For each definition, the constraints are the other causes and the domain of choice is defined accordingly.

The causal chains from the will or from reason to the free act can be more or less direct or pass through the intermediary of other parts of the agent (such as in training or learning) or through the external world (for instance, in investment). Reason-processes and the elements of the mind they mobilize receive themselves influences of various origins, yet they are characterized by a high degree of feedback. With any of these definitions, liberty is a particular structure of causality. This implies that the classical dilemma between determinism and liberty rests on an elementary misconception (or constitutes a misspecified question).

The concept of action, or of rational action, concerns us here only for understanding theories of justice and not per se. For instance, we do not discuss particularly such basic questions as the necessary meaningfulness of actions for the agent (Max Weber's criterion for acts constituting actions); the distinction of impulsive, compulsive, reflex, or akratic (that result from weakness of the will or *akrasia*) acts—that cannot constitute actions—from acts that result from habits, norm-following, or duty; acts performed for the mere feeling they procure as opposed to acts performed for more distinct effects; or the consciousness or unconsciousness of the various elements of an action. Discussions of certain of these aspects constitute a large part of theoretical sociology. Classic references include, in particular, Weber, Durkheim, and Parsons. Aspects of the theory of action within the context of justice are discussed by Gewirth (1978, 1982) and Phillips (1986).

16. The literature on rights is abundant. The historical landmark about the nature and logic of rights has been Hohfeld (1919); it considers only legal rights, however. A number of recent valuable works are mentioned in the references. Recent synthetic analyses of the concept of a right can be found in Waldron (1984), Wellman (1985), with extensions in Kolm (1985a, 1989a, 1993a).

A state of the world contains the Cartesian product of the uses of their rights by the right-holders, but it can also be defined as including rights themselves in its description (see chapter 15).

The aim of an agent's action can be either a "final aim" of this agent, or an "intermediate aim" of this agent that influences his final aims, for instance as a means to further action. Examples of final aims of individuals are happiness, the satisfaction of final needs, "self-realization," living a well-considered "good life," living a moral life, etc.

Wilfully choosing or influencing one's own motives of action, be they reasoned principles, desires, or tastes, increases liberty from its very definition.[17]

The Characteristics and Types of Liberties

The construction of the rational social ethics depends largely on the various characteristics of liberties and on the resulting types of liberties. These characteristics are the following which refer, respectively, to questions of *cause, agent, nature, extent, constraint, value, action, use,* and *conditions*:

1. The type of the *mental or physiological process or structure* that defines the freedom of the act in causing it: the will, reason, choice, desires, preferences, tastes, certain nervous processes, etc., and possibly more specific ones that consider particular influences.

2. The type of the considered free *person* or agent.

3. The nature of the considered acts or *domain* of choice or action.

4. The *extent* of this domain. Note that when a liberty of a new type is added to other ones without suppressing certain of their possibilities, this is both a complexification of the nature of the alternatives and a type of extension of domain.

5. The *nature and origin of the limits* or constraints that delineate this domain. In particular, these limits may be or may not be set by other agents' wills: This is *dependency* versus *independence*. The limits may also be set by institutions (themselves possibly set by wills, but with a

---

17. Correspondingly, this includes Kant's autonomy, Buddhist practice, and the widsom of Hellenistic philosophies.

certain stability and predictability). The effects of an agent's past acts may constrain his present acts, and this may or may not have been purposeful. In "self-restraint," an agent voluntarily limits certain of his acts; this can manifest an external constraint, as when this restraint aims to meet an external threat, but this self-restraint may also constitute a higher liberty, when it is more caused by the intraindividual entity that defines freedom, such as the will or reason, in the corresponding self-control. The set of constraints, and a given constraint, can have causes of various types.

6. The *reasons* for valuing freedom, or on the contrary for preferring it to be more restricted. These reasons are analyzed in the next section. A rough dichotomy distinguishes between instrumental and existential liberty.

7. The situation of the considered liberty in the process of *action*. An action consists of *acts* using *means* for an *aim*. This provides three types of freedom, whose distinction is essential both for the foundation and structure of basic rights and for the question of economic distributive justice (see below and the following uses of these concepts).

8. The *use* to which this freedom is put. In particular, the free agent can use this liberty in an individual choice, or he can use it in agreement with other agents, possibly in an exchange for something else.

9. The *defeasibility, alienability,* and *prescriptibility* of a liberty; that is, Can it be suppressed or transferred, or is it specified for a limited duration, or is this not the case, or under what conditions can this be the case? These properties can result from the nature of the freedom considered, or from social agreements or conventions, from an ethical choice, and so on.

The Values of Liberty

The Problems of Valuing Freedom

Liberty is a means for doing things and, in its most common and presently relevant conception, for the achievement of the aim of the action that uses it.

Now "liberty or death" is a motto with which many people died and which changed the world. It expresses an unconditional preference for death over a life devoid of liberty of a certain kind. But a dead person does not enjoy this liberty either. And among the other things that a living person can enjoy, there certainly are some that make life preferable to death. Hence this motto is irrational ... unless there is some other reason for valuing freedom, or certain freedoms.

Alexis de Tocqueville (1836) is peremptory: "He who wants freedom for anything but itself does not deserve it and will soon lose it." This beautiful and strong sentence rules out liberty-as-a-means from values and from possibilities: It has to be understood as a borderline case for the most basic of liberties.

Choosing between liberty and welfare is a standard topic of moral tales. In La Fontaine's fable *The Dog and the Wolf*, the hungry but free wolf pities the dog who is well fed and yet bears the mark of a collar. A country took as its motto and anthem "Let us prefer liberty in poverty to plenty in slavery."[18] A most vivid illustration is René Clair's film *A nous la liberté* where a wealthy manager prefers the liberty of poverty. Buddhist wisdom enjoins abandoning material wealth so as to free oneself from "attachments." The general upshot is that liberty is not always valued only as a means for what it enables one to obtain.

But is this rational, or even reasonable? Liberty is by nature a means, a possibility of action. Can one sensibly take a means as an end value? This is indeed possible for a means of individuals and an end value of a conception of justice, as a mere sharing of responsibility between the individuals and the policy that implements redistributions or respects or protects the "spontaneous" allocation. However, the above remarks suggest that liberty can also be valued in its own right by the concerned individuals, who attribute to it an intrinsic, final, or end value,[19] sometimes with priority over other values, and this may be a reason for a theory of justice to value this freedom. But the value of a means is a priori only derived from what is done with it, and is thus subordinate to its use. Attributing an end value to a means is thus alienated hypostasis, fetishism. Even if individuals and cultures fall into such irrational illusions (as they commonly do with respect

---

18. This country soon had both extreme poverty and a bloody tyranny (Sékou Touré's Guinea).

19. The analysis and the logic of this intrinsic value of liberty for individuals is worked out in the book *Happiness-Freedom* (Kolm 1982a).

to selves or gods), should rational social ethics follow them on this ground?

Indeed, from its definition, liberty is *a structure of causality*. Now causality is a matter of fact which a priori lacks the intrinsic desirability or the transcendence on which values can be based.

Furthermore, whereas individuals often like and desire freedom, *they also commonly dislike and shun it*. They have a number of possible reasons for this. One is constituted by the various *costs of choosing*, such as obtaining information, considering all of the alternatives and reasons, weighing and comparing them, and deciding. A second reason is the deeper "*anguish of choice*," analyzed, for instance, by Kierkegaard and particularly by Sartre, which can be a deeply disagreeable sentiment, even a paralyzing one. A third reason relates to *responsibility*, which is sometimes valued and desired but is also sometimes disliked and shunned, and which can be an important cause of the anguish of choice. One can feel oppressed by a sentiment of having to choose or (and) of responsibility, as much as by a sentiment of helplessness and impotence elicited by the opposite absence of possible options. Moreover an individual may prefer not having to choose in order to avoid others' judgment about his choice (this may be related to responsibility). An individual may also prefer to leave his choice to someone else who, he assumes, has more information or wisdom. And so forth.

Then the attribution of an intrinsic or end value to such an undesired liberty is directly contrary to individuals' "welfare" in a broad sense of the term. These reasons for preferring to have less liberty, however, should hardly be a match when the reasons in favor of the considered freedom rest on the basic entities of existence, being, or indeed often dignity, to be presented shortly.

These various aspects and values of liberty should therefore first of all be disentangled.

The Various Reasons for Valuing Freedom

We now consider the various reasons why a liberty can be valuable for an individual (in his own view, in the view of other persons, or in a conception of social ethics or justice). We first note, as we will see again below, that the unavoidable word "means" can have various extensions and thus can be ambiguous. The following reasons for valuing freedom begin by going, in a sense, from those most commonly manifest to the deepest:

1. Liberty is a means to obtain the desired consequences of the act it permits, in the most direct and restricted sense.

2. Liberty is a means for exercising one's capacities for movement, action, choice, reason, decision, or willpower, as training for future action.

3. Liberty is a necessary condition for exercising one's capacities for action and choice for any motive, including for no further purpose. This has the value of actualizing the existence of these capacities. Liberty thus permits *activity*, which Aristotle, for instance, sees as the most necessary condition for *eudaemonia*, flourishing or deep happiness.

4. In its most common conception, which is the most relevant here, liberty is *choice* and (*intentional*) *action*. Indeed, first, liberty permits choice and choice requires liberty. But liberty also requires choice which constitutes its actualization, when choice is understood in a broad sense including choosing "inaction" and letting chance choose. Second, liberty is also a priori necessary for (*intentional*) *action*, since a coincidence of intention with a strict external necessity would be fortuitous (or would be the particular spiritual attitude of wilful acceptance). And liberty also requires action sufficiently broadly understood (including resting quiet and delegating action). An "agent" is a purposeful actor. Hence liberty is necessary for *choice* and *agency*, and therefore for the *existence of man as chooser and agent*.

5. Indeed liberty strictly defined by reason and intention, which can be elaborate, is characteristic of man. A deep philosophical tradition even makes it the essence of man (for example, "my freedom is not an added quality or a *property* of my nature: it exactly is the matter of my being," "freedom is the being of man"[20]—this tradition includes Rousseau, Kant, Hegel, the philosophies of existence, and others). In the classical terms "liberty," the essenceless existence, *is the essence of*

---

20. Jean-Paul Sartre, *Being and Nothingness*, IV-1-1.

man's existence.[21] Unfreedom thus is denial of humanity and reduction of the person to a thing, or *reification* (since the emphasis is on the acting and choosing being rather than on the sentient being). This constitutes the basis of the *existential and ontological values of liberty.* It is the first level of these values, the second being self-creation, to be considered shortly. Then, since freedom requires choice (in the broad sense), it is responsible for this predicament of man, who is inherently "forced to be free" and to choose. Yet certain freedoms are more important than others in this respect (they are basic rights and the opportunities provided by the satisfaction of basic needs; see chapters 4 and 11).

6. Liberty makes the chooser's will and the agent's capacities take place among the *causes* of the world. It thus makes man *a creator.* This in turn makes him *accountable* for a part of what exists—hence it makes him "count for something." It also possibly makes him *responsible* for it (see chapter 9).

7. In particular, liberty makes man *choose* and in part *cause his own acts and situation.* He can also in this way train, and modify or create his own capacities of all kinds. In particular, at the deep level of moral and mental freedom, he can choose or change his own end values (choice of a morals and in particular Rousseau's and Kant's autonomy), desires (Buddhism), or tastes (Hellenistic philosophies). In all these respects and in all possible degrees, liberty is self-choice, self-determination, self-causation, and self-creation. This is often seen as the deepest essence of man, his basic *ontology.*

8. Being a condition for existence, choice, action, and responsibility, liberty is also a condition for *awareness, respect,* and *esteem of oneself,* for *dignity* and for *pride.*

9. For the same reasons liberty is a major condition for counting in others' eyes, for eliciting their consideration in the form of expectations and interest, appreciation, respect, or esteem, or on the contrary fear, hostility, contempt, or hatred, in any case for having *social existence.*

---

21. Note that liberty, the pure existence (and also a priori void) *has* no essence but *is* essence . . . of man's existence.

10. The various types of liberty provide particular important reasons for valuing it. The first distinctions among liberties refer to the nature of that which is chosen and of the constraints. With respect to the nature of that which is chosen, the existential-ontological value is the reason for the unconditional priority of the respect of basic rights and the satisfaction of basic needs. As regards the constraints, a main distinction considers whether they are chosen by some other persons' will, or not. In the former case unfreedom is *dependency*, and the corresponding liberty, nondependency, is independence when it is sufficiently wide. Strong dependency is *domination* by the other. It is *subjection* when it uses threat or force (with the limit case of slavery when the whole domain is submitted to the will of one or several other individuals). Dependency can be mutual or unilateral, balanced or unbalanced. Excessive unilateral or unbalanced dependency may be particularly detrimental to dignity and personhood (although in other cases dependency provides the "honor of serving") —in addition to the common unpredictability of the other individual's acts, wishes or whims, and hence of the constraint. As Rousseau remarked, "it is not the nature of things that enrages us, but only bad will." Particular values are thus attached to *nondependency* and *independence*.

11. Liberty and its various effects elicit a spectrum of varied *sentiments* which entail various preferences. These sentiments can be of the free person or of other persons. Preferences concerning the aims that freedom allows one to obtain go without saying. However, one can also enjoy liberty per se, the activity it permits, the exercise of choice, or the consequences of liberty with respect to responsibility, importance, sense of existence, dignity, self-respect, others' views of one's choices and actions, independence, mastery of oneself, and so on. The lack of these benefits elicits opposite sentiments. Certain of these sentiments are very direct. Feeling free, being free, the pure sentiment of liberty, can produce serenity, joy, exhilaration or elation. Unfreedom can produce, on the contrary, painful sentiments of helplessness or unimportance. Furthermore the same aspect or consequence of liberty can produce both positive and negative sentiments, alternatively and even jointly: Choice can provide excitement and a sense of importance, or embarrassment, complication, and anguish; responsibility can be a burden or a dignity.

Priorities and Happiness

The foregoing reasons for valuing liberty constitute a rather complex set. Two major groups of reasons stand out, however. They are, respectively, freedom as a means to obtain the result of the chosen acts, and freedom as a condition for human existence and being, that is, the *instrumental* and the *ontological-existential* values of liberty, or *freedom for having* and *freedom for being*.

By its existential-ontological value, liberty is a condition for human existence, and for this reason it has often been seen as having *priority* over other values, including other reasons for freedom, and "welfare." This is what is expressed by the positions noted above, such as Tocqueville's indictment and the other examples. The cry "liberty or death," for instance, manifests this transcendence: It could not be uttered for a liberty that would only be a means for some extra enjoyment of life. Freedom as a condition for human existence has "a value but no price" or, in Kant's terms, "dignity" and no price. This applies particularly to the specific "basic liberties," that is, the essential Rights of Man and of the Citizen, whose priority is implied by their being declared "inalienable" (see chapter 4).

Finally, respectful justice can a priori be based on two types of individuals' values: those in the category of liberty and those of the family of happiness. These two groups have a number of relations between themselves. First of all, the comparison of happiness appears formally as the limiting and borderline case of the comparison of liberties—where comparison means that an individual has as much or more than another—when all means are jointly included in the comparison, including the capacities for being satisfied (this question will be considered again below; see chapters 6, 7, 8, and 9). More straightforwardly, all the above-mentioned reasons to value liberty can elicit the satisfaction or the happiness of the freer individual. We have also noted various reasons why an individual might be unhappy with liberty or with more liberty and might prefer to be less free. However, the anguish of choice and the fear of responsibility tend to vanish when more freedom in the category of mental liberty is obtained.[22]

---

22. See the analysis in *Happiness-freedom* (Kolm 1982a).

Therefore freer practically implies happier if the scope of the increased freedom is sufficiently broad. Conversely, the individual would normally like his dissatisfaction, pain, or unhappiness to be repelled or removed: The existence of these sentiments thus constitutes for him a binding constraint, and hence the alleviation of these feelings constitutes a liberation. Moreover certain mental states, such as satisfaction, happiness, and in particular the resulting serenity, are common necessary conditions for conscious free actions, in freeing the individual from more or less obsessional desires, dissatisfactions, tensions, or pains,[23] just as, on the contary, a certain dissatisfaction or unhappiness may spur rational and wilful action. To conclude, one cannot a priori and in general oppose an ethic of happiness and an ethic of liberty, eudemonism (or, perhaps, "welfarism"[24]) and eleutherism. Both values are inextricably tied by many links. The distinction can only refer to particular liberties, means, or problems.

The Three Types of Liberty with Regard to Action

Liberty can be of many types, of many things, and can have many manifestations. However, *the modern theory of justice is first of all structured by the following action-centered classification of liberties in the broad sense.* This basic classification is essential for the analysis of these theories, and it will underlie most of what follows.

An *action* can be seen as a set of *acts* using *means* for an *aim*. The acts, the aim, and the relation from the former to the latter constitute the *process*.

The *means* considered here can be *capacities* which are by definition part of the agent; *tools; social power*, a possibility to influence other agents' acts by force or inducement (that is, against their will or thanks to it); in particular *income* or *wealth* which are purchasing power— that is, power to induce without persuading—which can obtain voluntary services or transfers from other agents through exchange; other property. An action always uses some means, since the agent's will can influence the world only through certain capacities of the agent (to

---

23. The relations between freedom and happiness, and their causes, structures and consequences, constitute a notable part of the book *Happiness-Freedom*.

24. The term was coined by Hicks (1959).

begin with, his willpower, and others). The aim can in particular be a product or output.[25]

The constraints on an action can therefore bear on the *availability of the means*, on the *acts* given the means, or on the *aim* given the acts and means, that is, on the aim or product itself, or on its relation to the acts or to the means that cause it. Looser or fewer constraints of these types respectively constitute more *means-freedom* or just *means*, *act-freedom* and *aim-freedom*. Note that the understanding of "means" is restricted here so as not to include act-freedoms (and aim-freedoms). The corresponding act-freedom and aim-freedom together constitute *process-freedom*.

A social ethic that advocates a liberty is by definition a "liberalism." Hence there are act liberalism, aim liberalism, process liberalism which is both of the former, and means liberalism.[26]

These concepts underlie and structure the theory of justice as follows: full act-freedom, justified by the existential value of liberty, leads to the human and civil rights (basic rights or liberties) and their priority; then distributive justice is determined by choices and balances between process-freedom and equal means-freedom.[27] Act- and process-freedoms, however, are limited by others' basic liberties for a moral reason (forbidding direct violence).

2.5   The Structure of Means and Ends

When a theory of justice takes as its end values certain possibilities of a justiciable agent, this implies that it finds both *irrelevant for actions*

---

25. We have noted that the aim can be intermediary or final for the agent. It can also be more or less inherent in the act, as with the sensation provided by an activity, or with following a norm or obeying a duty (the aim can also be seen as having followed the norm or obeyed the duty).

26. "Liberalism" in former English and in all other European languages means full process liberalism. Modern English made the term shift toward requiring more means.

27. Means-freedom is akin to Marx's "real liberties." Note that "positive freedom," as introduced by Isaiah Berlin (1958, 1969), is something completely different as it refers to mental freedom, rational selection of one's own principles of choice, "autonomy" in the Rousseau-Kant sense, and to constraints imposed on people for the sake of a conception of liberty deemed to be superior in the name of rationality, of a deep Social Contract (see chapter 3), or of any other view. Berlin's opposite "negative freedom" consists of act-freedom and certainly also of a part of process-freedom (possibly all of it).

justified by justice, and *legitimate* when this justice is actualized, together *what this agent does* with these possibilities, the *other means* he uses in this process, the resulting *outcome*, and the *other causes* of this outcome (other aspects of social ethics and morals can evaluate these outcomes, acts, or means, and other aspects of this conception of justice, if it is purivalued, can attach to other means or outcomes). These possibilities thus define a respected "private sphere" of this agent's actions and appreciations (this sphere may, however, include influences and interactions among agents, in exchange and otherwise). These "other means" of the agent can a priori be of any kind, including the particular (and important) capacities for appreciation and for being satisfied with which he derives satisfaction from the world. In an extreme case, the theory of justice takes as end values individuals' satisfactions (which can have a variety of psychological forms).[28]

The instrumental variables of justice are chosen among the causes of any type of its end values. They can in particular be other possibilities of the agents that they use in creating the end values of justice among their final or intermediate aims or as other consequences of their actions. Instrumental variables are sometimes necessarily not the end values themselves—in particular, satisfaction or happiness cannot be directly implemented. The ideal equality entailed by the rationality of justice obtains for individualized variables defined in such a way that the remaining relevant characteristic parameters are the same across the justiciables. These variables can be individualized end values of justice. For other situational (and in particular instrumental) variables of justice, the relations among their just allocations to the various justiciables depend on the relations of these variables to the end values. They must be equal for equal end values only when there are certain identities or symmetries in the latter relations. In other cases they must compensate particular effects that may intervene (in particular from certain acts or characteristics of the agents).

The relations between the means and ends of the justiciable individuals, on the one hand, and of the social ethic, on the other, can present all the logically possible patterns. The rational ideal equality of individualized items that are end values of a respectful conception

---

28. Such as happiness, pleasure, well-being, sense of achievement, or relief in lower levels of pain, insatisfaction, disappointment, and so on.

Table 2.1
Means and ends

Individual ╲ Social	Means	Ends
Means	A priori unequal liberties, $L_i \neq L_j$	Equal liberties, "Equity," $L_i = L_j$
Ends	Utilitarianism, "social welfare," $\sum u_i$ max	End "Justice" or "Practical Justice," $u_i = u_j$, or max min u_i

of justice can apply to both the means or freedoms, and the aims or satisfactions, of the individuals. The questions raised by the *definition* of equality or of the appropriate egalitarian second-bests for these two kinds of variables will be considered in chapters 7 (they are *Justice* and *Equity*) and others. Furthermore both individuals' means or freedoms, and aims or satisfactions, can also be means for the social ethic. This relation can be either instrumental or conceptual. Instrumentally, individuals' means and aims direct and induce individuals' actions and hence influence their consequences evaluated by the judgment. Conceptually, a social ethical end might a priori be, for instance, "social income" or "social welfare" that aggregates (for instance adds) individuals' incomes or "welfares." These individuals' means or ends are then to be seen as means of the social ethic. Such aggregate ethics are neither direct theories of justice (they are indirect ones, though) nor ethically individualistic. They are in part epistemically individualistic, but, in the case of "social welfare," the general epistemic status is marred by the ambiguity of the term welfare (we are not told what part of evaluation by the concerned individuals it contains), by the general impossibility of making sense of the operation of addition (see chapter 14 on utilitarianism), and by the general problems of meaning, ethics, consistency and rationality raised by the concept of "social welfare" (see chapters 14 and 15). Table 2.1 summarizes these possibilities: L_i represents a liberty or means, and u_i a "utility" or end, of individual i.

3 The General Structure of Justice

The abstract and general principles outlined in the first two chapters are now applied to the essential actual questions of justice, and notably of distributive justice. This provides a general overview of the field of the simple theories of justice. Section 3.1 focuses on the most important (by far) of the issues of distributive and economic justice: the allocation of the benefits stemming from the human resources or capacities. Section 3.2 then presents an overview of all the main questions, which the rest of this book will analyze. Finally, a couple of synoptic tables show the position of the main theories or principles that have been proposed with respect to the major issues.

3.1   The Just Allocation of the Human Resource

Natural Liberty or Solidarity

The main question of distributive justice is the allocation of the benefits from the human resources or individuals' capacities. The application of the foregoing analyses to this issue provides an illuminating overview and comparison of the main simple theories of the just distribution, of their claims, and of their shortcomings with the respective remedies, and it also provides the actual solution of the problem of global distributive justice. One particular view may lead one to reject the very concept of distributive justice, but it may also be seen as one of the possible solutions (this will be "full process liberalism"). A capacity is attached to an individual (although complementarities of various types among capacities of various individuals are a major feature of the question). From an economic point of view, an individual's activity is either the direct satisfaction of his ends, called consumption, or it is production (which thus is the indirect satisfaction of one's ends or the satisfaction of other persons' ends). Hence individuals' capacities can be divided into productive capacities, used in production, and consumptive capacities, used in consumption (the question of whether they are intrinsically different or similar capacities, or the same capacities in different uses, will be discussed in chapter 6).

Capacities certainly constitute the main resource. Labor income in general, including wage income, which remunerates services from productive capacities, commonly account for some 80 percent of GNP in modern economies. If, moreover, the value of all capital is allocated to the primary resources used to produce it (labor and nonhuman natural resources), in historical perspective, this proportion commonly exceeds 97 percent.[1] In addition the rules of allocation of the other, nonhuman, natural resources relates to characteristics of the individuals that are in fact often capacities or other means obtained from them: allocation according to productive capacities and other means, either directly as a principle of best use, or indirectly through "first occupancy"; allocation according to the particular capacities used in reaching a collective agreement; allocation according to particular needs that are consumptive capacities or liabilities; allocation for either valorizing or, on the contrary, compensating, productive or consumptive capacities. Finally, consumptive capacities are no less important than productive capacities. They include final needs as assets or liabilities, various capacities to appreciate or to make sense of life, and indeed a number of intimate elements of personhood. A "handicap" is a relative lack of a capacity.

All capacities are, by nature, an integrated part of their holder. In addition, consumptive capacities serve only their holder, whereas productive capacities can a priori also provide benefits to other individuals.[2] Of course capacities cannot be transferred (this would be transplant), but the benefits from productive capacities can be transferred, and all capacities can be more or less compensated for by other allocations. The ethical question of the allocation of capacities or of the benefits derived from them therefore is, practically, that of the allocation of the product of productive capacities, and of possible dependences of any allocation on individuals' capacities (notably consumptive ones).

However, forced transfers of product or in order to compensate for capacities, or appropriation of others' services, constitute infringements on process-freedom (either on act-freedom in the case of forced labor or on aim-freedom in the other cases). Therefore the prima facie equality required by rationality (see chapter 2) can be applied in two possible ways: equality either of the benefits derived from capacities or

---

1. See Kolm 1985a.

2. This contrast constitutes a simplification that bypasses various aspects of direct personal relations (an individual's capacities for love, friendship, or other personal relations can be very important for certain others).

of the liberty to use one's capacities (as process-freedom). Different solutions can be applied to capacities of different types, if this is justified (or all capacities might be ideally amenable to only one of these principles). This issue constitutes the major and central question of distributive justice in the whole of society.

The opposition between these two principles is often presented as an antinomy between "equality" and "liberty." This rather superficial presentation is more confusing than enlightening, since the equal sharing of the benefits provided by a resource (by transfers of product, rights to product or compensations) constitutes an equal means-freedom, and the other solution is equal process-freedom.

The process-freedom solution allocating the benefits of a capacity to its holder raises a number of issues. Its acceptable justification rests on both a view of liberty and an emphasis on a conception of the individual's self, and on a discounting of the value of solidarity (or its relegation to the field of voluntary transfers). It constitutes an extension to process-freedom of the core and irrefutable justification of act-freedom by respect for agency (this is the very extension implied by the critical seventeenth and last article of the 1789 Declaration of Rights). This allocation relates to the classical concept of the "natural", which has itself various dimensions: The individual is entitled to his capacity because it has been allocated to him by "nature" (a secularized version of a theological argument); the capacity "belongs by nature" to its holder, that is, the factual belonging entails the normative one; the capacity also belongs to "the nature" of the individual (a conception of the self); and this allocation is "natural" (in a particular individualistic sense, since it may not be unnatural that I should help my neighbor and should be helped by the law to perform this duty).[3] Hayek's "spontaneous order" also implies this allocation. The various references to "nature" and the "natural" as a legitimizing device may yield different results, however, with very important discrepancies. For instance, it is *in the nature* of a capacity to be attached to an individual, but certain of these capacities were provided to the individual by

---

3. Note that classical deep contractarianism (that is, theories of the Social Contract; see below) opposes this legitimization by the "natural," since it sees the "nature of nature" as its being overcome by society, possibly in compliance with a Social Compact. Hence the present use of the "natural" follows, rather, views in the style of Locke's.

"nature" (say, his genetic abilities) whereas, by contrast, he received the others from culture, education, training, experience, and so on. The difference is crucial because the education, motivation, and information provided by the family and the social environment standardly account for the largest part of the inequalities of income and status, and this distinction is relevant for both income and education policies (see chapter 6). The word "natural" will, however, be used presently in its larger former sense.

By contrast, the opposite solution disregards the original or "natural" assignment of the capacity. It considers the capacity as a common resource whose benefits should be prima facie equally shared (equivalently, the cost of a handicap should ideally be equally shared).

The classification of each specific type of capacity either into the common pool or into the domain where the "natural" allocation is respected is made by the actual societies, and can be made by moral theories, according to a number of possible criteria that will be analyzed in the following chapters. These principles rest on the conceptions of solidarity, liberty, natural rights and natural duties, needs, community and the corresponding social entity, individuality and the self, balance between egoism and morality and between the self-centered and the objective points of view, responsibility, dignity, charity and compassion, reciprocity, incentive and efficiency, and so on. One can foresee that common views (those that object to income inequality) will see a difference between productive and consumptive capacities in this respect, notably because the services from consumption are essentially used by the individual himself, an individual's income depends also on others' demand and on their competing or complementary productive capacities, preferences and tastes are particularly integrated in the self, and indeed they define the very use the individual makes of his freedoms and means.

Hence this classification also defines the *great polar simple theories of justice*, which respectively either endorses or rejects the "natural" allocation of *all* capacities, or rejects it for productive capacities but endorses it for consumptive capacities.[4] These three polar theories have, as respective ideals (prima facie), *process-freedom*, equal *incomes*

---

4. The fourth case, which would be the endorsement of the "natural" allocation for the productive capacities but not for the consumptive capacities, is not really available

or *consumption*, and equal *satisfactions* (a concept that will be discussed in chapter 7). Each of these three polar views (1) has problems with Pareto-efficiency, (2) has solutions for these problems (respectively presented in Kolm 1971, 1985, and, for the two types of problems of the intermediate solution, 1973a–1987f–1991d–1993d–1993g–1995a–1995c–1996b for multidimensional equality, and 1966b–1991d–1993d–1993g–1995f–1996b for the disincentive effect), (3) has given rise to famous but logically problematic formulations because of the omission of crucial features.

Table 3.1 summarizes the issues, which will be discussed below and in the following chapters.

These three theories span the space of individualistic theories of distributive justice. The social optimum in any large and complex society necessarily has elements of all three (since one can find specific topics in which one principle and not the others obviously has to be followed). Yet the specific and detailed structure and combination, and even the aggregate proportions, have to be determined. These aggregate proportions can be represented as a point in a triangular diagram that indicates what fractions of the social output is allocated according to *work* (and hence notably to productive capacities), to *needs* (satisfaction), and to a principle of *equal* sharing of production and consumption. (This diagram bears a relation to the diagram concerning economic processes in Kolm 1984b, p. 72.) Each actual society and each conception of ideal distributive justice is represented as a point in this diagram. Possible ideals for a society depend on the level of economic development, among other things. Low global income entails a higher share for the support of the satisfaction of basic needs. Modern developed societies redistribute between one-fourth to one-half of earned income, and this spans a reasonable domain of choice (the status of social insurance, public goods, and various other questions should be considered here, and this issue will be considered further below).

---

since the evaluation of consumption rests on the resulting "satisfaction" which depends on both consumptive capacities and other means which result from production (the compensation for consumptive capacities alone would have to refer to counterfactual —not actual—individuals' consumption and would depend on the arbitrary reference consumption chosen; furthermore this case has no neat and common possible justifications as the other polar cases have).

Table 3.1
The three polar cases of distributive justice

Capacities – Consumptive – Productive	Natural Natural	Allocation Natural Equalize	Equalize Equalize
End value equalizand	*Process-freedom*	*Income, consumption*	*Satisfaction*
Principle	Full Process-Liberalism	Equal consumption or income	Needs or ends full Justice
Cause of inefficiency	Market failures	1. Multidimensional equality 2. Disincentive	Equality
Solution for efficiency	*Liberal Social Contract*, liberal Public Economics (Kolm, 1985)	1. *Efficient super-equity* (multidimensional maximim; Kolm 1973, 91, 93) 2. *Fixed-duration income equalization* (Kolm 1966, 91, 93)	*Basic needs* in *Practical Justice* (leximin in fundamental satisfaction, Kolm 1971)
Incomplete or irrational theories	Private full process-liberalism: – Locke – The 1789 Declaration – Classical "political economy" – Nozick	Equalizand as: (1) Consumption goods (Tobin 1970) (2) Spheres of justice (Weber and Walzer 1983) (3) Primary goods (Rawls 1971) (4) Resources (Dworkin 1983)	Utilitarianism, "social welfare"
Omissions	Market failures	– The inefficiency of multidimensional equality: (1), (2) – Exchange capacities: (2), (3), (4) – The ethical value of prices: (2), (3)	The rationality of equality

Full Process Liberalism and Practical Justice

The *endorsement of all the natural allocation of capacities* constitutes *full process liberalism* (see chapter 5). This is the historically original, founding and central theory of modernity, the means-individualistic social theory, the resource-based and liberty-based justification of the free market. This view was however conceived as purely private full process liberalism, which bypasses the existence of genuine market failures (which, in particular, impair Pareto-efficiency). The application of this social ethic to the case of failures of the markets, or of wider agreements, leads to the theory of the Liberal Social Contract (Kolm 1985a, 1987b,c, 1991e; see chapters 5, 12, and 13 below). The allocations of capital and of nonhuman natural resources are related to those of capacities by the consideration of production in time for capital, and by a number of possible devices for natural resources (see Kolm 1985a, ch. 10, 1986c).

In the opposite view, no resource is a priori due to any specific individual. This applies notably to all capacities (and in particular to consumptive capacities). Hence the prima facie or ideal resulting justice is an *equal satisfaction of individuals' ends or needs*, from the rationality of equality (see above). Whatever its definition, this equality is commonly inefficient (Pareto-wise) in large and complex societies for a number of reasons analyzed below and in chapter 6, so this equality is replaced by the second-best end-egalitarian (or need-egalitarian) principle of first best catering for the neediest or least satisfied persons. This maximin can be extended, if necessary, to a leximin, that is: if, when the neediest are best taken care of, there remains some possible choice, then best take care of the second neediest, and so on. This is *Practical Justice* presented and analyzed in Kolm 1971 (the corresponding *Justice* would be the equality). More exactly, the structure of the principle is the priority ordering: Best satisfy the least satisfied (or neediest); minimize their number; best satisfy the second least satisfied; minimize their number; and so on. In other words, between two states, prefer the one that provides the highest level to the first lowest satisfaction that differs between them. This principle is meaningful only if one can define the relevant least satisfied or neediest individuals, which is unfortunately often not too difficult in practice in large societies (and they often remain the same persons when the policy is applied). This question will be taken up in chapter 7 and the particular analysis of needs is the topic of chapter 11. Practical Justice is particularly relevant when certain basic needs are not satisfied. There also exist certain more balanced comparisons of individuals' pairwise preferences (and not only of levels of satisfaction), but their relevance is restricted to occasional cases of local justice, to microjustice rather than to macrojustice (see chapter 14).

However, a notable literature has considered all resources as relevant for defining the social optimum (and hence, indirectly, justice), and in particular, among these resources, all capacities and notably the individuals' capacities for "welfare" (that is, for deriving welfare from a given consumption), and it tried to *add*, or otherwise *aggregate*, individuals' welfare into a "*social welfare*" to be maximized. When it adds individuals' welfares or utilities (utilitrianisms), this literature misses the points of both the rationality of equality if individuals' welfares are end values and the general lack of meaning of cardinal utilities (see chapters 12 and 14). And when it assumes or requires *a priori* a "social welfare function" to be maximized, this literature raises a number of other logical issues, including inconsistencies with the reason for equality (see chapter 15).

The spirit of the opposition between the two extreme columns of the preceding table, if not its detailed analysis, is an old story. One can for instance read this in Blanqui's famous opposition between each receiving "according to" either "his work" or "his needs" once each has given "according to his capacities" (these two possibilities define respectively "socialism", free from capitalist "exploitation"—see chapter 9—, and "communism"; Marx helped make this distinction famous). Of course, if the joint full satisfaction of all needs is not possible, "according to one's needs" has to be understood as "as a function of the individuals' needs" (from rationality, it is the same function for all the individuals—a "functional equality"), which means something like providing the "same degree of satisfaction" of the individuals' needs (needs-Justice).

Lower Inequalities in Consumptions or Incomes; Efficient Super-Equity and Fixed-Duration Income Equalization

The middle column of table 3.1 also corresponds to common views. Its principle inspires, for instance, advocacies to diminish inequalities in the distribution of incomes. However, if, in the economic process "production → consumption → satisfaction," one takes out consumptive capacities, that which remains is the consumed bundle of consumption goods. Equality in consumption goods is indeed often advocated for goods that satisfy basic needs, or for certain scarce and directly enjoyed resources, and it is for all consumption goods by Tobin (1970). The irrelevance of consumptive capacities for justice has been recently elaborately argued under different forms by two philosophers: Rawls (1971) who discards individuals' "plans of life," and in more detail, Dworkin (1981) who discusses tastes (both admitted, in brief answers, exceptions respectively for severe handicaps and for certain physical capacities). Rawls advocates an ideal equality in "primary goods" which are "income, wealth, power, positions, and self-respect" (or the means to it)—this ideal equality is replaced by a maximin as an answer to disincentive effects (see chapters 6 and 8). Dworkin advocates an equal sharing of productive resources (see chapter 9). Finally, Walzer (1983) is also on the same line when, after Max Weber, he advocates—or rather argues that people's common sense of justice requires—specific equality within each of various "spheres of justice," which refer to final consumption or intermediary means, or both (material life, presumably with income as variable, and education, politics, justice, etc.).

Now, these proposals face three conceptual problems, separately or jointly.

First, an equal allocation in each of several consumption goods for several individuals is generally dominated by other allocations preferred by everybody, because of the differences in preferences (tastes, needs): It is not Pareto-efficient.

Second, an individual can benefit from resources that are not consumption goods only by exchanging or transforming them; he can benefit from his income only by buying consumption goods with it; he can benefit from his "power" only by using it; and he can also exchange consumption goods, which may be a way of solving the problem of the inefficiency of their equal allocation. These actions use personal capacities, such as capacities for exchange, dealing on markets or bargaining. Taking the considered items as end values of justice implies the endorsement of the natural allocation of these capacities. But these capacities are not consumptive capacities. They indeed constitute the productive capacities typical of exchange or market economies, and they are de facto very important for the production of all economies with an important division of labor. The direct transformation of goods also uses productive capacities. Now, the considered social ethical positions claim to consist of the endorsement of the natural allocation of only consumptive capacities including tastes, preferences and liabilities due to personal needs and aims, and of the ideal equalization of the benefits from all other resources. They thus a priori lack consistency. And the inequalities in exchange, market or bargaining capacities can produce large differences in the resulting wealth and consumption, as observation shows, especially if one considers the cumulative effects of these inequalities in time. This question will be further considered in chapters 6, 8 and 9.

Third, in addition, the use of incomes implies that of prices for computing them, and the ethical value of the prices used in normative considerations of incomes should be ascertained:[5] Are these prices the relevant "just prices"?

The solution of this central case consists of an efficient second-best egalitarian allocation of consumption goods, which can be left to the individuals' choices with given just incomes. This solution, *efficient super-equity*, rests on the comparison of the inequalities of multi-dimensional distributions.[6] It demands that no more equal allocation be preferred by one individual, and no allocation be preferred by all individuals; that is to say, any further equalization is opposed by everyone, and Pareto-efficiency, in admitting indifference for certain individuals. There result specific limits to the dispersion of individuals' incomes, that depend on which goods are desired or consumed by several individuals and which are not (in particular, an individual's

---

5. A fourth issue concerns the individuals being concerned by other individuals' consumptive capacities, tastes, needs or demands, in relation to their own and also to the relative bargaining capacities, because of the effects of these characteristics on the possibilities the individuals face in exchanges and markets. This will be discussed in chapters 8 and 9.

6. See Kolm 1973b, 1975b, 1977a, and chapter 10 below.

leisure can be consumed by this individual only, it is "individual-specific" in both nature and use). The classical "egalitarian" ideal of the equalizing redistribution of earned incomes is indeed a possible solution, which provides a possible rational justification to this view, but much larger dispersions are also admissible: This permits one both to avoid inefficiency-generating disincentive effects, and to use other criteria, notably the usufruct of a part of one's own productive capacities (see chapters 6 and 9).[7]

Finally, policies that aim at lowering income inequalities commonly use taxes (and subsidies) based on *earned* (and other) incomes, and they achieve only partial equalization. Such a tax is also based on the duration of labor, and the resulting inefficiency and disincentive is a classical topic in economics. Scholars explain the choice of this tax base, instead of "inelastic" productive capacities, by a lack of information on the latter. This is short of convincing, since wage rates that measure these capacities (for given effort) can often be either observed or derived from total earned income and the duration of labor. The basic reason for taking earned income as redistributive base is, rather, that productive capacities are conceived as capacities *used* in production (a full discussion will be presented in chapter 6). Furthermore the imperfect equalization is not only the consequence of this disincentive effect. It also represents ethical views in between the two first polar cases of full process liberalism (no redistributive tax) and ideal equalization of the product of productive capacities. The policy that best represents this ethic consists in fully equalizing incomes earned during a fixed duration, and in leaving untaxed the extra earnings. This policy is, in addition, efficient with respect to the duration of labor. For the extreme case of full process liberalism, this duration vanishes. The redistribution in present-day western developed countries corresponds to a duration of equalization of 10 to 18 hours per week (but with a different and wasteful structure). This policy is *fixed-duration income equalization*.

---

7. The theory of efficient super-equity is developed in a number of technical papers (Kolm 1973a, 1987f, 1991d, 1993d, 1993g, 1996b).

3.2   The Field of Modern Theories of Justice

Basic Issues and Theories

The distinctions presented structure the field of contemporary theories of justice in the following manner, as *will be explained in detail in the rest of this book* (this point, and the patience it may demand, should be kept in mind all along this section):

1. In the action-centered distinction of liberties presented in chapter 2, with a sufficiently exhaustive definition and a sufficiently precise specification of the means (in the strict sense), liberties of acts, aims, and hence processes, given the means, can be seen as essentially *nonrival* among the agents, in the sense that practically any actual rivalry can be attributed to the allocation of means and managed by it (chapter 4).

2. As a consequence unlimited, *full act-freedom* is possible. The ontological-existential reason leads one to give it priority (chapter 4). This is basically the core Rights of Man and of the Citizen (the rights of the 1789 Declaration *minus* the last one—article 17), Marx's "formal liberties," Rawls's "basic liberties," and so on.

3. *Full process-freedom*, advocated by *full process liberalism*, from its definition allocates the product to its producer, requires unfettered freedom of exchange, justifies bequests as gifts, and allocates natural resources by free collective or individual choice. This leaves no room for another distribution or redistribution of anything. Distribution reduces to retribution (and remuneration), and distributive justice to retributive justice. Chapter 5 will make precise the basic steps of this theory.[8]

This is the central and founding theory of the modern world. It powerfully says: "this is mine because I made it, because I bought it with well-earned money, or because I was given it." A partial application of this theory constitutes the ideology of capitalism (along with efficiency for welfare). This is the "proprietarianism" of Locke (*Second Treatise of Government*), of the full 1789 rights (including the last,

---

8. Its most *complete* exposition is to be found in Kolm 1985a. It is recalled in Kolm 1987c (and 1987b). A new presentation and further applications are in Kolm 1991e.

seventeenth article on "properties"), of nineteenth-century "political economy," and of Nozick (*Anarchy, State and Utopia*, 1974). In an apparent paradox, the most eager critic of this theory, Marx (who calls it "political economy" in accord with nineteenth century usage), makes his central critique, "exploitation," rest on the same premise of the "right to the full product of one's labor"; what Marx in fact does is to accuse this theory of self-contradiction (the difference bears on the unique point of whether the supply of wage labor is free, as it formally is, or is forced since the propertyless worker has no other choice all his life long, notably if he is paid at subsistence wage).

The complete application of this theory extends it to the vicarious public correction of "market failures" according to the putative free exchanges of "*liberal social contracts*" (Kolm 1985a; see chapter 5 below). This finally leads to a notable role for the public sector and notable transfers, which implement the public part of complete full process-freedom.

4. With less than full economic aim-freedom, some (*re*)distribution according to some other criteria becomes possible (thanks to taxation in particular). These criteria necessarily imply either *efficient egalitarianisms* or *social ends*.

5. Social ends provide *indirect distributive justice*. They either aggregate or transcend individual ends or means. Aggregation can be either of individual end-fulfillment into additive or more general "social welfare," or of individual means such as maximizing global income. Transcendence can be for nation, culture, etc.

6. Rational-ethical equality (chapter 2) leads to "egalitarian" theories. These theories are primarily distinguished according to the *items concerning the justiciables* they deem to be *directly ethically relevant*. For respectful justice these items can be either the *fulfilment of agents' ends*, or *means to fulfil* them. This distinguishes *end-egalitarianism* from *means-egalitarianisms*. These are what the study *Justice and Equity* (Kolm 1971) called respectively "Justice" and "Equity," or equality of "utility" and equality of liberty. End-egalitarianism is the particular, extreme and limiting case of means-egalitarianism in which the whole set of means is considered globally relevant for justice (including *all* individual capacities and their situations with respect to those of other persons in markets and society). (The equalities noted here

are direct rational-ethical equality, since spurious equalities can possibly result from other theories—such as social cnds.)

7. Means-egalitarianisms can focus on the following *various items and stages of the economic and social process* (for means in the strict sense of means-freedom):[9]

• *Nonhuman natural resources.*

• (Nonhuman) *capital* (related to exploitation; see *infra* and chapter 9).

• *Bequests.*

• *Human productive capacities*, or their *production and wage income.*

• (*Nonconsumptive*) *resources*. These comprise the four previous items. The first and the fourth one are emphasized by Dworkin (1981) (at least in intention since this author's particular proposals commonly rest in fact on process-freedoms; see chapter 9).

• *Income*. This is the money product of the first four items, equalized for *consumption*.

• Power, or *primary goods* (Rawls's term) that are either the purchasing power to induce provided by *income* (flow) or *wealth* (stock), or other *power* and status provided by social *positions*. These equalities are the most traditional egalitarian ideal, and they are the ideal of Rawls (1971).

• *Consumption goods* in *specific egalitarianism*, either for sharing rare and necessary items, or for all consumption goods (Tobin 1970).

• *Consumptive human capacities* (*correction or compensation*). These can include more or less severe handicaps, all capacities used in consumption except "capacities for being satisfied" (with problems for the distinction), and certain of these "satisfaction capacities."

• *Basic needs*. There should be fulfillment of these needs for all, and hence their equal fulfillment.

• Modification of *human capital* for its capacities used in production or in consumption, achieved by education, training, information or health care.

---

9. "Means," in the larger sense, includes all freedoms (see chapter 2).

• *Equality of opportunity*. This describes various views which emphasize various sets of items including, in order of decreasing frequency: access to positions (nondiscrimination), education at various possible levels (either opportunity for education or education for opportunity in life), various types of information, basic health, bequests, social relations, certain capacities for consumption.

• Benefits from the various institutions in "spheres of justice" (Walzer 1983). They can be political, judicial, strictly economical, educational, or concern health, information, various services, etc.

8. Implementing *unanimous preference* constitutes an equality of power that is supported by important moral, epistemic, and consistency reasons (it is "social liberty").[10] It in particular implies Pareto-efficiency (or, for short, *efficiency*): A state cannot be the best possible if another possible one is preferred by everybody (with possible indifference for some, but not all). The corresponding preferences may, however, be cleaned of nonrespectable aspects (malevolence, malicious envy, etc.).

9. Equality in various possible items may be *impossible*, or *inefficient*, or more generally *rejected* because it opposes certain other aims, which may be other equalities. This can come about for a number of types of reasons, among which the following ones are prominent:

• *Nontransferability and possible noncompensatability of human resources*. Individual capacities are not transferable. Educational, training, and health policies cannot compensate for many of the differences due to genetic endowment and the influence of the family, and equally available public education commonly magnifies rather than compensates these differences. Differences in capacities may be compensated for by transfers of other items. The possible effects of such a transfer depend on the type of the capacity: The compensation may sometimes provide an acceptable substitute to the lack of a capacity, but sometimes these items are too different for this to be possible.

This holds in particular for consumptive capacities. Even if one considers an overall evaluation of his situation by each individual,

---

10. A full analysis of the ethical and epistemic values of unanimity and Pareto-efficiency is provided in Kolm 1993e (see also chapter 6 below).

such as his unidimensional "satisfaction" (or happiness, or "utility" in economists' terms), an individual's lack of consumptive capacities may make him irremediably less "satisfied" than others, irrespective of the amount of transfer or help, and without possible ambiguity in this interpersonal comparison (a question to be discussed in chapter 7).

For productive capacities appreciated for the resulting production (the relative painfulness and interest of labor for different people is akin to consumptive capacities), the ideal equalization can be that of the output. However, there are two possible concepts, which can be seen as two definitions of a productive capacity: Either a productive capacity is a capacity *used* in production, or it is a capacity *usable* in production. This dilemma raises an important problem for theories of justice that take as end value consumption or income and not the allocation of consumptive capacities, and that respect the liberty of labor supply either because it is an act-freedom or because it is necessary for efficiency. Indeed, if the productive capacities considered include both capacities actually used in production and those that could be so used, the ideal equalization leads one to tax, and compensate for, capacities that are not actually used in production, some of which are in fact used in the complementary category which is consumption and nonlabor or leisure. These capacities are included in the availability of mind and body during the corresponding time, with intelligence, strength, energy, attention, imagination, creativity, capacities to relate with other people, and so on. Then, this contradicts the position that "consumptive capacities" are irrelevant for redistributive justice. For this reason, the popular view of justice that objects to the allocation of the full usufruct of his own productive capacities to each individual endorses the other interpretation: The productive capacities considered are the ones that are actually used in production (for instance, if someone who could be a successful manager prefers to spend his time fishing for his pleasure, it would not be considered just that his income tax be based on his potential managerial earnings). Then, however, with free labor supply, the base for the equalizing redistribution includes the decision to work (in time and effort), and if this choice is free it creates the well-known disincentive effects, lower labor (at least for the price or substitution effect), and Pareto-inefficiency which economists have intensively studied. These questions will be considered more closely in chapter 6.

• *Information*. Informational difficulties may lead one to replace a redistributive base that does not depend on individuals' choices, or that depends little on them, by a "proxy" that depends on these choices, or that depends more on them. Then the disincentive effects may forbid the relevant equality or may prevent its efficiency. For instance, fixed-duration income equalization requires that one knows the wage rates, but in certain cases, they are less observable than earned incomes (which depend, in addition, on the duration of labor), or than earned income and labor duration which permit one to compute the wage rates. Then, if only earned incomes provide the observation for estimating the wage rates, a policy ideally based on the wage rates leads to the disincentives and inefficiencies just noted. Similar phenomena may occur for tastes or for various aspects of the individuals' situations.

• *Multidimensional egalitarianism*. Equality in several consumption goods generally implies that other distributions of these goods are preferred by everybody, because of the differences in individual preferences or tastes; that is, this equality is generally not Pareto-efficient (see section 3.1 above, and chapter 6).

• *"Social nonconvexities"*. Certain values are better satisfied by the inequality of individualized (relative to the justiciables) items that are also end valued. For instance, an efficient organization may require a hierarchy, be it for production, defense, or any other aim. Or income inequality leads to higher global free savings (and hence investment, growth, and long-term incomes) or free grants (to the arts, research, or charity), and so on (sec chapter 6).

• *Indivisibilities* of the items (if, for instance, there are only unequal and indivisible goods, equality is impossible if the goods are necessarily allocated, and inefficient if they can be disposed of).

These phenomena may lead to *second-best justice*, and in particular *second-best efficient egalitarianisms*, with, for instance, compromises, or "maximins" (maximize the smallest) such as of "Practical Justice" of *Justice and Equity* (chapter 7), Rawls's "difference principle" (chapter 8), the multidimensional "super-equity," or maximin in liberties (chapter 9 and Kolm 1991c, 1993d,e, g, 1996b).

10. When equality in some items is an ideal but is set aside for any reason, the ethical judgment commonly has to *compare various pat-*

terns of unequal distributions. For goods or incomes, notably, this elicits a particular family of properties, introduced in this ethical discussion in *The Optimal Production of Social Justice* (Kolm 1966a) and abundantly studied since, and which constitute by far the most elaborate contribution of logic to ethics (chapter 10).

11. *Minimal needs satisfaction* and the alleviation of *misery* can justifiably be seen as the most important criterion of justice. Beyond physiology, *basic needs* are cultural, which makes their definition difficult *in abstracto* but easy in practice since the very culture that creates these needs defines them as such (Kolm 1977b) (chapter 11).

12. Marx's influential *theory of exploitation* is marred by his theory of value (that is, of prices), but it can be reconstructed from either of the *inequalities* that characterize the wage relation: *unequal market power* (Robinson), *unequal consumption* (Weizsäcker 1972), *unequal ownership of capital* which both causes exploitation and results from it (Roemer 1982, the most elaborate work), or *unequal liberty* in the cause and especially in the nature of the wage relation (Kolm 1984a) (chapter 9).

13. If all individuals are essentially motivated by their own egoistic interest in the narrowest sense, there is no ethical implementer, and rules can only be the terms of a truce unanimously preferred to open war. The presence of "market failures" (which *neo-"libertarians"* omit) induces the constitution of a political sector which the studies of *"Public Choice"* analyze as a set of exchanges among various narrowly self-interested actors (Buchanan 1975). There is no moral motivation, yet Gauthier (1986) argues that the moral behavior of respecting act- and process-freedom and of following a certain rule for sharing surpluses would emerge (an important topic, yet with proofs and results that should be rectified, qualified, and modified). Furthermore the question of moral implementation offers in fact more possibilities than are considered by the common and opposed simple views about it. In particular, ethical motivations have some influence in common life and in the political process, and, probably more importantly, the fact that individuals care for other people's opinions concerning themselves permits ethical implementation at no cost to the holder of the moral judgment (chapters 12 and 13).

14. The classical concept of *cardinal utility* turns out to be psychologically meaningless (apart from its use for choice in probabilizable uncertainty and for the comparison of weak preferences—that is, of preferences between almost equivalent items). The bargaining or moral concepts that rest on it thus are meaningless, such as strict *utilitarianism* and the *bargaining* principles of Gauthier (Raiffa-Kalai-Smorodinski) and of Nash (which is also problematic for other reasons), except when this is justified by choice in uncertainty (Harsanyi's utilitarianisms). The various *utilitaromorphisms* are either flawed—when they lead to strict utilitarianism—or imprecise, or they are different ideas with a limited scope (chapter 14).

15. *"Social Choice Theory" in the strict sense* (Arrow 1963) can be interpreted as proving that utilitarianism remains impossible even if this cardinality and the addition of utilities are abandoned while all its other properties remain required. Yet this theory requires properties that are not required for the definition of the unique social optimum: Neither a social ordering, nor nonexisting sets of possibilities and of individuals' preferences are a priori needed or relevant. Hence the result of "impossibility" essentially criticizes these unnecessary requirements. Furthermore its proof uses only nonexisting sets of individuals' preferences (and of possibilities). (See chapter 15 and Kolm 1980a, 1986a, 1992a, 1995b, 1996c). Conversely, since this theory seems to take individuals' satisfactions as end values, it is a theory of justice. This implies an ideal of equality (chapter 2); hence it should imply the comparability of individuals' preference orderings (which remain ordinal). Maximin or leximin in these implied comparable preferences replaces equality in the common case where this equality would be impossible or inefficient. Now, while this equality raises notable informational and—in part—conceptual difficulties, pinpointing the most miserable people is unfortunately often too easy in large societies (and they commonly remain the same persons when the social policy is applied). These are the concepts of "fundamental preferences" and Justice and Practical Justice of *Justice and Equity* (see chapter 7). Furthermore liberties, means, or rights are readily and straightfowardly introduced in the theory in incorporating them in the very definition of the "social states" that the theories considers (see chapter 15). Finally, the original general social ethical problem of

"Social Choice" has also had important outgrowths in the analyses of voting processes and of informational implementation.

16. *Social Contracts* are the conceptual instruments of social ethics that define what is just, right or good in society as the result of putative (hypothetical, fictive, implicit) unanimous agreements among the concerned persons.[11] They thus in particular justify public constraints by implicit freedom and free choice. They differ according to the object of their choice, the supposed state of the persons, and the membership of their group. *Total Social Contracts* consider the choice of everything possible (Hobbes, Rousseau, Harsanyi, Rawls, Buchanan, Gauthier), whereas *limited Social Contracts* have a morally restricted field of choice, practically putting aside liberal rights (Locke, Kolm 1985a— Locke's Compact, however, is ultra-restricted to the rights-protecting "minimal government" whose duty is a priori and simply specified, whereas the Liberal Social Contract also concerns the correction, by putative exchange or agreement, of all market and agreement "failures"). Social Contracts also differ according to what they assume about the contracting individuals, and they can be more or less deep or shallow in this respect. In all cases but two, the contractants are the actual persons.[12] The exceptions are the theories of the *Original Position* where the individuals do not know their own actual identity and specific characteristics (Harsanyi, Rawls, with knowledge of the—unassigned—set of actual individuals for Harsanyi, and its ignorance for Rawls—"the thin and the thick veil of ignorance," respectively; see chapter 8). The theory of *"fundamental insurance"* (see chapter 9) constitutes an intermediate case between Social Contracts with actual persons and the theories of the Original Position, which applies to restricted scopes. Furthermore Social Contracts usually are among all people in a large group, while a single "liberal social contract" is a

---

11. A general theory and taxonomy of Social Contracts can be found in Kolm 1985a, ch. 23. Social Contracts have always referred to implicit agreements, but certain modern authors who use this term rather cursorily would probably also apply it to certain actual agreements (Buchanan, Gauthier; this would be the case of an actual constitution for Buchanan—see chapters 12 and 13).

12. In a number of Social Contracts of the seventeenth and eighteenth centuries, the Contract is presented as an actual one among ancestors, but these fables are certainly not meant to be taken literally.

Table 3.2
Social Contracts

Scope / Depth	Total	Restricted
Actual persons	Hobbes Rousseau Buchanan (1975) Gauthier (1986)	Locke Kolm (1985) Fundamental Insurance
Original Position	Harsanyi (1953) Rawls (1971)	

priori only among the people whose actual agreement is prevented by a specific market or agreement failure. Table 3.2 summarizes the main divisions.

Two reasons may lead one to reject certain Social Contracts as moral theories. The first concerns those that *rest exclusively on the threat of force* because violence as a founding device is a priori an immoral concept (and force and therefore threat can be very unevenly distributed). This is the case with Hobbes's Contract, but it does not show because of an implicit symmetry among the individuals—apart from the monarch. This nonmoral threat point is also the one in the Public Choice (Buchanan) Contract, which has to be considered an important descriptive and explanatory device. The second reason concerns *Original Position theories*, as has been suggested above. Indeed, an "original" individual, who may later become embodied into any of the actual ones and is assumed to be only self-interested, chooses to take the risk (for him) of sacrificing one actual individual if this makes it possible to render sufficiently many others sufficiently better-off: this can be very unjust for actual individuals. Such an actual individual cannot be held responsible for the choice of an "original individual" (they are all identical and have the same first best choice), since this original individual "is" any other actual individual as much as he is this specific one, and the interests of the actual individuals are by definition opposed to one another in the problem of distribution which is the topic of the theory (the continuity of self-identity that could ground responsibility is broken). In other words, the method and the phenomenology of choosing justly among the opposed interests of various individuals, which rests on impartiality, objectivity and equality (justified by reason as noted above), basically differ from an egoistic choice under uncertainty. (Chapter 8 will develop these points.)

17. The general necessary principle of *equal liberty* gives rise to a number of important elaborate analyses. The simplest case is that of a liberty that does not depend on others' use of their liberty (independent freedom), in particular when the agent values it only as a means (instrumental freedom). Such freedom is identical to the criterion that "no individual prefers any other allocation to his own," or Equity (see chapter 7).[13] This criterion does not describe a sentiment of envy in the most common use of the term, yet its logic and properties are important in an actual analysis of envy (Kolm 1991b, 1993f, 1995a; see chapter 9). From this simplest case the analysis develops in considering efficient maximin and leximin in liberty when equality is inefficient, and the theory of equal interfering liberties (Kolm 1993e, and chapter 9 below).

18. *Responsibility, merit, deservingness* are the names of the problem of the relation of justice to causality from the will, that is, of *retributive justice*, rather than a priori given solutions (see chapter 9).

19. Since several actual liberties can be chosen, the general principle of equal freedom is amenable to several applications, and, within this general principle, actual justice is *open, dialectical, rational and circumscribed moral polyarchy*. "Rational moral polyarchy" has been explained (chapter 1); "circumscribed" means that its criteria are taken from a specific set (prima facie equal means); "open" means that one cannot provide a priori the full list of the criteria to be used in all possible cases that raise a question of justice; and "dialectical," extending Plato's use of the term in *The Republic*, refers to the method of converging alternative consideration either between rival principles, or between a principle or theory and its parts and elementary components (as with Descartes's *Rules for the direction of the mind*), or

---

13. This criterion per se was proposed by Tinbergen (1946), noticed by Foley (1967), and its properties were analyzed in Kolm (1971) and then in many further studies (reviews showing how these results transform and are enriched when envy is actually taken into account can be found in Kolm 1991b, 1993f, 1995a).

between a principle and its consequences in application (as for Plato or with Rawls's "reflective equilibrium"). The solution of particular problems of justice also has at its disposition a tool-box of a number of precise concepts, criteria, polar cases, and theorems relating criteria and properties. Yet the ultimate choice in each case is obtained by the application of the *method* of justice, which contains both aspects of general procedural rationality, and techniques more specific to this particular domain (Kolm 1990b). This relates to the solution of questions of justice through the correct *discourse* (Perelman), *dialogue* (Ackerman), or *communication* (Habermas, Apel).

20. The outcome has to distinguish between the varied cases of local and specific microjustice, the more general but still specific issues of mesojustice, and the overall simple and general domain of macrojustice including the overall scheme of global distributive justice in addition to the standard priority of basic rights. This optimal overall global distribution is well defined as regards its central issue, and even its specifics for any given type of society, as a mix between the three alternative allocative principles of human resources: process-freedom, income or consumption justice, and the satisfaction of needs and basic needs and the alleviation of deep suffering. Preferences and related entities are *directly* relevant only in cases of deep suffering, of insatisfaction of final basic needs, and in particular situations of local justice. Other basic needs are instrumental (education, health, information, social insertion, etc.). The satisfaction of basic needs and, to a large extent, the alleviation of deep suffering are to have allocative priority. Yet, though this is the most important in necessity, the resources devoted to these needs, and those that should be used for this purpose by public policies, constitute a share of the global output that depends on the economic situation of society, and is rather limited in more or less affluent societies. There, the bulk of the volume of the global distributive issues consists of a division between process-freedom and income equalization. The corresponding policy is best implemented by fixed-duration income equalization. The optimal equalization duration among the possible ones depends on various ethical, economic, and sociological parameters of the society (average level and dispersion of individual productivity, sense of solidarity and justice, cultural homogeneity and sense of community, etc.). There can be different

scopes of redistribution for constituencies of different social and political scope. Finally, the equalization durations are to be chosen between one fourth and one half of labor duration in modern developed nation states (one-third is a standard outcome). Note that fixed-duration income equalization implies a minimal disposable income equal to the average wage during this duration.

3.3 Synoptic Tables

The three following tables summarize main points of the modern question of distributive justice. The detailed explanation of their content will be provided with the study of each theory in the subsequent chapters.

Table 3.3 focusses on the *situation of the social ethical end values in the overall economic process*, starting from primary resources and proceeding to income and other "primary goods," then to "spheres of justice" and specific consumption goods, to individuals' ends, and finally to nonindividualistic "social ends." Let us recall that an individualized end value of a conception of justice is rationally seen as the prima facie object of equality by this conception. Table 3.3 completes table 3.1 in being more detailed, broader, and more descriptive (less analytical).

Table 3.4 is more general and shows and compares main properties of main theories. It will be fully explained only in the rest of the text, but it may be useful to introduce it here so as to provide a condensed and comparative overview of the theories and properties, and for future reference. Among the properties considered, the "structure" refers to the fact that most theories consider several actual or hypothetical "stages." The questions of the "level" of the theory (the theory is either global or an aggregate of local solutions), of motivations, and of the government, will be analyzed in chapters 12 and 13. Market failures are defined and considered in these chapters and in chapter 5. Natural rights are considered in chapter 4, and the question of the allocation of human resources is analyzed in chapter 6. Natural resources are considered in chapters 5 and 9.

Tables 3.3 and 3.4 are not exhaustive: other theories and properties will be introduced.

Table 3.3
Liberties and equalities in modern social ethics

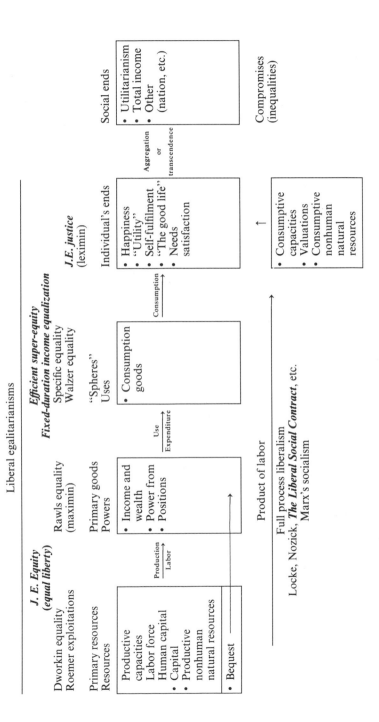

Table 3.4
Main theories and properties in modern social ethics (pages 78 to 81)

THEORY \\ PROPERTY	Neo-"libertarians"	Public Choice (Buchanan)	Morals by agreement (Gauthier's attempt)	Private full process liberalism (Locke, Nozick)	Liberal Social Contract
I. VALUES: **1. Justice**	Irrelevant	Morally irrelevant	From interest	From freedom	From freedom
2. Equalizand	Full freedom	Full freedom	Full freedom, then rights and relative concession	Liberal rights	Liberal rights
3. Status of liberty	Value (and means to welfare)	Fact and value	Fact	Value	Value
II: STRUCTURE: **1. Structure**	Amorphous	3 or 4 stages	3 stages	Recurrent in time	Recurrent in time
2. Initial stage	Undefined	War	War	Recurrent rights	Recurrent rights
3. Second stage	Allocation	Rules: constitution 3rd: market or choose government	"Peaceful interaction"	Allocation	Allocation
4. Level	Specific	Global	Specific	Specific	Specific
III. EXCHANGE: **1. Exchange**	All economic	All economic and political	Perfect market, plus specific bargaining	Perfect markets	Markets plus "liberal social contract"
2. Market failures	None	All: corrected by politics	Prisoner's dilemma	None	All: Liberal public economics

Specific, spheres, efficient super-equity	A Theory of Justice (Rawls)	Resourcism (Dworkin)	Full Justice (Practical) and needs	Utilitarianism, "social welfare"
Equal consumption, or equality in "spheres"	Basic liberties and "difference principle"	Equal resources	Leximin in "fundamental preferences"	Derived
Consumptions (possibly income)	Basic liberties and "primary goods"	Resources	"Welfare"	Marginal welfare
Possible means for efficiency	From equality: value and means	From equality: means and value	Personal value, means Needs: value	Means for welfare
2 stages	3 stages	2 stages	Amorphous	Amorphous
Specific equalities	"Original position"	Equality of resources	Allocation	Allocation
Allocation	"Principles of justice"	Allocation	—	—
From specific to global	Global	Global or specific	Global	Global
From equalities	Within "principles"	From equalities	Corrected	Efficient decentralization
(Inequalities)	Incentives (plus inequalities)	(Initial inequalities)	All	Welfarist public economics

Table 3.4 (continued)

THEORY ⟍ PROPERTY	Neo-"libertarians"	Public Choice (Buchanan)	Morals by agreement (Gauthier's attempt)	Private full process liberalism (Locke, Nozick)	Liberal Social Contract
3. Social Contract	No	Basic (Hobbesian)	Specifc basic	Rights protection (Locke)	"Liberal social contracts"
IV. GOVERNMENT: 1. Government	No (evil)	Political exchange	Omitted (institutions)	Rights-protecting "minarchy"	Protect rights, implements "liberal social contracts"
V. RIGHTS: 1. Natural rights	No	No (possible result)	No (result)	All	All
2. Human resources	Ownership or usufruct of onself				
3. Natural resources	Occupancy	Implicit in constitution or politics	Occupancy, nonviolence	Use, plus compensations	Agreement, (occupancy, other)
VI. MOTIVES: 1. People's motives	Amoral	Amoral	Amoral (but moral behavior)	Amoral	Self-interest plus some altruism
2. Motive of public action	Egoistic with bad consequences	Egoistic with good consequences	—	Owners' employees	Public service

Specific, spheres, efficient super-equity	A Theory of Justice (Rawls)	Resourcism (Dworkin)	Full Justice (Practical) and needs	Utilitarianism, "social welfare"
No	"Original Position"	Cases of "fundamental insurance"	No	No (or Original Position)
Implicit	"Institutions"	Implicit	Implicit	Maximizes "social welfare"
No for production	No for production (result for basic)	No for production	Implicit (or result)	No (possible result)
In production: public In consumption: private			All: justice-relevant	
Sharing of final outputs	Implicit in principles	Equal sharing	Consequential allocations	
Amoral, specific justice	Self-interest and agree with justice	Amoral	Self-interest and possible altruism Basic needs	
(Justice)	(Justice)	(Justice)	Justice	State-moralism

Table 3.5
Modern theories of the Social Contract (pages 82 and 83)

THEORY / PROPERTY	Harsanyi (1953)	Rawls (1971)	Exchange from equality (JE 1971; Dworkin 1981)	Buchanan (1975)	Liberal Social Contract (1985)	Fundamental insurance (1981, 1985)	Gauthier (1986)
Reason	Good allocation	Justice	Just allocation	Peace	All "market failures"	Different capacities	"Prisoner's dilemma"
Object of choice	Allocation	Principles of justice	Allocation	Constitution	Allocation	Compensation	Allocation (and rights)
Social level	Global	Global	Global or specific	Global	All local	Specific	All local
Realism	Hypothetical	Hypothetical	Actual or putative	Actual tacit consent	Putative from real	Putative	"Rational"
Time	Original or atemporal	Original or atemporal	Original or recurrent	Permanent	Real as unfolds	Anterior or atemporal	Permanent or atemporal
Number	1	1	1 or several	1 permanent	Many	Any	Many
Nature of contractants	Original individual	Original individual	Actual	Actual	Actual	Locally original	Actual
Information	Ignore self ("thin veil of ignorance")	Ignore self plus "thick veil of ignorance"	Actual	Actual	Best information of public sector	Ignore the capacity	Actual
Motivation	Self-interest	Self-interest	Self-interest or actual	Self-interest	Actual	Self-interest or actual	"Rational" self-interest

Nonagreement state	Irrelevant	Irrelevant	Equal sharing	War	"Market failures"	Irrelevant	1) War 2) "Peaceful interaction"
Nature of exchange	Direct unanimity	Direct unanimity	Actual free	Tacit consent	Vicarious of actual	Hypothetical	"Equal relative concession"
Implementation	Moral authority	Institution plus people	People from sharing	People	Public sector plus moral people	Public sector or moral people	"Rational" people

Finally, Table 3.5 focuses on the twentieth century theories of the Social Contract, in fact on the theories of the Social Contract that were developed in the second half of this century, which are also those that have been constructed since the late 18th century (essentially since Rousseau, completed by Kant's ethics). However, two older theories of the Social Contract have been and are the basis of important actual social philosophies: the Rousseauan basis of "republicanism," and the Contracts by tacit consent (from Plato's *Crito* on, and which have been given a modern development by J. Buchanan). The table shows comparatively the various properties of these modern theories. It is also provided here as a condensed and comparative overview and for future reference. Column 3 represents free exchange from equal sharing. These various theories are discussed in the following chapters. It will turn out that a number of these theories are either logically invalid, or not really moral theories. Yet they have been important landmarks in the contemporary debates and thinking in social ethics, and important stepping stones for further progress.

II ACT- AND PROCESS-FREEDOM

4 Act-Freedom

4.1 Freedom to Act

Full Act-Freedom

Let us now look more closely at the basic issues for social ethics and justice.

We have considered a justiciable agent's *act* using *means* for an *aim* (there may be several joint aims).

An individual agent's means are of two kinds. One is his *own human* means, or *personal* means, or *capacities*. These consist of his "mind and body." The other means are his *external means*.

We have noted that freedom can be separated into *act-freedom, means-freedom* (or simply *means*), *aim-freedom*, and *process-freedom* which is both the corresponding act-freedom and aim-freedom. Note that an act is not necessarily an "agitation": to rest undisturbed with the aim of being quiet for any reason is an "act."

The crucial distinction between the liberty to act per se and the availability of means is emphasized by the perceptive authors in various ways and words. Act-freedoms are the basic Rights of Man and of the Citizen of the 1789 Declaration (and of the earlier and contemporaneous American texts which are more practical but less universal and less philosophical),[1] Marx's "formal freedoms," John Rawls's "basic liberties," and so on. External means are what Marx wants to add in order to obtain "real freedom" and they include Rawls's "primary goods." Note that the "right to hold property" is an act-freedom which does not imply by itself any right to hold, as a means, any specific amount of property (the 1789 Declaration calls this ownership right "property" and it states it in its article 2, whereas it refers to specific holdings as "properties" and it protects them by its article 17, the last one—hence act-freedom can be seen as the content of the 1789 Declaration apart from the last article, and process-freedom as its content including this last article).[2]

---

1. See Kolm 1989a (1991) and 1993a.

2. See Kolm 1993a. This intended distinction between "property" and "properties" is brought out very clearly by the accounts of the debates that preceded the Declaration. It is now forgotten by the countries that use the 1789 Declaration as their basic constitutional text, yet engage in extensive redistribution policies (unless this redistribution can be justified by liberal social contracts; see chapter 5). Indeed, for the

A number of act-freedoms can be more or less devoid of actual content because of a lack either of the means necessary to make use of this liberty, or of the aim-freedoms necessary for benefiting from the consequences of the act. They are, for instance, freedom to buy when one has no money, freedom to work with a negligible real wage, freedom to produce when all the output is taxed away, freedom to publish without the means for it, freedom from arbitrary arrest when one is dying from starvation. This objection to "formal liberty" in the name of "real liberty" is well taken, and deriding equality restricted to act-freedom has a point ("the rich man and the poor alike have an equal right to sleep under the bridges," Anatole France writes).[3] Yet act-freedoms are necessary, even though not sufficient, for "real liberty." And a large part of modern history has been the use of this criticism as the major pretext for suppressing all liberties.

Rival means that more for one implies less for the other. This can apply to goods of various types, to aims, acts, rights, powers, or liberties of different agents or of the same agent, to these agents, and so forth.

A very important point is that, with a careful distinction between *acts* and *means*, the cause of rivalry among agents can be considered as resting in the agents' *external means rather than in the realm of act-freedoms* (for given aim-freedoms). For instance, my act-freedom to move cannot cause my hurting you if it is within a space—which constitutes an external means—that excludes where you are. In another example, competition depends on the means to compete. And so on.

---

common present view, articles 2 and 17 seem bizarrely redundant. In fact, August 26, 1789, was as importantly dramatic a day as the other main ones of this midsummer (July 14 and August 4), and a more important one for the future. Indeed the deputies hesitated up to the last moment as to the content of the last article, between "properties," on the one hand, and public "relief" for the needy, on the other hand. That is, they hesitated between the unhampered free-market and full process liberalism, on the one hand, and the introduction of a redistribution policy, on the other. A major step was thus taken every three weeks: After the power of the king and the birth-rights of the nobility were brought down, the bourgeois could establish their own way of ruling (yet the next revolutionary Declarations of rights introduced public assistance and—under Condorcet's advice—public education).

3. Robespierre and Marx were, for this reason, foremost critics of the 1789 Rights of Man. They at the same time criticized the full process-freedom of the "rights to properties."

Of course the means can be defined with all the required specifications as regards condition, time, space, and so forth. Certain particular aspects concerning offensive or misleading public expression do not prevent this conclusion from being the general property.[4]

This nonrivalry holds no matter whether the considered acts of the agents are, or are not, of the same type and nature. Furthermore, for the same agent, freedoms for different acts (of different types or of the same type) do not interfere with one another: more of one such liberty does not require less of the other. Only uses of these freedoms can be in competition because they would require the same scarce means (of any nature) of the agent. Hence *act-freedoms are essentially nonrival*, when they are carefully defined.

Therefore *act-freedoms can essentially be all and jointly unlimited for all agents*. Then they offer *infinite availability* to act, and the acts use this freedom *to satiety*. This is *full act-freedom*.

A classical idea is that act-freedoms should be "the largest possible consistent with equal liberties of others," that is, they should satisfy the following two conditions in order of priority: (1) equal for all, and (2) maximal. This is expressed by Rousseau, it is in the 1789 Declaration of Rights, Kant suggests it, and it is repeated by J.S. Mill and by Rawls, among others. Now these two conditions are *trivially* satisfied by the above-noted limitlessness, which constitutes these conditions (it is of course the liberty, not its use, that is equal, maximal, and infinite). This shows, incidentally, that these two conditions are consistent.

Furthermore, the Declaration states that these Rights of Man and of the Citizen are *inalienable, indefeasible, imprescriptible*, and have *priority* over all laws. This structure defines politically liberal regimes. Rawls also indicates this priority. Now, given the essential nonrivalry

---

4. However, it is sometimes not possible to assign the management of a means to a specific rivalry. For example, your right of free expression and my right not to be slandered, viciously insulted in public or gravely misled may lead to a rivalrous situation. One can restrict the paper material on which you publish your views (or any other medium you use). But this would also prevent you from writing something else on this paper. And if one restricts the paper-on-which-slander-is-written, this amounts to specifically and explicitly limiting slander, hence the right of expression. The same holds, for instance, for the right to shout "fire" in a crowded theater, and the right to affect the state of the air (which transmits the sound). However, there are not many other types of examples. The nonrivalry of act-freedoms holds *for the essential*.

of act-freedoms of any type and for any agent, act-freedoms can be limited only for the sake of something else (not for another act-freedom). Hence this priority implies that we choose full act-freedom. Conversely, full act-freedom implies that act-freedoms have priority if they conflict with any other rule. Therefore, the *essential nonrivalry of act-freedoms* entails that *their priority and their fullness amount to the same thing.*[5]

Note that full act-freedom can a priori be compatible with very different distributions of means and welfare. In particular, the redistributive taxation—whatever its form and its rationale—made possible by non-full aim-freedom can confiscate parts of products, transfers (exchanges, gifts, bequest), or assets and distribute incomes or services, without violating the act-freedoms to work, exchange, or give, and of course also those to be unmolested, to think, to write, or to vote. For instance, full act-freedom may be consistent with full process-freedom and its "generalized free market" (see chapter 5), as well as with the strong income redistributions implied by ideals of equal satisfaction or consumption and by the corresponding efficient second-best egalitarian maximins—"freedom-constrained Practical Justice" (Kolm 1971, 1985a; see chapter 7), certain cases of "efficient super-equity" (see chapter 6), or Rawls's "difference principle" (see chapter 8).

However, besides the "Rights of Man," these freedoms also include the "Rights of the Citizen," and notably the right to vote in a political

---

5. Certain presentations of these basic rights would probably require that they be accompanied by a certain amount of means which makes them "real" rather than merely "formal." This is not the case of Marx (the author of these adjectives) and of A. France (quoted above). This should logically not be the case of Rawls either, because his "difference principle" provides the largest means possible to the least endowed individuals (certain problems with this principle are discussed in chapter 8). Yet, it may be the case for other presentators (possibly the 1789 constituants), although this remains implicit, and, above all, unspecified. Now, for a number of basic rights, there is no "natural" level of these accompanying means. For instance, there is no satiety level (there is one for certain rights such as those to vote or to apply to positions, although even in these cases one may have various levels of relevant information, but there is no limit to the world diffusion of one's free writing, to the comfort of one's free travel, to the splendor of the cathedral where one freely practices one's religion, and so on). Then, the principle "equal and maximal with priority," applied to these liberties accompanied with means, would divert to these free activities all the resources of society, in opposition, in fact, to individuals' wishes (or, if these liberties are explicitly *all* act-freedom, this would amount to an equal allocation of everything, which is not the intent).

process having at least certain characteristics of democracy, including "no taxation without representation." This is bound to reduce the scope of a priori possible redistributions. For instance, a constituency of self-interested individuals will usually not vote for a "maximin" such as "Practical Justice" or Rawls's "difference principle" which cares for only few people—the most desperate or deprived—by transfers from the others, unless the distribution contains a sufficiently large number of people at about the lowest level. Such dilemmas are, however, solved in the rather common situation of "collective gift": people may be too egoistic to personally give if this does not influence others' gifts (or absence of gifts), yet they may realistically have the limited altruism or sense of duty that makes them want to give under the condition that the others give too; they then both do not give individually and vote (possibly at unanimity) for establishing the corresponding forced transfers (see also chapters 5 and 8).

The Reasons for Full Act-Freedom

The justification of full act-freedom (and hence of its priority) rests on two reasons: a basic *existential* and *ontological* one,[6] and a subsidiary one that rests on a consideration of *efficiency* (in Pareto's sense of unanimity), possibly extended to Practical Justice (help the most miserable; see chapter 7). Other justifications fail to provide this conclusion either with the validity or with the certainty and the universality required for this principle. We will see that this is in particular the case for justifications based on theories of the type of Social Contracts of various kinds.

Respecting Human Ontology and Existence
The basic justification of full act-freedom rests on the ontology of human nature. Classical variants of this position include "natural rights," the "sacred" character of the Rights of Man and of the Citizen, and the existential view. This conception sees full act-freedom as intrinsic to the "nature" and "essence" of man, as a part of his "being," a condition for his "existence" as genuine human being and for his "dignity," because man is an agent, characterized by his

---

6. See chapter 2.

performing actions which actualize his liberty. A violation of act-freedom deprives the victim of an essential part of his "self." This is akin to maiming him, and a step into the realm of slavery. To respect an individual's act-freedom is to take him and his will, or "humanity within him" (Kant), as the end of moral action.[7]

Act-freedom is thus founded in ontology, hence outside ethics proper. This provides incommensurability, priority, inalienability, and transcendence. The priority of act-freedom over values such as welfare or income is Kant's lexical priority of "dignity" over price. This transcendence causes the Declaration to qualify the Rights of Man and of the Citizen as "sacred." It must elicit sentiments of extreme respect for these rights and of indignation toward their violations, and a readiness to defend them "at all cost." This sacredness is not of the alienating kind, since it is only utmost mutual respect for one's alter ego, which globally simply amounts to overall *self-respect* of mankind for itself.

Only such conceptions can elicit and support the sentiments and attitudes of priority and deep obligation than can guarantee the respect of principles that, after all, amount to "thou shalt not kill, molest, arbitrarily arrest, confine in a gulag or in a concentration camp, condemn without due process of law, gag, rob, tax without representation," and so on.

Universal Act-Freedom
However, these latter arguments in favor of act-freedom are a kind of emotivism, rather than properly reason. Of course, the indictment of emotivism in the name of rationality has its limits. Imagine the rational philosopher who insists, before he admits that the Auschwitz camp is bad, that he find a proof that it is irrational. Yet many act-freedoms

---

7. This reason for act-freedom thus belongs to a family that includes the various classical concepts of "natural rights." The adjective "natural" in "natural rights" has to be understood as referring to "human nature" rather than to a "state of nature." Hence the argument that the concept of "natural rights" is meaningless because the existence of rights requires a law and there is by definition no law in the "state of nature" of the classical theories of the Social Contract, misses the point (this argument was expressed forcefully by Bentham—see chapter 14—and it is commonly repeated since). Natural rights are not "rights in a state of nature" but rights necessary to the existence or preservation of a functioning human nature. A recent elaboration of views belonging to the same Kantian family as the one presented here is provided by Gewirth (1978, 1982).

and basic rights are less extreme. But still other reasons support universal act-freedom. They rest on either the objective or the self-centered point of view.

By definition, an agent performs actions which are intentional. Hence he wants act-freedom for himself. If all individual agents are a priori equally worthy of consideration, from the rationality of equality (see chapter 2) this individual agent should also favor others' act-freedom if all these act-freedoms are copossible, which indeed they are for the essential. Hence morally rational individuals must want general full act-freedom, from this "Principle of Universality" derived from equal consideration ("objectivity" whence impartiality) and the rationality of equality. Therefore, globally, the rational person must want universal act-freedom from the conjunction of the following facts: objectivity and thus impartiality, the rationality of equality, the person's nature as a purposeful agent, and the essential nonrivalry of act-freedoms.

However, from a self-centered perspective (as opposed to the impartial viewpoint)[8] "I" am intrinsically different from "others," and universality loses its reason. Then it becomes relevant that individuals' act-freedoms affect in many possible ways the situations, desires, interests, etc., of others (from the fact that they move, speak, exchange, vote, apply to positions, and so on). But this may provide other reasons for act-freedom, not based on existence and being, and other reasons for desiring its universality, not based on impartiality.

Unanimity and Efficiency (and Practical Justice)
Basic rights may indeed also be commended for other reasons, which can be of many types. The most notable of these reasons, however, justifies these rights by individuals' interests. Considerations presented in other chapters lead one to emphasize, in particular, unanimous interest and efficiency, and care for the most miserable (and "Practical Justice").

Basic rights might be supported by unanimous interest. This would come from the fact that a certain theory of justice with full act-freedom is unanimously preferred to the state of society that would

---

8. The works of Thomas Nagel quoted in reference analyse with detail and subtlety the basic importance of this opposition.

have prevailed with the omission of full act-freedom (admitting in-difference for certain persons). This could result from the strongest property that for any social state without full act-freedom, there exists another social state with full act-freedom that everybody prefers to the former (with possible indifferences). Of course the two states com-pared may also differ by re-arrangements of various means or aim-constraints that compensate for the effects of act-freedoms (more act-freedom for an agent can produce effects of various types for other agents—for instance, more access to a market is appreciated by the other side but is regretted by the competitors, more access to the political arena is appreciated by people on the same side but regretted by opponents). A number of phenomena can prevent such unanimous preference with possible compensations, but they are not that com-mon, so that there is indeed a case for act-freedom based on efficiency. These phenomena are, notably, the following ones:

• "Nosy preferences" are direct individual preferences regarding others' use of their act-freedom. They reflect opinions about what other people say, think, or do that are held for this very fact, for instance, by reference to what is proper, moral, nice, adequate, either per se or in a certain situation. Full compensation for these prefer-ences may not be possible. Yet such preferences may have to be dis-counted on moral ground (a principle of "irrelevance of nosiness," or of "nonnosiness").

• The freer individual may dislike this liberty, because of the cost or "anguish" of choice, or because of a fear of responsibility (see chap-ter 2).

• The transfers that would compensate for the various effects of higher act-freedom may have economic and behavioral limits or may cause excessive efficiency losses, as will be discussed in chapter 6.

• These transfers may be prevented by the political process enacting the political Rights of the Citizen.

• A larger act-freedom for the individuals' choice of variables which are a base of public policy measures introduces efficiency losses (for example, bases of taxes and subsidies; see chapter 6). Yet the alterna-tive act-constraints, if they are to be efficient, require information on individuals' preferences and possibilities that is commonly not avail-able. Indeed this lack of information is a classical reason for choosing this observable policy base as a second-best proxy. Higher act-freedom may also have important favorable effects on motivation (we would, for instance, have to compare shirking and lack of initiative under forced labor with working more willingly in the case of free labor, apart from the effect of the income tax).

In the end, the efficiency advantage of act-freedom—in particular of full act-freedom—is not warranted, yet it is by no means unlikely and it certainly holds for a wide domain.[9]

Furthermore, even when full act-freedom does not permit unanimous improvement, it may permit one to improve the fate of the most miserable. In particular, it may be necessary for the corresponding efficient "leximin" of "Practical Justice"; see chapter 7, section 7.2. Relatedly, full act-freedom may permit the satisfaction of basic needs (see chapter 11). It may indeed be needed for any other social ethical objective.

The Dangers of Total Social Contracts

However, justifications of full act-freedom of basic rights that bypass the "ontological" priority are too unsure, speculative, shaky, and risky. Classical and recent history of thought lead us to note that this is notably the case for justifications that rest on ideas belonging to the family of Social Contracts, that is, for "contractarian" justifications. A Social Contract is a putative agreement that chooses certain rules or facts of the society. We must distinguish here between two kinds of Social Contracts (see chapter 3). Certain leave the choice of act-freedom out of the scope of this justification, whereas others include this choice among the objects of the Contract. The former category includes (indeed, consists of) Locke's theory and the theory of the

---

9. Consider the example of the limit, extreme distributional case where one individual owns all the others as slaves (they thus have no act-freedom). He extracts from them all they can produce minus the consumption necessary to their productivity. But the same result can be obtained from free workers in taxing them of the same amount and transferring the product of the tax to the former master (questions of information concerning the ca,)acities to work would exist in both cases). In this second case, the formal act-freedom to work is present, and the resulting distribution is about the same. A tax, of course, infringes upon *aim*-freedom. However, with priority of the basic rights, a tax is submitted to the political "Rights of the Citizen." Then no democratic vote (certainly no self-interested one) would choose to allocate all the product (above subsistence) to a single individual.

Liberal Social Contract (Kolm 1985a; see chapter 5 below), both of which state act-freedom for another reason. The theories that, on the contrary, submit the choice of act-freedom to the Social Contract, are in fact theories of *total Social Contracts*, that is, everything is left to this contractarian justification. Yet these theories have the following properties: First, it is by no means warranted that they will obtain this result, that is, that the considered contracting parties would actually decide in favor of act-freedom. Second, the status of these theories as moral theories is sometimes problematic. Third, if they are moral theories, these theories may not be very compelling for modern minds. We can consider, for example, the first and the last of the classical Social Contracts (Hobbes and Rousseau) and the three modern total contractarian theories that explicitly justify act-freedom in this manner (Rawls, Buchanan, and Gauthier).

Hobbes's argument is that everybody's submission to an autocratic, absolute ruler is better for everybody than the war of all against all. The contrary of act-freedom is obtained (unless the ruler's benevolence, or interest, decides for it, but that is another story).

The contracting parties in the total and communitarian Social Contract of Rousseau may well abandon their "natural" act-freedoms. This is clearly suggested by Rousseau, although he became, after Locke, the second inspirer of the 1789 Declaration. This possibility had indeed dramatic historical consequences, since Robespierre and his friends could see themselves as faithful Rousseauans, and the Terror could establish its own legitimacy merely by erasing the Lockean "natural rights" concept of 1789 in favor of the fully Rousseauan contractarian theory of 1793: The execution of an individual could then be seen as the social body correcting itself (this of course misinterprets Rousseau, for whom nothing can justify a single drop of blood).

The modern *total* contractarians are Harsanyi (1953), Rawls (*A Theory of Justice*, 1971), Buchanan (see notably *The Limits of Liberty*, 1975) and Gauthier (*Morals by Agreement*, 1986). Their theories will be discussed in following chapters. We will see that the different justifications they present are, for various reasons, not really apt for founding *normative* theories of justice (yet their recommendations may be *justified otherwise*, as is the case for that of Rawls with certain precisions—see chapter 8—or their theories may in fact have *other*

objectives and interests, as should be the case for that of Buchanan—
see chapter 12). Furthermore these justifications may not produce
act-freedoms.

For Rawls, "basic liberties" and their priority would be adopted
by the individuals "in the original position," "behind the veil of ignorance" (see chapter 8). Harsanyi does not mention these rights, and
indeed the maximization of the sum of utilities that he obtains does
not have this structure with priorities. Yet his founding theory is the
same (Rawls, however, argues that the "original ignorance" he assumes is deeper than Harsanyi's). Now the general possibility and
remark that have been pointed out in chapters 1 and 3 apply in particular to basic liberties. An individual "in the original position," who
knows that he may become any of the actual individuals (or perhaps
still others) and is assumed to be only self-interested, may well choose
the rules or allocations of the actual society in sacrificing one actual
individual, if this permits him to give sufficiently more to sufficiently
many others. He may find it worthwhile to take this risk. This prima
facie casts doubt on the appropriateness of this theory as a theory of
justice. In particular, this "original individual" might thus deprive
certain actual individuals in certain situations of certain basic liberties:
There is no a priori guarantee against this eventuality. For instance,
nothing guarantees that an individual "in the original position" would
not choose that one actual individual be a slave, in the appropriate
circumstances—not to speak of the "more moderate" rights to vote or
of free expression. Of course it may be that de facto such a choice
would not have been made. Rawls indeed argues that de facto the rule
of "basic liberties" with priority would have been adopted. He more
precisely argues that this would be the case with a sufficiently deep
"original ignorance" (and that this suffices for providing the justification). But these are reasoned conjectures rather than proofs. There
are far too many unknowns for it to be possible to provide an answer
with certainty. And certainly we should not take the risk of letting the
condemnation of slavery depend on the uncertain outcome of such
scholarly exercises. Furthermore we have noted that actual individuals
can hardly be held responsible for the choices of the undifferentiated,
identical "original individuals," in particular for questions where individuals' interests may be opposed. Finally, still another difficulty
is raised by Rawls's globally nondeductive Original Position theory

where it suffices that "there exists" a structure and depth of original ignorance that would (might) provide the outcome (this aspect does not belong to Harsanyi's conception and will be further discussed in chapter 8).

Another kind of total Social Contract, a basically opposed one, is that of Buchanan (1975; see chapter 12 below). Gauthier's theory (1986; idem) is in fact a subcase of Buchanan's, but since this is somewhat hidden by a number of specific additions (some interesting, some invalid, and some both) and a particular presentation, it will also be considered in itself. Buchanan's constitution is the set or rules actually adopted by the individuals, which manifests a unanimous preference over open fighting. Such a constitution *may* contain basic rights (the constitutants of 1789, on the contrary, undertook to *deduce* the constitution from the basic rights). Such a constitution can include, in addition to the Rights of Man, the political Rights of the Citizen, since it explicitly sets the rules of a political process. However, the constitution may also not contain any of these rights. Indeed many actual constitutions and sets or rules do not include such rights, and this constitutes the proof since they are Buchananian constitutions. This may in particular happen when the distribution of forces is sufficiently unbalanced.

Gauthier, however, argues that if the individuals were sufficiently aware of their self-interests (which he calls being "rational"), this motivation would lead them to respect the "classical rights to person and property," and to share the surpluses made available by market failures according to a certain rather specific rule ("equal relative concession" over a state of "peaceful interaction"—this state, however, is not completely defined). This, indeed, would be necessary and sufficient for ascertaining the beneficial cooperation of the others. The "classical rights to person" certainly includes the Rights of Man. The political Rights of the Citizen, however, have no place since Gauthier's full solution completely defines the outcome ("peaceful interaction" is assumed to be completely specified), so that there is no decision left for politics. Yet "equal relative concession" is logically void of sense because it requires a meaningless concept of cardinal utility (see chapter 12). But the "classical rights to property" logically imply that this rule for sharing surpluses made available by market failures is replaced by "liberal social contracts" (see chapter 5). Furthermore

Gauthier a priori errs in believing that situations of the "prisoner's dilemma" type would find a spontaneous "rational" solution in this way, but this may indeed happen if one adds a number of possible and rather realistic things such as: repeated or sequential interaction; an ethic of cooperation or of objective social rationality[10] either in the actor's motivation or through a taste for a favorable opinion of others; or coercive implementation either by an institution that can enforce promises and promises conditional on promises (see chapter 1) or by a public sector with the required power, political incentives and morals (see chapter 13), which are unanimously welcome and may be installed by a previous agreement. Gauthier, finally, does not prove that basic rights will be implemented, more than Buchanan does—and for the same reason—, and for both a *moral* "should" is basically out of place. Yet the modifications suggested, associated with the preceding discussion of the efficiency reason for respecting these rights, provide reasons that can explain the actual scope of these rights and of certain cooperative duties to respect them.

4.2   Process-Freedom, Aim-Constraints

In the economic sphere, *full act-freedom* forbids forced labor of all kinds (from slavery or *corvée* to conscript labor or "socialist" obligation to work or assignment to jobs), barriers to entry into markets, and discrimination that is not relevantly based on capacities. It implies the right to hold property, to exchange, sell and buy, and so on. Yet it does not imply that returns of all kinds are not taxed.

On the contrary, *full process-freedom* in addition implies *full aim-freedom*. Therefore, when the aim of labor is to benefit from the product, the aim of an exchange to benefit from that which one receives, the aim of a gift that the receiver benefit from it, in particular the aim of bequest that the heir benefit from the inheritance, then full process-freedom implies respectively the classical "*right to the full product of one's labor*," the right to *unhampered and untaxed exchange*, the right to full gift and *full bequest*. These are the starting points of

---

10. See Kolm 1993e.

full process liberalism, presented axiomatically in the next chapter. This complete theory indeed ends up with certain taxes, but these taxes implement this liberty in situations of "market failure" or "agreement failure." All transfers represent payments or gifts under various forms. This complete theory allocates capital to its producers in being intertemporal, and it allocates nonhuman natural resources essentially by collective agreements (actual or putative ones) which may accept first occupancy. Then nothing is available for redistribution according to any other criterion.

Without full aim-freedom, some redistribution of this sort is possible. This possibility provides the room and necessity for another theory of distributive justice.

As has been discussed in chapter 3, these other theories of justice consider as directly ethically relevant either something that favors the justiciable agents' own ends or some global social end. These social ends either aggregate or transcend the items favored by individuals. The aggregation can be either of agents' fulfillment of their ends, and this is a kind of utilitarianism in a large sense, or of agents' means, such as global social income. Transcendent aims can, for example, refer to group, nation, culture, nature, or to more specific aspects.

End-valuing categories of items that refer to individuals necessarily leads one to some sort of egalitarianism (see chapter 2). These items can be either the agents' *fulfillment of their ends* or agents' *means to fulfill their ends*. These are respectively *ends* and *means direct justice*. The means *stricto sensu* can be at various stages of man's social action of transforming the world: primary resources, incomes, consumption goods, human capacities used in production or consumption (with compensations). As has been pointed out earlier, choosing a set of means as end-values for justice amounts to deciding that both what the agents do with these means, and the other means they use for this, are *irrelevant for redistributive justice* but are thus implicitly *legitimized*. Note also the two particular, extreme and limiting cases of means-justice. One is *end-justice*, which obtains when all means (or, equivalently, all means *stricto sensu*), including all personal capacities, are jointly considered as relevant (this is "Justice" and "Practical justice" of *Justice and Equity*; see chapter 7). The other case is *full process liberalism* where no means *stricto sensu* (and no personal end) is an end value of justice. Yet full process-freedom implies equal full process-freedom for all and hence it is also an equality of a particular kind, namely an equality of rights to act and to enjoy the result of one's acts. This of course differs from benefiting from equal other means for acting or enjoying. These various theories of the just distribution and the problems they raise will be the topics in the next chapters.

5 Full Process Liberalism and Liberal Social Contracts

Full process liberalism is the founding and historically central reference for the social and economic ethics of the modern world. Its logic must, however, be made precise, notably with respect to the fact that its basic principle implies a specific notable role for a public sector. This chapter presents the core of its rational construction (complete analytical presentations are to be found in Kolm 1985a, 1991e). Basically, full process liberalism has only one principle: *full process-freedom*.

1. The consequent "right to the full product of one's labor" (see chapter 3, section 3.1, and chapter 4, section 4.2) implies that individuals have the *usufruct of themselves* (this is short of the classical "self-ownership").[1]

2. Full process-freedom implies the full freedom to transfer one's non-basic rights, to commit oneself, to exchange, to give, to make bequests, to make a collective agreement with any number of other persons, a priori without limit, constraints or taxes.[2] Basic rights (see chapter 4) are inalienable because they are necessary to the very existence of the agent as such, a condition of his being rather than a part of his having. Note that the outcome of a collective agreement or of an exchange is *completely determined* by the participants' resources of all kinds—material, rights, information, bargaining skills, intelligence, speed, and so forth.[3]

3. The set of the *fully liberally legitimate* rights in a society at a point in time is defined as full process-freedom plus the means that would have obtained if the fully liberally legitimate rights (including full process-freedom) had always existed and had never been violated nor influentially expected to be violated. "Influential" means that this

---

1. This principle does not imply, for instance, the right to destroy oneself by suicide or drugs, or to sell oneself into slavery, or even to engage in very long term labor contracts (which are indeed forbiden in most countries).

2. Remember that a "property right" is a set of rights concerning an object.

3. This determinacy has a number of consequences, notably these three: (1) The rivalry of surplus-sharing in an exchange or agreement can be assigned to the mentioned means that determine this sharing: free exchange or agreement is a case of act-freedoms and the general remark about the assignment of rivalry applies (see chapter 4). (2) The time path induced by the respect of full process-freedom is unique, as is, consequently, the corresponding allocation at each moment in time. (3) The "liberal social contracts" defined below are, in this respect, well-defined.

expectation has an influence on actions and the course of things. This expected violation can be at any moment in time (including after the date of existence of the rights mentioned at the beginning of the first sentence of the paragraph). The condition concerning expectations rules out in particular the influence of credible threats of violations of full process-freedom. The actions of the "liberal social contracts" and of the allocations of non-human natural resources, defined below, are by definition included in the actions considered in this process. Since the conditions of the definition have not been actually satisfied in the past, the establishment of the fully liberally legitimate set of rights requires the corresponding *rectifications* of the effects of the past. The rectification of effects of past actions, and in particular of past violations of rights, is a common object of court decisions and ethical debates, with recent scholarly discussions notably by Nozick (1974), Philip (1979), and Kolm (1985a). Rectification theory can justify transfers between broad classes of the present population whose situation depends on a historical violation of legitimate rights, even if a lack of information prevents the precise specification of each individual violation and of its consequences.[4]

4. The allocation of *initial rights to non-human natural resources* is amenable to several rules that have always more or less been used. These are the following:[5] (a) Collective unanimous agreement leading to sharing with possible side-payments and compensations, in which people use their various legitimate bargaining means. Collective agreement may also lead to any of the other following solutions. (b) First occupancy by people using their legitimate means for this occupancy. (c) Equal sharing justified by the rationality of equality (see chapter 2). (d) Use of the resources, or of the proceeds of their sale or of their rent, for the satisfaction of other distributional principles, such as helping the most miserable while respecting full process liberalism (fully liberally constrained "Practical Justice," see Kolm 1971, 1985a, and chapter 7) or the alleviation of basic needs (see chapter 11). (e) Use of these

---

4. One difficulty is that a number of past violations of rights have affected by various ways the very composition of the population.

5. A complete discussion of the question of the liberal allocation of natural resources is provided in Kolm 1985a, chapter 10 (see also Kolm 1986c).

resources, or of the proceed of their sale or of their rent, for collective purposes such as the provision of public goods and services (including collectively desired assistance to people in need—see below). This latter solution is often called the "socialization" of natural resources. First occupancy has been discussed for millennia. Locke (1689) and Nozick (1974) propose a sort of first occupancy qualified by equality. Steiner (1978) and Cohen (1986) are modern proponents of equal sharing. Walras (1898) is an elaborate proponent of socialization. A unanimous collective agreement can be the putative one of a "liberal social contract" (see below). Unanimous collective agreements seem to constitute the basic full-process liberal principle and method. Note finally that nonhuman natural resources produce only a couple of *percent* of GNP in modern economies (even counting their value that is accumulated in capital).

5. Since fully liberally legitimate rights are not defined by the force of the right-holder (they are not defined by "might") they generally have to be protected by a particular dominant "public" force. This includes rights born from agreements. This is the role of the minimal, "night watchman" *state* described by Locke (1690) from a Social Contract among owners and by Nozick (1974) through a hypothetical evolutionary process. Yet this is a minute part of the full-process liberal public sector (this "minarchy" falls short of the full-process liberal "optarchy"), for the following reason.

6. "Market failures" (or, more generally, "agreement failures") result from three types of causes, which are often interlocked: (a) difficulties in information and communication; (b) difficulties in the setting of constraints; and (c) difficulties due to certain strategic behavior in the process of cooperation itself. Whenever a liberally legitimate free act, exchange, or agreement (that is to say, one respecting the full liberal set of rights) is thus impeded, full process liberalism requires the implementation of whatever the outcome would have been in the absence of this hindrance, as well as possible. This hypothetical, putative agreement among any number of persons is *a "liberal social contract."* The set of the liberal social contracts is called "the Liberal Social Contract." The duty to implement a liberal social contract is one that can be taken up by any person, but since some use of the public force is usually implied, the state ordinarily has at least some role to play.

What the *public sector* should do is then indicated by the liberal theory itself, together with theories of bargaining, and information revealed by actual exchanges and political processes (Kolm 1985a, 1987c, 1991e). "Failures" of markets or of direct agreements are in fact defined relatively by the fact that another type of decision process can make things better for all the participants (this will be discussed in chapters 12 and 13).

7. The payments by private agents in publicly implemented liberal social contracts appear as *taxes*. These taxes are both voluntary and forced: Each taxpayer prefers the set of specific taxes and the action it finances to their absence, yet each would usually prefer not to pay himself if what the others do is given. Extracting tax payments is then nothing more than the enforcement of a voluntary contract, albeit a hypothetical, putative one. This applies in particular to the finance of *nonexcludable public goods* (items that concern several agents who cannot be excluded individually from this specific benefit). One particular very important application concerns *collective gifts* where several persons give to the same ones with the intent that the latter have more (other motivations may be superimposed, that lead one to value one's own gift in itself for a number of possible reasons).[6] Then the income, welfare, consumption, or needs satisfaction of a receiver is a "public good" for the givers (who derive from it the "benefit" of knowing the improvement, a particular type of benefit from which one could be excluded only by hiding the information to him, which would ipso facto also suppress his actual motivation to help). Thus the existence of even quite moderate levels of altruism or of a sense of justice leads full process liberalism to advocate public (and apparently "forced") redistributive transfers that can be substantial.[7]

8. The theory of the Liberal Social Contract enables one to determine the actions and institutional structures of the full-process liberal public sector. These include the general principle of *benefit taxation* for

---

6. See the analysis of the various reasons and motivations for giving in Kolm, 1984b.

7. For example, it will be explained in chapter 9 that the Liberal Social Contract, complying to general public opinion about "human resourcism" or "fundamental insurance," leads to public social insurance and public education in most western European countries, which constitutes a significant transfer.

public goods; the general *progressivity of taxation as a function of income* (this structure results from the fact that the benefit tax for each public good is often a rather linear function of income above a threshold that represents the income at which the complementary private goods are acquired,[8] from the effect of rectificatory transfers, and also from the taxation of externalities); the theory of the *public debt as retro-payments* (retro-buying and "retro-gifts")[9] and the determination of the optimal public debt; the management of externalities by transfers relative to the liberally-determined rights; the determination of the *political institutions and processes* that are optimal for the revelation of preferences (and for implementation, given the motivations); an advocacy of a decentralized public sector; and so on (Kolm 1985a, 1987c, 1991e).

Finally, let us note that liberal social contracts for the correction of market and agreement failures can be associated with another basic distribution, one that is not the full process liberal one (for instance, from an equal allocation of resources or of "primary goods," or from efficient maximins in these distributions, as will be discussed in chapters 6 to 9).

---

8. This specific tax schedule is piecewise linear convex. The "sum" of these schedules along the tax axis is therefore a convex schedule, and this represents progressive taxation.

9. An individual may wish that he had paid at a time before he actually could have done it (possibly before he existed, for example, he may wish to enjoy decades-old trees, or that his poor grandmother had been supported in her youth). This desire can be implemented by the government of the time which more or less foresees it, and makes the corresponding expenditure out of borrowing, thus creating a public debt later redeemed by taxes paid by this individual (this is another case of taxes that are generally actually forced, since the initial payment has already been made, though they are basically—here intertemporally—voluntary). This is a basis of the full-process liberal theory of the public debt, but in other and important cases the public expenditure also contains elements of public goods.

III EQUALITIES

6 Second-Best Justice, Human Resources, and Income Justice

6.1 Presentation

We have seen that rational justice consists in prima facie equalities of liberties. Liberty is here very broadly understood; it has to be all sorts of agents' means depending on the case, and in the borderline case it transmutes into agents' ends when all personal capacities are included. Symmetrically equality is implicit in liberty but is hidden by it in the cases of full liberties (the agents equally have in full the liberty considered). The two preceding chapters presented essential instances of full liberties, full act-freedom and full process-freedom respectively; a third instance will be considered in part V with the introduction of liberty that a priori does not have to stop where other people's liberty begins and is bounded only by people's relative force. In the meanwhile, we will focus on issues where the rational ideal of equality appears explicitly. The next part (part IV) will consider apart the question of the pure logic of the comparison of inequalities and of poverty, and the question of needs, basic needs and misery, since they use specific concepts and tools. The present part III gathers the other theories, most of which face basic problems drawn from the same cluster: the definition and properties of equal liberty, the inefficiencies of equality in several goods or with disincentive effects, the legitimacy of the unequal endowments in capacities for consumption and for exchange, and so on.

The opposite extreme case from full process liberalism (chapter 5) is full redistributive justice, or end justice, where all resources are jointly considered as relevant for redistribution, including capacities to produce and to consume, which can be compensated for, or, for the former category, whose product can be transferred; this is considered in chapter 7 (with the solutions of Justice and Practical Justice from Kolm 1971). Given the prevailing importance of human resources—including by the past production of present capital—(see chapter 2 and below), the intermediary cases consist largely of transfers to satisfy certain needs, form or support certain capacities, and diminish the inequality of incomes, notably labor incomes. The latter objective answers the very common criticism of excessive income inequality, which manifests a concern for *income justice*, where income, or the consumption it permits, is the end value of the conception of justice. In *full income justice*, the *ideal* is a complete equalization of incomes, which amounts to a complete pooling and socialization of productive capacities, even though one may stop short of this ideal for other reasons, notably because of the disincentive effect of redistribution on labor. In *partial income justice*, the ideal is the equalization of only part of incomes, and notably the pooling of only a fraction of the capacities used in production.

The present chapter 6 presents the solutions of the problems raised by the implementation and the justification of income justice. The justification concerns first, the opposite moral treatment of capacities used in production and in consumption, and second, the income form (with the moral justification of prices).

Two problems consist of incompatibilities between ideal income justice and Pareto-efficiency (whose justification is provided). The first problem is raised by the fact that, when preferences and satisfaction capacities are deleted from the classical economic process from resources to production, consumption and satisfaction, what remains are consumption bundles, whoses equality (demanded by rationality; see chapter 2) is generally inefficient (other possible allocations are preferred by everybody). The solution consists of the efficient second-best egalitarianism of a multidimensional maximin that leads to *efficient super-equity*. The result imposes certain limits to the discrepancies between disposable incomes which can, however, present notable differences.

The second problem concerns the celebrated disincentive effect of income taxation (and subsidies). This question has given rise to serious misunderstandings in both economics and political philosophy. The effect on output and the (Pareto-)inefficiency should be distinguished. The reason to base taxes on earned income rather than on mere capacities is much less an informational convenience than a conception of justice. Yet if this ideal is only partial income justice, its best representation is not a partial tax based on the totality of each earned income but, rather, the complete equalization of incomes earned during a given fraction of total time (a given duration). This *fixed-duration income equalization* is efficient with respect to the duration of labor.

The two questions of inefficient equality and the distinction between capacities are extended in this chapter into the more general ones of second-best justice, on the one hand, and the relation between justice and the human resources, on the other hand.

Other theories that basically rest on an ideal of full income justice, but offer other notable discussions and proposals, will be presented and discussed in further chapters. This is the case for the ideas of Rawls (chapter 8) and of Dworkin (chapter 9).

Chapters 7 and 8 will present respectively two works, published simultaneously, that rest on both equal liberties, and maximin as second-best efficient egalitarianism (but that are very different in other respects): *Justice and Equity* and Rawls's *A Theory of Justice.*

Chapter 9 will finally gather a number of other related and important theories and properties such as "fundamental insurance," efficient maximin and leximin in liberty, the role of social sentiments such as genuine envy, the modern theories of exploitation, the place of merit and responsibility in distributive justice, the concepts of equality of opportunity, and more formal criteria.

6.2   Second-Best Justice

Second-Best Egalitarianisms

Equality, as was noted earlier, is the a priori general form of rational direct justice. However, egalitarianisms of various kinds may often have to settle for less than strict equality of the relevant items, either because strict equality is not possible or because it interferes with other objectives—some of which may be equality in other items. The reconciliation of these various ends and possibilities requires associations of principles that can be of various types, such as compromises, priorities, superimposition (whereby one criterion is applied from the outcome of another), and so on.[1] In particular, certain equalities result from particularly deep reasons, and hence have priority, leaving only second-best solutions as possibilities for the others. One of them is *full act-freedom*, for the existential, logical and moral reasons presented in chapter 4, but which is often also commendable because of the efficiency of "decentralization" due to better local information, lesser coercion in implementation, and motivation by responsibility. The satisfaction of basic needs also has priority both for the same

---

1. A full analysis of the combinations of criteria is presented in Kolm 1990b.

existential reason as basic rights and for the alleviation of deep suffering (see chapters 7 and 11).

Still another case is the particular equality of power constituted by the principle of *unanimity*, which imposes the priority of *Pareto-efficiency*. The pervasiveness of this criterion makes it worthwhile to consider its reasons a little more closely.[2] Assume that the two alternative states A and B are possible and that everybody thinks that A is better than B (the costs of implementation are taken into account in these definitions, possibilities, and opinions; there is no further problem of information about these states and no further constraint imposed by somebody outside this society; and "better" describes a view that takes everything into account). Then implementing B rather than A cannot be the doing of any consistent, sane member of this society (since he thinks that B is better). If the implementation of B rather than that of A results from interactions between the actions of several members, this situation can be imputed to particular constraints on interpersonal relations that limit the scope of collective action, and that are insufficient information about others' preferences and situations, or insufficient possibilities of communication, of joint and integrated action, or of commitment (for instance, *a promise-enforcing institution that can enforce promises and promises conditional on enforceable promises eliminates the strategic causes of inefficiencies*, as noted in chapter 1). Yet these limitations can exist and induce the inefficiency, notably during provisional implementations of threats in a dynamic setting. Such an inefficiency is collectively self-inflicted harm and limitation of liberty. It can be seen as collective irrationality and social *akrasia* (weakness of the will), in any case a social disease. Furthermore, for the all-inclusive society, the idea that B is better than A is just *not thought* and thus cannot be sincerely expressed. Note that these reasons do not refer to "welfare," which may intervene indirectly as a personal reason for the preferences of welfare-seeking individuals.

In addition, one may have to consider only individual freedom obeying sane motivations, and individual preferences for only sane reasons, as for any ethical use of these concepts: one may thus have to ignore insane unethical causes and reasons such as malevolence, envy,

---

2. Detailed analyses of this topic are to be found in Kolm 1991b, 1993a, 1993e.

jealousy, malice, *schadenfreude* or gloating, and so on. Technically, this is achieved by cleaning ("laundering," "ironing") preferences for the corresponding structures (see Goodin 1986). Chapter 9 provides an example of how this is precisely done for the sentiment of envy.[3] This operation can in particular be applied for determining the conditions and consequences of Pareto-efficiency.

There are important instances where *equality is either impossible or such that another possible, unequal state is preferred by everybody*. This depends on the nature of the equalizand (what should ideally be equalized) and on a number of factors that basically refer to difficulties or impossibilities in the *transferability of individual capacities* or of *information* concerning them, to *social nonconvexities* in the effects of individualized items, to *multidimensional equalizations*, or to *indivisibilities*. Rather commonly, several of these factors intervene together.

Such circumstances lead one to resort to *second-best efficient egalitarianisms*. These second-best solutions rest on criteria that would yield equality in the relevant items when equality can be efficient (which implies its possibility). Among these criteria are the "maximins" or "leximins"[4] in comparable end-fulfillment ("fundamental preferences") of "practical justice" (Kolm 1971), in "primary goods" of the "difference principle" (Rawls 1971), in multidimensional equalizands (Kolm 1991d, 1993d, 1996b), and in liberties in general (Kolm 1993e) —see also chapters 7, 8, and 9.

Multidimensional and Income Egalitarianisms, Super-Equity

The Inefficiency of Equal Consumptions
If several individuals must have the same quantities of a consumption good, for each of several such goods, this is generally not Pareto-efficient for individuals with different tastes: they all prefer some other allocations where one individual has more of one good and another individual has more of another good.

Letting these individuals, or all the individuals, freely *exchange from a state with these equalities* has several drawbacks. (1) First, the result

---

3. The complete analysis is in Kolm 1991c, 1993f, and 1995a.
4. See chapter 3.

may not be Pareto-efficient either, for two reasons. (a) As with most exchanges, it may not be Pareto-efficient as a sharing of the total quantities of goods initially allocated. (b) Furthermore, even if it were Pareto-efficient in this sense (distributive efficiency), and even if one could not produce more of the initial quantities of one good without diminishing those of another good (productive efficiency), there generally are other possible allocations, with different but possible total quantities of these goods, that are preferred by all the individuals (since consumptions goods are generally not, or not all, primary resources, that is, they are produced, and different alternative bundles of total quantities can be produced). (2) A second and major drawback, also present in most exchanges, is that the free exchange considered gives an advantage to the individuals who are better endowed with *exchange capacities*, that is, bargaining skills and other capacities for dealing in exchanges and markets. This may make a large difference in the result. Now "to each according to his cunningness and his capacity for dissimulation" may not be considered an acceptable principle of justice. (3) Third, the individuals do not face the same set of *other* individuals, and hence the same *exchange opportunities* (other's supplies and demands, plus others' exchange capacities). (4) One may want to add that this exchange favors individuals who have more original tastes for more common goods, and discriminates against individuals who have more common tastes for rarer goods.

Another possibility would be to replace the equal allocation considered by the allocation corresponding to a *competitive equilibrium from this allocation*. It is a priori reached spontaneously only when the individuals are all relatively very small, among other classical conditions (including divisibility of the goods). The effects of exchange capacities disappear. The result is Pareto-efficient for the allocation of the given total quantities, but it generally is not if one considers the possibility of another *production* of these goods (or one would have to choose a particular initial allocation). The initially equal allocation of all consumption goods provides the individuals with equal incomes computed with the corresponding competitive prices, and the individuals can thus be seen as facing the same exchange opportunities with these competitive prices. With possibilities of production and of transformation of goods, efficient equal-income competitive equilibrium can be reached by full competitive equilibrium, with production and transformation of goods, with an equal sharing of both all initial resources and the profits of all firms. Yet in all cases *the competitive prices have a priori no reason to be considered fair or just.* In particular, the caveat concerning the situation of the individuals' tastes with respect to others' tastes and to the goods available (or the resources necessary to produce them) still holds. We will, however, obtain below certain possible justifications for efficient equal incomes.

The Possible Justice of Equal Allocations

Now, an equal allocation of goods, for several goods, simply results from the rationality of equality when these goods are the end values of justice (see chapter 2). It is thus normal to hear such demands from both people and scholars, although not all these goods are consumption goods or only consumption goods (for instance, education is only in part a consumption goods). Indeed end value of justice, and hence specific egalitarian claims, attach standardly to goods that are conditions of normal existence such as necessities in case of dire scarcity, human capital (education and health care or access to them), basic public services of security and justice, aspects of housing and of culture, and so on; see also the analyses of basic rights (chapter 4) and basic needs (chapter 11). Among scholars, Tobin (1970), Rawls (1971), Dworkin (1981), and Walzer (1983) respectively demand equal allocations of consumption goods, of "primary goods," of resources, and of goods in "spheres of justice" (for Rawls and Dworkin this is a prima facie first best, and Walzer—and similarly Max Weber—rather describes his view of people's views of justice).

In particular, the position concerning distributive justice that consists only in the endorsement of the "natural" allocation of consumptive capacities, tastes, preferences, life-plans, and so on, implies, as we have seen, the prima facie equality of *all consumption goods.* Rawls and Dworkin, who emphasize this view but choose other ideal equalizands, face a priori a problem of consistency (which will be analyzed in chapters 8 and 9).

Uncompromising Justice

Justice in a field or with respect to a good is often considered as something not tradable, something that cannot be sold or compromised for some advantage, even for unanimous satisfaction. It is then deemed to have the nature, and the requirements of precedence, which are characteristic of properties like honor and dignity. This sometimes results from the fact that the considered goods per se are seen as morally improper for trade-off (such as the sale for money of basic liberties, votes, court decisions, or honor). Yet specific and segmented justice is often appreciated beyond these cases (for health care, education, culture, etc., which can otherwise be bought and sold without suspicion of immorality). Then justice for each of such goods requires the relevant equality, from the rationality requirement. With several such goods, justice requires multidimensional equality. If several *consumption goods* must be equal, this is a case where specific conceptions and sentiments of justice tend to impair Pareto-efficiency (another very important instance of seemingly inefficient sense of justice will be encountered in shortly). Note that equality in nonconsumption goods does not a priori induce such inefficiency since these goods must at any rate be transformed or exchanged in order to yield goods that can be consumed. Furthermore the relevant preferences would probably have to be the full ones, encompassing the moral views of justice, notably the views just considered, and hence the corresponding indirect concern for other persons' allocations.

This segmented aspect of justice among goods or fields has been pointed out by Max Weber. This is the basis of Walzer's "spheres of justice" whithin which the relevant equality should prevail. These "spheres" encompass broad domains, such as "economic consumption" (probably with income as an aggregate), health care, education, the political process, the judicial system. Walzer also considers it likely that there will be inequality in each sphere, with different people being favored in each. He sees this as an ethical advantage of the "spheres" approach over the global one where the inequality would favor or wrong the same people across the board. Furthermore, social pressures and conflicts are likely to lead to people being favored in the "spheres" they relatively care for the most. This tends to create an efficiency advantage over the situation of strict equality in all spheres.

Yet Walzer lumps "economic consumption," rather narrowly understood, into one "sphere" represented by "income." Rawls also lumps economic consumption goods into disposable income. He moreover considers a kind of generalized income in advocating the maximum of the lowest level of a weighted sum of "primary goods" (they are, in addition to income or wealth, the individual's power, social position,

and self-respect or the means to it—all of which have to be measured
in the first place), when he considers the inefficiency of equality for
another reason to be discussed below (it is also another inefficiency,
defined in terms of primary goods). And Dworkin obtains about equal
income from exchanges of resources initially equally allocated.

Income Justice

To be sure, income equality, or lower income inequality, is the most
standard economic "egalitarian" ideal. Comparisons and measures of
income inequalities are the standard corresponding information. Progressive income tax is the standard tool of economic policy established
in the name of justice.

If, however, "income" means the value of consumption (present or
future) computed with certain prices, the justice of these prices has to
be ascertained. With income justice, the scholastic question of the
"just price" is much alive. The use of market prices may be justified by
freedom (of exchange) or by the related efficiency. Yet in this case
income equality discriminates against tastes that are more common or
for rarer goods, and in favor of tastes that are more original and for
more abundant goods. This situation depends, for each individual,
both on his tastes and on the tastes of others. Now the main idea
behind the use of income as the variable for direct justice is that the
specificities of an individuals' tastes are not relevant to justice toward
this individual. This reason, however, says neither that an individual
could justly be favored or victimized by others' tastes nor that his own
tastes could justly favor or victimize other people. Yet, truly, these
effects of others' tastes or of the relative abundance or scarcity of
resources on an individual depend on his own tastes. But, more basically, the irrelevance of an individual's tastes implies that his bundle of
consumption goods, rather than his income, is the end value of justice,
and this assumption does not lead to equal incomes but to identical
bundles of consumption goods.

Equal incomes, however, can also be seen as a case of equal means:
equal purchasing power, equal real freedom to buy (with free access to
markets). In this view, income is an amount of money (say) used to
buy goods. The noted effect of relative tastes and resources remains
unchanged, with the same conclusion. In addition, this income equality is really not equal purchasing power, since this power also depends

on exchange capacities (bargaining skill, market abilities); nor is it equal opportunities to buy, since these opportunities also depend on the supplies and demands of the set of other persons, a set that depends on the specific person considered. All these inequalities can be substantial. Only in the *theoretical* case of perfect competition (numerous small agents acting individually with the same relevant information and no transaction cost) do these two views of income, as a measure (or value) or as a mean, amount to the same.

Since the irrelevance of individuals' preferences leads to equality in consumption goods, can this in turn justify the focus on the limitation of income discrepancies? Can this transformation make room for Pareto-efficiency or, indeed, result from it? What is the corresponding relevant measure of disposable income?

Efficient Super-Equity

Multidimensional Egalitarian Maximin   We thus consider a set of "economic" consumption goods for which equality is ideal because of the assumed irrelevance, for justice, of preferences, tastes, and consumptive capacities, but such that unanimous preference and Pareto-efficiency standardly defined have priority. Pareto-efficiency is valued here as the exhaustion of the possibilities of unanimous desired changes and hence for freedom, as the implementation of collective freedom of choice or "social liberty" noted earlier, rather than for "welfare" (although an individual's "welfare" can motivate his preferences). Since multidimensional equality is generally inefficient, an efficient second-best egalitarian solution is sought for. The straightforward answer is: Loosen the requirement of equality as long as everybody favors this change, or move toward equality only if it is not against everybody's will; that is, choose a state such that no individual prefers a more equal one. This solution is a "multidimensional maximin." With efficiency, the maxim is: Choose a state such that no other possible state is preferred by all and no other more equal state is preferred by one.

This concept requires a concept of "more or less equal" for distributions of *bundles* of quantities of different goods, that is, for multidimensional distributions. The case where there is only one good, that is, one type of quantity, a unidimensional distribution, is a particular case. Chapter 10 will show the various reasons, meanings (and limits) for the consideration that a small transfer from a richer individual to a poorer, which diminishes the inequality *within the pair*, also diminishes the *injustice of the inequality* of the distribution with a larger number of people. The various, rich ethical and logical properties of this view (analyzed in Kolm 1966a, sections 6 and 7) will also be recalled. This comparison of unidimensional distributions has three or four natural and meaningful extentions for the comparison of multidimensional distributions (Kolm 1973b, 1975b, 1977a; see chapter 10). The strictest of these multidimensional comparisons, which implies all the others, is considered here. It implies in particular that the above unidimensional comparison holds for the quantities of each type of goods taken separately, and also that it holds for all the sets of individual incomes that one can compute from the two considered multidimensional distributions with any set of given prices.[5]

Then the property that no individual prefers a "more equal" (less unjustly unequal) distribution is shown to be equivalent to *super-equity* (Kolm 1973a), that is, no individual prefers any (weighted) average of the individuals' allocations to his own allocation (Kolm 1991d, 1993d, g, 1995a, c, 1996b). Super-equity implies in particular that no individual prefers any other's allocation to his own (Equity; see chapter 7), and unanimous preference to the complete equal sharing of the existing goods (the mean of the individual allocations).

Efficient Super-Equitable Allocations   Then, *efficient super-equity* is shown to possess the following properties.[6] We consider the prices corresponding to efficiency (the individual allocations would in general be chosen by the individuals facing these prices with their given incomes), and values computed with these prices. We say that an

---

5. The strictest concept, presently used, consists in considering that a distribution becomes "more equal" when each individual transfers to each other a given proportion of any quantity he has (this proportion depends only on the two individuals), and equal distributions are unchanged. It also consists in each individual bundle of goods in a "more equal" distribution being an average (generally weighted) of the individual bundles in the other distribution, with the same total quantities. It is finally equivalent to the sum of the values taken by any concave function for all the individual bundles being higher for a more equal distribution. See chapter 10.

6. See the proofs in Kolm 1987f, 1991d, 1993d, 1993g, 1996b. Individuals' preferences are assumed to be "smooth" (differentiable), and, for property 1 and its consequences, to present "satiation" (convexity, quasi-concavity of indifference loci).

individual "can buy" a certain bundle of goods merely as an image to express that his income does not fall short of the value of these goods.

1. *An efficient allocation is super-equitable if each individual can buy the quantities consumed by any other of the goods that he himself likes.*

2. *If an allocation is efficient super-equitable, each individual can buy the quantities consumed by any other of the goods of which they both consume some amount.*

Note that an individual "liking" a good means that he would enjoy to receive some (more) of it for free. He may not actually consume this good in any amount (say that he then finds it too expensive to buy any quantity of it). Property 1 implies that *an efficient allocation with equal incomes is super-equitable,* since then each individual can buy any other's whole bundle of goods—a property that is also directly obvious (this proves that efficient super-equity is possible in classical economic conditions, since equal income competitive equilibrium is efficient and exists, resulting as it does from perfect competition with equal sharing of both all initial resources and all firms' profits). Property 2 implies that individuals who consume the same goods (in types of goods, not in quantities) must have the same income for efficient super-equity to hold. More generally, efficient super-equity tends to require less unequal incomes if tastes are more similar and if the people are poorer (since they then tend to spend a larger share of their income on the same "necessities" and basic staple). However, the major question when one considers global justice for a whole society, and one that puts to the forefront both unequal incomes and the qualification about "liked goods," appears when one considers one very important and particular good: leisure, that is, each individual's consumptive use of his capacities.

Leisure and Distributive Justice   An individual's leisure is the availability of his capacities, for something else than labor. An individual "buys" his own leisure in working less at the cost of the income forgone, and hence the market price of an individual's leisure is his wage rate (per unit of time, but effort and intensity of labor can also be considered). An individual's capacities generally differ from those of others. This entails different wage rates, for capacities used in labor. But the capacities a priori also differ when they are used in leisure.

Both labor and leisure are individual-specific goods in nature. Furthermore leisure is also individual-specific in use. That is, one individual has no use for another's leisure. For instance, another's hour of sleep cannot provide rest for him. Individuals sometimes compare the duration of their leisure time, but just as they commonly compare quantities of different goods of the same type but of different qualities.[7] We might call "total income" and "ordinary income" an individual's disposable income respectively including and not including the value of his leisure. Property 1 entails, in particular, the following Property 3: *An efficient allocation is super-equitable if no individual's ordinary income exceeds any other's total income.* This condition is in particular satisfied by *equal ordinary incomes*, the classical ideal. It is also satisfied by equal total incomes, but we will see that this is an abusive equality because it values at the individual's wage rate, that is, at his productivity, large pieces of leisure that have no reason to be compared by this value (this constitutes most of his time, and it includes, for example, the time for the satisfaction of vital needs). But the condition of Property 3 may furthermore permit notable discrepancies in individuals' incomes. It says that no ordinary income exceeds any other by more than the value of leisure of the individual with the latter income. If, as an order of magnitude, the individuals work during about one fifth of their total time, and if the primary incomes consist only of earned or wage incomes, no redistribution is necessary for reaching super-equity if no wage rate exceeds five times the value of another (the figure could be six for taking account of retirement). This result can be compared with Plato's assertion, in *The Republic*, that justice require that no ratio of incomes exceeds four (this may amount to the present result, with the figures of this time). The condition still imposes a certain income redistribution in most large societies, yet the admissible discrepancies may be notable (the condition is only a sufficient one). From property 2, the *converse* of property 3 holds if all individuals consume the same nonleisure goods. This is generally not the case, and this still widens the income gaps permitted by efficient super-equity.

The margin of possibility in the conditions for efficient super-equity can be put to a few important uses. First, one can introduce a certain

---

7. A full analysis of this issue is provided in Kolm 1993d, 1993e, 1993g; see also 1996e.

amount of other criteria in the choice of the allocation, such as allocation according to the product of labor, to needs, to the painfulness of
labor, or to gifts and bequest received. Second, one can reach the
distributional objective while avoiding the inefficiency of the disincentive that results from strictly basing redistributive transfers on earned
income, by using other characteristics, even if they are not perfectly
known (this question will be analyzed in detail shortly). Less important, this margin may permit one to neglect the differences in individuals' capacities in buying goods with their income (see section 6.3).

The Justifications of Equal Incomes   Efficient super-equity provides
the *only justification of the classical ideal of equal* (ordinary) *incomes*
when the situation is *not one of very small agents in very large number*.
When, on the contrary, this kind of situation holds, there are two
other possible justifications of income equality, which indeed leave
no other possibility than strict equality. One justification is *freedom
of exchange from an equal allocation of all resources* (including
profit shares) in the conditions of *perfect competition* (divisibilities and
other required convexities, no collective agreement of sufficient size,
no transaction cost, perfect information on prices; in particular, differences in individuals' exchange capacities have no effect, and the
differences in the sets of other individuals' supplies and demand that
an individual faces vanish). Freedom of exchange from an equal allocation of consumption goods is also possible, yet this initial allocation
has to be well chosen so as to warrant overall efficiency taking into
account the production of consumption goods from the primary resources. The second justification is equal independent instrumental
liberty, or *Equity* (see chapter 7), plus *efficiency*, when the mass of
consumers present certain properties of continuity[8] and they consume
the same goods.[9]

---

8. Individuals' preferences must be smooth (differentiable) and parametrized in a
connected set; see Varian (1976), Hammond (1979), Kleinberg (1980), and Champsaur
and Laroque (1981) for this effect of what they call "no-envy" (see chapters 7 and 9).

9. Other justifications of equal-income competitive equilibrium exist when it is conceived as a rule applicable to different populations (works of Thomson, Magahisa,
Maniquet, Suh, etc.). On the question of the meaning of such pluralities, see chapters
9 and 15.

"Social Nonconvexities"

Inefficient equality for reasons of "social nonconvexities" refers to phenomena of the following type. With the standard increasing average propensity to save, higher global free saving is promoted by a more unequal income distribution. Now, higher national savings may permit having higher levels of investment, capital and growth, of future national income, of national power, and also of everybody's intertemporal income and welfare after the redistribution of this income flow (with, generally, inequality of these intertemporal achievements);[10] these results may (or may not) mobilize the effects of higher investment that result in higher employment or faster technical progress. As another example, the argument that the rich segment of an unequal distribution of income and wealth is necessary for the development of the arts (from which the poor *may* benefit) is not only a classical hypocritical defense of inequality: It is just a de facto reflection of how elaborate art came about in almost all of history. In other examples, most organizations, of all types, require certain hierarchies that imply unequal powers, statuses, and often incomes; these inequalities may thus be required for the efficient production of all types of goods, including safety and survival (defense), and for overall efficiency.

Noncompensatabilities

A number of important differences in capacities used in the general enjoyment of life cannot be fully compensated for by transfers of specific goods or services, or of income. This often prevents the efficient equalization of possibilities that include these capacities, or of individual end-fulfilment (see chapter 7). This is clear for the case of "handicaps," but this is also a rather common situation (we could indeed define a "handicap" by the impossibility to compensate it fully). Then, equalization would require that one introduce artificial impediments for the better endowed: this would be adding cruelty to Pareto-inefficiency.

---

10. The resulting "Practical Justice" (maximin in fundamental—comparable—utility) distribution and policy are studied in Kolm 1974a (see also Phelps 1977).

Redistributions with Act-Freedom

Efficient Equalization

Act-freedom enables the agents to react to interferences with the aim or the means of their acts. This applies notably to the economic liberties to exchange, work, save, spend, hire, and so on, while distributive policies that try to implement conceptions of justice affect incomes and the levels of wages or of various prices faced by the agents.

The preceding examples concerning savings and the arts, as well as the situations of free exchange in general and nonforced labor in particular that will intervene shortly, are cases of act-freedom (saving and supporting the arts are assumed to be noncompulsory). Act-freedom is respected either for the basic existential or moral reasons discussed earlier or for implementational efficiency. This efficiency is the frequent advantage of "decentralized" information, choice, and action, over implementation by "central" command. This "decentralization" can indeed save costs, and avoid impossibilities, in information about local possibilities, preferences, supplies, demands, and performance, as well as in computation and coercive implementation. It can also increase or enhance responsibility, and hence motivation, awareness, and effort.

Now act-freedom may constrain equalizations implemented by aim-constraint. For instance, an announced forced equalization of earned income in a large society where people work freely and only for income suppresses all work and all production, since each individual keeps virtually nothing of any amount he earns when it is divided among all. This standard remark, however, fails to count the direct consumption of resources in leisure (or consumption of one's own product), which increases when production or exchange decreases. Yet this inefficiency still exists if we take account of the inefficient mix of goods that results (such as too much leisure and too little of other goods) or of the loss resulting from suboptimal (nonexistent) division of labor.

Inefficiencies due to incentives have indeed attracted much attention from economists and philosophers alike, yet they need careful treatment. For instance, a common idea (often repeated in presentations of Rawls's "difference principle"; see chapter 8) is that if we redistribute too much income away from highly paid skilled people, they would produce less. This assertion elicits two remarks.

First, if these people work less, they consume the leisure made available, and they value the new units of leisure at their wage rate (for moderate changes) if they choose freely their working time. If the redistribution is made by an income tax, these persons' "total income" (including the value of leisure) is lower excluding tax but higher including tax, and the transfers benefit those who receive them. Similarly the people who cease to receive the direct or indirect services of this labor economize, by the same token, the cost they would have paid for them. There may thus be no notable loss in welfare. This at least holds for relatively limited changes, and it would not for large changes (beyond the "first order" approximation). Now, is the extra leisure taken by professionals because of the part of their income tax that they cannot pass on to their customers beyond the relevant "first order"?

Second, and most important, the opposite consequence may occur: taking money away from these people may induce them to work and earn more in order to make up for this loss. Indeed it is always possible to make them produce more by this "tax" and redistribution, in choosing a tax sufficiently high and independent of the amount of work they put in (yet this tax could depend on their abilities, as revealed by their earning per unit of time, their type of work, or their diplomas, etc.). Even if the tax is a function of the income actually earned, the result depends on the well-known balance between the "price effect" and the "income effect"; it in particular depends on the tax rate and more generally on the tax schedule. Furthermore, even though the abilities are not completely known, there usually is by far sufficient information involving them so as to establish a "lump-sum" tax of the noted type. But of course labor can adjust by all its chosen characteristics such as duration, intensity and effort, location, training and education (the choice of which, however, depends on life-long forecasts). In the end, redistributive taxes based on *earned* income introduce the classical economic inefficiency in terms of "satisfactions" (Pareto-inefficiency), but they do not necessarily and a priori induce a lower marketed output (the kind of so-called "inefficiency" that noneconomists and notably philosophers often have in mind), and lump-sum taxes are often possible, they produce no "satisfaction" inefficiency, and they can a priori require any labor.

Fixed-Duration Income Equalization[11]

The objective, however, is not to extract labor but to set up a just and Pareto-efficient social system and in particular redistributive and fiscal system. This is perfectly possible for one of the few most common conceptions of distributive justice (possibly the most common one). This conception is manifested by the desire to lower the income inequalities that result from the "spontaneous" working of the market. It holds notably this view with regard to the labor market and wages, and we will focus on this resource here, since labor accounts for a very large part of the value of the resources and of the output (notably considering its indirect and accumulated contribution) as will be emphasized in the next section. Notice that this view demands only partial equalization of incomes, rather than complete one, irrespective of any disincentive effect and as a purely moral stand. That is, this view holds that the "natural" allocation of productive capacities is unjust but only partly so. It holds that the individuals have some particular partial title in the usufruct of their own capacities, even when they choose to use them to produce, for reasons that refer to process-freedom and to conceptions of the self.

The natural interpretation of this conception of justice is that the income earned during a certain fraction of the time is completely redistributed to equality, whereas the individuals are free to keep untaxed and unsubsidized any extra income they choose to earn. That is, individuals are taxed by the excess of their wage over average wage for this reference duration, or similarly subsidized if their wage is below average. These taxes and subsidies do not depend on the individuals' actual duration of labor, and hence they induce no inefficiency with respect to this variable (but the further effects of effort, training, or education might also have to be considered). Hence this fiscal structure permits at once justice, Pareto-efficiency and a free labor market.

Practically, this structure can say that the individuals work for the collectivity during the first x days, or y working hours of the week, and that they own the rest of their time (or the benefits they derive from it) and are free to allocate it between leisure and labor for an untaxed and

---

11. This concept is analyzed in Kolm 1966b, 1991d, 1993d, 1995e, 1996a and b.

unsubsidized benefit. For example, the actual redistribution in present western developed countries corresponds to an equalization duration of 10 to 18 hours a week, but of course the tax structure is very different, and wasteful, since the tax is based on actually earned income (this estimation takes account of the distributive effects of social security systems, of public goods, etc.).

The *equalization duration* k constitutes a degree of collective usufruct of society's human resources, and a *degree of solidarity* within society. Its complement $1 - k$ (if total time is measured as 1) constitutes a degree of the individuation (or "naturalness" or "spontaneousness") of society. The case $k = 0$ corresponds to full process liberalism. A k equal to the official duration of labor, in societies where there exists one, approximates the polar case where the usufruct of productive capacities is fully shared whereas the "natural" allocation of consumptive capacities is endorsed. If overtime labor is possible, the policy amounts to leave it untaxed. We will also see below why higher k and notably $k = 1$ are meaningless. A very egalitarian, yet realistic, society would have a k of the order of magnitude of half the average working time or the official duration of labor, for instance, 20 hours per week. Half this level holds for the most process-liberal modern western developed societies.[12]

The actual tax system should superimpose taxes for other reasons on this redistributive system. This would notably be the case of a benefit taxation to finance public goods, and more generally of the payments determined by "liberal social contracts" (see chapter 5), since the partial equalization takes care of distributive justice. The redistributive scheme can theoretically be implemented in a decentralized manner without a priori knowledge of the wage rates determined by the market, in allocating to each of the n individuals the fraction k/n of the time of each other (he can sell this time on the labor market

---

12. Let i, j denote individuals, and let w_i, l_i, y_i, and t_i denote respectively individual i's competitive (or efficiency) wage rate, labor duration, disposable income, and tax (if $t_i < 0$, this is a subsidy of $-t_i$). Fixed-duration income equalization with the equalization duration of k is the set of taxes $t_i = (w_i - \overline{w})k$, where $\overline{w}$ is the average wage rate, $\overline{w} = (\sum w_i)/n$ if n is the number of individuals. Then individual i's disposable income is $y_i = w_i l_i - t_i = (l_i - k)w_i + \theta\overline{w}$. Full process liberalism correspond to $k = 0$, $t_i = 0$ for all i, $y_i = w_i l_i$ for all i. Fixed-duration income equalization is a "concentration toward the mean" of the distribution of full incomes (productivities), a property introduced and analyzed in Kolm 1966b and applied to risk (see also chapter 10 below).

or use it to receive direct services, and an individual can use his own time, received or bought, in labor or in leisure). Perfect competition from this allocation achieves the result, in the classical conditions that it requires. Efficient super-equity is satisfied by fixed-duration income equalization with levels of k not too small (the lower limit depends on all the parameters of the problem).[13] Nonlabor incomes can be similarly equalized by the initial equal sharing of the rights in nonhuman resources and in firms' profits.

Why Disincentive Redistribution?
These efficient redistributions, however, are not actual practice. The actual tax base is *earned* (and other) *income* rather than wage rates, productivities, or income earned during a given duration. The subsidy base for low incomes is not just earning capacities, but, rather, the actual income gap that the subsidy or assistance aims at filling in order to satisfy basic needs or to obtain a minimal level of income (the rare negative income taxes are also based on earned income). The tax base is also earned income when the proceed is used for general public expenditures, possibly with the intention that the tax has an equalizing effect through progressive taxation. Even if the resulting reactions in labor supply do not lower actual output because of the income effects, at least these transfers based on elastic items impair Pareto-efficiency. This is "irrational" since everybody could be better off otherwise. Why are such policies pursued?

The economic literature says that the reason is information, specifically that earned income is taken as a proxy for inobservable productive capacities. This answer is a priori puzzling on two grounds. First, capacities are indeed inelastic and would provide an efficient base (with due qualification for education and training), but the policy aims at reducing income inequalities, so why would capacities constitute the first-best base? The answer commonly suggested is that the knowledge of capacities would permit one to take, as base and ideal equalizand, total income, including the value of leisure. But we will see that this constitutes a misconceived ideal, and that even including a part of leisure is against the conception of justice that leads to an equalizing

---

13. See Kolm 1991d, 1993d, 1995f, 1996b.

income taxation. A policy base for redistribution concerns justice and not only efficiency (yet fixed-duration income equalization uses capacities).[14] Second, the explanation by difficulties of information is a priori unsatisfactory. The competitive wage rate, which is the (marginal) value of these capacities for given effort, is often readily observable, and in other cases it can be computed from observable earned income and labor time; in a number of cases, the wage rate is more observable than earned income and labor time. The informational reason presumed sometimes exists, but it is not very general and it does not suffice to provide the explanation—at least it does not suffice by itself. Furthermore, if the costs of information are included within the possibilities and constraints of the economy, as they should, then the use of the resulting proxies may in the end not be Pareto-inefficient.

There is, however, a more important reason to base redistributive taxes and policies on earned income, as far as labor is concerned. It consists of the widespread moral and conceptual view that does not endorse the "natural" allocation of productive capacities and only of these. This moral stand wants lower inequality in the disposable incomes produced by the productive capacities. These incomes do not include leisure in any amount. Leisure, indeed, consists of the use of consumptive capacities. Hence the inequality in productive capacities that is objected to concerns capacities used in production rather than capacities usable in production. This moral view is concerned with what individuals "give to" and "receive from" society, and it does not see leisure as included in these items but, rather, as a private and personal matter a priori irrelevant to redistributive justice.[15] Indeed no leisure is included in the standard concept of a disposable income. Similarly this common redistributive view does not hold that the leisure time (or part of it) of the productive engineer or manager should be taxed at the value of this person's high wage rate, or that the

---

14. In the particular model of "optimal taxation" of Mirrlees (1970), productive capacity happens to be the only parameter that differentiates the individuals and hence can differentiate first-best taxes (with a "welfarist" objective), since the individuals are assumed to have identical utility functions.

15. Note that this view also results from efficient super-equity (see above) where leisure is excluded from the conditions that constrain incomes.

leisure time of a person with low productive abilities should be subsidized in function of his low wage rate (note that taxing a skilled person's leisure in order to induce him to work would be a practical matter, not based on an ethic of redistribution).[16]

The inefficiency induced by this choice of an elastic base thus results from a moral and conceptual view concerning the items relevant for justice. It may remain if the individuals' moral views are included within their preferences. The existence of the inefficiency can be explained by the fact that another system of redistribution that would make everybody better off would lose meaningfulness in distributional ethics, require new information (this, however, can be part of the constraints), and introduce a tax reform that disturbs the understandable existing social compromise. Yet the limitation of this inefficiency accounts, at least in part, for the considered redistribution being de facto only partial (the arguments actually provided refer more to the elasticity of labor supply). However, the fact that this redistribution is only partial certainly also has a moral ground: The "natural" allocation of productive capacities is seen as having *a certain* degree of legitimacy. But, then, fixed-duration income equalization constitutes the efficient equalization of this ethic. It dominates partial redistribution based on earned income such as progressive income taxation (the comparison requires that benefit taxation for public goods be added to fixed-duration income equalization). And it has a clear and rational moral meaning. This solution, however, requires information concerning productivity or wages. The question of this information would then indeed acquire a certain relevance. Income is more observable than the wage rate in certain occupations, notably because the duration of labor may not be well defined; this is in particular the case for a number of high incomes and independent occupations. Moreover, effort is quite less informationally dissociable from capacities than

---

16. The work that an individual performs directly for himself can be included either in labor or in leisure, thus providing two possible conceptions, but this is often not an important issue. Moreover, the distributive policy may consider as relevant other characteristics of labor than its productivity, notably its relative painfulness which it would compensate for (if the corresponding relevant differences are the durations of work, the policy amounts to an equalization of wage rates), or indeed the effort or merit in the formation of capacities, which it would reward.

duration is. All relevant sources of information should be considered, but they have to be used to estimate the morally relevant variables.

Total Income

We have noticed the suggestion to equalize total income, including the value of leisure reckoned, for efficiency, at its competitive market price; this price is, for each individual, his competitive wage rate, since the wage rate measures the income forgone by working one unit of time less. The problem is the meaning of such a device. If this equality stands for the equalization of the effects of all capacities, the solution is, rather, full, complete, or end justice, that is, Justice and Practical Justice of *Justice and Equity* (Kolm 1971), with the interpersonally comparable and ordinal "fundamental preferences" (see chapter 7). If total income equalization stands for equal bundles of final consumption goods including leisure time, then the efficient solution is efficient super-equity described earlier, which is satisfied by total income equalization but is also by certain limited but substantial inequalities. In all cases the mistake consists in imposing a priori that the equalizand has the form of an income, which implies that all the inframarginal units are reckoned at the value of the marginal one. For instance, in the equal total incomes the durations of the satisfaction of vital needs are valued at the individuals' wage rates or marginal productivities, which is devoid of reason (and is unfair toward the most productive people). This solution thus is irrational, unjustified, arbitrary. It is thus no surprise that it entails transfers of extravagant amounts (if, as an order of magnitude, people work about one-fifth of their total time, total income equalization implies transfers that would be five times those required by the total equalization of normal, earned incomes).

Undominated equality may be possible

Redistribution based on earned incomes (whatever its reason) may elicit avoidance, with its effects on *total output, possibilities of transfers*, and *Pareto-efficiency*. The effects on total output and Pareto-efficiency can be due to the reactions of both the individuals who yield the transfer and of those who receive it (subsidies for income maintenance or needs satisfaction that complement earned income constitute a 100 percent rate, but milder "negative income taxes" also create a disincentive). Yet the overall effects are much stronger with respect to the tax side, especially when taxes also finance general public goods.

With respect to Pareto-efficiency, the first remark is that its existence, form, and seriousness cannot be asserted off-hand, without an actual consideration of all the relevant variables. This holds for both possible reasons to base redistribution on earned income. With respect to the informational reason, as was noted earlier, the restriction of actual possibilities due to costs and impossibilities in information should be considered (available information on both the wage rate and earned income should be used, and we have noticed that their relative observability depends on the type of occupation). With respect to the moral and conceptual reason, these views of the public may have to be introduced in the overall preferences of individuals for considering the possible Pareto-inefficiency: This generally tends to attenuate this inefficiency.

The effect on the volume of social output is a priori ambiguous, since the income effects of taxes may compensate or overcompensate the disincentive consequence of their price effect. For the receivers, however, both effects lead to lower production. Note that one can say that the amount of some fixed-time *overall* income including the "consumption" of some leisure time does not change, but its value at the actual wage rate increases and its value at this wage minus the marginal tax rate decreases (this latter effect also expresses that the value of this income's use decreases because of a distorted product mix, due to the fact that the tax subsidizes leisure).

Avoidance clearly limits the amount of transfers that one can achieve thanks to the taxation of earned incomes. This is, for instance, shown by the "Laffer curve" celebrated in other contexts. The possible amounts may or may not suffice for reaching an objective of justice. They *may or may not, for example, permit an equality in the (post-transfer) disposable incomes that is not dominated by possible higher incomes for all.* The possibility depends on the *elasticities of labor supplies* and on the *distribution of capacities in the population.* It is by no means always ruled out. The distribution of capacities appears notably as a crucial variable. If, for instance, there are many individuals with similar high capacities and only very few with low capacities, the equalizing taxes can be only a very small fraction of the former's incomes because of their relatively high number, and undominated equality is possible. (This small tax rate moreover induces a vanishing of the "product mix" inefficiency loss due to the sharing of one's time between labor and leisure, caused by this incentive for the high income earners).[17] In another, more balanced case where the population divides into two categories of similar size, with similar individuals in each with high and low productivity respectively, this undominated equality is commonly possible, since the most productive individuals commonly do not diminish very much their labor even if they are taxed by up to 50 percent of their earnings. Note that taxes on the highest incomes reach this order of magnitude and more (especially if one includes taxes on inheritance and property, and various indirect and other taxes) in countries that are globally among the most productive (such as Scandinavian countries). The main reason for dominated equality thus is the asymmetry in the distribution of capacities, with many more individuals who receive than individuals who yield if there is to be equality, which requires a tax that takes away a much larger proportion of high incomes.

6.3   Distributive Justice and the Human Resource

Human Resources

The main end, man, is also the main means. As was pointed out earlier, wage income standardly accounts for 60 to 90 percent of GNP in modern economies, labor income is still higher, and most of the rest is income from capital which is mostly income from past labor (and generally needs labor to be obtained). Natural nonhuman resources provide only a couple of percent of GNP, and the rules of their allocation is related to individuals' capacities or properties in various possible ways. Furthermore the human resource is also used directly by its holder in homework, consumption activities, rest, leisure time (nonlabor), or leisurely work (noneffort), even though "rest" is a particular use of a resource. Most of the human resource is in fact used this way in the sense that nonwork time is usually much longer than worktime, and these final uses include the invaluable ones of the satisfaction of basic, vital needs (such as minimal sleep and eating). Indeed

---

17. This loss is of "second order of smallness" because of the individuals' free choice under this income constraint.

the very capacities for willing, acting, feeling, and enjoying, the essence of the person or of the individual, are human resources. Therefore a priori a main part of the distribution problem in society concerns the distribution of the human resource, and at least certain aspects of this question are bound to raise particularly deep and delicate issues.

Now this resource comes, for humans, as housing does for snails: Each person carries a share with him. The free agent, the enjoyer, the planner, is indeed but a chunk of human resource. This allocation therefore constitutes a "natural" allocation of this resource, where natural rather means individualistic (see the discussion in chapter 3). Then each person owns himself (or at least enjoys the usufruct of his own human asset). This is both the basis of capitalism for the Lockean tradition, and the definition of socialism for Marx and before him for the "Ricardian socialists," Blanqui, and many others—"from each according to his capacities and to each according to his work," therefore to each according to his capacities (assuming that "work" does not only mean effort in intensity or time). The consequence is *full process liberalism* (even the allocation of nonhuman natural resources is delegated to the individuals' uses of their capacities by the methods of collective agreement or first occupancy, which use human resources both directly and through means acquired thanks to them). The transfer of product away from this "natural" distribution is condemned as exploitation by Smith and Marx when this is done by capitalists thanks to low wages, and as theft by free-marketeers when this is done by the state's taxes. All see these transfers as akin to the direct ownership of others' human capital, or slavery.

Other people see this "natural," individualistic, allocation as arbitrary, in various possible degrees, and they see humankind, or its subgroups, as communities that have to share this resource or its product among their members, according to criteria that are not merely who happens to have received it in the first place. Hence just distribution in this respect amounts to a duty of *solidarity*, with the resources of the better endowed benefiting others. The criteria of this distribution, however, are bound to mobilize not only legitimacy and equality from rational justice, but also needs and compassion (see chapters 11 and 16).

Especially after education has been received, individuals' capacities differ widely. This is the main basis of the division of labor and of the fabulous increase in social productivity it creates. Yet by the same token this raises acutely the question of the justice of the distribution of this social product and of the capacities that create or use it, and it gives their fullest impact to the basic questions of justice: When is a difference an inequality? When is an inequality an injustice? When should an injustice be remedied? How?

Furthermore, human capacities cannot be transfered. The products of labor can be transfered, but the effects of the capacities used in consumption cannot be transfered—these capacities can differ substantially from one individual to another. If differences in capacities used in consumption, and for enjoying or making sense of life in general, are deemed to be unjust, compensations can be used. However, one should then find an interpersonal common ground for this comparison (see the theory of "fundamental preferences" in chapter 7). Furthermore, since a number of these "final" capacities are an integrated part of the personality, they are more something one *is* rather than something one *has*, and for this reason compensations in terms of consumption, "welfare," or money are often seen inadequate: "Being" and "having" constitute different "spheres," one has a dignity and the other a price. Capacities can of course be modified by education and training, or assisted by specific devices, for both their consumptive and productive uses, but this possibility has limits. Finally, someone can also of course have a right to decide on the activity of someone else and to appropriate the product of the corresponding labor, within certain limits concerning the types of activity and the duration of the right, as in wage labor (slavery is the extreme and sometimes limitless case).

Education

Yet human capacities are formed: Much of the human resource is human capital. Education, training, information, and health care, of different kinds, provide the tools for forming capacities. The corresponding policies therefore seem to be essential instruments of justice in this respect—along with their role in fostering efficiency. They are indeed commonly used for trying to limit inequalities. They can affect capacities not only for production but also for consumption and life in general, through health, physical abilities, culture, awareness, the education of sensitivity, proposals for making sense of life, and, hopefully, teaching the means of mastering one's own mood, desires, and character. Furthermore education, training, or care are the essential tools of compensation when general material compensations are felt to be inadequate for differences in human capacities, especially for capacities used in consumption and life in general, because these capacities and welfare (and, still more, money) are seen as incommensurable and in different "spheres." Material specific devices for assisting low capacities are also sometimes a possibility, but they have limited scope and are inferior substitutes to capacity itself. Finally, to form capacities rather than compensate their effects by transfers respects process-freedom which is impaired by transfers: this can be valued per se and is advantageous for economic efficiency (yet the financing of education and training also has to be considered). Education constitutes the basic means to reconcile liberty and equality when they conflict and when fraternity is insufficient (as Condorcet emphasized in a much more dramatic setting than the one we consider here).[18]

However, the general effects of genetic endowments and, most important, of the education and motivation acquired in the family, can hardly be all compensated for by further education, training and information.[19] Indeed these factors commonly command what people make of public education. Public education on the one hand, and genetic and family-induced capacities on the other, are, on the whole, more complements than substitutes. As a consequence egalitarian educational policies, although they have provided basic skills and opened opportunities, have also magnified a number of original inequalities and often led to greater overall inequality (the scope of specific compensatory education is relatively limited). There thus necessarily remain large inequalities in capacities.

---

18. Condorcet explained the violation of liberty in the name of equality by the Terror (that eventually killed him) by the lack of public education. Whether true or not, this view led him to lay down the basis and the essentials of the social philosophy of education. A very good review of his work in this domain is provided by Christine Kinzler (1984). Another analysis is proposed in Kolm 1989a (1991). An interesting study of the relations between education and justice can be found in Peters (1966).

19. The question of injustice and the family is of course often considered (see, for instance, the works of Boudon, Bourdieu, and Fishkin 1983).

End Justice

The position concerning human capacities that is the opposite extreme from the general "natural" allocation and the ensuing full process liberalism consists in the ideal equalization of the consequences, for the individuals, of the whole stock of capacities, or rather, indeed, of the whole stock of resources of all kinds. This is full or complete redistributive justice, or full resourcism, or, in fact, end justice, considered in chapter 7 (and in Kolm 1971). The crucial question is of course what to compare across individuals given that the capacities for being satisfied are included, and the answer will be made easier by the fact that, de facto, requirements of possibility, efficiency, and satisfaction of basic needs lead one to replace this equality by a second-best egalitarian maximin. Then, for example, it is generally not too difficult to identify the neediest or most miserable or desperate people in a society.

This solution is interesting both because it constitutes an extreme in the spectrum of possibilities and because it is to be applied in a number of circumstances. This is, however, not the relevant solution in other circumstances, either because certain satisfaction capacities are irrelevant, or because one must not greatly sacrifice many people for a minute advantage of a least satisfied person who is not in a bad situation (this limitation has been emphasized since the mentioned initial presentation where this principle was not presented as the unique and universal dogma).

Income Justice

The Nature of Income Justice
However, the most standard "egalitarian" complaints in our societies concern the inequality of incomes. The corresponding equality of incomes, although strongly egalitarian, can be seen as substantially less so than the preceding "end justice" with regard to the scope of the *equalizandum*, since it wants to disregard the differences in personal capacities directly used in consumption, for enjoying, enduring, or making sense of life.[20] Yet it intends to redistribute the benefits from

---

20. With respect to the policy, however, this principle is more redistributive than the other when individuals' productive and consumptive capacities are inversely corre-

all other resources, notably including all human capacities used in production. This income is used for the present or future acquisition of consumption goods, not counting individual leisure time as such a good (however, the value of actual production directly used by the producer should be included). This ideal is taken up in recent philosophical debate by, for instance, Rawls (at least in *A Theory of Justice*: income is one of the "primary goods").[21] This proposal has to face a number of questions, apart from that of efficiency and second best discussed above: Why income? What is the justice of the prices used to compute income? Why earned income? Should not the exchange capacities in using income be treated the same as productive capacities? Why discriminate between productive and consumptive capacities or uses of capacities? Is it a question of the nature of these capacities, of the nature of their use, of means and ends, of responsibility, or of the definition of the self?

Before we turn to these problems, the basic intent of this theory with regard to human capacities should be emphasized. In the classical economic process, production is an indirect means for consumption; hence consumption uses human capacities both directly and indirectly (through production). This makes a great deal of difference for the theory considered here. Indeed the claim of equal (or less unequal) disposable incomes means an ideal of equality in consumption goods which result from production. Correlatively, it reveals an indifference, as regards active policy of distributive justice, toward capacities (directly) used in consumption, and a neglect of their differences (if not an active endorsement of their "natural" allocation). In so focusing on the *external* means of consumption rather than on its ends, this view focuses on the human means of production and ignores the human means of consumption. Making something for oneself is seen as outside the scope of active justice when it is done *directly*, and within it when it is done *indirectly* (essentially through exchange). This

---

lated, and less when they are positively correlated. It is indeed common to find individuals good at consumption and bad at production, and conversely. But positive correlation is not unfrequent either.

21. The qualification is due to Rawls's endorsement of fundamental utility or preferences (or at least his interest in these concepts) in Rawls (1982).

ideal places, in a sense, all of its concern on the *quantity* of consumption and none on the *quality* of consumption. It sees the "natural" allocation of capacities as *arbitrary* when they are used for production and ... "natural"—that is, *irrelevant* to the question of redistributive justice—when they are used for consumption. In other words, the *legitimate owner* of an individual's capacities is *the collectivity* when he uses them for production, and *himself* when he uses them for consumption. An individual is accountable for the relative shortcomings of the capacities he uses in consumption, whereas the individuals are collectively accountable for the weaknesses of the capacities they use in production.

The Income Metric

Let us first consider the question of the *income* metric. This unidimensional quantity enables one to define equality, inequality, maximins, and so on. Yet people do not consume income: They consume goods. Income is the value of these goods measured with certain prices. As was pointed out earlier, income can be considered in two possible ways, as do, for instance, income equality. Either income is just this value irrespective of the method of allocation of these goods, or it is an amount of money allocated to individuals and with which they go and buy consumption goods. This raises the two possible questions of the *justice of the prices* and of the *skills used in buying* goods with this income. The price question is always present, whereas the question of market skills occurs only in the interpretation in which people receive income with which they buy goods for consumption. In this latter case, indeed, what people can obtain depends on supplies and demands, and on their bargaining and market skills relative to those of others. Yet these skills are used in acquiring goods, and not in consuming them. They are not tastes, and this bargaining is neither play nor exercise. If anything, these bargaining skills belong to capacities used in production—in the broad sense—in a market economy. Yet they are not compensated by the ideal equality of income. The conclusion is that the end values for justice and prima facie equalizands of a conception that merely finds arbitrary the "natural" allocation of productive capacities and endorses that of consumptive capacities should be the bundles of consumption goods, as discussed earlier. Furthermore in both interpretations incomes depend on the prices used for computing them or faced in buying.

These prices are of course very important. An individual is advantaged if the goods he needs, wants, or likes are cheap, and he is handicaped if they are expensive. If these prices are market prices—for instance the efficient, market-clearing competitive prices (market clearing is a priori necessary for efficiency)—they may depend on all resources, scarcities, preferences, tastes, and capacities used in production and consumption. Now, deciding that an individual is accountable, as regards justice, for his own tastes, for any capacity he uses in consumption, for his ambitions and for the life-plans he sets up, does not say, for instance, that it is irrelevant to justice that he suffers from many people demanding the same (private) goods as he does (which raises their prices), or that he benefits from the opposite situation (which makes for low prices). Indeed, is it consistent to demand that an individual should not benefit from the fact that many people directly or indirectly like his productive talents (the ideal of equal income), but that he could derive a particular advantage from the fact that few people like the consumption goods he likes or needs? Can it be both unjust that I benefit from many people wanting what I have, and just that I suffer from many people wanting what I want? These questions conflate the two issues of the use of the income metric and of the scope of the equalizand.

The justification of the use of the income metric for justice endorsing the "natural" allocation of consumptive capacities, tastes, preferences, and personal aims, and only of them, is provided by the theory of efficient super-equity (section 6.2): The ideal is equal bundles of consumption goods, but this is generally inefficient while Pareto-efficiency has priority, and the resulting efficient multidimensional maximin limits the discrepancies in disposable incomes. No strict equality is required, however, and this margin can accommodate, among other things, differences in buying capacities if incomes ex ante are considered, especially since these differences are often relatively limited for markets in consumption goods in normal economic situations.

There remains, however, to consider the possible reasons for such an antagonistic treatment between the two kinds, or uses, of human capacities.

Why the Dichotomy?
A common view therefore favors limiting inequalities in the benefits derived from productive capacities, has no such preference for

capacities used in consumption in general, and, to begin with, distinguishes between these two types of capacities. Why does it consider this distinction and these opposite treatments? There are a number of possible reasons, which are more or less related but also more or less different.

1. The most common implicit and popular reason is certainly that the activity of consumption is something *private* and that therefore the personal capacities used in this activity are not a proper subject of public concern, and in particular of justice. Thus there is no reason either to compensate for their low levels or to tax their high levels so as to compensate the more poorly endowed persons. An individual's consumption and his related use of his capacities are nobody else's business. This is related to the ethic of respect for privacy. This privacy takes the particularly acute form of intimacy for this part of consumption that consists of the sensations and feelings of satisfaction, relief or enjoyment. The same view sees production, on the contrary, as a public activity, especially when it is performed collectively, with the division of labor which engenders earnings, and hence it sees productive capacities as amenable to a sort of collective usufruct. The two positions opposed to this one on either side extend respectively one of these two conceptions to the other category of capacities or of their uses: One sees exchanging one's labor as a private activity, and the other sees notably the alleviation of needs that are consumptive liabilities as a collective responsibility (see chapters 7 and 11).

2. Relatedly, as alluded to earlier, an individual's return from his labor depends not only on his capacities for production (and selling) but also on the *demands* for them addressed to him by the rest of society, and therefore also on the corresponding available substitutes or complements. Even if the individual were entitled to his productive capacities, one might consider that this effect of the rest of society on his income is not legitimately his own, that he should not benefit or suffer from it more than is the case for other individuals. This view does not value per se the process-freedom of free exchange, even if an individual's capacities are considered his property because they belong to his self. It a priori provides a reason for the equalization of only part of the incomes. However, the supplies and demands of an individual's productive capacities are joint causes of the income they yield,

and hence causality does not provide a "natural" allocation. The allocation thus has to be chosen, with the two extreme possibilities of allocating all to the individual or of ideally equalizing all.[22] Consumption does not provide as clear an equivalent reason for compensation, although it is in part and in various ways a social activity raising questions of this type by the consumer's appreciation of the others' view of his following norms or fashion, of his conspicuous consumption,[23] of his generosity or personal attraction, and so on. Education provides an external influence on both types of capacities.

3. The private aspect of preferences, tastes, consumptive capacities, and personal ends would come from the fact that they are parts of, or even constitute, the relevant conception of the *self*, of which productive capacities would be only an "external" instrument. For this reason they would belong to a private "sphere" for which material compensations would be morally inappropriate as they would violate the integrity of the self, fail to respect its independent existence, and possibly interfere with dignity and self-respect. The question of the self will be emphasized shortly.

4. An individual would be accountable for his *aims* or ends, which his preference represent, whereas his income and his productive and earning capacities are his *means* which are amenable to redistributive justice. This distinction underlies, for instance, Rawls's view. This justification, however, seems to miss the point: What is at stake is not the individual's choice but his capacity to derive satisfaction or happiness from it (and more generally from any situation). One may hold that individual differences in these capacities are irrelevant for justice, but this has to be based on one of the other arguments (such as privacy or selfhood).

5. This accountability would result from *responsibility*, since an individual "chooses his objectives." This would also apply more specifically to consumptive capacities such as tastes (as argued by Dworkin,

---

22. A simple rule would be: Each individual's disposable income is the fraction α of the income he earns plus the fraction $1 - \alpha$ of the average income, with $0 \leq \alpha \leq 1$ ($\alpha = 1$ for full process liberalism). This issue can also provide a reason and a base for the determination of the parameter k considered above.

23. See "Taxing conspicuous consumption," Kolm 1972.

for instance). Yet individuals rarely choose their tastes and can generally not change them easily. Responsibility is a particular notion, analyzed below and in chapter 9.

6. The output of productive activities can be readily redistributed. For consumption, on the contrary, compensation constitutes an indirect equalization, which may meet questions of incommensurability, and which does not have a priori a clear and obvious base.

7. Productive and consumptive capacities would be different by nature (a "preference" does not look like a means), and this would base the possibility of treating them differently as regards justice.

These reasons show that the issue is ambiguous on at least five grounds: the distinction between means and ends, their identification with productive and consumptive capacities, the assignment of capacities to these categories, responsibility, and the integrity of the "self." The first three questions concern the use of capacities, whereas the last two raise more "metaphysical" issues.

Productive and Consumptive Uses of Capacities
The argument that "people are responsible for their ends, and therefore their external means should be equalized" indeed raises questions.

Mental and physical capacities that are necessary for any nonproductive activity and that can substantially influence its performance are certainly also means. Capacities to appreciate, enjoy and endure, and tastes are, in a sense, definitely means of eudemonistic or cultural ends. One can even see means as completely determining ends in considering a "capacity for being satisfied" or "satisfaction-capacity." Indeed *an individual's preferences are but the structure of his satisfaction-capacity* over the domain of the possible objects of satisfaction, and, classically, preferences determine the choice of ends. With a more tangible psychology, an individual's preferences are the structure of his capacities for happiness, sense of fulfillment, contentment, enjoyment, pleasure, and the like, and of his "handicaps" in being prone to dissatisfaction, discontent, displeasure, grief, sorrow, sadness, confusion, anguish, disappointment, depression, and the like, or in being sensitive to pain and suffering (particular needs can be either handicaps, or assets of a valuable life, or both; see chapter 11). The minimal conclusion is that the distinction between means and ends cannot be taken as obvious.

Even apart from the formal identification of ends to means, an individual's ends are inextricably intermingled with his personal means. For instance, a productive activity (labor) always elicits satisfactions or dissatisfactions apart from its output (painfulness, sense of achievement, pleasure, interest, many aspects of social insertion, etc.). Indeed "life plans" and self-actualization are much more generally achieved in the category of labor than in the category of leisure, in usefully influencing the world rather than in enjoying it, in meaningful effort rather than in pastimes, hobbies, or the satisfaction of vital needs.

Furthermore, *one cannot establish a strict distinction between capacities used in production and "final" capacities used in consumption and other activities.* The elementary mental and physical capacities of an individual are used in more or less simple or complex clusters. The same elementary capacities are used in different clusters that can be applied in production, and in consumption, leisure or nonproductive life in general. These elementary capacities can refer to aspects of memory, intelligence, attention, imagination, willpower, sensitivity, body, for example, and they can be qualities of strength, speed, resistance, size, for example. Most elementary capacities are used on both sides. Even capacities that seem to belong to one side occasionally appear on the other: For instance, the sensitivity of the senses, which are the paradigmatic capacities of consumption, are used for production and income by artists, cooks, stylists, and experts of all kinds, as well as for motivating artistic production. And even strictly specialized capacities often depend on others that have effects on both sides—as sleeping capacity depends on general health, for instance. In addition, not infrequently the same fully patterned clusters of uses of elementary capacities are found on both sides. The leisure activities of play or exercise often use capacities in ways quite similar to certain productive activities. This happens for comprehensive activities: hunting, fishing, and gardening, once the basic productive activities, are common leisure activities. Furthermore production directly for oneself, rather than for sale, certainly is production, but when it produces a service it is not different from one category of consumption activity. Finally, a number of capacities are of course often more used on one side than on the other, but this is a matter of statistical distribution that depends on the types of production and consumption, and hence on most of the economic and cultural features of society. One conclusion of these remarks is that there is a certain arbitrariness in compensating personal capacities when they are used in production but not when they are used in consumption.[24]

Self and Responsibility

One reason to propose that the benefits or liabilities from a characteristic of an individual should be attributed to this individual is that this characteristic is a constitutive part of his *self*. This would legitimize the drawing of a transfer-proof "sphere" around or within each individual. The popular notion of privacy, as well as the classical notion of natural rights, are akin to this view. The main question is that the notion of "self" is amenable to a large variety of extensions. At one extreme, Buddhist and Jain philosophies deny the existence of an inner, core "self" (somewhat akin to Kant's or Jung's "transcendental I"). Yet they also consider "persons" (*pugdala* as opposed to *atma*) which, as in European eighteenth-century philosophy (Locke is a case in point) adds, to the individual, the basic means of his living. The self, if one is considered, should certainly include the "will" (with a relation to the next topic, responsibility), and the general principles of its decisions and choices. Sensory, mental, and then other physical capacities would then have to be considered. Finally, this can be used to build a case in favor of endorsing the natural allocation of preferences and final capacities, but not a definitive one (this will be further analyzed in chapter 9).[25]

The last criterion we must consider here is responsibility. Responsibility is and has always been considered as a major and central concept of the question of justice. It is also one of the most subtle, and it

---

24. For instance, assume someone has a capacity for having very quickly a global view of a situation and for making a prompt decision on this basis. He can use this capacity at the stock exchange and make money with which—let us assume—he buys masters' paintings. Or he can use this capacity for hunting for the pleasure of it. Why would an equalization of income include the value of paintings and not that of hunting time?

25. The question of self, the many possible concepts of self, the relation of this notion to desires, to happiness, to suffering, and to the deep and durable alleviation of suffering constitute an important part of the book *Happiness-Freedom* (Kolm 1982a, new ed. 1994).

will be analyzed in detail in chapter 9. The main point is that the assignment of responsibility is an ethical choice generally submitted to a necessary condition of causality. Responsibility thus cannot be the purely nonethical determinant of an ethical judgment. Even the condition it requires leaves wide-open moral possibilities. The relevant causality, for instance, admits of "omissions" and not only action ("commission"). It says, indeed, that a person can be held responsible for something only if his will *could have prevented* this occurrence. Another wide-open choice is the assignment of responsibility among the several causes of a fact, hence possibly among several persons, with the disappearance of responsibility assigned to causes that are not themselves caused by wills directly or indirectly.

For personal characteristics, the causality condition is sometimes clear. People indeed sometimes choose carefully their aims and objectives. They also willfully train a number of physical, mental, or sensory capacities. There are also a number of things that are certainly beyond their possibilities. Yet the domain of uncertainty in between is large, notably for various mental characteristics. A crucial issue, for instance, is whether or not willpower is itself caused by the will. In fact the logical limits do not even exist. For one thing, an individual could always be held responsible for all of himself because he could have suppressed his own existence. For the other, an individual has been created and educated, he is influenced and caused, so he might have to be exonerated from all responsibility. Such views can rely or sociological, psychological, physiological or even physical causalities. Even if one considers the simple problem of influencing one's own preferences, desires, tastes or aims, the views differ widely. On the one hand, for example, a common present western assumption considers tastes as given to the individual. On the other hand, the philosophies of life are based on the exactly opposite view. They include, for example, Hellenistic philosophies for the mastery of pleasure, the philosophical psychology of Buddhism for the control of the birth of desires and the decrease of one's suffering, all moralities that demand that one have or have not certain sentiments, desires, or aspirations, Rousseau's and Kant's views that freedom is choosing one's principles of choice and action, or the existentialists' maximally extended conception of responsibility.

Indeed, to make things more difficult, certain past conceptions of responsibility, and a few modern authors such as Sartre, do not even require the causality condition for responsibility (Sartre's "responsibility beyond oneself"). Responsibility then becomes a purely ethical concept, and in no way an external base for the ethical choice.

The Actual Ethic of Solidarity for Personal Capacities

Finally, the choice between the right to "natural" liberty and the duty of social solidarity with respect to the unequal allocation of human resources is so large a part of the overall problem of justice, in volume as well as in the depth of the issues, that it is bound to mobilize most of the questions of justice, including many that are specific to this choice. Thus, for capacities as well as for justice in general (see chapter 1), the surest result is that any specific proposal that presents itself as the solution to all actual cases and questions can only be mistaken, but the various cases are very different from each other both in global volume and in necessity, and the overall distributive optimum presents a clear and simple global structure. For macrojustice, the volume is essentially determined (in developed societies) by a sharing of the benefits from the productive uses of capacities, which is conveniently summarized by the single parameter of the equivalent duration of complete redistribution of earned income. The optimal possible values of this parameter are within a well-defined margin, and actual fixed-duration income equalization provides the most efficient implementation (section 6.1). Yet the alleviation of deep suffering and the satisfaction of basic needs is more important in necessity (see chapters 7 and 11). Mesojustice intervenes in issues that are specific in nature but particularly important in volume and in significance, concerning, notably, education or health that are not sufficiently taken care of by uses of private incomes in various forms. And the cases of microjustice raise all possible issues. Process-freedom and self-usufruct keep a large place both by the nonredistributed share of earned income and by the part of consumptive capacities that is not a concern of redistributive justice.

With respect to intrinsic social and moral importance, after the respect of the essential basic liberties and the avoidance of remediable deep suffering, and related to them, the issue having priority is the satisfaction of basic needs, with its indissociable cultural dimension; this will be analyzed in chapter 11.[26] The second basic point is the reconciliation of all freedoms by social sentiments in the category of community, mutual responsibility, reciprocity, solidarity, altruism, compassion, and so on[27] (notably in their realistic application in collective gift-giving, which requires only moderate levels of these sentiments and, often, public implementation[28]). A third basic issue is the formation of personal capacities by education and related policies, previously discussed[29]. This is, in particular, the main issue in the political debates concerning "equality of opportunity" (see chapter 9). For the rest, several characteristics of personal capacities are bound to be relevant, notably their origin, their use, their nature, and their specialization or generality (the extent to which they can serve several ends). The origin refers to assignment of accountability according to causes, notably as regards merit and responsibility. With regard to use, the collective and equally shared usufruct of capacities used in production has relevance, but it cannot constitute the only relevant principle. Indeed freedom, respect of the self, and merit make the producer the legitimate owner of his product to a certain degree and fully in certain cases, and, on the other hand, severe handicaps in final capacities obviously require assistance. Another important issue is the intrinsic social ethical end-value of culture, which leads to education and to subsidize particular types of consumption at the expense of other consumption and possibly other people (a general externality of the cultural aspects of individuals' behavior might provide part of the justification, but this bypasses the transcendent dimension of the culture of a society). Furthermore, compensation concerning human capacities, when it is relevant, for capacities used in production but still more for final ones (and certain may have both uses), is often morally adequately implemented only by specific training or devices that augment this capacity, or possibly by a similar action concerning another capacity, rather than by something that would aim to com-

---

26. This question is also developed in Kolm 1959, 1977b.
27. These questions are analyzed in Kolm 1984b.
28. See chapter 3 and Kolm 1985a.
29. For final and consumptive capacities, see Kolm 1982a.

pensate at the level of general welfare. Indeed, capacities and welfare, and often various types of capacities, are commonly considered to belong to different "spheres"; being so close to the person, capacities often have "a dignity" rather than "a price," to use Kant's distinction. This aspect also elicits particular "vicarious needs" (to be discussed in chapter 11). In the end, almost all ethical considerations and analyses are relevant, and we will not even be able to avoid resorting to wisdom in order to fill up the provisional incompletenesses of rational analysis.

The anchors of this analysis are constituted by the polar theories. Full process-freedom is one of them. The opposite is end justice, or full redistributive justice, presented in chapter 7. The intermediary polar case is income justice, analyzed in the present chapter with respect to its justification (the dichotomy of capacities), its form (income), and its accommodations with efficiency (efficient super-equity and fixed-duration income equalization). This standard conception of distributive justice underlies the view of a few scholars who, however, introduce other aspects (and create other problems), and thus deserve to be considered in themselves by the history of thought. Among them Rawls and his focus on "primary goods" (one of which is income) will be the topic of chapter 8, and Dworkin's "resourcism" will be considered in chapter 9. Chapter 9, more generally, presents the other solutions that are justifiable or have elicited fruitful arguments, and the overall view of distributive justice is completed in chapter 10 for inequalities and in chapter 11 for needs and misery.

7 Equal Liberty and Maximin: Justice and Equity

7.1 Outline

The study *Justice and Equity* (Kolm 1971) analyzes the properties of the basic necessary forms of justice. The issue is respectful justice for individuals, the essential question of the field (with possible extensions). The end values of justice are either means or ends of the individuals, or their liberty, on the one hand, and their happiness, satisfaction, utility, or welfare, on the other. The two basic topics are thus *end-justice* and *means-justice* (or eudemonistic justice and eleutheristic justice). The basic difference is that preferences, tastes, or satisfaction capacities, and the choices they induce, are relevant for direct distributive and comparative justice in one case and are not in the other. Furthermore rationality requires a prima facie equality of these individual values (for relevantly equal individuals, see chapter 2). The two topics are thus necessarily equality of liberty and equality of utility (or of happiness, satisfaction, or welfare), or the corresponding second-best egalitarianisms. They correspond respectively to the two terms "Equity" and "Justice," which are thus given here specific meanings, and suitable ones. This eudemonistic Justice is full or complete justice, where the allocation of all resources is considered the relevant variable for the ideal equalization, including all capacities and in particular satisfaction capacities. This end value is particularly relevant when the lowest satisfactions correspond to substantial suffering and pain and to unsatisfied basic needs.[1] Then, when the possibilities or the requirement of Pareto-efficiency manifestly impose an inequality in satisfactions (irrespective of the difficulty to define equality), the relevant second-best justice is maximin or leximin in satisfaction (and it is then rather easy to point out the relevantly least satisfied individuals, who commonly remain the same persons when the policy is applied): this is *Practical Justice* (where the adjective "practical" is to be taken in its Kantian sense of imposed by the constraints of the actual problem). The other, dual principle, equality in liberty, has equality of independent instrumental liberty, or *Equity*, as its simplest case, which is also a central concept and building block in the analysis of the other cases.

---

1. The question of basic needs is analyzed in Kolm 1959, 1977b; see chapter 11 below. For the issue of suffering, see Kolm 1982a.

This corresponds to the criterion that no individual prefers any other's allocation or situation to his own (see chapters 2 and 9, and below). A number of other criteria are also considered in this study, such as equal allocation of several goods or resources followed by free exchange, unanimous preference of a state to all possible equal allocations, (Pareto-)efficiency and "fundamental efficiency," "fundamental dominance," "Adequacy," "fundamental majorities", "realistic" Equity and Adequacy, etc., and other closely related criteria were introduced in follow-up works.

7.2 "Equity" and Equal Liberty

Equal liberty can consist of, or can include, equal human and civil rights ("basic liberties"), equal income, equality of resources, equality of opportunity with a more or less extensive definition (in particular with a larger or smaller set of personal capacities included in the "opportunity" by formation or compensation), equal income or wealth and power (Rawls's "primary goods"), equal market possibilities due to the equality of tradable resources and of exchange opportunities, and so on. The property of equal liberty considered in this section is a logical and formal one which can apply to any of these as well as other cases. The *ethical* meaning depends on the specific nature of the allocations, situations, or domains of liberty considered.

The social ethical analysis of liberty begins with two distinctions. First, liberty is *instrumental* when it is valued *only as a means* for what it enables the free agent to choose and obtain; such a freedom is not also an end in itself;[2] this opinion can be that of this agent, of the social ethic, or both. Second, an individual's freedom is *independent* when the domain of choice it defines does not depend upon other agents' choices and actions. **Equity** is defined as **equal independent instrumental liberty** of various justiciables (for instance, individuals) in a defined choice space, or as *an equivalent situation*. It is the basic and simplest concept of the analysis of equal freedom, and the basic tool of the analysis of more complex situations.[3] (The word "equity" de-

---

2. For the possible reasons presented in chapter 2.
3. Equal interferring liberties, and maximin in liberties, are studied in Kolm 1993e.

rives from the latin word for *equal*, and *equal liberty* is the general ethical equality;[4] semiotically, the word Equity stands here for *EQUal Independent Instrumental liberTY*).[5]

This Equity can also be expressed as "**no individual prefers another's allocation to his own**." Indeed this latter property holds *if and only if there exists a domain of choice such that, if each individual is given a domain of choice identical to this one (hence unaffected by the others' choices), one of his best choices is his considered allocation*. The proof notes that the existence of such a domain implies the property since each individual could have chosen an allocation identical to that of any other, yet he preferred his own choice. Conversely, if the property holds, then there exist such domains, since *one of them is provided by the set of the individuals' allocations* (the property expresses that each individual's allocation is one of his best choice in this set).[6] The property of instrumental freedom is expressed by the fact that each individual's preferences bear only on his allocation and neither directly bear on his domain of choice nor are influenced by it; hence two domains that lead to the same choice are equivalent, and equivalent to this choice, and the social ethic respects this view (it is easy to introduce additional non-instrumental or intrinsic preferences of the individuals for their domain of choice, or influences of their domain on their preferences for allocations).[7]

This form of Equity, referring only to individuals' comparisons of their allocations with others', was directly proposed by Tinbergen (1946) for evaluating the wages of various occupations (after a suggestion from Ehrenfest—his physics professor—in 1925); he calls this

---

4. It even theoretically yields the equal satisfaction of the next section if individual tastes are notionally included in the domain of choice.

5. By contrast, the word *fair* comes from the Germanic word *faga*, which means beautiful. Now, rationality is certainly a safer base for ethics than aesthetic is (Procrustes was probably motivated by the beauty of equality).

6. See Kolm 1973a.

7. Identical domains still entail the property. For the converse, it suffices to complement "no individual prefers any other's allocation to his own" by "for a domain of choice, the same for all, that includes the individuals' allocations and such that no individual prefers any of its elements—individual allocations—to his own allocation" (this domain can thus be taken as the equal liberty; it may be the set of individuals' allocations).

criterion the "exchange principle." It was mentioned in passing and cursorily by Foley (1967). Its various technical properties were then analyzed in the book *Justice and Equity*, and later in an abundant further literature.

This formulation of Equity, however, can be misleading, and has misled people, for two reasons.

First, this enunciation uses only individuals' preference orderings. One could thus say that this is a principle based only on individuals' preference orderings, hence only on individuals' preferences. However, this is a principle of individualistic *justice*. Hence it has to be based on some *equality* (see chapter 2). This equality is indeed the equality of liberty just noted. But then, since this liberty is the ethically relevant item, this implies that the rest is not considered directly ethically relevant for justice, and the only other items that are explicit in this framework are the individuals' preference orderings. The principle thus basically consists in saying that *individuals' preferences are irrelevant for justice*, contrary to the appearance. This irrelevance says both that preferences or satisfaction capacities are not among the end values of justice (notably for compensation), and that they are not among the parameters and conditions for justice about liberties (since the basic rationality principle is equal treatment of relevantly equals). Note that this irrelevance concerns direct justice. Indeed judgments of indirect or derived justice can evaluate any variable of the setting, in relating them to the end values. Notably the set of individuals' allocations can be evaluated in this manner. And their relations to the equal freedom (possibly a putative one) uses individuals' preferences. But if the end values of justice were the individuals' allocations, the principle would be their identity, and if the end values of justice were the individuals' satisfaction (or welfare, or happiness), the principle would have to be the eudemonistic Justice considered in the next section. However, Equity can be, for the allocations, not only this derived first best justice, but also direct second best justice: ideal equal allocations may be impossible (because of indivisibilities or nontransferabilities) or inefficient (because of differences in tastes), and Equity, which may then be possible and efficient, would be the second-best replacement of equal allocations by an equal domain of choice, which can be the set of individuals' allocations (this is the smallest set among those possible that give the same result). This second best can also be interpreted directly: among the properties of equal allocations, only the fact that no one prefers another's allocation to her own is kept.

Second, the principle bears a relation to an absence of *envy*. Tinbergen noted it. *Justice and Equity* discusses the relation to the absence of envy or of jealousy. However, the criterion itself came to be called "no-envy" or "envy-freeness," and this is an unfortunate confusion because envy is essentially (and notably for the morally relevant kind of envy) an externality where an individuals' preferences are affected by others' allocations (the relation will be shown in chapter 9).[8]

An important property of Equity is its *consistency with efficiency* under classical economic conditions, including when production and transformation of goods are possible.[9] The proof is provided by the example of one case: the equilibrium of *perfect economic competition with equal incomes* is efficient, equitable, and possible. This efficiency is well-known (see, for instance, Debreu 1959). Equity results from the fact that the individuals choose from budget sets with equal incomes, which are therefore identical (the individuals face the same given competitive prices). Finally, the possibility of an equal-income competitive equilibrium is obtained by an equal division of all initial resources and of the profits of all firms, for the resources and firms (technological transformations) that are involved in the problem considered.[10]

---

8. This envy externality has been noted for decades by a number of economists, and it is analyzed in Kolm 1972, 1991c, 1993f, 1995a.

9. This precision is made necessary by the fact that the property has been denied in this case (see Pazner and Schmeidler 1974, and Varian 1974). Yet this denial is based on an example where the "units of leisure" (it has to be time) of different individuals are considered as being the same commodity, which is hardly acceptable for individuals with different individual-specific capacities used in consumption (see chapter 6, and Kolm 1993d, 1993e, 1993g, 1995f, 1996a, 1996b, 1996e).

10. The obtained property can be used in many specific questions of "local justice". It is, however, useless for overall justice if all individuals' leisure times are among the goods considered. Indeed, each individual leisure is a specific good (the availability of different consumptive capacities) used only by this individual and of which the individual must consume some amount to satisfy his vital needs (rest, sleep, and so on). Then, for consumptions including leisure time, each individual has to prefer his bundle to any other's, and the situation is always trivially equitable. Other criteria of justice have to be used in this case, and the relevant ones bear a relation to Equity, such as efficient super-equity, fixed-duration income equalization, eudemonistic Justice (Equity when consumptive capacities are joined to the compared consumption goods; see Kolm 1971), or equal process-freedom.

A unanimously agreed-upon change from an equitable situation need not be equitable, as it was noted.[11] Yet such a change cannot occur from a Pareto-efficient situation, by definition. And the property to be applied is *efficient Equity*.

The book *Justice and Equity* then analyzed the other rich logical properties of this concept of Equity, notably its geometrical structures, and, in the various cases of the nature and structure of the items to allocate (notably with or without indivisibilities and transferabilities), its possibility, its consistency with efficiency, and the implementability of Equity or of efficient Equity by a number of processes with various structures of information, among which free exchanges and markets. Equity was thus analyzed in its relations with other normative principles, such as, in addition to efficiency and freedom of choice and of exchange, unanimous preference to equal allocations and a number of important concepts of justice closely related to Equity and which were introduced and analyzed along with it.

One of these principles is the classical conception of justice in antiquity: A thing should be allocated to the person who makes the best of it (see Plato, Aristotle, or "give the flutes to the flute player"). With a conception of "the good" that is either eudemonistic with interpersonal comparability (see the next section) or refers to specific criteria in particular problems, the concept is that of **Adequacy**: An allocation is *adequate* if each individual allocation is attributed to the person who makes the best of it. The central relation between Equity and Adequacy is: *If one assignment of the individual allocations is equitable, and one is adequate, all assignments that have one property also have the other.*

Restricted Equity or Adequacy restrict the set of compared assignments, and the same relation as with the unrestricted case holds between them. In particular, *Realistic Equity* and *Realistic Adequacy* consider only possible assignments. Notably in Realistic Equity each individual compares his allocation only to the others' allocations that he can actually have. A notable reason for not being able to have another's allocation occurs when the "allocation" includes a productive occupation that requires special skills. This concept is sometimes the ethically relevant one, and *efficient Realistic Equity* is possible

---

11. *Justice et Equité* (1971), p. 82 of the 1972 reprint.

and implementable by a decentralized free market in important cases where this does not hold for simple efficient Equity (the above noted sufficient conditions for existence and market implementability of efficient Equity do not hold when there are certain nontransferabilities or indivisibilities).

In a series of concepts, each individual prefers his allocation to certain averages of individuals' allocations that are here bundles of divisible quantities of goods. These averages can be an equal division of the existing goods (an equal sharing when the total quantities are a priori given), all weighted averages (super-equity, Kolm 1973a), the arithmetic average of all of the others' allocations (Thomson 1979, 1982; Baumol 1986) that can stand for the holdings of the "representative other," and a number of other meaningful cases.[12]

Among the other related concepts that were analyzed are the situations where no individual feels he has the worst of individuals' allocations (*minimal Equity*), each individual is seen as having the best of these allocations (vs. as not having the worst allocation) in the view of at least one other individual (*external Equity* and *external minimal Equity*), each individual is seen by at least one other as having a better allocation than this other's (*"minimal status"*), each individual is indifferent between the allocation and an allocation having anyone of the other properties considered (a situation denoted as this property followed by "equivalence"—equitable or Equity equivalent and equivalence, etc.), and so on.[13]

Finally, when Equity cannot be efficient, one efficient second-best freedom egalitarianism can be a *maximin in liberty* or a leximin in liberty, with concepts to be summarized in chapter 9.[14]

Equity, its related concepts, and their relations with other normative or implementational concepts, have many remarkable and important properties. These properties often result from the basic one of equal liberty. This has been the source of a vast and flourishing literature in the deductive economic theory of justice.[15] On the basic

---

12. An exhaustive presentation is in Kolm 1993d (summarized in 1996b).

13. See Kolm 1971, 1973a, 1987e.

14. See Kolm 1993e.

15. A review is included in Kolm 1991c and 1995a, where all of these properties are extended so as to actually deal with the sentiment of envy (see chapter 9). See also Kolm 1973a, 1974a, 1987e, 1991a, b, d, 1993b, d, e, f, g, 1994a, b, 1996b, e. Thomson (1997) provides an important survey in book form.

conceptual ground, the next advance was the analysis of the more general central concepts of justice, *equal interfering liberty, equal non-purely instrumental liberty*, a combination of both, and their various properties (possibilities, consistency among various specifications of these principles, second-best solutions, implementational processes, in the various cases of structure of the possibilities).[16]

7.3   Full Justice and Practical Justice

The extreme, borderline case of respectful justice occurs when all that influences the individuals' (justiciables') ends is considered globally as ethically relevant for the redistributive policy. In this sense, this is *full justice*, or *complete justice* (or all-inclusive justice). This amounts to taking the individuals' ends themselves as the social ethical end values of justice and this is therefore also *end-justice*. Then, minimal irrationality requires that this justice compare individuals' fulfilment of their ends, with an ideal of equality, which obviously has in general to be widened into an efficient second-best, such as a maximin. The concepts developed and analyzed in *Justice and Equity* are those of **Practical Justice** or *leximin in "fundamental preferences"* (or in ordinal "fundamental utility"), which becomes *Justice* or *equivalence in fundamental preferences* (or equality in—ordinal—fundamental utility) when this property can be (Pareto-)efficient. (The adjective "practical" refers to its use by Kant as meaning determined by the constraints of the actual problem of choice for action.)

Only the form of Practical Justice is analogous to the maximin in income which is one of the concepts analyzed in *The Optimal Production of Social Justice* (Kolm 1966a), and the difference in substance is crucial. However, the income considered there is the "leisurely equivalent income," that is, the income which, with no labor, is deemed equivalent, by the individual, to his actual disposable income with the actual work he performs, and so individual preferences between goods and labor or leisure are taken into account (this discards the absurdities of general maximin in simple disposable income as will be pointed out in chapter 8).

---

16. See Kolm 1993e.

First take care of the most miserable people, is simply what Practical Justice says. "The last ones will be the first ones." First relieve the deepest sufferings. The fact that this is not morally new does not make it morally flawed. And finding out who the worst-off (all included) or most desperate people are is commonly not too difficult a task, unfortunately, at least in a sufficiently large society (and they commonly remain the same people when the relief policy is applied). Of course particular pathological cases may have to be considered separately (one cannot spend most of the resources of a country for eliciting a faint smile on the face of its most atrabilious citizen).

The principle of Practical Justice is to be appreciated in reference to its meaning in practical applications. One aspect refers to the question of *needs*, which will be the topic of chapter 11. In a society where *basic needs* are not satisfied, Practical Justice amounts to give priority to the satisfaction of basic needs (basic liberties can be seen as a part of basic needs, and they in addition require means to make them "real" freedoms to a minimal extent). The domain of relevant application of Practical Justice may indeed be limited to this case. The question of the definition of basic needs will be considered in chapter 11. The identification of Practical Justice with the best possible alleviation of basic needs rests on the fact that these needs are not "vicarious needs" (that is, considered as needs only by persons other than the needy themselves). Then Practical Justice, and the related concept of "fundamental preferences" (see below) permit the selection and classification of basic needs according to their urgency, for each concerned person and across these persons.

One other major aspect is that Practical Justice commonly means the alleviation of pain and suffering rather than the promotion of satisfaction, pleasure or happiness. This makes a difference, since these two aspects are by no means a question of symmetrical presentation. For instance, suffering is a constraint and its alleviation is a liberation. Nonsuffering is satiable and a state of painlessness is often a possibility. By contrast, satisfaction, pleasure or happiness rarely have such a natural bliss-point.[17] The classical contemners of the corresponding positive values, such as Kant for eudemonism, Tocqueville for welfare

---

17. For a complete analysis of the difference, see Kolm 1982a.

or well being, or Nietzsche for happiness (which he dubs "chewing the cud") have no such harsh words for the decrease of suffering.

This being said, we can, for convenience and generality, use the point of view of eudemonism and the vocabulary of happiness, satisfaction, or preferences to cover all the types of situations considered. Aristotle, in *Nichomachean Ethics*, provides both the logical justification and the single most acceptable and general concept (Aristotle's eudemonism is not Kant's). *Eudaemonia*, says Aristotle, is the only human aim that cannot also be a means. Furthermore, he adds, other aims either are conscious means for *eudaemonia* or turn out to favor *eudaemonia* anyway. These latter ends can thus be seen as unconscious means to *eudaemonia*. Hence Aristotle practically implies that man has *eudaemonia* as a unique aim. Finally, Aristotle emphasizes the essential importance, for *eudaemonia*, of freely chosen *activity* for the mere sake of exercizing one's capacities for choice and action because it manifests their existence (hence one's existence as agent). Note that this activity implies some liberty: This shows how far this "eudemonism" is from the promotion of purely passive sensory pleasure or even of the ill-defined "welfare" (of which we do not know which satisfaction capacities it takes into account). Now *eudaemonia* is translated as "happiness" and we will follow this use (this is almost inevitable for a translation by a single word), although of course this Greek concept is at once broader, deeper and more specific ("flourishing," "self"-fulfillment, etc.). Note that in all languages, the word that is translated by "happiness" has quite different connotation, meaning, and scope ("happiness" is commonly both less deep and more restricted in scope).

We furthermore need interpersonal comparisons. The answer proposed to this end was the concept of *fundamental preferences*, that is, the following.[18] The basic relevant question is: can one say that one individual (in situation) is happier (or more satisfied) than another? Facts tell us that sometimes we can, and often we cannot. This suffices for most actual applications of Practical Justice, since, commonly, the most miserable people are rather clearly identifiable, at least in a sufficiently large society, and their misery in different states can be

---

18. Kolm 1966a, 1971, and a number of other presentations, with recent ones in 1992d and 1994a.

compared—often because the same people remain at the bottom under the considered choice of policy. Furthermore the relation "happier" is likely to be transitive. Anyway consider a set of individuals-in-situation connected by possibilities to answer the above question in an "objective" way (in particular all informed observers agree on who is "happier"), and such that these pairwise comparisons do not constitute "cycles" or "loops." Then, this set of comparisons constitutes an ordering that we label "fundamental preferences." What are ordered are pairs of an individual and a situation (that is, what he is and what he has or is in). They include in particular pairs for the same individual in different situations (or with different allocations)—on which the fundamental ordering normally coincides with this individual's eudemonistic preference ordering.

The domain of definition of the fundamental ordering extends if one assumes full information about the persons compared. Indeed information plays a role since the happinesses of different persons can sometimes be ranked, while this of course cannot be done if one knows nothing about these persons.[19] However, in a class of cases the comparison may also require some specification and precision of the concept of happiness. Much can be said, and has been said, on this topic.[20]

This fundamental eudemonistic ordering is also what psychology and sociopsychology consider when they study how properties such as happiness, satisfaction and the like depend both on what is happening

---

19. A common close friend or mother may be able to say which of two individuals is happier or more satisfied, while more foreign observers cannot tell. Some people have argued that one can never tell if one person is happier than another, because happiness or satisfaction is a purely individual experience (the French scholarly tradition bizarrely labels this hypothesis in English as "le no-bridge"). These persons refuse to guess whether an inmate in Auschwitz in 1943 is more or less happy than a Malibu beach surfer. They would not admit that someone's bliss suggests a higher happiness than some other person's despair. This position is usually a conscious or unconscious pretext to refuse to help other people in need. But the rejection of this view of course implies in no way that one could actually say which of two persons is happier or more satisfied, or if they are as happy or satisfied as each other, for any pair of persons, although the possibility extends with more information about these persons and their situation, and possibly with further specification of the type of satisfaction or happiness one wishes to consider. Yet the point is that the domain of the eudemonistic ordering or preordering need not be complete for the most important applications.

20. A complete discussion and analysis is provided in the book *Happiness-Freedom* (Kolm 1982a).

to the individual and on the various factors and causes of his propensity to experience these sentiments, such as his background, education, culture, past experiences, and sui generis psychological features, both as they provide general tendencies to happiness or unhappiness and as they correlate with the specificities of the individual's situation. Psychology is scientific, hence general; it studies laws of the human being in general, and in particular it studies causes of happiness or satisfaction in general, in taking into account both "external" and "internal" causes of the individual state and their interactions.

Therefore fundamental preferences are defined from the consideration of *tangible satisfaction or happiness* (with a structure of more or less and an ordinal scale) as they *attach, relate or are correlated to* what individuals are and have (or are in), and, as a secondary confirming and supporting addition, from the consideration of the *causality* from the latter items to the former.

By contrast, the fact that individual preference orderings (or ordinal utility functions) depend on the individuals' characteristics, or are caused by them, do not yield per se a fundamental preference ordering (or utility function).

However, one could try to define a structure of fundamental preferences from the consideration of the pure fact of preference. Then an individual would have preferences jointly over what he has (or is in) and over what he is. Of course individuals obviously do have preferences over their own characteristics, tastes, preferences concerning certain items, and causes of their tastes and preferences, along with the items of their situation or allocation: they wish they were taller and possibly know how much they would be ready to pay for it, they wish they were more intelligent or otherwise more able, they wish they liked items that are inexpensive or that ravish other people, they regret their expensive or embarrassing tastes or habits, they wish they had received or not the education corresponding to these tastes, they wish they were such other person and they would give so much for that, or they would dislike to be some other person unless they be duly compensated for, and so on. Indeed people do try to affect these characteristics of theirs by training, education, control of habit formation, reasoning, and the like. Of course, people's preferences about what or who they are depend on who or what they are. But for eudemonistic preferences and for comparisons among cases where happiness is comparable as described earlier, all people have the same preferences, the fundamental preferences.[21]

Philosophers, however, are allowed more "poetical license" than economists, since the pure preference approach is very similar to that of the "original position" (see chapters 1, 4, and especially 8). Only starting from actual individuals' preferences is to start from realism, whereas the "original position" plays games in "dreamtimes" from the onset. Indeed, in a theory of an imaginary "original position" where the individuals have not yet been attributed the "selves" that differentiate them but have preferences and could choose (Harsanyi, Rawls), these identical a priori individuals cannot but have identical preferences on both what they will be and what they will have. If these preferences represent "more or less satisfied" or "happy," they are the fundamental preferences. If furthermore one considers that these identical individuals decide on the future rules or allocations while they are uncertain about who they will be, it is legitimate (although not necessary) to assume that they have a behavior and preferences under this uncertainty of the type described by von Neumann and Morgenstern. This implies that they maximize the mathematical expectation of a cardinal utility (that is, a utility function defined up to any linear-affine increasing transformation) that specifies their preferences. Now, one can show that this cardinal utility specification of the fundamental ordering is a "fundamental cardinal utility" (Kolm 1992b). This justifies Harsanyi's (1953) assumption of such a cardinal utility. However, we have noted that even if one accepts their concept and plays their game, Original Position theories are not acceptable theories of justice (chapters 1, 4, and 8; hence the conclusions of the authors who rely on them have to be justified otherwise, and this is sometimes possible).[22]

---

21. Exclusive direct reliance on individuals' particular preferences, without the above consideration of the comparison of satisfaction or happiness, came to be called "extended sympathy" (Arrow) and is commonly doubted (J. Broome and D. Hausman, in particular, have expressed particularly explicitly this reservation; unfortunately, Broome at a certain point and, following him, Roemer, have mistaken fundamental preferences for extended sympathy). By contrast, the early remarks of Tinbergen (1957) refer to a comparison of happiness (he suggests to ask external observers professionally expert on well-being, happiness, and suffering, such as nurses, to provide interpersonal comparisons).

22. The theory of fundamental preferences is related to a number of philosophical analyses, in both Eastern and Western traditions, such as the theory of no-self of

When the fundamental preference ordering is representable by a utility function, this function is the *fundamental utility*. This utility depends both on the situation or allocation of the individual, and on his personal characteristics that influence his evaluation of this situation or allocation. It is, by construction, both interpersonally comparable and ordinal (i.e. defined only up to any increasing transformation—the same transformation for all individuals if we need to maintain the meaningful comparability). Social and economic analysis using fundamental preferences or utility is *fundamental analysis*. It has been practiced by hundreds of studies in both positive and normative economics (sometimes using a cardinal specification of the fundamental utility)—without discussion of the justification of the concept, however.[23] Fundamental preference or utility is also necessary in other structures, such as equality or symmetry in individuals' utilities, or, with cardinal utilities, in individuals' differences in individual utilities (the symmetry can be of a possibility set or of a social evaluation

---

advanced Buddhism, hermeneutics, and the egology of the philosophies of existence. Philosophical Buddhism (see Kolm 1982a) implies fundamental preferences in the following way. It holds that there is no "self" (that is, no "transcendental self," no specific, hardcore, individualized entity that is a "self," and to believe in its existence is to be the victim of an illusion). An individual is only a flow of physical and mental elementary items related by causal influences and also in causal influences with other items. Certain of these elements constitute suffering (*dukkha*) that should be decreased, which implies that "more" or "less" suffering is defined (an ordering structure). This suffering is causally determined by other elements. This latter *relation* is valid for each individual, and it constitutes a eudemonistic fundamental preference ordering. (The Western intuitions of "no-self," such as Hume's or Sartre's, have nothing of the Buddhist's extremely elaborate analysis; Sartre's extreme "total choice" of oneself, however, also suggests a fundamental preference). On the other hand, empathy, and the elaborate tradition of *hermeneutics* (Dilthey, Gadamer, Ricoeur, etc.), permit one to respectively feel like others and "understand" as they do. Yet reaching fundamental preferences in this way requires the further stage of comparison, something like comparative empathy or comparative hermeneutics. The existence of the sentiment of compassion proves the possibility of comparative empathy.

23. We should also note here that the very concept of an individual preference ordering or utility function (not the fundamental one), which is extremely widely used in economics and is also present in other social sciences, is not a "falsifiable" concept (in Popper's sense). Indeed its experimental falsification implies the assumption that these preferences guide choice and then the presentation of intransitive choices (such as *a* is preferred to *b*, *b* is preferred to *c*, and *c* is preferred to *a*), or of choices that imply such an intransitivity (by "revealed preferences"). Yet this implies experiments at various points in time (perhaps close to each other), and one can always say that these preferences are dated and have change from one point in time to the other (perhaps quite quickly). Only an additional hypothesis of stability over time can be tested (see Kolm, *Philosophy of Economics*, 1986a).

function), though most authors forget to state these conditions (several examples will be met in chapter 12).

End-justice evaluates the world through the persons' judgments, and therefore all factors that influence these judgments can participate in the possibility that the corresponding equality be impossible or inefficient. For end-justice alone, however, this impossibility or inefficiency of equality can be the direct result of differences in tastes, preferences, satisfaction capacities, or ambitions, notably when they present uncompensatable differences. But this situation of end-justice can also be due to all the other factors which can intervene in the various means-justices (see chapter 6). The interference among these factors of various types can produce reinforcements of the effects, as well as compensations in various possible degrees depending on the correlations of their distributions among the persons.

Fundamental preferences lead to a number of criteria of justice having each its domain of relevant application ("fundamental dominance," "fundamental efficiency," "Adequacy" or "Platonian justice"—see section 7.2—a number of "fundamental majorities," "Practical Justice").[24] The most extreme is Practical Justice, the "lexical maximin" or "leximin" which says, as recalled in chapter 3: Choose the possible state where the least "happy" or "satisfied" individual is the most "satisfied" possible; if there is more than one solution of which that is true, then choose the state that best "satisfies" the "next-least-satisfied" individual, and so on. This choice can furthermore be performed under the added constraint that the basic rights be respected, but this constraint is commonly not binding, since Practical Justice commonly entails this respect (and can constitute one of its auxilliary justifications) plus the provision of means that give some "reality" to these "formal liberties" (see chapter 4).

One can then introduce the notion that a number of personal causes of unhappiness or insatisfaction may not be relevant for justice. The fundamental preference ordering must then be cleaned up for the effects of these causes.[25] This is technically well-defined and easy in a number of important cases (for instance, in the case of envy, the cleaned concept is that of "envy-free preferences" presented in chapter 9).[26]

---

24. See *Justice and Equity* and complements in Kolm 1987e, 1991a, 1992d.
25. See Goodin 1986.
26. See Kolm 1991c, 1993f, 1995a.

Practical Justice has then been considered and applied in a number of studies. Hammond (1976) and Arrow (1977) interestingly deduce it from an axiom that is its application to the comparison of pairs of states differing only by two utility levels. However, the direct consideration of Practical Justice as the primary concept has the advantage that one need in general consider only the worst-off people, and find meaning and information only in comparing them to the other individuals, and among themselves across states. This is a much smaller number of comparisons, and often the clearest and easiest of comparisons, in contrast with the axiom "in the small" that requires all pairwise comparisons both within each state and across states, and thus meets fully—at the conceptual level—the difficulties concerning the meaning of these comparisons and the existence of the relevant information. In particular, for "global" justice in large, actual societies, certainly the fully egalitarian Justice would be ruled out even if it were definable and conceivable, and only the indicated limited comparisons are required. Furthermore, Practical Justice "in the small" is not more "compelling" or basic or, indeed, simpler than its general consideration. On the contrary, Practical Justice "in the large" is much more justified when it is applied for the relief of unsatisfied basic needs or of particular suffering. The concept of Practical Justice has been applied to a number of specific questions. The eudemonistically just and practically just taxes were determined for the case when the constraint on public policy is freedom of saving in Kolm 1974a. This question was developed by Phelps (1977). Atkinson (1973) studied the Practically Just tax based on earned income—and thus with disincentives for higher incomes—and concluded that it displays surprisingly low progressivity.[27] Practical Justice has since become a standard criterion. Let us note, finally, that economists commonly refer to Practical Justice as being Rawls's view, whereas Rawls's *Theory of Justice* opposes very strongly any use of individual utilities (this attribution thus reveals an ignorance of the essentials of modern political philosophy).

---

27. We therefore have the surprising conclusion that the practically just income tax—the most redistributive one in intention—is likely to be less progressive than the taxes resulting from the Liberal Social Contract which implies no redistribution (if we omit collective gift-giving and rectifications); see chapter 5 and Kolm 1985a, 1991e.

8 Equal Liberties and Maximin: Fairness from Ignorance

8.1 Two Sources of Morals

The most celebrated contemporary work in social ethics is John Rawls's *A Theory of Justice*. This work even became a social phenomenon in itself. However Rawls writes in the preface: "I must disclaim any originality for the views I put forward. The leading ideas are classical and well-known." But his use of these ideas as the alternative needed to make effective his strong moral criticism of utilitarianism— the very particular theory that dominated the limited circle of English-language political philosophy—doubtlessly disturbed this circle and accounts for a large part of the initial impact of Rawls's work. Moreover, if, on the one hand, the principles of justice proposed are indeed standard as they consist, roughly, of the inalienable human and civil rights that define liberal democratic states, of "first help the poor" that standardly defines leftist (or Christian) views, and of the acknowledgment of the disincentive effects of redistribution that is commonplace in political arguments and in economics, on the other hand the justification that Rawls offers for these views is on the contrary highly original notwithstanding his modest disclaim. This justification, the theory of the Original Position, resuscitated in this circle the theory of the Social Contract, yet it constitutes the most audacious form of a Social Contract and of the corresponding reasoning. Rawls offers the needed elaborate developments, includes economic realism (and one economists' concept), and more generally provides interesting and insightful discussions of a number of related questions.

The initial presentations of this theory have continually been improved upon. This confirms that this construction constitutes a philosophy rather than a dogma. The final perfectings should now be considered. They have to face four kinds of related tasks that I state now although their meaning requires the presentation of the theory that will come only shortly after.

1. The definition of the *principles of justice* should be precise and justified, with respect to

a. the logic of the *multidimensional maximin* of the "difference principle,"

b. the *interdependences in the individuals' uses of their "primary goods,"*

c. the distinction between *human capacities* for production and for consumption or life in general, respectively,

d. the allocation of the advantages derived from the *capacities to buy* and the capacities to *use power*,

e. the justification of the need for the *second-best egalitarian "difference principle,"*

f. the structure of *"basic liberties."*

2. The ideal of equal liberties and means (goods) should be justified directly from rationality in social choice (see chapter 2 above). This eliminates criticisms that propose that the justification initially offered, the theory of the Original Position, leads to something else (indeed, to utilitarianism). More generally, this justification frees these principles of justice from the reasons why a theory of the Original Position will not a priori yield any principle of justice and hence can hardly justify them (see below). Rawls explains that he proposes the theory of the Original Position in order to justify classical principles more firmly than by "intuitionism" (see his preface). Yet the valid justification of the improved principles is neither of these but rather the direct rationality of justice.

3. The domains of relevance of the principles should be specified (these domains are not all a priori universal and they are not the same for all the principles).

4. The question of the implementation of the principles should solve consistency issues involving motivations, the various principles, and their justification.

The contrast between the epistemic statuses of Rawls's principles and of the justification he offers for them is well grasped by the philosopher Bergson's famous distinction between clear ideas and enlightening ones (*idées claires* et *idées éclairantes*). *A Theory of Justice* proposes an idea in the field of clarity—the "principles of justice"—and it defends it with an argument in the style of enlightenment—the theory of the "Original Position." According to Bergson, "A new idea can be clear because it presents, simply arranged in a new order, elementary ideas that we already had. Our intelligence, then finding only ancient in the new, feels in familiar country; it is at ease, it 'understands.' Such is the clarity that we desire, and we are always grateful to he who brings it to us." By contrast, enlightening ideas begin "by being internally obscure; but the light they project around comes back to them by reflection, and penetrates them deeper and deeper; they then have the double power to enlighten both others and themselves." We will see that Rawls's "principles of justice" are so clear that even their priorities are very familiar. Yet they raise a number of *logical* questions, just noted, and their proposed justification does not really shed its light on justice, as will be shown below.

Now the rough framework of Rawls's "principles of justice" can be deduced from the general and necessary rationality of justice presented above (see chapters 2 and 3). However, abstracting from specific circumstances, situations, and problems, a number of other, different theories of justice also fit this rationality. Therefore Rawls's framework is one of the possible ones, that is to be applied when the circumstances are appropriate (indeed the various elements in Rawls's principles have various scopes of relevance, the "basic liberties" having the largest).[1]

A consequence is that the theory of the Original Position is *not needed* to justify Rawls' framework. This is fortunate since we will see that, as a general conclusion, a theory of the Original Position cannot be a theory of justice, that is, it cannot justify as being just the rules it can yield. This result concerning Original Position theories has itself two fortunate consequences.

First, the critiques of Rawls that argue that an Original Position theory cannot justify his "principles of justice" because it leads to another principle—such as Harsanyi's utilitarianism—are not relevant to justice (it thus does not matter who is right).

Second, since the role of rational thinking can be seen to roll back "enlightening ideas" in order to replace them by "clear" ones as much as possible, then we have greatly advanced in rationality, and this progress has *not* undermined Rawls' framework for justice but has, on the contrary, vindicated it. Furthermore, this progress improves the presentation of this framework with respect to its scope and to its various logical problems.

---

1. Paradoxically—and most unfortunately—basic liberties is the only principle that Rawls admits could be abandoned for the sake of economic development in poor countries (hence reversing his basic priority).

8.2   The Principles

Let us first note the following facts about the social ethics of modern times:

1. The Rights of Man and of the Citizen constitute the most basic legal principle of free countries. Their declaration is commonly the opening of the constitution of these countries; it constitutes their most basic official text, that legally prevail over all others. These rights are deemed to be "inalienable" by this declaration; in particular, they cannot be traded for any other benefit. This property implies that these rights have *priority* over all other considerations. The particular "right to properties," however, is understood in modern time as *not excluding democratically chosen redistributive taxation* (hence, the original intent of article 17 of the 1789 Declaration is forgotten).

2. The 1789 Declaration states that these human and civil rights should be equal for all (article 1), and that they should be maximal consistent with equal rights for other individuals (article 4). This "equal and maximal" structure of basic liberties had been proposed by Rousseau ("the citizen should not be limited in his freedom except when this is necessary for an equal freedom of others"), it is suggested by Kant, and it is repeated by J. S. Mill and many others.

3. Nondiscrimination is included in these rights.

4. "First take care of the poorest" is probably the most commonly heard principle of social ethics and justice.

5. Equality of income, wealth, power, positions is the most common ideal of "leftist" views throughout history. Aristotle says: "Justice is equality."

6. The idea that letting the better-off have more can be beneficial to the poorest, or to everybody, has been repeated innumerable times. Let us for instance note the following in bulk. Too high tax rates in the highest income tax brackets induce less work from useful professionals (like physicians who heal the poor). Progressive taxation, in diminishing high incomes (and possibly the return to capital), deters global saving and investment, risk-taking and innovation, and entrepreneurship, and hence impairs employment and incomes for the poor. It also deters the acquisition, by education and training, of skills that can be

beneficial to all. These are also standard arguments against inheritance taxes. The rich are necessary for defense and science (in certain societies) and culture and the arts, from which all can benefit. The money spent by the rich "trickles down" to the poor in various ways. The general argument is, for instance, developed by Hume in his critique of the "levellers" in his *Enquiry Concerning the Principles of Morals* (1752), where he describes equality as destroying the wealth of all as well as liberty and the rule of law.[2] It can also be found in a number of authors such as Bentham, and Lenin (for the NEP), among others. It is derided by Anatole France as a hypocritical defense of the privileged in *Penguins' Island,* and it is dramatically implied by the Roman *fiat justicia pereat mundus.* The first article of the Declaration of Rights—again—states: "Social distinctions can only be based in common utility" (where "common" clearly means "of each").

7. However, although a decrease in the rates of redistributive taxes that produce rather equal disposable incomes is indeed likely to augment actual output,[3] it may well be that these lower tax rates applied to this higher product result in lower transfers and lower income for the less able. It is even furthermore possible that a decrease in these tax rates leads to a lower output because of the "income effect." Scandinavian countries jointly have the highest transfers, the most productive economies, and the richest poor (see chapter 6).

8. Self-respect is a standard value, firmly grounded in theory by Kant.

---

2. "But historians, and even common sense, may inform us that, however specious these ideas of *perfect* equality may seem, they are really at bottom impracticable; and were they not so, would be extremely *pernicious* to human society. Render possessions ever so equal, men's different degrees of art, care, and industry will immediately break that equality. Or if you check these virtues, you reduce society to the most extreme indigence and, instead of preventing want and beggary in a few, render it unavoidable to the whole community. The most rigorous inquisition, too, is requisite to watch every inequality on its first appearance; and the most severe jurisdiction to punish and redress it. But besides that so much authority must soon degenerate into tyranny and be exerted with great partialities: who can possibly be possessed of it in such a situation as is here supposed? Perfect equality of possessions, destroying all subordination, weakens extremely the authority of magistracy and must reduce all power nearly to a level, as well as property." (Hume 1792, sec. III, pt. II).

3. Not counting the value of leisure and of lower effort in this output, or, if they are included, in taking account of the inferior "product mix" (see chapter 6).

9. Normal people in normal situations are responsible people. In particular, they are responsible for their choices and for the consequences of these choices concerning themselves. Therefore distributive justice toward them can only be concerned with the allocation of external means. It is indeed commonly considered that what people do with their liberty or with their income is their own concern; it is irrelevant to justice as long as they respect others' rights. "All that is not forbidden is permitted," says, once more, the Declaration of Rights. In particular, it is most commonly considered that people are "responsible" for their tastes, or at least accountable for them: certain persons having expensive tastes (for instance, they like caviar) does not seem a valid reason for transferring income from others to them, or for their receiving a higher income in general.

10. Relatedly, income taxes are based on earned income (plus, more or less, income from nonhuman assets). They tax neither the "psychic income" that people derive from their particular capacities for enjoying consumption and life nor their unused potential productive capacities. They tax only the productive uses of human assets, the capacities used in production but not those used in consumption. Since progressive income tax is the central tool for the implementation of distributive justice in modern societies and economies, this choice of base reveals the standard conception of justice in these societies (we have indeed seen in chapter 6 that this choice of earned income as base is essentially made for an ethical and conceptual reason rather than for informational convenience—or only for this reason).

11. There results the possibility of the deterrence of the labor supply that is often said to occur, notably for the ablest people in case of redistributive progressive taxation. Economists study few things more than the ensuing "welfare loss." Yet, the result can also be higher labor supply and output because of the "income effect" (see remark 7).

12. A classical method for the determination of principles of ethics, in particular social ethics and notably justice, is "dialectics" as described by Plato in *The Republic*, that is, iterative consideration and evaluation of the general principles and of their applications and consequences, with the resulting adjustments, until an equilibrium is reached.

13. The classical republican ideal holds that public institutions must be based on secularism and toleration and must permit peaceful coexistence and practice of various cultures, values, and beliefs.

14. Utilitarianism has always been strongly rejected and criticized, except in two limited academic circles: most of English-language political philosophy, and a part of economics.

Rawls defends these views, with the priorities they imply (although he does not point out all of the facts: See chapter 4 and below for the necessary priority of basic rights, and chapter 6 and remarks 7 and 11 for the disincentive effect of redistribution). The basic Rights of Man and of the Citizen are called *basic liberties*, both personal (man) and political (citizen). Income, wealth, power, positions, self-respect (or the means to it), and sometimes "opportunities" are called *primary goods*. They are essentially the flow and stock of purchasing power, and other power and status. Basic liberties should be equal for all and maximal. Inequalities in primary goods such that the lowest endowments are as high as possible constitutes the *difference principle*. There is the following order of priorities: basic liberties, nondiscrimination, and the difference principle. Individuals use these liberties and goods for pursuing their own "plans of life." A central method for determining the principles is *reflective equilibrium* reached by alternate consideration of the adjusted principles and of their implications. The work of Rawls posterior to *A Theory of Justice* emphasizes the fundamental role of just institutions in permitting cultural pluralism. Finally, *A Theory of Justice* begins by a strong criticism of utilitarianism on moral grounds, and by the statement that its own aim is to replace it because this criticism can be efficient only if an alternative is offered.[4]

8.3 Logical Difficulties with the Principles

Despite their being common and "clear," these "principles of justice" raise the following questions and problems.

---

4. My complete analysis of Rawls's theory is in *The Liberal Social Contract* (1985a, part 5, pp. 350–405). Rawls's theory has been presented in surveys by Daniels (1975), Pettit (1980), and Kukathas and Pettit (1991). The page numbers of the quotations from *A Theory of Justice* presented below refer to the 1971 edition.

Basic Liberties

We have seen in chapter 4 that equal and maximal basic liberties are *limitless* basic liberties because they are act-freedoms with essentially no rivalry across liberties and across individuals (the means bear the rivalry, for the essential). Furthermore this boundlessness *implies the priority* of the basic liberties, and it is implied by it. The statement of the "principles" thus contains a redundancy. This is a virtue for so important principles—the priority deserves at any rate to be explicitly recalled. In addition this actual structure of basic liberties makes irrelevant a number of qualifications proposed by Rawls (such as the proposal of a maximin in basic liberties) and a number of criticisms that could be addressed to his formulation.[5]

Multidimensional Maximin

Since there are several primary goods, the minimum and the maximum of the "difference principle" are not a priori defined. With respect to the minimum, one individual may have the least of one good and another may have the least of another good. Rawls says that de facto this does not occur. It is indeed true that the poorest and the least powerful are often the same person. Yet this is not general. Many societies have rich merchants excluded from political and administrative powers, and poor and influential wisemen. This, however, is probably not common in modern Western societies and for the lowest levels, where there is indeed a rough coincidence, and Rawls later added that his theory is only for these societies. At any rate, *maximizing* a bundle of goods is a priori undefined. Rawls says we should choose weights and maximize the weighted sum. But he does not say

---

5. For instance, why equal liberties rather than sets of liberties adjusted to specific needs or preferences of the various individuals (one individual's "plans of life" may need freedom of expression while the other's rather requires freedom of movement)? Rawls also admits "less extensive liberties" when they "strengthen the total system of liberty shared by all," and "less than equal liberty" when it is "acceptable to those with lesser liberty" (p. 302). But how does one define these terms, in particular how does one compare extents of liberty in general? (The answer is provided in Kolm 1993e; see chapter 9 below). Finally, we have noted in chapter 4 that the priority and maximality of basic liberties makes it impossible to make sense of an interpretation that would include, in each basic liberty, not only the corresponding act-freedom but also certain means that would make this liberty a "real" one in Marx's sense.

how we should make this choice. He presumably assumes that these weights should be constant, at least that they do not depend on the allocations of primary goods (that of the poorest individual and those of the others), but we will see that this undermines attempts to rationally define these weights. Furthermore "power," "positions," "self-respect," and "opportunities" have no a priori defined measure. These points will be further discussed shortly. Note that certain individual "plans of life" require relatively more wealth, others relatively more power of some sort or a higher status, and others relatively more "means of self-respect."

On the contrary, the maximin is well-defined with "fundamental preferences," as was noted earlier, and it constitutes "practical justice" of *Justice and Equity*.

Consumptive and Productive Capacities, Leisure and Work

The ideal equality in *primary goods* among the individuals, containing as it does the equality of incomes, implies that the differences in the market returns that the individuals could obtain from their *productive capacities* are seen as arbitrary (this income is standardly defined and hence it does *not* include the implicit value of leisure). By contrast, the ideal equivalence in fundamental preferences, that is "justice" of *Justice and Equity*, implies *in addition* that the differences in the benefits or handicaps stemming from *consumptive capacities* are considered as arbitrary from the point of view of justice. Now Rawls insists that the relevant subject matter (or "substance") of justice is primary goods including income (and basic liberties and nondiscrimination in addition to primary goods), because they are the *means* with which each individual can pursue his life plan. This raises several questions.

First, leisure time also is an important means for an individual's pursuit of his life plan. It is indeed an indispensable means for his being able to make something with his income. However, the introduction of leisure time among primary goods raises problems for the whole theory, no matter how this introduction is made. There are, indeed, two possible ways to introduce leisure time in this theory. First, leisure time is taken as a good in itself, and the ideal thus implies equal leisure time for all individuals. But this amounts to equal labor time for all (since this is by definition the complement of leisure time). Then, each individual is no more free to choose his own labor time.

This has several consequences: An individual cannot choose to work less (or more) in duration as a result of the redistribution of income, and this basic cause of the "difference principle" disappears; this imposition of the duration of labor violates the act-freedom of labor supply, and hence possibly a "basic liberty;" it also hampers the efficiency of the free choice of labor and leisure times; and the equality certainly introduces such an inefficiency. The second solution remedies these shortcomings in counting leisure as a good that the individual can choose to buy with his income. This is done in including the value of leisure time within the relevant disposable income, and in letting the individual choose his consumption of leisure by his choice of labor time. The market value of the individual's leisure time is just the market value of his time, namely his wage rate, or his marginal productivity. This income thus is the market value of the individual's capacities during all the time, which can be seen as the market value of his productive capacities during all the time, hence including both the actual and the potential (during leisure time) use of these capacities. The ideal relevant income equalization then is that of this income, that is, the taxation (or subsidy) of the excess of the individual's wage rate over the average wage rate, multiplied by total time. We have seen in chapter 6 that this ideal is extravagant and irrational. With respect to the incentive effect, the duration corresponding to this income is again given (it is total time), and the individual cannot decide to adjust this duration, which suppresses this essential reason for the "difference principle." On the contrary, the individual can adjust the allocation of his time between work and leisure, and this tax induces him to work a *longer* time in order to compensate more or less for this loss (the "income effect," since the "price effect" is absent),[6] and indeed simply to pay for the tax. A similar result obtains with the more realistic device of not counting a given time of leisure in the extended income. In both ways of introducing leisure the same conclusions are reached if leisure time is completed by lower work effort and lower time, effort and cost of education and training.

Rawls's principles imply that the "natural" endowments of capacities used in production are arbitrary—given society's demands for

---

6. Leisure normally is a "normal good."

productive capacities—and should see their proceed redistributed (and ideally equalized) because this income is an individual's means, while other capacities are irrelevant to the consideration of justice and thus have no reason to be objects of compensation. Chapter 6 has presented the various possible reasons for this distinction and for these opposite treatments, but it has also shown the large part of arbitrariness they contain. For one thing, these two categories are often not different in nature and even in use. These capacities are commonly the same ones. Even those that are more specialized are also put to uses of the other category: various mental and physical capacities that are essential in work are "consumed" in play, sport, or for planning and organizing one's private life; capacities to appreciate savor or beauty are marketed by artists of all kinds, cooks, designers, stylist, various experts, and so on. The identity of the two sets become much more pronounced if one considers the basic, elementary capacities rather than, globally, the clusters of these capacities that are used in the various activities. Furthermore, Rawls's basic criterion seems to ideally equalize individuals' *means*, but there is no logical limit to the consideration of all capacities as means (as we saw in chapter 6): even willpower, capacity to "make sense," and satisfaction capacities of various kinds can be seen as means.

The distinction used by Rawls also coincides with that between capacities used for obtaining an income and the others. But why discriminate between the benefits one derives from one's capacities when they are obtained indirectly through labor and income and directly in leisure? Indeed the differences between income-earning capacities and consumptive capacities are only those between capacities that are rented out in exchange or otherwise used to earn income, and capacities that are directly used by the person or for services provided free to others, notably within the family. Now a number of choices between providing a service to oneself (or to the family), and buying the corresponding services or a substitute equipment are a matter of contingent institutional development and individual decision (influenced in fact by the income tax, notably that which aims at redistributing income). Rawls admitted compensations for the "obvious" case of handicaps, and often the same handicaps affect both earning capacities and private life, but the line between what is a handicap and what is not is not a priori clear-cut.

However, the basic reason for the ideal equalization of income *may be* that what is deemed arbitrary with respect to justice toward an individual is not really this individual's intrinsic capacities (when used in production) but rather *society's demand of these capacities*, that is, the corresponding *"situational resource"* (see chapter 9). Indeed the individual's wage rate and labor income depend on both his supply and others' demand for his capacities, in a joint manner that does not permit any a priori assignment between these two factors (wage rates for standard capacities are furthermore usually given for the individual). One can then choose to assign the differences in earning rates to the demand side and see this as arbitrary, rather than to the embodied individual capacities. For example, the extraordinarily high income of a popular singer may be seen as arbitrary not because of the assignment of larynxes in the population but rather because of peoples' enthusiasm for this particular sound. More generally, the overall demand for an individual's productive capacities can depend on all tastes and other resources of all kinds, including other's capacities and technology. Then, since the perceived arbitrariness is reduced to the economic "situation" of the individuals, one can "endorse" consistently the "natural" allocation of *all intrinsic* capacities: Incomes are ideally equalized only to compensate for the unequal demands of other people, which in a sense hides and supersedes the "natural" allocation of productive (uses of) capacities, whereas the "natural" allocation of consumptive (uses of) capacities remains actual, on the contrary.

However, an individual with his disposable income is a buyer of consumption goods (and hence of "satisfaction") who benefits from low prices for the goods that best serve his ends and suffers relatively if these goods are expensive. These prices depend on the economy, namely on supplies of resources of all kinds and demands. Even if they depend also on this individual's demand, they can be morally assigned to the corresponding supply since these are joint causes. Now, if the economic environment is seen as arbitrary when it demands productive capacities, consistency probably requires one to see it as arbitrary when it supplies consumption goods. Then the ideal equalizand should be either the bundles of consumption goods or satisfactions according as one considers that other's supplies and demands determine the individual's buying or his satisfaction. In the former case, a priority of efficiency may then lead one to resort to the second-best efficient super-equity, which restores the role of income but is less demanding with respect to equality (see chapter 6). In addition consumption itself depends on the rest of society. Not only does technology interfere very closely with consumptive uses of capacities, but others' tastes are also present there, in consumptions necessary for social respectability, in fashion, in imitation or distinction, and so on. Comparable preferences can of course encompass all these effects (see chapter 7). The remarks of this paragraph remain valid if the "situational resources" are assigned only a part of the arbitrariness.

Furthermore, even if individuals are not entitled to their own productive capacities and to the demand for them, they may be entitled to the results of their efforts, notably in production. These efforts can be manifested by the intensity and duration of labor, or by previous training and education. This view, based on notions of merit, deservingness, and responsibility, is in fact much more entrenched than the view that people own their capacities (or should enjoy their product or usufruct) for reasons based on notions of process-freedom or of the self. A distinction between effort and capacities raises again a problem of joint production for defining the corresponding allocations. The problem is futher compounded by the consideration that people may have different capacities for effort.

The painfulness of different works, related to the intensity and duration of labor among other factors, is also something for which compensation is widely seen as justified. The compensation may or may not take acount of capacities to endure the corresponding hardship.

It should also be remembered that often the important part of an individual's life-plan is pursued in work rather than in consuming income and leisure, and hence directly thanks to the use of productive capacities. A meaningful, useful, socially rewarding labor, that provides activity, social relations, status, room for creativity and responsibility, is certainly much more a means to fulfilling life plans than is comfortable rest, gadget appliances, hobbies, and pastimes. The "primary goods" of status, position and the means of self-respect can indeed account for part of this question, but aspects such as room for creativity, the possibility to have a meaningful activity, and the absence of alienation probably deserved more explicit consideration.

The conceptual, moral, and practical difficulties to discriminate between capacities used in production and in consumption are compounded by the fact that commonly the same policies affect both. Health, education and information improve both capacities to earn and capacities to enjoy and to live a good, meaningful life. In particular, important public policies in health, education and sometimes culture aim in part to improve all kinds of consumptive capacities of people with poor health, poor family education, or a narrow cultural outlook.

Finally, in his 1982 article "Social Unity and Primary Goods," Rawls refers approvingly to "fundamental utility" and the corresponding "Justice", and thus considers compensating for consumptive capacities. We will in fact see below that the theory of the Original Position implies the consideration of fundamental preferences rather than of primary goods.

Capacities and the Difference Principle

Now, if one tries to equalize the benefits from all capacities—either producing a money income or used directly—then the transfers will no longer be based on earned incomes, and they will thus not produce the disincentive effects that are the reason for Rawls's "difference principle." (This question, related to the previous remarks concerning leisure, has been analyzed in full in chapter 6).

Interdependences

Because of social interactions of various types, an individual's fulfilment of his plans depends on others' acts and situations. Therefore, this fulfilment also depends on others' ends and means, and hence on others' endowments of primary goods, basic liberties, situations with respect to discrimination (and discriminating tendencies), personal capacities of various kinds, tastes and life plans. Indeed an individual's fulfilment of his plans encounters others' competition, cooperation, supplies, demands, and so on, in all spheres of life (the economy, politics, the family, in relative statuses, in social recognition, etc.). This occurs even if the individuals take no direct "interest in the others' interests" for reason of envy, altruism, malevolence, benevolence, and so on—as Rawls assumes for the individuals "in the original position," which implies that this is also the case for the actual individuals (as discussed below). Their interest in others' means and ends can result from mere self-interest alone. Individuals interact in spending their income (for instance they compete with one another) and in using their power (they can either oppose one another, compete, or cooperate). A social position is, almost by definition, relative to others' social positions, and this aspect is often the crucial one (such as in hierarchies). The means of self-respect are also often relative to others' means, situations and acts (see chapter 11 below). The outcome of the interactions depends on all their conditions, such as bargaining powers of all sorts. Finally the resulting interdependence also results from indirect effects by all ways of influence and at all degrees.

An important consequence is the question of the consistency of the different treatment of various situational resources, already met but that deserves explicit consideration. With the same income or power one individual may be unable to fulfil his life plans because this requires commodities that are much sought after by others, whereas another individual can fulfil his very easily because few people need the same commodities as he does. Prices reflect these relative scarcities. Therefore this fulfilment depends in particular on having tastes and ambitions that are either common or original. The ideal of equal incomes erases the effects of demands for particular personal productive capacities. Yet it leaves similar effects from others' demands for commodities that the individual requires more or less. This asymmetry seems arbitrary: Why should it be unfair that other people want what I have, and fair that they want what I want? Why should I be compensated because my skills are common and penalized because my tastes are common, why could I benefit from my originality in tastes but not in skills? Others' consumptive capacities of all sorts, and not only one's own, may matter for the individuals and may introduce differences between them, possibly unjust ones.

Furthermore, Rawls argues that justice cannot result from exchange because it cannot be "to each according to his threat advantage." This is his first reason for considering identical individuals "in the original position" (see below). Yet threats can occur in using income or power and not only in acquiring them, and the power of threats depend on the individuals' needs and tastes and not only on their endowments of primary goods.

In addition that which the individuals can make and obtain with their incomes or powers depends on their capacities for dealing in markets as buyers and in other sectors of social life. This may mobilize capacities of various kinds, such as forecasting, various information, and bargaining capacities of several types. But bargaining and market capacities are among the main productive capacities in most economic systems. Now a central tenet of Rawls's view is that the "natural" distribution of productive capacities is arbitrary and should be compensated. This raises a question of consistency.

Finally, the fact that an individual's possibilities and fulfilment of his plans depend on others' endowments of primary goods and not only on his own, in ways that differ among individuals, provides possible bases for questionning the validity of both the equality in primary goods as the ideal and the maximin in primary goods as the appropriate "second-best" efficient egalitarianism.

"Practical Justice" and the "Difference Principle"

In summary, the "difference principle," or maximin in "primary goods," faces a number of problems. These problems concern either the pure logic of this definition, or the way in which this principle realizes its basic intent. Logically "more," "less," maximum, minimum, or maximin is a priori not defined for a bundle of goods, and "more," "less" (and *a fortiori* a quantity for defining a weighted sum) are not a priori defined for "goods" such as power, position, or self-respect. Furthermore individuals' primary goods leave aside a number of means for fulfilling one's life plans. In economists' classification these primary goods are *intermediary* goods rather than *final* consumption goods. This has a number of consequences. Capacities for buying with income (market, exchange or bargaining capacities), or for using other power, differ across individuals; the former are usually classified as productive capacities, and Rawls wants to ideally equalize the benefits from this category of capacities. Furthermore individuals' possibilities to fulfil their life plans depend on others' endowments of primary goods because of interferences in markets and otherwise. For the same reason they also depend on others' capacities to use power and markets, and on their life plans, tastes and preferences. Finally, they also depend on the individual's leisure time and/or on a number of his consumptive capacities that are often basically the same as his productive capacities.

All these problems are solved if one replaces the "difference principle" by "practical justice" and "primary goods" by "fundamental utility." This solution should of course be *full act-freedom constrained practical justice* (Kolm 1985a), that is, leximin with fundamental preferences under the constraint that act-freedoms are respected; yet in many cases this constraint is not effective because "practical justice" implies act-freedom.

Informational problems for implementation exist in both cases. They may be more delicate for "practical justice" since this also considers individuals' capacities that are practically specialized in consumption. However, it is generally not too difficult to find out the minimum (the most distressed person) and its maximum as long as the criterion is relevant. At any rate the definition of the theoretically correct solution must precede the consideration of implementational problems, since these cannot be solved or even correctly considered if the theoretical objective is mistaken or ambiguous.

However, this solution to all these problems implies the theoretical difference between both concepts: "Practical justice" finds unjust certain differences in consumptive capacities that the "difference principle" deems to be irrelevant for justice. Now, in most large actual societies the people at the lowest level taken care of by "practical justice" are there because certain of their basic needs are not satisfied, rather than because they have demanding fancy tastes or abusive expectations (the cases of pathological suffering often have to be put aside: they should be helped with priority but not necessarily with absolutely maximal relief at any cost). Fancy tastes could cause certain individuals to be at the lowest level only if one considers the distribution within certain limited subsocieties. One would then have to justify this restriction, and "practical justice" would not be the appropriate criterion. Basic needs are described by the concerned individuals' preferences if they are not only "vicarious needs," that is, needs estimated as such only by others (see chapter 11). Then, in the general case of unsatisfied basic needs, "practical justice" and the "difference principle" are likely to designate the same people as being at the bottom. The difference, however, appears with regard to that which should be maximized, since the "difference principle" points out to a bundle of "primary goods" (for which the operation "maximize" is not properly defined), whereas "practical justice" proposes a unidimensional index defined from these persons' preferences.[7]

Note that Rawls's "weights"of primary goods for solving the multi-dimensional maximin problem of the "difference principle" cannot be deduced from a linear approximation of the lowest individual "funda-mental utility" (lowest for the same specification of the fundamental utility). Indeed, first, this function *qua* function of this individual's allocation of primary goods depends on this individual's specific characteristics (tastes) and situation (for the effect of others' primary goods, tastes, and demands, notably through the intermediary of prices), and this individual may not be the same one in different states—even when he is the same, his situation and the effects of others generally differ, and the linear approximation of his utility function may thus also differ. Second, this function also depends on others' allocation of primary goods by the various noted interdepen-dences; hence these "weights" would a priori depend on the overall allocation of primary goods. Let us finally recall that most of these "primary goods" do not have an a priori well-defined measure.

Universality

Furthermore *Justice and Equity* emphasized that "practical justice" is only one criterion among others—indeed an extreme and limiting case—which has to be considered, and applied in a number of very important cases but not necessarily always. By contrast, the "differ-ence principle" is offered as a universal principle (at least in modern societies). Now, there can be no doubt that in certain cases room must be made for certain other principles. For example, merit or process-freedom would be considered as the relevant ethic by practically every-body in a number of questions and situations: "This is mine because I acquired or earned it with much effort" is an argument that must certainly sometimes be considered and even obeyed, in particular

---

7. The relation between this "respect of preferences," basic needs, and the case of "vicarious needs" is discussed in chapter 11.

when the basic needs of the poorest people are largely satisfied (in the considered society).

8.4   The Original Position

Reasons for the Original Position

At any rate, Rawls's principles correspond to classical positions. Hegel would praise their virtue of "Minerva's owl" and appreciate that the novelty resided in the justification.

However, these principles were presented in just about the only circle in the modern world that considered it a mistake to take rights and equalities as primary ethical positions. This is English-language philosophy, which has been dominated for the last two centuries by the sentiment that utilitarianism is the self-evident moral truth. We will see in chapter 14 that utilitarianism in the strict sense is in general an impossible social ethic for logical reasons because, in the expression "maximize the sum of utilities (or of pleasures minus pains, or of happinesses)," either the word sum is meaningless in its strict sense, or what is added cannot be justified as measuring pleasure or happiness, or the derivation of the utilitarian form in not really justified. Utilitarianism also presents severe moral vices. For all these reasons, utilitarianism never had importance in other philosophical traditions, which dubbed it an "English fantasy," or "merchants' philosophy," and rested instead on concepts of rights, liberties, equalities, solidarity, Social Contracts (often of the types of Rousseau's or of "tacit consent", that is, as in Plato's *Crito*), Kantian duties and humanism, or philosophy of history. Similarly, lawyers and commonsense everywhere thought of justice in terms of rights and various types of equality. Only a number of academic economists had been attracted by utilitarianism, dating back a few decades, because of its use of "utilities"—including, in a sense, one for society itself—and of maximization, of its formal simplicity, and of its (misleading) similarity to "surplus" theory (see chapter 14).

Now, Rawls begins his work by a radical attack on the ethic of utilitarianism. Therefore this deeply stirred the *milieu* of English-language philosophers. Rawls indeed adds that a criticism can be definitive only if it offers an alternative, and that this is why he presents his own theory of justice. The results of this theory are the above-noted principles. The justification is the theory of the Original Position.

Rawls's Original Position theory says that the rules of justice are those chosen by self-interested individuals "before" they know what specific actual individuals they will be. They then are "in the original position," or "behind the veil of ignorance" of who they will actually be and other things.

In the justifications Rawls provides for his theory of the Original Position, one can distinguish three different reasons which refer to three aspects of the choice of principles of justice for society: to avoid the effects of the inequalities and contingencies in relative powers that could influence this collective choice, to avoid self-interested biases in the mere enunciation of the principles, and to provide a tool of thought for testing a priori ethical intuitions.

The individuals "in the original position" are all identical. This suppresses the effects of both different means and different ends of the actual individuals on the choice of principles.

The theory has indeed the noted objectives:

1. The suppression of the effects of different individual means on the collective choice is actually one of the reasons for the theory. "No one should be advantaged or disadvantaged by natural fortune or social circumstance in the choice of principles" (p. 18). The theory wants to "nullify the effects of specific contingencies which put men at odds and tempt them to exploit social and natural circumstances to their advantage" (p. 136). Indeed, "to one according to his threat advantage is not a principle of justice." These "threat advantages" or different "bargaining powers" of course also depend on the various differences in desires, needs, and individual objectives.

2. "It should be impossible to tailor principles to the circumstances of one's own case. We should ensure further that particular inclinations or aspirations, and persons' conception of their good do not affect the principles adopted. . . . For example, if a man knew he was wealthy, he might find it rational to advance the principle that various taxes for welfare measures be counted unjust; if he knew that he was poor, he would most likely propose the contrary principle. To represent the desired restrictions, one imagines a situation in which everyone is deprived of this sort of information. One excludes the knowledge of

those contingencies which sets men at odds and allows them to be guided by their prejudices. In this manner the veil of ignorance is arrived at in a natural way" (pp. 18–19). Indeed an individual cannot propose objective, fair, and unbiased general principles of justice—especially distributive justice—if what he says and chooses is influenced by a desire to promote his own individual, particular self-interest. There are two possible ways to avoid this bias: The individual, when he enunciates principles of justice, either disregards his self-interest or does not know it. That is, either he forgets about his self-interest or he is not informed about it in the first place. Yet the former way may be impossible (to believe in its possibility may be utopian), and the latter is against the facts. Both may thus have to be theoretical reconstructions. In particular, one could think that the second option is safer, but it is not realistic when the individuals know the specifics. This ignorance has thus to be introduced as a special theoretical assumption. This is the "veil of ignorance." When it is drawn, you cannot hear the butcher say that justice is a higher price for meat, the able man argue that it is "to each according to his work," the lazy one propose that it is "to each according to his needs," and so on, since no one knows if he will be an able man, an idler, or if he will want to be a butcher.

3. Rawls sees the Original Position theory as a tool of thought and an "expository device" (p. 21) for testing or extending our "considered convictions of justice" (pp. 19, 20) until a "reflective equilibrium" is obtained.

These three reasons for the Original Position theory must be carefully considered and compared. First, reasons 1 and 2 a priori seem to build up a morally self-contained deductive theory, whereas reason 3 introduces a dialectical method and other sources of moral "intuitions" or "convictions." Second, reason 1 is superseded by reason 2, since "behind the veil of ignorance" all individuals have identical objectives, want the same thing and make the same choice, so possible differences in individual means to influence the collective choice ("threat advantages," bargaining powers, etc.) are irrelevant (see p. 139). But all these reasons are valid only if the Original Position constitutes a valid theory of justice, and hence if the choices in an "original position" can be considered as just ones.

The Problem with the Original Position Theory

We will see that theories of the Original Position present the following interrelated problems:

1. They are heavily counterfactual.

2. They yield a priori unjust outcomes.

3. They are at odds with the way in which rational choices of justice are made.

4. They cannot rest on individuals' responsibility.

And in the specific case of Rawls's theory,

5. It a priori does not yield Rawls's principles.

6. It is not a deductive theory.

The individuals "behind the veil of ignorance" say, want, and choose the same thing because they are identical and in identical situations (though they might need trivial coordination for choosing among equivalent solutions, of the type concerning on which side of the road people should drive).

As regards the motivations of the persons in the original position, "in choosing between principles each tries as best he can to advance his interest" (p. 142). "The persons in the original position are assumed to take no interest in one another's interests" (p. 147), for any reason. There is "mutual disinterestedness" (pp. 146 and 148–149), and in particular neither altruism nor envy.

The hypothesis that the "original" individuals are self-interested economizes on assumptions. It leads to a nice derivation of the ethics of justice, its impartiality and its concern for others from *self-interest under uncertainty*.

Section 8.6 will present a detailed analysis of this question of the motivations of the individuals, for both actual and "original" individuals, and in particular with respect to these motivations being either purely self-interested or more or less moral or concerned with others' judgments. We will then conclude that these possible qualifications do not remove the basic difficulty with the Original Position theory, to which we now turn.

Indeed, the theory of the Original Position has the following problem.

Consider a self-interested individual in the "original position." He sets the rules of society that will determine the specific situations of the actual individuals. He does not know who he will be, what kind of individual he will be, including what he will want, what he will be able to do, what he will have, and so on. He takes this ignorance into account in his self-interested choice of the rules of society. Then he may well take the risk of sacrificing certain of the future, possible actual individuals if this permits to sufficiently improve the situation of sufficiently many others. That is, he considers that the chances he has to become a beneficiary individual overcompensate the risk he incurs of becoming an ill-treated one. But, when now the actual individuals materialize in these categories, this result can be quite unfair or unjust for the ill-treated or sacrificed ones. Therefore the choice in the Original Position cannot a priori be called just for the actual individuals, and hence *the theory of the Original Position cannot be a theory of justice*.

That is, the fact that the imaginary ex ante self-interest, and hence the judgment and the choice in the original position, are not biased by a specific actual position and self-interest, does not imply that this choice is just or fair with regard to the actual, ex post individuals. Justice cannot result from self-interested, egoistic ignorance. *Two vices do not make a virtue*. The theory of the Original Position provides justice for the individuals in the original position (indeed the best is the same for all) but not justice among the actual individuals. It provides justice ex ante but not justice ex post, and the real world is ex post.

Another conclusion is that the theory of the Original Position does not a priori and in general provide Rawls's principles of justice. Indeed it does not necessarily provide the difference principle: The choice in the original position would sacrifice the poorest if this permitted sufficiently many others to have sufficiently more. And it does not even necessarily provide the priority of basic liberties and nondiscrimination: The choice in the original position would deprive one individual of his right to vote or to publish in a type of situation if this permitted others to have sufficiently more of other goods; it would advocate that a service firm discriminate in hiring if this satisfied the strongly felt prejudices of sufficiently many customers (who also are possible future embodiments).

The individual in the original position may prefer to try his chance with a society of four capitalists and one bum rather than becoming surely one of five *petits-bourgeois*.

The origin of the confusion rests in two complementary questions: (1) the phenomenology of the choice of justice; (2) the individuals' responsibility for the original choice.

An individual choosing principles of distributive justice (or just outcomes) must abstract from his own particular interest as far as it opposes others' interests, so as to take the "objective" impartial point of view of justice. This viewpoint consists of fairness, equity, balance, equality, symmetry among interests (means or other), based on comparisons, and stemming basically from rationality in the sense of providing a reason applied to the a priori equality of consideration which defines the objective viewpoint (see chapter 2). Since this objective view implies not being influenced by one's specificities, this could indeed be described as a hypothetical loss of information about who one is. One can then imagine oneself as being "in the shoes" of the various individuals in order to have the best understanding of their interests, so as to evaluate the required comparisons, balances, and equalizations. This is however very different from choosing with one unified self-interest in assuming that one will become any of these actual individuals—the Original Position theory. The choice of justice considers that *all* the individuals exist, and it rests on this coexistence. By contrast, the choice in the original position takes care of the existence of only *one* individual, only he does not know who he will be. The choice of justice is objective and ethico-moral in considering the interests of the various individuals. By contrast, the choice in the original position is only self-interested. Thinking as if one did not know who one is does not have the same consequences with these two intentions. The existential or fully fundamental self-oblivion discarding of one's specific interests and prejudices that induces the impartial objectivity of the "view from nowhere" is not the "veil of ignorance" of an individual "in the original position." From the classical iconography of justice, the theory of the Original Position keeps the blindfold but forgets the balance. One can say that the Original Position theory mistakes ignorance for uncertainty: My ignoring who I am is not my being uncertain about who I will be. Indeed the whole assimilation of objectivity and impartiality to lack of information turns out to be a misleading metaphor. Justice is objectivity, not uncertainty. It is impartiality, not ignorance. It is abstracting from self-interest, not from information about self. Self-oblivion in interest is not self-oblivion in information. The two things are quite different and bound to lead to very different conclusions. Introducing uncertainty invites confusing issues, and substituting it to morals and impartiality completes the confusion. Justice stems from greater knowledge of relevant facts and reason, not from greater ignorance. The just choice comes from abstracting from self-interest, not from eagerly promoting it, even behind a "veil of ignorance." Justice is open-eyed and informed objectivity, not blindfolded egoism. (And, as we will see, it is the non-Rawlsian method that can justify—approximately—Rawls's principles, while the Original Position theory in fact opposes them.)

Of course an actual individual cannot be held responsible for the hypothetical choice of the hypothetical zombie in the hypothetical original position. He cannot recognize himself in this ghost who by definition has none of his characteristics which make him different from his competitors in the allocation of resources. Even if the story were true, the embodiment would constitute a discontinuity of the relevant self, and hence no responsibility could arguably be carried across it. We will see that this is inherently related to the very particular type of Social Contract that an Original Position theory is.

The described choice by an "original" individual is a perfectly *individually "rational"* choice, given the assumptions ("original" is taken to mean "in the original position"). It is indeed the only "rational" one (in this sense of "rational," commonly used in these discussions). The depth of the possible resulting injustice depends on the structure of possibilities for the society. Yet this unjust result, and the failure to yield the principles, can a priori occur with any general type of relevant ignorance in the original position. They can occur with the minimal ignorance where the "original" individuals know everything about the actual society and the individuals who inhabit it except which of these actual individuals they will be (the "thin veil of ignorance"). They can also occur with the deeper ignorance about the actual individuals that Rawls assumes (the "thick veil of ignorance"). Note that, in the latter case, a relevant materialization is not that of a single individual but that of the whole society with all its members, since the principles of justice are to be applied to the actual constraints on society as a whole; an "original" individual can then materialize into any of the individuals of this society, so his "original" view of this society is the same as that with a "thin veil of ignorance" where there is only one such society (and only the assigment of actual individuals is originally unknown).

The "Original" Information

Rawls argues that de facto the choice in the original position yields the conclusion he states, but he actually says much more, namely that there exists a possible definition of the original position such that this holds: "We want to define the original position so that we get the desired results" (p. 141), and "the original position has been defined so that it is a situation in which the maximin rule applies" (p. 155). There is indeed one possible parameter to be chosen in the definition of the original position: the information, or lack of it, of the person in this position. This person must be ignorant about whom he will be, but he may otherwise have different possible information and ignorance about society and the world. That is, the various cases differ according to the patterns and degrees of transparency and opacity of the "veil of ignorance." Then Rawls's view only requires that there exists one such veil that elicits the choice of principles he states.

Therefore Rawls's Original Position theory is not a *deductive* justification of the "principles of justice," as it would be were the "veil" given—for instance the "thin" veil considered below. If we are allowed sufficient latitude for choosing the likelihood of the various features of the world seen from the original position, then there exists a "veil" that yields the principles, as well as other "veils" that yield different and opposed principles (for instance, we show in the next subsection one way of obtaining the improved principles, and they are even reached through a utilitarian form). Such a "veil search" is not "reflective equilibrium," however, even though it is adjustment for justifying the principles, for several reasons: The two poles of the adjustment are not the principles and its applications but rather the principles and their "origin" in the original position (one might say that the "original" choice is the "principle" and the "principles of justice" its application, but this is not the definition presented of the "reflective equilibrium"); more important, this "veil search" is not moral evaluation at both ends and adjustment of the principles and hence of their consequences, as in a "reflective equilibrium," but, rather, the search for the possibility—and not the morality—of a "veil" that yields the "principles of justice" which are morally approved but a priori given.

However, the reasons provided for choosing a theory of the Original Position make it rational to choose a particular "veil of ignorance." Indeed among the Rawlsian reasons noted above, reason 2 supersedes reason 1 (as we noted) and is required for reason 3. Hence the reason for choosing this theory consists in displaying the choice of rules that is fair, objective, unbiased, and untainted by the specific and particular interests of the actual individuals that may be at odds with the interests of other actual individuals (see p. 136). Therefore all that is required, of this ignorance, is that each original individual does not know which of the actual individuals he may become, but this uncertainty must be complete. This informational structure, which constitutes the "thin veil of ignorance," is necessary and sufficient for the purpose of the Original Position theory. There is no *reason* for introducing any other conceptual uncertainty. Therefore, the principle of minimal irrationality (where rationality means here "for a reason") leads to the choice of the "thin veil of ignorance."

Original Position Utilitarianism

Then, the *form* of what the Original Position delivers is that of utilitarianism. Indeed, first, these "original" individuals care only about the outcome of their choice and of this uncertainty: They are *consequentialist*. Second, they have "a coherent set of preferences" (p. 143). Third, their complete uncertainty about which of the actual individuals they will become is a case where Laplace's principle says that these alternatives must be considered as having the same probability (this principle is the very basis of the definition of probabilities). These three conditions imply that the theory of choice under uncertainty of von Neumann and Morgenstern (1944) applies (see, for instance, Savage 1954). That is, this choice maximizes the mathematical expectation of a cardinal specification of the utility function that represents these preferences (these preferences and choice are the same for all the "original individuals" since they are identical). The equal probabilities imply that this maximand is the average of the values of this utility, each value being the level taken for a specific actual individual. This is therefore equivalent to maximizing the sum of these individual utilities. The complete explanation can be found in *The Liberal Social Contract*, but this basically constitutes the justification of utilitarianism that Harsanyi proposed in 1953 (and that Vickrey suggested in 1948). This theory is in fact the only valid justification of a utilitarian form (see chapter 14). This conclusion is ironical, since Rawls' explicitly proposed his theory of the Original Position in order to eliminate and replace utilitarianism!

This utilitarian form might itself about yield Rawls's principles, if the utilities and possibilities had the required structure. The priority of "basic liberties" can, for instance, result from the possibility that it is better for everybody, under the conditions stated in chapter 4. "Practical justice" (chapter 7), which could be seen as the difference principle with a solution to its various problems described above, can result from a utilitarian maximization, if social possibilities and individual utilities have the appropriate structures (Kolm 1992b—nondiscrimination can also easily be introduced). Yet there is no a priori guarantee that utilitarianism will yield these principles.

However, the result obtained has a utilitarian *form* but *cannot really be utilitarianism*, because utilitarianism is a theory of social ethics, and this result was obtained from a theory of the Original Position which we have seen cannot be a theory of social ethics (it would be more specifically a theory of justice, and it cannot be one). Similarly this result cannot be opposed to Rawls's principles of justice and used as a criticism of these principles because these principles state a position of justice, whereas the obtained "utilitaromorphic" theory results from a theory of the Original Position which cannot yield consequences concerning justice, as we have seen.

The Rational Place and Problems of Rawls's Principles

More generally, the fact that the Original Position theory does not a priori and in general yield Rawls's principles of justice cannot be taken as a criticism of these principles because the Original Position theory cannot be a theory of justice.

Therefore Rawls's principles may be valid, but they must then be justified otherwise. Now, this ordered set of principles indeed constitutes a particular case of the equality of liberties and means which is, as we have noted, the necessary form of rational justice. However, first, these principles have to be completed, in particular for solving the problems of the "difference principle" pointed out in section 8.3. Second, and more important, one can easily show that this set of principles cannot claim universal validity—as one can indeed show for any limited set of principles. That is, one can always find, as counter-examples, cases of questions of justice for which the answer provided by the considered set of principles is obviously not the good one (in particular, everybody would agree with this conclusion). For instance, justice sometimes also requires certain rights to the product of one's labor, certain compensations for differences in capacities when used in consumption, equality (or maximins) in certain basic more specific consumptions, considerations of needs or of merits, and so on. However, one can certainly build an ideal of justice where Rawls' ordered set of principles (with their required logical perfectings) has a dominant position, for instance where it constitutes the general rule with respect to which the other principles or priorities constitute either specifications, or exceptions which support the burden of the proof and require specific justification. In fact this ideal is a common one of the liberal left, shared by many people who have never heard of philosophy.

Yet in actual application it is standardly no more possible to discard other principles or to confine them to such a secondary role. This of course occurs when everybody thinks that some other principle has to be applied in a certain class of questions and situations. But, more generally, people's opinions interfere with implementation by the very nature of Rawls's principles. For instance, these principles contain the priority of "basic liberties", which include basic political liberties, that is, the right to vote and to participate in politics, certainly in a more or less democratic political setting. Then self-interested voters will not chose the "difference principle" except if sufficiently many of them are at the lowest level in primary goods (or "fundamental utility"). If, by contrast, the individuals are not self-interested and care for the situation of the poorest, this introduces two problems of consistency in the theory. First, the individuals in the Original Position would have to consider this altruism or sense of justice of the actual individuals, and their own choice would thus not be the self-interested one under uncertainty that the theory considers. Second, the ablest people would want to help the poorest, hence the disincentive effect of redistribution may disappear, and along with it the Rawlsian reason for the "difference principle" will vanish. Hence the difference principle is prima facie either unimplementable or irrelevant. This will be further considered below.

Social Contracts and the Original Position Theory

The basic reason for the inadequacy of the Original Position theory as a theory of justice or social ethics is well displayed in noticing its relation to theories of the Social Contract. The Original Position theory was indeed presented as a Social Contract theory. Like other Social Contract theories, it is a legitimizing hypothetical, putative unanimous agreement (the unanimity is among a group of individuals depending on the specific theory, such as a nation, or property owners for Locke, or people directly concerned by a given "agreement failure" in a liberal social contract). Yet, the unanimity does not have the same nature in an original position and in other Social Contracts. In the former case it is *"preference unanimity"* due to identical preferences, whereas in the other Social Contracts it is *"exchange unanimity"* where each individual accepts a deal (among any number of persons). This difference is indeed related to the following basic difference.

In fact, the Original Position theory rests on an exchange (an imagined one), but this exchange is of a particular kind: It is a *mutual insurance* where the risk is nothing less than *who one is* (or is going to be, in the colorful language of the theory). Since everything that differentiates individuals is then completely entrusted to chance, the "original individuals" are identical and thus choose with preference unanimity. That is to say, they take the same insurance against bad luck, and they make the same commitments to help others if they themselves happen to be more fortunate. Then the flaw of the theory noted earlier in this section amounts to the individuals possibly being underinsured; too little insurance may have been taken. Yet can one say this, since the individuals have freely chosen the insurance they take?

The point is that the individuals who have made this choice cannot be considered as being the actual individuals, since they have by definition been deprived of their personality as individuals different from the others (while distribution according to the differences is the issue).[8] This is not the case in the other Social Contracts where the contractants to the generally implicit Contract are the actual individuals who exchange restraints, contributions to other public goods (other than peace), or acceptance of rules or rulers. Actual individuals cannot be held responsible for the choice of the identical individuals "in the original position." This existential and egological discontinuity of the self interrupts the responsibility for the free choice, an issue that is absent in the other Social Contract theories.

What Would Be Chosen in an Original Position?

Furthermore there is no reason why individuals "in the original position" take insurance only against the risk of receiving small amounts of "primary goods" and not against any of the other harm or inconvenience that are also a priori uncertain. These other facts have been analyzed above in the discussion of the difference principle. They include: having expensive life plans or tastes, or life plans or tastes that require particularly certain primary goods, or being poorly endowed with personal means to live a happy, fruitful, and meaningful life such as sensory capacities, constructive intelligence and so on (the fact that Rawls excludes tastes from the topic of justice cannot prevent the self-interested "original individuals" from being concerned by them); having poor capacities to obtain good bargains with one's income or to use one's power; being unfavorably placed with regard to other individuals' competing demands or skills in the use of income or power, and hence with regard to others' tastes or life plans, endowments in primary goods, and skills in exchange and social interaction; and so on. The "original individuals" would establish certain rules of compensations for all these possible handicaps.

As a consequence a *partial application* of the theory of the Original Position can be used to solve the logical problems of Rawls's principles. Indeed, an individual "in the original position" has "a consistent set of preferences," according to Rawls. Since all the individuals "in the original position" are identical, these preferences are the same for

---

8. For this very reason, the interesting model presented by Varian (1980) cannot be a theory of justice.

all. These preferences can only bear on the items of the problem, that is, both what an "original individual" will possibly be and what he will possibly have as final goods and social situation. That is to say, they are the "fundamental preferences." Interpersonal ordinal comparison is defined with these preferences and hence so is the maximin (see chapter 7). This maximin may require a priority of basic liberties (see chapter 4), or this priority may constitute a further principle (a case of the *freedom-constrained practical justice* of Kolm 1985a).

We can furthermore choose Rawls's "primary goods" as the considered situational variables of justice (see chapter 2; for Rawls they are also the end values of justice). These primary goods, along with basic liberties, are means for the individuals' consumptions or fulfilment of their ends or "pursuit of their plans of life." With these means the individuals act, choose their consumption goods, and "pursue their plans." Hence the individuals' preferences on these latter final variables induce their "indirect preferences" on these means and in particular on the allocations of primary goods. However, the interactions of all possible types described above entail that an individual's fulfilment of his plans depend not only upon his own means but also upon the various means and ends of the other individuals. Hence an individual's "indirect preferences" bear on all these items, in particular on others' allocations of primary goods and not only on his own. (The outcome of interactions depend on all the conditions of the interactions— including bargaining powers of all sorts—and if there is uncertainty about it, utility under uncertainty can be introduced.) The maximin says that *the whole social allocation of primary goods should be the best possible one for the least "satisfied" individual.* This is well defined in theory. Yet, as we have seen, one cannot in general define the outcome as maximizing a function of the allocation of primary goods of one individual only, since the lowest utility depends on the individual's characteristics and situation and on others' allocations of primary goods—in particular, one cannot define Rawls's weights as those that would result from the linear approximation of such a function.

However, this "practical justice" maximin also tries to compensate for interindividual differences in consumptive capacities, from the definition of fundamental preferences. This is more "utilitarian like" than Rawls seems to wish in *A Theory of Justice* (1971), in the sense of using a certain concept of the type of "utility," even though there is no addition of such "utilities" of the various individuals—Rawls indeed criticizes both the use of a "utility" concept and the aggregation over all individuals. Yet we noticed that Rawls later (1982) quotes approvingly the "fundamental preferences" of *Justice and Equity* and admits compensations for interindividual differences in consumptive capacities. On the other hand, "practical justice" allows for a certain "cleaning" of preferences or utility functions in order to eliminate from them certain structures that are deemed to be irrelevant to the considered ethical question. For instance, this cleaning has been explicitly and precisely performed for erasing immoral envy and jealousy,[9] and Rawls states explicitly that the individuals in the original position should be considered as immune from these sentiments. This cleaning can or must be performed for a number of other features. Then these two maximin theories of justice may in the end be close to each other, if at all different, although they would still differ as regards the scope of relevance and application and, above all, in their justification (but one could say that the important thing is to end up with the right conclusion).

8.5 Rawls and Kant

For criticizing notions of "individual utility," Rawls in particular appeals to the authority of Immanuel Kant. This is well taken and legitimate.

Yet the bulk of the reaction of non–English-language philosophers to the work of Rawls, apart from the surprise of the absence of surprise in the principles, was a great surprise indeed at Rawls's claim that Kant inspired him. "Pursuing one's life plans" seemed awfully utilitarian and consequentialist, compared to obeying the duty one builds within oneself under the rule of reason and against one's happiness and inclinations. However, the law of justice edicted by the "noumenal" individuals "in the original position" is probably assumed by Rawls to be conceived and obeyed as a moral law by the actual individuals. This certainly is Kantian.

---

9. See Kolm 1991c, 1993f, 1995a.

That is, Rawls's theory is based on a *double "preference unanimity"*
(not a unanimity of the kind that would result from an agreement or
an exchange among any number of individuals). First, the individuals
"in the original position" are unanimous because they are identical.
Second, the actual individuals are unanimous because they are moral.

This moral motivation, however, raises problems for Rawls's
theory.

First, we have noted that Rawls's Original Position theory cannot
be a theory of justice or of ethics. Then obeying the resulting law could
not claim to be Kantian. However, the argument rested on Rawls's
assumption that the individuals in the original position are self-interested. This prima facie implies that the actual individuals they envision
they could become are self-interested too. But if the actual individuals
want to follow a Kantian moral law, they are no longer self-interested.
Then the individuals in the original position cannot be self-interested
either.[10] If, for instance, the actual individuals are completely moral
persons whose only concern is to obey the moral law of justice to be
determined, if indeed they are integrated persons with this "coherent
set of preferences," and if this general characteristic is known to the
"original legislators" who therefore take it into account, then the
noted handicap of the Original Position theory as a theory of justice
disappears. However by the same token the resulting moral law is
undetermined, since these actual individuals equally submit their will
to anything that constitutes the moral law, and this view is reflected in
the "original" individuals' preferences (hence the law chosen in the
original position is always the best one, whatever it is). However, the
actual individuals may be short of these "rational saints," and they
may be partly self-interested, partly moral in intention. This is indeed
Kant's actual conception of actual men. But then the initial vice of the
Original Position theory as a moral theory of justice still remains
(although perhaps in an attenuated form). Yet the "original" legislators of justice may have to discriminate among the various actual
motivations, keeping some and discarding others. In particular, if they
saw that they produce morals, they might want to discard the immoral

---

10. This can be in line with a late suggestion of Rawls that the "original" individuals
may have some "sense of justice" (see chapter 1, note 43).

motivations on the ground that one cannot base morality on immorality, and a Kantian view of morality leads them to discard individuals' egoistic self-interest. But then we end up with the noted indetermination. Rawls, on the contrary, implies that he wants the "original" legislators to discard the moral, law-abiding part of the actual individuals he assumes. But this has to be justified, and it reintroduces in full the noted reason why the Original Position theory cannot produce principles of justice.

8.6   Individuals' Motivations

The second problem raised by Rawls's assumption that actual individuals want to follow the law of justice introduces one more difficulty in Rawls's derivation of the principles, in particular for the "difference principle." Indeed, the basic reason for settling for less than an equal allocation of "primary goods" is that equality would have a disincentive effect on the most productive producers (forcing them to work presumably violates a basic liberty, and it may be inefficient for reasons of information, costs and limits of coercion, and motivation). However, if the producers are moral individuals who share this egalitarian ideal, they may work voluntarily for others. Then they would not reduce their output in response to redistributive policies or institutions that implement precisely what they themselves desire (and hence do not impose a binding constraint on them). There would then be no problem of efficient "second-best egalitarianism" and no place for a "difference principle." This was pointed out by Grey, Narveson, Barry, and Cohen (see references).[11]

The problem exists if the egalitarian ideal is obtained for a reason other than by a basically inappropriate Original Position theory. It exists, for example, for a "second-best egalitarianism" implementing an ideal equality derived from the rationality of justice (see chapter 2) if the more efficient individuals share this ideal. Indeed we will see that the problem is even more general. Furthermore, this problem also exists if the individuals are prompted to act morally by others' opinions concerning them rather than by (or, perhaps, in addition to)

11. A discussion of this issue is provided in Kolm 1993b.

a genuine moral motivation (this question will be analyzed in chapter 13).

However, we observed that the very existence, possibility, conditions, form and consequences of this incentive problem need to be considered explicitly and seriously (section 8.3 and chapter 6). Indeed, first, the disincentive effect considered, which is due to the redistribution of *earned* income, vanishes if we want to compensate for the "natural" allocation of productive capacities as capacities to earn income rather than restricting to capacities actually used in earning income. Such a capacity constitutes a possibility that the individual freely uses in labor in order to obtain income and various goods, or abstains from using in order to have more leisure according, for instance, as which suits better his life plans. This interpretation thus seems to be the one in tune with the most basic aspect of Rawls's overall conception. Furthermore, the result is exactly the same if we want to (apparently) depart from this conception in compensating for the allocation of individual capacities without discriminating according to whether the individual benefits from them directly or indirectly through labor income. Note that the leisure time considered can be only a part of total nonwork time. With these conceptions the distributive tax is based on inelastic personal capacities, and it normally tends to induce *more work*, rather than less, in order to compensate more or less for this loss in money income, which amounts to a lower consumption of leisure as a result of this lower total income. However, it is indeed a standard view in distributive justice that the ideal equality and the corresponding compensations are due for the benefits derived from the productive uses of the human resource, whereas its consumptive uses are seen as a private matter that justifies no compensation—this is an ethical view that may induce Pareto-inefficiency and may lead itself to be a second-best ethics (for instance to the replacement of equality by maximin). Yet fixed-duration income equalization (see chapter 6) also introduces an inelastic tax base with regard to labor-time and to all aspects of labor when suitably extended, and a higher tax then also induces more work rather than less. But earned incomes are *sometimes* more easily observable than wage-rates which value capacities. Second, the most productive individuals may at any rate work and produce more, rather than less, as an effect of the redistributive tax, in order to compensate more or less for this loss of income. Third, even with the considered disincentive effect, the best possible equality is not unfrequently the possible state that gives the most to the least endowed individuals (this depends on the elasticities of labor supply and, most important, on the distribution of personal capacities). Fourth, this distribution of earned income does not coincide with that of preferences; it omits the value of leisure and the cost of an inappropriate product mix of goods and leisure; its undominatedness thus is not Pareto-efficiency; now, the cause of the disincentive rests in the preferences of the ablest people, which should be considered explicitly and fully, including their moral preferences. Hence, the self-interested disincentive effect that makes everybody richer with a certain inequality is not that general. Yet it may also exist.

One possible vindication of Rawls's consistency in assuming both this effect and individuals convinced by the rule of justice consists in assuming that the individuals have two standards: a moral one for approving the general rules of society, and a self-interested one for their own behavior. However, this may not be consistent with the other assumption of a "coherent set of preferences" (at least in the strict sense in which economists would understand it).

More consistent explanations rest on the assumption that the productive individuals are ready to give to some extent. If this extent does not suffice for the equalization, coercion is required and it entails the considered avoidance. Yet in the most interesting and likely situation there are several most productive individuals who collectively contribute to help the poorest. Then each is generally ready to give much more under the condition that the others give too than he would be ready to give independently of the fact of the others' giving (this collective gift giving might even achieve the required transfers).

In such a case all these individuals would welcome an institutional or public obligation that transfers income from all of them to the poorest. In their own individual behavior, however, they would still behave egoistically subject to the constraint imposed for this transfer (an income tax, for example). Consequently, the transfers may actually induce them to reduce output. This may give rise to a problem of "second-best egalitarianism" despite the fact that everyone accepts the general rules of justice and is ready to accept some sacrifice for their implementation.

Technically this situation is one of "collective gift-giving" (already considered in chapter 5 and fully analyzed in Kolm 1984a, 1985a and related technical studies), a particular instance of "the problem of collective action." The end in view (be it characterized as "maximizing the income of the poor" or "promoting the rule of justice" in the abstract) is a "public good," in particular for the "givers." It is even a "nonexcludable" public good in the sense that they cannot be personally denied benefit from it, since this benefit is merely the information concerning what the poor receive or whether the law of justice is implemented. This raises the classical problem of "free-riding." The underlying game-theoretic structure is standardly here of the "prisoner's dilemma" kind, but it can also involve more refined social sentiments of fairness in contribution. The free-riding aspect of social rules in general is the basis of all Social Contract theories that derive a justification for public coercion from a putative voluntary unanimous agreement. Rousseau (1762) is the keenest expositor of this view, and this is what his famous remark that people "must be forced to be free" refers to.[12] Kant is very much aware of this kind of problem that he learnt from Rousseau, and this is the very reason why he proposed his categorical imperative: The free-riding problem disappears if everyone "does as if the others were doing the same." Hence the "collective giving" solution to Rawls's dilemma vanishes if the productive individuals' morals are genuinely Kantian (even though these individuals remain partly self-interested, in line with Kant's view of actual prople).

More generally, any efficient redistributive policy requires information about individuals' capacities or preferences that are known only to the concerned individual, whose interest is often not to reveal them truthfully. Yet moral adhesion to the ethic of this policy induces truthful revelation. In this case there is no conflict between efficiency and justice. The conflict remains, however, if the individuals have a double standard—one ethical and one individualistic—or if they are only partly moral, especially since providing the information is in fact a contribution to the nonexcludable public good of the actualization of justice in society.

---

12. A full analysis of this issue can be found in Kolm 1989a (1991), 1993a.

8.7   Culture, Pluralism, and Toleration

Rawls's focus on individuals' means has been opposed concerns with group, communal, or cultural values (Nagel, Taylor, Kymlicka, Sandel), with individual virtues (MacIntyre), or with the nature of the self (Sandel; see also Kolm 1982a).

From Rawls's later writings (1985, 1987) it is clear that he views the maintenance and development of cultures and traditions as he does individuals' "life plans". Justice in society only aims at providing means to these ends. It in particular provides the required liberties. Indeed Rawls emphasizes that his proposal is "political, not metaphysical" and aims at enabling various cultural traditions to coexist within the same polity in a spirit of pluralism and toleration.

This view, however, poses a problem with regard to the actual, political implementability of the strongly redistributive and egalitarian Rawlsian distributive justice. Most commonly the poor come disproportionately from certain distinct communities, and making them as well off as possible would require substantial transfers across those communities. Yet the sense of solidarity across communities that would be politically required to sustain such transfers is conspicuously lacking. In the United States (which Rawls obviously has in mind) white communities are not about to do everything they possibly can to raise living standards in the poor black community, which is what the "difference principle" would require. Similarly in old countries where the culture is deeply embodied in the historical places, recent immigration of poorer people with an originally different culture is rarely accompanied by the extended sense of solidarity and responsibility that permits the political implementability of the "difference principle." Most "third world" countries present a similar problem.

Finally, the aim of the present volume is to restrict theories to their essentials, and Rawls's work is about organized as a proof that the "principles" are validly justified by the "Original Position." However, all scholars who have scrutinized Rawls's work the most closely strongly tend to view its actual essentials in various developments used along the way and that are important reflections in themselves (even when these scholars adhere to the spirit of the "principles" of maximal intelligent egalitarianism within basic freedom). That is, in order to make the best of it—and this can be a great deal—Rawls's work should be appreciated through a Buddhist eye: The aim is in the way. Brian Barry (1989) remarks: "To push the matter to the edges of paradox, one might say that by his heroic efforts to building his insights into a single system, Rawls runs the risk that his sheer fertility as a political philosopher will be underestimated." This may, however, have the opposite effect in terms of impact on a heterogeneous audience: The people who know little enjoy the "dogma" and the others appreciate the various analyses.

Rawls's contribution is, finally, like edible animals: It is nourishing by its flesh rather than by its backbone, although the backbone has been necessary for supporting the flesh. The backbone was also necessary for the salutary but idiosyncratic task of standing against utilitarianism in the particular circle of English-language philosophy. The analytical flesh, the rightful and deep insights derived from it, and the rightful and courageous brandishing of the flag of the primacy of liberty and equality in a logically hostile territory, account for the vast impact and enduring inspiring power of the work. They make it utterly unimportant that the backbone itself could be seen as consisting of banal principles, invalidly justified and mistakenly presented, which had an impact because of the moral criticism of an illogical theory: The priority of the basic Rights of Man and of the Citizen, the ideal equalities, and the effect of disincentives; with logical problems raised by the multidimensional maximin, interdependences, the distinction of productive capacities, the natural allocation of capacities to buy and to use power, the measurement of primary goods, the neglect of the cases where equality can be efficient, and the motivations for implementation; with also justification by an Original Position theory; and which shocked its *milieu* because of its presentation as being anti-utilitarianism (with in addition a summary dialectics in reflective equilibrium and a problematic use of Kant). This reduction to backbone, which the author had to encourage for heuristic, organizing, didactic, and argumentative purposes, has now played its important historical role. On the contrary, the ideas that concluded the Enlightenment, the dialectics between liberty and equality, the choice of the limit between public justice and private freedom, the determination of equalizands, the definition of the necessary maximins, which are actual central topics of justice, are now recognized as such by an enlarged group of scholars.

9 Equalities and Liberties

9.1 Issues of Justice

This chapter proceeds with the presentation of the issues and solutions of respectful justice. After the presentation of the bases and of an overview in part 1, chapters 4 to 8 have presented certain of these issues and solutions that are particularly important in social life and/or in contemporary thought in social ethics. These solutions were *act-freedom* (classical basic rights or liberties), full process-freedom and *full process liberalism, Equity* as the general form of equal independent liberty, *end-justice* or *full or complete distributive justice* and the corresponding leximin *Practical Justice*, multidimensional and income equalities with *efficient super-equity* and *fixed-duration income equalization*, the "*difference principle*" and the questions it raises, and the theories of the *Original Position*. Justiciables will again essentially be individuals, because this is important and the literature emphasizes this case, but many issues and solutions can apply as well to problems with other justiciables. I will first point out the main issues, and then consider the various cases and solutions. Since the general form of justice is equality of certain means followed by free action which can be interaction or exchange, the analysis will begin by the general case of *free action, interaction or exchange from a situation of equality* of any kind, in emphasizing the various hidden ethical assumptions it entails. This will then be applied to the main equalizands such as *consumption, primary resources, capital* (exploitation), nonhuman *natural resources, "opportunities," and specific human resources* whose equality contrasts with "fundamental insurance." The very important relations of justice with *responsibility* and *envy*, the other modern theories of exploitation, the general theory of efficient maximin in freedom, and other concepts, will then be presented and discussed. Finally, the two following parts of the book will focus on, first, the ethical comparisons of *inequalities* and the questions of *needs* and of *misery* and, second, the various theories that use *freedom* as either a *right* or a *power*.

The Structure of Justice

In view of the general analysis of the various principles of justice, the present section complements the previous presentation of their general properties. The concepts presented here in their generality have often been met earlier in application in particular theories.

Justice is derived from rationality. One consequence is that it consists of principles or rules, since "this is done for this reason" implies that the same circumstances described by the reason entail the same conclusion; this can also be presented as a necessary property of nonarbitrariness. A further consequence is that several justiciables endowed with the same relevant characteristics should prima facie (a priori, ideally) be treated equally if one adds the requirement of a unique choice among mutually exclusive alternatives (see chapter 2). The precise derivation of this "equal treatment of equals" has been recalled in chapter 2 and is trivial only when a justiciable's "treatment" should depend only on his own characteristics. Then the result is a "functional equality" of the form "to or from each according to his or her...." The final concern of a principle of justice constitutes its end value. Respectful justice chooses its end values among justiciables' means of action or ends. A specific problem or question of justice can be solved by the application of a single principle, but justice in any large society has to rely on many specific principles. However, particular "theories of justice" advocate one or a few principles. A conception of justice is univalued (or pure) when it has only one principle or one category of end values, it is plurivalued (or mixed) when it has several of them, and it is "simple" when it has no more than a few. Plurivalved conceptions have a priori to solve the problem of the adjustments among principles, and even a single principle may not be possible; this leads to second-best justice and second-best egalitarianisms (see chapters 2 and 6). Adjustments among principles follow a number of well-defined structures, among which are compromises of various types, priorities, and superimposition (whereby a principle is applied from the outcome of another).[1]

A question of central importance is that of the actual intervention or nonintervention of the policy motivated by justice. Apart from practical limitations or impossibilities due to scant means, insufficient information, or hostile politics, or from seeing interference as an intrinsic evil, an absence of intervention implies the endorsement of

---

1. The full analysis of these relations is presented in Kolm 1990b.

what happens to be, or of what happens, in this situation. This domain of noninterference is thus well described by terms such as "spontaneity" or "spontaneous," borrowed from Hayek's "spontaneous order," that is, the absence of any interference in the name of "social justice," extended to the whole of society. The domain of endorsed "spontaneity" can of course be more restricted. As regards distributive justice (and hence beyond mere act-freedom), this domain coincides with the respect of process-freedom by the policy, and it includes the "natural" allocation of human resources. The question of the possibility or forbiddance of violation of act-freedoms by acts or threats among agents will be discussed in chapters 12 and 13. Intervention for achieving process-freedom (liberal social contracts) is to be counted in the domain of spontaneity. Equal process-freedom can be required by the general rationality of equality (and it corresponds to a basic intention of the classic principle "free and equal in rights"). In particular, a full process-freedom for a type of acts and of agents is an equal process-freedom for these agents (this can be in particular all acts or all individuals). The domain of endorsed "spontaneity" can also be defined in terms of functional equality, as it amounts to "to each according to how things happen to be, and in particular according to what he manages to obtain by the permissible means such as action, exchange, and so on." We have also seen that means-freedom is a type of liberty (a "real" freedom; see chapter 2). Nevertheless, it is customary to oppose the "freedom" of full process-freedom to the alternative "equality" of equal means or ends. The basic task of the theory of justice is to delineate the domains of respected "spontaneity" and of intervention.

Within individualistic respectful justice, full process liberalism, libertarianisms, or Hayek's spontaneous order occupy one extreme (left-anarchism is somewhat different as it emphasizes not an absence of distributive justice but its implementation otherwise than by state coercion); see chapters 12 and 13. The other extreme is the end-justice of Justice or Practical Justice (chapter 7) which submits jointly all possible distributional variables to its aspiration of equal satisfaction or to the help of the most miserable. In this conception, free choice can only be a policy instrument for information or implementation, or an intrinsic desire of the individuals (see chapter 2). The other principles of respectful justice occupy the intermediary ground.

The sectors of respected "spontaneity" are sometimes explicit in the form of a principle of noninterference, but they are also often implicit, notably in theories that focus on equalities in means in the strict sense or resources. In all cases the explicit or implicit choice of this domain amounts to the *legitimization* of the corresponding acts, of the consequences of these acts, of the other means used by these acts (notably resources and in particular capacities), and of the other causes of these consequences. When the endorsement of this domain is only implicit, this conception of justice must verify that this legitimization does not raise, in its eyes, moral problems that would lead it to qualify, modify, or even abandon its primary principles. In particular, these legitimizations could violate the basic reasons of these principles, ending up with a moral inconsistency. Indeed very famous theories of justice happen to lack consistency as a consequence of such a neglect. This is the case of theories that translate an irrelevance of individuals' tastes or preferences as an equal sharing of productive resources, an ideal equality of incomes or of "primary goods," or an equal allocation of consumption goods followed by free exchange, as they endorse the "natural" allocation of "situational resources" and of "transaction capacities" (see below) in addition to that of individuals' own preferences, choice and tastes. More generally, taking a means or a liberty as end value or as situational variable is like a coin with this means or liberty on one face and, on the other, the legitimacy of the other means and causes of the acts that use this means and of their results. For instance, "end-valuing" a certain freedom of exchange, or an allocation of goods that can implicitly or explicitly be exchanged, implies accepting and finding legitimate the outcome of these exchanges for each individual, and therefore the fact that it depends on the supplies and demands and hence on all the tastes and resources that determine them, as well as on the relative bargaining skills and market powers.

It should be noted that "resources" include the "negative resources" constituted by costs, liabilities, or relative handicaps. This is often a matter of point of view, as when one emphasizes, in a resource, its insufficiency with regard to a norm, a "normal situation," or an average. Yet this vocabulary or point of view sometimes also refers to the fact that a cost will be incurred because of the state of the feature considered. Finally, other aspects are naturally seen negatively such as, in human resources, certain needs (see chapter 11), addictions, or expensive tastes.

Human Resources and Capacities: A Summary

Previous analyses and examples concerning the human resource can be summarized as follows:

As soon as one leaves full process liberalism and hence one questions the justice of the "natural" allocation of the human resource, certain particular, deep, and major issues are raised. Pointing out the importance of this resource is trivial as it is synonymous with humankind, and hence with the concerns of justice. However, this resource remains by far the most important by the narrowest standard, that of marketed output. Yet it is also the "most particular" of resources, a large part of this particularity being due to its intricate relation with the ends.

Human capacities can be distinguished according to their *nature*, their *use*, their *origin*, and their *transferability* across *uses* and across *persons*. Their nature is related to the essential question of the self (chapter 6 and below). The origins are discussed with respect to education and training, responsibility and accountability, and genetic and environmental (notably family) influences (chapter 6 and below). Yet the uses provide the most discussed distinctions. Identification between nature and use has been a common source of misunderstanding. Each use of a human resource mobilizes a number of types of more basic capacities. A major property of a capacity is its degree of transferability across uses, or flexibility, or, on the contrary, the degree and scope of its specificity. A resource can be more or less adapted to a use. All uses utilize time, most make use of some effort and of some attention. All employ mental, physical, and perceptive capacities which are more or less general or specific. Denoting capacities by their use is helpful in discussions of justice, yet we must not forget that this tends to hide reality, since such a capacity for a type of application of the human resource is in fact a bundle of more fundamental capacities of broader use.

Human resources and capacities are sometimes conceived as reduced to those used in activities of production, or *productive capacities*. "Production" essentially means useful (serving human ends) but *not directly and immediately useful to the producer* (it may be indirectly useful to the producer—through his exchange or consumption of the product—and directly useful to others—in personal services). Yet many human resources and capacities are also directly useful or, more generally, valuable, to their holder. One can call them *consumptive* or *final capacities*, although "consumptive" sounds a little degrading when they serve the highest aims in life, or, indeed, when they determine these aims, and "final" strictly refers to the economic process. Among them are *capacities for being satisfied*, or *satisfaction capacities. Preferences* are the structure of satisfaction capacities considered in the set of the (other) means of this satisfaction: They are structural capacities. Being satisfied may result from enjoyment, need satisfaction, fulfilment of one's plans, "self-realization," and so on. Needs, tastes, habits, conception of life and of the world, ambitions, culture, are among the determinants of preferences. Other consumptive capacities are physical and mental capacities used in leisure (apart from production for oneself), in exercise, play, cultural activities, and so on. Hence many of the same actual capacities can be used both in production and in consumption or life in general, as we have noted. The imbrication is furthermore compounded by the facts that activities and performance in labor are also objects of direct preferences of the laborer, and that even subjective and intimate satisfaction capacities are put to production use by experts and artists.

Human resources cannot be physically transferred, but economic and legal transfer of productive capacities is possible in the form of rights to decide their use and to receive their service or their proceed. This is indeed the case of wage labor where the wage earner sells such a right for a certain duration (and usually for labor acts in a certain defined category). Such rights may be transferable. They are limited in duration and type of activity (short of slavery). Of course, proxies for the transfer of a productive capacity can be transfers of material or monetary product. And all capacities can be more or less compensated for by means that can be more or less specific (education, various substitute devices, and so on) or general (such as money transfers for welfare).

Relational, Exchange, Market, Bargaining and Transaction Capacities; Situational Resources

Relational capacities are the capacities used in relations of all kinds with other individuals and institutions. They are obviously of prime importance in society. Exchange is such a type of relation, mobilizing *"exchange capacities"* among which *bargaining capacities* or skills are important. In particular, *market capacities* are the capacities for dealing in markets, an activity which indeed requires information, forecasting, an ability for swift decision, and so on, in addition to pure bargaining skills. *Transaction capacities* are similarly defined. Different market capacities can produce large inequalities in wealth, notably when their effects cumulate over time. As we have noticed, bargaining, exchange, and market capacities are not consumptive capacities (although one may enjoy the game). In a market society, market capacities and capacities for economic exchange and bargaining certainly belong to productive capacities (although the direct effect of a specific case of bargaining is more the sharing of a surplus than its production).

A *situational resource* (or handicap or liability) is a resource constituted by the possibilities, advantages, and disadvantages offered by a particular situation. One can consider either the possibilities offered by a situation—a "freedom situational resource"—or these possibilities with respect to the preferences (needs, desires, tastes, ends, etc.) and means and possibilities of the "situated" agent—a "full situational resource." Economic situational resources refer to the situation with regard to economic resources and to others' supplies and demands and hence to other's preferences, tastes, etc. along with their other capacities and endowments. The corresponding freedom situational resource can include or not various productive capacities and other assets of the situated individual considered. One can also include exchange capacities or not. For instance, the full economic situational resource indicates that it is beneficial to have a rare talent with few substitutes and much in demand, and to have original tastes for private goods and common tastes for public goods—and in both cases for something common. One is "handicapped," on the contrary, by the opposite situations. The issue concerns one's place in the network of supplies and demands, epitomized by prevailing prices. The various theories considered here often raise the question of partial and limited situational resources, for instance only for tastes and preferences (and not any other resources), or only for the *opportunity* offered by others' supplies and demands irrespective of the situated individual's own preferences (a freedom situational resource). Relative supplies and demands also belong to the conditions of bargaining, and bargaining power itself results from relative bargaining skills of the protagonists.

Efficiency; Defining Equal, More or More Equal

We have seen in chapter 6 that (Pareto-)efficiency should have priority because unanimity represents free choice (not directly for reasons of "welfare," and the preferences may have to be "cleaned" of unethical features). Then, when the relevant equality is impossible or inefficient for the reasons noted in chapters 3 and 6, one has to resort to some efficient second-best egalitarianism.

The relations "equal," "more," "less," and "more equal" often pose problems of definition. "More" or "less" may be needed for efficient second-best maximins or leximins. Fundamental preferences have been constructed for defining more, less, and equal for end-justice. The extended analyses of the concept of "more equal" for whole distributions of quantities (such as incomes) will be recalled in chapter 10,[2] with the extentions to multidimensional inequalities.[3] One such multidimensional comparison is the basis of the super-equity solution to the problem of the definition of the multidimensional maximin, and hence to the problem of the inefficiency of multidimensional equality (see chapter 6).

9.2 Basic Principles and Pure Theories of Distributive Justice

Basic principles, and the corresponding pure theories, of (respectful) justice are distinguished by the individuals' (or justiciables') means in the broad sense that they choose as end values. The main logical distinction is between the principles that choose as end value a process-freedom (since the topic is distributive justice, pure act-freedom being something else) and those that choose the allocation of a resource (irrespective of its "natural" allocation in the case of a human resource). Such a resource belongs to the category of means-freedom (in the classification of chapter 2). These two kinds of theories are,

---

2. See Kolm 1966a sections 6 and 7.
3. See Kolm 1973b, 1975b, 1977a.

respectively, *liberalisms* and *resourcisms* (where liberalism stands now for process liberalism, the meaning of the term in the English of the past century and in other languages). This distinction rests on the nature of the ethical judgment and is de facto important because the pure rationality of justice demands a prima facie, or ideal, equality of the similar end values of justice relative to the justiciables (possibly qualified by a functional equality that determines the just allocation when justiciables' characteristics relevantly differ). Indeed, in other respects the views do not actually differ but are, rather, *dual* from each other, since the justice of a process-freedom legitimizes the allocations of the resources of various types used in the corresponding action, and the just allocation of a resource legitimizes its use by its beneficiaries.

There is furthermore a special category of liberalisms in which the considered individuals' free choice is hypothetical, implicit, assumed, or putative rather than actual. The choice can be individual or by collective agreement. This includes all Social Contracts in the traditional sense,[4] and the modern theories of the liberal social contracts, of the Original Position, and of "fundamental insurances" considered in section 9.6.[5]

The possibilities are the following:

The two extreme cases are *full process-freedom* and *full resourcism* or *end-justice* which were analyzed in chapters 5 and 7 but can be presented with the present concepts.

full process-freedom for all, and hence equal full process-freedom, legitimizes the individualistic "natural" allocation of the human resource, that is, the usufruct of oneself (or possibly self-ownership), including the capacities to produce, to appreciate and to interfere with others in respecting their corresponding rights. It can allocate non-human natural resources by the human process of collective agreement (or first occupancy). It allocates capital according to its origin. It overcomes exchange failures by liberal social contracts (chapter 5).

Seeing the whole world as a distributable resource, or *full* or *complete resourcism*, amounts to taking individuals' ends as end values for

---

4. Since it seems that J. Buchanan would also call Social Contract the agreement of an actual constitution (see chapters 12 and 13). For a general theory of Social Contracts, see Kolm 1985a, chapter 23.

5. See Kolm 1985a, ch. 19, and relatedly Dworkin 1981.

justice, since consumptive capacities are included (as well as all others). It can also be called *respectful ressourcism*, or *fully respectful resourcism*, in order to indicate that it follows completely the individuals' evaluation of the resources: Not only does it not omit certain resources valued by the individuals (as does particular or partial resourcism), but it also values the relative importance of the various resources as the individuals do. This ethic also is *end-justice* or *full justice* (Justice with the efficient second-best Practical Justice of chapter 7).

The resources possibly available for allocation or compensation are, in more detail: nonhuman natural resources and capital (produced resources), human productive and consumptive capacities, and situational resources.

Natural resourcism advocates the equal sharing of all *nonhuman natural resources* (section 9.9).

Primary productive resourcism takes as end values both *nonhuman natural resources* and *human productive capacities*. For individualistic justice these human capacities should include those formed by family and other social influences, and education and training that is not chosen and paid for by the individual (in terms of money, time, forgone income, effort, and the like—of course, even when an individual does not pay for his education and training, he provides some payment in terms of effort and time). We have seen and will encounter again below the question that exchange capacities (among which bargaining and market skills) are an essential part of productive capacities for an economy, and their omission from this group is a common inconsistency of a number of theories. Note that a nonhuman natural resource can be either used in a production process or directly consumed.

Productive resourcism adds *capital* and all the rest of education and training for production to the latter position. The *social capital* (relations, statuses, etc.) used in production should also be added.[6] Dworkin's (1981) very interesting discussions lean toward productive resourcism, although they do not describe this solution for a number of reasons and omissions, and in fact they should describe still something else for representing the author's basic intent (see section 9.10).

---

6. The notion of "social capital" is analyzed in Kolm 1966a.

Nonhuman resourcism criticizes the unequal allocation of capital and of nonhuman natural resources. The emphasis is on capital. This amounts to Roemer's (1982) theory of exploitation (see section 9.8). In a prolongation of this theory, Roemer adds productive human capital (that is, human resources that are productive and produced—by education and socialization). In further work (1985, Moulin and Roemer 1989), he reaches full resourcism (Justice of *Justice and Equity*; see chapter 7); see also section 9.7.

More or less *specific human resourcisms* choose as end values specific capacities or certain classes of them. The choice of these resources is justified by a number of possible seasons considered in section 9.4 (see also chapter 6). However, what can be seen as unjust is either the actual distribution of capacities of a certain type, or the fact that an individual was not given the chance to choose his own (for instance because it constitutes a natural endowment or results from family influence and education) or at least to take insurance against the bad luck of an unfortunate allotment. This leads to two different theories. One is a proper resourcism, with an ideal of equal allocation. The second is the theory of the implicit *fundamental insurance*, a putative liberalism (section 9.5).

Equality of opportunity is a human and situational resourcism described by its dual liberalism (section 9.7).

Another negative principle is *"nonconsumptive resourcism,"* that is, the view that the only items that are not relevant for redistributive justice are individuals' consumptive capacities or perhaps satisfaction capacities. As we have seen, this logically leads to equality in consumptions, or *consumptionism*, replaced by the second-best super-equity for efficiency (see chapters 3, 6, 8, and below).

9.3   Free Interaction from Equality

From its very definition, respectful justice has the general ideal structure of a *superimposition of liberties over equalities* (of means, aspects of the domain of choice, etc.). Liberty vanishes, at the *notional* level, only in the cases of end-justice and, if the question of the choice of one's own tastes and preferences is put aside, of equal consumption—that is, de facto, with Practical Justice and efficient super-equity—although it may be present there as means of implementation (but not generally from equality) or because of direct preferences for freedom (see chapter 2).[7] At the other extreme of the spectrum, equality dissolves into liberty in the equal rights to one's own capacities of full process-freedom. The other cases are clearly, and usually explicitly, situations of free action, possibly interaction, and possibly exchange, from a certain equality (or from a second-best egalitarian situation). This "initial" equality can be, for example, that of consumption goods (notably because of an assumed irrelevance of individuals' specific preferences), nonhuman or human primary resources, incomes, "primary goods," goods within "spheres of justice" (without exchanges of the "sphered" goods in the Weber-Walzer view, but not without interactions in their use), the resources considered in "equality of opportunity," or rights, powers, capacities, and endowments of all types. The questions raised encompass both *general* questions that exist in all cases, and questions that are *particular* to the various cases. We consider here the basic general questions, while the specificities of each theory are analyzed in the particular relevant sections or chapters.

In all cases, the statement of liberties and of the equalizands *leaves implicit the endorsement and legitimization of the "spontaneous" situation* of the other facts. These facts include the *personal characteristics used in the uses of these liberties.* These characteristics matter for the individual himself, as is the case with various skills or with consumptive capacities. In addition, however, these liberties are most commonly used in interactions with other individuals, so that each individual can be more or less concerned by the others' characteristics. These interactions can be competitions or cooperations of various types and in various domains. There are basically two types of such relevant characteristics: An individual in an interaction is concerned with others' *desires* (aims, preferences, etc., manifested by *demands* and *supplies*) and with their various *relational skills.* Among these relational skills are exchange or transaction capacities and in particular bargaining skills (capacities to seduce, induce, threaten, anticipate, perceive others' desires and moods, manipulate information, react swiftly, and various qualities of patience, intelligence, memory, self-mastery, and so on). All the aspects of desires and relations, of oneself

---

7. And the full analysis in Kolm 1982a.

and of others, can interfere. An individual's consumptive capacities determine both his own satisfaction and the supplies and demands he presents to others. The value of an individual's relational skills depends on their relation to others' such skills, as well as on his and others' desires, supplies and demands. An individual's actual domain of liberty depends on others' supplies, demands and relational capacities. But, for each individual, the set of the other individuals is a priori different. Therefore, *an apparent equal freedom of interaction or exchange hides generally different actual freedoms.* Such inequalities disappear only in particular cases, notably when each individual is small in a sea of relevant others as in the theory of perfect competition. Furthermore the value, for each individual, of this fully understood liberty encompassing others' supplies, demands, and relational skills depends on his own particular desires and relational skills. At any rate *the formal equality of means and freedoms entails unequal situational resources.* The free fox and the equally free chicken in the free poultry yard do not face the same opportunities and do not have the same situational resources.

These facts have to be emphasized because *many views of justice by-pass them and, as a result, often end up with inconsistencies which may be serious.* In particular, a number of views emphasize that individuals' consumptive capacities, tastes, or ends are irrelevant for distributive justice, which should respect their "natural" allocations. From this, they think they can conclude that justice consists of the ideally equal allocation of certain things that the individuals then use in interactions and in particular in exchanges. These equalizands are, for instance, primary goods for Rawls (income and wealth are spent, power is used, positional status is relative, and self-respect also is sometimes), primary resources for Dworkin (see section 9.10), and consumption goods that are then exchanged in the proposals of "free exchange from equal division" (see chapter 6). Two interlocked problems are thus created. First, *an individual's actual freedom depends on others' supplies and demands, and hence tastes or preferences.* The basic view of these theories is that preferences should not be relevant. Yet the reasons provided for this position are that individuals should be held accountable, or even responsible, for their own tastes or ends in life. Hence this irrelevance is meant only for the effects of an individual's own's preferences for himself (these effects are of two different types: in consumption and satisfaction, on the one hand, and for interaction and in particular exchange, on the other hand). These reasons do not apply to the effects of individual preferences on other individuals. These effects intervene in direct interactions, or indirectly, notably through market prices. Second, *an individual's possibilities depend on his and others' skills for exchange, bargaining, or dealing on markets*. Previous remarks have concluded that these skills, which interfere with individuals' supplies, demands (and hence preferences) and can make an important difference, are not consumptive capacities but rather crucial productive ones in economies with exchange and division of labor, so endorsing their "natural" allocation contradicts the stance that restricts such an endorsement to consumptive capacities. Of course the final effect, on an individual, of others' preferences, and of all exchange capacities, depends on this individual's specific preferences, but the latter are precisely deemed to be irrelevant as regards this effect by the theories considered. The solution to these problems that keeps the basic intent of these theories is equal consumption, attenuated into super-equity for the sake of efficiency.

However, with clear and full awareness of the implications, *free* action with certain *equal* means is the standard structure of justice, and, in particular, *free exchange from an equal allocation* of each of several goods is a standard concept of both micro- and macrojustice. For instance, the cases where the allocated goods are consumption goods (chapter 6) and productive resources (section 9.10, and about Dworkin's actual theory) are considered here. The *nature of the goods* is quite important for the structure of the problem, for *two reasons* which concern respectively *individuals' preferences* and the *possibility set*, and which distinguish respectively *final consumption goods* and *primary resources*. Goods that are not for final consumption have in any case to be transformed in order to be useful (this can be taken as a definition of final consumption). The first issue is that only if the goods are *final consumption goods* do an individual's preferences bear on this *individual's allocation alone* (in the absence of consumption externalities, and in particular psychic externalities such as benevolence, malevolence, envy, jealousy, desires for conformity or for distinction, and various sentiments of injustice). Individuals' preferences concerning goods of other kinds are indirect preferences: They thus depend on all the conditions of the interactions, exchanges and production, and therefore they depend in particular on other individuals' allocations of these goods. The second issue is that *primary resources* alone are *given* in the whole economic process from their very definition. By definition also, capital is a primary resource at a given date but a produced good in time perspective. Therefore the equal allocation of primary goods is merely the equal sharing of the available quantities (if no quantity is wasted). By contrast, for other goods there are several possible equal allocations, depending on the choice of production of their total quantities. For intermediary goods (which, by definition, are neither primary resources nor consumption goods) one has both individuals' concern for others' allocations and the problem of the choice of total quantities.

As a result of this possible choice of quantities, which exists in particular for the allocation of consumption goods, efficiency of the process requires, in addition to *exchange efficiency* in the redistribution of the equal allocation, *production efficiency* in the production of these goods (no good can be in larger quantity without another good being in smaller quantity), and particularly *efficient coordination between production and exchange*. One can, however, entrust the whole question to exchange by the following *process*, which is the *extension of free exchange superimposed on equal sharing that allows for production choices*: the individuals have to agree on both production and the sharing of the output, and there is a given possible equal allocation of consumption goods that each individual has the right to impose on everybody by his own decision. This equal allocation then is the "disagreement allocation", both a reference and a threat used by each individual. The outcome is unanimously preferred to this equal allocation, and it may be efficient for the usual reason found in exchange and interaction. Yet, generally, exchange per se does not a priori guarantee efficiency.

9.4   The Human Resource, the Self, and Self-accountability

The prime importance of human resources or capacities demands that some of the issues they raise concerning justice and its policy be given closer consideration. The first issue concerns whether capacities of a certain category should be supported, formed, palliated, or compensated for, or perhaps taxed in order to support other people. Moral justifications in this domain refer to the use, the origin, or the nature of the capacities, and to values such as utility, legitimacy and dignity. Use intervenes notably for capacities that are necessary for using or actualizing basic liberties, whose maintenance constitutes a basic need, or that enable one to have a certain autonomy, a standard objective for both welfare and dignity. The policy then consists of support and, often, education. The nature of the capacity is related to both it use and its origin. Use provides a consequentialist principle, in contrast with the two other basic concepts of the problem that are the self and responsibility.

The basic idea is that an individual is entitled to his own capacities and is liable for their possible shortcomings when these capacities belong to his self in a certain sense or when he is responsible for them. Self and responsibility constitute two complementary principles in the sense that an agent can normally be responsible for something only in the measure in which this item is caused by his choice (of action or abstention), whereas the self normally includes the choosing part of the individual. In fact, two concepts of the self have to be distinguished. One is the "ontological self" (the "transcendental I" of philosophers), whose meaning, nature, and existence are dubious.[8] The other, relevant here, is a social self that delineates the accountability, entitlement, ascription or imputation of personal characteristics. The idea is that an individual is entitled to his capacities that constitute his social self, or is liable for their shortcomings. The conception of justice is then one of respect of social selves and of the personality they define. For example, one individual may not have to pay for another's expensive tastes due to genes or upbringing. These tastes then belong to the social self in this conception. An individual may or may not be entitled to the proceeds of his high productive capacities due to innate ability or to family education, according to different views of the social self. For full process liberalism, the social self includes all capacities and even, one can say, all liberally legitimate rights and properties. For end-justice, social selves in this sense are void. The intermediary polar case defines the social self by individuals' aims, preferences or life plans, and explicitly excludes productive capacities from it. The social

---

8. A general analysis of the question of the self can be found in Kolm 1982b.

self is a concept of core personality that is seen as a private matter beyond the scope of social and distributive justice.

An individual is by definition accountable for the effects of his social self on himself, but not necessarily for its effects on the rest of the world and notably on other individuals. However, the self, embodying the personality as it does, has to include the will, and the concept of responsibility, in its normal understanding, is an accountability for consequences of the will on any relevant entity—oneself, other individuals, or anything else. Responsibility will be analyzed in section 9.6. Its domain includes the effects on oneself, and in particular on one's capacities, that result from the will by purposeful action (such as training), conscious neglect, or conscious secondary effect of an action. Hence these effects are added to the social self in the individual's self-accountability.

The consideration of social selves permits in particular the assignment to the individuals of the accountability for their own preferences, tastes, and satisfaction or consumptive capacities, even though they do not choose most of these elements and hence cannot be held responsible for them. It is indeed a common view, and often a justified one, that the specificities of an individual's ends, preferences, desires, tastes and consumptive capacities are irrelevant for active justice policy toward this individual. An individual may not have to support the consequences of another's chosen aims, expensive tastes, particular education, past experience, bad habits, lack of willpower to accustom himself to other consumptions (and of course his envy or malevolence). And he may not have to share the advantages of his own thrift, easy-going nature, delicate tastes and capacity to enjoy life, just as he may be entitled to no compensation in the opposite cases. Individuals may be entitled to the advantages that their preferences or tastes bestow upon them and liable for the shortcomings of these features.

The general phenomena that underlie such a view have been noted in chapter 6. One is the idea that an individual's preferences, tastes, values, ends, desires, or drives are properly constitutive of the individuals' personality rather than mere means to his satisfaction (or happiness, fulfillment, etc.). In the consumer (economic) model of man, preferences indeed constitute the personality. Productive capacities, by constrast, are not so integrated a part of personality because they can provide useful services to other people. As a consequence each individual is seen as having a *natural right to his satisfaction capacities*, or more generally to his consumptive capacities. That is, he has a right not to pay compensation in any form because these capacities of his seem to exceed the similar capacities of others. *Ipso facto*, this individual is *naturally accountable* for any relative shortcomings of these capacities of his, these defects constitute a *natural liability* for him, and thus he is entitled to no corresponding compensation. This is the *natural ascription, imputation, assigment, or accountability* of these capacities (that full process liberalism extends to all capacities). This conception of the person provides a reason to include these capacities within the social self described earlier.

However, self-accountability of ends, values, tastes, desires, or preferences may also result more or less from an assumption of *self-responsibility* for these features. This responsibility implies that the individual could intentionally manage these aspects of his personality, that is, that his will in this respect can have such consequences and, indeed, that he *can will* such things. A discussion of this requirement should consider the various cases and possible conceptions. If this causality is deemed to hold for only a part of these elements, responsibility cannot be ascribed for more than this. Now individuals often choose willfully, and sometimes carefully, their aims in life, their ambitions, or their conception of the good. They sometimes cultivate or even create a number of their tastes. They can be seen as indulging in others, which implies that they could have prevented their existence. One can even assume that an individual can always willfully change his tastes, preferences or desires, by mobilizing sufficient willpower (assumed to be available, and with more or less time and effort, plus the required information on how to do it). This is indeed the main topic of a number of important philosophies, such as Sartre's—specifically for ascribing responsibility—or Buddhist and Hellenistic philosophies for eudemonistic improvement. As we have noticed it and more dramatically, an individual can always be held responsible for his very existence, since he abstains from suppressing it. But the individual's will is de facto, by commission or omission, only one of the possible joint causes of the considered items, and the assignment of responsibility to joint causes constitutes an ethical choice which is a priori open.

These two reasons for self-accountability, the self and responsibility, a priori apply respectively to given and to chosen elements of the person's evaluation and choice system, hence to different items, though the flow of time can transform a self-chosen item into an ingrained and core element of the personality (and a cause of further choices).

9.5 Specific Human Resourcism and "Fundamental Insurance"

It has been emphasized that the bulk of the distributional problem stems from the allocation of the human resources, and we have considered the three great polar conceptions where justice endorses the "natural" allocation of either all capacities, or none of them, or only consumptive capacities. Yet a number of moral views are more subtle and denounce the injustice of the "natural" individualistic allocation of more specific capacities. This can nevertheless provide very important topics, since, for example, these views may concern health, a number of productive capacities, or education (which is given to individuals when they receive it in childhood).

Two types of moral reasoning can then be used, a "fundamental specific resourcism" leading to an ideal of equal resources, and the "fundamental liberalism" of "fundamental insurance" which rests on a hypothetical equal process-freedom of acquiring this resource or, rather, of obtaining a compensation for a low endowment. The practical outcomes are policies of compensation for correcting either the relative handicap itself or its general effects (for instance, on income or welfare).

Specific resourcism takes the considered resource as an end value and hence sees its equality as the ideal to be reached by compensations as long as no other consideration intervenes (such as disincentives and possibly inefficiency when the ideally compensated benefits from this resource require some action from the individual).

The other approach takes an altogether different view. Indeed the unequal allocation of human resources is good or bad luck for the individuals. Yet luck is a priori amenable to *insurance*. An insurance is an exchange. When it is free, it is morally justified by process liberalism, as any free exchange is. When something impedes this free exchange, the logic of process liberalism requires its vicarious implementation as a *liberal social contract* (see chapter 5). But when this hypothetical exchange is *an insurance*, what *actually appears is only the transfer* received as compensation, from the people who pay the premium or provide the mutual assistance. This justifies a number of transfers.[9]

In particular, people commonly take out insurance against the disability caused by accidents (and by disease, old age, etc.). Should they not also be insured against relative disability due to poor education, training, and motivation provided by the family environment, or due to physical and mental characteristics determined by genetic endowment? Since people cannot actually have taken this insurance (this would have taken place before they were responsible adults or even before they existed), such and insurance can only be a kind of liberal social contract (see chapter 5), and we will discuss below whether it can be so justified or not. This is a "fundamental insurance." Such an insurance a priori is for a specific capacity or a specific consequence of capacities (such as earning power), but various possible sets of capacities can be so "insured." The insured capacities can a priori be both productive and consumptive capacities (one could for instance be insured against having various handicaps, demanding needs, or even expensive tastes and ambitions). We will see below that this view is related to the rationale of very important actual public policies, justified by the fact that this rationale is accepted practically at unanimity (including by the payers).

A fundamental insurance is thus an "insurance" against having received poor genetic abilities at birth or poor education or motivation in the family, which lead to low earning or "enjoyment" capacities. It proposes a justification for certain compensations of certain capacities. Yet it is *not a resourcism but a process liberalism*, because its end values are not the human resources that it more or less compensates for but, rather, a hypothetical liberty (the liberty to take out this insurance, a particular case of freedom of exchange). With regard to these resources, it is a concept of derived or indirect justice. Relatedly

---

9. The various types and causes of these implicit insurances are presented in Kolm 1985a, ch. 19.

the compensation is not complete, even ideally and notionally, but only that which would have resulted from the insurance. These compensations therefore depend on individuals' risk-aversions and preferences (about the considered capacity and its consequences).

Being as it is an hypothetical exchange used to justify a measure of social ethic, a fundamental insurance is, by definition, a type of Social Contract. In scope, it is more specifically a limited Social Contract (see chapter 3). In depth, it is in between a liberal social contract (where the limited putative agreement is essentially among actual individuals) and an Original Position theory,[10] a point to be discussed shortly.

A fundamental insurance has several possible variants, along several dimensions. The compensation can either be for the effect of the relative handicap on a general individual value such as income, welfare, or happiness (it is then usually provided in money income, which in particular can compensate for poor earning ability), or it can be specific in providing some correction of the considered relative handicap in the form of education, training, or specific assistance. The payers of the compensation can be either only the people who are well-endowed with the particular capacities considered—this is then a fundamental *mutual* insurance—or another group of people, possibly all people, who are assumed to have taken the risk to insure and have lost. The nature and scope of what is so insured constitute the basic ethical choice. The compensated capacities may depend on the social and economic environment (talents *in demand, expensive* needs, etc.). Being a kind of free exchange with equal liberty, fundamental insurance has all the properties of such schemes presented in section 9.3. The particular, extreme, and borderline case of fundamental insurance where the *whole* of the individuals' capacities are so insured is the theory of the Original Position.

Now, since we have shown that a theory of the Original Position cannot be a theory of justice (see chapters 1, 3, 4, and 8), this a priori seems to cast doubt on the validity of fundamental insurance in general as a theory of justice. On the other hand, a fundamental insurance is a free exchange that did not occur because of a particular impediment, which is here an inversion of timing (that is, the insurance would

10. See chapters 5 and 8, respectively.

have been taken by a responsible adult before he existed as such a person). In similar cases the theory of liberal social contracts justifies that one implements that which this exchange would have achieved. This latter analogy, however, faces two problems.

First, the consequence of a fundamental insurance is *purely distributional*—the better endowed or a less specific group pay to help the beneficiaries of the insurance—whereas, in the vicarious exchange of a liberal social contract, all parties gain by definition (although there is in addition the distributional issue of sharing the surplus).[11] In particular, the choice of what is putatively insured and of what is not is the distributional reference point about which the interests of the various actual individuals oppose one another (since the risk-aversions, the relevant preferences, and the resulting intensity of the insurance are given in theory). The only obvious objective solutions are the two extremes: nothing, on the one hand, and an Original Position, on the other.

Second, if that which is so insured is to be seen as part and parcel of the *individual's personality*, a potential buyer of this insurance (if he could indeed make such a choice) cannot be considered as really being the *same* person as an actual one. This holds both for the "unfortunate" persons who have to be helped and for the other participants to a fictitious mutual insurance scheme who have to provide the assistance. Then actual persons cannot be held accountable and responsible for this decision and, therefore, for the liability of the transfer on the one hand, and for a possible insufficiency of the compensation (only partial insurance) on the other—this lack of continuity in personality, and hence of responsibility, is one aspect of the impossibility of Original Position theories as theories of social ethics and justice. Now, possible items of fundamental insurance may either be or not be necessary for characterizing the individuals' personality, with undoubtedly certain capacities or certain aspects of education being necessary.[12] However, answering this question is unnecessary in the following very important situation.

---

11. Recall that in general these parties are not all the individuals. For others, only the respect of their liberally legitimate rights is required. By contrast, the scope of contractants extends to all in an Original Position theory.

12. This may be a reason for restricting fundamental insurance to productive capacities and for not considering it for tastes and preferences (thus justifying Dworkin's limitation).

A number of societies consider, practically with the unanimity of their members, that the allocation of very important human resources, such as health or the education one receives from one's family or derives from family-provided opportunities, is very unjust and should be more or less corrected. A certain implementation of the compensating measures and transfers is then justified by unanimity and Pareto-efficiency. These transfers may be direct gifts from people, but centralization may be helpful or necessary, either for reasons of information, or because the payers dissociate their view of justice from their private behavior, or again because they are ready to abide by this ethic only if the others do too—which may justify a "noncoercive coercion," that is, a coercion that guarantees to each person that the others contribute, making him willing to contribute.[13]

For instance, public social security is desired by practically everybody in Western European nations because it compensates not only actually insurable bad luck—as private insurance would do—but also differences in *propensities* to become sick, which are capacities of the individuals. Indeed the basic objection to private health insurance is that people with higher propensities to be sick would be asked higher premia: Not only do they have this bad luck, but in addition they would have to pay more! Uniform premia, which are possible in the name of justice in a nonmarket scheme, in part compensate these differences in health capacities. Similar views led to the establishment of free and compulsory primary education, and to free education in general (the compensated occurence being here family-supported education). Hence policies undertaken for this kind of reasons amount to a large part of public budgets and, indeed, of GNP, in these societies.

However, it is not easy to say whether the motivating reason behind such ideas and hence behind the corresponding policies is a fundamental insurance or a specific resourcism. On the one hand, the fact that individuals did not choose their genetic abilities or their family environment (and hence cannot be held responsible for them; see the next

---

13. Note that all these motivational questions differ from the case of collective gift-giving (chapter 5, Kolm 1984b and 1985a). Remark in particular that someone who wants to implement a fundamental insurance desires to pay the premium he owes putatively, rather than preferring the beneficiary to have a better situation per se (as would be the case for collective gift-giving). All these motivational questions are analyzed in detail in Kolm 1984b and 1985a.

section) is deemed important. On the other hand, there is no attempt to discriminate according to that which the individuals would have chosen in the corresponding insurance given their specific risk-aversions and preferences. One can say that the policies are motivated by both resource inequality and fundamental insurance, but implemented according to an ideal of resource egalitarianism (with various options, such as compensating for family education or also, jointly, for abilities).

The concept of fundamental insurance is proposed and analyzed in *The Liberal Social Contract* (Kolm 1985a) as a particular case of liberal social contracts or a direct extension of standard ones, and hence as a case of specific policies justified by process-freedom. One of Dworkin's (1981) proposals for defining equal productive capacities amounts to a fundamental insurance. This, however, is at odds with Dworkin's basic intent which is resourcism. Furthermore, fundamental insurance does not provide the abstraction from preferences that Dworkin seeks to obtain by this device.[14]

9.6 Responsibility

Retributive justice provides important principles of distributive justice. It consists in establishing, or endorsing, relations from an agent's act or action to advantages or costs (in the broad sense) for this agent. The central concepts are those of merit or desert, aim-freedom and responsibility. The crucial relations from acts to moral consequences for the agent may be completely set up for a moral reason, for certain cases of merit or desert, but they may also rely on certain other, existing relations, that are causal relations of various kinds, and may be dubbed "natural" or "spontaneous" with the same use of these adjectives as earlier. Let us focus here on the principle of responsibility.

A very large part of justice considered in societies rests on the notion of responsibility. This holds for legal, court, and retributive justice as well as for important general social ethical concepts. The notion of responsibility has had historical importance in applied social

---

14. As has been pointed out, for instance, by Roemer (1985) among other criticisms of Dworkin's use of this concept.

ethic and applied conception of justice, since the oponents to the introduction of social insurances opposed them in the name of responsibility. Indeed, in the classical political array of redistributive arguments, reponsibility plays for the liberal right the role that needs play for the left (see chapter 11). Both concepts are as important as they are delicate. And, in fact, the left bases its morals on the responsibility for catering for others' needs, and its claim for social liberty and dignity on a need for responsibility.

An agent A is responsible for a fact X when his free autonomous actions cause X by commission or omission, and he can for this reason be blamed for X or be assigned the corresponding costs. The equivalent concept is more rarely applied to praises and benefits, but the difference is often merely a choice of the state of reference. The concept can be for omission as well as for "commission"; that is, the action can be an abstention from acting in a certain way. The ethical choice about responsibility concerns both the consequences and uses of responsibility such as blame, cost ascription, and so on, and the relation to causality. This latter aspect would offer no possibility of choice if the agent's will were the only cause of fact X. But this is never the case, although there are various degrees: others' wills and non-will items may be other causes of X, and A's will may not be fully autonomous. The origin of all these causes can be at various dates of the past. Responsibility has to be assigned to these joint causes, and the shares assigned to non-will causes have no consequence. Responsibility thus is not determined by the mere reference to "mechanical" causality, although one can be more or less close to this situation. Then the choice to assign costs (and benefits) according to responsibility is not in itself a solution of the problem of justice: it is only the indication of an intention to base accountability on causality from the working of the agents' wills, and then responsibility is the name of the problem.

The application of the notion of responsibility raises a number of issues. Responsibility by omission requires the definition of the relevant domain of possible acts for each agent, the ascertainment of the actuality of the possibility (with possibly the requirement that the agent tries to intervene), and it opens a wide scope for the notion of collective responsibility. In all cases, the responsibility for the information that leads to the act or to inaction has to be specified (see for example the legal principle that everyone is assumed to know the law).

A main issue is the degree of autonomy of the agent's will and of its violations for various reasons (influence, education, past experience, weakness of the will, and so on). We of course discard here odd uses of the term responsibility, such as its metaphoric use for a cause that is not a will, or for an accountability not based on causality as in certain ancient uses or even modern ones (such as Sartre's "responsibility beyond oneself").

Accountability from responsibility and aim-freedom (see chapter 2) constitute "natural" retributive justice: "to or from each according to that which he causes." It has a natural place in distributive justice, since justice requires rationality, that is, providing reasons, and the most standard of reasons is reliance on natural causality. Retributive justice is primarily a deontic moral concept, referring to what is due (to or from) as a primary judgment, but its influence on action also gives it the consequentialist dimension of an incentive.

Responsibility by omission can a priori apply to all that an individual could do to improve the world. The choice of assignment of responsibility in general is thus a major variable in the moral link between the individual and others, society and the world. Hence responsibility in general is much more than legal quiblings in courts or even a principle of distributive justice. It is the deontic basis of adhesion and contribution to the rest of the world, of engagement and free solidarity. This view has been developed by the great ethics of responsibility.[15] However, this refers more to justice in the ancient sense of behaving justly toward others than to the distributive justice considered here.

Responsibility may intervene in all allocations resulting from choices and actions (or inaction) of all kinds. An individual may be held accountable for something because he is responsible for it. This gives rise to compensations for torts from harm inflicted to other persons. But a particularly important application concerns effects unto oneself. An individual may have to be helped only if he is not responsible for his unfortunate situation. Now, one particular domain is at once very

---

15. For instance, by Bouglé, Braunschwig, with a special place for Sartre, and recently by Jonas. The most elaborate and deepest analysis of the concept of self-responsibility (responsibility for oneself) is the philosophical theory of the *karma* developed by advanced (analytical) buddhism (see Kolm 1982a).

important for allocation, inherently problematic for responsibility, and such that the opinions concerning the possibilities differ widely. This is the complex of individual characteristics that includes both the internal causes of choice and the capacities to appreciate. Both are closely related: for instance, the concept of "preferences" encompasses both aspects. An individual can more or less choose or influence his aims, ambitions, duties, principles, desires, preferences, tastes, capacities of appreciation, and so on, with more or less effort, time, advice and information. He may at least have prevented the actual state in these respects (responsibility by omission). He can thus be held responsible for the corresponding part of his satisfaction, and hence be held accountable for it, while the effect of the other part may fall in the domain of general distributive justice submitted to the compensatory measures already discussed (possibly limited or specific ones because of incommensurabilities or "sphere" effects, and if the "natural" allocation of these characteristics is not endorsed for another reason such as selfhood or process-freedom). The extent to which the individual cannot choose causes of his choices correspondingly diminishes his possible responsibility.

However, we have already alluded to the striking differences between classical views concerning the possible scope for such willful choice of oneself. Economists see preferences as given to the individual;[16] however, self-formation of preferences is analyzed and modeled in Kolm (1980b, 1982a, 1986b, 1987a). Economists also see choice as determined by preferences and given possibilities. Therefore the classical man of economics could not be held responsible for his preferences (and possibly not for his choices and actions either). On the contrary, for Sartre the individual chooses fully and instantly who he is, and he is fully responsible for this, for what he does and for much more (by "omission"). Stoicism considers that an individual can fully choose his preferences. Epicure advocates improving one's appreciation (indeed all Hellenistic philosophies put ideas of this type at their center). All personal morality consists in choosing one's principles of action, a

---

16. Even in the relatively rare studies that do not take preferences or tastes as a priori fully given to the analysis and that consider their formation or transformation, for instance, in habit formation or addiction (see the references and discussion in Kolm 1982a).

choice that should be guided only by reason in Kant's *autonomy*.
Kant indeed, following Rousseau, calls liberty the obedience to a law
chosen by oneself (chosen from reason rather than from tastes or
preferences, so that there is no further regress). The most remarkable
philosophy on this ground, based on unmatched (by far) psychological
knowledge, is that of Buddhism: one can master the birth of one's own
desires, provided one is taught how to do it and properly advised
and trained—a process that requires time and effort and for which
individuals' abilities differ greatly.[17]

9.7 Equalities of Opportunities

One of the most discussed principles of justice in political debates is
that of *equality of opportunity*. The idea is that all people should
receive equal chances in life, that they will use according to their
wishes, willpower and other capacities. The central theoretical point is
that these latter elements are thus implicitly not equalized or compensated for, and one needs to know where to draw the line. Practically,
however, these political debates are quite clear about what they mean.
What is deemed to be unjust is the inequality in the means of economic
activity (in particular competition) with which society provides the
individuals. Hence the focus is on discrimination, education (opportunity for education or result of education), inheritance, and secondarily
on social relations and various information.

Opinions that are closer to end-justice, and that value the quality of
social relations,[18] deride equality of opportunity as "good for horse
races but not for justice." Equality of opportunity is, however, also
sometimes invoked beyond the social cause of possibilities and limits,
for the alleviation of individual handicaps, and beyond productive
use, in education for culture. The notion of equality of opportunity
has also been called upon in various attempts to define an objective
domain for equalization. Much of this is to be found in discussions
concerning basic needs, most of which are means for action and some
of which are personal capacities (health, information). This question

---

17. For a complete analysis, see Kolm 1982a.
18. See Kolm 1984b.

will be taken up in chapter 11 where the concepts of needs and basic needs are analyzed.

The vocable "equality of opportunity" has also recently been used for meaning equality in liberty or means in general, by studies that attempt to justify this equality, as opposed to equality in outcome, by the concept of *responsibility*, and possibly to deduce from this the specific relevant equalizand. This was initiated by Cohen (1989a,b) and Arneson (1989).[19] Roemer notably emphasized the political definition of the extent of responsibility. Although this is stepping down from pure ethical analysis and rationality, at least it permits to define practical and workable solutions. Moreover, since distributive justice is generally to be implemented through politics anyway, this method permits to build a well-rounded and consistent program for a redistributionist political party. Fleurbaey (1995) points out a number of logical difficulties such as the question of joint causes. The general idea would be: Equalize that which the agent is not responsible for. We have, however, seen that the necessary causal condition for responsibility leaves a very wide range for the moral choice of ascribing responsibility. Hence the appeal to responsibility enables one to use the nonmoral fact of causality for solving the question of justice, but this provides only a small part of the solution, and the rest remains ethical choices. Yet the concept of responsibility in general is prominent in people's sense of justice and sentiment of injustice, as well as for institutions dealing with justice, and hence its full incorporation into the theory of distributive justice is an indispensable enterprise.

9.8 Theories of Exploitation

The view that someone is "exploited" by someone else is a common and often powerful cause of indignation and sentiment of injustice. It

---

19. Cohen and Arneson otherwise largely react against Sen's proposition for "capacities" and "functionings" that they see as well-meaning but ad hoc and lacking analytical justification (the fullest discussion is in Cohen 1989a). This relates to the basic needs issue (see chapter 11). It should also be emphasized that considerations of tastes, culture, and dignity cannot be separated from the provision of human needs or "capabilities." For instance, human "nutrition" can be satisfied by dog food.

is closely related to equality and to liberty. It indeed refers to an asymmetrical and unequal relation, which necessarily also has certain inequalities among its causes and in its consequences. Furthermore, if the "exploited" person objects to this exploitation, this implies that his liberty to avoid it is limited.

Following suggestions of Adam Smith and of the "Ricardian socialists," Marx developed a theory of exploitation of wage labor by capital owners which had a powerful influence, as it integrated a positive analysis of the economic development of capitalism with an indignant and highly moral-sounding indictment of this system. Marx describes capitalism as transferring a part of the product of labor, thanks to low wages, to capital owners who mostly invest it in means of production, that is, more capital (they also consume a part of it). He calls this transfer "theft," a word that implies both involuntariness and a concept of legitimacy. The workers are indeed seen as being forced to this transfer because they have no other choice but to sell their labor—or, rather, to rent out their labor power—at this price, or to starve. Yet "theft" furthermore seems to imply a moral adhesion to the principle of the "right to the full product of one's labor" or the usufruct or ownership of oneself. Marx, however, sees morals only as an endogenous ideologization of interest, and he denies that his scientific undertaking contains a moral stand, except perhaps in so far as he chooses to consider things "from the point of view" of the exploited. Indeed the principle of distribution that Marx quotes the most approvingly is "to each according to his needs" rather than the second-best "to each according to his work." Marx's theory of exploitation, however, is not a mere attempt to positively describe or explain the source of capital accumulation. What it also and basically intends to be is a *critique* in the philosophical sense (Descartes, Kant, Hegel) of the ideology of capitalism based on private full process liberalism, that is, the uncovering of a logical internal contradiction (inconsistency) of this theory. This is achieved by showing that the system so justified by self-ownership and free exchange rests crucially on forced transfers, that is, theft, at the very original level of the use of labor force. The difference essentially rests on only one basic point: the status of the market supply of labor with respect to liberty. Indeed a propertyless laborer is formally and legally free to work ... given that the alternative is to starve. And this happens all his life long for maximal labor time if the employers offer only subsistence wage for maximal work. (The subsistence level—the "iron law of wages"—was not an unrealistic hypothesis in the "hungry 1840s," and Marx's theory became more confused when he later considered higher wages which he explained as determined by the sociology of workers' consumption habits). The worker then also remains propertyless. Furthermore Marx saw freedom as being violated during the past "primitive accumulation" by war, looting, or slavery. These various unfreedoms are due to unequal means, notably the unfreedom of the wage earner is due to his lack of property since "he has nothing to sell but his labor." This entailed, for Marx, both the disgraceful human relation of the wage labor of the type he considers and exploitation proper.

Marx, however, would not have stopped at a concept of exploitation as "taking unfair advantage," since he wanted "scientific" concepts, and hence objectivity, precision, and, if possible, measurement. A straightforward solution consists in considering that the gain of capital owners, profit, "comes from" labor, rather than only being the remuneration of waiting (abstension from consuming capital), risk-taking, and the organization of production. Yet this would result from a theory of prices and market values that disregards interest and differences in time, as well as the heterogeneity of labor. This "labor theory of value" takes "labor" as a sort of industrial Spinozian "substance" rather than as an actual entity, and its construction encounters a number of logical difficulties.

However, since exploitation is the object of a powerful and widespread sentiment of injustice, several writers proposed rebuilding its theory on sounder bases. Each emphasizes one feature or the other of the Marxian vision. Joan Robinson (1933) provided perhaps the most direct answer, in considering a monopoly in the demand for labor, with exploitation being the excess of the marginal productivity of labor over the wage rate. This monopoly is not properly Marx's view (who at least emphasizes competition between firms on the product market). It is indeed sometimes a reality, but this restricts the scope of exploitation probably more than one wants, since there may also be exploitation of only inframarginal labor units. Weizäcker (1972) concentrated on the inequality of intertemporal consumption. Roemer (1982) offered an elaborate full-fledged theory of exploitation. He defined exploitation by the inequality in the ownership of nonhuman productive resources (capital and natural resources). This enabled him to consider other relevant kinds of exploitation which derive from the unequal distribution of the human capital formed by socialization and education. Now, Marx's basic value is not equality—which he derided as a "petit-bourgeois" ideal—but rather liberty (or, better, liberation, based on a Hegelian view of the "unfolding" of history): The unpaid excess labor over workers' consumption which constitutes the "surplus-value" (which becomes profit when the product is sold) is forced labor that leaves nothing for the worker, and hence pure worker's unfreedom, people in communism will be free to do what they want, and so on. Yet inequality is indeed also a necessary and intrinsic aspect of the exploitative system he describes.

An altogether different reconstruction focusses on Marx's direct condemnation of the wage relation (Kolm 1984a). The wage relation is the renting of the labor force, or the buying of the flow of its availability for a certain time. Buying a stock about amounts to buying the flow of its availability for the duration of its life. A propertyless worker at subsistence wage has no choice but to rent out his labor force all of his life long. This is much like selling the stock, that is, slavery (the worker could quit a master only to rent himself out to another, similar one). This comparison was indeed common in the late eighteenth and early nineteenth centuries (Adam Smith pointed out that employers prefer wage labor to slaves because they can dismiss employees when necessary). Furthermore, by its nature, wage labor (as slavery) is an unequal, asymmetrical relation of domination and direct dependency where the employer decides the actions of the employee /in a certain domain)—this differs from a craftman's sale of specific services. The salaried worker thus is in a sense twice unfree (he is forced to yield his labor, and what he yields is the disposition of his labor force). Now, (process) liberals condemn slavery, but they accept wage labor as free exchange. When it comes to man, they refuse trading in stock but accept trading in flow. In Marx's eyes, this is both illogical and hypocritical. Marx, on the other hand, does not object to the trading of goods, and hence of products of labor, per se (although a qualification may come from his theory of the alienation of labor). Therefore liberals and Marx agree on both the condemnation of slavery and the acceptance of markets for products. They oppose each

Table 9.1
Trading in labor

Buying labor force	Stock (slavery)	Flow (wage relation)	Product (product market)
Liberalism	Condemnable	Acceptable	Acceptable
Marx	Condemnable	Condemnable	Acceptable

other on the middle ground which is basic for industrial societies: wage labor is accepted as commodity trading by liberals and condemned as de facto akin to slavery by Marx. Table 9.1 shows this difference. The ulterior historical evolutions of wages and of the wage relation, and indeed their future from now on, are of course relevant.

Note that an absence of dependency and domination through exchange is also the reason for Rousseau's egalitarian ideal: "No one should have either so little as to have to sell himself or so much as to be able to buy someone else."

9.9   Equal Sharing of Natural Resources

Equal sharing of nonhuman natural resources is a classical position, with applications throughout human history (often as a result of collective agreements such as those noted in chapters 5 and 12). In theoretical work, Locke (1689) subjects his theory of the appropriation of natural resources by "mixing one's labor" with them (or one's servant's labor, or one's horse consuming them) to the egalitarian "proviso" that "enough and as good" is left for others (he thought that this was always satisfied thanks to America—a view that glosses over locational characteristics and, perhaps, indigenous right-holders —and that this egalitarian condition can be completely abandoned when "money," that permits wage labor, is introduced). This inspired Nozick (1974) who adds the possibility of compensations. A unanimous agreement indeed permits compensations, and it actually determines their value. The various schools of the "socialization" of land or rent (see, in particular, Walras 1898) are in part motivated by an equal distribution of the benefits provided by natural resources. An equal sharing of these resources has also been recently advocated by Steiner (1978) and Cohen (1986). (A complete analysis of the question of the allocation of natural resources is to be found in chapter 10 of Kolm 1985a).[20]

9.10   Productive Resourcism

In a two-part study Dworkin (1981) presented, first, an epoch-making criticism of "welfarism" (a term due to John Hicks 1959) which amounts to denying the relevance of individuals' tastes and ends for distributive justice, and second, a proposal conceived as being both the necessary implication of this criticism and productive resourcism. This proposal thus sees justice as the equal sharing of productive resources (note that a nonhuman natural resource that is also a consumption good should belong to these resources). The problems encountered are solved by free exchange. There are questions indeed, since most of these goods are nonfinal (not ready for consumption), equality in several final goods would generally be inefficient, indivisibilities prevent equal sharing, human resources are not directly transferable and vary greatly across individuals, and other problems will be noted below. Dworkin then proposes: free exchange from equal multidimensional sharing; auctions for indivisible goods with the same initial endowment of cash for all individuals; the equal sharing of each individual's time of disposal of his human resource among all individuals, followed by free exchange of these rights; and "fundamental insurance" for productive human capacities (see section 9.5).[21]

All these devices consist of free exchange with certain identical initial allocations for all individuals. Since fully free exchange is equal freedom of exchange, this situation from identical starting endowments seems to define equal possibilities. However situational resources and transaction capacities differ. Each individual faces a different set of others' desires, supplies and demands, and capacities for dealing in exchanges and markets and for bargaining. Furthermore the individuals' own endowments of these later exchange capacities

---

20. See also Kolm 1986c.

21. Dworkin also uses what he calls the "envy test," that is, no one prefers any other's allocation to his own. Chapter 7 and section 9.11 below note the history of this criterion, its moral meaning and value, and its relation to "envy."

differ. Only in particular situations such as a perfectly competitive equilibrium do these differences vanish, but the consideration of these situations should be possible and justified (see below). In particular and for example, the set of possible allocations that an individual can have given that no other accepts an allocation if he prefers the initial one, differs from one individual to the other. Now, the point is whether all these differences are relevant or are not, notably in Dworkin's philosophy of which we are rather well informed—that is, whether they should or should not be considered relevant in this philosophy since the answer is not given explicitly. Furthermore most resources are not final, consumption goods, and thus they must be transformed into such goods before they can be appreciated by the individuals' irrelevant tastes. This production also uses exchange capacities and opportunities (and hence supplies, demands, and preferences)—it could solve a problem for equal allocation when indivisible resources produce divisible goods, in dividing the output, but this is not in Dworkin's proposal. There are, finally, two groups of issues: unequal exchange capacities and opportunities created by others' exchange capacities, and unequal opportunities created by others' preferences. They are related, since the application of exchange and bargaining capacities depends on supplies and demands (including, for an individual, his own, that manifest his own preferences and tastes).

First, there is the effect of all exchange, market, and bargaining capacities. We have already noted its relevant features (chapters 3 and 8, and section 9.3 above). To recap, actual situations show that these capacities can make a large difference in the outcome. These capacities are obviously not in the category of "consumptive capacities," tastes, or needs. Indeed these capacities are essential in the overall production of an economy with exchange, markets, bargainings, and division of labor (although each bargaining case shares a surplus rather than produces it). In the dichotomy of the uses (and, in part, the nature) of capacities between "productive" and "consumptive" ones, they have to be classified among productive capacities. Now Dworkin wants to share equally all productive capacities and the benefits from them, whereas his schemes imply, on the contrary, the endorsement and the legitimization of the very unequal "natural" endowment of exchange, market, and bargaining capacities, which fall in this general category.

One can try to use Dworkin's own schemes to avoid the resulting inconsistency. An exchange capacity (including for bargaining and generally dealing on markets) is a human resource, and there are two possible ways. In one of them, these capacities are compensated according to the principle of the "fundamental insurance" (see section 9.5). However, these exchange capacities would themselves be used in the hypothetical exchange that determines this insurance. This is an infinite regress (which, however, can be provided a solution as a fixed point). Yet, as was pointed out earlier, fundamental insurance is basically *a liberalism* rather than a resourcism (an equal sharing of a resource), and therefore it is basically at odds with Dworkin's deepest outlook and intention. The fact that this free exchange is putative and vicarious does not affect this conclusion. The second solution consists in the individuals using others' capacities for exchange as one of the possible uses of others' time either received in initial allocation or bought in the labor market. Yet the individuals with good exchange capacities will then have to use them ... against other uses of these very capacities when their services are used by different others, and also against their own personal interests (and they will have an exchange advantage in renting out their exchange capacities in the first place). Note also that by nature an individual cannot check easily his employee's use of his higher exchange capacities.

The second inequality is the one induced by others' demands, supplies and underlying desires, needs or preferences. The basic view is that redistributive justice toward an individual should not depend directly on his own preferences, tastes, aspirations, desires, needs, drives, or consumptive capacities. Differences in capacities for being satisfied should not be a reason for compensatory redistributions. But this per se does not imply that these individual characteristics are altogether irrelevant for justice, since they also intervene in other ways. Indeed an individual's external, material possibilities depend on others' supplies and demands, and hence on others' preferences of all types, including when these others have the same Dworkinian resources, and in exchanges that accompany the necessary transformations of goods. In addition, as was noted earlier, the effects of capacities for exchange or bargaining discussed above depend on all individuals' supplies, demands, and desires (and hence, for each individual, both on the others' and on his own). For all these reasons also, Dworkin's schemes do not provide equal external means. In particular, an individual's preferences, tastes, and supplies and demands from the initial allocations considered, constitute, for the other individuals, the *situational resource* of an *exchange opportunity*. And the set of the other individuals is not the same for each individual. The proposition that an individual's tastes cannot be a source of injustice for himself implies neither that they cannot be a source of injustice for others nor that others' tastes cannot be a source of injustice for this individual. Practically, only in cases of large numbers of small individuals without transaction costs and with the same relevant information (for instance in competitive equilibria) could this overall exchange opportunity be considered as identical for all individuals.

Indeed both problems of unequal capacities and opportunities for exchange vanish in situations of competitive equilibria. However, the various conditions of this situation should be satisfied. In particular, Dworkin considers the case of indivisible items, which are excluded in such situations. And there should be the relative smallness of all agents, the absence of nonsmall coalitions, the perfect relevant information, the processes necessary for reaching the equilibrium, etc. Then freedom of exchange from an equal allocation is indeed an equality of possibility sets for all agents. But, of course, what set this is, and hence the set of equilibrium prices, is not a matter of indifference for the agents, and their having different preferences for goods implies that they have different and in part opposed preferences for the set of prices. These prices themselves depend on all supplies and demands, and hence on all preferences, tastes, or individual ends.

Therefore in all cases, irrespective of the equality or inequality of individuals' possibilities, an individual's satisfaction depends on the relative situation of his preferences with regard to others'. The philosophy considered holds each individual "responsible" (in fact accountable) for his own preferences. Yet these preferences intervene not only in using and enjoying consumption goods but also in the exchanges which determine the production and allocation of these goods. This moral assignment is clear for the first effect. But what about the second? The individual, being responsible for his tastes, probably also has to be held responsible for the goods that these tastes induce him to acquire, given the market conditions. Hence he is responsible for his demands and supplies induced by his tastes. But these demands and supplies also influence others' acquisitions, and therefore their satisfaction. Individuals thus bear a certain responsibility in others' satisfaction and welfare. But this does not seem in tune with the basic intent that holds each individual to be responsible for his own satisfaction given the endowment of resources.

Apart from the partial possibility of treating the question of exchange capacities by Dworkin's own devices, all these difficulties in Dworkin's proposal are similar to those met with Rawls's, yet they are often more extensive because the exchanges start from resources, while in Rawls's case the *ideal* equalization is already achieved at midway, with income (and other "primary goods"). This in particular affects the roles of exchange capacities, and other problems such as that of indivisible primary resources that produce divisible outputs.

The answer to all these difficulties, and the implementation of Dworkin's (and others') ethics, consist in taking the allocation of consumption goods as end-values of justice, and in resorting to second-best egalitarianism to avoid the inefficiency of equal consumption bundles (or the impossibility entailed by indivisible consumption goods that cannot be made divisible by the consideration of the duration of use). With divisibility the standard solution is efficient super-equity, and in all cases fired-duration income equalization can play a role (see chapter 6; free exchange from equal consumption goods, or auctions of the indivisibles with the same amounts of money or of divisible goods, would suffer from a number of the same drawbacks as primary resourcism, as noted in section 9.3).[22]

Finally, Dworkin's basic claim of the direct irrelevance of individuals' tastes, preferences, etc. for justice is to be considered on both logical and ethical grounds. This has been presented in chapters 6 and 8 (since this is also Rawls's view). In particular a number logical limits to this view have been highlighted and discussed. In brief, the same elementary capacities are used in production and in consumption and

---

22. Equitable efficient allocation and compensation for indivisible items are presented and analyzed in Kolm 1971 and 1991a (see also the references in this second work).

life in general. To mobilize personal resources for putting them to production use or for the pursuit of other aims is often quite similar. Why distinguish between benefiting directly and indirectly from what one can do? Individuals are given most of their tastes, desires and needs, from nature or past experience. It is not a priori obvious that they could be held "responsible" for them. Furthermore, production thanks to "productive capacities" is a physical, mental, and social activity that is also directly "consumed": Work is commonly the most important way through which people make sense of life, set and achieve aims, relate to others, and find a place in society, and its pains and joys are also directly felt. Sensual capacities are often put to productive uses—as noted. Moreover no *formal* distinction between these two types of capacities appears to be relevant (Roemer 1985 extensively discusses this formal aspect).

The distinction between the capacities that are "naturally" justly and unjustly allocated must thus rely on what it is used for, namely *ethical* considerations. However, it turns out that one should help the satisfaction of certain *needs* created by the lack of consumptive capacities to withstand certain harshnesses (these needs are "consumptive liabilities"), and that the benefit of *certain* productive uses of capacities should be left to the producer. Therefore the principle of equalizing all productive capacities and no consumptive one cannot be held as a universal theory of justice. It is nevertheless an important polar case, and the relevant one in a fair number of situations, but then it should be treated as previously described (chapter 6).

9.11 Justice and Envy

Egalitarians are commonly accused of camouflaging sentiments of envy and jealousy under an ideal of justice. The most despicable and the noblest of social sentiments indeed entertain close relations. Equality erases envy. So does, more generally, the Equity situation considered above (equal liberty, chapter 7) where *no one prefers any other's allocation to his own*. Indeed the very first scientific mention of such a criterion was followed by a praise of an envy-free society (Tinbergen 1946), and this criterion was later often called "envy-freeness." Yet calling envy my preferring your allocation to my own misspecifies envy. Indeed, first, I could have this preference without experiencing any sentiment of envy, either because it is not in my nature to be envious or because I deem these allocations, or these individuals, to be insufficiently comparable. Second, if I envied you, I would be affected simultaneously by both our allocations, rather than alternatively by either one or the other as when I say that I prefer one to the other. In by far the most common use of the term "envy," and probably in all uses of the term "envious," the person who envies is less satisfied or less happy because of this fact (hence he would be happier if that which he envied were less good, yet commonly an *additional* moral sentiment of nonmalevolence prevents him from explicitly desiring that the other person become worse-off without a material or "objective" benefit for anybody else). In rare uses only, the word "envy" does not imply this negative effect on "welfare" (such as admiring envy, "I envy your youth," etc.). The universal moral condemnation of envy (very strongly pronounced by Kant and J. S. Mill, for example), refers to the former, common conception of envy. Indeed another economic literature considered this aspect and correctly modelled envy as a negative consumption externality.[23] This literature, however, sometimes failed to specify the limits of envy, and in particular the fact that "there is something" in the idea that I can envy you only if I "prefer your allocation to mine" in some sense.

This sense is obtained by an individual preferring an individual allocation to another one given that, in each alternative, the other individuals are assumed to have allocations identical to that of the individual.[24] This identity suppresses any possible sentiment of envy, and the corresponding individual's preference can be called his *"envy-free" or "intrinsic" preference.* Then the noted condition of envy is that *an individual cannot experience envy if he envy-free prefers no other's allocation to his own.* This situation for all individuals can be shown to be *equivalent to equal liberty,* as in the case without externalities (chapter 7), and it just boils down to this case when this externality is absent: it thus is also called *Equity.* Hence *Equity (equal liberty) is a sufficient condition for an absence of envy,* with a proper theory of envy.

---

23. See Kolm (1964, 1966a, 1972), Brennan (1973), Boskin and Sheshinski (1978), etc.
24. The theory of envy is presented in Kolm 1991c, 1993f, and 1995a.

The consideration that "strong" envy is a disagreable sentiment completes the analytical framework. The resulting structure entails many remarkable properties. As an example, whereas externalities usually prevent the Pareto-efficiency of individual free choices, this is not the case with the envy externality if individuals' incomes are not too unequal (in a competitive equilibrium with such incomes, for instance). The resulting situation is furthermore actually envy-free. This is a case where more equality is favorable to efficiency.

More generally, all the properties that have been obtained for the property of Equity with individuals who experience no envy (see chapter 7, section 7.1) have equivalent properties in the logic of envy, but these properties are now richer (there commonly are several meaningful properties with envy for each property for Equity), much less obvious and more subtle to prove, and actually about envy and about its absence in a nontrivial sense. Other important properties are specific to this case. Finally, a number of other social sentiments have been analyzed with similar methods and results, and some of them are related to the questions of justice and of equality, such ad the sentiments of superiority and inferiority, the desire (or pressure) for conformity or on the contrary for distinction, various aspects of benevolence and reciprocity, and indeed the sense of justice and resentment for injustice.[25]

9.12   Maximin in Liberty[26]

We have seen in chapter 7, section 7.1, the identity between equality in instrumental freedom and Equity. Yet in certain circumstances the property of Equity may be impossible or necessarily inefficient. A possible solution consists in resorting to maximin or leximin in liberty. This requires the definition of the relation that one individual is more or less free than another and the designation of the least free. This can indeed be achieved by an extention of the concepts of both Equity and "Realistic Equity" (that is, no individual prefers any other's allocation

---

25. See Kolm 1993f.
26. The complete analysis is in Kolm 1993e.

that he can have to his own—a concept that is notably useful for the allocation of tasks to be performed, which may require particular capacities).[27] The concepts and results are as follows, all of which concern instrumental freedom.

In a given overall allocation, an individual is said to be *no less free* than another when there exist two individual possibility sets, one for each individual, such that each individual's allocation is one of his best choice on his possibility set, and the set for the former individual includes the set for the latter one.

Then, *an individual is no less free than another one if and only if he does not prefer the other's allocation to his own* (indeed "no less free" implies this preference since the individual could have chosen the other's allocation, and this preference implies "no less free" in taking as possibility sets respectively the pair of allocations and the other individuals' allocation).

We then naturally say that: Two individuals are *equally free* when each is no less free than the other; an individual is *less free* than another when he is not "no less free" than him—he prefers the other individual's allocation to his own; an individual is *freer* than another when he is no less free than him and both are not equally free—equivalently, he is no less free than him and the latter is less free than the former, or the individual does not prefer his allocation to the other's and the latter prefers the former's allocation to his own. (Hence for the same individual freer is better off and less free is worse off.)

If each individual can have each other's allocation and if the number of individuals is finite, then one can show that if the overall allocation is Pareto-efficient, there is at least one ranking of the individuals such that each individual is no less free than the individuals of lower rank. There are thus, in particular, individuals such that all individuals are no less free than them. They are equally free among themselves. They are said to be the *least free* individuals. If there is only one least free individual in the considered efficient overall allocations, the criterion says that an efficient overall allocation is *not chosen if there exists another such allocation in which the least free individual is freer than the least free individual in the first allocation.* A notable property is that the

---

27. See Kolm 1991a.

individual who is least free in the allocation not chosen is better off or freer in the other allocation. This criterion can be extended (by a leximin) to the cases where there can be several least free individuals in each overall allocation.

More generally, this analysis extends to the "realistic" concepts, when individuals cannot necessarily have others' allocations (we noted the example of the allocation of jobs requiring capacities). The individuals' domains of choice for defining *"realistically" equally free and no less free* are the intersection of the notional ones considered in the above definitions and of the actual possibility set of each individual. Then one shows that an individual is realistically no less free than another if he either does not prefer the other's allocation to his own or could not have this other's allocation (instead of his own). One also shows that a number of individuals are realistically equally free if an only if each one is realistically no less free than the other. *"Realistically less free"* is "not realistically no less free", that is, the individual both can have the other's allocation and prefers it to his own. *"Realistically freer"* is realistically no less free and not realistically equally free; or, equivalently, realistically no less free while the other is realistically less free; or, again, the individual either does not prefer or cannot have the other's allocation, while the other can have the individual's allocation and prefers it to his own. Then the above properties and concepts for *efficient* overall allocations also hold with these "realistic" concepts: the ranking such that each individual is realistically no less free than individuals of lower ranks; the existence of a class of *realistically least free* individuals such that all others are realistically no less free than them; for allocations where this class contains only one individual, the elimination of allocations such that another allocation's realistically least free individual is realistically freer than the realistically least free individual of the allocation; the result that this realistically least free individual prefers the other allocation or is freer with it; the extension to the cases where there are several realistically least free individuals and to leximin.[28]

---

28. Varian (1976) considers the case of the allocation of bundles of goods—such that any individual can have any allocation—and implicitly a finite number of individuals. He points out the existence of an individual that "no other envies" in efficient allocations, and says this could be used for a "Rawlsian" maximin. This "no envy" does not

9.13 Other Criteria, the Egalitarian Equivalent

Egalitarian Equivalence

"Egalitarian equivalence" is *unanimous indifference to an equal alloca-tion* (which need not be possible, and an individual allocation of which need not be possible by itself). If an agent cares only for his own allocation, the (overall) allocation is egalitarian equivalent if each is indifferent between his allocation and the same individual allocation. This neat and simple criterion was proposed by Pazner and Schmeidler (1978)[29] for the allocation of private consumption goods to con-sumers, each consumer caring only for his own goods, with possible transformation of these goods into each other (production) and per-fectly divisible goods. These conditions, which will be assumed here, have been relaxed by further studies that consider concerns for others' bundles (envy in Kolm 1991c, 1993f, 1995a), public goods, etc. Let us denote as the "equal equivalent" the equal allocation which is un-animously indifferent to an "egalitarian equivalent" one. There exist (Pareto)-efficient egalitarian equivalent allocations; there even is one for each given set of proportions of the goods in the equal equivalent, as it is shown by a progressive increase of an equal allocation in these proportions, which increases all individuals' utilities until the Pareto frontier in utilities is reached—same reference—(the actual allocation that gives these utilities is a different one, and the obtained equal equivalent is in general impossible). If the total quantity of goods is given, one can take an equal equivalent proportional to it (same refer-ence). With possibilities of transformation of the goods, salient egali-tarian equivalent allocations are those where the total quantities are

---

describe envy (see section 9.11 above) but, rather, "no less free". Yet, it is not said how the comparison with other allocations is made (if we only want the least free individual to be better off, then the least free of *each* allocation can be better off in the other). Furthermore, it is neither pointed out that there can be several such individuals nor, therefore, indicated what should be done in this case. Finally, considering that the individuals can have different possibility sets (the "realistic" cases) can be very important.

29. In order to replace Equity when it cannot be efficient (although production, labor, and leisure do not per se impair efficiency given the individual specificity of leisure).

proportional to those of the equal equivalent,[30] where the ratio of the equal equivalent to a possible proportional vector of the goods is the lowest (this can describe the "least impossible" or "more realistic" equal equivalent) or the highest, where the value (at efficiency prices) of the equal equivalent is the lowest or the highest, where the ratio or the difference between this value and that of the actual goods is the highest or the lowest, and so on. However, our first concern should be the meaning and reason of this principle.

An allocation can be egalitarian equivalent with one individual having more of all goods than another individual. Then any individual, with any preference, prefers the allocation of the former to that of the latter. This is unfortunate if equality in allocation is a valuable ideal, and this is certainly the case for the egalitarian equivalent principle, since it refers to an equal allocation that is equivalent to the actual one for everybody. This possible dominance is, for instance, banned by income equality, by Equity, and by super-equity (which implies Equity).

This possibility leads one to wonder about the rationale of egalitarian equivalence: What are its reason, its morals, its justice, its end values? This criterion rests on two axioms: (a) Equality of bundles of consumption goods is just; (b) indifference for individuals entails indifference for the moral judgment, that is, that which matters is only the levels of "welfare" of the individuals. Hence the final variables that concern the ethical evaluation are individuals' welfare, yet equality in consumption goods is just. Now, finding just this equal allocation of consumption goods implies, given the items and variables considered, that these individual allocations are considered to be the end values for justice (see chapter 2). This in turn implies that individuals' consumptive capacities are seen as irrelevant for justice. But these capacities define the maintenance of individuals' welfare in the comparison between the allocation and the equal allocation. And this corresponds to the fact that the end values are individuals' welfares, and indeed it implies such an ethic. A priori this constitues an inconsistency, which

---

30. See Kolm 1993e where *equitable equivalence* (unanimous indifference to an equitable allocation) is also considered and analyzed (also independently studied by Thomson).

is the cause of the noted problem. However, we will notice that the principle's end values cannot be welfare in the end, and there can also be mixed criteria.

Note, indeed, that the criterion, though it appraises an individual's situation only by this individual's welfare level, does not aim at welfare justice which implies an ideal equality in welfares. An individual who has lower satisfaction capacities than another receives no compensation for this handicap. In this respect, what egalitarian equivalence does is to enact the inequalities in satisfaction capacities that exist for the equal equivalent allocation.

Hence egalitarian equivalence is certainly to be considered as having equality in allocation as ideal, and as being a corresponding second best criterion permitting efficiency. Its problem then is that the equal equivalent can a priori be anything. Hence the satisfaction or violation of the criterion depends on preferences of the individuals in domains that may be far away from any actual relevance. The equivalent overall equal allocation may be impossible. Each of its individual allocations may be impossible by itself because of the resources, of the characteristics of each individual, or of available social processes. A change in these irrelevant preferences can make the actual allocation pass or fail the test of this criterion. Indeed the individuals may not even have clear views and preferences in these domains. They are not required to as is the case in domains where they have to choose. Nor are they induced to as when they compare their allocations with others'. Therefore the criterion demands a priori *a large amount of information* some of which may be *meaningless*, and it is extremely dependent on *individuals' preferences on irrelevant alternatives* (contrary, for example, to a classical requirement of Social Choice Theory; see chapter 15). The other principles that have been considered have altogether different properties. In Equity, in its related criteria, in superequity, in free choice or exchange from equal allocations, resources, incomes or domains, and so on, preferences are for actual choices, or for comparison with or between actual individual allocations (possibly others' allocations that one can have for the "realistic" criteria), or for averages of actual individual allocations which are in a neighboring domain. Moreover these preferences often manifest freedom of choice rather than welfare (for instance, choice or exchange from equality of certain items, choice in equal domains, and so on).

The structure of egalitarian equivalence is a kind of superimposition (application of one criterion from the outcome of another). It can thus be compared to free exchange from equal allocation considered previously. Free exchange from equal allocation implies unanimous preference to an actual equal allocation. Egalitarian equivalence is individuals' indifference to an equal allocation that can be impossible. Yet the formal similarity conceals deep differences. Free exchange from equality is justified by freedom of exchange rather than by unanimous preference. It is a superimposition of two interindividual equalities of different means (the second is a process-freedom). On the contrary, the second step of egalitarian equivalence is an equality of welfare (indifference) for each individual between two states (and the equal allocation of the first step need not be possible). Other free choices, actions, or exchanges with various initial equalities of allocations or of domains of choice are also superimpositions of criteria that are interindividual equalities of different means, hence that belong to the same category.

Other Principles and Criteria

Finally, a number of other specific principles or criteria of justice have been proposed, as well as properties for these criteria and relations among these properties and among criteria. Most of the author's works in social and economic ethics and in public economics contain a number of such principles, properties, and theorems concerning their logical relations (see the references). Others appear in the literature. The essential point to be made here is that each of these properties, principles, or criteria must have its relevance, importance, deep meaning and scope of validity evaluated and justified by an analysis of "philosophical" nature. The basic maxim of such studies should be "no axiomatics without hermeneutics" or, logically, "hermeneutics should precede axiomatics" and formal analysis. Reliance on a shallow intuitionistic impression of interest or meaningfulness of a property can be utterly midleading. Examples of such cases have been shown and will be shown (chapters 12, 13, 14, and 15). This analysis for all possible criteria and properties is not included here but, in a number of cases, the arguments are the same as those presented here for principles that are explicitly analyzed.

Among the main general issues that should be raised for each principle or criterion are those that concern its relation to the general theory
of justice and to equality (see chapter 2). In what sense is this criterion
justice? Is it direct or indirect justice? What are the end values? What
are the equalizands? Is it a simple or a mixed or complex criterion? In
the latter case, what are the component principles and how are they
associated? Is it a first-best or a second-best criterion? And so on.

Another important issue concerns the justification of the consideration of *counterfactuals*, that is, items that do not exist but may influence what exists, for instance, in the problems at hand, in influencing
the choice of criteria. These counterfactuals can be, for example, other
possibility sets, resources, individuals' preferences, or populations than
the actual ones. Counterfactuals can be used to define properties of the
criterion, notably in comparing the outcomes with various alternative
actualizations of the data, some or all of which are counterfactuals.
This question is discussed in this book *a propos* of the Theory of Social
Choice (chapter 15 below),[31] and the reasonings presented there can
be applied to other uses of counterfactuals.

A few excellent recent books present criteria of justice and their
properties, in being both surveys with a certain scope and didactic in
presentation. The contents of these books have its logical place here,
and they are of course recommended. These books include William
Thomson's *The Theory of Fair Allocations* and the books by Hervé
Moulin quoted in reference (see also the references mentioned in
chapter 1).

---

31. The fullest analysis is in Kolm 1992a (see also 1995b).

IV INEQUALITIES, NEEDS, AND MISERY

10 Pure Distributive Justice: Comparing and Measuring Unjust Inequalities

10.1 A General Overview of the Topic

When the prima facie equality required by the rationality of justice (see chapter 2) is set aside because this equality is not possible or because other aims or values are also relevant, one generally has to evaluate and compare situations of inequality of the considered individualized values with regard to social ethics, that is, to the imperfect justice or the injustice of their pattern. This comparison of the injustice of inequalities that are unjustified per se requires new reasons. The structural aspects of these reasons constitute *pure comparative justice* (they are twice comparative, across individualized values and across states) and also *pure distributive justice*, notably when the distribution is not only statistical but also actual concerning scarce resources or their benefits. The possible properties of these judgments depend on the structural nature of the considered values. The problem and its history have been considered when these values are domains of liberty and ordinal satisfactions.[1] In the very important cases where these values are quantities (for instance, incomes or wealths) or bundles of quantities, the logical meaningfulness of the operations of multiplication by numbers and of addition entails a vast array of economically and ethically meaningful properties. *This chapter proposes the simplest complete presentation of the fundamental ideas, concepts, properties and results of this question of quantitative inequalities.*

The essentials of the modern analysis of the justice or injustice of quantitative inequalities was presented in a series of papers in the 1950s and early 1960s, whose concepts and results were gathered in the 1966 essay *The Optimal Production of Social Justice* (Kolm 1966a, sections 6 and 7) and in a book published the same year (Kolm 1966b).[2]

---

1. Chapter 7, section 7.2, and chapter 9, section 9.9, for liberty, and chapter 7, section 7.3, for ordinal satisfaction or happiness (see Kolm 1971, 1991a, 1992d, 1993e).

2. The book applies the results to choices in uncertainty, notably the concepts and properties of what was later called second-order stochastic dominance. These basic concepts and results, applied to the comparison and measures of inequality, were presented in numerous seminars and conferences in the late 1950s and early 1960s. They were applied to the comparison and measure of poverty in African countries in the late 1950s (including comparison and measure of multidimensional underdevelopment). Questionnaires concerning these properties of inequality comparison and measures were used in the early 1960s, notably concerning the perception of the different

A number of these concepts and results have been often repeated since. However, it is essential not to lose sight of the meaning of the concepts. These fundamental concepts and properties will be recalled below in the simplest possible way, but their basic meaning and their scope of validity will be emphasized when these issues are relevant. The present section offers an overview of ideas that will be presented more in detail in further sections.

The Example of Progressive Transfers and Returns in Proximity

One of the simplest (and also most central) examples concerns the transfer of one dollar (say) from a person to a poorer one when nothing relevant justifies the difference in their incomes. At all times of history, in all societies of all sizes, you can meet more or less frequently the view that such a transfer is *just* and *good* and that it should be done. This can manifest charity, solidarity, a sense of justice, and notably a certain application of the rational ideal of equal treatment of equals which, however, is either segmented and myopic or justified as it will be explained below. Hence, it would be rather ludicrous to attribute such a view to a particular person (should it be Christ, Robin Hood, or a leveler?). By contrast, the assertion that such a transfer *diminishes inequality* in society constitutes a strong, particular, and specific assumption proposed by a few scholars (among whom Pigou and Dalton). Indeed this transfer certainly diminishes the inequality within the considered pair of incomes. More generally, the inequality between two incomes decreases according to any rational account if the former interval strictly includes the new one and the order is preserved (see section 10.2). But, then, the transfer also augments the pairwise inequalities between the decreasing income and higher fixed

---

but mathematically equivalent properties. The essay *The Optimal Production of Social Justice* was prepared for the International Economic Association conference on Public Economics held in Biarritz in 1966, where it was presented, distributed, and discussed (all in English; the list of participants at this conference is available in both editions of the proceedings). These results contained a number of new mathematical properties (the concentration curve dominance equivalences is one of them), yet mathematical interest was aroused by Ostrowski's proof of the equivalence between Schur concavity and symmetrical rectifiance (1952), by Berge's synthesis (published in book in 1959 in French), and by the classic results of Birkhoff, Karamata, Schur, and Hardy-Littlewood-Pólya (the only early mathematical work in English—the others used French, German, and Spanish).

incomes and between the increasing income and lower fixed incomes. The issues behind this difference can be shown by the following story.

Say you meet a beggar. You are going to hand out a coin to him. It is indeed just that you help out someone clearly poorer than you— thus reducing the inequality between both of you. Yet you stop short of dropping the coin, arguing: "but this would increase the unjust inequality between me and my wealthy friend Mr. A." "You have four good reasons to drop this coin anyway," the beggar supposedly replies. "First, why care about inequality? I am hungry and you are not, that is all. Second, why care about Mr. A? This is an affair between you and me. Mr. A's wealth does not change. He is unconcerned and irrelevant. Then you should give me the coin both because I need it more than you do and because it does not seem just that I am so much poorer than you. Third, your alm will also diminish the unfair inequality between Mr. A and myself. Hence two pairwise inequalities will decrease while only one will increase. Fourth, the gap between Mr. A's wealth and mine will decrease by exactly the same amount as the increase in the gap between Mr. A's wealth and yours. This decrease thus exactly compensates this increase. It indeed overcompensates it because the decrease is in the larger, unbearable gap and inequality, while the increase is in the smaller gap and inequality which is still rather acceptable. You could of course object that the last point might go the other way, since a variation in a larger gap and inequality may be less important than the same variation in a smaller gap. But my first two reasons should suffice for the following reason. I am sure you agree that it is preferable that you keep this coin rather than throw it away into the river, although this latter act would reduce the inequality between us. Indeed, being benevolent, you are a moral and hence nonenvious person, and therefore you would not approve the destruction of Mr. A's property for the mere sake of diminishing two inequalities. This means that you consider that welfare has priority over inequalities, or that people whose income does not change should be disregarded in the judgment. But these are precisely the bases of the first two arguments. Consistency requires that you apply them to the alm also, hence disregarding either inequalities or Mr. A, which leads to the same final conclusion. Hence, in the end, your initial intention to give me the coin is doubtlessly rational and should certainly be carried out. Thank you."

Note that the first argument ("priority of welfare over inequality") just gets rid of the inequality issue, although the difference in welfare it emphasizes is intrinsically linked to inequality. The second argument (the "principle of independence of irrelevant individuals") also gets rid of inequality issues as a result of discarding the fixed terms of inequalities, but this leaves, as possibly relevant, the pairwise inequality between the two changing incomes. Then the transfer can be recommended for a reason of comparative welfare between these directly concerned persons, as in the preceding case, but it can also be recommended because it unambiguously diminishes the only possibly relevant inequality, that between the two affected incomes. With this latter reason the transfer is justified purely as decreasing inequality. Yet these reasons rest on discarding inequalities, either directly or through discarding "irrelevant" individuals, in opposition to the other two reasons, the compensations in numbers of varying pairwise inequalities or in the sizes of gap variations, which focus on all the variations in pairwise inequalities. Note that these various reasons suggest different measures. The compensation in gaps speaks of a Gini index. The over or undercompensations in gaps are satisfied by Schur-convex or Schur-concave (see below) functions of the gaps. The first two reasons can be satisfied by additively separable social welfare evaluations (hence a kind of utilitarian form).

We have noted that the last argument (overcompensation in gap variations) can turn the other way around and be an undercompensation. This happens when there is a decreasing (marginal) cost of gaps, that is, "increasing returns in proximity." This provides reasons why transfers from a richer to a poorer of no more than half the difference in incomes—called *progressive transfers*—might increase overall inequality with certain perfectly legitimate conceptions. The extreme form of this structure consists in distinguishing only between strict equality, on the one hand, and nonequality, on the other (at least for pairs). Then, in the three-person society with income distribution (4, 4, 1), a progressive transfer of 1 from the second individual to the third increases inequality, since the new distribution (4, 3, 2) contains no equal pair while the initial one contained one such equality. For instance, a measure of inequality that would be the number or the proportion of unequal pairs would decrease as a result of this transfer. With this proportion as measure, inequality decreases when identical populations are joined together. Increasing returns in proximity favors clusters as causes of low inequality. Increasing returns in proximity is also implicitly quite common in sociological conceptions that focus on groups with a certain homogeneity rather than on individuals.

For instance, well-traveled observers usually say that Australia is a much more egalitarian society than France. But the Australian Lorenz curve of income distribution is everywhere below the French one.[3] And one can pass from a distribution with a lower Lorenz curve to one with a higher by a sequence of progressive transfers (average incomes being similar; see details in theorems 1 to 6 in Kolm 1966a). Hence the common view opposes the idea that progressive transfers diminish inequality. And if progressive transfers attenuate injustice, Australia can be both more equal and less just. What happens, of course, is the conspicuousness of the large, characteristic, and rather equal Australian middle class (while the poor most ancient and most recent populations and the international richest may not even be thought of as "Australians" at first glance, at least they are not "typical Australians").

Of course a sequence of progressive transfers that exhausts all the possibilities of such transfers ends up in complete equality. But this does not imply that there is a continuous decrease in inequality along the process. One can also certainly say that a progressive transfer diminishes inequality if it is between the two extreme incomes and the ranking of the incomes is not altered (no pairwise inequality increases) —at least it does not augment inequality even in the qualitative case where only strict equalizations are counted as progress in equality. A progressive transfer in a two-person population is a particular case. These are the only three cases where single or sequential progressive transfers unambiguously diminish inequality (given the preceding qualification).

A sequence of progressive transfers constitutes one of a dozen of equivalent properties which are separately meaningful and whose meanings should thus be added to appraise the effect on inequality or on injustice (Kolm 1966a, b). These properties will be recalled below. Let us just note here that they imply concentration curves, Lorenz

---

3. Excluding foreigners.

curves, evaluation functions, sum of functions of each income, "averages," "mixtures," "averagings", "dispatchings," linear transformations, etc. To these properties are added innumerable effects of sociological and psychological nature (envy, class structure, distinction and conformity, and so on).

The only transformation that always diminishes inequality is a complete equalization of the same fraction of all incomes (a "concentration"—see below). A progressive transfer amounts to such an operation restricted to a pair of incomes.

The Example of Proportional and Additive Covariations

It is often thought that the mutiplication of all incomes by the same number does not change inequality. Then inequality is what the natural sciences call an *intensive* property (see Kolm 1966a). But consider a two-person society with incomes 0 and 1. Multiply both by the same number 10. The incomes become 0 and 10. I have met nobody who says that inequality has not changed. Indeed everybody thinks that inequality has increased, and I have met only two kinds of people: those who say that it has increased by 9 and those who say that it has been multiplied by 10. Both expressions imply that inequality is measured by the difference between the incomes. Such a measure does not change if all incomes are added the same amount. But add now the amount 9 to each of the initial incomes 0 and 1. The incomes become 9 and 10. And many people say that inequality is now lower than it was initially, although thoughtful people feel ill at ease with this answer and say that it depends on which inequality one considers: absolute inequality has not changed, while relative inequality has been brought down to manageable size (same reference). Practically everybody makes this distinction when asked by how much the inequality has decreased, and more people make it when they have previously been submitted to the former experiment (the multiplication by 10).

Of course zero is a particular level, but the result should not change if it were replaced by a sufficiently small number, say 0.01, so that the incomes 0.01 and 1 become 0.1 and 10 in one case and 9.01 and 10 in the other. At any rate we are a priori particularly interested in inequality for particularly unequal incomes, and, possibly, for particularly low lower incomes (when incomes tend to be similar and not very small, the difference between equal multiplication and equal addition vanishes).

Consider also that New York City, with its very rich and its very poor, strikes one as a more unequal society than Burkina Faso, where all incomes are crushed down toward the bottom. Yet both places have the same Lorenz curve, the same proportional distribution, just with a multiplicative factor of about fifty as the difference. In general, a distribution that is substantially proportionally crushed down, notably if it contains a fair share of very low levels, is seen as becoming more equal in its general new poverty; and a substantial proportional blowing up of all incomes, which also blows up all income differences, commonly appears as increasing inequality (especially if there are very low incomes which do not gain many dollars in the operation). Both direct and statistical observations elicit such views. However, if people are then explicitly shown that the distributions are proportional, they commonly conclude that relative inequality remains unchanged but wonder whether this is the presently appropriate concept.

The dilemma revealed by the experiments admits of two kinds of solution: the *synthetic* solution and the *compromise intermediate* solution. Let us denote as *"equal-invariant"* a function of the incomes that is invariant when all incomes vary by the same amount. Experiments first show the necessity of distinguishing both the *relative* and the *absolute* forms of a measure of inequality, where relative is absolute divided by average income. An intensive measure has to be a relative form, since if it were an absolute form the relative form would decrease under an equiproportional increase in all incomes, an unlikely property of inequality. Similarly, an equal-invariant measure has to be an absolute form since, if it were a relative form, the absolute form would increase under an equal increase in all incomes, an unlikely property of inequality.

The synthetic solution says that one can have both intensive relative inequality and equal-invariant absolute inequality. The family of measures that satisfy this property includes the Gini index, standard deviation, etc. (the absolute and relative measures are a function homogeneous of degree one of respectively the absolute and relative differences between the incomes and the average; see Kolm 1966a, b).

The compromise intermediate solutions force the mind to be less refined and to compromise between its various rationales, logic and "intuitions." It proposes, for instance, that the distribution (3, 10) is as unequal as the distribution (0, 1). The variations of inequality with equal and proportional increases in incomes are discussed in Kolm

1966a (with reference to views of classical scholars such as Cannan, Loria, Taussig, Tawney, and Dalton), with a particular interest in the compromise measures that increase when all incomes increase in the same proportion and decrease when they all increase by the same amount. The cases of invariance to scale or to equal variations are extreme cases of a spectrum of families of solutions. The simplest such families apply properties of proportional covariations to "augmented incomes," that is, incomes all augmented by the same constant: the two polar cases are obtained when this constant is zero and tends to infinity, respectively. This, however, gives two families according as the properties of proportional covariations are the effects on the relative or on the absolute forms of inequality injustice, and these cases have different other notable properties (Kolm 1966b and 1976a, b; see below).[4]

Independence

We have seen that the evaluation of a change of one income, or of a transfer between two incomes, may not be affected by the levels of the other, unchanging incomes. If this is a basic property rather than a consequence of the other noted reasons, then it has no reason not to apply to other changes of the pair of incomes, and indeed to any set of changing incomes, the others remaining constant (one shows that if it holds for pairs, it holds for larger groups, and that it also suffices that it holds for larger groups for incomes with the same sum). This property of "independence of irrelevant individuals," or, for short, "independence," is not a necessary property of evaluations, yet it is a meaningful and significant property, at least worthy of consideration. If the evaluation is represented by a function that takes higher values for better distributions, a known mathematical property is that this independence is equivalent to the fact that a specification of this evaluation function is a sum of functions of one income each, that is, this specification is "additively separated" and the ordinal evaluation function is "additively separable."[5]

---

4. For instance, with one of these concepts, the new incomes are $x_i' = \lambda \cdot (x_i + k) - k$, where the x_i are the initial incomes. The example is for $k = 0, 5$ (the average income suggested in Kolm 1976a) and $\lambda = 7$.

5. See the discussion and the references in Kolm 1966a, section 6.

Basic Properties

Progressive transfers are equivalent to a dozen properties which, although they are not as meaningful as such a transfer, add their own meaning to the concept (and can themselves be given meaning by these equivalences). These equivalences were presented in Kolm 1966a (see also 1966b and a number of earlier papers) which also showed the corresponding measures of injustice, justice, inequality (and risk). This subsection recalls a sample of these results, and sections 10.5 and 10.6 will provide a more complete (though summarized) presentation. Most of these results constituted new mathematical properties, but the most important thing is the meanings that were provided to these concepts, structures, and relations.

Since equality is the rational ideal when the individuals are not relevantly distinguished among themselves (otherwise than by their incomes), this nondistinction or "impartiality" holds for most of these properties, and it is a priori presently assumed (in a few instances this is a conclusion).

Elementary statistics textbooks call *concentration curve* the sum of the m lowest incomes as a function of m (or of m/n if n is the total number of individuals). The Lorenz curve is the curve of these numbers divided by the total sum, as a function of m/n.[6] A curve is said to be higher than another (or above it) when it is somewhere higher (above) and nowhere lower (below), and similarly for lower and below. A "strong progressive transfer" is a transfer from a richer individual to a poorer of no more than the difference in their incomes (this includes transferring the difference, that is, permuting the incomes).

The three following properties are equivalent (Kolm 1966a, section 7, theorems 4, 5, 6, 8, and 9)[7]:

- A distribution has a higher concentration curve than another.
- It can be obtained from it by a sequence of progressive transfers,

---

6. The concentration curve (an old and classical concept and term) was bizarrely re-labeled the "augmented Lorenz curve" or the "generalized Lorenz curve" by the article and literature that repeated without reference and seventeen years later parts of theorems 4, 5, 6, and 9 of Kolm 1966a (section 7).

7. All the cases of strict and weak forms were considered, along with other different equivalent properties.

increases and permutations in incomes (or of strong progressive transfers and increases in incomes).

• It gives a higher sum of the values taken by any concave increasing function for each income.

Therefore, for distributions with the same total sum, the three following properties are equivalent (idem, theorems 1, 2, and 3):

• A distribution has a higher Lorenz curve than another.

• It can be obtained from it by a sequence of progressive transfers and permutations in incomes (or of strong progressive transfers).

• It gives a higher sum of the values taken by any concave (or concave increasing) function for each income.[8]

These latter relations are also equivalent to each of several transformations whose definition will be recalled below, and which are averages of permuted distributions, "mixtures" or "slice reshuffling," sum-preserving averaging, equality-preserving dispatching, both averaging and dispatching, and linear or affine transformations that preserve both the sum and equality. These transformations (defined on the relevant domains) have different empirical meanings, they preserve total income, and as the concentration or Lorenz curve dominance in this case, they neither diminish the lowest income nor augment the highest income (each extreme may correspond to different individuals in the two distributions), and they preserve an equality in all incomes. Each of these transformations plus income increases provides an equivalence with a higher concentration curve.

The increase in the sum of the values of a concave function of income can be replaced, for the corresponding equivalent property, by the increase in more general functions of the set of incomes.[9] The concavities of these functions relate to the variation in inequalities. The possibility of the additive form is highly significant, since it amounts to the property of independence (see above). This sum pro-

---

8. This particular constant-sum case amounts to a theorem of Hardy, Littlewood, and Pólya, but the noted theorems of Kolm 1966a added a number of qualifications, distinction, and variants, and other equivalent, though very different, properties.

9. Schur-concave and symmetrical concave or quasi-concave functions (Kolm, 1966a, section 7, theorems 1 to 6).

vides a utilitarianlike form (see chapter 15), which can be interpreted as a sum of evaluations of individuals' welfares (the function of income whose values are added will be increasing, and its concavity represents satiation or decreasing marginal utility): this can constitute the welfare justification of the justice of progressive transfers and of independent income increases.[10]

A measure of inequality is diminished by progressive transfers ("rectifiance") and is symmetrical ("impartiality") if and only if it is Schur-convex. From the above, a higher Lorenz or concentration curve for distributions of same total amount entails a decrease in such measures. If such a measure is, furthermore, intensive, a higher Lorenz curve entails a lower inequality even for distributions of different total amounts, since each distribution is as unequal as the distribution obtained by dividing each income by the total sum.

But the consideration of evaluation functions in general led to the definition of specific measures of the injustice of inequalities.

The *equal equivalent income* of a distribution was then defined as the individual income which, if everybody had it, would constitute an equal distribution as good as the considered distribution (Kolm 1966a, section 6). An equal distribution's equal equivalent income is equal to its average income and to the individual incomes. Hence absolute and relative excesses of the average over the equal equivalent are absolute and relative measures of the injustice of the distribution's inequality, and hence the ratio of equal equivalent to average constitues a measure of the complementary relative justice. With an additively separable evaluation function (from independence of irrelevant individuals), the positivity of these measures of inequality injustice for unequal distributions implies both impartiality and an appreciation of progressive transfers (because it implies that the added functions of individuals' incomes are the same[11] and are concave).

An intensive (invariant to scale) relative measure, and an equal-invariant absolute measure, were shown to amount, for an additively separable evaluation function (independence), to added individual

---

10. Since the added functions are the same, they cannot represent the individuals' different capacities to enjoy, and at any rate adding individuals' utilities is generally meaningless (see chapter 15).

11. Up to arbitrary additive constants.

evaluation functions that are respectively power or logarithmic, or exponential (up to a linear-affine transformation). There resulted the corresponding measures (Kolm 1966a, b).

Hence one cannot have jointly both these covariational invariances and an additively separable evaluation function, that is, independence. These three properties can only hold by pairs. In particular, independence precludes the synthesis of these polar covariational invariances noted above. But independence is consistent with compromise intermediate measures of inequality injustice, notably of the augmented-income types (Kolm 1966a, b, 1976a, b).

Compromise measures of inequality injustice in general (that increase with proportional increases and decrease with equal increases) can be *intermediate* between the invariances to proportional and to equal variations that they reach as particular cases. But we have seen that the two polar cases are respectively a relative and an absolute measure. Hence intermediate measures have to consider both their absolute and their relative forms, or be hybrids passing from one form to the other. In the latter case the measure loses the meaningful relation with the evaluation function and with meaningful properties it may embody, such as independence. This applies in particular to augmented-income families of measures (same references, and see section 10.5 below).

The effects on all measures of variations and aggregations of populations, and of general additions, subtractions, variations and averagings of distributions, were shown in Kolm 1966a (see also 1966b for variations in distributions).

The 1966a work also introduced the general absolute and relative marginal inequalities and injustices, and it showed their particular form with an independent evaluation (see below). With this independence, the absolute marginal measure is inversely proportional to the characteristic ratio of the first derivative of the individual evaluation function to the second, which is a linear (affine) function for the general evaluation-consistent intermediate case recalled above, reducing to a proportional function and to a constant for the polar cases of invariances to scale and to equal additions (same references).

Later work added that progressive transfers might reduce injustice or inequality more if they take place between lower incomes, the related properties of dominance of the integral functions of successive orders, and the corresponding properties of the evaluation functions (Kolm 1974b, summarized in 1976a, b).

The injustice in the distribution of income and wealth consitutes a major issue in the views of social justice. Yet all the discussions of this chapter can be applied to the distribution of the quantities of any good, and the term "income" is used here as illustration and because it is an important case. However, previous chapters have emphasized that to take incomes (or wealths) as end values of justice—which would justify the justice of their ideal equality and of the corresponding impartiality—should be justified. In a welfarist view, the ideal equalizands are individuals' satisfactions or utilities (see chapter 7, section 7.3). If individuals' tastes or preferences are irrelevant for justice, the end values become the bundles of consumption goods. The end values can also be or include other goods, when the justiciables are deemed accountable for what they do with them (see chapter 9). The consideration of income adds a relevance of prices and hence should be particularly vindicated (see chapter 6). Therefore the basic case for the consideration of the justice of quantitative inequalities is that of multidimensional inequalities. This is also the general case since it includes the unidimensional case as a particular instance. However, the theory of multidimensional inequalities uses the concepts and results of the unidimensional case. Multidimensional quantitative inequalities and their injustice have been analyzed in Kolm 1973b, 1975b, 1977a in considering the three basic cases of more equal or just independently for each good, similarly for all types of quantities, and for incomes computed with any prices—which constitutes an intermediate case. Atkinson and Bourguignon (1984), Maasoumi (1986), Mosler (1995), and others provided interesting contributions of various types. The multidimensional ideal equality in consumption goods is generally Pareto-inefficient, and the requirement of efficiency is bound to provide the justification for the consideration of income or wealth, as with the conditions of efficient super-equity which is based on a concept of comparison of multidimensional inequalities (see chapter 6).

Issues and Summary

The general problem posed is very simple, though its analysis mobilizes a number of properties that can be rather elaborate on the grounds of logic, mathematics, psychology, ethics, or sociology. It consists in the consideration of the way in which the structure of a distribution influences its value, its justice or injustice, or its inequality relevant for justice or for certain related sociological issues. These moral judgments on mathematical properties reveal the mathematical structure of moral judgments, which constitues the essential conclusion.

The judgment may only order distributions, or it may provide quantitative measures. The issues are comparison of distributions, effects of transformations, comparisons of transformations or of comparisons. Certain of these properties do not depend on the nature of the items, such as "impartiality," the number of changing individual situations, "benevolence" (approval of an individual improvement if nobody loses), "independence of irrelevant individuals," the use of evaluation functions, the size of populations, the distribution of homogeneous subclasses, and aggregations or divisions of populations. But other properties rely on the fact that the items are quantities, and hence on their properties of addition and of multiplication by scalars. These comparisons can be classified according to a number of criteria, such as the number of incomes that change (from one to all), the maintenance or variation of the total sum, the fact that there is a single change or a sequence of changes, the fact that the populations are the same one, different ones, or partially the same, and the comparison of their size. Then the specifics of the comparison or change define the issue.

A number of issues refer to very practical questions such as the effects on justice of growth and slumps, of savings, of taxation, of redistributions of various types, of the addition of new agents or of the disparition of former ones, of the scope of the considered population, of the addition of incomes of various types, and so on. But the answers rest on properties defined for more specific and simple variations.

The foregoing examples have pointed out a number of these elementary issues. For instance, is an increase in one income alone, or any increase in incomes, a good thing given that it may create or augment unjust inequalities? If it is good, is a given increase the better when applied to lower incomes? Hence, is it good to transfer a dollar from a richer to a poorer, as has been proposed at all times and places (charity, redistributive justice, etc.), given that it may create or increase other inequalities? If such a progressive transfer is good, is it the better the lower both incomes are (with the same difference or ratio)?

Relatedly, does a Lorenz curve represent more equality when it is higher or when it has flatter parts?

Relatedly again, when an income becomes closer to another one by one dollar, is the decrease in their inequality or in its injustice higher when they are already close to each other or when they are more distant? Does a progressive transfer of a given amount diminish more inequality or injustice when the two incomes are closer or when they are farther apart?

More generally, inequality certainly decreases when the same fraction of all incomes is equally redistributed. But does it decrease by more or by less than this fraction?

Is not the inequality or the injustice of a distribution expanded by an increase of all incomes in the same proportion, which blows up all the differences or gaps? Are not inequality and injustice multiplied by the piling up of identical unequal and unjust distributions (each individual having the same income in each distribution)? Are they not reduced, on the contrary, by an equiproportional shrinking of all incomes and hence of the gaps between them? Is not, for instance, half the distribution also half unequal (inequality would then be what the natural sciences call an "extensive" property)? Does, in general, the inequality or injustice change when all incomes vary in the same proportion? If it did not, does this also hold when certain incomes are zero (so they do not actually change) or small? Is inequality or its injustice affected by the neutral addition of the same amount to all incomes, which leaves the differences or gaps invariant and adds an equal distribution? If it were not, does this also hold when incomes are all diminished by the level of the lowest income, which then becomes zero?

Can equal addition maintain an "absolute" inequality or injustice that is per person or total, whereas proportional variations maintain an inequality or injustice that is relative or "per dollar"? Or should each of these two variations either augment or diminish inequality or injustice? Can in particular inequality or injustice be both augmented by a proportional increase and diminished by an equal increase? How do these properties of joint income increases or decreases interfere with the property of independence of irrelevant individuals of the overall evaluation?

Does the replacement of each income by a weighted average of the initial incomes diminish the inequality? How does the inequality of a sum of distributions depend on the inequalities of these distributions? The same question can be asked for the average distribution. How is the inequality diminished, if it is, when the gaps between each income and the mean income are halved, or diminished in any given proportion (this amounts to the equal redistribution of the same fraction of all incomes described earlier)? How do the variations in inequality compare when the same distribution is successively added to an original one with different proportions? How does the variation of income inequality depend on the inequality in the variations of incomes or in their growth rates (or how does the variation in wealth inequality depend on the inequality in savings)? How does post-tax income inequality relate to the inequalities in pre-tax incomes and in taxes? Does a progressive income tax diminish income inequality?

How does the inequality in an aggregation of populations relate to the inequalities in its subpopulations (such as the overall inequality in the US and the inequalities within states): Is it some average, or some sum, or something higher because intergroup inequalities are now added? Does then the aggregation of identical populations maintain inequality, or does it lower it because there are more people with equal incomes in number or in proportion, or does it augment it because there are several of the initial inequalities?

Should the comparison when only a subset of incomes change depend on the other, unchanged incomes? Does a reassignment (permutation) of the incomes among individuals affect the evaluation (this amounts to taking his income from an individual and giving him another's income)? The corresponding property of neutrality, "impartiality", is to be set aside because it is only a question of the evaluated items exhausting the relevant individualized variables, plus the same necessity from rationality as that requiring equality (see chapter 2).

The rest of this chapter constitutes the simplest complete presentation of the essential concepts and logical properties of the topic, along with the explanation and evaluation of these concepts and properties. It thus amounts to the simple presentation and explanation of the central ideas, propositions, and theorems of sections 6 and 7 of *The Optimal Production of Social Justice*, plus a number of further discussions and examples.

Section 10.2 considers the possible justifications of the properties of *benevolence* and *rectifiance* which respectively approve of an increase in one income and of a progressive transfer even though they may augment pairwise inequalities. Rectificance can be justified by about a dozen logical reasons, which also provide grounds for denying it. An endless number of further reasons of psychological or sociological nature support or oppose the property. Benevolence is also approved or denied by several reasons with, however, most commonly a final positive judgment. The crucial basic concepts are independence of irrelevant individuals, decreasing or increasing returns in proximity, and priority of welfare over equality.

Section 10.3 considers the invariances under proportional or equal variations in all incomes, and the synthetic and intermediate cases.

Section 10.4 focuses on the effects of "concentrations" (to the mean), that is, of equal redistributions of the same fraction of all incomes.

Section 10.5 considers the evaluation function, the derived measures of inequality injustice, their form corresponding to the various properties (benevolence, rectifiance, independence, intensive and equal-invariant justices and the synthetic and intermediate cases, and the marginal inequality injustices), the relation with preference for higher concentration curve ("isophily") or Lorenz curve ("constant-sum isophily") without and with intensive justice. The effects, on inequalities, of additions, concentrations, and sequential equal variations of the income distribution will be briefly summarized.

Section 10.6 recalls the equivalence of a sequence of equalizing transfers, or of Lorenz curve dominance, with the meaningful transformations of sum-maintaining averaging, equality-maintaining dispaching, both averaging and dispaching, sum- and equality-maintaining linear or affine transformations, mixtures, and averages. It then recalls the "principle of diminishing transfers" and the concept of rectifiances of higher degrees. This section finally recalls and discusses the effects of aggregation and separation of population on inequality.

Finally, section 10.7 recalls the basic concepts of the comparison of multidimensional inequalities.

10.2   Benevolence and Rectifiance

Basic Properties: Impartiality, Benevolence, and Rectifiance

Impartiality
Only a very small part of the ethical logic of inequality is the direct extension of the logic of equality—this part constitutes, however, an

essential property. This property is that of symmetry in the sense of permutability: if the evaluated variables relative to several justiciables encompass all that which relevantly differentiates these justiciables, then permuting these variables among these justiciables yields ethically undifferentiable situations. This is a logical necessity, but one that rests on the ethical choice of the considered relevance. This property of "impartiality" just means that other possible differences among the justiciables do not influence the judgment.

Variations and Transfers: Benevolence and Rectifiance

The ethical judgments considered here are concerned with the comparison of patterns of distributions (and not with the way in which they are arrived at), a position which can be called "consequentialism" in this particular sense of the term. This position in particular enables one to assimilate transformations and comparisons of the extreme states, and to obtain judgments on the effects of sequences of transformations from judgments on each of these component transformations with an assumption of transitivity of the evaluation.

We begin by considering the case where an individual's allocation is *one quantity* of the same good for all, which we call his *income*.

If a number of incomes change, this has an effect on the individuals' welfare, or on the means for it, which we call "welfare effect" (the name "income effect" would elicit confusion with another classical topic), and an effect on the inequalities among sets of incomes (from pairs to the overall distribution), called the "inequality effect(s)."[12]

The inequality *between two incomes* (or *pairwise inequality*) certainly unambiguously increases if the higher income increases or if the lower one decreases, decreases in the reverse cases that do not reverse the relative position of these incomes, increases if both the higher increases and the lower decreases, and decreases in the reverse cases that do not reverse the relative position of these incomes. "Unambiguously" means according to whatever justifiable criterion (including, among others, the difference relative to any of the changing incomes—either

---

12. Note that another possible effect, which would be changes in the ranking of the incomes, can be discarded, since each transformation of the distribution can be considered as a sequence of similar transformations without reversal of the ranking but where two incomes possibly become equal or cease to be (which is only an inequality effect): A change in ranking is thus transformed into shifts from decrease to increase in pairwise inequalities. Furthermore, rankings are a priori irrelevant when *impartiality* holds.

the highest, or the lowest, in both measures—, as one can easily check). A pair of incomes is said to be inclusion more equal than another if the interval between the latter strictly includes the interval between the former. A pairwise inequality inclusion decreases if the final pair is inclusion more equal than the initial one. Less equal, more or less unequal, increase, augment, or diminish is used similarly with the qualificative "inclusion."

Let a *progressive transfer* (*PT* for short) denote *a transfer from a higher income to a lower one of no more than half the difference between them.* Then the foregoing property implies that *a PT unambiguously diminishes the inequality between these two incomes.* There results that *to add a given extra amount to a lower income rather than to a higher one unambiguously produces a more equal pair* if the amount does not exceed the difference. If furthermore these two incomes are only relevantly distinguished by their size (this is implied by impartiality), then *a transfer from a higher income to a lower one of less than the difference between them unambiguously diminishes the inequality between these two incomes,* and *to add any given extra amount to a lower income rather than to a higher one unambiguously produces a more equal pair* (easy verification).

Now, first, these properties say nothing about the variation in inequality if there exist *other* relevant incomes than the two considered, and second, the relevant issue is the *ethical* evaluation of society and not just "inequality."

Hence the studies reported in *The Optimal Production of Social Justice* considered in particular the two following properties:

Benevolence: *to give an extra amount to an individual is good.*

Rectifiance: *it is better to hand out a given small extra amount to one individual than to another if the former is poorer than the latter.*

At all times in history and in all societies, these two principles have been considered and applied. Benevolence is nonwaste. Rectifiance is the reason for charity, for helping first the most miserable, for charging costs or liabilities to those who can pay (or can pay more easily), for redistributive transfers from richer to poorer. However, these principles have not been considered as universally good, even when more for someone is prima facie good and when nothing else relevantly differentiates the individuals, for obvious reasons to be recalled shortly.

Given the consequentialist assumption, rectifiance can equivalently be stated as:

To transfer a small amount from a richer individual to a poorer one is good (note that this does not say that this transfer "diminishes inequality"; it certainly does for the pairwise inequality between these *two* incomes, as a special application of a preceding remark, but it can also augment other pairwise inequalities).

Rectifiance can also be stated as:

A PT is good,
since a PT can be made by a series of successive small PTs.

One easily checks that, with *impartiality*, rectifiance can furthermore be stated in the two following ways:

It is better to hand out a given extra amount to one individual than to another if the former is poorer than the latter (there is no restriction on the size of the amount).

A transfer from a richer individual to a poorer of less than the difference in their incomes is good.

Again, it is not said that these transfers "diminish inequality," for the reason noted above. This assertion by economic scholars such as Cannan, Taussig, Loria, Pigou, Tawney, Dalton, and Divisia rests on an unclear view of the question (less unclear for Pigou than for others) to be discussed shortly. Note also that these scholars mention this concept without analyzing its properties.

The objections to benevolence and to rectifiance, even for individuals who are not relevantly differentiated in other ways (hence with impartiality), rest on the effects of the operations they imply on unjustified inequalities, as it is straightforwardly seen for pairwise inequalities between a changing income and a fixed one. Indeed an increase in an income creates inequalities between this income and those equal to its initial level, and it unambiguously augments the pairwise inequalities between this income and the incomes lower than its initial level. A decrease in an income unambiguously diminishes pairwise inequalities between this income and those lower than its final level, and it may suppress certain pairwise inequalities. A PT unambiguously augments pairwise inequalities between the highest changing income and incomes not lower than its initial level, and between the lowest changing incomes and incomes not higher than its initial level, and it may replace certain pairwise equalities by inequalities. A similar remark can be presented for transfers from poorer to richer. These effects that oppose the effects of the changing incomes alone are absent for transformations that do not affect the ordering of the incomes in size and are changes in either the smallest income alone or both the extreme incomes of equal amounts in opposite directions.

Therefore the study, or the recommendation, of both benevolence and rectifiance should be justified. One could be content with the fact that they are commonly considered and desired, and perform a mercenary's job in presenting their consequences. Yet even then we would do a better work if we knew why they are desired, and why they are not in other cases, be it for explicit reasons or for implicit, nay, unconscious ones. But we have to be particularly clear on these possible reasons if we furthermore recommend these principles or on the contrary advise against their use.

These principles can be supported by a number of different reasons. A couple of reasons for benevolence and a dozen reasons for rectifiance rest essentially on logic, whereas a limitless number of other reasons call on various more or less specific psychological or sociological phenomena. Among the basically logical reasons, three hold for both principles; they can be called *welfare priority*, *independence of irrelevant individuals or incomes*, and *irrelevance of opposite reasons*. The mostly logical reasons specific to rectifiance refer, first, to elementary views of inequality that *match variations in pairwise inequalities in number or in gaps*, and second, to its *equivalence to a number of other properties that describe differently comparisons of inequality*. These reasons specific to rectifiance, and particularly the pairwise match in gaps (see below), explain why rectifiance is not unfrequently more readily accepted than benevolence. We now successively consider welfare priority, matching pairwise inequality variations, independence, irrelevance of opposite reasons, and equivalent comparisons.

The various reasons for rectifiance lead to specific and different types of measures of inequality (or injustice). Rectifiance cannot be assumed a priori and without a reason. And when a reason is provided, it more specifically requires a specific type of measure, as we will see. Hence rectifiance cannot be adopted in general for measures having any other type of property. Rationality and justification requires that it be associated with specific alternative other properties.

When there is a single individual, we consider here the standard assumption that things are better if his income is higher and worse if his income is lower (we disregard presently the psychological value of a certain poverty).[13]

The Basic Reasons for Benevolence and Rectifiance

Priority to Welfare

We consider evaluations of comparisons or of transformations that give priority to certain properties or structures. The above remarks about consequentialism and about the distinction between welfare effects and inequality effects are relevant here.[14]

To give *priority to welfare effects over inequality effects implies benevolence*, since increases in one or several incomes is then seen as more important per se than any resulting effects on inequalities, including possible increases or negative effects for any reason.

Similarly *rectifiance* is implied by the following two-level priority:

1. *Welfare effects have priority over inequality effects.*

2. Given this priority, *a lower income has priority over a higher one for an increase of the same small amount.*

Condition 2 is for individuals not relevantly differentiated for another reason (other than their incomes). Condition 1 eliminates the relevance of inequalities for the comparison of condition 2.

Note that the priority considered in condition 2 is for the same amount. If this priority held whatever the amounts received by each individual, this would be a maximin principle (for each pair but hence also for the whole distribution).

This reason for rectifiance does not consider variations in inequalities. On the contrary, it rests on a disregard of these variations. By contrast, the reasons for rectifiance presented in the next two subsections rest on notions that relate a PT to a decrease in inequality. Then the variations in the inequalities between the two incomes that

---

13. This is analyzed in depth in Kolm 1982a.

14. The reduction of possible "ranking effects" to inequality effects (or their elimination by impartiality) is also relevant.

change in a PT and the other incomes are seen as either matching one another or irrelevant.

Matching Pairwise Inequalities

The basic idea is that, in a PT, *any increase in inequality between a changing income and a fixed income is* (*at least*) *matched by a decrease in inequality between this fixed income and the other changing income*, so that this increase does not oppose the decrease induced by the PT itself (and possibly by other decreases in pairwise inequalities). Thus this reason builds up its case from the only a priori unambiguous variations in inequalities: variations of pairwise inequalities when the two incomes do not change in the same direction. The compensation is one-by-one in *two* types of variables: the *number* and the *gaps*. By *gap* between two incomes we mean the absolute value of their difference. The fact that *compensation is in gaps* results from the fact that the two incomes that change in a PT vary by the same absolute amount. Thus these compensations justify rectifiance as an opinion on the injustice of inequalities.

More precisely, first consider small changes in income distributions, where "small" means sufficiently small so as not to affect the ordering of the incomes (yet equalities can be broken up or introduced). A PT can be constructed as a sequence of successive small PTs. In a small PT, the incomes outside the interval of the final levels of the two changing incomes see their pairwise inequalities increase with one of these two incomes and decrease with the other, in each case of the same absolute amount of difference (gap). The incomes within this interval (limits included) see their pairwise inequality decrease with both changing incomes. The pairwise inequality between the two changing incomes decreases. And the other pairwise inequalities are fixed.

One can produce similar, indeed de facto identical, reasonings in considering directly a PT that is not small, or in comparing the effects of increases (or decreases) in two incomes, of the same amount, for either small changes or directly not small ones. For instance, for alternative small increases in two incomes, the only differences with respect to either the direction of changes in pairwise inequalities, or the variations in their gaps, concern the incomes in between the two levels that change, and for them the inequality increases with the highest changing income and decreases with the lowest one. Or, again, with a non-small PT, the only new cases concern fixed incomes that are crossed by the level of a changing income. The pairwise inequality between such a fixed income and this changing income can either increase, decrease, or remain the same (with reverse positions), whatever its measure. But the pairwise inequality between this fixed income and the other changing income decreases. And this gap decreases by the amount of the PT, whereas no increase in the gap with the former changing income can exceed this amount. The same conclusions are similarly reached in comparing the effects on pairwise inequalities of the same non-small absolute increase in two different incomes.

These compensations account for the fact that PTs are commonly seen as being less able to augment an overall inequality than a simple increase in a relatively high income does, and that oppositions on this ground commonly affect more benevolence than rectifiance.

These pairwise compensations in gap variations show that a PT diminishes a larger number of gaps than it can augment, and produces a total decrease in gaps larger than the total increase it can produce. This latter effect amounts to a decrease in the Gini index, that is, in the sum of the gaps. Yet the conclusion is the same if an increase in any gap is seen as increasing more the inequality or the injustice when this gap is larger. This can be called *increasing (marginal) cost of gap or distance in inequality or injustice*, or *decreasing returns of proximity in equality or justice* (the closer the two incomes, the smaller the effect of a given variation). Indeed a gap with a fixed income that is augmented by a small PT is smaller than the gap with this income that the PT diminishes. Hence the sufficient condition is *nonincreasing returns of (or in) proximity* (the case where the effect of the gap variation does not depend on the gap is "constant returns" of gaps or proximity, that gives the Gini index if it is satisfied for all gaps).[15]

---

15. The conception of inequality or injustice implicit in the above considerations corresponds to indexes of the form $I = F(\{g_{ij}\})$ where $g_{ij} = |x_i - x_j|$ is the gap between incomes x_i and x_j of individuals i and j, with F being a weakly Schur-convex function; that is, it is increasing, symmetrical (as required by impartiality) and such that $g_{ij} > g_{kl}$ implies $\partial F/\partial g_{ij} \geq \partial F/\partial g_{kl}$ (only cases where i or j is k or l are used). We will also choose $F = 0$ if $g_{ij} = 0$ for all i, j. In particular, there can furthermore be gap separability implying $F = \sum f(g_{ij})$ with $f(0) = 0$, $f' > 0$ and $f'' \geq 0$, or F is any increasing function of such a sum. The Gini index corresponds to $f'' = 0$ and $\sum_{i<j} g_{ij}$. The function F can be homogeneous of degree one, so that the relative index $I/\bar{x}$, where $\bar{x} = (\sum x_i)/n$ is the average income, is invariant to equiproportional variations in all incomes (I is invariant to equal absolute variations in all incomes). This property implies that $F = [\sum g_{ij}^\alpha]^{1/\alpha}$ with $\alpha \geq 1$ if F is to have the foregoing form, and the Gini form $\alpha = 1$ if F is to have the additive form. The case $\alpha = 2$ corrresponds to the standard deviation.

Increasing costs in distance can mean that a certain tolerance for gaps becomes exhausted. It can also reveal that larger gaps become more conspicuous so the effect of their variation is larger. Decreasing returns in proximity can describe a relative satiety in equality or in justice. Opposite effects will be considered shortly. The above properties need to be satisfied only for pairs of gaps corresponding to one interval being included in the other (and hence producing a lower pairwise inequality for any reasonable measure).

The Principle of Independence of Irrelevant Individuals (PIII, or P3I, or the 3I Principle)

This principle is that *the individuals' allocations that do not change when the distribution changes are irrelevant for the evaluation of this change*, or, *the evaluation of a change depends only on the individual's allocations that actually change*.

This principle applies to any kind of allocations (see also chapter 14 on utilitarianism). It is an ethical principle that represents something like nonnosiness. Of course purely formal conceptions of inequality have a priori no reason to follow this principle.

The 3I principle is amenable to several qualifications which refer to the type of either the evaluation or the change in the allocation. For instance, an *ordinal P3I* applies to evaluations by more or less, or better or worse. The specification of the changes in allocation can refer to the number of individual allocations that change, or to other aspects. The *singleton 3I principle* (1-P3I) applies to cases where only one individual allocation changes in each change. The *pairwise 3I principle* (2-P3I) applies to cases where only two individual allocations change in each change. These three qualifications can apply with allocations of any kind. With allocations of quantities (unidimensional or multidimensional) we will have to consider the *constant-sum 3I principle* (S-P3I) where the changes considered do not affect the total sums. The *pairwise and constant-sum 3I principle* associates the last two cases, and it therefore concerns *progressive transfers* (PT-P3I). We have recalled, and we will use again, for ordinal evaluations, the identity of the general P3I with additive separability and "independence," and its being implied by the 2-P3I and by the constant-sum P3I. But we focus here, on the contrary, on the PT-P3I and on the 1-P3I.

The P3Is permit one to deduce the overall evaluation of simple changes within small societies from their evaluation within the small societies where they take place, where this evaluation may be unambiguous (such as certain changes in one or two individual alloca-tions). Furthermore the consequentialist assumption permits one to deduce the evaluation of certain sequences of such simple "local" changes from the evaluation of each of these changes. One can thus obtain overall evaluations of certain overall changes.

The two local changes considered here will be an increase in one income and a PT.

In a one-person society, an increase in this person's income is a good thing, we assumed. In particular it has no inequality effect. With 1-P3I this provides *benevolence*. The P3I has suppressed the inequality effects.

In a two-person society, a PT has the three following effects. (1) It *diminishes the inequality* (see above). (2) If nothing else but incomes relevantly differentiates the individuals, a PT *diminishes the arbitrari-ness* of choosing one allocation rather than the other deduced from it by the permutation of the incomes between the individuals; it thus *diminishes the irrationality of inequality* in this sense. (3) Favoring a PT amounts to *favoring lower relative poverty*, to *give priority to the poorer* for allocating a given extra amount (we do not need a particu-lar assumption of "priority to welfare" here). For these three reasons, and when nothing else relevantly distinguishes the individuals, cer-tainly *a PT diminishes the injustice between the two individuals*. Since the total sum is constant, it certainly has to be favored in the condi-tions considered. Then in a larger society, with the additional assump-tion of PT-P3I, this justifies *rectifiance*.

If we consider the first effect—a PT in a two-person society dimin-ishes the inequality—and a PT-P3I applied to the evaluation of "more or less equal" (rather than to "just" or "good"), we have the result that a PT diminishes the overall inequality. This consequence is the view expressed by the scholars noted above. These scholars, however, provided no reason, no justification for this view (they take the "prin-ciple of transfers" as materializing from thin air, as a self-evident truth parachuted from a superior wisdom or taken from their "intuition" as the rabbit out of the magician's hat). The unconscious mechanism that led to this view was probably an oversight of the other incomes, which is equivalent to an "inequality PT-P3I." Indeed the reason could not be the property of compensated *gaps* discussed above, since, if this were the case, these scholars would have considered a Gini index measure of inequality (the sum of the pairwise gaps) or the form presented in the preceding note, while they proposed other indexes, and properties that the indexes just noted do not possess. The reason could not be either that the *number* of increasing pairwise inequalities is at least compensated by the number of decreasing ones, since this motivation alone leads one to advocate maximin (a small increase in the lowest income lowers all gaps), which is not their proposal and does not refer to inequality per se. Yet these scholars do not mention the P3I, which is the strong assumption since the consideration that a PT lowers the pairwise inequality between the two changing incomes is logically unavoidable, necessary, and trivial. But the P3I is here neither a priori necessary nor a property justifiable by the mathematical logic of inequalities, but rather a property considered on social and ethical grounds that is amenable to the discussion presented below. This helped to maintain a confusion.

The Evaluation of Opposite Reasons

Oppositions to an increase in one income alone among a number of approximately equal incomes commonly rest on sentiments of envy or jealousy, or on desires to avoid such sentiments. This might raise opposition to benevolence. But strong envy and jealousy are the typical antisocial sentiments. They are commonly condemned on moral grounds, and certainly rightly so. They should therefore be discarded in an ethical evaluation. These sentiments, or the desire to avoid them, can also motivate oppositions to rectifiance in comparing the increasing income with fixed incomes initially roughly equal to it. However, if these sentiments cannot be suppressed by education or argument, they may have to be taken into account in second-best policies. Then equality, even at the cost of some waste in distribution, may be favorable to an absence of these sentiments, or of resentment due to a sense of unfairness, and for these reasons be favorable to peace, social harmony, friendship, and cooperation.

More generally, income distribution elicits a variety of social views and judgments that refer to various sociological and psychological considerations and depend on various structures of the distribution. This can provide reasons against benevolence or against rectifiance. A number of examples will be provided below (and in the next chapter). Certain reasons may be invalid, or may be valid for purposes other than an ethics of inequalities (such as sociological descriptions). Others may have direct or indirect ethical relevance. The scientific position consists in the close consideration, analysis, evaluation, and modeling of these specific phenomena, which has been done for the main ones. It is probably justified to draw the general conclusion that, for their *ethical* purposes, benevolence and rectifiance can be seen as the central and normal case, against which others have to be checked, and that exceptions should bear the burden of the proof. They are, at any rate, expressed moral views in numerous situations.

Equivalent comparisons, isophily (Lorenz and concentration curves dominance)

Finally, a study that led to *The Optimal Production of Social Justice* (1966) had to analyze the variety of people's opinions for comparing the injustice of unequal distributions, and a main aim of sections 6 and 7 of this work was to show that a number of meaningful comparisons, which do not seem to imply one another at first sight, happen to be mathematically identical. These equivalences reinforce the meaning of the property. These different equivalent properties are impartial benevolent rectifiance, isophily or preference for higher Lorenz or concentration curves, averages preference, mixture preference, averaging, dispatching, linear and affine transformations, and so on. We consider only isophily at this point (other equivalent properties will be recalled below).

Of course, if a distribution has a higher Lorenz curve, and a not lower average or total sum, than another, it also has a higher concentration curve (from affine transformations; see also the following references).

A distribution can be obtained from another one with the same total amount by a sequence of progressive transfers if and only if its concentration or Lorenz curve is above that of this other (a known mathematical property—see above—whose strict and weak variants and equivalence with other meaningful properties are presented in Kolm 1966a, section 7, theorems 1, 2, and 3). I showed that a distribution can be obtained from another one by a sequence of strongly progressive transfers (or progressive transfers and permutations) and income increases if and only if its concentration curve is above that of the other (Kolm 1966a, section 7, theorems 4, 5, and 6). Since a higher Lorenz curve for distributions of the same total amount is commonly seen as corresponding to a less unequal distribution, a preference for a higher concentration curve was labeled isophily (from the Greek word *isophilia*, liking equality), with the special case of constant-sum isophily for the comparison of distributions with the same total amount. Hence the above properties constitute, for an impartial evaluation, the equivalences of rectifiance with constant-sum isophily, on the one hand, and of benevolent rectifiance with isophily, on the other hand. Furthermore these equivalences hold if the evaluations are restricted to independent evaluations, that is, to cases where the evaluation function has an additive specification, justified by the general ordinal P3I; impartial independent rectifiance is the concavity of the function of one income whose values are added (the "individual evaluation function") —note that independent rectifiance implies impartiality. This equivalence again resulted directly from a known property for the constant-sum case (idem) and it was shown for general isophily and concentration-curve dominance (Kolm 1966a, section 7, theorems 8 and 9, which also adds other equivalent properties and considered the strict and weak cases). The structure of evaluation functions will be further considered in section 10.5.[16]

The Reasons against Rectifiance (and Benevolence)

The various possible reasons in favor of rectifiance and benevolence provide also, by their possible failures, the various possible reasons to reject these properties. We will consider each of them successively before presenting a series of simple illustrative examples (the property of impartiality is altogether of a different nature, since it results only from the consideration of variables sufficiently exhaustive to describe all the morally relevant differences among the individuals, and we thus assume it here).

Dependence on "Irrelevant" Individuals

There are a large number of possible reasons why the P3I may not hold. These reasons can have consequences in various directions. They can rest on various psychological, social, economic, or political considerations that are often more or less specific to the case or type of cases considered. The ethical relevances would have to be checked in

---

16. A part of theorems 1, 2, 3, 8, 9 of Kolm 1966a was later sometimes called Atkinson's theorem, after the didactic presentation of Atkinson (1970), and a part of theorems 4, 5, 6, 8, 9 of Kolm 1966a was later sometimes called Shorrocks's theorem, after Shorrocks (1983, seventeen years later).

each case. The phenomena considered below are either consequences or causes of dependences on "irrelevant" individuals.

Priorities

If the welfare effect does not prevail over the inequality effect, benevolence may be rejected because an increase in one income may augment an unjust inequality. Similarly, the priority justification of rectifiance may fail under the same condition because each change in one income may elicit specific increases in unjust inequalities.

Increasing Returns of Proximity

The compensation of gap increases in a PT may not be seen as reflecting the effects on inequality (or injustice). Indeed, in a PT, an income that lies outside the original levels of the changing incomes sees an *increase* in the *smallest* of its two gaps with the changing incomes and a *decrease* in the *largest*, by the same amount (the amount of the PT). Therefore, if an increase in a pairwise gap from a given income and of a given amount is seen as more detrimental when this gap is smaller than when it is larger, in a PT the gap decrease from a given fixed income outside the original values of the changing incomes fails to compensate the effect on inequality of the gap increase between this fixed income and the other changing one. Then such effects on inequality may overpower the other decreases in gaps and in pairwise inequalities, and the "gap compensation" justification of rectifiance vanishes. The noted property can be called a *decreasing costs of gaps or distance*, or an *increasing returns of proximity*. One dollar more in the gap augments less inequality (or injustice) when it is added to an already large gap than when it is added to a smaller one.[17] This is plausible, although the contrary effect of an increasing marginal inequality (or injustice) effect of distance is also a meaningful possibility. A large gap may be seen as so large that small differences do not matter much, or as much as they would for a smaller gap. Also, closer incomes may be thought of as more comparable than distant

---

17. This corresponds to measures of inequality injustice that are strictly Schur-concave functions of the gaps $I = F(\{g_{ij}\})$. All the remarks of note 15 are maintained in changing $\partial F/\partial g_{ij} \geq \partial F/\partial g_{kl}$ into $\partial F/\partial g_{ij} < \partial F/\partial g_{kl}$, $f'' \geq 0$ into $f'' < 0$, and $\alpha \geq 1$ into $\alpha < 1$.

ones, and hence given variations in their distance may be seen as more important for inequality or injustice. The key structuring effect of increasing returns of proximity is to induce clusters (if one income is variable between two fixed ones, inequality or injustice is lowest when it takes the level of one of these two incomes). In particular, reaching equality may be particularly valued, or breaking it may be particularly detrimental (examples will be presented and discussed below). Again, the above properties need to be satisfied only for pairs of gaps corresponding to one interval being included in the other (and hence producing a lower pairwise inequality for any reasonable measure).

Comparative Social Sentiments

Pairwise inequalities are bound to elicit a number of comparative social sentiments such as envy, jealousy, sentiments of inferiority or of superiority, preferences for conformity or on the contrary for distinction, and the sense of injustice or unfairness. These sentiments may be morally irrelevant, but they may also have to be considered because of their various effects on society. Any change in pairwise inequalities can affect them. There can result all types of overall effects for changes in one income of for PTs.

Group Size, Commonality and Originality

The number of people with similar incomes can have a number of various effects on inequality, its perception or its injustice, which result not only from proximity or distance but also from issues of relevance, conspicuousness or discretion, and commonness versus either originality or eccentricity (oddity, abnormality).

By definition, a cluster of incomes of similar size (into an income "class") exhibits low intraclass inequality. Yet the remaining intraclass inequalities may seem particularly relevant because they compare similar incomes which are for this reason deemed to be particularly comparable, while other incomes belong, in a sense and more or less, to "another world." But the focus may on the contrary insist on taking an integrated view of society, and thus emphasize the inequalities between the incomes of this class and the others.

Attention is bound to be attracted by a larger class size per se, and by extremes in both class size and income levels. This may emphasize, for the class one focuses on, inequalities with other incomes, or intraclass equality, or the limited remaining intraclass inequalities especially for larger classes (for the reason just noted). Attention may be irrelevant for justice or "objective inequality," but it may influence the sentiment of injustice which may have relevance for social reasons.

An individual's income is common if it belongs to a large class, it is original if it belongs to a small class, and it is eccentric, odd, bizarre, abnormal if it belongs to a very small class. These features influence attention but they differ from it. Originality and eccentricity are particularly accentuated for extreme levels (highest or lowest). Originality may underline the inequality with other incomes. The "isolation of the poor" and "elitism of the rich" measured by G. Field (1993) belong to this category. But still smaller classes may lead to the opposite effect as odd or abnormal cases are discounted as irrelevant in an overall view (the effect on attention can go both ways).

Consider, notably, the extreme groups, of the poorest or of the richest (or both together in considering PTs between them). When such a group decreases (say) in size, this can have at least three different effects on "inequality," with the new effects appearing successively if one starts from a relatively large group. First, in all cases the shrinking of an extreme group prima facie tends to diminish inequality. Yet, second, when this group becomes sufficiently small, their members become "originals," and the shrinking accentuates their originality. This per se tends to foster the impression of inequality. However, third, when the group becomes sufficiently smaller again, it may cease to have an actual relevance, as its members become not only original but eccentric, bizarre, odd, abnormal, or socially pathological cases.

Furthermore the members of an income class tend to develop a collective consciousness, a common culture, and various solidarities among themselves. These social phenomena commonly influence awareness, sensitivity, judgment, and action about inequalities, and they are influenced by them. This can concern both inequalities with other groups or the smaller intraclass inequalities. Such social phenomena are particularly sensitive to both differences and clusters or group size. They are essential for the quality of society, the impressions of solidarity, and the sentiments of injustice. It is to be noted that income class is the main feature of social class and is closely related to the other parameters of the social hierarchy: occupation, education, political influence, and so on. People with similar income levels tend to have analogous consumption patterns, comparable places in the production process and in society in general, and common interests. These subgroup cultures tend to increase social proximity within the subgroups but also distance and alienation, and sometimes hostility, with regard to other subgroups. Solidarity among the poor may help relieve the extreme cases, although one often has to distinguish between misery, poverty, low income, etc., which correspond standardly to different classes and possibly to different cultures. Among the rich, solidarity defends privileges. Just seeing more other poor people may relieve a poor's sentiment of isolation. A poverty culture may provide explanation, meaning, and self-respect, but it can also brood over the hardship and develop a sense of shame, guilt, or sentiments of inferiority. It may develop either envy or resignation. This may make poverty more or less bearable, and affect views and actions that could lead to change. Upper-class culture commonly fosters prejudice, sense of superiority, and the related status consumption. Now, the influence of income distribution on these phenomena of consciousness and culture is varied. Higher absolute and especially relative differences in levels are favorable to their development, as are the existence of clusters of levels. The effects of group size, absolute or relative, can go both ways. Culture requires communication and diffusion, reinforcement of views, and behavioral feedbacks that reinforce behavioral patterns. Thus its fabric, development, and duration require sufficient size of class. However, small relative size reinforces sentiments of particularity and specificity, and possibly the need or desire for their self-assertion, in addition to the possible defense of common interests.

Averagings, Dispatchings, Linear or Affine Transformations, Preference to Mixtures or to Averages

The transformations of distributions called "constant-sum averaging," "equality-preserving dispatching," both averaging and dispatching, sum and equality preserving linear or affine transformations, "averages of permutations," and "mixtures" or "slice-reshuffling" (see *The Optimal Production of Social Justice*, sections 6 and 7, and section 10.5 below), all are transformations that present aspects of equalization and turn out to be equivalent to benevolent rectifiant preference. Then a limit of this property is exhibited by the fact that all these transformations are *linear* ones.

Examples

Increasing Returns of Proximity

1. *Lorenz curves.* We have seen in section 10.1 that common impressions of inequality can attribute more inequality to a distribution whose Lorenz curve is above that of another, as a result of the attachment of a particular importance to the size of clusters and of the corresponding classes.

2. *The simplest example.*[18] Consider two individuals whose respective incomes are 1 and 4. Transfer one unit from the latter to the former, so the incomes become 2 and 3. Inequality has decreased. Add now a third individual with an income of 4. The initial set of incomes is (1, 4, 4). Proceed now to the same transfer between the first two individuals. The set of incomes becomes (2, 3, 4). If rectifiance for inequality holds, inequality has again decreased. Yet, one could also see inequality as having increased. Indeed no two incomes are equal in the latter situation, whereas at least the former situation contains two equal incomes (a situation that may be less equal than if all three incomes were equal, yet more equal than when all incomes are different as in the latter case). The number (or proportion) of pairs of equal incomes has decreased from 1 (or 1/3) to 0.[19] It indeed suffices that the gap increase from 0 to 1 is seen as more detrimental than the decrease of the other two gaps from 3 to 2 and 1 is favorable. The same reasons and conclusion can hold if the third income is 1. Of course, if the third income, instead of being 4 or 1, were 2, or 3, then the same views would reverse their conclusion. Indeed the transfer between the first two individuals would transform the distribution from (1, 4, 2) to (2, 3, 2), or from (1, 4, 3) to (2, 3, 3), and hence one equality between two incomes would be introduced where there was none initially. Furthermore all the pairwise gaps would be diminished. In these cases,

---

18. See Kolm 1993a.

19. It goes without saying that individuals having *exactly* the same income—a feature of these simple examples—is not the relevant issue. This may be relevant for the distribution of indivisible goods. One could also consider the number of incomes in an interval. Favoring equal incomes merely epitomizes, for this simple example, the increasing returns in proximity.

these views reinforce the pure effect of the transfer, whereas they oppose it in the former case. The P3I is clearly violated.

Similarly a view favoring equality in incomes (possibly for a certain type of incomes) should prefer that an extra dollar be handed out to the poorer rather than to the richer ... at least if there are only two individuals. Were the incomes 1 and 3 and were we to distribute 1, then distribution (2, 3) would be preferred to distribution (1, 4). Add a third individual with income 4 and these alternative treatments of the first two may be judged otherwise. Indeed they create the two distributions (2, 3, 4) and (1, 4, 4) respectively, and the latter may be preferred because it contains one pair of equal incomes (the number or the proportion of pairs of equal incomes is higher) or, more subtly, because the smallest pairwise gap reaching zero instead of 1 is seen as overpowering the fact that the others are 3 rather than 1 and 2. If instead the third income were 1, handing out 1 to the first individual would break down one equality since (1, 3, 1) is transformed into (2, 3, 1), while this is not the case if this extra unit is handed out to the second individual, yielding the distribution (1, 4, 1); the more subtle reason based on increasing returns to proximity also works for this case. If, on the other hand, the third income is 2, giving 1 to the first individual creates an equality since the distribution becomes (2, 3, 2), while giving it to the second yields the completely unequal distribution (1, 4, 2). Finally, a third income of 3 implies that giving 1 to the second individual breaks down an equality in transforming the distribution from (1, 3, 3) into (1, 4, 3), while this is not the case if the beneficiary is the first individual since the distribution becomes (2, 3, 3). Furthermore in these two latter cases handing out the extra income to the poorer rather than to the richer provides lower levels for all gaps.

All these remarks can be reinforced by the consideration of the possibility of psychosocial sentiments of envy, sentiment of inferiority, and sentiments of superiority, and of course of the social concept of conformity (or on the contrary of distinction).

Sociological and Ethical Inequalities   The following examples illustrate a number of the above considerations about the various effects of equalizing transfers.

Transfer 100 dollars from someone who has 300 to someone who has zero. Does this decrease inequality? Assume the other persons all have 300 each. Previously one person *deviated from the crowd*. Now two do (who are not even equal between themselves). The *number or proportion of pairs of people with the same income* has decreased. One can thus consider that inequality in society has increased, in line with the previous example. Furthermore the people who keep 300 may focus more on the loss of 100 by their former alter ego than on the equal gain by the *distant and possibly rather foreign* poor. Of course, if the other people all had 200, or all had 100, the transfer would augment the mass of equals, and more precisely the number and the proportion of pairs of people with the same income. It would also diminish all the gaps. These effects thus reinforce that of the transfer per se.

Assume now that individuals are envious or jealous of people who have an income higher than theirs, or experience a sentiment of inferiority toward them. Now, in the first case of the preceding paragraph, where one person has zero and all the others have 300 each, a PT of 100 doubles the number of people feeling envious or inferior, and increases the number of envied incomes. This may be a reason to oppose it.

Consider now a society consisting of the same number of rich and poor people, and proceed to a sequence of successive PTs between one rich and one poor each, so the persons affected leave these groups (the following remarks apply if only one of these groups changes). These two extreme groups decrease in size, which a priori diminishes the inequality. At a point each of these groups becomes smaller than the intermediary "middle class." Still further, they become rather limited minorities and to be rich or poor is rather an originality that becomes exacerbated when these groups shrink still more. Such isolation, per se, tends to foster the impression of inequality. This would, for instance, begin when each group is, say, 20 percent of the population. As their size still decreases, the originality becomes an oddity and then an eccentricity. When the size shrinks to a couple of percent, the members tend to be seen as exceptional cases, outside normal society, not to be considered by evaluations of the state of this society, and hence with no influence on its inequality. Other effects of group size will be considered in chapter 11 about poverty and misery. These effects superimpose on those, already discussed, concerning the effect on inequality of transfer per se, of breaking equalities, and of the variations of the various gaps.

Other examples can similarly illustrate the various effects of the allocation of extra amounts or of their withdrawal (such as by taxation).[20]

Conclusions on Rectifiance and Benevolence

A higher income is good (so we assume) in a single-person world, and a PT is just in a two-person world whose individuals present no other relevant difference as it unambiguously diminishes unjustified inequality while preserving total income. But the world is more populated than these cases assume. Even if an implicit assumption of "independence of irrelevant individuals" leads one to consider only a subpopulation, the number of relevant individuals is often larger than one or two. Then one cannot say a priori and in general that an increase in one income or a PT is good, or that a PT diminishes inequality, since the comparisons and inequalities involving also the other, fixed incomes are a priori relevant. An increase in one income or a PT surely diminishes all pairwise inequalities only if the increasing income is the lowest of all or the changing pair consists of the two extreme incomes, and rankings are preserved.

In general situations, benevolence or rectifiance can be promoted or opposed by a fair number of possible reasons which refer either essentially to ethical logic or more intensively and explicitly to psychological and sociological phenomena. Yet the reasons of the former category have been exhaustively presented in this section and the others have also been discussed, so these analyses can be used to appraise benevolence and rectifiance in each kind of situation. Examples show

---

20. (Added in proofs.) These effects of the size of groups or income classes (Kolm 1993a) can be complemented by the interesting examples of "polarization" provided by Esteban and Ray (1994). Polarization, an important sociological structure, is clustering into groups that are larger and more equal in size, more apart in income levels, and consequently smaller in number but remaining several. Polarization implies group size which is a more elementary, more basic, and more general phenomenon. Esteban and Ray consider polarization as a phenomenon different from inequality which they see as restricted to cases of inequality-rectifiance, whereas we see here polarization as one aspect of the general inequality-equality structure of the distribution. Interestingly, the first example provided by these authors is the opposite of the above-noted "Australo-French Lorenz curves syndrom," since it is a bipolarized distribution that Lorenz-dominates one with more evenly spread inequalities. Other relevant discussions can be found in Temkin (1993, but with a less than accurate report of the history of ideas).

straightforwardly that benevolence or rectifiance should sometimes prevail and should be discarded in other cases. No universal adoption or rejection of any of these principles can hold. Assertions of the type "progressive transfers diminish inequality," or "they are just or good" (for otherwise relevantly identical individuals), or, on the contrary, "they have no reason," or again "an increase in one income is good," if they are meant for all cases, can only result from insufficient reflection. Hence the general analysis consists in considering the various relevant phenomena and issues, and in pointing out the various types of cases of application and the conclusions they lead to.

More than a dozen reasons for or against rectifiance or benevolence have been shown and discussed, and the number is much larger if the psychological and social effects are considered more fully or more in depth. Certain reasons can provide only support or only opposition whereas others can produce arguments in both ways. Certain reasons are the same or similar for both benevolence or rectifiance whereas others are specific to one of these properties. For example, among the logical reasons, the "priority of welfare effects over inequality effects" suffices for benevolence and provides half a reason for rectifiance. Or the P3I, used as 1-P3I and 2-P3I respectively, suffices for benevolence and practically also for rectifiance. And many inequality effects of all kinds raised by the inequalities between changing incomes and fixed ones are or can be active for both properties. On the other hand, the matchings in gaps and in numbers, and the logical identities with a number of other principles, can only support rectifiance or jointly benevolence and rectifiance. Conversely, only benevolence can be fully justified by the priority of welfare over inequality. These specificities explain why, in a number of cases, only one of these two properties is retained while the other is discarded.

The variety of the nature of possible reasons is conspicuous, and these reasons rely more or less on the pure logic of justice or social ethics, on more specific ethical assumption, and on psychological or sociological considerations. The equalizing effect of a PT in an isolated pair, and matching variations in number or gaps of inequalities, rest on pure logic, but the P3I, the priority of welfare effects over inequality effects, the preference for increases of lower incomes, increasing returns of proximity, increasing marginal cost of distance, or preferences for clusters all require moral justifications that can be more or less based on psychological and social effects. And psychology and sociology can be intensively mobilized in considerations of sentiments of envy, jealousy, unfairness, inferiority, superiority, isolation, elitism, rejection, exclusion, togetherness, solidarity, distinction, conformity, opposition, and so on, or in the analysis of the cultural effects of group size or of comparisons. These phenomena must then be related to the effects concerning justice and social ethics.

The particular strength of the case for benevolence rests on the fact that the avoidance of waste or the priority of the welfare effect over inequality effects suffices for it. They are reinforced by the "nonnosiness" justification of the P3I (1-P3I suffices), and by the common ethical weakness of possible opposite reasons. These properties underlie the common strong support for benevolence and the opposition, sometimes the indignation, against its violation. One should favor improvement of an individual's situation even if this increases unjust inequalities with others. To diminish inequalities should not justify worsening one individual's situation for nobody's benefit. The contrary view often seems to imply a kind of malice. It leads to waste. It would often result from unreasonable clinging to equality, immoral sentiments of jealousy or strong envy, abusive egalitarianism, perverse and inhumane conceptions of justice, or, at least, misplaced aesthetism enjoying the symmetry of equality. Its extreme is Procrustes' justice. We have noted, however, that balking from benevolence can sometimes have indirect justifications when there is no other way to prevent envy, jealousy, sentiments of injustice or of inferiority, resentment, and so on, and all their various mental, relational and behavioral negative effects on the fabric and the workings of society. Yet it seems that such justifications should be carefully provided while benevolence remains the prima facie principle. Moreover, in the absence of these externalities benevolence is supported by the reasons for Pareto-efficiency (see chapters 1 and 6).

The strength of these moral reasons in favor of benevolence reveals and manifests the strength of the two logical basic principles on which they rest: the P3I and the priority of welfare over inequality. These principles are thus bound to bring the same force to other structures that they can support, and in particular to rectifiance. They are, however, not sufficient for rectifiance as they are for benevolence. Yet for the P3I—that is now necessary as the 2-P3I rather than as the 1-P3I—

the complementary property is the pairwise equalizing effect of a PT, which is necessary. For the priority of welfare, the complement cannot be this pairwise equalizing effect, since it is a priori no more important than other variations in inequality (and such effects are by assumption secondary). It thus has to be the second welfare assumption for rectifiance, namely the preference for giving extra amounts to poorer persons. This certainly also has some strength. This strength is particularly justified when the low income corresponds to misery and fails to satisfy vital needs, especially if this is not the case for the higher income. The welfare case for PTs between two such incomes tends to resemble that of benevolence with much of its strength. But rectifiance has, in addition, its own possible reasons. The compensations in gaps and in number of the variations of pairwise inequalities justify rectifiance by reductions in overall inequalities entailed by PTs, if there is no "increasing returns of proximity" for the gaps. Moreover the various properties equivalent to rectifiance provide further information about the inequality-reducing effects of PTs and hence about rectifiance (they also show other aspects of the limits of rectifiance). One can also note that rectifiance amounts to pairwise constant-sum maximin, that is, maximin for each pair and for given extra amount or total amount, and hence its justification is related to that of maximin from both points of view of inequality reduction and of differential welfare effects.

Finally, the various specific psychological or sociological effects that might lead one to oppose rectifiance—as well as benevolence—should be specifically considered. They may have no ethical relevance, or no ethical relevance as regards justice. They may have to be faced with specific means in the fields of suasion or compensation. Yet they may finally be relevant for direct or indirect reasons discussed above, and in this case they should be analyzed and modelled specially and precisely.[21]

---

21. As for instance in Kolm 1971, 1991c, 1993f, 1995a, for envy, jealousy, sentiments of inferiority or of superiority, preferences for conformity or for distinction, malevolence, etc. G. Field (1993) also goes some way in this direction for originality ("isolation of the poor" and "elitism of the rich") in his process of building an index of inequality that incorporates these effects. See also the preceding note about polarization.

The final conclusion is that a number of principles and properties for the moral evaluation, comparison and measure of unjustly unequal distributions should be given prima facie status (adoption in the absence of an explicit overpowering reason), favorable prejudice, or systematic consideration as to whether or not they should be retained. Yet the force of this a priori interest depends on the property. Setting aside *impartiality* which is logically necessary for the suitably defined variables, the two practically necessary properties are *concentration-decreasing inequality* (Kolm 1966b, see section 10.4 below) and *benevolence*. *Rectifiance* comes behind. Then come properties of the type of decreasing returns in proximity such as *concentration-subdecreasing inequality* (Kolm 1966b, see section 10.4 below), and the *principles of diminishing transfers*, or 2-rectifiance (or 2-isophily), and rectifiance of further order (see below). For variations of all incomes in the same direction, inequality should certainly be *weakly superintensive and subequal* (hence possibly intensive and equal-invariant; see Kolm 1966a and section 10.3 below). And the general ordinal P3I, hence an additively separable evaluation, is an important property. A number of these properties lead to specific forms of the measures of inequality or of its injustice. Note, finally, that the status of being a prima facie property applies to the reason for equality itself (see chapter 2) and hence provides the basic logical reason for resorting to the comparison of inequalities.

10.3 Covariations

Equiproportional and equal variations of all incomes are the elementary logically meaningful transformations because incomes are quantities and given impartiality-symmetry that demands the consideration of equalities, and they are also actually (socially, ethically, etc.) meaningful changes. *The Optimal Production of Social Justice* (1966a, sections 6 and 7) thus analyzed all the cases of variation of a measure of inequality or injustice with equiproportional or equal variations in all incomes. It in particular emphasizes measures that are *intensive* (invariant to scale), *equal-invariant* (invariant to equal absolute variations), *superintensive* (augmented by an equiproportional increase), and *subequal* (diminished by an equal increase). Given the actual meaningfulness of the consideration of both relative and absolute forms of the measure, an intensive measure has to be a relative form and an equal-invariant measure has to be an absolute form (to avoid measures diminished by an equiproportional increase or augmented by an equal addition).

The two polar cases of intensive and equal-invariant measures are amenable to a synthesis and a compromise.

In the *synthesis* the relative measure is intensive and the absolute measure is equal-invariant. This amounts to the measures whose absolute and relative forms are linearly homogeneous functions of absolute and relative income deviations from the mean, respectively (the absolute deviation is the income minus the mean and the relative deviation is the absolute divided by the mean). Equivalently, the absolute measure is a linearly homogeneous function of income differences. For instance, the Gini index and the standard deviation belong to this class of measures of inequality.[22]

The *compromise* consists of measures that are both superintensive and subequal. Such measures are *intermediate* when they constitute a family that contains the two polar cases as extreme limits. But, since the polar cases are respectively relative and absolute forms, intermediate measures either consider both forms ("dual" measures), or are hybrids that are also intermediate between the forms whose actually meaningful distinction then fails to be expressed. The augmented-income families of these measures were considered in Kolm 1966b. They consist in adding a constant to all incomes in the measure that is either the intensive measure for the hybrid intermediate compromise, or the corresponding extensive measure for the absolute form of the dual intermediate compromise. Both measures give the relative intensive measure when the constant is zero and the absolute equal-invariant measure when the constant becomes infinite.[23]

---

22. If x_i is the income of individual i, n the number of individuals, $\bar{x} = \sum x_i/n$ the average income, $g_{ij} = |x_i - x_j|$, absolute measures can be $\phi(\{|x_i - \bar{x}|\})$ or $F(\{g_{ij}\})$, where ϕ and F are linearly homogeneous, and if they have an additive specification they have to be $(\sum |x_i - \bar{x}|^\alpha)^{1/\alpha}$ and $(\sum g_{ij}^\alpha)^{1/\alpha}$ up to a multiplicative constant. The standard deviation is the former with $\alpha = 2$ and the Gini index is the latter with $\alpha = 1$, with $\alpha \gtrless 1$ for respectively decreasing, constant, or increasing returns in proximity to the mean or between incomes.

23. They are the measures I (relative I^r and absolute I^a) and J such that

$$I^a = \bar{x}I^r = \frac{\bar{x} + c}{1 + c}J = F(\{x_i + c\})$$

Measures derived from the equal equivalent of independent evaluation functions (from the P3I) can be neither synthetic (1966a, theorems 11 and 12) nor augmented-income hybrid intermediate (see section 10.5 below).

The meanings of the effects of these covariations of incomes on inequality have been discussed in Kolm 1966a, 1966b, 1976a, 1976b, 1993a, in considering a number of sources of information. One source is a classical political dispute between people who see an increase of all incomes in the same proportion as a fair change and those who see this as utterly unjust because it provides more to the already rich and less to the already poor. Indeed a few classical economic scholars such as Cannan, Taussig, Loria, Dalton, and Tawney have noted some of the issues. Systematic enquiries by questionnaires were then made, along with ethical, psychological and sociological analyses of the issues. The conclusion is that the view concerning the comparative justice of covariations in incomes depends on the setting of the question, and, of course, on the political reading of this setting. It depends on the levels of the real incomes, and in particular on the average level and on the levels of the lowest and of the highest; on the conceived solidarity or duty of solidarity; of course on the origin of these transformations; on past and expected history; on the fact that the considered variation is an increase or a decrease; and so on. One important aspect of the issue concerns whether the relevant measure is a relative or an absolute measure (if the question concerns inequality rather than injustice, this precision has to be provided).

---

where F is a linearly homogeneous function. When $c = 0$, $I^r = J$ is intensive. When $c = \infty$, $I^a = J$ is equal-invariant. J is invariant, and I^a varies proportionally, along rays issued from the point of coordinates $-c$, but these geometrical properties have no actual understandable meaningfulness, except in the two polar cases (for instance, the property defined as "if one adds 10,000 dollars to all incomes, then multiplies all the proceeds by two, and withdraws 10,000 dollars from each result, inequality would be the same," is not "actually" significant). When $c \to \infty$, the helix $J(x)$ and the cone $I^a(x)$ both tend to the cylinder describing equal-invariance. All these measures are compromise if they are concentration-subdecreasing, although concentration-decreasingness suffices for J, and for I^r to be subequal, and I^a to be superintensive (see section 10.4). The forms for independent measures were explicitly provided (see section 10.6).

Another notable class of hybrid augmented-income compromise intermediate measures rests on functions of relative income deviations from the mean and are of the form $\phi[\{1 + c)(x_i - \bar{x})/(\bar{x} + c)\}]$ where $c \geq 0$ is the augmenting constant. The measure ϕ is intensive for $c = 0$ and equal-invariant for $c = \infty$. If ϕ is homogeneous of degree one, these two cases are the two forms of a synthetic measure.

The idea that inequality is maintained by equal proportional variations in all incomes is one relevant case among others, which was
studied and for which measures or indexes were provided, notably
those implied by the definition from the equal equivalent income and
independence (additive separability in the evaluation function), as it
was done for the other relevant cases (*The Optimal Production of
Social Justice*, 1966a, and Kolm 1966b). Since the standard scientific
qualificative for a property that is invariant to scale is *intensive*, this
term was used for magnitudes having this property: intensive measure
of inequality, intensive justice, and so on. Now a number of people
consider this property as particularly compelling. However, they reject
it, as everyone does, when they are presented with a number of comparisons, as noted in section 10.1. This happens notably with large
inequalities and very low lower levels. And scale invariance and equal-
invariance tend to amount to the same thing with nonsmall incomes
that do not differ much, and properties intermediate between them
and others also tend to them. Hence the attachment to scale invariance
is the compounded result of four things. First, this can be an actual
conceptual and moral view which, however, has to be restricted to a
limited domain of application. Second, this view often results from
insufficient reflection, as shown by the preceding considerations and
experiments notably for very different incomes. Third, when the incomes are on the contrary not very different (and not very small), scale
invariance may in fact approximately be a number of other structures,
among which is equal-invariance. Fourth, this view also often rests
on a confusion between scale invariance proper and unit invariance.
Indeed, scale invariance makes the measure immune to a common
change in units for the incomes. Notably the measure is immune to
inflation and we may indeed want to consider inequality in real incomes. But the parameters of a measure need not be dimensionless:
they can incur the adequate compensating contravariant change when
units change.

10.4 Concentration (Kolm 1966b)

From the above, a PT cannot a priori and in general be said to
diminish inequality or its injustice. Hence rectifiance in the sense that
a PT diminishes inequality (and Schur-convexity of inequality indexes

that amounts to this property and impartiality-symmetry—see below) is not the most general and basic property of the type of convexity of such indexes. This general property is *concentration decreasingness*. A distribution is said to incur a concentration when all the gaps between each income and the average income decrease in the same proportion. This is equivalent to the equal redistribution of the same fraction of all incomes, a clearly meaningful and meaningfully equalizing property. The inverse of a concentration is a (mean-centered) expansion. For instance, the fixed-duration income equalization recalled in chapter 6 amounts to a concentration of "total" income. Inequality is *concentration decreasing* when a concentration lowers it. A concentration of course maintains total and average quantities. Rectifiance and impartiality (Schur-convexity of inequality) implies concentration decreasingness. One can also consider concentrations restricted to subsets of the incomes, and this gives PTs for pairs of incomes.

Measures of inequality are also normally assumed to be zero at equality and positive elsewhere. A measure of inequality is *concentration subdecreasing* or *superdecreasing* when a bridging of the gaps between incomes and the average income in a certain proportion diminishes the inequality in a larger or in a smaller proportion.[24]

10.5 Evaluation Functions, Equal Equivalent, Measures and Indexes

Evaluation Functions

An *evaluation function* is a numerical function of the overall allocation or distribution, that takes a higher value when the allocation is better. If "better" is the only relevant qualificative, this function is *ordinal*, that is, it can be replaced by any increasing function of itself. Any of these functions is called a *specification* of the ordinal function.

An *equal distribution* is a distribution with equal individual incomes.

---

24. The distribution defined by $\xi_i = \bar{x} + \lambda \cdot (x_i - \bar{x}) = \lambda x_i + (1 - \lambda) \cdot \bar{x}$ with $\lambda \geq 0$ is a concentration of distribution x for $\lambda < 1$ and an expansion of it for $\lambda > 1$. The measure $I(x)$ is concentration decreasing when $I(\xi) \lessgtr I(x)$ according as $\lambda \lessgtr 1$. It is concentration subdecreasing when $I(\xi) \lessgtr \lambda \cdot I(x)$ according as $\lambda \lessgtr 1$, and concentration superdecreasing in the opposite case.

Equal Equivalent

The Optimal Production of Social Justice (1966a, section 6) defined the **equal equivalent income** of a distribution as the individual income of the equal distribution that is as good as the distribution under consideration.[25]

The *minimum average equivalent income* of a distribution was defined as the smallest average income of a distribution as good as the one under consideration. It however coincides with the equal equivalent income for the evaluation having the specific properties considered (impartiality and rectifiance).

The equal equivalent income is a specification of the evaluation function.

Measures and Indexes of Inequality, Injustice, Equality, and Justice

The equal equivalent income of an equal distribution is equal to its average income, and to its individual incomes. Therefore, if the injustice of the inequality of a distribution lowers the evaluation of this distribution, the equal equivalent income of an unequal distribution is below its average income, and their *difference* is a measure of this injustice. Thus, this was labelled *injustice* in *The Optimal Production of Social Justice*, and *absolute* (per person) *inequality* in *Unequal Inequalities*.

The ratio of this measure to the average income was labelled in these studies *relative injustice* or *relative inequality*.

These two measures measure respectively *inequality per person* and *inequality per dollar* (or per unit of quantity), as they were also called.

One minus relative injustice or relative inequality is *the ratio of the equal equivalent income over the average income*. This ratio, lower than 1 which it reaches for equal distributions, measures a *relative degree of equality* or relative justice and was called "*justice*."

The "total" inequality or injustice was defined as the absolute, per person, inequality or injustice multiplied by the number of individuals and was also considered and analyzed.[26]

---

25. In his article of 1970, Atkinson uses the name "egalitarian equivalent income."

26. If x_i is individual i's income, and n the number of individuals, $\bar{x} = \sum x_i/n$ is the average income. Then, if $F(x_1, x_2, \ldots, x_n)$ is the evaluation function, the *equal equiva-*

The Optimal Production of Social Justice (1966) then produced these measures, and in particular the *relative inequality*, their form and their properties, in the various cases of the properties of the evaluation of the inequality injustice of the distribution.

Impartiality, Benevolence, Rectifiance for Evaluation Functions and Measures of Inequality and Injustice (*The Optimal Production of Social Justice*, 1966a, section 6)

The properties considered previously give the following structures to the evaluation functions and to the various measures presented in the previous section. In the following, the mention of a derivative implies the assumption of its existence.

Impartiality means that all these functions and measures are *symmetrical*, that is, invariant under any permutation of individuals' incomes.

Benevolence means that the evaluation function, and in particular the equal equivalent income, are increasing functions of individuals' incomes.

Rectifiance means that, for a given distribution, the first derivative of the evaluation function is higher for an individual's income than it is for another's if the former income is lower than the latter (and the reverse for the derived measures of inequality).

Impartial rectificance was also called Schur-concavity, since rectifiance plus symmetry was shown by Ostrowski (1952) to be equivalent to another property used under the corresponding form of convexity by the German mathematician I. Schur in the 1920s (the uses of this other property are recalled in section 10.6 below).

Intensive Justice and Inequality, Absolute Invariance, the Synthesis and the Intermediate Compromises (*The Optimal Production of Social Justice*, 1966a, section 6)

Intensive justice means that the above defined measures of *justice* and of *relative inequality* or injustice do not change when all incomes

---

lent income (Kolm 1966a and 1966b) is defined as $\bar{\bar{x}}$ such that $F(x_1, x_2, \ldots, x_n) = F(\bar{\bar{x}}, \bar{\bar{x}}, \ldots, \bar{\bar{x}})$. The defined measures then are $\bar{x} - \bar{\bar{x}}$, $(\bar{x} - \bar{\bar{x}})/\bar{x} = 1 - \bar{\bar{x}}/\bar{x}$, $\bar{\bar{x}}/\bar{x}$, and $n \cdot (\bar{x} - \bar{\bar{x}})$.

are multiplied by the same positive number. That is, these measures are intensive, or only *ratios of incomes* matter for them.

Absolute invariance means that the measures of absolute inequality or injustice, per person or total, do not change when the same amount is added to or deducted from all incomes. That is, these measures are equal-invariant, or only *differences of incomes* matter for them.

These two properties also mean, for measures derived as indicated from the equal equivalent income (and as it is straightforwardly checked), that the equal equivalent income incurs the same variation as individual incomes when they incur respectively the same relative or the same absolute variation. Geometrically these properties mean that, in the space of the individuals' incomes, the hypersurfaces of equivalent distributions are respectively homothetic from the origin and translated in the direction of the line of equal distributions (the measures are invariant along rays issued from the origin or parallel to this line, and their graphs are the corresponding helix and cylinder).

These two properties are amenable to either the synthesis, or the intermediate compromises, recalled in section 10.3.

Independence: The Principle of Independence of Irrelevant Individuals (P3I)

The (ordinal) general P3I (see section 10.2 above) holds if and only if *the evaluation function has a specification that is a sum of functions of one income each.* The pairwise 2-P3I and the constant-sum P3I are necessary and sufficient for this property (see *The Optimal Production of Social Justice*, section 6, and also chapter 15 below and the references to the related works of Leontief, Debreu, and Gorman quoted there). Note, however, that the constant-sum pairwise P3I, that is to say the PT-P3I, is not sufficient for this property; it only leads to rectifiance.

A conception of justice or inequality that satisfies the P3I, and hence this additive structure, was called *independent*.

The functions of one income that are added are called *the individual evaluation functions*. They can be replaced each by any linear (affine) increasing function of themselves, with the same positive multiplicative term for all, since this transformation preserves the ranking of the values of the sum for various distributions (and this is the largest class of transformation that does this for all distributions): This is expressed by these individual functions being "cardinal co-multiplicative."

With independence, the various properties have the following relations with the structures of the individual evaluation functions (in sufficient domains).

Benevolence is equivalent to the fact that the individual functions are *increasing*.

Impartiality is equivalent to the fact that the individual functions differ only by the *addition of constants*, or equivalently (because of their co-multiplicative cardinality), they *are the same* function.

Rectifiance implies impartiality (*Unequal Inequalities*, section XId). Hence rectifiance *implies the identity of the individual functions* (up to arbitrary constants), and Schur-concavity.

Rectifiance is equivalent to the fact that the individual functions are identical (*up to arbitrary constants*) *and concave* (same references).

Rectifiance is equivalent to the quasi-concavity of the evaluation function.

Rectifiance is equivalent to the fact that the measures of injustice and inequality defined above are positive out of equality (*The Optimal Production of Social Justice*, 1966a, section 7, theorem 8). In particular, *this sign implies impartiality*.

For the measures derived from the equal equivalent as above, *intensive relative inequality*, and *equal-invariant absolute inequality*, are equivalent to the facts that the individual evaluation functions can be taken as proportional to the same *power* or *logarithmic*, and *exponential*, functions respectively, and the further property of impartiality means that the proportionality coefficients are the same (*The Optimal Production of Social Justice*, 1966a, section 7, theorems 13 to 17).[27] These power or exponential functions depend on one parameter which defines the degree of injustice of the inequality or of inequality aversion, that is, the intensity of the egalitarianism of the considered conception of justice. In both cases the two extremes are the same: extreme egalitarianism with *maximin* (benevolence precludes favoring equalities dominated by unequal distributions where all incomes are larger) and no egalitarianism where, with impartiality, the evaluation favors only total sums.

---

27. The case of power functions was later considered by Atkinson (1970), and the corresponding relative measure of inequality was sometimes labeled Atkinson's index by certain authors.

There result consequences for the effect of independence on the two solutions that associate the two polar cases of intensive justice and absolute invariance, the synthesis and the intermediate compromise.

Independence precludes the synthesis, as it is shown by the form of the measure obtained for this synthesis, or by the impossibility that the power or logarithmic, and exponential, individual functions coincide (except in the trivial case of linear individual functions, which precludes rectifiance, implies that the inequalities or injustices are everywhere zero if they cannot be negative, and, then, that the evaluation is merely the total sum of individual incomes; see *The Optimal Production of Social Justice*, theorems 11 and 12). That is, the three following properties cannot hold jointly: (1) independence, (2) intensive justice or intensive relative inequality or injustice, and (3) absolute invariance or invariance of absolute (per person) injustice or inequality under equal increases. Yet these properties can hold by pairs: The evaluation functions are sums of powers or logarithms, and of exponentials, for property 1 and either property 2 or property 3, respectively; and for properties 2 and 3, the absolute and the relative injustice or inequality are a linearly homogeneous function of incomes' absolute and relative deviations from the mean, respectively.

By contrast, independence allows and specifies compromise intermediate measures of inequality injustice, notably of the augmented-income families. However, this then has to be the dual measure rather that the hybrid one, since the hybrid can be derived from the equal equivalent of an independent evaluation neither as a relative nor as an absolute form.[28] Yet both measures were provided and used, as the augmented-income measures derived from the intensive (for J) or extensive (for I^a) independent measure (hence with power or loga-

---

28. With a measure J defined as in note 23, $\bar{\bar{x}}$ defined from $J = 1 - \bar{\bar{x}}/\bar{x}$ or from $J = \bar{x} - \bar{\bar{x}}$ cannot be a function of a sum of functions of each income (if $J > 0$ for unequal distributions). By contrast, this is possible for the measure I with $I^a = \bar{x} - \bar{\bar{x}}$ and $F = \bar{\bar{x}} + c - f^{-1}[(1/n) \cdot \Sigma f(x_i + c)]$. Then the intermediate measures are obtained with a power or a logarithmic function f. Indeed, the following measures I (I^a and I^r) and J were used:

$$I^a = \bar{x} I^r = \frac{\bar{x} + c}{1 + c} J = \bar{x} + c - \left[\left(\frac{1}{n} \right) \cdot \Sigma (x_i + c)^\alpha \right]^{1/\alpha} \qquad \text{with } 0 < \alpha < 1,$$

$$I^a = \bar{x} I^r = \frac{\bar{x} + c}{1 + c} J = \bar{x} + c - [\Pi (x_i + c)]^{1/n}.$$

rithmic individual evaluation functions; Kolm 1966b). Rectifiance is then necessary to have nonnegative measures. But, among the possible reasons for rectifiance, the priority of welfare over inequality implies a disregard for inequality, the comparison of changes in number or gaps of pairwise inequalities in a progressive transfer leads to measures of other forms, and there thus only remains the P3I. But the only possible reason for the required PT-P3I is the general P3I, that is, independence. And the hybrid measure cannot be consistently derived from an additive evaluation function, either as a relative or as an absolute measure. The study *The Optimal Production of Social Justice* (1966a) introduced the compromise intermediate measures which are fully analyzed for independence in the book Kolm 1966b, and in this case and in the general case in *Unequal Inequalities* (Kolm 1977a, b).[29]

In *The Optimal Production of Social Justice* (1966a, section 6), the *marginal injustice* (or *marginal absolute or per person inequality aversion*), and the *marginal relative injustice* (or *marginal relative inequality aversion*), were defined as the limit of the ratio of the absolute injustice or inequality to the variance, and the ratio of the relative injustice or inequality to the variance divided by the square of the average, respectively, when the variance tends to zero (in particular, if all incomes tend to the same value). With an *independent and impartial* conception, they were shown to be minus one half the ratio of the second derivative to the first derivative of the individual evaluation function, and this value multiplied by the variable, respectively, for a value of the variable such as the average income. Then, the constancy of these two marginal injustices corresponds respectively to the exponential and power or logarithmic individual evaluation functions, that is, to equal-invariant absolute and intensive relative inequality measures. The *generalized and intermediate* cases were shown to correspond to *linear*

---

29. In this latter study, the income-augmented compromise intermediate measures are geometrically characterized by blow-ups (or downs) from points of the "generalized bissector" in the space of incomes with equal (negative) incomes, which correspond to the invariance of the hybrid measures and to the same blow-up of the absolute form of the dual measure. This study then worked explicitly with the relative and absolute measures for the various indicated reasons (meaningfulness of this duality and of the derivation from evaluation functions, meaningfulness and necessity of independence from the P3I, actual meaninglessness of ray-invariance as well as of ray-proportionality). But all the properties of the compromise intermediate measures proposed in both parts of this study are valid for all these types of measures.

(affine) functions for the ratio of the first derivative to the second derivative of the individual evaluation function. (This property was also applied to choice in uncertainty and portfolio selection in Kolm 1966b, and in a subsequent literature). Of course, ratios of the first two derivatives of the individual evaluation function completely characterize this function because it is only cardinal (and this kind of differential equation obviously characterizes the arbitrary linear transformation).[30]

Independence and Concentration Curve Dominance (*The Optimal Production of Social Justice*, 1966, section 7, theorem 9)

A distribution has a higher concentration curve than another if and only if it is preferred for all independent impartial benevolent rectifiant evaluations.

As a corollary, the same holds for distributions with the same sum and Lorenz curve dominance.[31]

Independence can be dropped from the foregoing statements, and the resulting benevolent Schur-concavity can also be replaced by impartial quasi-concavity (or concavity). Since a higher Lorenz curve and a not lower total or average income entails a higher concentration curve, this also implies a higher value for all these evaluation functions.

Inequalities or Injustice When Incomes Are Added, Averaged, Concentrated, or Sequentially Varied

One often has to consider the effects on inequalities (and on injustice or justice) of additions of various types of incomes, of deductions from incomes (such as taxes), of growths of various kinds of the incomes, of the addition of savings to wealths, or of other operations or trans-

---

30. $\sum f(x_i)$ is the additive specification of an independent, impartial evaluation function. $f' > 0$ is benevolence. $f'' < 0$ is both satiation (concavity of f) and rectifiance. $-(\frac{1}{2}) f''/f'$ and $-(\xi/2) f''/f'$, where ξ is the variable, are respectively the per person or absolute and the relative injustice or inequality aversion. $\bar{x} - \bar{\bar{x}}$ is convex when f'/f'' is convex; it corresponds to the intermediate measures when f'/f'' is linear (affine), and in particular to absolute invariance when f'/f'' is constant and to intensive justice when it is proportional to the variable.

31. The case of distributions with the same sum, and for nondecreasing evaluation functions, was a known mathematical property. For all cases, *The Optimal Production of Social Justice* considered weak and strong forms and a number of other equivalent properties.

formations. The answers depend on the structure of the comparisons and measures of inequalities. *The Optimal Production of Social Justice* provided the bases of this analysis (section 7, theorem 22), and *Unequal Inequalities* presented the full general theory and applications.

For instance, for independent rectifiant inequality measures whose relative form is intensive, for the absolute form (per person) the inequality in a sum of distributions is lower than the sum of the inequalities of the component distributions, with the special case of equality when these distributions are proportional to one another ("subadditivity"), and for the relative inequality the same property holds for the sum weighted by the relative shares of the total income of each distribution ("weighted subadditivity"). For these conceptions (independent rectifiant with intensive justice or relative inequality), for the independent rectifiant equal-invariant absolute measures, more generally for the dual intermediate independent rectifiant measures defined above, and indeed for all independent rectifiant measures with a *concave inverse of marginal injustice* (inequality aversion), then, for the absolute or per person measure inequality decreases less and less under the successive addition of identical distributions from an unequal one and toward an equal distribution. This property is "decreasing returns to equality". The "added" distribution in this result can have positive and negative components (that is, there can be decreases in certain incomes, possibly all). In particular, the total sum may be constant, that is, the added distribution is a mere redistribution and the moves are concentrations. In this case the property also holds for the relative measures of inequality. The assumed properties also imply concentration subdecreasingness (section 10.4), and a similar property for the absolute forms when moves are toward an equal distribution that is not a simple redistribution.

10.6   Averaging and Dispatching, Linear or Affine Transformations, Preferences for Mixtures and Averages, Diminishing Transfers, Variable Populations

Averaging and Dispatching

We consider now transformations of distributions into other ones. A transformation can be applied to several distributions (possibly all)

that constitute its domain, but, by definition, it is defined by parameters that do not depend upon the distribution it transforms. That is,
the ethical evaluation evaluates *processes*, in comparing the outcome
to the initial state. "Average" means here a possibly weighted average
(a linear convex combination). We first consider the two following
transformations:

1. *Averagings:* each final income is an average of the initial ones.

2. *Dispatchings:* each final income receives a relative share or fraction of each initial one.

These weights and relative shares depend, and depend only, on the
concerned initial and final individuals.[32]

We also consider two properties of transformations:

1. *Sum maintenance:* the total sum of incomes is preserved.

2. *Equality maintenance:* if the initial distribution is equal, so is the
final one.

Clearly averaging respects equality maintenance, and dispatching
respects sum maintenance.

Now, *rectifiance is identical to favoring transformations* that are
either of the following three:

1. *Sum-maintaining averaging.*

2. *Equality-maintaining dispatching.*

3. *Both averaging and dispatching.*[33]

This is also identical to favoring *linear or affine transformations of
any distribution,* that *satisfy both sum and equality maintenance.*[34]

---

32. If x_i and x_i' are individual i's initial and final incomes, and a_{ij} are nonnegative
numbers between zero and one (limits included), averagings and dispatchings are,
respectively,

$x_i' = \sum_j a_{ij} x_j$ with $\sum_j a_{ij} = 1$ for all i,

$x_i' = \sum_j a_{ij} x_j$ with $\sum_i a_{ij} = 1$ for all i and all j.

33. Proposition 1 requires that the domain of the transformation has a sufficient
dimension (it can be all incomes). Proposition 2 requires that this domain contains one
equal distribution with nonzero incomes.

34. The nonnegativity of the a_{ij} then results from that of the x_i and x_i' and universal
domain. The a priori form of the transformation can be with or without a constant
term.

Mixtures and Averages Preference

Impartial rectifiance is also equivalent to finding better, less unjust or less unequal the results of the two following operations that are equivalent to a sequence of PTs (*The Optimal Production of Social Justice*, sections 6 and 7, theorems 1 to 6).

First, *mixtures* are the result of *slice-reshuffling*, that is to say, the following transformation: All incomes are divided into slices of same proportions (that is, for each income we take, say, 30 percent of the income, 5 percent, 3 percent, etc., adding up to 100 percent); then we reshuffle the slices with same percentage among the individuals, in permutations that can differ for each case.

Second, we consider the $n!$ reassignments or permutations of the individual incomes among the individuals. From impartiality, they are all seen as equivalent. Then the new vector of incomes is any average of these reassigned distributions (they are vectors of incomes) that is not one of these permutations.[35]

The Principle of Diminishing Transfers

The priority justification of rectifiance extends to a next degree in *favoring more a PT when it is between lower incomes*. This constitutes the "principle of diminishing transfers" or "rectifiance of degree or order 2" (2-rectifiance) for the same differences among incomes.[36] This comparison can be considered when the first degree (isophily) does not discriminate (intersecting concentration curves). This extends to further degrees. The limit is maximin (there is thus always a discriminating degree—equivalence being possible). These comparisons are related to the dominances of the successive integrals of the concentration curves (or of the ordered distribution), and, for independent evaluation functions, to the successive derivatives of the individual evaluation function alternating in sign (which is the case for the cases

---

35. Mixtures and averages preference both result from the theorem that bistochastic matrices (the $\{a_{ij}\}$) are the convex hull of the permutation matrices.

36. The same ratios were also considered (the "principle of relatively diminishing transfers").

with "intensive justice", "absolute injustice", and for the dual compromise intermediate cases, considered in section 10.4).[37]

Aggregation and Separation of Populations

Considering together two individuals, who individually of course present no inequality, introduces an inequality if their incomes differ. However, if two individuals with different incomes are joined by an individual whose income is equal to one of the former two, then one inequality is introduced, but, also, one equality is introduced. More generally, lumping populations together adds inequalities across populations to the inequalities within populations, but it may also make people meet new others with similar incomes. Lumping together identical populations, or populations with the same proportion of people in each income class, may be conceived as not affecting some sort of average inequality—this is Dalton's principle of *proportionate addition to population*. This property, applied to the general measures of relative or absolute inequality defined in section 10.5, is *equivalent to independence*, and hence it furthermore implies *rectifiance* if these measures of inequality are nonnegative and can be positive. With this structure of the evaluation, the inequalities in an aggregation of any populations exceed the sum of the corresponding inequalities for the component populations, weighted by the relative shares of, respectively, populations for the absolute (per person) measures and total incomes for the relative measures, except if all the aggregated populations have the same proportion of incomes in each class (see *The Optimal Production of Social Justice*, section 7, theorem 21).[38]

This "proportionate addition to population" has, however, the possible limits implied by its equivalent structure, namely independence, that is, the P3I. This may notably come from properties of increasing returns of proximity, which favor clusters. The simplest example is provided by the extreme case of increasing returns to proximity, which only discriminates between strict equality and inequality (and does not

---

37. These principles and properties are analyzed exhaustively in Kolm 1974b and summarized in Kolm 1976b.

38. Other properties of aggregation of populations were also shown (*idem* and Kolm 1976a, b).

discriminate among different inequalities in pairs). Then, straightforward indexes of equality and of inequality are the proportions of pairs of equal and of unequal incomes, respectively. Consider a population of n individuals with different incomes, replicated m times. There are nm individuals, and hence $nm(nm - 1)/2$ pairs of incomes. Each income is replicated m times, which gives $m(m - 1)/2$ equal pairs, and since there is on the whole n such incomes, there are $nm(m - 1)/2$ pairs of equal incomes. Hence the equality index is $e = (m - 1)/(nm - 1)$, and the inequality index is $i = 1 - e = m(n - 1)/(nm - 1)$. This inequality depends on m, and hence the "principle of equiproportionate addition to population" is violated, except if n is very large and then $e = 0$ and $i = 1$. i decreases and e increases when m increases. They vary from $e = 0$ and $i = 1$ for $m = 1$, to $e = 1/n$ and $i = 1 - 1/n$ when m becomes very large. These latter values are $1/2$ for $n = 2$.

10.7   Multidimensional Inequalities

The relevant items may be bundles of goods rather than only quantities of the same good (income in particular). This is in fact a general, direct, and very important case, whereas the relevance of the unidimensional case, and in particular of income, should be established by a specific justification. Indeed, if preferences, tastes, and the like, are deemed irrelevant for respectful justice, and only they are, then the end values of this justice are the individuals' bundles of consumption goods. If furthermore certain exchanges or transformations of goods are also deemed irrelevant for justice and are left to agents' free choices, then the end values contain other resources (see chapters 6 and 9). Therefore the inequalities of quantities relevant for justice are a priori multidimensional rather than unidimensional. In fact major justifications of the interest of the study of unidimensional inequalities rest on the multidimensional case. There are two types of such reasons. First, the analysis of the multidimensional case rests on concepts, properties, and results of the unidimensional case. Second, the consideration of incomes, of their equality and of the limitation of their inequalities can be justified by multidimensional egalitarian considerations and concepts (the theory of efficient super-equity is a case in point—see chapter 6).

The comparison of multidimensional inequalities is a much richer question than that of unidimensional inequalities (see Kolm 1973b, 1975, 1977a). Each property in the unidimensional case can extend into several meaningful properties in the multidimensional case, and the relations are more varied.

In particular, the various properties that amount to rectifiance, isophily or the dominance of concentration curves and Lorenz curves have been extended into three concepts (see the above references):

1. *Specifically more equal:* the unidimensional comparisons apply to *each type of good separately.*

2. *Income (at all prices) more equal:* the unidimensional comparisons apply to each set of income distributions obtained from the given multidimensional distributions for *each given set of prices.*

3. *Uniformly more equal:* the unidimensional comparisons apply to each type of good, but with the *same* transformation to pass from one distribution to the other. For instance, in averagings the new *vectors* of individuals' bundles are averages of the former ones; in dispatchings the fraction of any quantity held by an individual that is transferred to another individual in the equalization depends only on the two individuals and not on the good. The transformation is again quantity-preserving averaging, or equality-preserving dispatching, or both averaging and dispatching.

The relation among these three comparisons is that "uniformly more equal" implies "income more equal" which implies "specifically more equal."

The uniform comparison (3) is the one that provides the multidimensional extension of the property concerning the sum of values of concave functions (see section 10.5): An allocation is uniformly more equal than another if and only if, for each strictly concave function of individual allocations, it provides a larger sum of the values taken by this function for each individual's allocation. If we add that these functions are sums of functions of one variable each (the quantity of one good), that is, they are additively separated, the property characterizes the relation "specifically more equal" (1).

Lorenz hypersurfaces and concentration hypersurfaces have been defined.[39] They constitute the multidimensional extension of Lorenz curves and concentration curves. The corresponding dominances (hypersurfaces above or below) are equivalent to the comparison by the relation "income more equal" (2).

The strictest of these comparisons, relation (3), is the one used for the definition of the multidimensional maximin which leads to efficient super-equity, and hence to the justification of equalizing incomes or of restricting their inequality (chapter 6).[40]

10.8 Conclusion

The comparison of inequalities has developed into the study of the properties of other specific indexes, applications notably to progressive taxation (Jakobsson 1976; Fellman 1976; Kakwani 1977), and empirical comparisons.[41] The properties considered above constitute the essential, the core and the basic ground of this domain. We have also discussed the various facets of their meaning, their limits, their degree of necessity, and the reasons why they should or should not be retained. Apart from the sign of inequality by assumption, impartiality as a consequence of the definition of the relevant vairables, and concentration-decreasingness, none of these properties is universal by necessity. Even the generally recommendable ones are prima facie

---

39. Kolm 1993g. If $x_j^i \geq 0$ is the quantity of good j held by individual i, with $\xi_j \geq 0$ for all j and $\xi = \{\xi_j\}$, the concentration hypersurface is the graph of

$$\lambda(\xi) = \max\{\sum_i \lambda_i : \sum_i \lambda_i x_j^i = \xi_j, \forall j; 0 \leq \lambda_i \leq 1, \forall i\}.$$

The Lorenz hypersurface is obtained in replacing x_j^i by $x_j^i/\sum_k x_j^k$. "Income more equal" corresponds to a surface everywhere below (the standard definition of the curves, for one good, reverses the axes).

40. Section 10.1 has provided references to further works.

41. Among the books that synthetize this domain, one can mention Chakravarty (1985) and Lambert (1993 edition), where, however, the history and origin of ideas is not presented exactly about a number of concepts and results. Furthermore a number of studies have systematically asked people how changes in distribution of the kind studied above affect inequality. The whole analysis of the basic properties of pure distributive justice indeed started from such enquiries in the late fifties and early sixties. Recent interesting studies of this type are those of Amiel and Cowell (1992) (who, however, do not present exactly the history of ideas) and of Harrison and Seidl (1994).

properties, possibly overpowered by stronger reasons. However, the organization of this set of properties, and their hierarchization by the degree and scope of the necessity to consider and to retain them have been presented at the end of section 10.2. This field constitutes the pure theory of distributive justice, along with the analyses of Equity and related properties presented in chapters 7 and 9, the consideration of the distribution of variables of different structures such as "fundamental" ordinal utilities and domains of choice recalled in section 10.1, the analysis of the general logic of justice,[42] and the related comparison and measure of poverty (see next chapter). Progress comes now from the integration of the logical structures of the relevant ethical, psychological and sociological properties, as suggested by the preceding discussion. Yet, the set of basic properties presented in this chapter and related ones constitute by far the most elaborate relevant contribution of logic to ethics.

---

42. Kolm 1990b, 1994b.

11 Needs and Misery

11.1 The Economics of Poverty or the Poverty of Economics

When we think it better that an extra dollar be given to the poor rather than to the rich, the reason typically has less to do with the fact that this attenuates inequality and more to do with the fact that it alleviates poverty.[1] Too low incomes have particular relevance. Suppressing dire misery is indeed both doubtless the most important problem of justice, and seemingly the easiest to define and identify. The alleviation of poverty has in fact been the basic objective of "social policies" and "development policies." However, decades of such policies show a large number of failures and, most importantly, very damaging negative effects, all of which have the same cause in the misconception of the nature of the problem and of its causes. The most damaging of all are the "development" policies that, in the name of modernization, wipe out balanced and invaluable traditional civilizations ("ethnocide") and transform their members into "poors" and beggars of the industrial world.[2] The people concerned are often forced into this transformation by a variety of political and economic means, and they are often unaware of the final outcome at the onset of the process.[3] A major cause of these dramas is the ignorance of the cultural and social aspect in both defining the problem and understanding its causes. In addition "measures of poverty" were considered, and although certain correctly described misery or want, others added their own challenges to logic.

Discussions of "poverty" have conflated (and sometimes confused) a number of distinct concepts such as low incomes, misery, inequality, needs, and exclusion. "Poverty" can apply to a number of quite different situations, which call for different policies or nonpolicies (that is, respect). Indeed in ordinary situations the people with the lowest incomes often feel that their needs are perfectly satisfied, because they live in stable traditional societies where all the needs they know of are

---

1. This is the welfare reason for rectifiance (see chapter 10).

2. Probably the most perceptive sociological analysis of this process is to be found in Germaine Tillion (1960) who calls it *clochardisation* ("bumization," one might say).

3. See the theoretical and empirical analysis of this process in Kolm 1982a, 1984b, 1994d. Let us emphasize that the foregoing remarks concern "development" and not help in accidental exceptional situations.

satisfied—or even because their philosophical-ethical-religious views lead them to value poverty. Hence what raises problems is not poverty or low incomes per se but rather misery or wretchedness, which cannot be separated from the reasons of the problem. And these reasons, when they are not directly in the domain of physiology, pathology and medicine, have to introduce the social, psychosocial and cultural context.

11.2 Needs

Misery and wretchedness are not topics to analyze but evils to oppose. They are to be fought rather than thought. Only their causes require understanding. *Needs* are altogether different. Which needs are to be satisfied, with others' help if necessary, and why, constitute a major social question. The answer is of course unambiguous for strictly vital needs. It is, however, a priori not obvious not much further above, in particular for those of the *basic needs* that are not strictly vital. The difference is important, as shown by the example that the nutritional content of a minimal "decent meal" can be provided otherwise at about one tenth of the cost. And a decent meal in one culture can be adject food (or forbidden food) in another. Should, however, taxpayers subsidize particular eating habits? The circus became a subsidized basic need in Rome (on a par with bread). Do TV sets and cars satisfy basic needs elsewhere? Does schooling? At what level? Innumerable lists of needs and of basic needs have been provided by development agencies. The political debate seems to discover a new basic need every month. Psychologists' contributions, such as Maslow's "hierarchy of needs," are illuminating but usually remain at the nonoperational level of broad categories. When practical, the lists of needs that should be satisfied, by others' help if required, are usually asserted with well-meaning and commonsense remarks rather than argued for from analysis.

The concept of need is characterized by a series of properties. The situation of each particular need in certain of these dimensions determines its property of "basicness" and the possible reasons for its being relieved by others' help. The duty to help alleviate others' needs can indeed rest on several rationales. Certain reasons derive from the respect of humanity in individuals or from the relief of suffering. An important reason rests on the interference between the *objective* aspect of needs and a certain sense of *community* inducing co-accountability. This constitutes the dual of the conception of community of (productive) *capacities* described above (chapter 6). Individuals are—roughly —given both their initial capacities and a number of their needs. Hence they cannot be held responsible either for these capacities or for these needs, and this view holds that they should not be accountable for them. The "natural" allocation of these characteristics to individuals is seen as being morally arbitrary. Hence justice requires the sharing of both the benefits of these capacities and the burden of these needs. The need liabilities are pooled just as the human assets are. This reason, comparison and duality is most clearly expressed by Blanqui's motto (taken again by Marx) expressing the ideal relations between individuals and the community: "From each according to his capacities, to each according to his needs." This view can also be applied to only certain of these needs, and also of these capacities. In a less communal setting, only the satisfaction of "basic needs"—for instance —is guaranteed by the group. More generally and for any reason, the satisfaction of certain needs can then be end values of justice, which entails ideally their equal satisfaction for persons in the same relevant conditions.

The relevant properties of needs are the following: degree of *necessity* of the satisfaction of the need for the person, for relief, material subsistence, social existence, culture, or self-realization; *objectivity or subjectivity* for the person (external vs. internal, in a sense), where objectivity for the person can be either subjectivity for others or for society (for instance, "proper" food, clothing or type of education), or objectivity with respect to society (for instance, purely physiological needs); *intensity* (either for the person or in others' eyes); *nature*, either physical or cultural or otherwise induced by others, or indeed being considered a need of the person only by others ("vicarious needs"); *origin*, such as physiology, education, experience, acts or choices of the person, or social pressure; *responsibility* or nonresponsibility, of the person, and possibly of other people, of society or of culture; *satiability* as opposed to *expandability*, with also perverse expandability when satisfaction uncovers or suscitates other needs; and is the need a *value* or a *liability*. These properties are quite distinct, yet related.

The satisfaction of certain needs is *necessary* for the very *existence* of the person as such. These are physiological needs for—above survival—the adequate and normal functioning of mind and body, and the requirements of social existence in norm-determined forms of consumption and in means of social relation. This is the main criterion for defining *basic needs*. The duty of satisfying these needs of others who cannot do it themselves rests on an *existential justification* similar to that presented for *basic liberties* and complementary to it (chapter 3). Both "basics" are indeed closely related. A basic liberty can be a basic need. They are also commonly complementary: Satisfying basic needs prevents basic liberties from being purely "formal." At the most basic level, physical integrity has to be protected from both starvation and aggression. Yet above this level cultural and social requirements make these needs substantially dependent on culture.

The intensity of a need is another reason for helping. However, the actual reason in this case is, rather, that another reason becomes sufficient (for instance, the alleviation of pain, or some social effect).

Other people, or the culture of society, may designate, as an individual's need, something that he would not have considered as such by himself, because they hold the corresponding consumption to be proper, adequate, etc. The individual himself has no direct responsibility for this need (he may however have put himself in the situation that elicits this judgment of others). The individual must then be coerced into the corresponding consumption either out of his own resources— for instance, by law or by the general social pressure of approval or disapproval—or, if the corresponding goods are provided to him, by a material impossibility or an interdiction of selling them. Such *vicarious needs* are akin to Richard Musgrave's (1959) "merit wants" (these are government's desires, and the term is rather odd).

The morals of *responsibility* and retribution (see chapter 9) entail that others have a lesser duty to help an individual satisfy a need of his when this individual is more responsible for this need (other things being equal). An individual cannot be held directly responsible for his basic needs and for his vicarious needs, since he cannot avoid them—although he may have avoided, and hence be held responsible for, certain acts that led him into a situation where these needs are not satisfied. A common reason behind the advocacy of pooling the satisfaction of certain needs, discussed above, is that individuals cannot be held responsible for these needs that they cannot avoid (at least directly and easily). Similarly the intensity of a need is commonly seen as beyond the reach of the individual's will, and hence not the (direct) responsibility of this individual, and a reason to help him. "Objective needs" are conceived as more related to "human nature", and thus less the responsibility of the individual, than "subjective needs" are (although, again, they may materialize in situations for which the individual bears a responsibility). "Subjective needs" are more on the side of desire, even though a rather compulsive kind of desire; now, desires are seen as largely within the realm of the individual's responsibility (or, at least, accountability), although not for strongly compulsive desires (notably when they reach pathological levels).

The *structure* and the *dynamics* of needs and of the set of needs are also important considerations. The aspect of necessity of needs tends to give them two related basic structural traits. First, most needs are more or less *satiatable*. "Insatiable needs" tend to be either pathological, or a misnomer as they really are cravings or genuine compulsive desires rather than needs. This is of course a favorable feature for defining need satisfaction. Second, needs tend to be ordered by priorities and in a hierarchy (as Maslow emphasized). Therefore, satisfying a need is likely to bring to the forefront another need crying out to be taken care of. "Basic needs" are by definition first in the order of priority for ordinary persons. The aim of the satisfaction of basic needs can be seen as making room for needs of quality which manifest the value of man and implement the values of civilization, with the risk that some different drive takes the place.

The needs that are or should be considered as basic in a society, and hence whose satisfaction should be supported by others if necessary, depend in particular on the means of this society, say on its average income. This relation has a specific structure. Basic needs tend to be rather constant when society's means are low, as they consist essentially of basic physiological needs (they cannot all be satisfied when the means are very low). Then they tend to increase with society's means. But they possibly tend to be rather constant again in rich "gadget societies" whose extra wealth is spent in nothing really "basic." In this latter case, even if further "objectively valuable" needs are supported, the would probably not be "basic."

Determining objective needs is often considered a difficult task. It is indeed even an impossible task if one hopes to find a definition that is independent of culture and history. Purely physical and physiological needs are relatively easy to define. But most needs are determined, either in totality or for an essential part, by culture-determined tastes, habits, social relations, and various norms. Furthermore the types and levels of needs that are or should be considered as basic in a society at a certain time cannot but depend upon this contingency, both in themselves and in relation to the availability of means. Thus one cannot overemphasize the importance of culture in needs of all types, above the physiological basis and closely intermingled with it. Since this physiological basis is relatively clear, the whole question refers to culture (or "civilization"). But this also provides the key, since *culture, which creates the need, by the same token defines it as such.* As a consequence an objective (acultural) definition of an objective need is usually impossible, but the sociological determination of such a need is usually rather clear, and its political revelation is commonly easy and available. Contrary to many others, this problem is difficult (impossible) in theory but easy in practice. Indeed at a moment in time and in a given culture, there typically is a rough consensus about what the important or basic needs are. When different views exist in this society at a given time, it is usually only a matter of delay between the different political families, all following in the end the same general trend of their common civilization.[4] This of course does not say everything. There can be collective mistakes. Yet this argument has been so often "cultural racism" (rather than paternalism) which ignores, disparages or despises cultures, notably in the name of "modernization" and "development" (for instance, as regards a certain education), and it has so often been misused to destroy cultures more or less directly and rapidly, that it should be faced with a priori suspicion and requirement of complete justification.

On practical grounds, alleviating needs can be achieved through the transfer of general purchasing power (income) when the individual's

---

4. See Kolm 1977b.

considered needs coincide with his preferences. This is commonly the case for basic needs (apart from various questions of information). case for basic needs (apart from various questions of information). On the contrary, specific intervention is required for purely vicarious needs or for vicarious orders of priority in the satisfaction of needs.

Finally, having needs of quality is the essence of a man of quality, in particular of a man in tune with a culture and a civilization. In contrast, desire is beastly. Even short of giving "to each according to his needs" in a society of men "rich in needs" (Marx), conscious and autonomous need-building takes precedence over the mere satisfaction of these needs. The right way to fully pose the economic question is not "how can we derive the greatest satisfaction from what we can do and have," but rather "given what we can do and have, what set of satisfiable needs should we build into ourselves so as to be the best people possible."[5]

11.3 Measuring Poverty: The "Progressive Deficit" or "Weighted Head Count"?

The cultural dimension has been well understood and emphasized by analyses of "relative deprivations." "Relative," indeed, means here compared not to others' incomes or consumptions, but to what the individual considers "normal" (Runciman 1966), or to cultural standards, to the means of carrying out a good personal life as the society understands it (Townsend 1971).

The income value of this minimal normal standard is a "poverty line". This "line" is indeed a basic concept of most of the "measures of poverty" that have been considered for a very long time and notably of those that accompanied the "ideology of development" since World War II (certain measures do not have such a "line," however, as it will be noted below). The question of this "measure" is interesting, as with inequalities, because it pinpoints in the most precise way the logical side of all the issues raised by the concept that one attempts

---

5. Further analyses of needs can be found in the works of Maslow, Barry, Soper, Braybrooke, Thompson, Doyal, and Gough (see references). See also Kolm 1959, 1977b, 1982a.

to grasp.[6] The concepts have in general been properties of the distribution of incomes below the "poverty line," with the two exceptions of measures without a "line" and of the multidimensional comparisons used in certain early studies of poverty and development.

The simplest measure is the *number* of people whose income is below a "poverty line," that is, the number of "poor" or *unweighted head count* (sometimes used as proportion of the total population). This measures the *extent of poverty* (rather than its depth). It is a relevant measure when the poor constitute a rather distinct category, in particular when they all have about the same income level (if we do not want to also measure the possible psychosocial phenomena due to size discussed in chapter 10 and below, and which tend to be specific to society and culture and not very relevant for international comparisons, for instance). This is then a sufficient statistic of poverty when this level is known. This level is often a "subsistence level" (more or less qualified by cultural considerations). When the poor have various levels of income, this measure is standardly refined, when needed, by providing the number of people (in proportion) for various levels of the poverty line (or, equivalently, the poverty lines that correspond to several numbers). However, this is no more a unique measure.

Since the number or proportion of poor is the normal and a priori correct index of poverty for the comparison of states of society with all poors at about the same income level, a normal and correct measure of poverty should be proportional to this number *for such comparisons*. This is the case of both the "social deficit" and the "progressive deficit" or "weighted head count" described below (but not of the "poor's Gini" described in note).

A full measure of poverty can aim at measuring either one of two basic concepts.[7] In the strict sense, poverty refers to low means, and hence, equivalently, to the lack of means or consumption for reaching the non-poverty level, which is a "deficit" such as an "income deficit." Then, the appropriate measure of poverty in society is the total lack, the sum of these deficits for all individuals (or other relevant economic

---

6. Certain proposals were also blatant nonsense, as it will be noted below.

7. These two measures are discussed and applied empirically to West African countries in Kolm 1959.

units), that is, the *social deficit* (notably in income). On the other hand, the reason for the moral objection to poverty is the hardship it imposes on the poor. One can try to represent this hardship. The measure would then grasp something like "misery" or "wretchedness" rather than poverty in the proper sense of the term. In particular, it has to express something in the area of the following: Since an individual (or a family) satisfies with priority his more urgent needs (as he sees them), then an increased lack of his means (such as income) leaves unsatisfied new needs that are more urgent than those that were already unsatisfied; that is, there is "increasing marginal hardship"—as a function of the deficit in means or consumption.[8] The corresponding measure is the "*progressive deficit*," or "*weighted head count*."

The *social deficit* measures *shortage* or *lack* of allocation, consumption, or means. This is in particular an operational concept: The "social deficit" of a good is merely the amount to be distributed to those who have less than a certain level so that they reach this level. The reference can be individuals, families or other groups. The "income social deficit" is the same notion applied to income. The "social deficit" bears a close relation to the *comparisons of inequality* (Kolm 1966a, sections 6 and 7; see chapter 10): A higher social deficit at each reference level is equivalent to a lower concentration curve (sum of the n lowest incomes as a function of n). Of course, the social deficit relative to a given level that is seen as the "poverty line" could not a priori measure the "hardship" of poverty. Indeed, first, if a poor's income steadily decreases, all units equally increase the measure (in particular, there is no "increasing marginal hardship"). Second, and consequently, 1,000 almost-not-poor individuals below the poverty level by 0.1 percent of its value, contribute the same amount to the social deficit as does one individual at zero income—who therefore dies from starvation. This does not describe the relative "badness" of the two situations, and if they are alternatives one should certainly not prefer one death to 1,001 almost-not-poor (at the indicated level) because it provides a lower social deficit.

---

8. This standard structure can of course be violated by a number of psychological phenomena, such as becoming accustomed to poverty or losing sensitivity to further hardship.

The indicated standard "hardship" of poverty is simply grasped by attributing more weight to "deeper" units of deficit. Uncertainty concerning the specific differential psychology of the various poor leads one to attribute the same weight for the same depth below the poverty line for all individuals. Then these weighted units of deficit are added. This measure can be seen in two ways, according as one focusses on levels of income (or of deficit), or on individuals: the *weighted head count* and the *progressive deficit*. The weighted head count adds the numbers of incomes below each level weighted by a decreasing function of this income level, from the bottom up to the "poverty line."[9] This amounts to dividing individuals' deficits into small "brackets" and adding across both brackets and individuals in weighting each bracket by a weight that is an increasing function of the corresponding level of deficit. This also amounts to adding the values of an increasing and convex function for the various individuals' deficits, that is, the "progressive deficit" measure. This function is called the *poverty function* (it generally takes the value zero for a zero deficit).[10]

A measure of poverty has this form if and only if a given addition to a poor's income disminishes this measure by an amount that depends only on this income level (and not on others' income levels or on the poor's other characteristics) and is the larger the lower this level; and only if a transfer of one dollar from a poor to a poorer diminishes the measure by an amount that depends only on these two income levels. Furthermore, the progressive deficit of a distribution is higher than that of another, for a given poverty line, and for all convex poverty functions, if and only if the social deficit is higher for the first distribution than for the second for all poverty lines lower than the one considered.[11] An "equal equivalent" deficit is defined as the deficit that would give the same measure of poverty if all the poor had it (as in Kolm 1966a, section 6). This equal equivalent deficit is also a possible measure: It is the deficit measure of poverty as hardship (the additive

---

9. These are differential weights for a continuous addition.

10. In empirical work, the weights were often a linear function of the deficit or income, corresponding to a quadratic poverty function.

11. See Kolm 1959, 1993g (higher means here higher or equal; the cases with strict inequality are easily introduced).

form makes it a mathematical "mean" of the deficits). This is an increasing function of the previous measure. The equal equivalent deficit is higher than the average deficit per poor, because of the convexity of the poverty function, and hence because of increasing marginal hardship. The difference or the ratio of their levels thus measures this increasing hardship. This equal equivalent is multiplied by a number if all deficits are multiplied by this number, or is added an amount if all deficits are added this amount, if and only if the poverty functions are linear functions of either power or logarithmic, or exponential, functions, respectively. Most concepts and results developed for measures of inequality are meaningfully and readily transposable for poverty such as, for instance, absolute and relative measures, absolute and relative increase in marginal hardship, diminishing transfers, intermediates between the power and the exponential cases (power functions applied to deficits plus a constant), addition of incomes of various types, aggregation of populations, comparisons of multidimensional poverties, and so on (see Kolm 1966a, sections 6 and 7, and chapter 10 above).[12]

---

12. If d_i is individual i's deficit, the weighted head count approximates $\sum f(d_i)$, with $f(0) = 0, f' > 0, f'' > 0$. The power case is $\sum d_i^\alpha$, with $\alpha > 1$. The mean with power is $\bar{d} = [(1/n) \sum d_i^\alpha]^{-\alpha}$. The linear weights case amounts to $\alpha = 2$; in this case the poverty index can be computed from the social deficit and the variance of deficits. Indexes of poverty of these families have been studied by Clark, Hemming, and Ulph (1981), and by Foster, Greer, and Thorbecke (1984). A review of indexes of poverty can be found in Chakravarty (1985).

Another proposal has been to measure poverty by a sum where the deficit of the nth least poor among the poor is counted n times: It is the deficit of the richest poor, plus twice the deficit of the second richest poor, plus three times the deficit of the third richest poor, and so on (Sen 1976). By analogy with the Gini index, this is appropriately called the *poor's Gini*. Higher deficits have greater weight (which is the intent). Yet the difference with the weighted head count or progressive deficit measure is that the poor's Gini applies this larger weight to all the inframarginal units, whereas the weighted head count or progressive deficit counts more highly only the units that correspond to deeper poverty. Since these poverty measures intend to measure hardship for the poor, the case against the poor's Gini and for the progressive deficit is clear.

This can also be seen as follows. Assume that the poor are about equally poor: Incomes below the poverty line have about the same level. With the weighted head count measures, poverty with n poors is n times poverty with one poor. By contrast, the poor's Gini measures poverty with n poors as $n \cdot (n - 1)/2$ times poverty with one poor. For instance, it sees poverty with 10 poors as being 45 times poverty with one poor, poverty with 100 poors as being about 5,000 times poverty with one poor, and poverty

An adequate choice of the convex poverty function can make very low incomes have a very large effect on the measure. It even permits one to avoid the choice of a particular "poverty line" which is often rather arbitrary. Poverty then is the sum of the values taken, for each individual income, by a "poverty function" *of income*, a function that is positive, decreasing, and convex, and that takes sufficiently low levels for incomes that are certainly not poor's incomes so as to make their global contribution to the measure negligible. Such a measure of poverty is higher with one distribution than with another for all convex poverty functions if and only if the concentration curve of the second distribution is higher than that of the first. The equal equivalent income corresponding to such a measure is the "poverty income" (this is the mathematical mean of individuals' incomes with the poverty function). The poverty income falls short of the average income because of the convexity of the poverty function, that is, because of the increasing marginal hardship of poverty. Therefore the difference between the average income and the poverty income, or their ratio, measures this increasing hardship. The poverty income is multiplied

---

with 1,000 poors as being about half a million times poverty with one poor. With a weighted head count, one extra poor always adds the same amount to poverty. By contrast, with the poor's Gini the nth poor adds n times more than the first one. For a poverty measure that intends to describe the hardship to the poor, these properties make the poor's Gini completely out of place, and they confirm the weighted head count as the normal and central measure. The poor's Gini presents an extremely negative size effect of the number of poor. If it intended to describe some outsider's impressionnistic view of poverty, first, this would not be the viewpoint of the poor, and second, one could not justify this steady acceleration with the number of poors (there might be a jump once, when one becomes aware of poverty). If anything, a larger number of poor, in lowering the isolation of each poor, might rather attenuate certain aspects of the hardship of poverty (there may be other effects—see below—but certainly not capable to explain this structure and intensity).

Finally, again with similar incomes for all the poor, the poor's Gini is proportional to the individual deficit: A lowering of the income of the poor by some amount augments the poor's Gini by an amount that does not depend on the level of this income. More generally, for the case of possibly different poor's incomes, if all the incomes of the poor decrease by the same amount, the poor's Gini increases by an amount which does not depend on the initial levels. This violates the notion that additional hardship is higher for deeper poverty, which the progressive deficit measure grasps by definition (and which was in all cases the reason for not using the social deficit as measure).

In short, *what should be added with weights is not the rank of poverty (weighted by deficits) but the rank of deficit brackets (weighted by number)*. The poor's Gini index mistakenly reverses the axes.

by a number when all the individuals' incomes are multiplied by this number, or is added an amount when all the individuals' incomes are added this amount, if and only if the poverty function is a linear function of a power or logarithmic, or of an exponential, function, respectively.[13] Indeed, again, most concepts and results developed for measures of inequality are meaningfully and readily transposable to these measures of poverty, such as absolute and relative measures, absolute and relative increase in the marginal hardship of poverty, diminishing transfers, intermediaries between the power and the exponential cases (power functions applied to incomes plus a constant), addition of incomes of various types, aggregations of populations, and comparisons of multidimensional poverties.

In fact, this case is identical to the analysis of inequalities with an independent (additively separable) symmetrical rectifiant evaluation function, with the individual evaluation function being any linear (affine) decreasing function of the poverty function. Furthermore, the case with a povery ligne is the particular limiting case where the poverty function is constant and zero for incomes above the poverty ligne. Hence all the relevant concepts and their properties have been considered with the analyses of inequalities (essentially in Kolm 1966a, sections 6 and 7; see chapter 10 above). This also holds when independence-separability is abandoned (see below).

A number of further refinements lead to the abandonment of the convexity or the continuity of poverty functions for certain deficits and incomes, the additive separability, the nondifferentiation of individuals, or the aggregated representations using a single variable for each individual and a single aggregate index. Each of these changes is justified by psychological, social or ethical reasons that provide the specific structure. For instance, the form of the poverty function may have to depend on the use of income (such as the fact that people cease to consume certain types of goods when income is too low, which may possibly induce a structure with poverty threshholds), on the social

---

13. If f is the poverty function, with $f > 0$, $f' < 0$, $f'' > 0$, and x_i is individual i's income, poverty is $P = \sum f(x_i)$, and the poverty income is $x^p = f^{-1}(P/n)$, where n is the number of individuals. The power and exponential cases then are $f(y) = y^{-\alpha}$ and $f(y) = e^{-\alpha y}$ with $\alpha > 0$.

structure of society (within the poor), on past experience, and so on. Nonseparability may in particular result from the special effects of the extent of poverty.

The extent of poverty can indeed have a number of effects on its hardship. The poor may lose hope of getting out of poverty when they see more poor around them. On the other hand, this diminishes their socially relative poverty which may be painful in itself. Seeing other's misfortune may help one to endure one's own, just as it may draw attention to it with the opposite effect. A culture of poverty may be fostered either by a larger number of poor, which favors interaction among the poor and consciousness of their existence as a group, or by fewer poor who are aware of their common singularity and may cling together in defense. It may soothe poverty by providing explanations, meanings, examples of similar misfortune, the reconstitution of sub-societies and mutual comfort, and possibly help, but it may also worsen it by collective brooding over misfortune and by developing a sense of helplessness or guilt. The fact that more extended poverty draws general attention is hardly relevant because poverty measures harshness for the poor rather than an observer's impression influenced by his particular information or attention.[14]

Basing the measure on individuals' incomes which they freely spend is valid if no vicarious need demanding other priorities is relevant. Measure by a single index has obvious limits, however, especially for so deeply social a phenomenon as poverty and its consequences. Poverty and underdevelopment have thus been compared in using several variables (income, life expectancy, education measured by years of schooling, etc.). Indexes have been constructed with weights for these various aspects, and overall indexes of underdevelopment have been computed as previously in replacing income by these indexes. This has been related to the multidimensional concentration dominance (see chapter 10): Underdevelopment is higher with all (nonnegative)

---

14. If only additive separability of the measure is abandoned, and there remains nondifferentiation of the individuals (symmetry) and rectifiance (a small transfer from a poor to a poorer diminishes the measure), then the measure is an increasing Schur-convex function of the deficits, and the relation with social deficit dominance, noted above, still holds.

weights and all convex underdevelopment (or poverty) functions if and only if the concentration hypersurface is higher.[15]

---

15. See the preceding references. Let x_j^i be the quantity of the favorable item j for individual i. The property is that $\sum_i f(\sum_j \alpha_j x_j^i)$ is larger for all numbers $\alpha_j \geq 0$ and all decreasing convex functions f if and only if $\lambda(\xi)$ is larger for all relevant vectors $\xi = \{\xi_j\}$ with $\xi_j > 0$, with

$$\lambda = \max\{\sum_i \lambda_i : \sum_i \lambda_i x_j^i = \xi_j, \forall j; 0 \leq \lambda_i \leq 1, \forall i\}.$$

The graph of the function $\lambda(\xi)$ is the concentration hypersurface (for one quantity j only, the classical concentration curve is obtained by inverting the axes).

V LIBERTIES, MORALS, AND THE STATE

12 Freedom, Morals, Market Failures, and the State

12.1 The Social Theories of Process-Freedom

Presentation

In the general principle of "equal freedom" (see chapter 2), equality is emphasized for means-freedom (and end-justice), whereas, for act- and process-freedoms, equality is commonly only implied in the statement that everyone should enjoy the corresponding liberty (although the Declaration of Rights emphasizes "free and equal in rights"). Chapters 6 to 11 have analyzed a variety of concepts of equal means and ends. We now revert to act- and process-freedoms already considered for the two essential cases of *basic rights* which must have priority (chapter 4) and of *full process-freedom* which is the founding theory of modernity (chapter 5). The emphasis, furthermore, is on interdependent free acts (in contrast with the concept of Equity; see chapters 7 and 9). We want to know what consequences such principles entail for society. Since the principles refer to freedom, the consequences will often be legitimizations, explanations, or requirements of processes and institutions, rather than explicit end-states. We thus now examine, evaluate and compare all the conceptual uses of the liberty of processes or acts as founding or legitimizing the basic allocative institutions. This will emphasize the roles of *markets*, of the *public sector*, and of *morals*.

These views constitute a field of theories, spanned by alternative possible hypotheses about the *basic criterion*, man's *motivation* (such as being egoistic or moral), and the extent of *market failures*, with varying conclusions concerning the places of the market and of the public sector, and the nature of the theory (moral, explicative, or prudential). A number of these possible theories have been elaborated, and this includes, notably, *private* and *complete full process liberalism*, the school of *Public Choice* and the work of James Buchanan which inspired it, neo-*"libertarians"* and classical *Libertarians* ("right" and "left" "anarchists"), the proposals of scholars such as Friedrich Hayek and Milton Friedman, David Gauthier's "morals by agreement," and the roles of the theories of *Public Economics* and of the *redistributive state*. Furthermore, this investigation requires us to elucidate the basic questions of the possible motivations and of the nature of the criterion of liberty.

The joint and comparative consideration of these theories provides a great advantage, first because each position on each specific issue is common to several of them, and second, more important, because the contrasts of their differences concerning both assumptions and conclusions are particularly enlightening. This set of theories constitute the topic of both the present chapter and the next.[1] The present chapter presents the basic features of these theories. Chapter 13 will deepen the analyses on two aspects. First, it will emphasize the essential comparisons among these theories, in the various relevant dimensions. Second, it will analyze the possibilities and ways in which ethics can have an actual influence on the acts and facts in society. These latter considerations are essential here, notably because one of these theories, "Public Choice", has posed a fundamental challenge to all ethics in arguing that the lack (or insufficiency) of moral motivation precludes that moral views have a significant influence: Were this conclusion fully true, ethics would be an essentially useless exercise, at best something like a song, an incantation, or medieval scholastics, and hence to begin with an inconsistent endeavour, since it is a priori intended for application (that is, it is "practical reason" in Kant's terms).

As we will see, the possible influence of ethics is in between this impotence and the classical "state-moralism" which assumes that the government can implement any ethics that is proposed (subject only to informational limits). This is in part due to the fact that people seek the appreciation of others and shun their reprobation, which separates the persons who act morally from those who judge morally, enables one to have moral views implemented at no cost for oneself, and, to begin with, contributes to make "self-interest" a deeply ambiguous concept. At any rate, a crucial consequence of the noted position is that a theory that deems ethics to be useless and wants itself to be useful cannot be an ethical theory. All it can try to do is either to explain moral-looking behavior or rules, as well as immoral ones, or to advise people in their own narrow "self-interest." That is, it can only be either *explanatory* or *prudential*. This affects essentially the

---

1. Recall that chapter 5 constitutes a summary of full process liberalism.

theory of Public Choice (and "morals by agreement" which is indeed a part or an extension of it).

As a result, in particular, for this view, freedom cannot be a moral value (this would be an impotent concept); it is only an explanatory principle or a personal means. Consequently freedom does not mean the same thing for this view and for the theories that take liberty as an a priori principle of social morals, which is the case of all the specific theories described in previous chapters. This difference between both concepts of liberty is both in nature and in scope, since the difference in nature (moral versus nonmoral) entails a difference in the boundaries and hence in the scope and in the distribution of liberty: When the amoral view mentions freedom, this cannot imply that one agent's liberty is limited by the requirement to respect others' liberty-rights, as it does for the moral conceptions. That is, this view's freedom is also that of the egotistic conceptions of Nietzsche, Spencer, or Rand, but with an altogether different use of the concept. We will see shortly that the neo-"libertarian" school is also to be attributed this conception of liberty, although not without problems of consistency.

These different definitions of liberty constitue the deepest divide among the whole set of theories considered here. For the moral or principled freedom-based theories, "one man's freedom stops where the other man's freedom begins." One is not morally free to hurt, enslave, or, possibly, rob one's fellow man. Nothing of the sort exists as an a priori principle in the other view. The argument would be that nothing, in the meaning of the word free, precludes that hurting or enslaving someone be a free act; on the contrary, preventing hurting constitutes, by nature and definition, a limit to this liberty; but so is the prevention of preventing, and so on. That is, freedom is power and is limited by the agent's weakness rather than by his duty, and by others' strength rather than by their right. One can say that this view considers power rather than liberty; or that the two sides consider freedom respectively as right and as power; or that for one side freedom provides power while for the other power provides freedom; or, again, that for the principled view freedom includes a priori and by definition "freedom from" others' aggressions, while for the other view freedom is basically only "freedom to" (including to defend oneself if one can). In an eighteenth-century vocabulary, these unprincipled and principled liberties would, respectively, be *natural liberty* and *natural rights*. Of course interacting people may, or may have better, end up respecting others' rights because of others' self-defense or retaliation, because of the police, or because of a rule agreed upon tacitly or explicitly, but this is neither an a priori rule nor necessarily moral behavior in the sense of morally motivated behavior. The principled theories see the other theories as amoral, but they are themselves seen by them as either utopian or incomplete.

The views recently revived under the name "libertarian," giving this word a new sense (Murray Rothbart, David Friedman, etc.; see section 12.15 below),[2] rest on the unique principle that "the state is evil because the state is violence and violence is evil." But if the unique principle is that the state is evil, then individuals' freedom that is not a priori morally constrained is acceptable or good. An if violence is evil, then freedom should be a priori morally constrained to exclude violence. This a priori constitutes a contradiction. But moral constraint cannot be the state's doing, given its members' assumed motivations and situations. And from what this school says of private protection, one should infer that its view is that what is good is unprincipled liberty, and private protection prevents it from actualizing into violence. This, however, constitues a petitio principii that cannot be said to be fully supported by historical evidence. The neo-"libertarian" basic view is prudential, for people who suffer from the state's repression and hypocrisy, it sounds moral in its indictment of the state and its condemnation of violence, and it may indeed be moral, and it offers an explanatory principle, notably for state actions which are seen as maximally predatory. The implementation of bringing down the state would be by formal and informal politics. Individuals can a priori be moral (except if they work for the government), altruistic, for instance, although they are seen as essentially self-interested, and this provides the mechanism of the superior private courses of social life.

Still other views see freedom with a moral eye but only as a means to some other ethical value, such as "welfare" for the views con-

---

2. The choice of this name violates this theory's own favorable view of property rights and of the right of first occupancy, since this name has been preempted for over one century by "left anarchism," a very different view, which is no less opposed to the state but holds opposite conceptions of the value of capitalism and of human nature. This is all the more unfortunate as certain scholars add to the confusion in extending the name "libertarian" to full process liberalism (at least private one) in spite of its resting on the opposite view of liberty.

sidered here (thanks, for instance, to the efficiency potential of free exchange).

However, similar views about freedom or motivations can lead to very different outcomes, and opposite views can lead to comparable outcomes, because of other differences, notably, as concerns government, as a result of the views about of "market failures." For instance, the public sector seen by Public Choice is exactly the actual one which it explains (apart from possible prudential advice), and complete full process liberalism also ends up with a notable public sector, because they both take full account of market failures, although both views are opposed as concerns freedom, motivation, and the nature of the theory. Conversely, neo-"libertarianism" and private full process liberalism both discount market failures and advocate no or minimal government, although they have opposite views of freedom and different ones as regards motivations.

Therefore a large part of the understanding of the field consists in making explicit the various issues and in situating each theory on the grid constituted by the various options for each issue, so as to see the kinships, the differences and oppositions, the general problems and possibilities, and the effects of the answers to each specific question. The basic assumptions concerning motivation, market failures, the nature of the question, values, and the concept of liberty, lead to the differences concerning the nature, role, and quality of the public sector, the morality of behavior and motivations, the level and type of the agreements (local or general, effective or fictive), and the very nature of the conclusions. Although this grid of interrelated issues makes these theories constitute a very integrated set, each issue displays a large variety of actual or possible positions.

Indeed, the theory may be either moral, or explicative, or prudential. Liberty may be an end value or a means for social ethics, or an acknowledged fact. Individuals may be either only egoistic, or largely capable of moral behavior, or at least sufficiently moral in the government or as voters, or moral in the government and only egoistic outside it, or egoistic but acting morally by explicit or implicit exchange for others' similar behavior, or, again, induced to moral acts by their quasi self-interest in the others' judgments. The public sector may either be the endogenous product of the process, or it may use its dominant force to act as a moral protector, implementer or corrector, or on the contrary as the utmost immoral despoiler and oppressor; it may be *deus ex machina* and savior, or the very incarnation of evil, or again a more realistic social process where politics does not preclude a variety of motivations. Agreements among individuals may be local as in ordinary markets, or society-wide as in classical Social Contracts; they may be actual, and then either explicit or implicit, or they may be putative as in (almost) all Social Contracts. Finally, the morals of a theory can refer to either one or several values, and, for instance, either keep consistently to process-freedom or complement it with other values such as welfare, equality, or altruism.

The differences among the various theories can be introduced in the following constructive way. Assume that several agents using their liberties have aims that set them in opposition to one another. Then there are several possible cases. The agents may have sufficient concern for the others so as to adjust their desires accordingly (this possibility may depend on the "social proximity" of the agents,[3] and the concern may in fact be for others' views of oneself). Alternatively there may be moral rights limiting the agents' freedom so that their actions that respect these rights are consistent (these rules can be either internalized by the agents as duties, or enforced on them, or supported by others' opinion for which the agents care, and their possible origin will be discussed below). But also none of these may exist.

Foundational Theories

In the latter situations without rules nor altruism, the agents consider using force against one another. If one agent is unquestionably stronger than the others, he will have his way. If this is not the case, either fighting erupts or the individuals acknowledge that they can save the costs, harm, and losses of fighting by agreeing about the contentious issue. The potential fighting then constitutes a priori a state of reference and threat. Two things must now be considered: exchange and a more general level.

First, agreement always involves yielding up about something *in exchange* for a similar behavior by the other(s). And what is exchanged can be more than just abstention from violence. With several goods and different preferences, the superior alternative to quarellous force-

---

3. The scope for this kind of behavior in general is analyzed in the book *The Good Economy, General Reciprocity* (Kolm 1984b).

ful acquisition can be mutual yielding up something, that is, exchange in the strict sense. Then, with a sufficient set of possible exchanges, other threat points in an exchange can be provided by the possibility of other exchanges, that is, by competition. A full market can develop. At this point the neo-"libertarian" ideal is reached. But of course this outcome of force alone may also a priori yield slavery or anything else odious, and when the outcome is exchange, it can be blocked into inefficient states by "market failures". However, another scholar in the field, David Gauthier, argues more optimistically that people should find fruitful and possible to agree on terms that are the respect of the liberal rights, from which a perfect market develops, plus, in case of market failures, a particular sharing rule to be discussed shortly. This is his "morals by agreement," which explores an important research program (although this specific conception departs from logic on two basic issues noted below).

Second, agreements may a priori involve any number of people, and certain arrangements will be beneficial to all the members of a larger society. A foremost case of this larger social scope consists of the pooling of the means to enforce local agreements. A number of public goods constitute other cases. These arrangements take the form either of a written constitution or of a set of various rules, conventions, laws, habits, etc. Buchanan calls these the constitution, which can be either implicit or explicit. This constitution sets various rules for dealing with the specific cases that may occur in the future and cannot be foreseen in detail. It has no moral content per se—other than being a state of peace and being unanimously preferred to open war. It may adopt liberal rights in general, and hence let a market develop, and choose the rules of a political process for dealing with the various cases where this process can do better than the market. The domain of "Public Choice" is basically the study of this political process as a set of exchanges among its participants of various types.

Market Failures

Recall that we termed a "market failure" a situation where some non-market way of doing things can outperform the market (chapter 5). The "performance" of reference can vary with the theories considered. In a number of important cases, the performance of this nonmarket course can be preferred by everybody (Pareto-inefficiency). Yet full process liberalism is content with unanimous preference within a subset of persons with the respect of everybody's liberally legitimate rights (chapter 5). There are, however, two very important aspects that may or may not be included within "market failures." First, the protection and enforcement of any right *can be seen* as a domain of market failure when it is not provided in the best possible way by self-restraint, self-protection, and the market for services of security. Second, the distribution that results from the market *can be seen* as a market failure by the appropriate theories. Yet these last two cases are not commonly included under the vocable "market failure."

Principled Theories

In the cases where there are *a priori moral rules and rights*, these requirements often have to be enforced by coercion (or by the threat of coercion). The coercive agent cannot behave exclusively in his narrow egoistic interest, since this would lead him to use his power in violation of these rights. He then has to have some kind of moral behavior, and he is assumed to be in the public sector (the question of moral behavior and motivations will be discussed in the next chapter). Assume now that these rights include the process-freedom of liberal economic rights to own and exchange. Then a market develops.

The ensuing theories are distinguished from one another according to two aspects: the extent and nature of *market failures* they see in the market, and their fundamental *ethical criterion*, which can be either full process-freedom or "welfare" (in the latter case, liberty may be a means for welfare through adequate markets and policies). Apart from market failures proper, there is on the one hand the protection and implementation of rights for which all these theories require a public force, and, on the other hand, the question of distribution. Full process-freedom considered in the full dimension of time generates its associated distribution (see chapter 5).

The two first following theories see *no market failure proper*.

First, the tradition of Locke, and in particular Nozick nowadays, values full process-freedom. This is *private full process liberalism*. The public sector is restricted to the protection of the liberally legitimate rights. This is also *minarchy*, that is, minimal government or the minimal state. Government is reduced to the police (and the army), and the police requires a budget which is only a very small fraction of GNP (the addition of courts of justice would not affect this conclusion). The resulting distribution, which is determined by the natural allocation of capacities, the extension of the process over time and the rules for allocating other natural resources, is seen as legitimate.

Second, any other theory of justice may appreciate markets for their possible Pareto-efficiency, yet it may find unjust the resulting distribution since it does not consider process-freedom as the ethical end value. Distribution is therefore entrusted to the public sector (in addition to the protection of rights), and performed through transfers or through the allocation of rights to resources—with possible delicate problems of information and incentives if the end values imply the outcomes of markets and in particular final satisfactions. This is the theory of the *distributive state*. Pareto offers the first precise suggestion of this view. His particular ethical ideal is a special utilitarianism including individuals' sentiments of altruism and of justice (Pareto 1913). Yet other criteria of justice may be used, such as equal sharing of certain resources, fixed-duration income equalization (see chapter 6), efficient super-equity as a second-best equality in consumption (idem), the maximin or leximin of Practical Justice (chapter 7), or satisfaction of needs.

Other scholars admit that there can be certain market failures, yet on a quite small scale, as is for instance the case with Hayek and Milton Friedman. Still others see a much larger scope for market failures, and this is generally the case with *Public Economics* of various kinds. Views differ widely, however, according to which *moral principle* should be followed for the correction of these failures, and for the praise of the market in the first place.

Two principles are considered: liberty and "welfare." Public economics is consistent in choosing the same criterion for praising the market and for the public correction of its shortcomings. This, however, leads to two theories: Liberal Public Economics which rests on liberty (see chapter 5), and Welfarist Public Economics which takes welfare as its objective. Both demand Pareto-efficiency but they a priori differ as regards distribution. For this purpose, Welfarist Public Economics mainly relies on a Social Welfare Function, a problematic concept which will be discussed in chapters 14 and 15. Scholars like Hayek and Friedman are less consistent—or more eclectic—as they want the market first and foremost for freedom (of exchange), yet their measuring rod becomes welfare when they see the market fail and they admit a (small) role for government. Welfarist Public Economics alone, among these theories, praises the market for its efficiency for welfare (the Adam Smith–Pareto tradition).

Government and Markets

All these views see the corrections of market failures as the *raison d'être* of governments—if we include the protection of rights and distribution. The principled theories of all kinds see these corrections as constituting the moral duty of governments. Yet Liberal Public Economics emphasizes both the virtues of public decentralization for efficiency, clarity, and responsibility, and the actual dispersion of moral motivations at all stages of the political and administrative process.

Finally, the authentic, historical Libertarians (or "left anarchists") oppose both the repressive state and the exploitative and egoism-reinforcing market, and base their ideal on the basically moral relations of free reciprocity, solidarity, community and participatory democracy.[4]

Synopsis

As table 12.1 shows, related dimensions of morals, markets, and the public sector span a wide field of views which are both comparable and yet sometimes very different and opposed to one another. A common ground of these theories is that they are more or less individualistic—yet with possible altruism and a sense of community for some (and certain qualifications for "social welfare" and "community anarchists"). Relatedly, most see the public sector as the substitute for the market when it "fails" for specific reasons (and this may be a large role). On the other hand, morals may be either self-interested collective behavior (Gauthier), irrelevant in general and absent in government ("libertarians"), de facto negligible (Buchanan), necessary in the public sector (from minarchy to Public Economics), or possibly widespread (original Libertarians). The market may be perfect (Locke-Nozick and Pareto), even capable of providing the protection of rights

---

4. For a recent development of this social philosophy, see Kolm 1984b.

Table 12.1
The theories of liberty, markets, morals, and the state

I. Principled (a priori moral)

Theory / Characteristic	Liberal Public Economics	Welfarist Public Economics	Minimum-plus (Hayek, Friedman)	Minarchy (Locke, Nozick)	Distributive (Pareto)
Markets	Failures		Small failures	Perfect	Perfect
Moral criterion	Freedom	Welfare	Freedom for markets, welfare for state	Freedom	Welfare
Government	Liberal social contracts, public sector	State-moralism — Protects, corrects, distributes	State-moralism — Minimum-plus	Minimum, protects rights	Distributive, state-moralism, protects rights

II. Basic

Theory / Characteristic	Public Choice (Buchanan)	Neo-"libertarians"	Morals by agreement (Gauthier)	Classical Libertarians
Level	Overall constitution, politics	Local: anarchies Exchanges		Reciprocity
Markets	Failures	Best	Failures	Moral failure
Moral agents	No moral motivations			Moral motives Moral behavior

("libertarians"); or it may exhibit failures which can be remedied by other means, and which are either quite limited (Hayek, Friedman) or possibly substantial (Public Economics, Public Choice, Gauthier); and it may be a model for the public sector either for the analysis (Public Choice) or for the choice of public policy (Liberal Public Economics). The resulting size of the public sector can vary widely, from zero (the "libertarian" ideal), not much more than 1 percent of GNP for the police of the "minimal state," probably less than 10 percent (without the army) for Friedman's and Hayek's recommendations, up to its actual levels for Public Choice and possibly this order of magnitude for Public Economics.

We will now briefly consider and evaluate each view. The comparisons between them will be analyzed more in depth in chapter 13.

12.2 The Two Public Economics

The normative correction of market failures by the public sector is studied by *Public Economics*, which is either "liberal" or "welfarist." *Liberal Public Economics* studies the implicit agreements and exchanges that result from complete process liberalism, described above as "liberal social contracts" (chapter 5), and it determines the corresponding government actions, taxes and transfers (Kolm 1985, 1987a,b, 1991c); the distributional base can be of any kind, including full process freedom, income redistributions for lower inequality, catering for needs, and so on. By contrast, the much-studied *Welfarist Public Economics* uses "welfare" as its ethical criterion (see, *inter alia*, Kolm 1964, 1968a,b, 1969b,c, 1970a,b);[5] this includes many studies concerning aspects of the justice of distributions, such as inequality and poverty (see chapters 10 and 11).

Both types of Public Economics are concerned with Pareto-efficiency. Indeed, for Liberal Public Economics, its absence constitutes a market failure that calls for a liberal social contract—since it implies that there is a unanimous preference for another state. Hence many results of Welfarist Public Economics which refer only to Pareto-efficiency are also valid for Liberal Public Economics. These results are indeed much more interesting for Liberal Public Economics since this also implements a type of Pareto-efficiency restricted to subsets of agents as long as its attainment only requires the use of their liberally legitimate rights (other persons may lose, as long as their legitimate rights are not violated). The final difference between the two Public Economics resides in the distribution. One cannot say a priori that one is more redistributive than the other (we have noted in chap-

---

5. The term "public economics" was first introduced in the book entitled *Foundations of Public Economics* (Kolm 1964). The following year, Leif Johansen (with whom I discussed the topic) titled his book *Public Economics* (1965). (The topic is of course much older, and the scientific economic analysis of the economy of the public sector, notably with a normative intent, can neatly be dated back to Dupuit 1844; see chapter 14, section 14.9).

ter 5 that overall optimal taxation is certainly much *more progressive* with complete full process liberalism, and even only for the financing of public goods by Liberal Public Economics, than it is with Welfarist Public Economics). Yet the main point is that the theoretical tools of Welfarist Public Economics *for dealing with distribution* have various and serious problems of meaning, logic, and ethics. This is the case with the sum of utilities (see chapter 14), a politically given Social Welfare Function (politics hardly provides such a thing),[6] an a priori Social Welfare Function (this may violate reason and justice; see chapter 15), the approximation of utility by income, or the maximization of the "surplus" (the surplus' comparison of willingnesses to pay a priori cannot determine the good distribution, and it classifies this criterion within Liberal Public Economics when it is extended to actual compensation; see chapter 14, section 14.9). However, two kinds of distributional uses of welfare concepts can be meaningful and justified in certain cases: the maximin Practical Justice (chapter 7, section 7.2) and the comparison of pairwise preferences (chapter 14, section 14.7).

12.3   Hayek and Friedman: Free Market and a Minimal-Plus State

Certain influential economists like Friedrich Hayek (1976) and Milton Friedman (1962; see also Friedman and Friedman, 1981) advocate an economy that is, say, about 95 percent market and 5 percent government. The large market role is for the sake of freedom, the small government role for the sake of welfare. The government's job is to take care of certain weak market failures (externalities, nonexcludable public goods) and to alleviate severe poverty, in addition of course to the protection of rights (the comparisons in the next chapter will pinpoint differences between both authors; Friedman furthermore wants all money to be public, whereas Hayek wants it to be only private).

Both Hayek and Friedman suppose that giving any larger role to government would necessarily diminish freedom, although both concede that officials can be well meaning. Hayek, in particular, argues

---

6. The use of the preferences of an elected politician must consider the normative worth of the electoral process, the actual actions of this politician and their aims, etc.

that "social justice" is a meaningless and undefinable "mirage." He praises the development of a social "spontaneous order" in opposition to "constructivism." But can his view not be seen as a particular conception of social justice? And are not dictatorships the "spontaneous" outcomes of history? Friedman concedes that the existing distribution came about by chance anyway and is therefore always unjust;[7] his point is that to rely on a government to correct it can only make matters worse. The practical upshot is much the same either way.

12.4   Private Full Process Liberalism

Full process-freedom with a perfect market is, as we have noted, the central social ethical justification of the market system and capitalism, the view that socialists of various kinds opposed. The consequentialist justifications of the market by wealth, welfare or Pareto-efficiency, including those developed by Adam Smith and by Pareto, have been only of secondary importance in history (although this may be changing nowadays). Private full process liberalism is thus, with nationalism, the main ideology of the last two centuries, that is, of modernity.

An early expositor of this view is Locke (1689). Dozens of writers elaborated its implications during the nineteenth century. Then, the expression "political economy" meant or implied private full-process ideology. Marx, for instance, set out to "criticize political economy" in this sense, as the titles of subtitles of most of his works indicate (see chapter 9). Recently Nozick (1974) elaborated several points. A systematic logical construction of the theory can be found in Kolm (1985a and 1991e, along with the public part of full process liberalism). Locke notes no "market failures" (no systematic analysis permitted this in his time), and Nozick denies their existence (he discusses the case of a public good, yet of an *excludable* public good for which an access price can be demanded). The government is reduced to its so-called "minimal"—or "night watchman"—role of protecting liberally legitimate rights. This requires the police, possibly courts—hence much less

---

7. In a personal discussion.

than 1 percent of GNP—plus the army. Locke justifies this government by a Social Contract among property owners. Nozick explains how it could spontaneously emerge as a "dominant protective association" to which people buy the service of protecting their rights. Yet he adds a slight moral tinge in the end, which crucially differentiates him from his neo-"libertarian" inspirers. Indeed, the all-powerful members of this "association" have to be *morally* motivated to respect peoples' rights, since, otherwise, they would just seize this payment and more.

Two other views accuse private full process liberalism of betraying its ideal of full process-freedom and of being inconsistent, in very important ways. These two views, which are very different from each other are Marx's theory of exploitation and complete full process liberalism. Marx's theory of exploitation denies that propertyless workers are actually free when they rent out their labor force for a wage. This is certainly a fair use of the term "freedom" when the wage is at subsistence level and the workers' alternative is starvation (one has, however, to consider the nonindustrial occupations that workers may have left). But the case is less clear for higher wages which permit the worker to chose a shorter worktime one way or the other (in the day, the week, the year, or in life)—Marx then explains wages by workers' consumption habits, which thus induce a kind of sociological bondage. In addition Marx's further elaboration of the notion of exploitation is problematic (see chapter 9). *Complete full process liberalism*, on the other hand, accuses private full process liberalism of not seeing the various cases of market failures, where process-freedom should be implemented by public vicarious actions that actualize the corresponding liberal social contracts and constitute *public full process-freedom*, the necessary public part of (complete) full process-freedom (see chapter 5). This makes a very large difference with respect to the role and size of the public sector.

12.5 "Libertarians"

A number of authors calling themselves "libertarians," such as Murray Rothbart (1973) and David Friedman (1978), advocate only freedom and *define* liberty as the absence of government. Hence their position comes to be exclusively against anything that is government. We have seen above this view's ambiguity (or inconsistency) as regards the kind of liberty considered, which basically amounts to discounting the possibility of private violence. These authors furthermore emphasize "property rights" and their free exchange. This antigovernment stance makes this position an anarchism. It is, indeed, the age-old "anarcho-capitalism," very different from other brands of anarchism which take a richer and deeper view of human relations, motivations, and institutions and whose basic question is the extent of the possibilities of the nonegoistic motivations they consider (for a recent work and analysis in this latter trend see Kolm 1984b).[8]

These authors provide a number of important arguments showing that a variety of actual government activities could be performed by the market, and might be performed better by the market than by government (although the "deregulations" they more or less inspired have also shown a number of unforeseen drawbacks). They thus provide salutary indictments of arguments used by the political class to enlarge and maintain its domain of power, and also a healthy and necessary challenge to the scientific vindications of publicness. These authors also propose a number of different variants of their basic position. Yet their view meets problems, one of which is the following. Living in organized societies as they do, these authors see that coercion is mostly monopolized by government police. They forget that if this institution is ruled out, as they advocate, and if the individuals remain essentially self-interested (as they see them), then coercion and violence by private agents would a priori rule the land. Indeed these authors want the protection of persons and property to be left to self-defense, or entrusted to private profit-making protection firms. Yet why would such a firm demand payment for its job? It would just take this money (and more), since it has the force and it lives for profit. Logically, such firms can only engage in racketeering and in gang warfare against other such firms. And if one wins over the others, it will probably end up calling itself a "government" (yet it will not submit itself to democratic elections)! This unprincipled liberty may well resemble the freedom of the free fox in the free poultry-yard. Even

---

8. As we have already noticed it, this use of the name "libertarian" is quite unfortunate, for the name had been preempted for a century and a half by the other, "left," anarchists. This is especially problematic, since some people now extend this name to private full process liberalism.

the term "property" is misplaced here, since all there can be is possession (using lawyers' and Hegel's apt distinction).

This school should also explain why governments monopolizing force are not always maximally exploitative, and it should see a difference between despots and more or less democratic systems, between a dictator and a Swiss canton. This shows an insufficient analysis of politics, of the constraints on the public sector and of the motivations of its members.

Finally, this "libertarianism" thus brings an important and stimulating voice in the dialogue that constitutes society's search for its own best forms. Given that man's motivations commonly make him look more eagerly for arguments when he knows the answer in advance and "believes in it," this kind of division of the collective labor of argumentation may well be efficient. Yet given the very simple view of man and of society taken by this school, its conclusions have to be taken for what they are: pleas rather than judgments.

12.6 Public Choice and Buchanan's Constitutional Social Contract

Fighting individuals may *all* avoid harm, save the resources used for combat and defense, and possibly benefit from cooperation, by accepting a *truce*. When the issue is the state of society at large, this unanimous agreement inevitably takes the form of rules to be followed, because of the informational difficulties of agreeing on all of the specifics in advance. These rules, explicit or tacit, constitute what James Buchanan calls a constitution (*The Limits of Liberty*, 1975). They may include basic rights and a political process for dealing with the frequent market failures. This political process is a market substitue —or a "political market"—whose rules are unanimously accepted with the constitution, and which can be seen as a set of self-interested exchanges—for instance, of government services against votes. The important field of study called *Public Choice* sets out to study political processes as free exchanges generally among *exclusively self-interested individuals* (such as power-seeking politicians). Distribution, and in particular public redistribution, results from this whole process.

This constitution, and its consequences, are accepted by unanimous *consent* (either an explicit or a tacit one). This seems to give them a sound and important moral justification. The authors furthermore often pronounce injunctions on practical matters, which also have a very moral overtone. However, in this theory, the alternative to consent is the actualization of the threats to use force, coercion and violence. The explicit contractarian reference is indeed Hobbes. And the theory says that the constitution is changed if the forces, or the willingness to use them, change (see, for instance, Buchanan, op. cit.). That is, a priori this consent may well be consent at gunpoint. Unanimous preference sounds good, but the unanimous preference to war may be surrender. Definitely "might makes right" in this theory. Hence this theory *cannot* be considered as pertaining to the realm of morality, or ethics in the strict sense. It is *not an ethical theory stricto sensu*, but only a theory that could *explain* certain moral-looking rules or acts, as well as immoral ones by any account. Its outcome is anything that exists in society: possibly certain *behavior* with a moral form or certain equalities, but also any inequality of any kind, and serfdom or slavery if that be the case. This theory can *explain* the outcome, but it can hardly *justify* it, and still less legitimize it morally. It is an amoral theory, and an immoral one *if* it were used as justification.[9]

The "Public Choice" authors do not deny this. On the contrary, they pride themselves on it. Indeed they argue that *there exists nobody who could implement an ethical view* because "all political and social actors are only self-interested for what matters" (this notion of "self-interest" will be discussed in the next chapter). Therefore they see ethical theories of all kinds as useless and pointless, and they commonly deride them as mere noises.

One might then be surprised by certain moral-sounding injunctions coming from the same authors (for instance, for suppressing public

---

9. Hobbes's Social Contract can be said to justify, by unanimous advantage, the autocrat's rule over pacified subjects who become *equal* in submission. In fact Hobbes's individuals are envisioned as roughly equal in force before the Contract (they fight rather than one completely dominating and exploiting the others) and in status after it. This prevents one from applying the preceding remarks to Hobbes's scheme. If, however, the autocrat is included within the considered society (in our modern views, he has to be), then, first, the choice of the ruler is relevant (it could, for instance, be successively everybody in turn, in Athenian theoretical fashion), and, second, defending oneself against one's neighbor may not be worse than being exploited by an all-powerful, purely self-interested (in the Public Choice fashion) monarch—this later remark is the point of La Fontaine's answer to Hobbes in the fable *The frogs who demand a king* (God sends them a hungry crane).

deficits). But I think this is quite explicable. These views are to be seen as technical ones. Their conclusions are prudential in that they indicate how certain people can be made better off. But furthermore the normative overtone can probably be justified by the fact that the advocated measures could possibly make everybody better-off (a "Pareto-improvement"). These positions are then "technical-unanimist" rather than "moral-distributional." Or, possibly, deserving people would be better off, or everyone's opportunities would be increased, and so on.

Given its extreme simplicity, the basic psychological hypothesis of Public Choice is sufficiently realistic for it to be worthwhile or necessary to consider its social consequences. This approach therefore certainly constitutes an important research program. However, the analysis of motivations presented in the next chapter shows that there also exist other important behaviors that can more or less implement moral principles because their motivation has a moral side or because the actor is concerned with others' opinions about himself. Then, the conclusion that normative analysis should draw from the view of Buchanan and Public Choice is to propose only theories for which the motivations that can lead to their implementation can exist, along with the required power and information. That is, realism and implementability require that we only propose motivationally constrained second-best theories of ethics, social ethics, and justice. The proposition that this qualification renders the set of these theories empty is unwarranted. Man clearly is not angel but nor is he beast, and especially he rarely likes to pass for one.

12.7   Morals by Agreement

However, even bluntly exploiting one's threat advantage may not in the end best serve one's interest in the narrowest sense. One may gain from eliciting full cooperation from others, and this may require that one imposes certain constraints on one's own behavior. Indeed in certain situations, noncooperation produces outcomes such that certain other possible ones would better serve everybody's interest ("inefficiency"; the "prisoner's dilemma" structure is a case in point, and it constitutes, indeed, the general a priori situation of all mutually fruitful exchange when cooperation fails to actualize). There may exist a rule of behavior such that each individual's best interest is to follow it, assuming the others follow it too. This rule may be called "rational." David Gauthier, in his book *Morals by Agreement* (1986), believes that these suppositions are the case, and he describes this rule as follows: First, respect full process liberal rights. When this gives perfectly competitive markets, this is the solution. Second, in cases of market failure the solution builds up in two stages: imagine a reference state of "peaceful interaction"; by assumption, certain possible states are preferred to it by all the concerned persons. Choose among these the state that corresponds to the well-defined rule of "equal relative concession" above this state of reference.[10]

The general idea of deriving moral behavior from the narrowest self-interest in cooperative situations is a very important one. Note that behavior is classified here as "moral" by virtue of its acts and not of its underlying basic motivation. Narrow self-interest is of course not the only actual motivation, notably in cooperative situations, yet it is obviously very important to know what it can lead to and what it can explain, since this is sometimes (or often) the unique or main motivation, and since other motivations are often too uncertain to be relied upon and the moral ones are commonly more asserted than actual. Explaining rules in this manner is indeed an important program for game theory. It is, in particular, very important to know if and how the respect of liberal rights and of certain rules for sharing can be obtained in this way. Hence Gauthiers' overall intent is of major importance.

However, the particular theory and proofs provided turn out to have problems with logic about a couple of basic points. They can be rescued with other hypotheses, elements and specific results, but this more or less changes the theory. In particular, and most important, if Gauthier's general outlook is true, then what it proves to be "rational" is full process liberalism, liberal social contracts and Liberal Public Economics. This is indeed the direct consequence of Gauthier's argument that the solution respects liberal rights and of his acknowledgment of the existence of market failures.

---

10. Two collective books discuss this proposition of Gauthier, respectively edited by E. Frankel Paul, F. Miller, J. Paul, and J. Ahrens (1988) and P. Vallentyne (1991).

Gauthier, however, insists on a couple of points that have to be replaced.

One such point is the principle of *equal relative concession* for sharing surpluses and its use of *individual utility*, two aspects that Gauthier deems to be central to his theory. This particular theory—a "solution" of the bargaining problem that had been formally considered by game theorists Raiffa (1953), Luce and Raiffa (1957), and Kalai and Smorodinski (1975)—will be recalled in appendix C along with other such "solutions," but the first point about it is that it *requires the use of a concept of cardinal utility which is hardly meaningful*—as it is shown in the next section. This, however, also invalidates a number of other well-known theories, such as utilitarianism (see chapter 14) and the "Nash bargaining solution" (whose proposed justifications are also otherwise erroneous, incomplete, or arbitrary; see appendix B).

Now, replacing "utility" by gain or income would render all these uses of a cardinal utility logically possible. Doing so might even be justified by the view that what is relevant for justice or fairness is not individuals' ends but the means to them. However, all these theories definitely want "utility." This is the case for utilitarianism, of course. But it is also the case for bargaining theories such as Nash's or Gauthier's who want to use "subjective utility" rather than an objective payoff—a point that Gauthier forcefully emphasizes.

Second, a problem of the prisoner's dilemma type played once among several self-interested players cannot be solved by the individuals' mere choice, without commitment, to follow a rule given their knowledge that the other people reason as they do—as suggested. These individuals indeed would have an interest in breaking such a rule. However, one can introduce modifications into this game that can indeed solve the problem. They are of three possible kinds. (1) One can decide ex ante to create an institution that can enforce promises and promises conditional on promises (see chapter 1). (2) The game can be repeated, a situation whose effects have been much studied by game theory and which can substantially improve the efficiency under certain conditions (such as uncertainty in termination to prevent "backward induction" if there tends to be any); more generally, the game can be sequential, and this is definitely realistic for the choice of general rules of social life. (3) The individuals' mentality may be different; in particular, if they are rational in the sense of choosing "for a reason" with a certain objectivity, several reasonings can solve the problem[11] (the introduction of elements of altruism or of reciprocity constitutes a more classical possibility[12]).

Third, *Morals by Agreement* presents a number of other shortcomings that can be more or less easily corrected and are more or less detrimental. For instance, there are other causes of "market failures", and other strategic behaviors leading to such "failures", than situations of the "prisoner's dilemma" type; these can be introduced. The time dimension is also necessary to define the ownership of capital. "Peaceful interaction" does not suffice to define a precise state unless types of effects and ways of appropriation are made more explicit (Gauthier, for instance, admits the pollution of one's neighbor as a "peaceful interaction," but the line between pollution and aggression is not always easy to draw). There may be several competitive equilibria. And so on it goes.

Morals by Agreement is also extraordinary, notably in the eyes of Public Economics of all kinds and of Public Choice, in that it speaks only of market failures, "public goods," externalities and the like without once mentioning government, the state, the public sector, politics, voting, or elections.[13] Gauthier however mentions "our institutions and practices" for sharing surpluses. Whether the noted rights and sharings are enforced by public constraint is not mentioned. The game-theoretic interest of Gauthier probably leads him to answer negatively. Yet we have noted that the one-shot "self-interested" game does not solve the problem. A number of phenomena would make people *demand* or establish coercion: the need for a promise-enforcing institution; the prevention of free riding (one free-riding problem concerns the collective punishment of deviators in a sequential game with more than two players); the ascertainment of others' behavior in certain game-theoretic situations (then the constraint is not actually binding for each individual); people's desire to be coerced so that their

---

11. See Kolm 1993e.

12. See, for instance, Kolm 1975a, 1984a and Collard 1978.

13. These terms are absent from the index of this book. In fact "government" appears once in the text ... in the remark that utilitarianism requires one.

short-run impulses do not jeopardize their long-run interest (notably with regard to repeated or steady cooperation); and so on. Furthermore, education can more or less inculcate motivations that induce cooperative behavior.

Gauthier's final outcome is a possible theory of justice (except for the meaninglessness of "equal relative concession") since it defines equal rights or liberties (and equal "relative shares"), and their arrangement, namely liberal rights and the sharing of surpluses above a "peaceful interaction" that respects these rights. We have noted the necessary precisions and corrections.

The justification of this outcome is an implicit agreement, and hence a Social Contract. This agreement is among actual persons, as are all Social Contracts except Original Positions and Fundamental Insurances (see chapters 3, 8, and 9 above), and in particular as are Buchanan's constitution and the Liberal Social Contract among present-day theories.[14] It is, however, a Social Contract implemented by self-interest (as are many others, including Buchanan's in modern times) rather than for a moral motivation of either keeping an implicit promise or realizing the good state of society defined by the Contract. One of its most important features, however, is that it is a *total* Social Contract (see chapter 2) that *derives* liberal rights, and in particular act-freedoms and the Rights of Man, rather than postulating their moral rightfulness—Gauthier barely mentions the "classical rights to person and property," yet he discusses "peaceful interaction" and relies greatly on property and market rights.

This kind of overall idea may be the best explanation of the fact that certain societies actually respect these rights. Then, however, the global theory should be perfected and the most straightforward manner is to emphasize that the game is repeated or sequential without a clear termination. More generally, Gauthier "moralizes" the Buchananian outcome by having the contractants find it beneficial to respect others' liberal rights, to consider sharing surpluses from a baseline of "peaceful interaction," and to accept a type of equality in sharing. Yet these outcomes and their self-interested "rationality" are asserted rather

14. See a note of chapter 3 for the case of certain pre-Rousseauan classical Social /ontracts.

than proved. As it stands, the theory offers no proof of the irrationality of violating others' liberal rights, of sharing from an unpeaceful
baseline, of making no concession at all, of taking rather than exchanging. When fully worked out, a theory of this kind may provide
the respect of liberal rights and a certain symmetry in the sharing
of surpluses, but it may also lead to something else under threat.
The determination of the conditions for the various outcomes is an
important research program, which, however, should also introduce
the possibility of more complex motivations (see next chapter) and
the conception of rationality appropriate to questions of justice (see
chapter 2).

12.8   Generally Meaningless Cardinal Utility

"Cardinal utility" refers by definition to *utility functions* defined *up to
any increasing linear transformation.*[15] This is equivalent to the *actual
meaningfulness of the numerical value of the ratios of differences in
utility levels*, and also, in very common cases, to the actual meaningfulness of the fact that *the difference between two utility levels is larger
than another such difference.*[16]

Cardinal utility has been widely used in economics and game theory, and it is necessary for a number of concepts used in social ethics.
Among these concepts are utilitarianism—discussed in chapter 14—
and a number of possible solutions to bargaining situations which
include, among others, those proposed by Raiffa-Kalai-Smorodinski,
which is also Gauthier's "equal relative concessions," and Nash. The
Nash bargaining solution has been used by Braithwaite (1955), and it
is discussed by Barry (1989) with an important more general discussion of two-stages theories of justice.

If a theory that uses a cardinal utility makes sense, this cardinal
utility has to make sense. This meaningfulness of a cardinal utility is
implied by the theories that assume such a function. The various

---

15. "Linear" means here "affine" rather than proportional.

16. This second property requires a further topological hypothesis of connectedness on
the domains of variation that need not detain us here (see the discussion and general
proofs in Kolm 1992b and 1993c, and the works of K. Basu (1983), M. Lebreton
(1984), and W. Bossaert (1994)).

theories sometimes present explicitly this assumption and sometimes imply it by the properties they use. Two cases have to be distinguished.

In one case, the theory considers choices or preferences in uncertainty with the von Neumann–Morgenstern theory and the corresponding use of a cardinal utility. This is justifiable by considerations of rationality, although of course it by no means describes universal behavior. The risk is assumed to be representable by probability distributions, and the cardinal form results from the structure of the calculus of probability. This theory's maximization of the expected value of utility results, notably, from what should be called *probability-consequentialist preferences*, that is, lotteries whose prizes are lotteries are appraised only by the resulting probabilities. A couple of theories that are or can be relevant for social ethics rest on this uncertainty-relevant cardinal utility. They are the two theories proposed by Harsanyi to justify utilitarianism and which will be analyzed in chapter 14, and the derivation of one structural aspect of the "Nash bargaining, or cooperative, solution" suggested by Harsanyi and Selten (1972) (note here that the derivations of Nash's full solution do not abide by logic irrespective of their use of cardinal utility, as shown in appendix B).

Other theories use no such uncertainty and their use of cardinal utility has to be justified on other grounds.[17]

We will now consider the question of the general meaningfulness of a cardinal utility, in trying to appraise whether its equivalent properties noted above can make sense.

Utility functions have been taken to mean preference, preference "revealed" by choice, satisfaction, happiness, with more or less close relations among these possible meanings.

---

17. Distributional solutions defined with cardinal utilities can be implemented by mechanisms that rely on the valid von Neumann–Morgenstern cardinal utilities because they use randomizations, but the moral judgment bears directly on the solution rather than on the properties of the implementational processes that are often particular and are considered valuable essentially because they lead to the solution with rather sound behavioral assumptions. Then the basic problem of the meaning of general cardinal utility remains. If, however, the process is sufficiently natural and meaningful by itself and can be morally appraised, it can participate to the moral justification of the solution (this is for instance the case for the aspect of the Nash solution derived by Harsanyi and Selten 1972). Essentially implementational processes have been provided for the Kalai-Smorodinski solution by Moulin (1984; see also Binmore 1986 for the Nash solution).

There may thus be a "utility function" that takes a higher value in A than in B whenever I prefer A to B.

It is also sometimes meaningful to say: "I prefer A to B more than I prefer C to D" (for example, this expression is certainly meaningful whenever I am almost indifferent between C and D and not between A and B), or even "my preferring A to B is higher than my preferring C to D," or, perhaps, "my preference for having A rather than B is higher than my preference for having C rather than D."

However, in this case there is *no reason* to translate "my preferring A to B" or "my preference for having A rather than B" as the *difference* of the values taken by the utility function, or as any increasing function of this difference, or as any increasing function of the differences of the values taken in these two states by some increasing function of the utility level; and there is no reason to translate the whole expression by the ordering of the magnitudes of such differences. Now, this translation is how one can make sense of a cardinal utility, since the meaningfulness of the ordering of differences of the utility function characterizes that of a cardinal function in the generally interesting cases.[18]

Even if there exists both an ordering of states and an ordering of pairs of states, for the representation of preferences and of comparisons of preferences, and if the ordering of pairs of states can be expressed as an ordering of the pairs of the corresponding utility levels, and if one adds all the other possibly meaningful mental structures (ordering of pairwise orderings of preferences, regret, and so on), one obtains no psychologically meaningful structure that implies the property of cardinal utility in the full or generally required domain (see appendix A).

Furthermore, cardinality is equivalent to the invariance of the ratios of differences. Hence to make sense of cardinal utility by the comparison of preferences between pairs also requires that it be meaningful to say for instance "I prefer A to B 2.7 times more than I prefer C to D"

---

18. The ordering of differences is invariant under increasing linear-affine transformations, and, reciprocally, this invariance implies that the function is defined only up to such transformations (under a condition of domain that needs not detain us here, as noted in a preceding note).

(and this is sufficient). Such a comparison doubtlessly lies beyond the limit of meaningfulness, although one can sometimes order comparisons of comparisons and differentiate between preferring A to B more, or much more, than preferring C to D.[19] At any rate this justification of cardinal utility requires again the same arbitrary translation of this expression by the comparison of *differences* in utility levels.

The simple comparison of pairwise preferences becomes hard to make sense of when preference is replaced by satisfaction or happiness, because preference is already by itself pairwise. "I am more happier in A than in B, than I am in C than in D," or the same expression with "satisfied," constitutes an expression with problematic understandability. And cardinal utility also requires "3.8 times more" to be meaningful, and at any rate it requires the unwarranted expression of pairwise comparisons by *differences* in levels. The case for "the rise in my happiness from B to A is greater than the rise in my happiness from D to C" may be better, but a hint that this could refer to differences would be mistaking a metaphor for the actual psychology.

The observation of choosing behavior of course does not "reveal" comparisons of preferences (if I am given the choice between "choosing between A and B" and "choosing between C and D," I choose the alternative that contains my preferred state, without comparing pairwise preferences).

Therefore neither introspection nor observation of behavior and nor reason can justify the concept of cardinal utility or make sense of it as an entity endowed with general actual meaningfulness (and not only formal-mathematical meaningfulness). That is to say, any concept that uses a utility function and that logically forbids its transformation by all nonlinear functions cannot a priori make sense. However, concepts of cardinal utility can be meaningfully used for particular domains, reasons or issues. Then this use is legitimate, but

---

19. It is even sometimes meaningful to say: "I prefer A to B more than C to D" more than "I prefer E to F more than G to H" (for example, assume that I am almost indifferent between C and D, between E and G, and between F and H). Other meanings can be provided by the expression of *regret*: "I would regret to have B rather than A more than to have D rather than C," with similar remarks and conclusions.

the specific justification has to be provided and ascertained in each case. These possible justifications are of several kinds.

First a cardinal utility can be meaningfully derived from comparisons of *weak* preferences, as shown in appendix A. A weak preference is of the type "I prefer A to B and I am almost indifferent between A and B."

Second there may be reasons for an ordinal utility function to have a specification that is a (possibly weighted) sum of partial utility functions of items that have the same nature except for a particular characteristic. Then if these partial functions are the same, they have to be a cardinal utility for the additive structure to be meaningful. The risk case described above can be classified in this category. In other cases the characteristic can be time, although the justification is then more problematic and much more restricted in scope.

Third, in other cases the relevant variable is in fact a quantity (rather than usual utility). Then the comparison and ratios of differences have meaning (this may be a quantity of money).

Finally, cardinal utility can be considered for the sake of the history of thought, so as to analyse other features of theories that use it (such as Nash bargaining or cooperative solution in appendix B).

More generally, the structure of utilities is a question of psychological meaningfulness, and within this domain, for normative applications, of choice of ethical relevance. Hence certain economists' use of the term "information" to denote this structure, implying that utility is intrinsically a quantity about which we know or do not know certain things, is a revealing nonsense.

12.9   Appendix A: Comparison of Preference Comparisons

Consider a set of alternatives X, and a classical complete preference preordering on X denoted as p (is preferred to), i (is equivalent to), and r (p or i), which may possibly be represented by an ordinal utility function $u(x) = u_x$ for $x \in X$. If, for x, y, z, $t \in X$, xpy, and zpt, the expression "I prefer x to y more than I prefer z to t" is meaningful, it formally constitutes a pairwise comparison on pairs (on ordered pairs) of alternatives, which will be denoted as $(x, y)P(z, t)$. The comparisons p and P are respectively the *preference comparison* and the *comparison of preferences.* Then the following properties are natural properties to consider, and they are necessary if cardinal utility is to make sense.

1. The comparison extends to the cases where either *trz* or *yrx* as follows: *xpy* and *trz* $\Rightarrow$ $(x, y)P(z, t)$, *yrx* and *zpt* $\Rightarrow$ not $(x, y)P(z, t)$.

2. Antisymmetry: $(x, y)P(z, t)$ $\Rightarrow$ not $(z, t)P(x, y)$.

3. Comparability and indifference: for *xry* and *zrt*, neither $(x, y)P(z, t)$ nor $(z, t)P(x, y)$ means that x is preferred to y *as much as* z is preferred to t, and this is written as $(x, y)I(z, t)$ (a symmetrical relation from its definition). R denotes P or I. We consider the relation R on the domain of weakly ordered pairs, (x, y) such that *xry*. From the definition of I, *xiy* and *zit* implies $(x, y)I(z, t)$ (since P has not been defined for these cases); this holds in particular if $x = y$ or $z = t$ (or both).

4. $x', y', z', t' \in X$ and *xix'*, *yiy'*, *ziz'*, *tit'* implies that $(x, y)P(z, t) \Leftrightarrow$ $(x', y')P(z', t')$ (one can in particular have $x' = x$, $y' = y$, $z' = z$, or $t' = t$). A similar property is assumed for the relation I.

5. *xrz* and *try* without *xiz* and *tiy* implies that $(x, y)P(z, t)$.

Properties 4 and 5 express that the comparison of preferences P is *compatible* with the preference comparison.

6. Transitivity: the comparison R defines a complete preordering on the pairs of its domain. This assumption does not seem more audacious than the similar one for the preferences.

If this ordering is representable by a numerical function $\Gamma(x, y)$, where Γ is an ordinal function (defined up to any increasing transformation), $(x, y)P(z, t)$ is $\Gamma(x, y) > \Gamma(z, t)$; hence $(x, y)I(z, t)$ is $\Gamma(x, y) = \Gamma(z, t)$, and in particular $\Gamma(x, x) = \Gamma(y, y)$. Then property 4 implies that $\Gamma(x, y)$ can be written as $C(u_x, u_y)$ for any given specification of the ordinal function u. The "comparison function" C is an ordinal function defined for $u_x \geq u_y$ (and possible values of u_x and u_y), such that $(x, y)P(z, t)$ is $C(u_x, u_y) > C(u_z, u_t)$, $(x, y)I(z, t)$ is $C(u_x, u_y) = C(u_z, u_t)$, and hence $C(\alpha, \alpha) = C(\beta, \beta)$ where α and β are any real numbers that can be values of u. Property 5 implies that the function C is increasing in its first argument and decreasing in its second argument. The "isocomparison curves" $C =$ constant can be drawn in the plane (u_x, u_y), in the domain $u_x \geq u_y$. The "indifference line" $u_x = u_y$ is an isocomparison curve. If the function C is differentiable and C_1 and C_2 are its first order partial derivatives, $C_1 \geq 0$, $C_2 \leq 0$, and $C_1(\alpha, \alpha) +$

$C_2(\alpha, \alpha) = 0$. One could specify $C(\alpha, \alpha) = 0$ for all possible α, so the function C becomes "zero-preserving ordinal" (defined up to any increasing zero-preserving function), and $C \geq 0$ in all its domain of definition with $C > 0$ if $u_x > u_y$.

If there is a specification of the function u such that $u_x - u_y$ is a specification of the function C, then this specification of u is a meaningful cardinal utility (with sufficient domain). But there is no particular reason that such a structure holds. For example, it does not hold if, with a specification of u, a specification of C has the form $(u_x - u_y)(u_x/u_y)$ in the domain $u_x > k, u_y > k$ for some $k > 0$. A family of isocomparison curves in plane (u_x, u_y) cannot in general be expressed as $f(u_x) - f(u_y) = $ constant for some increasing function f.

However, the *ordinal comparison of pairwise preferences provides a meaningful cardinal utility for comparisons restricted to weak preferences*. Alternative x is said to be weakly preferred to alternative y if it is preferred to it and they are almost indifferent. Indeed, if x is weakly preferred to y and z is weakly preferred to t, then the relation $C(u_x, u_y) \geq C(u_z, u_t)$ is equivalent to the relation $v_x - v_y \geq v_z - v_t$ where $v = f(u)$ with a function f such that $f' = C_1(u, u) > 0$, assuming C to be differentiable and $C_1(u, u) \neq 0$. This holds because $C(u_y, u_y) = C(u_t, u_t)$, hence the first inequality is $C(u_x, u_y) - C(u_y, u_y) \geq C(u_z, u_t) - C(u_t, u_t)$, that is, if $u_x \to u_y$ and $u_z \to u_t$, $(u_x - u_y) \cdot C_1(u_y, u_y) \geq (u_z - u_t) \cdot C_1(u_t, u_t)$, while the second inequality is $(u_x - u_y) \cdot f'(u_y) \geq (u_z - u_t) \cdot f'(u_t)$ in the same conditions. The function v is cardinal from the ordering of differences; specifically, the arbitrary additive constant is the constant of integration of f' into f, and the arbitrary positive multiplicative constant is $F'[C(\alpha, \alpha)] > 0$ when the ordinal function C is tranformed into $F(C)$ with an arbitrary increasing function F. The function u itself is a meaningful cardinal utility for weak preferences when $C_1(u, u)$ is a constant. This happens when $C_1(\alpha, \beta)$ is a function of differences of functions $\varphi_i(\alpha) - \varphi_i(\beta)$, for example if $C(\alpha, \beta) = \sum [\Psi_i(\alpha) - \Psi_i(\beta)] + k$ where k is a constant. For instance, if $C(\alpha, \beta) = (\alpha - \beta) \cdot \varphi(\alpha, \beta)$, for $\alpha \geq \beta$ and with $C = 0$ for $\alpha = \beta$, then $C_1 = (\alpha - \beta) \cdot \varphi_1(\alpha, \beta) + \varphi(\alpha, \beta)$ where $\varphi_1 = \partial\varphi(\alpha, \beta)/\partial\alpha$, and $C_1(\alpha, \alpha) = \varphi(\alpha, \alpha)$. Then, for comparing weak preferences, the function u itself is meaningfully cardinal if $\varphi(\alpha, \alpha)$ is a constant (for instance with $\varphi(\alpha, \beta) = (\alpha/\beta)^a$), and its power n is meaningfully cardinal if $\varphi(\alpha, \alpha) = \alpha^{m+n-1}/\beta^m$. When $C_1(\alpha, \alpha) = 0$ in the relevant domain, the result remains valid in considering developments of higher orders.

12.10   Appendix B. The "Nash Bargaining, or Cooperative, Solution": Logical Problems

Nash's axiomatic cooperation

The *maximum of the product of the excesses of individuals' utility levels over these levels in a reference state* constitutes the famous "Nash bargaining or cooperative solution". This is a solution to the "bargaining problem" where several individuals have both a common interest in cooperating and opposed interests as to the specific outcome chosen. A solution is one such outcome. Nash (1950; see also 1953) deduces this result from a set of basic assumptions (hypotheses, axioms). Another, different, deduction of the same result from basic assumptions has also been suggested. These deductions are logically flawed for several reasons that will be pointed out. (The behavioral processes that lead to this form or to a related one constitute another issue). The reference state is assumed to represent "the state without cooperation". Individuals' utilities are cardinal (they are even, for Nash, the von Neumann-Morgenstern utilities, although his theory entails no uncertainty). Nash presents his theory for two individuals, but everything holds for any number of individuals and we will consider this case here (for the sake of generality). The status of the axioms is not stated. They presumably represent "conditions of rationality". For one ("equality from symmetry") Nash says in 1950 that it represents equal bargaining power but he retracts from this assertion in 1953. Two other axioms are cardinal utilities and Pareto-efficiency (discussed in this chapter and in chapter 2). The last axiom (Nash's "independence of irrelevant alternatives", or "set restriction") is akin to a condition that will be discussed in chapter 15 about Arrow's theory. The other proof referred to above assumes the a priori existence of a social welfare function depending symmetrically on the excess utilities (this structure and its use contain several problems).

Apart from the status and acceptability of these assumptions, the logic of Nash's proof has two problems both of which come from the assumption of "equality from symmetry" which says: in the space of the excess utilities, if the set of possibilities is symmetrical then the solution is equality. The following statement of the nature of the problems will be followed by their specific explanation.

The first problem is that from this axiom as just stated and the other Nash's axioms, there results that any Pareto-efficient state is the solution. But Nash makes it explicit that the solution he states is the only one, of course. All the statements of this paragraph will be shown and explained shortly. In particular, it turns out that one obtains Nash's result in adding that "equality from symmetry" holds only for certain sets to which it applies and not for the others. In particular, it suffices that it holds for convex sets and does not hold for others. Now Nash says that the possibility set he considers, S, is convex; he uses this property to obtain the uniqueness of the utilities that maximize the product of excess utilities, and this is the only explicit use he makes of this property. But equality from symmetry is not applied to the possibility set of the problem, S, or to any representation of this set under any admissible transformation of the utilities. These sets are indeed a priori not symmetrical. This axiom is applied to another set that contains one of these sets. And Nash's statement of the axiom is ambiguous as to whether it applies under the assumption that the set to which it is applied is convex if this set is not the possibility set of the problem. This results from a statement of the type "if the set S were symmetrical, the outcome should be equal". But the set of the problem, assumed to be convex, is not a priori symmetrical. And the symmetrical set to which the axiom is applied is not the set of the problem. Furthermore, at any rate it is not said that the axiom does not apply to non-convex sets (or to certain of them), and this is the crucial issue. Now, logically, if the axiom holds for convex sets there is no possible reason to exclude that it also holds for non-convex sets sufficiently close to convex sets and of the form that leads to other solutions. Then Nash's axioms lead to a number of solutions of which the one he describes is only one.

The second problem is that the properties of symmetry and of equality can be meaningful only if one precludes the independent variations of individuals' excess cardinal utilities used in the proof (and if the reference state corresponds to the same utility levels).

In order to show these issues more explicitly, let i denote one of the n individuals, u_i his cardinal utility, u_i^o the value of u_i at the reference state, $v_i = u_i - u_i^o$ the excess utility, $v = \{v_i\}$ the vector of the v_i, and, in the space of the v, S the possibility set, $P(S) \subseteq S$ the set of Pareto-efficient states, and E the line of equal v_i's. Since u_i is defined up to an arbitrary increasing linear (affine) function $a_i u_i + b_i$ with constant a_i and b_i and $a_i > 0$, v_i is defined up to an arbitrary multiplication by a positive scalar $a_i v_i$ with $a_i > 0$. A *permuted* vector of a *vector* v is a vector obtained by a permutation of the coordinates of the vector v. A set of vectors v is *symmetrical* if it contains all the permuted vectors of each of its vectors. The *symmetrical extention* of a set T of vectors v, $\Sigma(T)$, is the set of all the permuted vectors of the vectors $v \in T$. One has $T \subseteq \Sigma(T)$ (the vectors of T correspond to the invariant permutation). $\Sigma(T) = T$ if and only if T is symmetrical. A symmetrical extention is symmetrical by construction. Nash's assumption that we call "equality from symmetry" is: if S is symmetrical, then the solution is in E. Adding Pareto-efficiency, the solution then is $P(S) \cap E$. The other particular Nash's assumption, called here "set restriction" (Nash's "independence of irrelevant alternatives", or Arrow's "axiom of choice" expressed in the domain of utilities) is: if S and T are two possibility sets, $T \subset S$, and the solution for S is in T, this is also the solution for T.

Then, take any vector $\bar{v}$ of $P(S)$. Transform each function v_i into the function $v_i' = k v_i / \bar{v}_i$ where k is any positive real number (possibly 1). Then $\bar{v}$ is transformed into $\bar{v}' \in E$ with $\bar{v}_i' = k$ for all i. S and $P(S)$ are respectively transformed into S' and $P(S')$. One has $\bar{v}' \in P(S')$ and hence $\bar{v}' = P(S') \cap E$. Take now the symmetrical extension $\Sigma(S')$ of S' as a possibility set. One has $\bar{v}' \in \Sigma(S')$, and even $\bar{v}' \in P[\Sigma(S')]$ (since if $\bar{v}'$ were not Pareto-efficient in $\Sigma(S')$, a vector of $\Sigma(S')$ would have all its coordinates not lower than k with one being higher, the corresponding vector of S' of which it is permuted would have the same property, and hence $\bar{v}' \notin P(S')$). Thus $\bar{v}' = P[\Sigma(S')] \cap E$. Therefore, if $\Sigma(S')$ were the possibility set, the "equality from symmetry" and Pareto-efficiency assumptions indicate the equal $\bar{v}'$ as the solution. And since $S' \subseteq \Sigma(S')$ and $\bar{v}' \in S'$, the "set restriction" assumption implies that $\bar{v}'$ is the solution in the possibility set S'. Hence $\bar{v}$ is the solution in the possibility set S.

But the set $\Sigma(S')$ is in general not convex. If "equality from symmetry" is assumed *only for convex possibility sets*, the above reasoning does not generally hold. But there is *no a priori reason for this restriction*, at least if the angles between E and the rays of the cone tangent to $\Sigma(S')$ at $\bar{v}'$ are not much smaller than 90 degrees. Nash takes as $\bar{v}$ the vector of S and P where the product $\prod v_i$ is maximum. Then $\bar{v}'$ is the vector of S' and of $P(S')$ where the product $\prod v_i'$ is maximum. If S is convex, S' also is and hence $S' \subseteq T$ where $T = \{v': \sum v_i' \leq \sum \bar{v}_i'\}$. Equality from symmetry and Pareto-efficiency imply that $\bar{v}'$ is the solution in T (which is convex with a flat border). From set restriction it is also the solution in S'. Hence $\bar{v}$ is the solution in S.

However, the properties of equality of the v_i (or v_i') for different i and of symmetry of sets in the space of the v (or v') are not independent of the multiplication of the v_i by *different* constants. These properties are thus logically meaningless with these excess utilities and the corresponding cardinal utilities. Their logical meaningfulness requires that the multiplicative factors be required to be the same for all individuals. Whatever the possibilities of actual meaningfulness of this restriction, which will be considered shortly, this restriction forbids the above formal transformation of the state $\bar{v}$ into the equal $\bar{v}' \in E$ except when $\bar{v} \in E$. One can then take $\bar{v} = P(S) \cap E$ if it exists ($\bar{v}' = \bar{v}$ with $k = 1$) and prove as above that this is the solution: $\bar{v}$ is the solution in $\Sigma(S)$ from equality from symmetry and Pareto-efficiency, and hence in S from set restriction (however, the set $\Sigma(S)$ is not convex in general). Hence the only solution is the efficient equality of the excess utilities, if it is possible (a condition implied by Nash's assumptions that the set S contains $v = 0$ and is compact).

Furthermore, the definition of the v_i up to multiplication by the same arbitrary positive constant means that the u_i are co-multiplicative cardinal, that is, are defined up to transformations $au_i + b_i$ with $a > 0$ and where a and the b_i are otherwise arbitrary constant. The only concept that could be called upon, with the required prudence, to make sense of this structure, is fundamental utility, taken in a cardinal specification.[20] This gives co-cardinal utilities, that is u_i defined up to the same arbitrary linear-affine increasing transformation $au_i + b$ with $a > 0$ and a and b are otherwise arbitrary constants. This can give meaning to the required $v_i = u_i - u_i^o$. Yet what remains problematic is the meaning of cardinal utility. Without it, equality, substitution, permutation and symmetry are not defined for the v_i. With ordinal (fundamental) utility, they are defined only for the u_i. This can be

---

20. See chapter 7, section 7.3, and Kolm 1992c, 1993c for the cardinalization. The outcome is the concept directly assumed by Harsanyi (1953).

meaningfully reported on the v_i only if the u_i^0 are all the same. Then, the efficient equality of the v_i is that of the u_i, that is, eudemonistic Justice.

This result obtains directly, with the co-ordinal fundamental u_i. Denote $u = \{u_i\}$. In the space of the u, with S as possibility set and E as line of equality, the Pareto-efficient equal vector $\bar{u} = P(S) \cap E$, if it exists, is the solution in the symmetrization $\Sigma(S)$ from equality from symmetry and Pareto-efficiency, and hence in S from set restriction. There is no other solution (if the u_i of u are not all equal, there is no admissible transformation of the u_i that transforms them into the equal coordinates of a point of E because these transformations transform the u_i into $f(u_i)$ where f is any increasing function, the same for all i). Note also that the convexity of S is now a meaningless property (not invariant under admissible transformations). Therefore what Nash's three axioms of Pareto-efficiency, equality from symmetry, and set restriction validly prove is eudemonistic Justice (see chapter 7 and Kolm 1971). For this result, cardinality of utility is fortunately irrelevant. Equality from symmetry in utilities is, with fundamental utility, both meaningful and justifiable from rationality (see chapter 2). Set restriction cannot be a universal principle, but it has a certain scope of validity (see the discussion in chapter 15). And Pareto-efficiency is largely necessary (see chapter 2).

Therefore, Nash's whole set of concepts is not logically meaningful, and hence his conclusion does not hold, but his interesting valid intuitions can provide a notable vindication of the welfare equality of eudemonistic Justice.[21]

---

21. Another, quite different and simpler "proof" of Nash's cooperative solution makes no assumption concerning possibility sets but assumes a priori the existence of a social maximand (Social Welfare Function), that is, a numerical function which takes higher values for better states. This function "respects individuals' preferences" in being an increasing function of the u_i, and, given the reference state and hence the u_i^0, it can be written as a function of the v_i, say, $F(v_1, v_2, \ldots, v_n)$ for any number n of individuals. This function is ordinal—defined up to any increasing transformation. Since, for any given i, v_i is defined only up to any arbitrary multiplication by a constant, there results that one specification of F has the form $v_i^{\alpha_i} F_i$, where F_i is a function of all v_j for $j \neq i$ and α_i is a positive number. Since this should hold for all i, there results that one specification of F should have the form $v_1^{\alpha_1} v_2^{\alpha_2} \ldots v_n^{\alpha_n}$. Then the argument says that there should be "impartiality" (see chapter 10), that is, symmetry of the social maximand, taken here as meaning that all the α_i are equal. In this case the product of all the v_i is a specification of the maximand, which amounts to "Nash's solution" for

Behavioral Bargaining[22]

Finally, Nash's result (for two persons) can be obtained by the bargaining process proposed by Zeuthen (1930) applied to the v_i, for which it is logically meaningful, but this process is not normative, it is behaviorally quite particular (and it would use cardinal utilities not particularly justified). By contrast, Harsanyi and Selten (1972) consider uncertainty-relevant cardinal utilities in a theory of bargaining with alternative offers and uncertainty, and they obtain the maximum of $v_1^{\alpha_1} v_2^{\alpha_2}$ with α_1 and α_2 that are a priori different (they are related to the individuals' risk aversion). Other particular bargaining processes lead to Nash's outcome for two persons and their scope and meaning has to be appraised in each case (see Nash 1953 and the more recent works, noted in reference, by Rubinstein, Binmore, Dasgupta, Thomson, Lensberg, Wolinsky, Safra, and others).

12.11   Appendix C: Equal Relative or Absolute Gains or Concessions, the Average Preferred State

A family of solutions to the problem of distribution consists of choosing Pareto-efficient states that correspond to equal increments from an inefficient reference state, or equal concessions from an impossible reference state, or increments from an inefficient reference state in

---

$n = 2$. This reasoning raises several problems: (1) Normally the function F is defined for a specification of the v_i so that when v_i is multiplied by a scalar, this function incurs a compensating contravariation and the above reasoning does not hold. (2) Even if it held, the symmetry assumed for the equality of the α_i implies that the v_i are all co-multiplied by the same scalar and that the function F is only required to have an homogeneous specification; Nash's product is a possibility, but there are many others, one of which is the utilitarian sum (the only case where the maximand and hence the optimum do not depend on the reference utilities u_i^0 and on the reference state). (3) The ethical symmetry can only be justified by the fact that the variables refer to a "fundamental" concept that encompasses all the relevant interindividual differences; but then it applies to the u_i assumed to constitute a fundamental cardinal utility, rather than to the v_i, and these cases differ when the u_i^0 are not all equal (except with the utilitarian sum); hence the symmetry in the v_i has to be justified. This problematic justification has certainly been repeated a number of times. Kaneko and Nakamura's (1976) elaborate proof of Nash's result rests on the valid probability-consequentialist cardinal utilities but is basically amenable to all the foregoing remarks. A recent direct restatement of the argument can be found in Roberts (1980).

22. As opposed to "axiomatic bargaining" as in the case of Nash's theory.

proportion to the differences with another reference state, or concessions from an impossible reference state in proportion to the differences with another reference state. These solutions need respectively either one reference state and interpersonally comparable units, or two reference states and meaningful ratios of differences for each individual. The latter condition defines the metric of cardinal utility, and the former corresponds de facto to fundamental comparable cardinal utility. In all cases, the distribuands can be quantities of a good, either the same good for all individuals in all cases, or possibly a specific good for each individual in the cases of equal proportions.

These solutions are then characterized by the definitions of the reference states, with one equal-variation solution for each reference state, and one equiproportional-variation solution for each pair of reference states.

There is a possibility set with a subset of Pareto-efficient states. We will define reference states from this set. In addition, there often is another given reference state, which can represent the nonagreement state (a threat point), the status quo, or a starting state. Given the reference states, the solutions exist most of the time. With the given reference state, they notably generally exist when this state is possible (which is necessary for a number of its meanings). Hence we will focus on the definition of the meaningful reference states from the possibility set.

The most important of these states will be the *average preferred state*, that is, the arithmetic average of the individuals' preferred possible states, which constitutes the natural compromise (but is often not efficient; its existence and possible nonuniqueness will be discussed below). Then comes the state whose individual utilities are the highest possible levels for each individual (the level at his preferred possible state): this is the "claim" or "utopian" state considered by Raiffa, Kalai, Smorodinski, and Gauthier. These states' definitions require no comparable utility and hold for any number of individuals. Hence efficient equal relative improvements of the average preferred state toward the claim state (or concession of the former from the latter if none is possible), or, in other words, efficient equal relative concession from the claim state to the average preferred state, constitutes a favored solution: it requires neither a given reference state, nor interpersonal comparability of utilities, nor restriction on the number of individuals. Efficient equal absolute variations from these states or from a given reference state are interesting solutions when there is interpersonal comparability of variations. With a given reference state, two other solutions are the efficient equal relative expansion (or other variation) of the average preferred state from (or to) the given reference state, and the efficient equal relative concession from the claim state to the given reference state; they require no interpersonal comparability; the latter is the Raiffa-Kalai-Smorodinski-Gauthier solution.

Let us consider $n \geq 2$ individuals i with utilites u_i (a cardinal utility, which can possibly be a quantity) constituting a vector $u = \{u_i\}$ that has a possibility set S in its space. $P \subseteq S$ is the set of Pareto-efficient states. We will want to choose a state in P. The relative or absolute equal variations correspond to the choice of states of P by the intersection of P with a straight line defined by two points (states) or by one point and the direction of equal variations in the u_i (this amounts to a second point at infinity in this direction). The states (points) used in such a way will be called the *polar* states (or points). Apart from a possible given reference state and from the state at infinity in the direction of equal variations when this equality is defined, the other polar points are all derived from the possibility set S. A couple of distinctions have to be made.

Either the individual utilities are noncomparable or they are comparable (fundamental co-cardinal). This latter case provides meaning to interpersonal equal variations and levels (since there is no actual reason for utilities with the same unit and not completely the same fundamental function), and to sums of utilities being higher or lower.

Either there is a given reference state (or several ones) or there is none.

Either one considers only "good" polar states, in the direction of Pareto-efficiency, or one considers also the symmetrically defined "bad" states, as it will become clear shortly. The "bad" states and values become all the same when the possibility set is truncated by a condition that all individuals are not worse off than in a possible given reference state, and then their specificities vanish.

Another relevant distinction is whether there are only two individuals or whether any $n > 2$ is admitted.

All the points and discussions can be straightforwardly represented in a two-dimensional diagram (for $n = 2$) representing the set S.

First of all, with comparable individual utilities, a solution is the state with equal utilities. And with interindividually comparable variations in utilities (implied by co-cardinal utilities) and a given reference state, a solution is the point of equal variations from this reference state.

The polar points derived from the possibility set S will mostly be derived from the preferred and worst points of S for each individual. Let $u^i \in S$ denote the *preferred state* of S for individual i, and $u^{i-} \in S$ denote the *worst state* of S for individual i. u^i and u^{i-} are the states u of S where u_i is the highest and the lowest, respectively. The utility levels u_i^i and u_i^{i-} thus are individual i's best and worst possible utility levels, respectively. In order to simplify the discussion, these points are here assumed to be unique (this happens, in particular, if S is strictly convex).[23] The states u^i generally exist because of the limitation of resources (and possibly satiety). The states u^{i-} do not exist in a number of problems.

A very important polar state is the *average preferred state* $u^a = (1/n) \sum u^i$. It represents the natural compromise. Yet it is generally not Pareto-efficient. It is often possible, notably when S is convex. The corresponding point $u^{a-} = (1/n) \sum u^{i-}$ is the "average worst state."

The polar state $u^m = \{u_i^i\}$ whose coordinates are the best possible utility levels on S for the individuals is the classical "utopian", "claim", or "ideal" state used by Raiffa, Kalai, Smorodinski, and Gauthier (for $n = 2$ for most of them). It is generally not possible. Similarly, the state $u^{m-} = \{u_i^{i-}\}$ is defined (an "anti-claim" state).

When $n = 2$, a remarkable polar state is the state of *worst efficient threats* u^t with $u_1^t = u_1^2$ and $u_2^t = u_2^1$. It is generally possible and inefficient. The symmetrical polar state is $u^{t-} = (u_1^{2-}, u_2^{1-})$. We have $u^a = (1/2)(u^m + u^t)$ and $u^{a-} = (1/2)(u^{m-} + u^{t-})$.

With comparable utilities, another notable state (possibly not unique) is the *utilitarian state*, the state u^u of S, and of P, where $\sum u_i$ is the highest. However, this state is already efficient and hence cannot be used as indicated above. By contrast, the *anti-utilitarian state* u^{u-}, the

---

23. We may at least choose Pareto-efficient u^i's. More specifically, if the u^i are not unique, one can choose for each i a (or the) particular u^i such that no other u^i for any i is in the half-space of higher coordinates limited by the hyperplane that passes through the chosen u^i.

state of S where $\sum u_i$ is the lowest, can play such a role (especially if it is unique).

A reference state provided in addition to S, u^o, defines, with S, the polar states of the border of S where all coordinates but one are those of u^o, and notably the states u^{oi} and u^{oi-} of S such that $u^{oi}_j = u^{oi-}_j = u^o_j$ for all $j \neq i$ and u^{oi}_i and u^{oi-}_i are the highest and lowest possible such numbers. The states u^{oi} may be Pareto-efficient or not. Other polar states are their averages $u^{oa} = (1/n)\sum u^{oi}$ and $u^{oa-} = (1/n)\sum u^{oi-}$. The state u^o also leads to the definition, from each subset of S in a subspace for which a certain numbers of coordinates are those of u^o, of all the polar states defined as those for the whole set S. Furthermore, all these states defined from S and u^o lead to other polar states in taking any of the polar state that have been or will he derived from S instead of u^o.[24]

Notable polar states are obtained as averages between preferred and worst values or states. In particular, denoting the averages between extreme values as $u^z_i = (1/2)(u^i_i + u^{i-}_i)$, the "average" polar state is $u^\alpha = \{u^z_i\} = (1/2)(u^m + u^{m-})$.

Similarly, the averages' average is $u^A = (1/2)(u^a + u^{a-})$. For $n = 2$, one also defines $u^T = (1/2)(u^t + u^{t-})$ and one has $u^A = (1/2)(u^\alpha + u^T)$.

Other polar states are the average utilitarian state $u^{au} = (1/2)(u^\alpha + u^{u-})$, and $u^{oA} = (1/2)(u^{oa} + u^{oa-})$.

With comparable variations in utilities, the states of the border of S from which the lines of equal variation are tangent to S can be interesting. Similarly, if the reference set u^o is not in S, the points of contact of tangents to S issued from u^o also have meaning. In both cases, with $n = 2$ there commonly are only two such relevant states. The averages between these pairs are other polar states.

Still other states averaging pairs of previously defined states can be considered, and either they or their averages can be other polar states.

In a number of problems, a condition of considering only states that are not worse than a given reference state for all individuals, plus, possibly, a condition of "free disposal" in resources and hence in utilities, lead to particular places for a number of the states previously

---

24. For each possible polar or reference state that is dominated by some efficient states, another solution is the highest product of excess utilities above this state, as with the Nash solution for a given reference.

considered. In particular, the most preferred states u^i may become u^{oi}, the worst states would be with $u_i^i = u_i^o$ for each i, and various polar states on the "worst side" would be the given reference state u^0. Note that reference states can also be on the side of larger utilities of the Pareto-efficient set.

From this set of polar states, one obtains an efficient solution aligned with each pair, and, with comparable variations in utilities, an efficient equal variation from each state. This provides a number of solutions (not all distinct for cases noted above and, when $n = 2$, because u^m, u^a and u^t are aligned). These solutions can be discussed as regards their existence, their relations, and their various properties, for the various possible n, s, and u^o. Most important, their moral meaning can be specifically discussed and vindicated, with finally various degrees of interest.

If the utilities considered are cardinal utilities justified as representations of weak preferences (see appendix A), the problem is local and "in the small" and, as a consequence, the relevant border of the possibility set is a hyperplane of Pareto-efficient states. Then, with solutions restricted to those where no individual is worse-off than in a possible given reference state, interesting particular properties hold. The average preferred state and the "equal relative concession" state (Raiffa-Kalai-Smorodinski-Gauthier) and others coincide and are Pareto-efficient.

13 Morals, Liberty, the State, and Ethical Motivational Implementation

This chapter considers the process-freedom theories of society and of social ethics presented in chapter 12 in analyzing their various properties and implications, essentially by comparisons. It also considers the basic issue of the motivational possibilities of implementing conceptions of ethics, social ethics, and justice.

13.1 Theories of Publicness

The consequences of process-freedom have led to a number of theories of the public sector, government, the state, or politics. These views have both much in common and much that makes them different. They lead to public sectors of very different sizes, indeed from zero (the "libertarian" recommendation) to the actual size (Public Choice by definition, but also, as a possible order of magnitude, the two Public Economics), and also very differently motivated (either "self-interest", or an ethic of liberty, "welfare" or something else). Yet, all these theories consider the public sector by comparison with the market, and they justify or explain it by its ability to perform better than the market in a certain domain (or they criticize it for its inability of doing so). They constitute the *"market failure" theories of the state.* They are also, ipso facto, the *economic theories of the state.* They are thus individualistic and constructivist theories of the state (rather than holistic, communitarian or culturalist theories)—although most of these views could admit that the individuals' sense of community induces particular public actions.

These theories divide into those that rest on publicly implementable a priori moral principles and those that do not and thus only rest on the existence of individuals and on their view of them. This division bears no relation to the size of the public sector, as table 13.1 shows.

Three of these theories present *substantial explicit theories of the public sector: Liberal* and *Welfarist Public Economics,* and *Public Choice theory* (views of the purely redistributive state are de facto mostly held by "welfarists," and hence can be included in Welfarist Public Economics, although this is by no means a necessity since other distributive criteria can be held such as equalities in means or ends, needs satisfaction, etc.). These three theories share an important common ground, yet they completely oppose one another on the two most basic issues. The common ground is that all three theories are

Table 13.1
Size and nature of the public sector

Public sector ＼ Size	Normal, market failures	Very low, no market failure
Principled	Public Economics	Minimal state
Unprincipled	Public Choice	Neo-"libertarians"

economic theories (by their view of man and by their method), which see important qualities in the *market*, yet acknowledge rather important causes of *market failures*, and see the prevention of these failures as the reason for a public sector. The two lines of opposition are the nature of the theory and of its principle: on the one hand, the theory is either *positive* or *normative*, and on the other hand its principle is either *liberty* or *welfare*. Indeed, first, Public Choice theory stands in contrast to the two Public Economics in that it is not a moral theory— as it has been explained—whereas the other two are. Second, Welfarist Public Economics rests on a principle of welfare, whereas both Liberal Public Economics and Public Choice theory rest on a principle of liberty, notably on freedom of action and in particular of exchange (although a morally constrained freedom in the former theory and not in the latter), and consequently on theories of the Social Contract among the actual individuals (yet, a restricted and notionally decentralized Social Contract for the principled Liberal Public Economics, and a total and a priori global one for the amoral and foundational Public Choice). Table 13.2 summarizes the differences.

Liberal Public Economics thus constitutes the (economic) theory of the public sector that is both moral and based on liberty.[1]

The size of the public sector implied by the various theories considered here is either known (the "libertarian" ideal, the "minimal state," the descriptive "Public Choice") or can be tentatively and very approximately guessed at. This suggests the orders of magnitude listed in table 13.3, which should be considered essentially for the comparison between themselves, for a measure that would be the share of GNP used by the public sector. For the evaluation of this attempt, one

---

1. From the above, these qualificatives apply to the theory, but they apply ipso facto to the reasons for the actions of the public sector it describes.

Table 13.2
Types of theories and of principles

Theory / Property	Public Choice theory	Liberal Public Economics	Welfarist Public Economics
Nature	Positive	Moral	
Principle	Liberty		Welfare

Table 13.3
Size of the public sector

Public percent of GNP	Principled	Unprincipled
0		Neo-"libertarians"
Low, decentralized, and diffused	Classical Libertarians	
1 or 2% (plus army)	Minimal state (Locke-Nozick)	
About 5% (plus army)	Hayek	
About 8% (plus army)	M. Friedman	
For example, 30%	Liberal Public Economics	
	Welfarist Public Economics	Public Choice
(For instance, 80%	Administrative "socialism")	

should remember, in particular, the following facts: The budget of the police (and of the judiciary) is known (for the "minimal state"); government share was 7 percent in England at the end of the nineteenth century; Milton Friedman proposes redistribution through a negative income tax and for the finance of schooling with "vouchers" distributed by the government (and a public monetary seignorage); Public Choice describes (and explains) what exists (unless we add the prudential advice, notably for efficiency, which would lower the figure); classical (left) Libertarians insist on the structure and modalities of the social and economic organization; this also holds in part for Liberal Public Economics; and the actual overall size does not primarily matter for most theories as it results from the application of their view for each specific question. The expression "unprincipled" refers to the preceding discussions about the relation to morals.

13.2 A Priori "Freedom to" Only

Three theories start from liberty, unconstrained by an a priori moral principle: that of the (neo-)"libertarians," Buchanan's constitution and

Public Choice, and morals from agreement in the spirit of Gauthier. They explain how society is formed, or should be formed for everybody's sake, from interactions among individuals, without any other a priori social requirement. Yet these theories separate among themselves along three lines: the *existence of market failures*, the *level of agreements*, and the resulting *moral behavior*.

Indeed, first, "libertarians" see nothing that can perform better than the free market in any case, whereas both Buchanan and Public Choice theory on the one hand and Gauthier on the other see very important market failures. Second, Buchanan's constitution constitutes an overall view of society and Public Choice theory often studies national political processes, whereas both "libertarians" and Gauthier are concerned by local levels only, for each specific question. Third, Gauthier ends up with a type of moral *behavior*—and the defects in his specific presentation can be corrected—, whereas non purely "self-interested" behavior is seen as an irrelevant issue by "libertarians" and as unimportant by Buchanan.

Figure 13.1 summarizes these differences.

The gaps in this set of theories define what should be its research program. First, the technicalities of the important Gauthier enterprise should be put right, essentially thanks to repeated or sequential games and other and more general forms of surplus-sharing. Second, "libertarians" should be careful to *explain* states, and in particular non-

Figure 13.1
"Natural" liberty: Three views, three properties

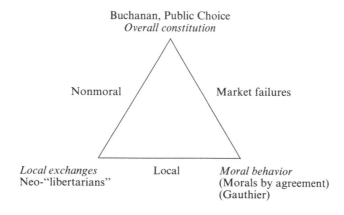

Buchanan, Public Choice
Overall constitution

Nonmoral   Market failures

Local exchanges   Local   *Moral behavior*
Neo-"libertarians"   (Morals by agreement)
                                           (Gauthier)

dictatorial states (not all states are dictatorial!). Third, and relatedly, the Gauthier enterprise should be applied to the overall level, for explaining governments and showing their moral or "rational" behavior. Indeed the classical reelection model of government behavior constitutes the repeated game that considers this question.

13.3 The Role of Morals

Morals play two kinds of role in the human sciences: they provide the evaluative criteria of moral theories, and they are a feature of the views, judgments, motivations or behavior of the observed agents. These two roles are related in a complete normative theory, since the application of moral principles generally requires morally motivated agents, or an influential morally motivated opinion,[2] unless this theory proves, as a moral Minerva's owl, that "all is the best in the best of possible worlds," possibly after better informing the nonmoral agents. This question of the influence of morals on behavior arises both for common behavior and for the choice and the enforcement of rules. The moral motivations of agents or opinions constitute one of the two hypotheses *on facts* that differentiate the various theories considered here, the other being market failures. A third difference is constituted by the *choice* that the theory be *more or less exhaustive*, since principled theories admit an *exogenous* moral principle in their views. These latter theories, however, then face the problem of *motivational implementation*—that is, of who is motivated to apply them—which completes the two other implementation problems raised respectively by the necessity to have the required information and power.

This question of power leads a number of classical theories in social ethics to assume unquestioningly that their views should—and hence could—be implemented by the state, the monopolist holder of public force. The corresponding *informational* implementation is an active field of study. But do the motivations of the individuals who staff a government permit or induce this use of power or this quest of information?

---

2. The only possible exception is that of nonmorally motivated agents who act for others because they care about these others' egoistic favorable opinion of these acts.

State-moralism, the theory of the moral state, is the hypothesis that the state implements the moral principles, possibly subject to limitations in information only. It assumes that the state *can* implement these principles, where "can" refers to both the various constraints and the motivation of the individuals who constitute "the state." This hypothesis is both crucial and usually implicit. In a strong version the state can thus implement any moral principle; in a weak one it can implement the principles under consideration; in intermediary cases it can implement several theories that are being compared or a set of theories that contains them. The people who staff the state are assumed to be sufficiently either convinced or induced or constrained, and they fear no other risk to be eliminated by election or rebellion than one that may participate in such a constraint. State-moralism where an all-powerful authority wants to implement the best social state is commonly referred to as the hypothesis of a "benevolent dictator," a name that certainly confesses a lack of seriousness.

Such an all-moral state is particularly conspicuous when the theory assumes that the other agents are or can only be, on the contrary, strictly amoral and "self-interested" (the ambiguity of this expression will be shown below)—a view that is particularly palatable to a majority in the sub-culture of economics. Then there seems to be an enormous contradiction between this view of man in general and the hypothesis about politicians (this criticism of the assumption of moral agents within the state constitutes the Public Choice indictment).

State-moralism is held by theories that advocate very different scopes for the government, from almost none to everything: the minimal state (Locke, and especially Nozick, see the government as employed by the holders of rights, yet they should at least explain why it does not violate these rights with its dominant force—a general remark that will be further discussed below); the minimal-plus state (Hayek, Friedman); Welfare Economics and in particular Welfarist Public Economics; Rawls (concerned with "institutions" and assuming a somewhat moral public, as discussed in chapter 8); up to the extensive state of the *moral statisms* or ethocracies imagined by ideal "administrative socialisms" or other views.

Two possible consistent alternatives consist in seeing moral motivation either relevantly nowhere, or in any place where it is necessary. These are respectively *amoralism* that assumes amoral individuals and thus is also *nonmoralism* (that is, not a moral theory since none can be implemented, including for setting rules)[3] and *all-moralism*. Then, since a state with dominant force can only be extortive with the former hypothesis (it is acquisitive and has no moral restraint) and is not needed with the latter (the public has moral restraint and behavior), these views lead to the two anarchisms: the neo-"libertarians," on the one hand (Rothbart et al.), and the classical Libertarians, on the other. When the amoral individuals find it necessary to make explicit or implicit general agreements, they set up a Buchananian constitution and a framework for Public Choice. "Morals by agreement" (the Gauthier enterprise) proposes that individuals who are amoral in their motivation can find it beneficial to behave according to certain rules of morals in voluntarily respecting others' rights (and accepting rules for sharing cooperative surpluses). Amoralism implies that moral statements or theories can have no actual influence (an issue for moral-sounding basically amoralist theories).

The next section will show that all these views are too extreme and are, in a sense, naive (this may or may not be a defect for developing an analysis), for the following reasons: (1) The importance that each individual attaches to others' views of himself makes "self-interest" a highly ambiguous concept and constitutes a powerful reason for moral behavior. (2) The repeated-game aspect of social interactions induces a certain moral behavior. (3) Internalized moral norms definitely exist and more or less influence behavior. (4) The political-public process offers particular opportunities for moral influence by voters, statesmen, and public officials.

The polar views discussed here are nevertheless interesting ones to consider, since each emphasizes or analyzes one aspect and can sometimes be more or less close to reality, and especially since their comparison and oppositions enlighten central issues. Their statements concern reality, ideals and normative judgments. The two implementative phenomena are morals and the state (or government, politics, or the public sector).

In the ideal they describe, "libertarians" have neither actual and relevant morals nor state, Public Choice has a state but no morals,

---

3. A possible exception is noted in the preceding note.

Libertarians have morals and no state (Gauthier has morals for a certain behavior but not for motivation, and he does not actually mention a state), and all the others have both morals and a state. The epistemic status of the elements differ, however: The views concerning states are moral for anarchists, descriptive for Public Choice, and both descriptive and moral for state-moralists (including Rawls, for example), and the views concerning motivations intend to describe the essential facts (plus a traditional concern for the relevant affects of education for classical Libertarians).

Tables 13.4 and 13.5 summarize part of the discussion.

Of the various contrasts and oppositions that divide these theories, those between state-moralisms and the theory of Public Choice (based on Buchanan's contractarian constitution) have been the most resounding in contemporary debates. These theories, of the moral and the amoral state, respectively, each holds a rather puzzling particular stance. State-moralisms are practical theories (that is, theories intended for application) which propose moral views intended implicitly or explicitly to be implemented by the state, without considering whether

Table 13.4
Morals and government

Morals \ Government	No: anarchies	Yes
No relevant morals	Neo-"libertarians"	Public Choice
Endogenous moral behavior	"Morals by agreement"	A possibility for Public Choice
Exogenous moral motives	Agreement from morals, anarcho-etharchy, Libertarians, reciprocity	State-moralisms

Table 13.5
Morals in society

Morals \ Location	The public	The state
No relevant morals	Classical state-moralisms, Public Choice, "libertarians"	Public Choice
Moral motives	Libertarians, (Rawls: in part)	State-moralisms, (Rawls: institutions)

the members of this institution can do it, want to do it, or can want to do it. On the other hand, Public Choice is a descriptive and explanatory theory which commonly pronounces moral sounding injunctions. This places these theories in complete opposition as regards the relations between *force and justice* and between *reality and morality*: For state-moralisms, *right makes might* and *ought implies is*, and for Public Choice, *might makes right* and *is implies ought*. Indeed state-moralism implies that if something is right and ought to be done, then a state produces the power to implement it and make it exist. For Public Choice, on the contrary, the balance (or imbalance) of power, playing both on and within the constitutional framework, produces an outcome which is tautologically the unanimously desired result of free, peaceful and voluntary interaction. These qualificatives elicit praise—which may misguide one into forgetting that they hold under the threat of the use of the force that each agent has. Furthermore the "ought" of amoral Public Choice can "only" be technical advice on how to satisfy better certain interests, possibly everybody's interests: Its amoral ethics stems from informed interest rather than from the a priori rights and duties of mutual respect.

13.4   The Ways and Means of the Implementation of Social Ethics

The Puzzles of the Amoral Hypothesis

The hypothesis that individuals have no moral motivations and that, as a consequence, social ethics cannot be implemented and is useless, it held far beyond the school of Public Choice (and the neo-"libertarians" for government) since it underlies the views of, for example, Marx, Nietzsche, Spencer, Hayek, and others (each with a particular and elaborate theory, though). This view has to face a number of challenges. First, it should certainly distinguish behavior within the family, where altruism is the rule, from behavior outside it, and accept "altruism within the family, 'non-tuism' outside it" (as discussed, for instance, by Wicksteed); the extent of the relevant "family" depends on the type of society; one might, however, see intrafamily altruism as merely extended egoism. Second, why do people speak so much of what is good, right or just and of what is not, if this talk has no importance or influence—a fact that, presumably, everybody should have become aware of ? (Would one resort to explanations by psycho-analysis?). How can one explain that people care so much to claim that their own political view is the good or just one, that politicians boast of taking electoral risks for moral reasons (attracting attention to these deeds may further endanger chances of reelection), that officials and voters commonly ask for moral advice regarding what is good or just, that moral theoreticians can survive and publish? Third, observation shows many instances of altruistic behavior (outside the family), from small ones in everyday life (is respecting one's neighbor only explained by fear of retaliation or of the police?), to charity toward individuals or causes and notably in publicly implemented and politically approved collective gift-giving (see chapters 5 and 8), to activism in politics or for particular causes when the individual's interest is not at stake or when his own action has only a negligible effect, and to self-sacrifice in cases of major accidents and, most conspicuously, war. The public good aspect of collective gift-giving may hide limited but possibly widespread altruism which either fails to materialize or appears as forced contribution when implemented by constraint. People commonly abide by rules or norms without being forced to, seek fair deals rather than good deals in exchanges, vote or take part in collective action while their own contribution has no actual influence. Moral or altruistic behavior is therefore a possibility: Is its neglect the best first approximation, or indeed a valid one, for the problems considered? Fourth, the state, with its police and army, possesses the monopoly of the dominant public force: Why, then, if there were no moral self-restraint, is it not always maximally exploitative, and how can democracies persist?

To answer these questions, and most important to evaluate the motivational implementability of theories of social ethics and justice, individuals' motivations should be closely considered. The result can in particular be applied to the public at large, to these people as voters, to politicians and statesmen, and to public officials and civil servants.

Moral Implementation without Moral Motivation

The relevant judgments of an individual can be of the following main types (for relations outside the family):

1. Strictly egoistic judgments or evaluations about one's own acts.

2. Moral judgments about one's own acts.

3. Egoistic judgments and preferences concerning other people's acts (hence acts that concern this individual).

4. Moral judgments about other people's acts.

5. Judgments or preferences about other people's judgments that concern one's own acts or about other people's sentiments elicited by these acts.

There are other, related types of opinions, such as judgments about judgments concerning other people's acts or about sentiments concerning them. Note also that an act can elicit judgments of several types at once—and it may be difficult to disentangle their relative importance. In particular, category 2 (I morally judge my own acts), when it exists, is commonly associated with category 5 (I feel concerned by other people judging me) where other people judge my acts for egoistic or moral reasons (types 3 or 4). The amoral hypothesis denies the existence (or the sufficient importance) of category 2. It bypasses, however, category 5 along with 3 or 4 as other people's judgments about one's acts. Categories 3 and 4 can also be intermingled (I praise someone who gives me because he gives and because I am the receiver). Category 3 by itself is a standard case for exchange, in "buying" the other person's act (this is occasionally, but not normally, done for the moral evaluation of case 4). Yet gratitude is an alternative to buying in this case, and gratitude can be a payment if the person who is the object of it appreciates it by the relevant sentiment of type 5. A kind of gratitude can also be elicited when there is a moral desire for the other person's act (this should be seen as belonging to case 4). Buying may be precluded by any type of "exchange failure," a particular cause of which is actor's benevolence.[4]

Now, other people's opinions concerning oneself is a main motivation of individuals in society. These opinions can be consideration, regard, esteem, respect, approval, admiration, gratitude, or contempt,

---

4. The exchange failure effect of benevolence and altruism is analyzed in Kolm 1981d, 1981e, 1983a, 1984b, 1994d, and Kranish 1992 (benevolence and altruism are a particular type of externality that preserves Pareto-efficiency only in quite special cases).

pity, reprobation, and so on. Others' views of oneself are often the main motivation when physiological basic needs are satisfied. This shows in everyday life, in professional and other achievements, in a number of types of consumption and expenditure that entail respect or consideration (conspicuous consumption is only the extreme case at the limit of insanity).

Furthermore, judging someone else is practically costless (a cost means here a sacrifice of any kind). Therefore motivations provided by case 5 associated with 3 or 4 for the others can have the following very important consequences:

i. *Moral acts are performed without moral motivation* of the actors.

ii. *Moral views are implemented at no cost for the holders of these views.*

iii. *Altruistic acts can be performed without any moral view by anybody* (this is the case where the other people's judgments are the egoistic ones of the beneficiaries—case 3).

Morals can thus be implemented without anybody making the choice to sacrifice his purely egoistic interest for the sake of his own moral motivation (Kant's necessary condition for morality), that is, choosing between reasons 1 and 2. The *moral social feedback* 5 and 3 or 4 is probably no less important a moral implementer than the *direct moral choice* 1 versus 2, although we will see below that they tend to be associated, reinforcing each other.

In particular, the standard expressions "self-interest", "self-centered" or "egoistic" are ambiguous in a basic manner when it is not made precise whether or not they include preferences about other people's opinion of oneself for the mere sake of this opinion (that is, not in view of obtaining further advantage from it). In other words, is "self-interest" only case 1, or does it also include case 5? The difference is essential for moral implementation. One may call "quasi self-interest" an interest in others' opinions concerning oneself for the sake of it.

One reason why moral social feedbacks and direct moral motivations are difficult to disentangle is that one's own, and other people's, moral judgments about one's acts commonly follow the same cultural standards and norms. Being judged favorably or unfavorably in others' eyes or in one's own eyes is not always very different. Let us also point out the particularly relevant case of gratitude, the absence of which when it is due elicits clear moral reprobation; eliciting gratitude and its manifestation is often a notable cause of moral or altruistic *behavior*.

In addition, and independently, behavior that is classified as moral can result from the strictest and narrowest egoism through social interaction, as explicit or implicit terms of a truce or agreement, notably in certain repeated or sequential gamelike situations. This is indeed likely to elicit acts of mutual respect or aid. Then a theory can help by providing information that makes people, or some of them, aware of this means for serving their narrow and egoistic interests. Furthermore, in the rather common case where such interactions have several stable solutions, moral reason can help to select one (for instance by reference to domination by unanimity or to rational symmetry); this selection may need no or sufficiently limited extra motivation that is moral or induces moral-like behavior, and global interactive behavior does not destroy this moral choice and, indeed, it implements it.

Finally, moral-like behavior can be genuinely moral and hence directly induced by the actor's moral motivation, it can be motivated by the actor's quasi self-interested concern for others' opinion, or it can result from purely self-interested social interaction. These three ways have each many kinds of modalities, and they can be associated in many manners.

Modalities of the Moral Social Feedback

This moral social feedback is an essential course of moral implementation. It acts through a spectrum of sentiments which are quite clear and obviously widespread, with various forms and intensities: An aversion for other people's negative judgments about oneself, for their reprobations or indictments, leads one to try to shun or limit the behavior that elicits such attitudes and opinions, or, on the contrary, a liking or a desire for other people's positive judgments toward oneself, for their appreciation, approval, approbation, admiration or gratitude, and for one's "good name," reputation or fame, leads one to seek such opinions and to try to arouse them. These sentiments *induce moral behavior of nonmoral persons*. They can act either by themselves or in association with other reasons for this behavior, with various

relative importances. These other reasons can be genuine moral motivation, fear of punishment, or narrow egoistic interest either direct or
through other people's reaction in social interaction. The social feedback, or whatever importance, can add to these other reasons and be
the extra cause that induces the moral action.

The fact that, through this moral social feedback, *the payer for the
moral act is not the holder of the moral judgment*, is of foremost importance, and it certainly accounts for a large part of the actual effects of
moral views, and therefore also finally for the enduring existence (and
importance) of such views. The "payer" for the moral act, by inconve-
niences or costs of various possible types, is the actor. The holders of
the moral opinion are the observers who thus have their morals implemented at no cost for them. To show or to express one's opinion
actually costs little, and indeed it suffices that the actor thinks that
other people think about him in the manner considered, or even perhaps that they could think so, or would think so if they knew. This
"moral judge" can thus become quite impersonal, with finally little or
no difference from a pure moral motivation. In any case through the
social feedback moral views are implemented for free by their holder.
Furthermore, since people approve of acts that are beneficial to them
(reason 3), the social feedback has an inherent tendency to foster
altruistic acts. More generally, in judging favorably acts that are
favorable to persons other than themselves, people can be altruistic
at no cost for them, while the giver acts altruistically without altruistic motivation (yet he can himself favorably appraise other people's
altruistic acts and induce the same behavior from them—then everybody gives without anybody directly wanting to give).

The classical opposition between "self-interested" and moral motivation misses this very important cause of moral behavior. For this
reason, among others, this opposition appears overly naive, superficial, and ill-defined. In the way just described, people act morally and
freely without experiencing a moral sentiment, and people feel morally
without acting so. Indeed a taste for fame or for other people's approval or gratitude, or a dislike for their reprobation or contempt, can
constitute sufficient motives of moral behavior, yet they are not moral
motivations. However, the individual is moulded by culture, and culture is shared values. Hence is being judged good or not-bad by others
that different from the same judgment applied to oneself? Can really

one be moral motivation and the other not be? On the other hand, individuals who are concerned by other people's view of them in itself (that is, not as a means for further purposes) are "interested" in this opinion. Yet this is quite different from the mere enjoyment of tangible goods. It can indeed induce moral behavior against one's more strictly defined self-interests. If, however, seeking others' approbation or non-reprobation were not "following self-interest," then seeking income is not either when it is for maintaining a standing or a minimum of dignity in others' eyes, for being judged a "good father" in supporting the family, for entertaining friends and thus obtaining their friendship, gratitude or admiration, for conspicuous consumption or "keeping up with the Joneses," and so on. These motivations account for much more spending than the nutritional or calorific power of consumption goods.

By contrast, the people who judge are morally minded. But they do not act, and they pay no cost for acting. The question of their self-interest is rather irrelevant. They may possibly be seen as deriving a particular type of moral satisfaction from the acts they induce which, on other grounds, may not affect them or may affect them favorably or unfavorably. Yet, this approval or disapproval is often of another kind, in another "sphere," than those of their other judgments or sources of pleasure or displeasure. This judgment may be more or less involuntary (it then results from various aspects of the individual's socialization) or the result of ethical reflection and choice. Its expression, however, is generally voluntary. Gratitude is motivated by a beneficial act which may be moral if the motivation is duty or benevolence, non-moral if the objective is to receive a "return gift," and something in between if its motive is merely to elicit gratitude appreciated per se. There may also be a kind of gratitude toward people who act morally in a way that the evaluer appreciates for this reason rather than for his self-interest in the strict sense. Finally, several persons may judge an act which becomes a kind of moral public good for them, this plurality may be necessary in order to induce the corresponding behavior (and, if the expression of the judgment is costly to any degree, free-riding problems may arise).

Notice that the same people can judge others and be judged by them. Then the same individual can have a moral view and act according to it, yet this act is not the consequence of his moral thinking but of others', and his moral judgment may induce others to act according to these principles. There can thus be a globally moral society without properly moral individuals.

Furthermore, the moral judgment about an individual is derived from the moral judgment about his acts. Therefore an individual who judges others for a certain type of acts judges himself similarly for the same kind of acts if the relevant circumstances are similar. This self-image may also be an incentive. Then, this motivation of behavior enters into the category of moral motives, although not of the purest kind of morality (the nuance would be between "I do this because this makes me be a good person" and the more directly and purely moral "I do this because this is a good action"). This judgment of oneself may be sufficient to induce behavior, or others' judgments may be required in addition.

And since morals are essentially shared values, part of a common culture, the others' judgments about one individual are bound to coincide with his own judgment about himself. Both can reinforce each other's influence in the same direction. Indeed, at a point, the others' and one's own images of oneself are not very different facts. The existing morals become an intrinsic entity, and to obey its precepts is of course a kind of moral behavior.

At any rate, others' opinions need only be imagined by the actor. He may not even consider really specific others. This opinion may become abstracted into that of the "generalized other" as George Herbert Meade puts it. This becomes about "society's view" of what is right or good, indeed something not far from the hypostasis of society into religion as seen by Durkheim.

Of course, other motivations of various kinds can be associated with the ones considered here, notably purely self-centered and purely moral motivations. The motivations considered here can constitute the addition that determines action-taking.

Finally, for the various reasons and motivations noted, moral behavior can and does exist. It is observed—outside family altruism—in everyday life, in exceptional events and situations, and for implementing, obeying and establishing the rules of society. The question of the role of moral behavior and motivations is particularly important with respect to politics and government. Indeed, first, these processes, institutions and persons control the dominant coercive force in society. Second, they are commonly seen as the implementational *locus* of social ethics and justice, a view followed by state-moralisms whereas amoralist and nonmoralist theories—classical Public Choice in particular—deny this possibility with commonsense remarks that probably seem plausible at first sight. State-moralism and "benevolent dictators" are obviously myths. Does this imply, however, that one should go to the other extreme and deny any notable role for social ethics and ideas of justice in the political-public process? But even if such ideas and ideals play or can play a role, they may be restricted in the social ethics that they can implement.

We thus need to consider in greater depth the question of the possibility of social ethical implementation by politics, and thus the three questions of the possible existence and role of moral motivation in politics, of the logic of power seeking, and of the role of public opinion.

Ethical Motivations and Possibilities in Politics

Political actors play various roles, notably, in electoral democracies, those of politicians and statesmen, elected and appointed public officials, voters, civil servants at all levels, activists, members and officials of political parties, lobbyists and purveyors of material means of political advertising, and opinion-makers notably in the media. Motivations of all kinds meet in this process. Can and do moral ones play a role? Is there a scope for moral influence in this essential part of social life where it is so commonly expected and demanded?

Propositions, arguments and discussions that belong to the realm of social ethics or justice constitute a very large part of the discourse of politics. Politics is, indeed, the place where these ideas are discussed (from common talk to elaborate "political philosophy"). Why would it be so if everybody cared only about his own interest in the narrowest sense, if no part of any ideal could actually be implemented, or if everybody's ideas were a priori settled?

Furthermore, citizens, voters, political organizations and parties, the media, statesmen, responsible civil servants, all ask for advice and guidance in the domain of social ethics and justice, and ideas in this field are received with eager interest and are the object of active discussions. The aim is sometimes to provide an objective justification for one's own narrow interest, but, not uncommonly, the attitudes and motivations reflect genuine moral concern. Even when narrow self-interest alone is the objective, the quest for moral justifications implies that they can influence other people, or, at least, it implies the belief that they can have such effect. And such a belief is so entrenched, durable and widespread that it cannot fail to contain some important .grain of truth. In all cases these moral interests and discussions would not exist, or would not last, if all individuals were only pursuing their narrow self-interest, or if their ethical views were only unmovable prejudice.

Political actors even all claim more or less that they act and choose ethically, and they demand that the other actors do so as well. It seems that all these claims would make no sense if restricted interest were the unique and universal motivation. They would make sense, however, for individuals who want to be judged favorably by moral opinions, as was discussed earlier. But then moral views can have an influence. Furthermore, politicians often boast of risking unpopularity (and hence of jeopardizing their chances of reelection) by doing what is right: why would they take this risk, or even say they do, if they were strictly self-interested (by definition an unpopular measure displeases many voters so that to boast of it is not a way to attract them)? Even moral approval of these actions is limited in this case since these voters would generally not morally approve what they vote against (although this is not impossible).

Now, moral behavior exists, as we recalled. Many instances of it can be observed, from grand sacrifice to goodness and rightfulness in common life. Indeed, if it were not the case, all ethical ideas would be useless and meaningless, both in the public and in scholars' work, and their presence could hardly be explained. Why, then could not people also act more or less ethically when they vote, govern, or administer?

A crucial case and test consists of the fact that the government has the monopoly of the public, dominant force, yet it often is nondictatorial. If it (or the military) were motivated only by pure and narrow self-interest, then tyranny, slavery and maximal extortion would prevail. This authority would, to begin with, cancel the bothersome next elections. The balance of force among various armed forces, or the possibility of general popular rebellion, do not suffice generally to explain why this does not occur, since several armed forces would still collectively exploit the people, and the people do not have matching weapons. Short of tyranny, there generally has to be ethical behavior somewhere in the line of order behind the trigger. The guardians can be guarded only by themselves, that is, by their moral conscience.

Furthermore, the various actors in the public-political process have notable domains of choice where their decisions are unrelated to what is considered to be their material interest. Then they can, and often do, fill this gap with ethically motivated behavior.

The most conspicuous case is that of voters, since a single vote has no effect in a large election (people do not think of the Pascal's wager situation of casting the unlikely but decisive vote in case of a tie). Now, the reason why people vote is essentially a sense of duty, mostly of the "popular Kantian" type ("what if nobody voted ..."). Hence, if the reason why people vote is ethical, and the way each individual votes has no consequence, why would the way they vote not also be ethical, at least in part? If duty makes people go to the booth, why could not is also influence their choice of the ballot, especially since this does not affect the self-interest of this specific voter? Furthermore people discuss their vote with their environment and are concerned with its opinion of it (although the secret ballot prevents the checking of the actual vote).

A similar situation exists for elected politicians. A president does not seek reelection during his last term, and this may be half his time in office; his motivation then is often his public image and his "place in history," and this is largely judged by moral standards. More generally, it is often said that the relevant memory of voters in an election is shorter than the duration of the mandate; then in a first period the mandate can be used for more or less autonomously moral government rather than for wooing voters. Furthermore, a politician who can have a majority larger that necessary to be reelected can use part of his surplus of votes in behaving for moral—rather than electoral—reasons.

With regard to civil servants, promotion largely by seniority, job guarantees, and other statutory advantages give them their well-known latitude in their constraints and incentives. Now, civil servants commonly fill up these gaps by following norms of behavior, and they can in this manner implement ethical ideals, as they sometimes do (indeed Public Economics was started by civil servants wondering what should be done).

In particular, democracy could not exist without the minimum of moral behavior that induces individuals to vote and holders of the public force to restrain its use.

Power Seeking

The question of the motivation of politicians is crucial in this debate. It is commonly argued (for instance by the school of Public Choice) that they are self-interested because they "seek power" in elections or otherwise. Seeking political power is indeed the definition of a politician. But why do politicians seek power? Power is not something you can eat or sit on. It is a means to do things. Then its value should depend on what you can have with it (especially with the view of man standard in economics, that Public Choice endorses to the extreme). If the final objective were wealth or consumption, then the politicians' skills and energy would usually be used much more fruitfully in private business—at least in democratic regimes. Now the power-seeking politician has the following interesting logic.

Since public power enables one to do public things and the politicians seek power, they use their power for doing things that will maintain them in power—through the next elections in electoral democracies. That is, they seek power to seek power, and so on. Hence there is no final output for them. Therefore, in the usual view of economics, this activity is useless for them and they should not seek it and waste energy in it, were they "rational" men. But politicians do engage in this activity, usually with much stamina, energy, and time. An explanation may be that they like the very process in itself, as a game or a "final" activity. But this process-liking is classically dubbed "irrational" in this view of man, and it is difficult and puzzling to make the explanation of the system rest entirely on irrational behavior.

Another alternative is that politicians seek power because it enables them to implement their conception of what is good or just for society, or to serve people or country, perhaps by educating the people in the process, or simply by implementing what the people want. Yet this is ethical political behavior.

In reality, the answer to the question of what do politicians seek is both rather obvious and not reducible to a simplistic assertion. They obviously and earnestly want job, status, fame, importance, the exercise of power, ideal, to be useful and recognized as such, activity, challenge, self-image, wealth, fringe benefits, and so on. This does not make them different from the rest of mankind. The relations of these elements among themselves and with other interests and desires are as often joint consequences, joint causes, or cause and effect, as they are competition among alternatives. Hence disentangling the various motivations and checking them against one another is often not the relevant exercise. However, the reasons why people engage in politics constitute a self-selection that may provide politicians with a somewhat particular mix of motivations. Among these motivations, those that are conducive to moral implementation are not, on the whole, negligible, such as moral motivation or a quest for celebrity.

Public Opinion

The opinions that other people hold about oneself constitute, we have noted, an essential and basic reason for human action. One seeks appreciation and approval and shuns reprobation and disapproval. This may be for the building of a reputation with a view to further aims, but it is also a very important final, direct motivation. In particular, politicians are often public men judged in this way by public opinion. The state of this opinion is often a means to future power by election or choice. Yet most politicians also value it in itself. Indeed public opinion is commonly a powerful drug for men engaged in public life and politics. Hence, as far as politics leaves them a choice of action, politicians often use this possibility to enhance still more their public image in the directions that suit this objective. These actions are therefore influenced by the criteria by which the public judges.

If each individual's judgment depended only on the way in which these actions foster his (narrow) self-interest, then public opinion would influence the public man's behavior as self-interested votes do. No social ethical motivation intervenes, and we are again in the end in a "Public Choice" world, even though fame-seeking or disapproval avoidance, per se, is not ordinary "self-interest."

If, however, people judged these public actions according to ethical criteria, and to the extent in which they did, then ethics can be influential. Now, people do not choose their own criteria as they do their acts (for instance votes). These criteria rather belong to the broad category of tastes (although their difference with ordinary tastes will be emphasized in chapter 16). They depend on the individual's culture, education, social milieu, and past experiences, and on the current political-social debate. When they change, this results from consideration or influence in ways that are usually more akin to religious conversion or *metanoia* than to consumer's choice. Politicians, statesmen, public men in general, try in fact to influence these criteria, sometimes in a moral direction ("ask not what your country can do for you, ask what you can do for your country" implies "praise the official who acts for aims higher than your own advantage.") However, opinion influences through its being known, and hence expressed, and people can choose to express their views or not to do so, when this opportunity exists. At any rate, as with votes, the opinion of a single ordinary individual among many has a negligible practical effect. This certainly helps opinions not to mirror exclusively the narrowest of self-interests, and hence this is conducive to each individual's opinion having a certain ethical dimension, thus to the overall aggregate public opinion having a moral dimension, especially since egoistic interests commonly oppose one another and may more or less cancel out in the global people's voice. This overall opinion is in the end what influences politicians and therefore the policy they choose. This effect might be stronger than the similar one for the case of voting, since casting a vote is an act, which therefore tends to mobilize a sense of responsibility that may make it mentally more difficult to vote differently from the choice one would have made if it had a decisive influence (even though this individual responsibility is illusory).

The roles of opinion makers and leaders, the media, and party activists, should also be considered, with results that essentially reinforce the general ones obtained so far.

Ethics and Politics

Therefore state-moralism which assumes that the government can have the will and has the power to implement any ethic, "Public Choice" which considers exclusively self-interested motivations, the other views holding that ethical reasoning can have no effective influence, the various possible "morals by agreement" that find certain moral behavior without moral motivations or judgments, constitute a number of extreme views that oppose one another, yet convene in neglecting important aspects of society, but also in emphasizing aspects that are important elements of actual life.

Rousseau's insight is more trustworthy, however, when he asserts that "morals and politics go together and he who wants to study them separately is bound to misunderstand both" (and who considers his work on politics, *Social Contract*, as a mere appendix to his work on education, *Emile*, published at the same time).

VI UTILITARIANISM AND SOCIAL CHOICE

14 Utilitarianisms, Strict and Metaphorical

14.1 Meaningless Utilitarianism and Utilitaromorphisms

Utilitarianism is the social ethic that advocates that the sum of individuals' happinesses, or pleasures minus pains, possibly described by "utilities," be as large as possible.

Utilitarianism as a general principle has ever been considered exclusively in two relatively limited circles, both of scholars: English-language philosophers and academic economists. It has always been ignored elsewhere, including by laymen and by other philosophers, it has never been applied practically, and it faces famous opponents in its two homes. Other ethical concepts are used in all these cases. Yet utilitarianism is very much discussed in its two circles.

Utilitarianism raises a number of problems, of philosophical, social, psychological, and logical natures. In particular, does the operation of summation make sense for pleasures, happinesses or utilities? Can an individual's despair be compensated by the sufficient happiness of others? Can the concepts of happiness, welfare, utility, interest, and so forth, be applied to society as a whole? Should we torture to please the sadist, deprive to please the envious, and starve the continent to approvision the greedy? However, the question of the possibility of the logical meaningfulness of utilitarianism supersedes other discussions, since it makes them pointless if the answer is negative.

Now, a state of society in which the sum of utilities is the highest keeps this property when each individual utility is replaced by an increasing linear[1] function of itself, with the same multiplicative term for all (this can be called a "co-multiplicative linear increasing transformation"). It does not generally keep this property when utilities are transformed otherwise. A set of individual utilities defined up to this transformation can be called "co-multiplicative cardinal." In this case an individual utility cannot be transformed by an increasing non-linear transformation. And it can be transformed by any increasing linear transformation provided the other individual utilities also incur a linear transformation with the same multiplicative factor. That is to say, these individual utilities must be *cardinal*. But we have seen in

---

1. "Linear" is taken in the sense of "affine" in the most common present-day mathematical vocabulary.

chapter 12 that the specific restriction that constitutes cardinal utility or amounts to it is in general devoid of meaning. Therefore utilitarianism strictly understood is a priori meaningless. This conclusion does not even need any consideration of *interpersonal* comparisons of preferences or of differences in utility: It suffices that individual cardinal utility does not possibly make empirical sense, or that writing an individual's preference for one state rather than another as the specific form of a *difference* in the corresponding utility levels has no psychological reason, justification, or meaning.

Hence utlitarianism strictly understood does not make sense: It is meaningless, that is to say, absurd. If we add the moral and social problems raised by utilitarianism (see section 14.3 below), we see that utilitarianism fits the judgment that its main promoter, Jeremy Bentham, had prepared for natural rights: *"absurd in logic, pernicious in morals."*[2]

However, if one is less strict about the meaning of either a "sum" or "happiness," or if one assumes particular situations or particular structures or conceptions of "the good" for individuals or for society, one may obtain theories that are *not* utilitarianism in this strict sense, yet possess certain of its properties and in particular sometimes a similar additive structure. These theories thus are not utilitarianism but, rather, *metaphorical utilitarianisms*, or *utilitaromorphisms*. A utilitaromorphism can be valid, invalid for several possible reasons, valid with particular assumptions, or imprecise.

There are ten utilitaromorphisms (UM, for short): (1) the *philosophers' UM*, (2) the *preference comparison UM*, (3) the *independence (separability) UM*, (4) the *Original Position UM*, (5) the *morally risk-neutral UM*, (6) the *consequential rational bargaining UM*, (7) the *efficient independent transferability* UM, (8) the *surplus theory UM*, (9) the *social income UM*, (10) the *Social Welfare Function UM*.

These forms are analyzed in this chapter or in others.

The last three, UMs 8, 9, and 10, are the *remote UMs* in the sense that, although they are akin to a utilitarian outlook (and historically inspired by it for the Social Welfare Function of UM 10), they definitely

---

2. Bentham 1843, iii, 221; ii, 497.

abandon one of the two features whose combination elicits the logical lack of meaning: the additive form for UM 10, and the nature of that which is added for the other two, since they add money units in evaluating the goods either with uniform prices (income) or by individuals' "willingnesses to pay" (surplus).

This Social Welfare Function, or, in better terms, the social ethical evaluation function or maximand, is a function of the social state that takes higher values for better states ("social ethical" stands here as the adjective for social ethics, and "ethical" can be implied by "maximand" which means "should be maximized"). Furthermore, this function is assumed to "respect individuals' preferences" in the sense that it depends on the social state only though the intermediary of the levels of individuals' utility functions. Three of the "stricter" UMs, "independence" (3), "moral risk-neutrality" (5), and "consequential bargaining" (6), assume a priori that there is such a function and they consist in proposing reasons for which it should have an additive structure. Note that (strict) utilitarianism does the opposite: It derives the existence of such a function (with its particular additive form) from its own theory. The question of the meaning of the a priori existence of a social ethical evaluation function will be included within the discussion of Social Choice Theory in the next chapter, since it is one of its central features. The conclusion is not encouraging in terms of rationality in the normal sense ("for a reason")[3] or of the common sense of justice: the social optimum need not be defined as a maximum, and very commonly it cannot be defined in this way with a social maximand independent of the set of possible states.

The "independence" UM 3 is the common *economists' UM*, the most common justification that modern economic theoreticians give for assuming "utilitarianism" (when they care to provide a justification). It is based on the conjunction of two or three hypotheses: a preference-respecting social ethical maximand (see chapter 15), the Principle of Independence of Irrelevant Individuals (P3I, see chapter 10), and possibly a fundamental utility (see chapter 7, section 7.2).

---

3. This precision is needed since the literature in this field commonly uses the word "rational" to describe the very hypothesis of a maximand or more generally of an ordering.

Two UMs, the "Original Position" (4) and the "moral risk-neutrality" (5), imply that the relevant cardinal utility is the one meaningful for choice in probabilizable uncertainty introduced by von Neumann and Morgenstern, which will be called (for reasons to be recalled shortly) the *probability-consequentialist* utility (PC utility). Both also need fundamental preferences (see chapter 7, section 7.2). Both have been introduced by John Harsanyi (1953, 1955). UM 4 is the valid form of the theory of the Original Position, the validity of which has itself been appraised in chapters 3, 4, and especially 8. UM 5 assumes a social ethical evaluation function. Then, it results from the assumption that the social ethical evaluation does not depend on whether the individuals are or not held accountable for the effects on themselves of the risk they incur (see section 14.6 below).

UM7 rests on Pareto-efficiency as ethical principle, and on a particular structure of individuals' preferences.

Finally UM2, which compares preference comparisons, is the most genuinely utilitarian in spirit, and yet it does not generally obtain a sum and its application is limited to certain cases of microjustice.

Table 14.1 gathers the hypotheses and the conclusions that will result from the discussion.

These properties show in particular that no case has jointly generality, nonarbitrariness, and an additive form, that can represent the social good, of added items that can represent individuals' "happiness."

The *Original Position* UM has already been presented and discussed in chapter 8, along with Rawls's theory. It was pointed out that its form is valid since it represents the expected utility of a single individual; that it is the justified theory of the Original Position (in contrast with Rawls's theory); but that no Original Position theory is a possible theory of justice.

When they use the words "sum" or "add" in discussing utilitarianism, most *philosophers* do not seem to mean these expressions literally as economists do or mathematicians would. They rather seem to use them as a sort of metaphor. They rarely use "Σ" or "$+$" signs. This immunizes them against the basic meaninglessness of utilitarianism, but at the cost of sacrificing precision and the determinacy of the solution when they do not consider only comparisons where all individuals become happier together (Pareto-improvements)—that is, for issues of distribution.

Table 14.1
Metaphorical utilitarianisms

Utilitaromorphisms / Characteristics		1 Philosophers'	2 Preference comparisons	3 Independence (separable)	4 Original position	5 Moral risk-neutrality	6 Consequential bargaining	7 Efficient independent transferability	8 Surplus	9 Social income	10 Social maximand
Hypotheses	Substance	Happiness, pleasure	Preference, happiness, pleasure	Utility	PC utility	PC utility	Excess utility	Money value	Money	Money	Utility
	A priori Social Maximand	No	No	Yes	No	Yes	Yes	No	No	No	Yes
	Fundamental Preferences	Probable	Fundamental comparison	Possible	Yes	Yes	Yes	No	No	No	Possible
	Uncertainty	No	No	No	Yes	Yes	No	No	No	No	No
Properties	Precise	No	Possible	Yes	Yes	Yes	Yes	Yes	Yes	Yes	Yes
	Sum valid	Cannot be	No	Not general	Yes	Yes	Yes	Yes	Yes	Yes	No
	Happiness valid	Yes	Yes	Cardinal	Cardinal	Cardinal	Cardinal	Quantitative	Means	Means	Yes
	Ethical valid	In rare cases	Possible	Not general	No	No	Particular	Efficiency	Efficiency, compensation	If distribution	Often not

The other UMs will be presented and discussed below, after the presentation of the basic issues concerning the history and the ethic of utilitarianism.

14.2   Relevant History: Sum of Utilities against Equality of Liberties

The highest total sum of happiness defines the best state of society: Since people seek happiness (and only this if understood in a sufficiently broad sense),[4] how else could the good and the best be defined? Furthermore, when something is to be allocated among people, should we not give it to the person who derives the greatest happiness or utility from it? Utilitarianism therefore seemed self-evident to a number of persons. However, when a piece of social ethics is both self-evident and undefinable, understanding it certainly requires the consideration of its sociology and history. A couple of facts stand out there.

First, utilitarianism is *restricted to two subcultures*: English-language philosophers for the last one or two centuries, and academic economists for the last few decades—and this view is far from unanimous in each of these two circles. All other people, including both laymen and other scholars and philosophers, think of distributive ethics with primary concepts of rights, liberties, equalities, entitlements, needs, merits, solidarities, social contracts (refined ones at scholarly levels), and traditions. Only the "comparison of preferences" utilitaromorphism is used in certain local and rather rare occasions, and this is quite far from full-fledged utilitarianism (see section 14.7).

Second, even in these two subcultures, most of the best people did not believe in utilitarianism, and they either contradicted themselves, or opposed this philosophy, or sought to modify it beyond recognition. For instance, Bentham sees the addition of pleasures of different people as devoid of meaning.[5] J. S. Mill sees the addition of pleasures

---

4. See the note on the vocabulary of "happiness" in chapter 7, section 7.2.

5. "'Tis in vain to talk of adding quantities which after the addition will continue distinct as they were before, one man's happiness will never be another man's happiness: A gain to one man is no gain to another: you might as well pretend to add 20 apples to 20 pears ... " (1802).

of different qualities as poor ethics (such as pleasures derived from poetry and from the game of pushpin). Sidgwick was fond of pointing out that his book[6] begins with the word "ethics" and ends with the word "failure"; he complained that where he looked for Cosmos he found only Chaos. Pareto both writes down one of the first explicit mathematical sums of utilities[7] and discovers ordinal utility[8] which makes this sum be an absurdity. Among contemporaries almost all major economists rely on other socioethical concepts than utilitarianism (often freedoms, sometimes equalities, and sometimes general Social Welfare Functions which abandon the meaningless sum but keep the rest of utilitarianism; see the next chapter), and we have already discussed the roles of Rawls, Nozick, and others, among philosophers.

Third, utilitarianism was given this dominating position in English political philosophy for an exclusively political reason, by someone who thought it does not make sense. When the enlightenment of the eighteenth century sought to replace tradition and divine right as the bases of social legitimacy by an ethic based on the individual, it did so along two lines, the "enemy twins" of equal liberty and the sum of happiness (the latter being developed notably by Saint-Pierre, Helvetius—in *De l'Esprit*—, Holbach, Beccaria, Palmieri, Hutcheson, Hume, Brown, Tucker, and Paley). The American and French Revolutions—two very closely related events[9]—chose the equal liberty of "free and equal in rights" and the inspiration of Locke to replace their kings' traditional and divine legitimacy (happiness appears with the "right to pursue" it in the American Declaration of Independence, and as the unanimous *"le bonheur de tous"*—"happiness of all," not global happiness—in the French Declarations of Rights). Bentham (1789) thus had to brandish utilitarianism as the modernistic, left wing of the British counterattack on the ideological battleground[10] (Burke

---

6. *The Method of Ethics* (1874).

7. 1913.

8. Independently co-discovered by Henri Poincaré in an answer to a question posed in a letter from Walras, at the same time and place (1910, Paris).

9. The very close relation was on all grounds: personal, ideological, political, military, financial, etc. See Kolm 1989a (1991), 1993a.

10. See Hart (1982) and Sumner (1987).

provided the right wing, a rational defense of tradition). Commenting upon the French Declarations of Rights, Bentham writes "Natural rights is simple nonsense; natural and imprescriptible rights, rhetorical nonsense—nonsense upon stilts" (1795; the adjectives "natural" and "imprescriptible" stand out in the preamble of the Declarations). Thus the historical reason for the *sum of utilities* is to oppose the *equality of liberties*.

Utilitarianism thus came to dominate English, and then English-language political philosophy. It later seduced many academic economists because of its "utilities," its maximization, its simplicity and its apparent analogy to "surplus theory" (developed since Dupuit 1844 but which sums addable money units). Yet it did not spread beyond these two relatively limited milieus, and it has also always met more or less opposition and doubt within them, for natural reasons.

It is thus no surprise that most of the noted contributions to social ethics and political philosophy since the midtwentieth century came as various reactions against utilitarianism. In one voice, Rawls, Friedman, the "libertarians," and Nozick said that you *must not* apply utilitarianism since what matters is liberty or primary goods, Buchanan argued that there is *nobody who would want to implement* a social ethical maximization, Hayek judged the assessment of end-states of society to be a *mirage*, Arrow proved that utilitarianism *cannot exist* even if you do not insist on the strict sum of utilities with which it *does not make sense* (see chapter 15), and Dworkin once suggested that utilitarianism is all right for deciding whether the stadium should be used for rugby or for soccer.[11] However, the fact that one could inflict so many mortal blows should imply that these blows are not really deadly. Indeed utilitarianism appears to be well and alive, and still rather dominating its two scholarly circles.

14.3   Outline of Moral Problems

Utilitarianism raises several types of problems, most of which remain with UMs: logical, epistemological (meaning), psychological (what is

---

11. In private conversation.

the added substance?), moral (what is good, just or right?), anthropological (conception of man and of society), and ontological (the essence of man).

Utilitarianism and Justice

Utilitarianism is a surprising mixture of individualism in its inputs of individuals' happinesses (it even usually considers tastes as exogenous) and of collectivism by being concerned only with their sum. In its view, sufficiently happy individuals can make up for the despair of others. It sees individuals as pleasure machines which add to the heap of global enjoyment. Can, then, utilitarianism claim to achieve justice? Is it, can it be, a theory of justice?

Utilitarianism often sees itself not only as a theory of the good but also, and as a consequence, as a theory of the just. It even classically sees itself as strictly egalitarian on the ground that it adds individuals' utilities with equal weights, as expressed by Bentham's redundant slogan reported by J. S. Mill (1863): "Everybody to count for one, nobody to count for more than one." And utilities, pleasures or happinesses are indeed the individual values for utilitarianism. However, if these individual values were the social ethical end values, the just state would imply their ideal equality, from a requirement of rationality (see chapter 2), and not their highest sum. It would be eudemonistic Justice, with the possible second-best Practical Justice (see chapter 7), rather than the outcome of utilitarianism.

Yet, since utilitarianism determines an optimum, it determines all possible variables at this optimum. Hence it can constitute a theory of *indirect or derived justice* (see chapter 2), for any situational variable one cares to chose. In particular, it is a theory of indirect or derived justice for individuals' utilities, pleasures or happinesses. But what are its end values, is it also a theory of *direct justice* for certain items? The answer is that utilitarianism is also direct justice in two ways, both with problems, though: it is "collective eudemonism" and balance of pairwise preferences.

Utilitarianism could indeed be seen as maximizing something like the total happiness *of* society (and not only *in* society). "Society" as a whole would then be the unique justiciable. This ethic would be eudemonistic but not individualistic. Yet such a eudemonistic collective egomorphism is very hard to make sense of (there are "happy societies" in the sense that its members are happy, notably with positive inter-relations, but this is something else).

But utilitarianism also allocates an item to the individual who pre-fers the most to have it rather than not (consider an indivisible item, or a small amount). It constitutes a balance of individuals' preferences between pairs of states. This is individualistic direct justice. But the end value, which is ideally equalized, is not individuals' happinesses but their preferences between pairs of states. This is related to satisfaction, happiness or pleasure but it is logically different. Utilitarianism represents these preferences as *differences* in utility levels, and this constitutes the logically unwarranted step, except for weak preferences (see section 14.7). The equality is well exhibited by the equality of marginal utilities in the allocation of a divisible and transferable quantity. At any rate, the corresponding individual "weights" are indeed equal. Hence utilitarianism is also *direct individualistic justice*, but for *preferences* or individual comparisons of satisfaction or happiness rather than for satisfaction or happiness, and it can be logically meaningful for this purpose if these (pairwise) preferences are weak, and hence only as marginal justice, for issues of local justice or micro-justice.

Eudemonism

The exclusive reference to pleasure or happiness met the steady opposition of ethicians of freedom of one brand or another. Kant sees eudemonism as the essence of immorality. Tocqueville despises welfare as an aim. Nietzsche derides happiness as "chewing the cud." Rawls sees it as an individual question, not one relevant for justice. Happiness, however, cannot be neglected either, especially if one considers its deepest meanings and its contrary in suffering or despair. The latter are in particular relevant for solidarity and public policy. The maximization of a utilitarian sum (if it made sense) may favor the lowest levels (of the same specification of a fundamental utility), depending on the structure of utilities and of the set of possibilities, but it need not lead to this result.

Rule-Utilitarianism

The various moral problems of utilitarianisms can be epitomized by the utilitarian possible advocacy of torturing a child in front of millions of sufficiently sadistic TV watchers. These problems were faced by a number of proposals. For instance—and this holds for any moral use of individual preferences—unethical aspects of utilities can be "laundered away" or "ironed away" (see Goodin 1986), and this can sometimes be done precisely (for example, for the case of *envy*, the "clean" preferences are the "envy-free preferences" defined in chapter 9).[12]

The most discussed proposal for remedying moral defects of this kind consists in replacing "act-utilitarianism" by *rule-utilitarianism* where what is appraised and should maximize the sum of utilities are *rules* rather than specific acts or facts.[13]

However, rule-utilitarianism can be different from act-utilitarianism only in submitting itself to requirements that are not derived from utilitarianism, and hence in abandoning the status of unique and universal principle usually claimed by utilitarianism. These requirements involve both the scope of application of each rule and the content of the rules (one could say that a rule is a consistent pair of a maxim and a scope or domain of validity, but "rule" is usually used for the maxim).

First note that whatever the scopes are, the sum of utilities (were it meaningful) would always be maximized by the following rule applied in all domains: "act or choose so as to maximize the sum of utilities." Then rule-utilitarianism with any definition of the scopes of rules would amount to act-utilitarianism. This trivial remark shows that there should be a priori given constraints on the rules (maxims). The minimal obligation that avoids this trivial solution consists of the requirement to provide *explicit* rules of choice or behavior. However, if this is done without obligations concerning the scope, then the solution is back to act-utilitarianism again, since the sum of utilities (if it made sense) would be maximized by restricting the scopes to single acts or facts. But now one cannot get rid trivially of this trivial solution. The scope of the rules must be given exogenously (at least for certain rules). Hence this essential part of the choice cannot be utilitarian.

---

12. The full analysis is in Kolm 1991c, 1993f, 1995a.
13. This proposal dates back at least to Paley (1785).

Finally, the whole discussion of utilitarianism usually bypasses one aspect which, however, it could accomodate, namely the fact that the effects (on the sum of utilities) of various acts or rules are generally *not independent*: The specifics of a particular act or rule that maximize this sum depend on what the other acts or rules are. The utilitarian principle can therefore a priori only be "choose the set of all acts, or of all rules, that maximizes the sum." Yet all the discussions can easily be adjusted to take this interdependence into account.

However, all these problems are *superseded* by the *logical—or meaning*—problems of utilitarianism, which suggest that the very definition of utilitarianism cannot even possibly make sense. The various UMs constitute attempts to provide solutions to this question.

14.4   A Preference-Respecting Social Maximand

Three UMs, 3, 5, and 8, assume a priori a preference-respecting social ethical evaluation function or maximand, that is, a classical Social Welfare Function which is an increasing function of the levels of individuals' utility indexes (and not otherwise a function of the state of society—and of course not a function of the possibility set if it can vary). The justification is classical: (1) There exists a social ethical evaluation function of the state of society, a higher value of which characterizes a better state; (2) this function "respects individuals' preferences" in the sense that (a) if all individuals' are indifferent, it takes the same value, and (b) if certain individuals prefer and the others (if any) are indifferent, it takes a higher value.

If furthermore we can consider a "fundamental (ordinal) utility" for all the individuals (see chapter 7, section 7.2), and if we consider the same specification of this function for all the individuals, then a permutation of the values taken by this function for the various individuals produces a situation which is undifferentiable for the social ethical evaluation, that is to say, this social maximand is a symmetrical function of these values.

Classical utilitarianism justifies such a social maximand, with a particular additive form, by its theory of the highest sum of "happinesses." The UMs considered here reverse the order: They a priori assume the maximand (but not a priori one with the form of a sum), and this is the end for UM 10, whereas UMs 3 and 5 find a reason why this function could be written in the special form of a sum of individuals' utilities. The a priori assumption of this maximand will be discussed critically in the next chapter on Social Choice Theory.

14.5   The Independence (or Separability) Utilitaromorphism

UM 3 adds, to the assumption of a preference-respecting social maximand, a hypothesis of *independence* in the sense discussed in chapter 10, from a general *Principle of Independence of Irrelevant Individuals* (P3I): The direction of the change in the social maximand resulting from a change in the utilities of a subgroup of the individuals does not depend on the utility levels of the other individuals, for each such subgroup (it suffices that this hold for pairs). Then, the social maximand can be written as a *sum* of increasing functions of individual utilities. But since these utilities are ordinal (defined only up to an arbitrary increasing function), these increasing functions constitute valid specifications of the utilities. (A property studied by Roy, Divisia, Leontief, Gorman, Debreu 1960, Kolm 1966a and b, Yaari, etc.). This is probably nowadays the main reason for "believing in utilitarianism" offered by academic economists.[14]

This justification of a utilitarian form meets, however, the three following questions:

1. The assumption of the a priori social maximand, and that of its considered structure of "respect of individual preferences," constitutes a problem with several facets which will be discussed with Social Choice Theory (next chapter).

2. The independence-separability assumption is a particular one. Its discussion presented in chapter 10 is valid here (and too long to be repeated). In particular, the examples provided there can be restated here by considering that the individual utilities are the same specification of a fundamental utility function (equality in levels is then defined, and we consider qualitative variations rather than quantitative "transfers"). These examples show that evaluations can have standard and normal reasons not to follow the P3I. For instance, a change

---

14. See, for instance, the presentation in book form in Broome (1992).

in a subset of individuals' utility levels can be considered unfavorable, yet become favorable if the other, unchanged utility levels are different in such a way that the change considered now introduces equalities. In another example, with four individuals, the prima facie requirement of equality may lead one to prefer the set of levels (3, 3, 3, 3) to (4, 1, 3, 3), and the set (4, 1, 4, 4) to the set (3, 3, 4, 4) (the former has three equal pairs), but this violates the P3I considered. However, the possible *ethical* defense of independence as "nonnosiness" (see chapter 10) can also be proposed here.

3. From the theory presented, one can as well conclude that what should be maximized is a *product* of individual utilities, or a sum of power functions of individual utilities (and not necessarily the same power for all) or of exponential functions of these (not necessarily with the same exponential coefficients), a possibly weighed sum, or sums or products mixing utilities and powers, exponentials, logarithms, etc., of utilities. It indeed suffices to choose the corresponding specifications of the ordinal utilities. Now, as far as *meaning* is concerned, utilitarianism is in terms of pleasures, pains, happiness, etc. Can one think of "my pleasure multiplied by your pleasure," or of "the cube of my pleasure multiplied by (or plus) the exponential of yours," etc.? If the individual utilities are the same specification of a fundamental utility, we are restricted to symmetrical social maximands. This leaves the product of utilities, the sum of powers (with same power), etc., and the case is about the same.

The sum obtained by the theory considered can hardly be seen as a *utilitarian* sum of pleasures or happinesses. If, for example, there existed a quantitative measure of an individual's pleasure or happiness, as the classical discourse often seems to assume, or indeed a cardinal measure of it as a number of more modern discourses seem to assume, these measures would be specifications of the utilities, and therefore an independent-separable respectful social maximand could be taken as a sum of functions of these individual indexes, but it could generally not be taken as a sum of these indexes (this remark also applies to a number of other utilitaromorphisms).[15]

---

15. Maskin's (1978) proof of utilitarianism from an independent (separable) impartial social welfare function of the indivdual values of a cardinal (without justification)

14.6   Risk and Justice: Harsanyi's Respectful Consequentialism or Moral Risk-neutrality

Respecting people's risk-taking preferences rules out trying to limit the resulting welfare inequalities and miseries; that is, it implies judging society by the sum of individuals' utilities. This is the essence of a justification of utilitarianism put forward by Harsanyi (1955).

Indeed, if a just policy leads to lower miseries and inequalities resulting from a risk, at the cost of lower benefits for the lucky people, it may be opposed ex ante by people who prefer to incur this risk, and to risk misfortune in exchange for the hope of a high gain. This policy may even be so opposed by unanimity, thus setting justice against democracy. But must one respect ex ante preferences (if one has a choice)? The point is that an individual's preferences ex ante and ex post a risk are inconsistent in a sense: If he loses, he prefers that a lower risk had been taken; and he may also prefer that the choice had been still more audacious if he discovers that he would have been on the winning side. The just policy considered may be opposed by unanimity ex ante, but not ex post when the losers appreciate being in a better situation. And justice ex ante and ex post can be completely at odds with each other: Equal ex ante levels of the individuals' satisfaction facing the risk may end up in a very unequal situation as the result of the risk, very unequal ex ante levels may result in ex post equalities (yet not at the same level in all eventualities, since this would suppress the risk), an individual with the gloomiest prospect may turn out the luckiest, and the most miserable ex post may have had the brightest prospects ex ante. Life is full of such destinies.

The issue, seen from the general theory of justice, is whether the final effects of the occurrence of the risk are within the responsibility of justice, or whether, on the contrary, the individuals are accountable for these effects of this occurrence on themselves. This is merely an instance of the central problem of justice, which consists of dividing the items of the world into those for which the justiciables are deemed

---

fundamental utility function $u(i, x)$, where i denotes an individual and x the state, is based on the omission of the fact that in the sum $\sum_i f[u(i, x)]$ the cardinal function f depends on the specification of the function u and incurs a compensating contravariation when this specification changes.

to be accountable for their effects on themselves, and the others, whose effects fall under the concern and responsibility of justice. Ex post justice amounts to the position that the occurrence of the risk and its consequences are within the scope of justice. This is *consequential justice*. By contrast, ex ante justice leaves the individuals accountable for the occurrence of the risk. If, however, this ex ante justice considers that everything else is within the scope of justice, notably including all of individuals' preferences, its end values are individuals' ex ante satisfactions, which encompass notably individuals' ex ante preferences about the risky prospect. In still other cases the accountability for the effects of the occurrence of the risky event can be shared, in various possible proportions, between the individuals and the justice policy.

These various alternative conceptions of justice provide generally different ex ante social ethical evaluations and policies (policy measures can be either ex ante, or ex post—that is, after the occurrence of the risky event—but considered ex ante; insurances of any type are included). This a priori assignment of the effects of the consequences of the risky event has no effect on the social ethical evaluation and policy only with a particular form of the social ethical evaluation. Indeed the ex ante social ethical evaluation is the same when it sees the risk directly and when it sees it through the individuals' evaluations that appraise it by average utilities (mathematical expectations) if and only if this social ethical evaluation is the (linear) average of individuals' utilities or evaluations, that is to say, given impartiality, with a utilitarian form (more on this below). However, this form eliminates all trace of the prima facie or ideal equality (of individuals' welfares) that is required by the rationality of justice (see chapter 2). But there is no a priori moral reason that the considered choice of allocation of accountability of the consequences of the occurrence of the risky event makes no difference, and that the evaluation and policy of justice be neutral with respect to this ascription.

This interesting issue constitutes the justification of utilitarianism provided by Harsanyi in 1955. The logic rests on the following assumptions: (1) There is a social ethical evaluation function respecting individuals' preferences. (2) Both the individuals and the social ethical evaluation evaluate risky prospects ex ante by the mathematical expectation of utilities or of the social ethical evaluation. That is to say, they evaluate according to the von Neumann–Morgenstern theory, which can be characterized by the rationality of *probability consequentialism*, that is, lotteries on lotteries are evaluated by the resulting probabilities of the final outcomes (although actual behavior departs frequently from this evaluation for various possible reasons in the domains of perception, such as focus on extreme values, or emotion, such as fear of regret or of disappointment, or others). The utility functions and the social ethical evaluation function are then specified as the corresponding cardinal functions. (3) The ex ante social ethical evaluation is neutral with respect to the assignment of accountability of the consequences of the occurrence of the risky event between the evaluation and policy of justice and the individuals themselves. Then the ex ante social ethical evaluation is both the mathematical expectation of its values in the various eventualities of the risk, and a function of the individuals' mathematical expectations of their utilities in these eventualities. (4) It is furthermore assumed that all these probability distributions for evaluating this risk are the same (they can be "objective" probabilities; this assumption is implicit for Harsanyi). We then consider the obtained equality for all the probabilities of a certain domain. These probabilities are taken as variables. A mathematical expectation is a linear function of the probabilities. Hence the equality (now an identity) assumed above says that a function of linear functions is itself a linear function of the variables. There results simply that this function is a linear functions of these linear functions, for a sufficient domain of variation.[16] That is, the ex ante social ethical evaluation is a linear function of the individuals' expected utilities. Hence, in certainty, the social ethical evaluation is a linear function of the individuals' utilities. Let us now assume, in addition, (5): The individuals' utilities are the same specification of a fundamental utility. There results that the social ethical evaluation function is a symmetrical function of these individual utilities. Finally, the social ethical evaluation function amounts to the sum of these individuals' utilities: This is utilitarianism. Harsanyi assumes the necessary symmetry

---

16. Since Harsanyi's theory intends to be general, it has to consider the full variability of probabilities, and any set of ex post states. The question of the necessary dimension of the domain of variation of the probabilities has been the object of a close scrutiny by Domotor (1979), Fishburn (1984), Weymark (1994), Mongin (1994, 1995) who also introduces other issues, and others.

without justifying it by the consideration of fundamental utilities, although he himself introduced such utilities in his other utilitarian theorem (1953).

However, the neutrality with respect to the assignment of accountability of the consequences of the occurrence of the risky event has a priori no reason.[17] The fact that the social ethical evaluation be an increasing function of individuals' expected utilities is a kind of Pareto-efficiency, and hence the conditions of the above result are often described as full consequential welfarism plus Pareto-efficiency. Then utilitarianism seems to be a consequence of Pareto-efficiency, which would be a strong property indeed. But this is ex ante Pareto-efficiency, while full consequential welfarism implies that the ex post Pareto-efficiency is the relevant one. An individual who has no luck in the lottery constituted by the risky event prefers that the public policy helps the unfortunate, or enforces more caution ex ante, and hence

---

17. Let u_i and W denote individual i's utility function and the social ethical evaluation function, with the specifications indicated in the previous paragraph. $u = \{u_i\}$ denotes the vector of the u_i. $W(u)$ is an increasing and symmetrical function. Ex ante, the world, and hence u, and hence $W(u)$, are stochastic variables. Let E denote the mathematical expectation operation. Full consequential welfarism evaluates ex ante according to $EW(u)$. The individuals' ex ante welfares are $Eu = \{Eu_i\}$. The social ethical evaluation that lets the individuals accountable for the consequences of the occurrence of the risky event thus is $W(Eu)$. The difference $R = W(Eu) - EW(u)$ is the social cost of the effects of the occurrence of the risky event. $R > 0$ for all actually risky events says that the function W is concave, which expresses, with its symmetry, the prima facie justice of equality (note that concavities of the individual functions u_i in their variables such as income may lead to a concavity of $\sum u_i$ in these variables, but the ethic presently considered is welfarist with the u_i as end values and prima facie equalizands). The ex ante social ethical evaluation is $EW(u)$ if the conception and policy of justice endorses this cost, and $W(Eu)$ if this cost is left to the individuals. There can also be a sharing of this cost, with the social ethical evaluation

$$EW(u) + aR = W(Eu) - (1 - a)R = aW(Eu) + (1 - a)EW(u),$$

with $0 \le a \le 1$, where a and $1 - a$ are the shares of R assigned respectively to the individuals and to the social policy. Harsanyi's theorem is that $R \equiv 0$ (for a sufficient domain of variation of the stochastic variables) if and only if $W = \sum u_i$ (up to an increasing linear transformation, and given that W is symmetrical and increasing). Hence utilitarianism results from what can be labelled "Harsanyi's condition": The social ethical evaluation does not depend on the assignment of accountability for the consequences of the occurrence of the risky event (that is, on the parameter a, and it suffices to consider its extreme values 0 and 1). Note that the criticism that was addressed to this theory and result of Harsanyi about its ethical meaning by-passed the crucial issue, which is the question of accountability and responsibility for the consequences of the occurrence of the risk (hence it needs not be discussed here).

lowers the final dispersion of individuals' welfares, whereas he may oppose these policies ex ante when he still has hope in his luck.

The basic point indeed is that ex post justice, by measures taken either ex ante or ex post, tends to lower the final dispersion of individuals' welfares and to increase the lowest welfares, in the name of the prima facie or ideal equality resulting from rationality (see chapter 2), and this tends to reduce the risk below what the individuals would ex ante prefer to incur in risking to end up in a poor situation in exchange for the possibility to obtain a much better one. As a result the best, just, and Pareto-efficient policy for full consequential welfarism may well be opposed ex ante by all the individuals. Consider, for instance, a society of two individuals, and two possible alternative prospects, with the evaluations and utilities considered in Harsanyi's theorem. One prospect is risky with utility pairs (for the individuals in a given order) of $(0, 10)$ with probability $\frac{1}{2}$ and $(10, 0)$ with probability $\frac{1}{2}$. The other prospect is sure with the utility pair $(4, 4)$. For many social ethical evaluation functions which are increasing (Pareto-efficiency), symmetrical (indifferentiability of fundamental utility levels), and concave (prima facie preference for equality), the sure prospect is preferable. This is, for instance, the case for functions that are the product, the sum of logarithms, the sum of square roots, or the minimum, of the two individual utilities. By contrast, the risky prospect is preferred by both individuals, since it gives them expected utilities of 5. The risky prospect is also chosen by the utilitarian sum. Finally, justice in risky situations is a possible reason for uncertainty-paternalism, that is, for the ex ante social ethical evaluation not respecting individuals' preferences toward risk (with the same information for the individuals and the policy). Note that when all individuals oppose ex ante the just policy, they would prevent its choice in a democratic setting. Risk may thus create an opposition between democracy and justice. However, the individuals preventing ex post justice would then be *responsible* for this choice.

Now, one may indeed hold that the policy of justice is not in charge of the effects of the occurrence of the risky event. These effects would then be imputed to the individuals who incur them. This, however, should be justified. The most standard reason for accountability is responsibility. In the standard sense of the term, an agent is responsible for a fact if he could have prevented its occurrence (by omission or commission). Responsibility is not consequentialist, since it is assignment according to a *cause*. Indeed the individuals can often affect the risks they incur by action, protection, voluntary insurance, and the like. However, the corresponding end values of justice would be individuals' means for these choices. They would not be the individuals' expected utilities, as required if the social ethical evaluation function is to be taken as a function of these expected utilities. This latter case would correspond to the individuals choosing only the ex ante dispersion of their utilities around these expected values, whereas by assumption they aim only at maximizing these expected values, and the ex ante dispersion is a consequence of this choice as the expected value is. When the risk considered cannot be influenced by the individuals, then, since the considered social ethic is otherwise completely welfarist, consistency probably requires that it be full consequential welfarism focussing on ex post justice. Then ex ante choices are bound to meet the noted difficulties with individuals' ex ante preferences, which raises issues such as justice requiring compulsory insurances, interferring with democracy, or requiring, for its implementation, nonegoistic individuals concerned with ex post justice.

Note, finally, that the Original Position utilitarianism (Harsanyi 1953; see chapter 8) consists of an ex ante choice with the risk being the allocation of individuals' specific selves (all the individuals are ex ante identical). Utilitarianism then results from another property than the one considered in this section, although the setting is a particular case of the one considered here.[18]

14.7 Interpersonal Comparison of Preferences

The following expressions, which express a reason for favoring an individual rather than another, are not uncommon and hence reveal a meaningful moral concept: "Give this to her rather than to him be-

---

18. The relations between risk and justice are analyzed in Kolm 1996d. It is shown, in particular, how these considerations provide the solutions of the question of letting the individuals accountable for certain of their characteristics while the others are compensated by the policy, which can be either a "fundamental insurance" (see chapter 9) or a "resourcism" aiming at an equalization, by compensations, of the benefits or handicaps provided by these capacities.

cause she likes it more than he does, or because she would suffer from it less than he would"; "choose state A rather than state B because individual 1 prefers A to B more than individual 2 prefers B to A, and the other individuals are indifferent between A and B." These distributional choices are based on an interpersonal comparison of preferences (that is, of pairwise preferences, not of preference orderings or levels of satisfaction). It is often possible to express such a comparison of individuals' preferences for A over B by the levels of a function of the individual's utility levels in these two states. If this function could be written as a difference between these utility levels, the considered judgments would amont to utilitarianism for choices concerning two individuals. However, in general, this function cannot be expressed in this manner (no increasing function of this function and increasing functions of the utility functions lead to this form), except for *weak preferences*, that is, in the neighborhood of indifference.

This interpersonal comparison of preferences is the meaningful concept that is the closest to the utilitarian intention or "intuition." Yet, first, it does not yield utilitarianism as just noted. Second, it can be applied only for pairs of concerned individuals (this condition can be extended by the appropriate devices, so as to consider a larger number of concerned individuals, yet not to the point of obtaining a complete comparison of pairs of states and general transitivity among these pairwise comparisons).[19] Third, this interpersonal comparison of preferences between pairs of states exists and is meaningful only for specific questions of rather limited scope: it belongs to local justice not only as regards the relevant society (pairs of individuals) but also the topic, and it is one criterion among many that are occasionally relevant; this is microjustice, and indeed marginal justice with respect to overall distributive justice; this criterion in no way claims universal applicability as utilitarianism commonly does.[20]

---

19. See Kolm 1996g.

20. The relation between the interpersonal comparison of ordinal pairwise preferences and a utilitarian form is as follows. Let X be the set of social states and u_i be a specification of individual i's ordinal utility function on X. Let $x \in X$ be chosen in accord with the interpersonal comparison of ordinal pairwise preferences, and let $y \in X$ be a state such that $u_k(y) = u_k(x)$ for all $k \neq i, j$. Then x is socially preferred to y because individual i (say) prefers x to y more than individual j prefers y to x, a binary relation written as $(i; x, y) P(j; y, x)$ with $u_i(x) > u_i(y)$ and $u_j(y) > u_j(x)$. Let us now

14.8   Consequential Maximizing Bargaining

Consider the following conditions (each is discussed in other sections or chapters): (1) Individuals have a fundamental (see chapter 7) and cardinal utility, and we choose the same specification for all; (2) the solution is determined by a bargaining, hence by variables that are increases in utilities above a reference state; (3) the solution maximizes a function (it is "socially rational" in this classical economists' sense), which, by condition 2, is a function of these excess utilities; (4) from a unanimity-Pareto condition, this function is increasing; (5) the outcome is consequentialist in the sense that it does not actually depend on the reference state. Then the maximand is the sum of the individuals' utilities. Indeed conditions 2, 3, and 5 imply that it is a linear form of the excess utilities, which amounts to a weighted sum of utilities, and the weights have to be positive from condition 4, and equal if condition 1 requires the symmetry of this maximand.[21]

---

introduce a series of natural assumptions that are defensible as rather general. On the relevant domain for x and y, P constitutes an ordering representable by the ordinal function U such that the foregoing binary relation writes $U(i; x, y) > U(j; y, x)$. Then with natural assumptions $U(i; x, y) = V[i; u_i(x), u_i(y)] = V^i[u_i(x), u_i(y)]$, where U and V are ordinal, the V^i are coordinal (the change of V into V^i is a mere notation), and $V^i(\alpha, \beta)$ is increasing in α and decreasing in β. The $V^i(\alpha, \beta)$, defined for $\alpha > \beta$, are extended to $\alpha = \beta$ with $V^i(\alpha, \alpha) = 0$ (they thus become zero-preserving ordinal). One thus has $V_1^i(\alpha, \alpha) + V_2^i(\alpha, \alpha) = 0$, where V_1^i and V_2^i are the partial derivatives, assumed to exist, with $V_1^i > 0$ and $V_2^i < 0$. Then, assume the required connectedness, continuities, and differentiabilities; assume $y \to x$, and write $u_k = u_k(x)$ and $u_k + du_k = u_k(y)$ for $k = i, j$. One then has $V^i(u_i, u_i + du_i) > V^j(u_j + du_j, u_j)$, with $du_i < 0$ and $du_j > 0$. That is, subtracting $V^i(u_i, u_i) = V^j(u_j, u_j) = 0$ from both sides and letting $y \to x$ and hence $du_i \to 0$ and $du_j \to 0$, $V_2^i(u_i, u_i) \cdot du_i > V_1^j(u_j, u_j) \cdot du_j$ or $V_1^i(u_i, u_i) \cdot du_i + V_1^j(u_j, u_j) \cdot du_j < 0$. Denoting $f_k(\alpha) = \int_\alpha V_1^k(\beta, \beta) \cdot d\beta$, and $v_k = f_k(u_k)$, this condition writes $dv_i + dv_j < 0$. But this is the condition obtained for the maximization of $\sum v_i$, a utilitarian form and principle. The inequality $<$ is replaced by $\leq$ if one also considers the relation "as much as" for comparing individuals' pairwise ordinal preferences. The function v_i is a specification of the ordinal u_i, since $f_i'(\alpha) = V_1^i(\alpha, \alpha) > 0$. The v_i are comultiplicative cardinal with the added constants being the integration constants for the f_i and the common multiplicative positive constant beting $F'(0)$ when the V^i are replaced by $F(V^i)$, where F is any increasing zero-preserving function. Note that these meaningful cardinal utilities have only been defined in the small, that is, for weak preferences, in line with appendix A of chater 12. Hence only a necessary local meaningful uilitarian condition is obtained.

21. Condition 5 can be replaced by the symmetry of the maximized function in both the excess utilities, in order to express a certain "equal bargaining power," and the utilities, in order to express impartia¹ity, when the utility levels in the reference state can differ.

14.9 Efficient Independent Transferability

If the individuals' utility functions are quasi-linear, that is to say, one of their specifications has the form of the quantity of money (or any other given transferable good) held by the individual plus a function of his other goods, and these quantities of money are freely transferable, then at an efficient allocation the sum of these specifications of the utility functions is the highest possible (see Kolm 1987h, i, 1989e). The formal limitation of this utilitaromorphism is that this quasi-linear form is rather particular (it amounts to the classical assumption of "constant marginal utility of money" in standard economic analysis, and it is the way to make sense of the classical assumption of "transferable utility" in game theory; it is a good assumption for profit-maximizing firms, but utilitarianism considers individuals). Moreover, why would these additive specifications of utilities be the right specifications for representing pleasure or happiness?

14.10 Surplus Theory and Compensation

Since Dupuit (1844) economics has developed the *method of surplus* as a criterion for the choice of public projects to realize. The surplus of a project is the sum of all the individuals' willingnesses to pay for the project. The willingness to pay of an individual, or the money value of the project for him, is the highest amount of money he would be willing to hand out in order that the project be realized. If he dislikes the project for whatever reason, this money value is the negative of the lowest amount this individual should receive in order to accept that the project be implemented. We include the various money costs of the project as negative money values for the payers (for example, the taxpayers). The money values of any positive or negative "external effects" are of course included. The surplus is the algebraic sum of all the money values. The surplus criterion states that the project should be realized if and only if its surplus is positive, and that the alternative that provides the highest surplus should be selected (the latter condition encompasses the former, since the nonrealization of the project is one alternative).

A number of classical criteria can be derived from the surplus in the relevant conditions, such as choosing the investment with the highest "rate of return," maximizing the surplus under a given budget constraint, or implementing projects taken in the order of decreasing rates of return until either this rate reaches the relevant market interest rate or a budget constraint is exhausted.

This criterion raises a number of problems. One is that a project may give a positive total surplus when evaluated from its absence, and a negative total surplus when evaluated from a state where it exists, that is, its absence then provides a positive surplus (see Scitovsky 1941); a similar inversion may occur for the choice among variants; yet this dilemma (due to the "income effect") does not actually materialize in many cases. Another well-considered question is that if the project is paid with taxes that are not lump-sum for whatever reason (see chapter 6), their raising causes a loss that leads one to value a public dollar at more than a private one (see an exhaustive analysis and applications in Kolm 1969b, 1970a). Both questions are affected by the specific accompanying transfers and compensations considered below.

However, the first question to answer is: What is the meaning and justification of surplus theory? The maximization of a sum of individuals' values makes the theory look like utilitarianism. It would even be formally valid utilitarianism, since the added values, being measured in money terms, are formally addable. But the principle also means that the people who gain from the implementation of the project can compensate the people who lose, which makes it a criterion of potential unanimity (or Pareto) efficiency. However, the implementation of a project financed from a general public budget imposes a loss on general taxpayers who may benefit little from it, and on the victims of its negative external effects (monetary effects through markets, and others); then society often has more possibilities from the realization of the project, yet certain people lose from this, which may raise an issue of justice. These various questions and the answers they entail are considered now.

Surplus theory maximizes a sum of individuals' values expressed in money terms. The highest an individual's desire for the item, the highest his willingness to pay for it. And the addition of money values is logically meaningful. Hence surplus theory has an appearance of logically valid utilitarianism. This view may find support in Bentham's assertion that "Money is the instrument for measuring the quantity of pain or pleasure."[22]

However, an individuals' willingness to pay for an item measures the intensity of his preference for this item relative to his preference for other items, rather than relative to other individuals' preference for this item as standard utilitarianism would have it. Surplus theory relates to utilitarianism as "I like this more than that" relates to "I like this more than he does."

Surplus theory would nevertheless remain amenable to the social ethical indictments of utilitarianism, such as the criticisms that it "does not take seriously the division of society into individuals" (Rawls), or that it disregards the differences in the types of pleasures or of rights (see, for instance, J. S. Mill on both points, with "privacy rights" having priority over the utilitarian maximization).

Furthermore, an individual's willingness to pay for something depends not only on his desire for this item but also on his capacity to pay, on his income or on his wealth. Hence, if the distribution of income or wealth is unjust, it seems unfair to compare or add the unweighted willingnesses to pay of the individuals for the decision concerning the implementation of the project. Indeed the surplus criterion then seems to provide an unfair advantage to the unjustly richer and to discriminate against the unjustly poorer, thus exacerbating the existing injustice. Utilitarianism as a global social ethic is not amenable to this kind of issue since all variables, including distributional ones, are optimized jointly. The point here is that surplus theory is necessarily limited to partial optimizations, notably excluding the determination of the just distribution. Indeed, in a society of self-interested individuals, transfers among individuals always have a zero surplus from the definition.[23]

---

22. The full quotation is revealing: "The thermometer is the instrument for measuring the heat of the weather: the barometer for measuring the pressure of the air. Those who are not satisfied with the accuracy of these instruments must find out others that shall be more accurate, or bid *adieu* to Natural Philosophy. Money is the instrument for measuring the quantity of pain or pleasure. Those who are not satisfied with the accuracy of this instrument must find out some other that shall be more accurate, or bid *adieu* to Politics and Morals" (1973, p. 123).

23. The case where individuals are concerned by others' incomes, wealth, or welfare is analyzed in *The Optimal Production of Social Justice* (Kolm 1966a).

A positive surplus for the project means that its realization, accompanied by adequate transfers, can make everybody better off than in its absence. It is, in this sense, a criterion of social efficiency in the unanimity sense. The same holds for the choice among alternative variants. Making everybody better off means that the people who gain from this realization compensate those who lose from it in costs of realization or through any negative external effects. Let us not insist here on the technical point that the actual transfers affect agents' behavior, the surplus, and the ideally optimal variant;[24] we will also discuss the choice of a variant as the choice of a project.

Hence, if a positive-surplus project is not realized, the resulting state of society is not Pareto-efficient. Since we want Pareto-efficiency (see the discussion in chapter 2 and the references), we must want the realization of positive-surplus projects. However, if a project is considered by itself rather than as integrated within the whole budget, its realization makes certain people lose: the general taxpayers who do not benefit sufficiently or at all from the project, and the people who endure negative external effects. Therefore, there is no unanimity for the project by itself, although ad hoc accompanying transfers could guarantee this unanimity. Furthermore the project augments the possibilities of society in a sense, yet certain people lose as a result: This tends prima facie to be immoral for a consequentialist social ethic tuned on individuals' satisfactions, needs, or well-being.

The positive surplus permits one to face these questions in associating to the project the financial transfers that make the operation to be an improvement for everybody (at least, nobody would lose from it). This is the *principle of compensation*, which means actual compensation and is opposed to the simple surplus criterion which is the *principle of compensability*.

Compensation implies a principle of benefit taxation (including ad hoc ear-marked taxes or users' charges). It requires the same

---

24. The transfers affect agents' behavior both by "income or wealth effects," and by "price or substitution effects" because these transfers may have to be based on "inelastic" items both for intrinsic and informational reasons (see a similar discussion in chapter 6).

information as the ascertainment of compensability (positive surplus),[25] and it uses more this information since it uses individuals' values to implement the compensatory transfers. Yet the principle of compensation raises three basic types of issues: the sharing of the surplus above the compensation, the rights to receive compensation, and the scope of the "project" considered.

Various criteria of justice can be used to share the surplus. For example, the liberal (process-freedom based) ethic offers two levels of possible principles. First, the beneficiaries of the extra surplus would only be the people concerned directly or indirectly by the project, since this surplus is created by the meeting of their desires, needs or means. Second, the sharing could be achieved by direct agreement, possibly putative and vicariously implemented by the public sector in cases of "agreement failures"; this amounts to the endorsement of the existing allocation of means and capacities for bargaining.

Furthermore, the financial independence of the project under the compensation principle, and the unanimity for the project accompanied by the transfers, makes this realization akin to a direct agreement. However, in the usual private realizations, people who lose by external effects of any kind cannot claim compensation if their rights are not violated. This is for instance the case of the monetary external effects of commercial activities (such as losses incurred by competitors). The question of other external effects depends on the existing rights. Several alternative systems of entitlements to compensation can be considered. The particular case where the liberally legitimate rights are considered and the extra surplus is shared by free agreement leads to full-process liberalism, possibly vicariously implemented as a liberal social contract in case of "agreement failure" (see chapter 5). The solution so arrived at is about the opposite of utilitarianism.

Finally, another parameter is the scope of sets of "projects" considered together, from an element of an ordinary "project," to the whole of public actions and expenditures in a political system. With a certain pooling, smaller "projects" can be financed by global receipts, with different people being interested differently by various more particular projects. The extreme case of the whole of the public budget is particu-

---

25. The effects noted in the preceding note can make a difference, however.

larly relevant. Everybody may gain from the whole of the public sector as compared to its absence. If the decision is voluntary agreement, the scheme becomes Wicksell's "new principle of just taxation" if the agreement is between representatives,[26] and a Public Choice framework if the political system is also at stake and the threat of violence is a priori considered. In all cases, opposites of utilitarianism are again reached (yet all these process-freedom based solutions differ from each other).

14.11   Social Welfare and Social Income

Inspired by utilitarianism, a number of applications have put forward the concept of "welfare," and in particular of "social welfare" as a sum of individual welfares. However, the term "welfare" is often used in ways that make it a highly ambiguous concept. It is certainly meant to include means of happiness, but it is ambiguous about which personal consumptive or satisfaction capacities (see chapter 6) are included and which are not. This "welfare" basically oscillates between "utility" and income. The ideal seems to be utility, but interpersonal addition is then meaningless. On the other hand, income can be added, but it omits all the personal and in particular subjective causes of welfare. Yet, replacing utility by income may be the application of Bentham's indication that utility is practically to be measured in money (see the previous section)—of course the comparison of incomes with different prices raises well-known conceptual questions.

However, as with the surplus, maximizing the sum of individuals' incomes may not be a utilitarian proxy but rather a criterion of efficiency. If indeed lump-sum transfers are possible, a higher total income permits one to attribute a higher individual income to everybody.

For one reason or the other, national income is a widespread criterion for judging policies (Judge Posner, 1981, is one of its most articulate advocates, notably for application to judiciary decisions).

But transfers are limited by politics, by process-liberal ethics, by information, and by disincentives since both the ethics of income re-

---

26. In Musgrave and Peacock (1962).

distribution and information lead one to base transfers on elastic items (see the full discussion in chapter 6). The highest national income corresponds to a particular distribution of individuals' incomes. Then the highest total income is not justifiable by Pareto-efficiency any longer.

Income may, however, still be the relevant individual item, but with an ethic adverse to its inequality because of applications of the rationality of the relevant equality (see chapter 2), and for a number of possible reasons which makes it either the end value of justice because it is a means of the individuals, or a consequence of other principles involving efficiency, ideal equal consumption or liberty (Equity), competitive equilibrium, and super-equity. This income justice has been analyzed in chapters 6, 8, and 10.

14.12   Appendix: A Note on Oriental Utilitarianism

Utilitarianism is commonly accused of the misconception of seeing society as one big self, which induces the moral mistake of possibly sacrificing certain individuals to "society's objectives." However, the opposite extreme view a priori leads to about the same formal conclusion as utilitarianism (not to its practical conclusions, though). This view agrees that a self does not exist for society as a whole, but it emphasizes that it does not exist for an individual either. Each individual is a set of many causally related elements of various kinds, but it contains nothing that can be called a self in a strict sense (perhaps the "transcendental I" of Western philosophers). This is the basic tenet of advanced Buddhist philosophy (in the West, similar views are held by Hume and Sartre, in particular, but without anything approaching the Buddhist elaboration—by very far).[27] Now, the other tenet of Buddhism is the aim of the decrease of suffering (pain, insatisfaction, etc.)—sensations of pain are basic elements among others. Since there exist no suffering essences, this is decrease of suffering in general, without ascription to particular "selves." This looks much

---

27. Advanced Buddhist philosophy in fact distinguishes a number of *concepts of the self*, some existing either by definition or from psychology, others illusory (see Kolm 1982a, ch. 19).

like a kind of philosophical utilitarianism, in particular of the "negative utilitarianism" kind that has sometimes been considered.[28] However, Buddhism also adds that the only efficient and durable way to obtain this result is essentially through the control of the birth of desires, and that this can be done practically only by each individual for himself (others can basically only provide information on how to do it when they have this knowledge). This differs widely from the allocation of resources to satisfy given tastes. Furthermore this theory shows that suffering, unsatisfiable desires, and illusions of selves all decrease and eventually vanish together, so that actual awareness of no-self also erases the eudemonistic reference.

---

28. This similarity is analyzed in Kolm (1982a). It is also noticed by D. Parfit (1986).

15 Social Choice Theory

Social Choice Theory is a theory in social ethics which is very famous in economics, known to certain philosophers and other social scientists, frequently mentioned in general, and which has given birth to an abundant technical literature. Social Choice Theory in the strict sense is very interesting for three reasons. First, it may be appreciated in the *history of thought* because one might argue that it provides the definitive closure of the utilitarian digression on logical grounds, since it can be presented, in a certain sense, as a proof of the impossibility of utilitarianism even if one does not insist on the meaningless strict *addition* of utilities or pleasures (see section 15.1 below). Second, the logic of this theory is the *mathematics of the aggregation of orderings*, a general problem in pure mathematics, very simple in its formulation, elementary in its methods, yet with some richness: This provides the right degree of logical challenge to a field which is all the more enticing as one conceives it as representing the main problem of societies. Third, and not least, this theory has inspired valuable *side fields* of study analyzing voting procedures or informational implementation. Yet as a theory in *social and economic ethics* proper, rather than in the history of thought or in mathematics, the meaning of its formal framework, and the ways in which it seeks to define the optimum and reaches its conclusions raise crucial questions of logic, relevance, realism, sense, and rationality.

15.1 The Problems of and with Social Choice Theory in the Strict Sense

The Essence of Social Choice Theory in the Strict Sense

The *actual* question is the determination of the general social optimum in the unique and given *actual* set of possibilities, with the *actual* preferences of the individuals if these preferences are relevant, including as usual the *future* and *uncertainty*. This choice presents itself as structured into various subchoices, all *different* by their topics, their dates, or their populations.

Now, as we will see, the central results of this theory are reached by the following logic. Consider a particular set of nonexisting or false problems (all very different from the actual one on several grounds, and some of them shockingly absurd); require strong particular relations between the characteristics and the solutions of these problems, most of them comparing problems; conclude that, as a consequence, it is not possible that all these problems have a solution; and hence that it is not possible that all these problems and the actual problem (and any other imaginary ones) all have a solution. If you now define the term "problem" as the obtention of a solution for all of the previously noted problems, then this newly defined "problem" has no solution. This does not mean nor imply that the actual problem has no solution.

At any rate the mere requirement of false problems for obtaining the impossibility of a set of problems that includes them provides a result that has no relevance for the solution of the actual problem, except perhaps to confirm that this whole approach is not a possible way to define the optimum—a conclusion that could be straightforwardly inferred from the absence of explicit variables that permit the application of the basic social ethical concepts, as noted below.

However, we will also see that the use of rationality and of principles for solving a problem may require the hypothetical consideration of nonexisting problems and that they require it when there is a single actual problem. But the theory considered uses many more false problems than required. Furthermore the false problems that one should consider are restricted to problems that lead to a solution for the actual problem, since this is the reason for their consideration. They should also be sensible. In particular, very implausible imaginary problems cannot be let to interfere with the existence of the solution. Moreover, the relations across problems should not themselves violate rationality (see section 15.3), and their satus is problematic, especially when they need not even involve the actual problem.

We will note in the next section that the considered plurality of problems cannot mean, given the specifics of the theory, several issues, dates, circumstances, populations, uncertain occurrences, or a "theory of constitutions."

Specifically, in this setting, a problem consists in the choice of *a state of society* (or *social state*) among several *alternative* ones which constitute its *possibility set*, for a given preference *ordering*[1] of the social

---

1. In all the orderings that we consider here, there can be equivalent elements. That is to say, these entities are, more specifically, "pre-orderings." A pre-ordering may be representable by a function—a utility function for a pre-ordering that represents a preference—which takes a higher value for a state that is higher in the ordering, and which is ordinal (defined up to an arbitrary increasing function).

states by each *individual*. A set of one preference ordering for each individual, for all the individuals, is called a *profile* of individuals' preferences, or *preference profile*. The absence, a priori surprising for a definition of the social optimum, of any explicit item or variable with which one could define impartiality, equality, equal treatment of equals, liberty, right, and so on, will be dealt with below[2] (the introduction is *trivial and straightforward for liberties, rights, powers, duties, etc*; see section 15.4.)

The actual problem has one possibility set and one preference profile. Future and uncertain prospects should classically be included in the definition of social states. The various specific sub-problems all bear on partial "states of society" of different nature (topics, circumstances, dates, populations).

We will notice that the theory discussed above uses only very untrue preference profiles and possibility sets, and needs to consider unthinkable individual preferences. Indeed it considers choices in possibility sets with only two or three alternatives, whereas the mere question of the distribution among individuals requires much more, and there are continuous variables. Furthermore, the theory uses only preference profiles with false and impossible coincidences in the set of individual preferences (see the next subsection). Finally, the theory needs and requires that a solution be provided for cases where I happen to prefer, above all, that everything is objectively very bad for me (my family dies in a fire, I incur a dramatic life handicap, I lose everything, and everything else I value is destroyed).

The theory considered has a fair number of variants, which relax or qualify one assumption or the other or introduce other related ones. There is no need to present explicitly all these variants here (certain will be noted below), since all the logical issues raised apply to most of them, and at least one crucial set of issues applies to each of them.[3]

The same remark applies to interpretations of the theory that depart from its initial presentation as considering the general social

---

2. This reveals the utilitarian ancestry, although utilitaromorphisms that use fundamental utility can define equal utility levels (that is not their concern, however), and the utilitarian sum has the "marginal equality" property (see chapter 14).

3. The presentation of variants is usefully gathered in Kelly (1978) (but with almost no discussion of actual meanings).

optimum,[4] and aim at *more specific or "local" questions of collective decision*. There remains, in particular, the crucial question of the possible *meaning* of the consideration of *various specific choices* with *social states of the same specific nature* (not different topics, circumstances, dates, or populations), with *several preferences for each individual* (numerous and very varied ones), *numerous but particular possibility sets*, and *particular relations between these various choices*. This will be discussed in more detail below. Note also that *the general optimum is but the set of all more specific optima*. We consider below the definition of the general social optimum, as the theory presented itself, and only parts of the remarks apply to certain more limited applications; but they are crucial parts, and they generally include most of the remarks.

The relations standardly assumed by the theory among the various specific choice problems it considers, concerning their possibility sets and their solutions, amount to the existence of a *social ordering*. This is an ordering of the alternative social states, independent of the possibility set, such that the optimum (solution) for each possibility set is a maximal element of this ordering. This imposes, therefore, the following structure on the way of solving the problems: first, for each profile of individuals' preferences, define a social ordering; then, for each possibility set, choose a maximal element. We may call the *ordering function* the function providing a social ordering for each preference profile (Arrow calls this the "social welfare function," but others have used this name for a numerical representation of the social ordering). The requirement of a social ordering is sometimes replaced by subproperties of this structure or by other neighboring properties, but this leaves all the remarks presented here; apart from its possible intrinsic meanings, the social ordering also corresponds to the history of thought and the consideration of classical Social Welfare Functions (see below). One such alternative subproperty is the "axiom of choice": An optimum remains an optimum if certain other alternatives become impossible and no new possibilities are added. This is implied by the choice through an ordering. The "axiom of choice" implies in turn a condition which will be considered below, the "Chernoff condition":

---

4. This is in particular conspicuous from the situation of the theory in the history of thought, as starting from classical "Social Welfare Functions", or from Arrow's definition of a "social state" (1963, p. 17).

the common elements of two alternative possibility sets cannot include both a state that is an optimum for one set and not for the other, and another state that is an optimum for the latter set and not for the former. The other alternative conditions are variations on transitivity (see below).[5]

The other properties considered are properties of the ordering function.

Only one of these other properties concerns each preference profile separately. This is the unanimity or Pareto condition: If all the individuals prefer one alternative to another, the social ordering ranks it higher than the other; this "weak Pareto condition" can be extended to the standard Pareto condition where one alternative is ranked higher than another if at least one individual has this preference and those who do not have it are indifferent, and to the property that unanimous indifference leads to social equivalence. This can be said to manifest the "respect of individuals' preferences."

We will see below that the assumption of a social ordering, as well as the other weaker or alternative assumptions such as the "axiom of choice" or the "Chernoff condition," are at odds with standard conceptions of equity and justice, and with consequences of rationality in the normal sense of "for a reason" (see section 15.3). The requirement of a social ordering is indeed problematic at first sight: Why would we want to know the 193th best alternative?[6] Only the first best is required for the choice. An ordering is by definition equivalent to transitivity: For the three alternatives a, b, and c, if a is chosen in the set (a, b) and c is chosen in the set (b, c), then a must be chosen in the set (a, c), with the obvious extensions for the cases of ties. But this implies choices between pairs of alternatives, whereas the actual choice problem is unique and in a much larger set. The same holds for the other alternative conditions (the "axiom of choice" is applied to pairs and triples and applicable with all hypothetical possibility sets). We have already noticed that the economists' use of the name "rational" for choices derived from an ordering is eccentric and unwarranted. The

---

5. Such as "quasi-transitivities," "independence of paths," or "triple aciclycity."

6. This illustrative simple question is in fact not really possible since the actual social choice contains the choice of continuous variables.

basic argument in favor of a social ordering from the special consistency of transitivity is a weak one, notably since it involves so many and so unrealistic nonexisting problems for the question of social ethics (choices from pairs; a similar conclusion holds for the "axiom of choice" and for the other alternative conditions).[7] Expressions such as "the preferences of society", "society prefers", and similar ones are rather often used in this theory; at first sight, this may suggest an anthropomorphism of the collective, or a group mind, quite at odds with the otherwise very individualistic outlook of this field. However, thoughtful contributors (like Arrow) emphasize that this is to be taken as conditions among various choices, in the tradition of "revealed preferences" in the economic theory of the consumer, but this sound view then raises more acutely the issue of the types and plurality of the possibility sets and domains of choice. Note that all these remarks apply to the a priori *assumption* that the social optimum should be defined by the intermediary of an ordering (or with the equivalent properties). It is a completely different thing that a theory *deduces a social ordering from specific, tangible reasons*. This is, for example, what classical utilitarianism did (this is also the case of Practical Justice, for nonuniversal application).

Indeed the social ordering is a utilitarian relic, notably with the respect of individuals' preferences. The meaninglessness of the sum and of the cardinality of individuals' utility functions led several scholars to replace the sum by a more general function of the social state through the intermediary of the individuals' utility functions (Bergson, Divisia, Lange, Allais, Samuelson, etc.). Arrow (1951, 1963) added the requirement that this function be defined for *several* sets or profiles of individuals' utility functions (or preference orderings). Samuelson (1967) argued that the consideration of several profiles belongs to the field of political science while welfare economics is concerned only with a single profile. Arrow (1963) replied that the division between disciplines is indifferent (see also below the remark concerning "constitutions"). Bergson (1966) insisted that this Social Welfare Function

---

7. By comparison, an individual's preference ordering is a *psychological* property, and its existence is a psychological hypothesis (which raises its own questions, see Kolm 1986a, and also 1982a and 1986b, and chapter 7, note 23).

represents the social ethical view of a specific individual, such as a government adviser, and that it "respects individuals' preferences" in being a function of individual's utilities concerning their standard welfare only rather than also their ethical views (that is, Bergson's Social Welfare Function is what Pareto 1913 calls an individual's "utility" as opposed to his "ophelimity" or strictly self-interested welfare);[8] but this person's moral views are not exempted from the requirements of justice and of rationality which may not be consistent with an ordering (see section 15.3 below); furthermore the questions of the selection of this evaluer and of how he considers his own preferences are raised; note finally that Bergson considers only the actual individual preferences or utility functions. Little (1951, 1952) objected to the consideration of relations between different profiles but admitted the existence of a social ordering which implies relations among different possibility sets and the choices, a possible lack of consistency. Indeed all these criticisms accepted a social ordering, in contrast to, notably, Buchanan (1954), who argued that a preference ordering is meaningful for individuals but not for society.

The other properties of the ordering function that Arrow assumed for the result of impossibility referred to above relate several specific choice problems or situations. They are the following:

Independence of Irrelevant Alternatives. The ordering of any set of alternatives by the social ordering depends only on the orderings of this set by the individuals, and not on their orderings involving other alternatives. Note that Nash (1950; see chapter 13) used the same expression to denote what is called here classically the "axiom of choice": The solution remains the same if other alternatives are removed from the possibility set (Nash, however, considers possibilities for utility levels).

Nondictatorship. An individual is called a "dictator" if the social ordering always coincides with his own preference ordering. The condition rules this out. But such an individual could also be a *wiseman*

---

8. Pareto, however, considered a linear function, and he also considered a "utilitarian" sum of these utilities. He thus had a "cardinality problem," both for ophelimities and for utilities, which also shows in his definition or complementary and substitute goods, and is in a sense at odds with his co-discovery of ordinalism.

whose views should be followed (individuals' preferences are assumed to include "values," views of the good for society). Or he might also be a *democrat* who adjusts his preferences to the good social ordering (this "democratic dictator" will be discussed below).

Another condition is that the social ordering is not the same for all preference profiles (*nonimposition*). Finally, Arrow also considers a *monotonicity* property called *Positive Response*: If an alternative goes up in one individuals' preference ordering and nothing else changes, no alternative that was worse than this one in the social ordering becomes better than it.

We will see that Independence of Irrelevant Alternatives and Positive Response can also be at odds with standard views of justice or equity and with rationality (see section 15.3).

The *status* of all these properties of the set of problems and solutions —the "conditions"—constitutes another question, which notably raises the issue of whose view they are, especially since individuals' ethical views are assumed to be incorporated in their preferences considered (see section 15.4).

Nevertheless, all these conditions might seem sensible at the very first sight if one accepts the plurality of preference profiles and the definition of the optimum through both individuals' preferences and a social ordering.

Now, the fact that the fruitful way to consider these theory and results, apart from pure mathematics, is by their position in the history of thought is confirmed by the fact that *the utilitarian sum of individuals' utilities and the social ordering it defines satisfy all these conditions*, as can be easily checked. Of course utilitarians would find it bizarre to consider imaginary utility functions (and hence preference orderings), but their theory can accommodate these cases. Then the problem defined and the question posed by the theory considered can logically be presented as utilitarianism minus the logically meaningless sum and cardinal utilities. This is indeed how they came about in the history of thought, as we have noticed. The preference-respecting social ordering, with the noted conditions, could therefore be considered as "ordinal utilitarianism." Then the "impossibility" would mean that even the logically meaningful, ordinal, utilitarianism is not possible.

This requires of course the considered plurality of profiles. At any rate, this is the fundamental reason why this result of Arrow seemed important, challenging, and sometimes appalling to people trained in an overall utilitarian ethical outlook, and hence used to think that the optimum has to be defined through individuals' preferences and with a social maximand function, when they are furthermore aware of the dubious character of cardinal utilities (but not of that of the plurality of profiles). This describes notably a fraction of academic economists addicted to what Hicks called "welfarism" in a critical comment of 1959.

Then, since this problem was also mathematically interesting, notably as the problem of the aggregation of orderings, a number of studies focussed on this formal aspect of the question, and resulted in extending the initial scope of "impossibility" (to weaker or somewhat different "conditions"). The real challenge, however, laid elsewhere: in elementary and naive questions of meaning and necessity, and in general questions of social ethics some of which are obvious to everybody (certainly including these scholars outside their scholarly activity) and have been for centuries.

Indeed, what does it mean that each individual has several alternative preferences over the same alternatives in this context? Why consider absurd preferences? Why consider untrue preference profiles, and indeed use only these? Why consider several possibility sets with alternatives common to them? Why consider untrue possibility sets and indeed use only these? Why require a social ordering? What does "society prefers" mean? The correct consideration of rights, liberties, and powers raise no particular issue, since they can straightforwardly be included as features of each social state considered (with indirect preferences about them; see section 15.4).

Furthermore, if the social ethical end values are individuals' "welfares," then the optimum is their ideal equality (see chapter 2), which implies that they are compared, and hence comparable, and probably that one resorts to a second-best such as Practical Justice for efficiency (see chapter 7, section 7.2). In addition the social states can also be specified in distinguishing individuals' allocations of goods, rights, powers, etc., so that the end values can also include such items and hence the optimum can include their prima facie equality. We finally arrive at the full standard question of justice and social ethics, but one should probably consider that the initial problem has been altered beyond recognition.

The rest of this chapter develops or presents the points noted or suggested so far and related ones (other analyses and developments of this topic can be found in Kolm 1980a, 1986a, 1987a, 1992a, 1994b, 1995b, 1995c). The ideas considered can be said to constitute *Social Choice Theory in the strict sense*. It should be emphasized that the book of Arrow (1951, 1963), of which this field constitutes a close development, is practically the only work that discusses the crucial questions of *meaning* of these issues and of the related ones, and it also stands as a major study in social philosophy. We will barely mention the important side fields inspired by the framework of this theory but that either are not *ethical* in themselves, in the domains of informational implementation and, in part, of voting procedures, or are amenable to most of the basic questions considered here for the other part of the analysis of voting procedures.

Summary of the Twenty Problems of Social Choice Theory in the Strict Sense

To recap, the problems of the theory considered are the following (a number of points will be elaborated in further sections):

1. The theory considers nonexisting individual preferences.

2. The theory considers nonexisting possibility sets.

This use of *counterfactuals* (items that do not exist, and yet influence the conclusion and eventually choices or actions it inspires) will be considered closely in the next section. In addition, however, the theory considers *only* nonexisting possibility sets and preference profiles, as stated now:

3. The actual possibility set is not actually considered (used in the proofs). Indeed the only possibility sets considered in the concepts and proofs used contain only two or three alternative social states (four in certain related but misconceived studies).

4. The actual preference profile is not actually considered (used in the proofs). Indeed the only profiles considered in the proofs contain more similarities among individual orderings than is actually the case. For example, in varying income distribution, one can produce triples of

possible alternative social states such that each of the thirteen orderings of the triple (indifferences included) is its ordering by the actual
preferences of certain individuals. It suffices to consider standard cases
where each individual prefers to have a higher income (or where a
higher or lower income can compensate other influences on preferences). But the profiles used in the proofs contain a smaller number of
different individual orderings of each triple (in fact they need only
consider four such different orderings).[9] Note that this implies that the
theory rests crucially on the assumption that many people prefer to be
poorer.

5. Therefore, by points 3 and 4, the theory does not effectively consider the actual social choice situation. Hence the impossibility results
concern only a set of made-up situations and problems.

6. The possibility sets used by the theory are all very far from reality
(they contain only a couple of social states).

7. These possibility sets are very numerous.

8. The preference profiles used by the theory are all very different
from reality.

9. These preference profiles are very numerous.

10. The theory needs to consider absurd individual preferences. Indeed, for each individual, all preferences between any pair of alternatives are considered. Now, certain social states are obviously better
than certain others for an individual (the theory insists on defining an
optimum for the case where I would prefer that my mother dies under
torture).

11. Certain related theories remedy certain of these questions, but not
all of them. A few, in particular, have considered only one preference
profile,[10] in adding a further condition on the ordering function. Yet,
first, they replace the problem of the plurality of preference profiles by
more reliance on the problem of possibility sets since the conditions

---

9. Kelly (1994) considers this fact to be favorable because it shows a restriction of the
domain of preference profiles. But this shows that the domain effectively used for the
result excludes the actual problem.

10. Parks (1976), Kemp and Ng (1976), Pollak (1979), Roberts (1980), Rubinstein
(1981), Hurley (1985); see also Suzumura (1987).

rests on pairwise comparisons (anyway necessary for the definition of the social ordering). Second, the extra condition is not really acceptable.[11]

12. All the "conditions" considered (except Pareto) require either false preferences or false possibility sets.

13. The conditions about possibility sets (a social ordering, the "axiom of choice," etc.), and the set of conditions about preference profiles and the ordering function, violate standard conceptions of justice or equity, and rationality (see section 15.3).

14. The conditions considered by the theory are definitely arguable, in various degrees. We have discussed the Pareto or unanimity condition, by far the most rationally compelling one although possibly for "laundered" preferences.[12] All the other conditions require pluralities of possibility sets or of preference profiles, which constitutes a first problem in itself. Even when certain reasons for particular pluralities can be found, the various specific situations are generally alternative (only one can be actual), which weakens the meaning of these conditions (see section 15.2). And the theory applies the conditions to only non-actual and nonsensible specific situations (problems), as we have seen. Furthermore the conditions except Pareto oppose to the possible view that each specific social choice situation constitutes a problem in itself which has to base the reason for its solution on its own structure, for which other problems are irrelevant, and which is transformed into a possibly altogether different problem by an alteration of the data. The conditions of the axiom of choice and of transitivity (for the social ordering), on the one hand, and of Independence of Irrelevant Alternatives (and Positive Response), on the other hand, constitute assumptions of independence, separability, irrelevance, or "consistency" in particular senses, when either the possibility set or the preference profile varies. Specifically, the axiom of choice and the Independence of

---

11. The condition is that if each individual orders a pair as he orders another, then "society" orders one pair as it orders the other. Then, if we share a desired quantity in a society of two egoistic individuals, and consider the allocations (0, 2), (1, 1), and (2, 0), if "society prefers" the egalitarian (1, 1) to (0, 2) then, from the condition, it has to prefer the unequal (2, 0) both to the equal (1, 1) and to the symmetrical (0, 2).

12. See chapters 1 and 6, and a detailed analysis in Kolm 1993e.

Irrelevant Alternatives express an independence of the solution with regard to its *position* in the possibility set, on the one hand, and in individuals' preferences outside the set considered, on the other hand. These properties cannot claim universal ethical and logical validity, as examples straightforwardly show (see for instance section 15.3). Finally, the "nondictatorship" condition begs the question of the meaning of a "dictator" and of his "preferences" (which might represent well-considered wisdom).

15. The all-encompassing scope of the theory, and the fact that individuals' preferences include their moral *values*, raise the question of who holds the theories' "conditions" to be valuable requirements (the conditions become trivial if they are the individuals' views; see section 15.4).

16. This scope and this inclusion of values also raise the question of the endogeneity of individuals' values, and hence of their preferences, since an ethical theory—the theory considered is one—aims at influencing the world and it does this by influencing the values of individuals.

17. The theory is social ethics, indeed individualistic social ethics and hence a theory of justice. However, the most fundamental classical concepts of these fields (liberty, equality, fraternity) are a priori absent. There is no variable over which so basic principles as impartiality, equality of treatment and equal treatment of equals can be defined. Liberties, rights, and powers are not explicit (this is the utilitarian heritage).

18. However, the question of liberties, rights, and powers is trivial, since they are straightforwardly introduced in the very definition of a social state (in a given social state, an individual has this good, this right, this power, etc.). The preferences over these states are derived from the preferences over end states or over actions, as indirect or derived preferences, and they can also manifest preferences for other reasons over liberties, rights, or powers. An individual's preferences over these states depends a priori on others' preferences over end states or actions (and on others' liberties, rights, or powers, in addition to his own) because of interacting actions.

19. The theory certainly "end-values" individuals' satisfactions. It is thus the direct full or complete theory of justice. Hence rationality

requires prima facie equal satisfaction, which requires interpersonal comparability, and certainly has to retreat to a second-best such as Practical Justice for reasons of possibility and efficiency.

20. But the end values, and the ideal equalizands, can also be individual's means of various kinds: basic liberties and powers, rights, allocations, and so on. The full theory of justice is then reached. But is this still Social Choice Theory?

Let us come back to the first remarks of this list. Bypassing the actual problem of social choice, and proving the impossibility of non-existing problems only, raises a question of general relevance, if it is not a problem of basic logic. But the mere requirement of defining the optimum in these counterfactual situations begs questions: Why require an answer to nonposed questions, to so many of them, to ones so bizarre, and indeed only to bizarre ones? Even in the most standard presentation of the theory, where the problem is defined as the determination of a social ordering for all profiles of individual preferences, so that the actual social choice situation is included, one also requires the solution to provide answers to questions such as: What would be the 193th best choice if the possibility set were completely different from what it is and if the individuals' preferences were the opposite of what they are? (For instance, most people would be masochistic, prefer having less of all goods, enjoy their family being tortured, even prefer dying, and so on.) The theory indeed then seeks to answer this type of questions for all hypothetical possibility sets, all ranks of social goodness, and all hypothetical individual preferences, with particular relations between the answers. Is it rational to seek a rational answer to absurd questions? Or even to irrelevant questions (even if the cases were less extraordinary and outlandish)? Certain people would question the seriousness of the problem so defined. Fortunately, Social Choice Theory concludes that one cannot answer. This is sobering. But why did other people seem to regret this conclusion?

However, a few reasons for considering a plurality of settings or situations or specific social choice problems (each has one possibility set and one preference profile) have been alluded to (a priori uncertainty, various dates or populations), and others can be added. They are considered in the next section. It should be recalled, for this purpose, that the specifics of the theory require that the various settings (or specific problems) it considers are defined with *the same overall set of alternative social states*. This is required by all the definitions and the conditions of the theory (except Pareto or unanimity). Indeed the various individual preferences and social orderings in different settings are defined over the same overall set of alternatives and have to. And the conditions that define or justify a social ordering, or alternative conditions (such as the axiom of choice), require the consideration of possibility sets with common elements.

15.2   The Question of Pluralities

A priori Impossible Meanings

A number of possible meanings of the plurality of possibility sets and of preference profiles in this Social Choice Theory are commonly or sometimes alluded to. These are several dates, a priori uncertainty, several populations, several topics, a theory of constitutions, and individuals' freedom to choose their preferences. Can they make sense of these pluralities?

1. *Several dates.*   The various possibility sets and preference profiles would represent choice situations at various dates. Yet the choice is a priori *intertemporal*, for *all dates to come*. If there were a *sequential* choice, it would at each time consider all the future, and then it would each time bear on *different overall sets of alternatives* (and the problems would not be independent in various ways).

2. *A priori uncertainty.*   Uncertainty would justify the a priori consideration of what should be the social optimum in all or several of the cases of individual preferences and of possibility set. However, the application of this rule requires the knowledge of the actual preferences and possibility set. But then one can make the ethical selection of the social optimum when one knows these occurrences. Thus no Social Choice *rule* defining the optimum with *several* possible applications is necessary. However, one may have to implement an optimal *action* (a policy, for instance) while uncertainty subsists. But, then, to know the optimum in each of the sure cases is not the question posed, since there is only one optimal action facing the whole uncertain prospect. The same remarks can be applied separately to the justification by

uncertainty of an ordering function defined on a domain of several or all preference profiles, and of the possibility sets necessary to the definition of the social ordering or of alternative hypotheses.

However, an association of both several dates and uncertainty in a sequential decision provides a case for the consideration of several preference profiles and possibility sets, as noted below.

3. *Various populations.* The various profiles of preferences would represent different populations.[13] However, there is only one population for the global optimum. At any rate, a social state includes the situation of each individual of the population, for instance, his allocation of private goods, and therefore, if the population changes, the set of all the social states also changes. The number of individual situations (in particular allocations) is not even the same if the number of individuals is not the same, as is usually the case for different populations. Furthermore the definition of a "dictator" is impossible with different populations. The conditions of Independence of Irrelevant Alternative and Positive Response have no meaning either (except with the same size of populations and arbitrary assignments of the private bundles). In addition the possibilities also depend on the population, since they depend in an important way on the capacities of the individuals (which can even determine the nature of the goods that can exist).[14]

4. *Several topics.* The various choices would be on different topics. However, the overall sets of alternatives would be different.

5. *A theory of constitutions.* It has been proposed,[15] and it is often repeated, that this theory would be a theory of constitutions, where the constitution, which says how to make use of a preference profile, is the ordering function. But a constitution does not provide a social ordering. It provides laws, rights, obligations, or policies that agents' actions transform into a "social state," and with the appropriate

---

13. This interpretation is, for instance, suggested by Little (1951), it is admitted by others, and it is more or less implicit in the "constitutional" interpretations noted below.

14. The allocation of Picasso's drawings is an issue only in a world that contains Pablo Picasso.

15. By Kemp and Asimakopulos (1952).

definition and indirect preferences, one can consider that it provides social states (as discussed in section 15.4 below, including the issue that each indirect preference depends a priori on all direct ones). The constitution could then be the social state or its determinants as a function of the preference profile and of the possibility set (and the social ordering or the alternative properties would be requirements on this function). However, the applications of a constitution are for different topics, dates, subpopulations, total populations, or circumstances (a circumstance is an event that is not chosen but concerns the individuals so that social states identical but for certain circumstances have to count as different social states; varying circumstances are often the cause of an individual having different preferences over otherwise identical chosen items). These applications thus cannot constitute the pluralities of the theory for the reasons explained in the other paragraphs. Furthermore such a constitution (rule) would not depend on the society, whereas the classical concept of a constitution says that it should depend on the society (see, for instance, Montesquieu's classic *L'Esprit des lois*).

6. *Free to choose.* The literature of this Social Choice Theory often suggests a justification of the plurality of an individual's preferences in arguing that the individuals should be free to choose their preferences, tastes, or values or to order the social states as they want to, or that they should have the right to these choices. But one just has to take the actual, existing preferences of the individuals. An individual's preference ordering always "orders the states as this individual wants to," by definition. The individuals might well have "chosen" these preferences for themselves. At any rate, the model contains no variable about the causes, origin and formation of preferences, and it thus cannot describe the fact that the individuals have chosen or not their preferences, or in which measure they have. If the individuals' assumed choice of their preferences is not known, the issue is just a case of uncertainty, described above. In addition, of course, the idea that the individuals can chose their preferences, tastes or values, antinomic as it is to almost all economic thinking,[16] is a broad-minded tribute

---

16. See, however, the models in Kolm 1980b, 1982a, 1986b.

to Rousseau and Kant for values, Buddhism for desires, Hellenistic philosophies for tastes, and existentialism for all. It will however be argued below that this choice has to be considered at least for values.

Four Possible Meanings

However, pluralities of possibility sets or of preference profiles can find four kinds of partial justifications: "rationality counterfactuals," sequential choices under uncertainty, independent sequential choices, and endogenous values.

1. *Rationality or epistemic counterfactuals.* Rationality, in its normal sense of "for a reason," provides a reason for the consideration of counterfactuals, that is, of items that do not exist (are not the case) and yet influence a conclusion and hence possibly a choice, a judgment, or an action (and thus possibly that which exists or is the case). Indeed providing a reason, like "I choose x because y," implies that there exists a hypothetical y', different from y but substitutable to y, such that if y' were the case instead of y, then I would have chosen x' different from x instead of x. Item y' is a "rationality counterfactual".[17] Hence rationality requires (and hence justifies) that one consider choice in nonexistent situations, in particular, for this Social Choice Theory, with nonexistent individuals' preferences and possibility sets. However, the strict application of this theory of rationality requires only one counterfactual, whereas the working of this Social Choice Theory requires a very much larger number. Furthermore, when y is the possibility set and x is the chosen alternative in y (for given individual preferences), any set of alternatives y' that does not contain x constitutes a possible, but trivial, counterfactual. A nontrivial set y' should contain x. Now, as a general rule, if y' is a rationality counterfactual for the choice if y is the case, conversely y is a rationality counterfactual for the choice if y' is the case. But if we apply this property to proper (nontrivial) counterfactuality when y and y' are possibility sets, then the choices x and x' should be different and should both be in both sets y and y': This precludes that the social optimum can be

---

17. The full theory of rational counterfactuality is provided in Kolm 1992a.

determined as a maximal element of a general social ordering (independent of the possibility set); more specifically, this property constitutes, by definition, the violation of the "Chernoff condition," which implies the violation of the "axiom of choice," which implies the impossibility of a choice from an ordering. A specific example will be provided below.

2. *Sequential choices in uncertainty.* A sequential social ethical choice, with uncertainly in a first action and certainty in a second one at a later date when the formerly uncertain event is known, provides a reason for considering the best choice with several possibility sets or preference profiles. Indeed for the first choice one must consider ex ante the various uncertain alternatives, along with the best social ethical choice that will have to be made in the second step in certainty. However, this conclusion is valid only if there is an actual choice to be made in the first step, and hence the social choice question with pluralities considered cannot describe the *full* social choice, since it is restricted to the second step.

3. *Sequential separabilities.* Different problems of social optimality that are more *local* than the determination of the general social optimum (of which they are parts) may present similarities such that rationality (providing a reason) implies similarities in the corresponding solutions. This can provide questions with pluralities of settings. However, for the application of the full theory considered, previous remarks forbid that these similarities concern different topics or different populations. Then the only possibility left is that of sequential similar choices for the same group of people separated in all respects from the other people's situations and with periods that are independent from one another with respect to both preferences and possibility sets: myopic or separable preferences, no saving and investment, and so on. Hence, to begin with, this cannot justify the application of this Social Choice Theory to the overall social choice. One would also wonder about what makes these people's preferences change and about the possible scope of these changes: if this change resulted from the situations being different in some respect, then the alternatives properly defined do not have the same nature.

4. *Endogenous values.* It will be argued in section 15.4 that an ethical theory has to consider the influence of its propositions on individuals'

values (which are a priori also described by individuals' preferences). Thus a theory that uses these values has to consider several cases of them in order to determine its "fixed-point" final proposal. But the theory considered here is not such a complete theory. Even if it were so completed, it would have to consider only a limited set of profiles, excluding notably absurd preferences, tastes, and profiles. And this reason justifies no plurality of possibility sets apart from their possible dependence on preferences (through individuals' actions, and this would not justify the particular sets used by the theory).

In the latter three types of cases the set of actual or possible settings (different preference profiles and possibility sets) which should be considered is generally much smaller than what is required by the theory under discussion. In particular, these cases cannot justify the consideration of possibility sets or preference profiles that we are sure cannot be the case. Similarly, even if the consideration of a larger number of counterfactuals than only one may improve the epistemic strength of counterfactual rationality, this does not extend to counterfactuals that are absurd or a priori impossible. Therefore all these cases cannot justify the application of the theory to the overall social choice, and even their providing such an opportunity in certain very rare cases of specific questions of social choice isolated from the rest of the world is very doubtful (see also the next section). However, the justification of the consideration of several possibility sets or preference profiles, even in a very small number (two, for instance), can help the theory, given the generality it requires, in providing *possibilities of falsification* of certain of its hypotheses, as we will see. Now, falsificationism is as relevant in ethical theory as it is in "positive" theory (that is, for explaining what should be rather than for explaining what is).[18] Let us emphasize that such falsifications do *not oppose* the impossibility result; they rather *explain* it. They are especially useful for further work that tries to derive constructive results. For instance, most "conditions" of the theory can be so "falsified" by examples, as will be shown in section 15.3.

---

18. See Kolm 1990b.

Specific Social Choice

The overall social choice is de facto divided into specific choices, certain rather general, such as the choice of a national budget, others local, down to the interactions between two persons. Each interdependence, and notably each opposition, among the interests or values of several persons gives rise to a situation of social choice, possibly with coordination, application of rules, and concern for justice. Yet it must be emphasized that the overall social choice is but the set of all the specific social choices. Hence the optimum for the overall social choice is but the set of the optima for all the specific social choices. To define the optimum for the overall social choice, and to define the optima for all the specific social choices, constitute one and the same problem.

The specific social choices are a priori interdependent. However, a number of them are considered as ethically more or less independent from the rest. This is a view of specific justice, sometimes local justice, akin to justice within the Weber-Walzer "spheres" (see chapter 4) but at all possible levels (economizing on information about the concerned persons' situation in the other spheres of life is also a reason for such separations). Then issues of specific and in particular local social choices may be more or less amenable to separate consideration. Now, certain difficulties with Social Choice Theory applied to the overall social choice may not appear with certain specific and notably local social choices. However, most of the questions are bound to remain for these applications of the theory. For example, the various applications of the rule constituted by a voting scheme used for a kind of questions in a certain social setting usually cannot be taken as constituting the pluralities of possibility sets and of preference profiles considered by this Theory of Social Choice. Indeed the alternatives are usually not of the same specific nature (the theory demands that various possibility sets have common elements and that all the preference and social orderings bear on the same alternatives) because they are on different specific topics, or at different dates, or associated with circumstances that differ and are relevant for the definition of an alternative social state.[19] Second, the populations are often different

---

19. For example, in 1939 a country has to choose a head of state for one year among three candidates: Mr. A, Mr. B, and General C. It chooses Mr. B. In 1940 two new

(and hence most "conditions" cannot be defined, and this generally is
a further cause of differences in social states). In addition, choosing
one among several alternatives does not require that one can order all
the alternatives. There are indeed almost never the extensive choices in
pairs or triples that the theory considers. Furthermore these cases
manifest the inconsistencies between the "conditions" and rationality
and justice described in section 15.3.

When the social choice (for instance, the vote) is made sequentially
in choosing, first, a subset of alternatives and, second, one alternative
from this set, a social ordering guarantees that the final choice does
not depend on the choice proposed at the intermediary step. This is
path independence. But when such a sequential specification is used,
there are particular reasons for the specific choice proposed in the first
step, manifesting particular importance, priority, desire to obtain an
absolute majority in the last stage, unequal voters, and so on, which
introduces new issues in the problem.

Social Choice Theory presented itself as aiming to find the solution
to the general problem of the social optimum. This was explicit,[20] and
also clear from this presentation situating itself in the historical tradition of utilitarianism and of the classical Social Welfare Function.
This is also a main reason why the "impossibility" result struck many
people as very puzzling and important news (people who, however,
did not consider closely the possible meaning of what was proved).
Yet the theory discussed simultaneously examples of much more limited scope, such as voting on specific topics. Condorcet's "voting paradox" was noted and is akin to a central structure of the proofs. There
was then an important development of the analysis of voting procedures and of collective choices variously limited in scope. In the measure in which it uses the central concepts and topics of Social Choice
Theory discussed above, this field is affected by most of the same
problems, as shown by the previous remarks concerning more or less
specific social choices.

---

events occur: First, Mr. A is no longer a candidate, and second, a war erupts. Then
General C is preferred to Mr. B. This apparent "violation of the axiom choice" may be
rational.

20. See, for instance, the definition of a social state in Arrow (1963, p. 17).

15.3   Reason and Social Choice

Rationality and Justice against the "Conditions" of Social Choice Theory

Consider a relevant society consisting either of two individuals, or of a larger number of individuals but in cases where two groups of equal size are each made up of individuals with the same preferences over the considered alternatives while the other individuals are indifferent (in the latter case, the expressions "individuals 1 and 2" refer to these two groups, respectively). In the spirit of classical Social Choice Theory, let us assume that preferences have the structure of an ordering of the alternatives and that *nothing else is known and considered relevant*. The examples and their results are easily adapted to the cases where preferences have a richer and more specific structure. Let us also recall two requirements of the theory. First, an optimum should be defined for each subset of the alternatives. Second, the optimum (or the social ordering) on any subset of alternatives depends only on the individuals' orderings of these alternatives: This is the condition of Independence of Irrelevant Alternatives. Let us consider problems of choice, that is, in each case one and only one of the considered mutually exclusive alternatives must be implemented and therefore chosen.

First, consider three alternatives a, b, and c which individual 1 orders in this *increasing* order and individual 2 orders in this *decreasing* order. A very common view in this case is that alternative b should be chosen because it represents the balanced solution, the "just middle," or the "equitable" compromise, because it does not completely yield to one individual in sacrificing the other, and hence because it is "equitable," "fair," or "just." This represents a common "sense of justice." A particular but important application of "rationality" (in the common sense of "for a reason") leads to the same conclusion. Indeed, if one chooses alternative a, one can provide no reason for not choosing alternative c instead, since a and c are indiscernible (each is the best alternative for one individual and the worst one for the other, and we have assumed an absence of any other relevant and known fact that would differentiate them)—of course alternatives a and c can be very different for each individual. This indiscernibility implies that *one cannot give a complete reason* for choosing either a or c: Such a choice has this necessary arbitrariness and lack of rationality. This fact is indeed one reason for the "sense of justice" described above, as is revealed by the remark: "If I choose a, then why not the symmetrical c?"[21] Alternative b is the only one that does not present this arbitrariness, and this provides a prima facie reason in favour of its choice (this means that other reasons may overwhelm this one, when there is any such reason—which is not the case here by assumption—; for instance, if the two orderings in decreasing order were (a, b, c) and (b, a, c), alternative c is not to be chosen in spite of a similar position because it is Pareto-dominated). Note also that the fact that some arbitrariness necessarily remains if there is an even number of alternatives (or as in the last example) does not constitute a good reason for not eliminating arbitrariness when it is possible to do so.

Consider now the same individuals and alternatives, plus two alternatives d and e, such that the ordering becomes (a, b, c, d, e), in increasing order for individual 1 and in decreasing order for individual 2. As before, a standard sense of justice, fairness, equity, balance, and the like, prompts one to choose the midpoint c, and by a reasoning similar to the one presented above the choice of alternative c prevents an arbitrariness that exists in all other cases (in choosing between indiscernible a and e, or b and d, respectively): this provides a prima facie reason in favor of this choice.

Now, one of these two possibility sets is a subset of the other, and the choices b and c are possible in both cases. Hence the respective choices of these alternatives violate the *axiom of choice*, the *Chernoff condition*, and the possibility of defining the choice by a *social ordering that is independent of the possibility set*. Note that it has not been said that the choices will always be made as they have been described and explained but only that they are often and in common cases made in this way, which is sufficient for a counterexample. Indeed, in certain other cases, the choice from the possibility set (a, b, c) may consider the preferences on the alternatives d and e, if they are known, and then choose c (for example, if the alternatives are political parties ordered on the left-right axis). This, however, would violate the condition of Independence of Irrelevant Alternatives. Whether one type of choice

---

21. The possibility of choosing between a and c by a lottery cannot provide an objection, for the reasons indicated in the similar justification of equality in chapter 2.

or the other is made depends on whether the choice of justice focuses
more on preferences or more on the set of possibilities.[22]

Another example uses the same reasons for choices in the quintuplet
(a, b, c, d, e) and in the triplet (a, b, c) ordered with this ranking but in
reverse order by the two individuals. It also introduces the condition
of Pareto-efficiency. And it starts from the last considered situation:
the possible alternatives are (a, b, c, d, e) ordered with this ranking in
increasing order by individual 1 and in decreasing order by individual
2. Then the above-discussed reasons lead to the choice of alternative c.
Assume now that individual 1's preferences change in that alternative
c becomes his best one, while individual 2's preferences do not change.
Then alternatives d and e become worse than alternative c for both
individuals, and hence Pareto-dominated, which leads to their elimination as candidates for the optimum. The individuals' orderings of the
remaining alternatives (a, b, c) have not changed, and the same reasons
as above lead to the choice of alternative b. This shift from c to b
violates two conditions: *Independence of Irrelevant Alternatives* (the
social preference between b and c depends on individual 1's preferences concerning d and e), and *Positive Response* (alternative c has
jumped up in individual 1's ordering and nothing else has changed, and
as a result it has been displaced as the optimum, while this condition
says that, with such a change, all states worse than c in the social
ordering should remain so).

Transversalities

Furthermore the conditions that the considered theory imposes consist of relations between several different settings (possibility sets or
preference profiles), with the unique exception of Pareto-efficiency—
that is, they are "transversal" conditions.[23] Now, the transversality of
a condition impairs its meaningfulness for two reasons. First, this
transversality opposes the view that the solution of a specific problem
depends primarily on the whole structure of the situation. Second,
when the situations considered by the transversal conditions are mutually exclusive, the condition can be seen as lacking actual bases, and
still more so when both are counterfactuals (note that the situations

---

23. For a full analysis of this question, see Kolm 1992a.

are mutually exclusive in the justification of pluralities by sequential uncertainty or by epistemic counterfactuality).[24]

15.4   Equality, Liberty, and Endogenous Values

Equality

This Social Choice Theory belongs to social ethics, and it is or implies more specifically a theory of individualistic justice, since it considers explicitly individuals' preferences and implicitly individuals' situations in all respects. The theory's end values can only be the rankings of the chosen social state in the individuals' preference orderings or in the social ordering, or possibly the "conditions" of the theory. If the social ordering is justified by arguments of "consistency" of various social choices (transitivity, the axiom of choice, etc.), and given that it is to be determined by the theory, the intended end values are very likely the rankings in the individuals' preference orderings (or their ordinal "satisfaction" levels). Then the basic problem that this theory has to and fundamentally intends to solve is the determination of the individualistic "preference" direct justice. Consequently rationality implies (see chapter 2) that the solution to the problem of the definition of the social optimum rests on considerations of equality, with its successive levels of impartiality, equal treatment of equals, prima facie equalities, and second-best egalitarianisms. But this is precluded by the very definition of the variables explicitly considered by the theory, which permit one to define neither "equal individuals" nor "equal treatment." Individuals' preference orderings are all that the theory explicitly considers for both individuals' characteristics and possible individualized end values (which are then the places of the chosen social state in these orderings). But equal treatment of equals cannot consist in the trivial property that if two individuals have the same orderings of the social states, then the chosen state has the same place in both their orderings (as it is the case for any social state). Indeed what is normally called identical preferences is not identical orderings of the

---

24. Little (1951) rejected transversal conditions for preference profiles, but he admitted the plurality of profiles, and he admitted a social ordering whose definition and possible meaning rests on transversal conditions.

social states but identical orderings by each of his own consumption bundles (plus possibly a certain concern for others). For example, if an individual is egoistic and cares only for his own consumption, identical orderings of the social states would imply that the other does not care for his own consumption and is exclusively altruistic in caring only for the former's consumption. That is, the identity of preference orderings has to refer to the rankings of different "social states," obtained by the required permutation of individuals' situations. Then, for such "equal individuals," "equal treatment" means indifference of the individuals' situations with this common preference ordering. When individuals are not a priori "equal" in this sense, they are rendered so by the theory of "fundamental preferences" which, however, has to rest on a tangible concept of the levels of satisfaction (see chapter 7, section 7.2). Then what the theory really wants as optimum, or what it should want, is "end-justice" or "full justice," that is, the fundamental indifference of Justice, or the second-best maximin or leximin of Practical Justice for efficiency or for mere possibility (same reference) plus, possibly, a certain role for the interpersonal comparison of pairwise preferences (see chapter 14, section 14.7).

However, justice considers also, more generally, prima facie equality of means, allocations, liberties, rights, and powers. These concepts are not *explicit* in the theory. Yet making them explicit is trivial and straightforward.

Means, Liberties, Rights, Duties, Powers, Wealth

Ask anybody to begin a description of a "state of society," notably with the intention to define later the best one. This description will conspicuously include means, liberties, rights, duties, powers, incomes, and wealth of the individuals (there are of course overlappings among these categories). To begin with, we want to live in a society where the basic human rights are respected. We want other rights. We are concerned with incomes which are means rather than consumption goods. And so on.

Therefore the inclusion of these items in the definition of a "social state" is not only direct, obvious, trivial, and straightforward, it is simply the normal, standard, and everybody's way to conceive the world.

These means, freedoms, rights, duties, powers, incomes, or wealth define possibilities and constraints of individuals' actions. From all individuals' actions there result final consumption goods (and also the items just noted for future uses and actions). Hence, from the individuals' direct preferences concerning their consumption goods (private ones, including leisure, and public ones), and also concerning others' consumption goods if there are "consumption externalities," there result their indirect or derived preferences concerning these means and limits of their and others' actions. These consumption externalities are also considered when social states are described only with consumption goods. They can notably be psychic externalities due to social sentiments. These can be envy, jealousy, malevolence, sentiments of superiority or inferiority, or preferences concerning one's own or others' conformity or distinction, but they also have to include the judgments resulting from the fact that individuals' preferences also include their values: sense of justice, equalities, minimal need satisfaction for others, benevolence and altruism, conformities, and so on. Furthermore individuals can also value means, liberties, rights, duties, powers, incomes, or wealth for other reasons than the final consumption goods they lead to. These reasons are presented in chapter 2 (for liberties, but this extends to other kinds of means).[25] These more or less "direct" reasons can bear, for each individual, on his own allocation of these items. But the individual can also have more or less direct preferences concerning these items for others. This can be for reasons similar to those just noted for consumption externalities. In particular, direct preferences concerning these items for others and for oneself are implied by the consideration that individuals' preferences also describe "values," since most social values concern individuals' rights, freedoms, powers, duties, means, incomes, or wealths. Furthermore an individual may be directly concerned by others' activity, actions, and interactions with himself and with others for various reasons (direct evaluation, game, social relations, etc.), and this provides another indirect valuation of the considered items that permit or limit these actions.

The part of the individuals' preferences over the items considered that is indirect and derived either from final allocations or more directly from actions and interactions depends on others' preferences, as well as on their allocations of these items, since these preferences (and

---

25. See also the analysis in Kolm 1982a.

means) determine others' choices and actions and hence the resulting final allocations. These are others' preferences over final allocations, or more directly over actions and interactions, of themselves but also of others when they can influence them. They are combined with the other aspects of others' preferences, over that which their acts do not influence. This per se does not a priori restrict the possible domain of preference profiles that one can consider (except theoretically for special and particular structures that the theory can discard).

Of course, these interactions among individuals may result in the classical "market failures," or "failures" of agreements or interactions, such as those resulting from situations of prisoner's dilemma among others, with resulting Pareto-inefficiencies. These situations are classical and dealt with classically. There may be no actual Pareto-inefficiency when all the actual constraints are considered, including limits to communication and to the possibilities to coerce, to commit oneself, or to cooperate. Institutions for enforcing promises, or promises conditional on promises (for the prisoner's dilemma, notably), may eliminate the inefficiency (see chapter 1) and be set up by unanimous agreements. More generally, a public sector may correct these failures. It then has to make a distributional choice among various Pareto-efficient final states. If the state considered with rights, liberties, and so on, is optimal, then this determines the just Pareto-efficient final state, as the outcome of the "liberal social contract" consisting in the hypothetical agreement in the absence of the cause of the inefficiency (see chapter 5). Consistent liberalism is Pareto-efficient.[26]

Finally, the possible introduction of rights, duties, liberties, powers, and means in general in the definition of the "social state" enables one to consider the prima facie equality of these items among the individuals. We then reach the full theory of justice considered in this book (and in the related ones).

---

26. Of course an individual's freedom cannot be described as his choice among alternative social states, since a social state depends on the choices of all individuals. The various ex ante possible social states constitute the cartesian product of the possible individual choices. The description as an individual's choice among alternative social states constitutes a misspecification of what freedom, right, or power is (see, among others, the obvious criticisms of Sen 1970 by Gibbard 1974, 1980; Nozick 1974; Bernholz 1974; Nitzan 1975; Seidl 1975, 1986; Gärdenfors 1981; Sugden 1985; Gaertner, Pattanaik, and Suzumura 1992; in addition a social ordering was demanded, and for all preference profiles, which makes three features without a justification.

Who Holds the Moral-Logical "Conditions"? Endogenous Values

The basic and central presentation of this Social Choice Theory has a number of overall features that raise a few crucial inter-related problems. For one thing, the preferences of individuals encompass their *values*.[27] For another, the theory considers a number of *conditions* on the way in which the optimum depends on the possibility set and on the individuals' preferences. Furthermore the theory concerns a priori the whole society. Finally, this theory is an ethical theory, and hence it is meant for application (that is, ethics is "practical reason" in Kant's terms). But this application requires that certain persons want the result of the theory, and therefore the theory should influence certain preferences. Indeed any ethic is about convincing people, and individuals' values are the outcome of ethical arguments, rather than their inputs, or, at least, they are influenced by them.

To begin with, who holds the view that the "conditions" of the theory should be respected? The answer is "individuals," since no other entity who can have a view exists (with a tautologically individualistic conception of society). Indeed the considered preferences of the individuals are assumed to include their values, and hence their moral opinions concerning society. The social states considered by the theory do not include the rule that provides the solution and of which the "conditions" are features, but individuals' opinions concerning this rule are implied by their preference orderings of these social states. Now, the conditions take a strange and trivial form if we assume that they are held by the individuals whose preference orderings describe their views of the goodness of social states. For instance, all individuals agree that only individual preferences matter for determining the optimum in a given possibility set (since this includes their own preferences). All individuals agree that the social states can be ordered by their goodness (yet they generally disagree about what this ordering should be, since each thinks it should be his own ordering). Or consider the sufficient "weak Pareto condition": Each individual necessarily agrees that "if everybody thinks that a is better than b, then a is better than b," since he is one of these individuals who thinks that a is

---

27. This is explicit and much emphasized in Arrow's book, the title of which refers to "individual values."

better than *b* by assumption. Or, again, consider the so-called "dictator" question: All individuals agree that there should be a "dictator" (whose preference ordering becomes the "social ordering"), yet, fortunately, they disagree on who he should be, since each individual thinks he himself should be the dictator (since his preference ordering includes all his social and moral judgments). All individuals also consider that the good classification of two alternatives does not depend on views concerning any third one (Independence of Irrelevant Alternatives), that if an alternative becomes better than certain others in his or others' views and nothing else changes, this cannot make it become worse than any other (Positive Response), and so on. Arrow, however, suggests that, in another possible interpretation of the theory, individuals' preferences represent only their "material welfare," and a few scholars have analyzed this view, but this reduces the scope of the theory.

The actual meaning of the "conditions" has indeed been the source of much confusion. We have noted it for the pluralities of preferences of each individual and of sets of possibilities. This has also largely been the case for the social ordering ("society's preferences") or for the substitute conditions that relate various choices. But the maximum has been reached with "nondictatorship" and the corresponding concept of a "dictator," that is, an individual such that the social ordering always coincides with his own preference ordering. This vocabulary was initially used rather metaphorically, as the vocabulary of mathematicians is, if not tongue-in-cheek, but many people have understood it literally. What if, for instance, this individual is a sage who knows what is good for society and desires that it be implemented? Or else, there always is a dictator, and I know him, for the following reason. If I am shown the good social ordering, I agree with it because I am a rational, moral, and democratic person. I thus hold that the alternatives should be ranked in this order, and hence this order is my preference ordering. But this coincidence makes me "a dictator" in the sense considered. I am a dictator precisely because I am a democrat: This is the *"paradox of the democratic dictator."*[28]

---

28. See Kolm 1980a, 1986a, 1987a, 1992a, where this kind of moral feedback is considered and analyzed.

A problem of this type lies indeed at the heart of the logic of the theory. Social Choice Theory a priori means that its possible positive results be applied (as it is necessary for an ethical theory). But this implementation requires agents who desire it, be they dutiful officials, members of a government, or people in general who vote, have an opinion, or act otherwise (see chapter 13), and either for direct implementation or for the establishment of rules that lead to the result. The classical assumption is that of the celebrated "benevolent dictator" (a name and concept used with no relation to the theory under consideration). Indeed Social Choice Theory does not consider constraints created by the motivation for implementation. When a related field or subfield does analyze constraints for implementation (see below), the constraint it considers comes from the implementer's information about people's preferences, and not from the implementer's motivations. Then the "benevolent dictator" is indeed a "dictator" in the sense of the coincidence of objectives. More generally, implementation implies the existence of certain agents who want the outcome of the ethical theory (possibly for the establishment of rules) and act or judge accordingly, and hence certainly whose views influence particularly the conclusion of the theory or are influenced by the theory, or who are convinced of the value or legitimacy of the social process used.

Still more generally, moral opinions are the product of the search for the good rather than its inputs as presented by the theory considered. Or, at least, it should not be a priori excluded that moral theory can influence them. This influence is indeed that which moral theory directly aims at, most often in order to induce actions through its influence on the moral views of actors or of people who influence them, and sometimes merely to induce positive or negative moral judgments. Without such an influence, a moral theory is useless and powerless, and hence pointless. Without the hope of such an influence, it is contradictory. And without the consideration of such an influence it is either mistaken, or right but an inconsistent exercise, or, at best, incomplete and partial. There is the same basic epistemological opposition between values and tastes as between normative and positive analysis. Individuals' "values," notably their moral values, are endogenous in a moral theory rather than being exogenous data as classical Social Choice Theory takes them to be. Kant, Rawls (see chapter 8), Habermas (see chapter 16) are, for instance, among the many authors who variously emphasize this endogeneity, which is a necessary feature of any complete moral theory. Hence a normative analysis that uses people's values is involved in a two-way process, a basic feedback, a Heisenberg principle that is the essential of the exercise and is that which makes it meaningful. The corresponding *Social Choice with endogenous preferences* (*or values*) is indeed easily constructed: Individuals' preferences or values influence the social ordering or the social optimum, conversely the latter influences the former, notably by the rationality of its construction, and the corresponding "fixed points" are considered. The iterative process based on these relations (possibly leading to these "moral equilibria") can be related to the large family of classical iterative processes for determining justice.[29]

Finally, a good society is made of good people, not only of satisfied ones,[30] and hence the intrinsic value of individuals' values (and tastes), and preferences and values concerning them, are relevant for an overall social ethic (though possibly not for a theory of justice alone).

15.5   Informational Implementation

This theory has also inspired two fields of studies, apart from its own variants. One is the analysis of specific decision processes, essentially voting schemes, mentioned above. The other field concerns informational "implementation." The question is the application of a criterion that requires information about individuals' preferences or possibilities that these individuals have no interest to "reveal" truthfully. This topic is not properly ethical, and hence it would not be in its proper place here, although it can be important for the implementation of ethical principles, as well as for that of other objectives. Landmark studies such as those of Gibbard (1973), Satterthwaite (1975), and Maskin (1975, 1985) have been followed by a large literature (surveyed notably by Barbera, 1995). This topic relates to studies in public economics for the "revelation" of individuals' values of public goods (Kolm 1964, Groves and Ledyard 1977, see also Green and Laffont 1979, etc.), for the establishment of public tarifs or taxes on agents

---

29. Such as Plato's dialectics in *The Republic*, Rawls' "reflective equilibrium", Habermas and Apel's "communicational ethics", Ackerman's "rational dialogue", and so on.

30. This is the topic of the book Kolm 1984b.

whose specific preferences or possibilities are imperfectly known (Kolm 1969b, 1970a, and later studies), or for dealing with tax evasion, and to the well-developed analysis of the policy of a "principal" who wants to induce a better-informed "agent." The choice can consist of allocations, rules, schedules, iterative processes, or the form of games through which various agents interact.

However, implementation requires the three interdependent conditions of *motivation, power*, and *information*. The implementation of principles of social ethics, be they criteria of justice or social efficiency, can present particularities on all three grounds, but they are especially notable as regards motivation, a topic just noted and analyzed in chapter 13. Most of the studies noted assume the required power of action, and a particular, manicheistic distribution of motivations in society, with a powerful "center" who is fully and only moral and who only wants to implement the ethical rule ("state-moralism", see chapter 13), and a "periphery" of agents who are only strictly self-interested and lie and cheat accordingly without scruple. The focus on this cheating behavior, in this area of "Social Choice" and in the related literature in public economics, was evaluated as misplaced emphasis by Leif Johansen (1981), and it indeed bypasses a number of actual behaviors and motives (as shown by observation and experiments).[31] Yet, even though the assumptions of these studies are not universal and constitute an oversimplification of the human mind, they are nevertheless important to consider as more or less valid approximations in a number of cases, or as polar cases, or for partial studies. Furthermore the earliest analyses explicitly included the ethical preferences of the public at large, notably for the implementation of distributive justice seen as a collective concern or public good (Kolm 1964, 1966a).[32] In addition, in very important cases (voting, the provision of public goods, and so on) each individual or agent finds no advantage to lie because he is relatively small among many others and a "mass effect" makes his own situation practically independent of the information he provides if it is not used as a statistical sample; then mini-

---

31. These cooperative behaviors and motives are reviewed notably in Kolm 1984b.

32. An idea which was summarily considered again by Hochman and Rodgers (1969) and Thurow (1970).

mal truth-telling morality or the mere salience of truth suffice for truthful "revelation" (see Kolm 1964, 1967).[33]

15.6   From Social Choice Theory to the General Theory of Justice

Finally, the central body of this Social Choice Theory should be appreciated as it presented itself: in the context of the history of thought after utilitarianism and its ordinalization by classical Social Welfare Functions. For general social ethics, this theory constituted the crowning and the consumation of a field—utilitarianism—and by the same token its closure, rather than the possible opening of a new approach. It had a certain opening role in motivation and inspiration, but for the fields which have been noted and are either not ethical, or globally much less ethical and more modest in scope and ambition. The a priori unsuitability of the framework *as it was* for social ethics is obvious, as we have noted: The intention of this social ethic is certainly morally individualistic, and hence this theory should be a theory of direct justice, but it contains no variable with which a certain *equality* of treatment can be defined and indeed no variable that allow one to say that several individuals are "equal." Successive improvements can lead to the various aspects of the theory of justice, but they soon transform the approach beyond recognition.

First, this Social Choice Theory seems to want to consider individuals' satisfaction as end values (the social ordering is endogenous and a concept of "society's satisfaction" would raise a question of meaning). If this were the case, then social ethical rationality, which

---

33. It should be noted that rules that induce truth-telling or truthful "revelation" of preferences (or other private information), that is, "strategy-proof" rules, important as they are for implementation that requires this information, are by no means an important property of voting or other social rules that are seen as constituting in themselves the social ethical end value. For instance, with most actual voting rules people would vote for an outcome rather than for their preferred one when they know that their preferred outcome has no chance to pass, and this "useful vote"—as it is called—is not seen as condemnable "manipulation" but as the simple (and possibly intelligent) exercise of a right that all voters have and that everyone knows. Possibilities of this type, that are common knowledge, are integrated within the working of the rule, and they raise no a priori objection. The search for strategy-proof rules in such cases is an illegitimate transfer of this issue from the implementation field, where it is important, to this analysis of rules as end values, where it is irrelevant.

leads to a prima facie equality in end values (chapter 2), requires the expressions "more, less, and as much" to be ideally meaningful in comparing individuals' satisfaction. This fortunately permits preferences to remain ordinal. The minimal conceptual requirement is that of ordinal and interpersonally comparable individual preferences. Furthermore, unfortunately for social justice, but fortunately from the point of view of information on facts and concepts, possibility and efficiency preclude equality at the global scale and lead to its replacement by a second-best egalitarianism, and the existence of identifiable people affected by deep suffering, misery, and unsatisfied nonvicarious basic needs, which should be relieved with priority, makes the theoretically defined maximin in these preferences both the necessary principle and an operational one. These are the theories of "fundamental preferences," and of eudemonistic Justice and Practical Justice (the leximin), of *Justice and Equity* (Kolm 1971; Hammond 1976; Arrow 1977; Roberts 1980; and others; see chapter 7, section 7.2). This leximin in fundamental preferences constitutes a social ordering, but one deduced from the noted ethical tangible considerations rather than assumed a priori in the abstract.

This eudemonistic maximin meets two kinds of limits: the constraints on its implementation and the issue of its ethical relevance for justice. The former limits include the social and political oppositions to the implied redistribution. The ethical relevance is impaired by phenomena such as an extreme psychological propensity to distress and unhappiness. But the most important is that the priority to the highest satisfaction of the least satisfied (in maximin, or in leximin for higher levels) loses ethical relevance for sufficient levels of satisfaction. Then there still is some place for distributive justice based on satisfaction through interpersonal comparison of preferences (rather than of preference orderings, that is, through interpersonal comparison of intrapersonal comparisons of satisfactions; see section 14.7 of chapter 14); but this is mostly for certain cases of local or microjustice. Beyond these limits, full or end or eudemonistic justice ceases to be the relevant reference. This extends to most of distributive justice in societies that are not too poor.

The other principles directly value various possible individuals' means (allocations, liberties, rights, powers, etc.). The rationality of justice advocates the relevant equality in these means (chapter 2) which the individuals then freely use. The simplest structure is that of equal independent instrumental liberty, which coincides with the criterion of Equity (see chapter 7, section 7.1). Nonindependent liberties lead to interdependences and interactions. The existential-ontological reason imposes the inalienability, and hence the priority, of the essentially nonrival basic Rights of Man and of the Citizen (chapter 4), and the guarantee of the means of satisfying basic needs (chapter 11)— which are also advocated by Practical Justice. The equal power of veto and unanimity, and hence Pareto-efficiency, are also rationally compelling (although for individual preferences that may have to be cleaned of their unethical externalities; see chapters 6 and 9). Rights are to be protected by public coercive institutions. This includes an institution that can *enforce promises, and promises conditional on promises* when these promises want to be enforced (and respect all legitimate rights). The existence of this possibility can eliminate most Pareto-inefficiencies resulting from strategic behavior (see chapter 1). Other inefficiencies resulting from interactions constitute "exchange failures," which may have to be corrected by the implementation of the "liberal social contracts," which describe the corresponding efficient free exchanges or interactions (chapter 5). Finally, the main distributive choice is the division of an individual's production into his legitimate due and the share redistributed for solidarity (chapter 6), with the two extreme cases of full process freedom (chapter 5) and of equal consumption replaced, for efficiency, by the second-best egalitarian "efficient superequity", and the efficient intermediate case of fixed-duration income equalization (chapter 6). For global distributive justice in large actual societies, the possible optimal solution of this choice is rather well determined (chapter 6), as is, therefore, the whole of the corresponding macrojustice.

In summary, Social Choice Theory has provided (1) a close family of results showing the incompatibility of various possible properties in the aggregation of orderings, (2) a possible ethical interpretation of this result as the impossibility of a general ordinalist rescue of utilitarianism, (3) more broadly understood, a host of very notable studies and results concerning voting schemes and informational implementation. ("Social Choice" is sometimes understood in still larger senses, toward the theory of justice, or perhaps social ethics, possibly also including a big chunk of political science; then this makes it a problematic concept, the basic feature of which seems to be an original utilitarian prejudice, in particular a view of man as maximizer—called "rational"—associated with a taste for formalization which is definitely praiseworthy when it enlightens structure and unveils properties rather than obscuring meanings).[34]

---

34. The view that Social Choice Theory is social ethics leaving in its turn philosophy to become a science, as seducively expressed by Kelly (1992) where this statement precedes voting examples and the remark that mostly negative results are offered, was matched by the dictum that "a Social Choice theorist is an economist who tries to find the solution of moral problems in mathematics" (so much the better if he succeeds). There will doubtlessly be fast progress toward more complete views.

VII STRUCTURE AND METHOD

16 The Form, Method, and Situation of Justice

16.1 Macrojustice and Microjustice

This book has presented the judgment of rationality as regards both the answer to the issue of justice and the various proposed answers to this question. The positive answer has been summarized in the first chapters (see also chapter 6). It turns out to be necessary to distinguish between two problems. One is the question of global, overall, and general justice, or *macrojustice*, including, besides basic rights, the issue of overall distributive justice and the resulting determination of the optimal distribution and redistribution. This problem is by now roughly solved. The second question, *microjustice*, consists of the multifarious cases of specific and more or less "local" issues of justice. By nature this problem cannot be provided an a priori explicit complete solution, and its general consideration can only consist of methods, cases, distinction of issues, situations or variables, general principles, and a toolbox of specific principles and criteria. Finally, a number of issues of specific justice acquire a global distributive scope and importance because the problem they raise is widespread and factually important. This is notably the case of various questions concerning the human capital such as education or health, or various aspects of general basic needs. These issues can be said to consitute the intermediary field of *mesojustice*.

The solution of the question of global distributive justice, let us recall, consists essentially of a combination of the three rationales of rights and duties about capacities: process-freedom, partial income equalization by efficient means, and the satisfaction of basic needs and the alleviation of deep suffering. The proportions of these three rationales depend on the state of society. For instance, in modern developed societies, the largest share is for process-freedom (with qualification as regards the transmission of bequest and particularly of education to achieve a certain "equality of opportunity," and "liberal social contracts" for exchange failures); then comes efficient partial income equalization; and the public care of basic needs and deep suffering comes last in volume of transfers but not in intrinsic importance. In poorer countries the basic needs issue is due to mobilize a larger share of the redistribution through traditional or modernistic ways.

Basic issues of structure and method about justice in general are now summarized.

16.2   Liberty and Equality

For centuries, the dispute in political philosophy has centered around
the question of whether liberty and equality are opposed values or
identical ones, with "rightists" arguing that equality kills freedom, and
"leftists" replying that actual freedom requires equality[1] (and attention being particularly attracted by humane rightists who adopt leftist
values and by realistic leftists who acknowledge rightist necessities).
Such a problem is obviously not well posed. The answer depends on
liberty of or from what and on equality of what. All cases can be
found, from liberty and equality being identically the same thing in the
case of nondependency, to equal sharing destroying process-freedom
and permitting "real freedom," and so on. The point is that both
liberty and equality are properties rather than essences—they are of
(or from) something—and that they are neither values in the same
category nor even often genuine end values of social ethics. Indeed,
even when they are not clearly ethically instrumental structures (such
as liberty for implementation and equality for peace), equality results
from rationality by the particular structure noted in chapter 2, and
basic liberties or means are necessary for the mere existence of agency.
Then, we have noted, the general form of respectful justice is prima
facie equality of liberty in the broad sense, with adjustments of various
possible types to jointly accomodate several types of these freedoms,
powers, means, or ends. This, however, still leaves a priori a rather
large choice.

16.3   Open Rational Dialectical Moral Polyarchy

Consider any social ethic that claims to answer all specific cases by the
application of the same criterion, or of the same small number of
criteria, or even of criteria drawn from a larger but pre-established

---

1. The political distinction applies more to recent positions than to the various
"modernists" of two centuries ago. Classical views of the relations between liberty and
equality include Hume showing that the levellers' egalitarianism destroyed freedom
and law, Rousseau complaining that excessive discrepancy in wealth entails servitude
in wage labor, the 1789 assembly declaring men to be "free and equal" (in rights),
Tocqueville explaining the fate of the Revolution by equality killing liberty, Marx
exposing unfreedom due to and creating inequality, etc.

list. Or consider any social ethic that claims to answer the global distributive issue by the application of a single principle. Then, if the criteria or principles are sufficiently precise, it is possible to find counterexamples of either actual or realistic and possible cases for which the application of this ethic is obviously against reason and would be condemned by everybody informed (at the very least, for each observer, one can find a case for which he rejects this ethic).[2] Conversely, for each grand principle of justice (or set of principles) that neither is vitiated by a logical mistake in the domains of meaning or rationality nor violates basic rights to liberty, respect, and subsistence, it is possible to find cases where everybody informed agrees that this principle is the appropriate one (at the very least, for each observer one can find a case for which he would advocate this principle). Furthermore it is also possible to find counterexamples of actual or realistic cases where such an ethic does not suffice to provide the answer with the required precision—although it may indicate a direction, or suggest a method, for the solution. Indeed making the proposition operational requires the specification of a number of items, and this implies choices that are morally relevant (for instance, the definition of an income, a liberty, a need, etc.). This question of specification exists for any ethic, since an ethic has to rely on principles or "maxims" that have a certain degree of generality, because of the irrationality (lack of a reason) implied by not treating similar cases alike; yet, when it comes to practical applications, new questions arise that require the subsidiary criteria. Therefore an overall social ethic is necessarily a *moral polyarchy*, and if it also claims to answer all cases of microjustice, it is necessarily an *open-ended* moral polyarchy.

A number of scholars have indeed advocated moral polyarchy or found it necessary.[3] The latter case is in particular that of socio-

2. Fishkin (1979) provides a number of examples in this direction.

3. The expression "moral polyarchy" is found in Gallie (1956). Other terms are used for similar concepts, each emphasizing a particular aspect. Leventhal (1970, 1976, 1980), Schwinger (1980), and Mikula (1980) speak of the "multi-faceted approach"; Edel (1986) of the "network (of criteria) analysis"; and Brandt (1986) of the "coherence theory." Similar ideas are found in the "analytico-dialectical" conception of Weinberger and in the method of "prima facie obligations" of Ross (1930). This position is also endorsed by modern "ethicists," among them Isaiah Berlin (1956), Eugene Kamenka (1979), C. F. Delaney, Stuart Hampshire, Norman Daniels, Jane

psychologists who study empirically people's sentiments of justice, fairness, or equity (for instance, Leventhal, Mikula, and Schwinger). Moral polyarchy is also well defended in philosophy, and it is practiced by economists either in practical application—as demanded by the public—or for the theoretical analysis of relations among various criteria (which, however, belong to a definite class). Various authors emphasize different aspects of the polyarchic approach such as the multiplicity of criteria, the consistency between them, or the method for choosing a criterion. The issues that should be added include the determination of the domain of relevance and validity of each criterion, the various types of consistency or inconsistency (logical, logical in the relevant domain, belonging or not to the same *ethos* and the same conception of man, society and morals, etc.), the various ways of combination of criteria and of relations between them (precedence, criteria specifying the indeterminacy of other criteria, compromise, superimposition where one criterion is applied from the implementation of another),[4] the variety of methods,[5] and so on.

Moral polyarchy should of course not be interpreted as the suggestion that any criterion that has been proposed could eventually find a place in the overall moral framework. Previous discussions entail that a number of types of principles or criteria are ruled out for lack of meaning (such as many of those that use a "cardinal utility" in certainty), of rationality (such as arbitrary inequalities in the relevant variables), or of basic morality (such as views that imply violations of basic liberties). This both substantially restricts the field of available criteria and leaves a fair amount of latitude for further determination. Furthermore, for the important domain of *respectful individualistic justice* within social ethics, we have noted that rationality requires that the ideal structure be equality of liberty, in a large sense of the term, possibly including the limit eudemonistic egalitarianism, with the required adjustments for multiple criteria. This limits still more the field of possible ethics. The result is a *middle way* moral polyarchy, where "middle way" means that principles are not a priori and univer-

---

English, Kai Nielsen. Walzer's (1983) segmented egalitarianism within "spheres of justice" presents features different from those of the preceding philosophies.

4. The general logic of the combination of criteria is presented in Kolm 1990b.

5. Same reference.

sally determined, yet they are to be chosen for each kind of cases among a limited and well-defined overall set.

Moral polyarchy finally gives prominent importance to the *method* of social ethics, that is, to the rational ways of coming to a conclusion in each particular case and problem. This question divides into two, one concerning the ethical dialogue, argumentation and communication, the other concerning the method per se.

16.4   Method, Dialogue, and Communication

Perelman (1963) sees concepts of justice ingrained in the rationality of rhetoric. Ackerman's (1980) *Social Justice in the Liberal State* explores the rational constraints on arguments in a dialogue between competing claimants, so as to reach and determine a just solution. The *communicational ethics* of Apel, Habermas, and others is more ambitious, but perhaps less practical. It intends to derive the just or the good from the very conditions that make mutual understanding possible. The communicating persons speak from an objective and moral point of view. Their agreement is not an "exchange" agreement but rather the revelation of the meaning of moral terms, or indeed the very definition of these terms. What is just would be recognized in a situation of "ideal speech" with perfect and neutral communication (a fictitious device to be sure, but perhaps no more so than certain Social Contracts or impartial observers). Yet it is rather difficult to draw, from this theory, other practical conclusions than an emphasis on serene and informed dialogue about the issues. But since communication requires shared meaning and rests on similarities of individuals' thought processes, this theory should lead to a close analysis of the semiology and of the phenomenology of ethics. These obviously are necessary exercises, yet this deemphasizes the purely interactive and communicational aspect.

The method of justice applies the general method of rational judgment to the specific questions of justice. This domain includes the consequence of considering several comparable justiciables and the logical structure of ethical equality (*isology*); the analysis of the sentiments of justice and especially of injustice (*thymology*); ethical epistemology and in particular moral falsificationism (hold a moral principle as long as you have not found a case of application where it is repulsive, and actively seek such cases—an essential variable is the delineation of the domain of validity of the principle); the iterative induction concerning principles and their consequences (Plato's "dialectics" in *The Republic* or Rawls's "reflective equilibrium"); the similar comparison of alternative principles; the analysis of the relevant generalizations; the rational and organized use of introspection, empathy, and "objective subjectivity"; the development, in particular, of comparative empathy and comparative hermeneutics; and so on (see Kolm 1990b).

16.5   Judging Justice, and beyond Justice

Claiming justice for oneself may sound right, but it does not necessarily sound nice. Such claims may be motivated by a sheer sense of justice or by needs, but they may also be motivated by greed, egoism, jealousy or envy. Sense of justice and sentiments of injustice can accomodate second rate morality. This is, however, the modern sense of the term "justice," which makes it a quality of society independent of the intrinsic quality of persons' sentiments and attitudes. This gap did not exist in the classical sense of the term (before the sixteenth century but still so for Kant, with certain vestiges to this day) that designated the individual virtue of "behaving justly" toward others. This issue is essential for the actual implementability of justice (as discussed in chapter 13).

For instance, sufficient altruism can take conflict and coercion out of distributive justice, although it leaves the problem of defining the just sharing. There is indeed a whole field of social sentiments and behavior that mixes justice and altruism, or is intermediary between them, or is altruism or gift-giving motivated by justice, or, again, is voluntary actualization of justice: This is *reciprocity*, a central phenomenon of social life and an essential cement of societies (see the analysis and references in Kolm 1984b).[6]

Furthermore justice is an essential property of communities. It is defined by traditions and by shared culture, meanings, and practices.

---

6. See also Kolm 1984d, 1994d.

History brings about this idea as it maintains or changes it. Walzer and Taylor, inter alia, emphasize this angle among present-day scholars. Yet norms of justice, and their origin, maintenance, and changes, can also be explained.[7] These explanations, when they are sufficiently scientific, both rest on concepts and results of the "pure theory of justice" and provide the empirical material that feeds it.

However, general justice and macrojustice, as understood in "theories of justice," is by no means a universal conception but a Western one. Of course every society develops rules of microjustice for solving distributional problems of everyday life, and a social structure determining dues, duties, powers, rights, roles, and statuses. But non-Western languages do not even have a suitable expression for translating general and conceptual "justice," not at their common nor at their sophisticated level. A common rendering is "conformity with the Law"—this can be a metaphysical, yet well-defined, "Law." The Chinese render "that is unfair" by *pu kong ping*, "that is against public harmony." Confucian respect of family values has little to do with justice. The most elaborate knowledge of the mind, advanced Buddhism, aims at diminishing suffering through increasing awareness of the illusions of the self, resulting in "self"-mastering of one's desires. It sees this method as the only efficient and durable way of answering the valid reasons of concerns for justice (history is rather on the side of this view). It also sees other aspects of this concern as dangerous diseases, as they may foster appropriation, attachment, envy, and illusions concerning selves.[8] Even in the West, Léon Walras at the end of the nineteenth century—counting as theories of justice neither English utilitarianism and traditionalism nor German historicism and communitarianism—audaciously declared "Justice is a Graeco-Latin and French idea." Whatever truth this suggestion might have contained, the concept has obviously spread since. Yet it does not seem to spread as far as certain increasingly powerful non-Western industrial countries, and it is not certain that it will.

---

7. Social psychology has developed an abundant literature on this topic. This literature is presented in Kolm 1991a and, for application to just or fair pay or wages, in Kolm 1990a. A variety of criteria of just or fair allocation used in "local" problems are presented in Elster (1992).

8. See Kolm 1982a.

Finally, the classical contention that justice is "the first virtue of societies" ("in society" for Aristotle, "of institutions" for Rawls) can be doubted. Culture, rootedness, and the respect of history are not behind it. Altruism and fraternity overrule it when they are possible. And the consciousness of the articifiality of the self, hence self-creation and nonalienated spirituality, constitute the highest and deepest stage of humankind. Justice therefore is only the fourth or fifth virtue of society. This does not make its establishment less necessary, the fight for it less righteous, and understanding it less important.

Even the mere instrumental value of justice is no small contribution. Peace without justice is oppression, spoliation, and violation of dignity. Dignity without justice fosters wars for one's due and freedom. Justice alone permits the reign of both peace and dignity.

Bibliography

Ackerman, B. A. 1980. *Social Justice in the Liberal State*. New Haven: Yale University Press.

Ahrens, J., E. Frankel Paul, F. Miller, and J. Paul. 1988. *The New Social Contract: Essays on Gauthier*. Oxford: Basil Blackwell.

Amiel, Y., and F. Cowell. 1992. Measurement of income inequality. *Journal of Public Economics* 47:3–26.

Apel, K.-O. 1980. *Towards a Transformation of Philosophy*. London: Routledge and Kegan, Paul.

Archibald, G. C., and Donaldson, D. 1979. Notes on economic inequality. *Journal of Public Economics* 12:205–14.

Aristotle. *Nichomachean Ethics*. Loeb Classical Library. Cambridge: Harvard University Press.

Aristotle. *Politics*. English trans. by E. Barker, 1946. Oxford: Oxford University Press.

Arneson, R. 1989. Equality and equal opportunity for welfare. *Philosophical Studies* 56:77–93.

Arneson, R. 1990. Liberalism, distributive subjectivism, and equal opportunity for welfare. *Philosophy and Public Affairs* 19:158–94.

Arrow, K. J. 1963. *Social Choice and Individual Values*. 2d ed. New Haven: Yale University Press.

Arrow, K. J. 1977. Extended sympathy and the possibility of social choice. *American Economic Review* 67:219–25.

Arrow, K. J., and T. Scitowsky, eds. 1969. *Readings in Welfare Economics*. Homewood, II: Irwin.

Arthur, J., and W. H. Shaw, eds. 1978. *Justice and Economic Distribution*. Englewood Cliffs, NJ: Prentice Hall.

d'Aspremont, C. 1985. Axioms for social welfare orderings. In *Social Goals and Social Organizations*, ed. by L. Hurwicz, D. Schmeidler, and H. Sonnenschein. Cambridge: Cambridge University Press.

d'Aspremont, C. 1993. Economie du bien-être et utilitarisme. In *La Méthode et l'enquête*, ed. by L. A. Gérard-Varet and J. C. Passeron. Paris: Maison des Sciences de l'Homme.

d'Aspremont, C., and L. Gevers. 1977. Equity and the informational basis of collective choice. *Review of Economic Studies* 44:199–209.

Atkinson, A. B. 1970. On the measurement of inequality. *Journal of Economic Theory* 2:244–63.

Atkinson, A. B. 1973. How progressive should income tax be? In *Essays on Modern Economics*, ed. by M. Parkin. London: Longman.

Atkinson, A. B. 1983a. *Social Justice and Public Policy*. Cambridge: MIT Press.

Atkinson, A. B. 1983b. *The Economics of Inequality*. Oxford: Oxford University Press.

Atkinson, A. B. 1987. On the measurement of poverty. *Econometrica* 55:749–64.

Atkinson, A. B., and F. Bourguignon. 1982. The comparison of multi-dimensioned economic status. *Review of Economic Studies* 49:183–201.

Atkinson, A. B., and F. Bourguignon. 1987. Income distribution and differences in needs. In *Arrow and the Ascent of Modern Economic Theory*, ed. by G. Feiwel. London: Macmillan.

Baier, K. E. M. 1958. *The Moral Point of View*. Ithaca, NY: Cornell University Press.

Bailey, M. 1979. The possibility of rational choice in an economy. *Journal of Political Economy* 87:37–56.

Baker, J. 1987. *Arguing for Equality*. London: Verso.

Barberá, S. 1996. In *Social Choice Re-examined*, ed. by K. Arrow, A. Sen, and K. Suzumura. London: Macmillan.

Barnett, W., H. Moulin, M. Salles, and N. Schofield, eds. 1995. *Social Choice, Welfare and Ethics*. Cambridge: Cambridge University Press.

Barry, B. 1965. *Political Argument*. London: Routledge and Kegan Paul.

Barry, B. 1973. *The Liberal Theory of Justice*. Oxford: Oxford University Press.

Barry, B. 1982. Lady Chatterley's lover and doctor Fischer bomb party: Liberalism, Pareto optimality and the problem of objectionable preferences. In *Foundations of Social Choice Theory*, ed. by J. Elster and A. Hylland. Cambridge: Cambridge University Press.

Barry, B. 1989a. *Democracy, Power, and Justice: Essays in Political Theory*. Oxford: Clarendon Press.

Barry, B. 1989b. *A Treatise on Social Justice*. Vol. 1: *Theories of Justice*. Hemel Hempstead: Harvester-Wheatsheaf.

Barry, B. 1995. *Justice as Impartiality*. Oxford: Clarendon Press.

Barry, B., R. Barber, J. S. Fishkin, and R. C. Flathman. 1983. Symposium on justice. In *Ethics*, vol. 93.

Basu, K. 1983. Cardinal utility, utilitarianism, and a class of invariance axioms in welfare analysis. *Journal of Mathematical Economics* 12:193–206.

Battifol, H. 1979. *Problèmes de base de philosophie du droit*. Paris: LGDJ.

Baumol, W. J. 1986. *Superfairness*. Cambridge: MIT Press.

Bayles, M. D. 1990. *Procedural Justice: Allocation to Individuals*. Dordrecht: Reidel.

Beccaria, C. [1864] 1984. *Dei delitti e delle pene*. New edition, ed. by G. Francioni. Milan.

Bedau, H. A. ed. 1971. *Justice and Equality*. Englewood Cliffs, NJ: Prentice Hall.

Benhabib, S., and Dallmayr, F., eds. 1990. *The Communicative Ethics Controversy*. Cambridge: MIT Press.

Benn, S. 1988. *A Theory of Freedom*. Cambridge: Cambridge University Press.

Benn, S. I., and R. S. Peters 1959. *Social Principles and the Democratic State*. London: George Allen and Unwin.

Bentham, J. [1789] 1970 *An Introduction to the Principles of Morals and Legislation*, ed. by J. M. Burns and H. L. A. Hart. London: Athlone Press.

Bentham, J. 1843. *The Works of Jeremy Bentham*, 11 vols., ed. by J. Bowring. Edinburgh: William Tait.

Bentham, J. [1843] 1962. *Anarchical Fallacies*. In *Works*, ed. by J. Bowring. New York: Russell.

Bentham, J. 1973. *Bentham's Political Thought*, ed. by Bikhu Parekh. London: Croom Helm.

Bentham, J. [1802] 1978. Principles of the civil code. In *Property*, ed. by C. B. McPherson. Toronto: University of Toronto Press, pp. 41–58.

Berge, C. 1959. *Espaces Topologiques, Fonctions Multivoques*. Paris: Dunod. English trans. by E. M. Patterson. New York: Macmillan, 1963.

Bergson, A. 1938. A reformulation of certain aspects of welfare economics. *Quarterly Journal of Economics* 52:310–34.

Bergson, A. 1966. *Essays in Normative Economics*. Cambridge: Harvard University Press.

Berkowitz, L., and E. Walster, eds. 1976. *Equity Theory: Toward a General Theory of Social Interaction. Advances in Experimental Social Psychology*, vol. 9. San Diego: Academic Press.

Berliant, M., and M. Gouveia. 1993. Equal sacrifice and incentive compatible income taxation. *Journal of Public Economics* 51:219–40.

Berlin, I. 1956. Equality. In *Proceedings of the Aristotelian Society*, new series, LVI: 301–26. London: Harrison.

Berlin, I. 1969. *Four Essays on Liberty*. Oxford: Oxford University Press.

Berlin, I. 1985. *Two concepts of freedom*. Oxford: Clarendon Press.

Bernholz, P. 1974. Is a Paretian liberal really impossible? *Public Choice* 20:99–107.

Binmore, K. 1994. *Game Theory and the Social Contract*, vol. 1: *Playing Fair*. Cambridge: MIT Press.

Binmore, K., and P. Dasgupta, eds. 1986. *Economic Organization as Games*. Oxford: Basil Blackwell.

Binmore, K., and P. Dasgupta, eds. 1987. *The Economics of Bargaining*. Oxford : Basil Blackwell.

Binmore, K., A. Rubinstein, and A. Wolinsky. 1986. Nash bargaining solution in economic modelling. *Rand Journal of Economics* 17:176–88.

Black, D. 1958. *The Theory of Committees and Elections*. Cambridge: Cambridge University Press.

Blackorby, C. 1975. Degrees of cardinality and aggregate partial orderings. *Econometrica* 43:845–52.

Blackorby, C., and D. Donaldson. 1977. Utility versus equity: Some plausible quasi-orderings. *Journal of Public Economics* 7:365–81.

Blackorby, C., and D. Donaldson. 1978. Measures of relative equality and their meanings in terms of social welfare. *Journal of Economic Theory* 18:59–80.

Blackorby, C., and D. Donaldson. 1980a. Ethical indices for the measurement of poverty. *Econometrica* 48:1053–60.

Blackorby, C., and D. Donaldson. 1980b. Means testing versus universal provision in property alleviation programmes. *Economica* 57:119–29.

Blackorby, C., and D. Donaldson. 1984. Ethically significant ordinal indexes of relative inequality. *Advances in Econometrics* 3.

Blackorby, C., D. Donaldson, and J. Weymark. 1984. Social choice with interpersonal utility comparisons: A diagrammatic introduction. *International Economic Review* 25: 327–56.

Blair, D. H., G. Bordes, J. S. Kelly, and K. Suzumura. 1976. Impossibility theorems without collective rationality. *Journal of Economic Theory* 13:361–79.

Blocker, H. G., and E. H. Smith. 1976. *John Rawls' Theory of Social Justice: An Introduction*. Athens: Ohio University Press.

Borda, J. C. [1781] 1953. Mémoire sur les élections au scrutin. *Mémoires de l'Académie Royale des Sciences*. English trans. by A. de Grazia. *Isis* 44.

Bordes, G. 1976. Consistency, rationality and collective choice. *Review of Economic Studies* 43:447–57.

Bös, D., and G. Tillman. 1985. An "envy tax": Theoretical principles and applications to the German surcharge on the rich. *Public Finance* 40:35–63.

Boskin, M., and E. Sheshinski. 1978. Optimal redistributive taxation when individual welfare depends on relative income. *Quarterly Journal of Economics* 92:589–602.

Bossert, W., and F. Stehling. 1994. On the uniqueness of cardinally interpreted utility functions. In *Models and Measurement of Welfare and Inequality*, ed. by W. Eichhorn. Heidelberg: Springer-Verlag, pp. 537–51.

Bourguignon, F. 1979. Decomposable income inequality measures. *Econometrica* 47: 901–20.

Braithwaite, R. B. 1955. *The Theory of Games as a Tool for the Moral Philosopher*. Cambridge: Cambridge University Press.

Brams, S. J., and A. Taylor. 1996. *Fair Division, from Cake Cutting to Dispute Resolution*. Cambridge: Cambridge University Press.

Brandt, R. B. 1959. *Ethical Theory*. Englewood Cliffs, NJ: Prentice Hall.

Brandt, R. B., ed. 1962. *Social Justice*. Englewood Cliffs, NJ: Prentice Hall.

Brandt, R. B. 1979. *A Theory of the Good and the Right*. Oxford: Oxford University Press.

Brandt, R. B. 1986. The future of ethics. In *New Directions in Ethics: The Challenge of Applied Ethics*, ed. by J. P. de Manco and R. M. Fox. London: Routledge and Kegan Paul.

Braybrooke, D. 1987. *Meeting Needs*. Princeton: Princeton University Press.

Brennan, G. 1973. Pareto desirable redistribution: The case of malice and envy. *Journal of Economic Theory* 2:173–83.

Broome, J. 1991a. *Weighting Goods*. Oxford: Basil Blackwell.

Broome, J. 1991b. Utility. *Economics and Philosophy* 7:1–12.

Brown, A. 1986. *Modern Political Philosophy: Theories of the Just Society*. Harmondsworth: Penguin Books.

Buchanan, A. E. 1982. *Marx and Justice*. London: Methuen.

Buchanan, J. M. 1954. Individual choice in voting and the market. *Journal of Political Economy* 62:334–43.

Buchanan, J. M. 1975. *The Limits of Liberty*. Chicago: University of Chicago Press.

Buchanan, J. M. 1986. *Liberty, Market and the State*. Brighton: Wheatsheaf Books.

Buchanan, J. M. 1991. *The Economics and the Ethics of Constitutional Order*. Ann Arbor: University of Michigan Press.

Buchanan, J., and G. Tullock. 1962. *The Calculus of Consent*. Ann Arbor: University of Michigan Press.

Campbell, D. 1992. *Equity, Efficiency and Social Choice*. New York: Oxford University Press.

Campbell, T. 1988. *Justice*. London: Macmillan.

Cannan, E. 1930. *Elementary Political Economy*. London: Macmillan.

Chakravarty, S. 1990. *Ethical Social Index Numbers*. Berlin: Springer-Verlag.

Champsaur, P., and G. Laroque. 1981. Fair allocations in large economies. *Journal of Economic Theory* 25:269–82.

Chapman, J. 1964. Justice as fairness. *Nomos VI, Justice*. New York.

Charvet, J. 1981. *A Critique of Freedom and Equality*. Cambridge: Cambridge University Press.

Chaudhuri, A. 1986. Some implications of an intensity measure of envy. *Social Choice and Welfare* 3:255–70.

Chernoff, H. 1954. Rational selection of decision functions. *Econometrica* 22:422–43.

Chichilnisky, G., and W. Thomson. 1987. The Walrasian mechanism from equal division is not monotonic with respect to variations in the number of consumers. *Journal of Public Economics* 32:119–24.

Chipmann, J. S. 1987. Compensation principle. In *New Palgrave Dictionary in Economics*, ed. by J. Eatwell et al. London: Macmillan, pp. 524–31.

Clark, S., R. Hemming, and D. Ulph. 1981. On indices for the measurement of poverty. *Economic Journal* 91:515–26.

Coase, R. H. 1960. The problem of social cost. *Journal of Law and Economics* 3:1–44.

Cohen, G. A. 1986. Self-ownership, world-ownership and equality. In *Justice, Equality, Here, Now*, ed. by F. S. Lucash. Ithaca, NY: Cornell University Press, pp. 108–35; and *Social Philosophy and Policy* (Spring 1986):77–96.

Cohen, G. A. 1989a. Equality of what? On welfare, goods and capabilities. Mimeo. All Souls' College.

Cohen, G. A. 1989b. On the currency of egalitarian justice. *Ethics* 99:906–44.

Cohen, G. A. 1995. *Self-ownership, Freedom and Equality*. Cambridge: Cambridge University Press.

Cohen, M. et al., eds. 1980. *Marx, Justice, and History*. Princeton: Princeton University Press.

Cohen, R. L., ed. 1986. *Justice: Views from the Social Sciences*. New York: Plenum Press.

Collard, D. 1978. *Altruism and Economy: A Study in Non-Selfish Economics*. Oxford: Martin Robertson.

Condorcet, J.-A.-N. Caritat de. 1785. *Essai sur l'application de l'analyse à la probabilité des décisions rendues à la pluralité des voix*. Paris.

Condorcet, J.-A.-N. Caritat de. 1847–1849. *Œuvres complètes*, ed. by F. Arago and Mme O'Connor. 12 volumes. Paris: F. Didot.

Cook, K., and K. Hegtvedt. 1983. Distributive justice, equity and equality. *Annual Review of Sociology* 9:217–41.

Cook, K., and K. Hegtvedt. 1985. *Distributive Justice*. New Haven: Yale University Press.

Coulhon, T., and P. Mongin. 1989. Social choice theory in the case of Von Neumann-Morgenstern utilities. *Social Choice and Welfare* 6:175–87.

Cowell, F., and K. Kuga. 1981. Inequality measurement: an axiomatic approach. *European Economic Review* 15:287–305.

Crawford, V. P. 1977. A game of fair division. *Review of Economic Studies* 44:235–47.

Crawford, V. P. 1979. A procedure for generating Pareto-efficient egalitarian-equivalent allocations. *Econometrica* 47:49–60.

Crawford, V. P. 1980. A self-administered solution of the bargaining problem. *Review of Economic Studies* 47:385–92.

Crawford, V. P., and W. P. Heller. 1979. Fair division with indivisible commodities. *Journal of Economic Theory* 21:10–27.

Dalton, H. 1920. The measurement of the inequality of incomes. *Economic Journal* 30:348–61.

Dalton, H. 1925. *Inequality of Incomes*. London.

Daniels N., ed. 1975. *Reading Rawls*. New York: Basic Books.

Dasgupta, P., and P. J. Hammond. 1980. Fully progressive taxation. *Journal of Public Economics* 13:141–54.

Dasgupta P., P. Hammond, and E. Maskin. 1979. The implementation of social choice rules: Some general results on incentive compatibility. *Review of Economic Studies* 46:185–216.

Debreu, G. 1959. *Theory of Value*. New York: Wiley.

Debreu, G. 1960. Topological methods in cardinal utility theory. In *Mathematical Methods in the Social Sciences*, ed. by K. Arrow, S. Karlin, and S. Suppes. Stanford: Stanford University Press, pp. 16–26.

Del Vecchio, G. 1955. *La Justice*. Paris: LGDJ.

Deschamps, R., and L. Gevers. 1978. Leximin and utilitarian rules: A joint characterization. *Journal of Economic Theory* 17:143–63.

Deutsch, M. 1985. *Distributive Justice: A Social-Psychological Perspective*. New Haven: Yale University Press.

Diamond, P. 1967. Cardinal welfare, individualistic ethics, and interpersonal comparison of utility: Comment. *Journal of Political Economy* 75:765–66.

Domotor, Z. 1979. Ordered sum and tensor product of linear utility structures. *Theory and Decision* 11:375–99.

Donaldson, D., and J. A. Weymark. 1980. A single-parameter generalization of the Gini indices of inequality. *Journal of Economic Theory* 22:67–86.

Donaldson, D., and J. Weymark 1986. Properties of fixed-population poverty indices. *International Economic Review* 27:667–88.

Doyal, L., and I. Gough. 1991. *A Theory of Human Need*. London: Macmillan.

Dummett, M. 1984. *Voting Procedures*. Oxford: Clarendon Press.

Dupuit, J. 1844. De la mesure de l'utilité des travaux publics. *Annales des Ponts et Chaussées*. Séries 2, 2, 2ème semestre, pp. 332–75. English trans. (1969): On the measurement of the utility of public works. In *Readings in Welfare Economics*, ed. by K. J. Arrow and T. Scitovsky. Homewood, IL: Irwin, pp. 255–83.

Durkheim, E. [1893] 1964. *The Division of Labor*, trans. by George Simpson. New York: Free Press.

Durkheim, E. [1912] 1966. *Moral Education*, trans. by E. K. Wilson and H. Schnurer. New York: Free Press.

Durkheim, E. [1912] 1979. *Essays on Morals and Education*, edited with an introduction by W. S. F. Pickering. London: Routledge and Kegan Paul.

Dworkin, R. 1977. *Taking Rights Seriously*. Cambridge: Harvard University Press. New impression with a reply to critics, London: Duckworth, 1978.

Dworkin, R. 1981. What is equality? Part I: Equality of welfare; Part II: Equality of resources. *Philosophy and Public Affairs* 10:185–246, 283–345.

Eckhoff, T. 1974. *Justice: Its Determinants in Social Action*. Rotterdam: Rotterdam University Press.

Edel, A. 1986. Ethical theory and moral practice: On the terms of their relation. In *New Directions in Ethics: The Challenge of Applied Ethics*, ed. by J. P. de Manco and R. M. Fox. London: Routledge and Kegan Paul.

Eichhorn, W., ed. 1994. *Models and Measurement of Welfare and Inequality*. Heidelberg: Springer-Verlag.

Eichhorn, W., and W. Gehrig. 1982. Measurement of inequality in economics. In *Modern Applied Mathematics: Optimization and Operations Research*, ed. by B. Korte. Amsterdam: North-Holland.

Elster, J. 1985. *Making Sense of Marx*. Cambridge: Cambridge University Press.

Elster, J. 1992. *Local Justice*. Cambridge: Cambridge University Press.

Elster, J., and A. Hylland, eds. 1986. *Foundations of Social Choice Theory*. Cambridge: Cambridge University Press.

Elster, J., and J. E. Roemer, eds. 1991. *Interpersonal Comparisons of Well-Being*. Cambridge: Cambridge University Press.

Esteban, J. M., and D. Ray. 1994. On the measurement of polarization. *Econometrica* 62: 819–51.

Farrel, M. 1976. Liberalism in the theory of social choice. *Review of Economic Studies* 43: 3–10.

Fauré, C. 1988. *Les Déclarations des droits de l'homme de 1789*. Paris: Payot.

Feinberg, J., ed. 1969. *Moral Concepts*. Oxford: Oxford University Press.

Feinberg, J. 1970. *Doing and Deserving: Essays in the Theory of Responsibility*. Princeton: Princeton University Press.

Feinberg, J. 1980. *Rights, Justice and the Bounds of Liberty*. Princeton: Princeton University Press.

Feiwel, G. R., ed. 1987. *Arrow and the Ascent of Modern Economic Theory*. London: Macmillan.

Feldman, A. 1980. *Welfare Economics and Social Choice Theory*. Boston: Kluwer/ Nijhoff.

Feldman, A. 1987. Fairness. In *New Palgrave Dictionary in Economics*, ed. by J. Eatwell. London: Macmillan.

Feldman, A., and A. Kirman. 1974. Fairness and envy. *American Economic Review* 64: 995–1005.

Fellman, J. 1976. The effects of transformations of Lorenz curves in economic analysis. *Econometrica* 45:719–27.

Field, G. S. 1980. *Poverty, Inequality and Development*. Cambridge: University Press.

Field, G. 1993. Inequality in dual economy models. *The Economic Journal* 103:1228–35.

Finnis, J. 1980. *Natural Law and Natural Rights*. Oxford: Clarendon Press.

Finnis, J. 1983. *Fundamentals of Ethics*. Oxford: Clarendon Press.

Fishburn, P. C. 1973. *The Theory of Social Choice*. Princeton: Princeton University Press.

Fishburn, P. C. 1984. On Harsanyi's utilitarian cardinal welfare theorem. *Theory and Decision* 17:21–28.

Fishkin, J. 1979. *Tyranny and Legitimacy*. Baltimore: Johns Hopkins University Press.

Fishkin, J. 1983. *Justice, Equal Opportunity and the Family*. New Haven: Yale University Press.

Flathman, R. E. 1976. *The Practice of Rights*. Cambridge: Cambridge University Press.

Flathman, R. E. 1987. *The Philosophy and Politics of Freedom*. Chicago: University of Chicago Press.

Fleurbaey, M. 1994a. On fair compensation. *Theory and Decision* 36:277–307.

Fleurbaey, M. 1994b. L'absence d'envie dans une problématique post-welfariste. *Recherches Economiques de Louvain* 60:9–41.

Fleurbaey, M. 1995a. Three solutions for the compensation problem. *Journal of Economic Theory* 65:505–21.

Fleurbaey, M. 1995b. The requisites of equal opportunity. In *Advances in Social Choice Theory and Cooperative Games*, ed. by W. A. Barnett, H. Moulin, M. Salles, and W. Schofield. Cambridge: Cambridge University Press.

Fleurbaey, M. 1995c. Equal opportunity or equal social outcome? *Economics and Philosophy* 11:25–55.

Fleurbaey, M. 1995d. Equality and responsibility. *European Economic Review* 39:683–89.

Fleurbaey, M. 1996. *Théories économiques de la justice*. Paris: Economica.

Flew, A. 1985. *The Politics of Procrustes*. London: Temple Smith.

Foley, D. 1967. Resource allocation in the public sector. *Yale Economic Essays* 7:45–98.

Folger, R., ed. 1984. *The Sense of Injustice: Social Psychological Perspectives*. New York: Plenum Press.

Foot, P. 1978. *Virtues and Vices and Other Essays in Moral Philosophy*. Berkeley: University of California Press.

Foot, P. 1985. Utilitarian and the virtues. *Mind* 94.

Foster, J. 1984. On economic poverty: A survey of aggregate measures. *Advances in Econometrics* 3:215–51.

Foster, J. 1986. Inequality measurement. In *Fair Allocation*, ed. by H. P. Young. Providence: American Mathematical Society.

Foster J., J. Greer, and E. Thorbecke. 1984. A class of decomposable poverty measures. *Econometrica* 52:761–66.

Fried, C. 1981. *Contract as Promise*. Cambridge: Harvard University Press.

Friedman, D. 1978. *The Machinery of Freedom*, 2d ed. La Salle, IL: Open Court Press.

Friedman, J. 1991. *Game Theory with Applications to Economics*. Oxford: Oxford University Press.

Friedman, M. 1962. *Capitalism and Freedom*. Chicago: University of Chicago Press.

Friedman M., and Friedman, R. 1981. *Free to Choose*. New York: Avon.

Galston, W. 1980. *Justice and the Human Good*. Chicago: University of Chicago Press.

Gaertner, W. 1992. Rights and game forms, types of preference orderings and Pareto inefficiency. In *Mathematical Modelling in Economics*, ed. by W. E. Diewert, K. Spremann, and F. Stehling. Berlin: Springer-Verlag.

Gaertner, W., and M. Klemisch-Ahlert. 1992. *Social Choice and Barganing Perspectives on Distributive Justice*. Bonn: Springer-Verlag.

Gaertner, W., and L. Krüger. 1981. Self-supporting preferences and individual rights: The possibility of Paretian libertarianism. *Economica* 48:17–28.

Gaertner, W., P. Pattanaik, and K. Suzumura. 1992. Individual rights revisited. *Economica* 59:161–77.

Gallie, W. 1956. Liberal morality and socialist morality. In *Philosophy, Politics and Society*, ed. by Laslett. Oxford: Oxford University Press.

Gärdenfors, P. 1981. Rights, games and social choice. *Noûs* 15:341–56.

Gauthier, D. 1986. *Morals by Agreement*. Oxford: Clarendon Press.

Gauthier, D., and R. Sugden. 1993. *Rationality, Justice and the Social Contract*. Ann Arbor: University of Michigan Press.

Gevers, L. 1979. On interpersonal comparability and social welfare orderings. *Econometrica* 47:75–90.

Gevers, L. 1986. Walrasian social choice: Some simple axiomatic approaches. In *Social Choice and Public Decision Making*, ed. by W. Heller et al., vol. 1. Cambridge: Cambridge University Press.

Gewirth, A. 1978. *Reason and Morality*. Chicago: University of Chicago Press.

Gewirth, A. 1982. *Human Rights: Essays on Justification and Applications.* Chicago: University of Chicago Press.

Gibbard, A. 1973. Manipulation of voting schemes: A general result. *Econometrica* 41:587–601.

Gibbard, A. 1982. Rights in the theory of social choice. In *Logic, Methodology and the Philosophy of Sciences*, ed. by I. J. Cohen, J. Los, H. Pfeiffer, and K.-P. Podewski, vol. 4. Amsterdam: North-Holland, pp. 595–605.

Gibbard, A. 1986. Interpersonal comparisons: Preference, good, and the intrinsic reward of a life. In *Foundations of Social Choice Theory*, ed. by J. Elster and A. Hylland. Cambridge: Cambridge University Press.

Ginsberg, M. 1965. *On Justice in Society.* Harmondsworth: Penguin Books.

Goldman, A. H. 1979. *Justice and Reverse Discrimination.* Princeton: Princeton University Press.

Goldman, S., and C. Sussangkarn. 1983. Dealing with envy. *Journal of Public Economics* 22:103–12.

Goodin, R. E. 1976. *The Politics of Rational Man.* New York: Wiley.

Goodin, R. E. 1985a. Negating positive desert claims. *Political Theory* 13.

Goodin, R. E. 1985b. *Protecting the Vulnerable.* Chicago: Chicago University Press.

Goodin, R. E. 1986. Laundering preferences. In *Foundations of Social Choice Theory*, ed. by J. Elster and A. Hylland. Cambridge: Cambridge University Press.

Graaff, J. de V. 1957. *Theoretical Welfare Economics.* Cambridge: Cambridge University Press.

Graham, G. 1988. *Contemporary Social Philosophy.* Oxford: Basil Blackwell.

Gray, J. 1984. *Hayek on Liberty.* Oxford: Basil Blackwell.

Green, J., and R. L. Cohen, eds. 1982. *Equity and Justice in Social Behavior.* San Diego: Academic Press.

Green, J., and J.-J. Laffont 1979. *Incentives in Public Decision Making.* Amsterdam: North-Holland.

Greenberg, J., and R. L. Cohen, eds. 1982. *Equity and Justice in Social Behavior.* San Diego: Academic Press.

Griffin, J. 1986. *Well-being.* Oxford: Clarendon Press.

Gross, B. 1978. *Discrimination in Reverse: Is Turnabout Fair Play?* New York: New York University Press.

Groves, T., and Ledyard, J. 1977. Optimal allocation of public goods: A solution to the free rider problem. *Econometrica* 45:783–809.

Grzegorcyzk, C. 1982. *La Théorie générale des valeurs et le droit.* Paris: LGDJ.

Guest, S., and A. Milne, eds. 1985. *Equality and Discrimination: Essays in Freedom and Justice.* ARSP (suppl. 21). Stuttgart: Steiner.

Gutmann, A. 1980. *Liberal Equality.* Cambridge: Cambridge University Press.

Habermas, J. 1970. *Toward a Rational Society*, trans. by J. J. Shapiro. Boston: Beacon Press.

Habermas, J. 1975. *Legitimation Crisis*, trans. by T. McCarthy. Boston: Beacon Press.

Habermas, J. 1978a. *Communication and the Evolution of Society*, trans. by T. McCarthy. Boston: Beacon Press.

Habermas, J. 1978b. *Knowledge and Human Interests*, trans. by J. J. Shapiro. Boston: Beacon Press.

Habermas, J. 1981. *Theorie des Kommunikativen Handelns*. Frankfurt: Suhrkamp.

Habermas, J. 1983. *Moralbewusstein und Kommunikatives Handeln*. Frankfurt: Suhrkamp.

Habermas, J. 1992. *Faktizität und Geltung*. Frankfurt: Suhrkemp.

Halévy, E. 1901–1904. La jeunesse de Bentham. In *La Formation du radicalisme philosophique*, vol. 1. Paris: Alcan.

Halévy, E. [1903] 1960. *The Growth of Philosophical Radicalism*, trans. by M. Morris. Boston: Beacon Press.

Hammond, P. J. 1976a. Equity, Arrow's conditions, and Rawls' difference principle. *Econometrica* 44:793–804.

Hammond, P. J. 1976b. Why ethical measures of inequality need interpersonal comparisons. *Theory and Decision* 7:263–74.

Hammond, P. J. 1977. Dual interpersonal comparisons of utility and the welfare economics of income distribution. *Journal of Public Economics* 7:51–71.

Hammond, P. J. 1979. Straightforward individual incentive compatibility in large economies. *Review of Economic Studies* 46: 263–82.

Hammond, P. J. 1981. Ex-ante and ex-post welfare optimality under uncertainty. *Economica* 48:235–50.

Hammond, P. J. 1982. Utilitarianism, uncertainty and information. In *Utilitarianism and Beyond*, ed. by A. K. Sen and B. Williams. Cambridge: Cambridge University Press.

Hammond, P. J. 1983. Ex-post optimality as a dynamically consistent objective for collective choice under uncertainty. In *Social Choice and Welfare*, ed. by P. K. Pattanaik and M. Salles. Amsterdam: North-Holland.

Hammond, P. J. 1985. Social choice of individual and group rights. In *Social Choice, Welfare and Ethics*, ed. by W. Barnett, H. Moulin, M. Salles, and N. Schofield. Cambridge: Cambridge University Press.

Hansson, B. 1977. The measurement of social inequality. In *Logic, Methodology and Philosophy of Science*, ed. by R. Butts and J. Hintikka. Dordrecht: Reidel.

Hardin, R. 1982. *Collective Action*. Baltimore: Johns Hopkins Univesity Press.

Hare, R. M. 1952. *The Language of Morals*. Oxford: Oxford University Press.

Hare, R. M. 1963. *Freedom and Reason*. Oxford: Oxford University Press.

Hare, R. M. 1981. *Moral Thinking*. Oxford: Oxford University Press.

Harrison, R. 1983. *Bentham*. London: Routledge.

Harrison, E., and C. Seidl. 1994. Percepional inequality and preferential judgement: An empirical examination of distributional axioms. *Public Choice* 79:61–81.

Harsanyi, J. C. 1953. Cardinal utility in welfare economics and in the theory of risktaking. *Journal of Political Economy* 61:434–35.

Harsanyi, J. C. 1955. Cardinal welfare, individualistic ethic, and interpersonal comparison of utility. *Journal of Political Economy* 63:309–21.

Harsanyi, J. C. 1956. Approaches to the bargaining problem before and after the theory of games: A critical discussion of Zeuthen's, Hicks', and Nash's theories. *Econometrica* 24:144–57.

Harsanyi, J. C. 1963. A simplified bargaining model for the N-person cooperative games. *International Economic Review* 4:194–220.

Harsanyi, J. C. 1975. Nonlinear social welfare functions. *Theory and Decision* 6:311–32.

Harsanyi, J. C. 1975. Can the maximin principle serve as a basis for morality? *American Political Science Review* 69:594–606.

Harsanyi, J. C. 1976 *Essays in Ethics, Social Behaviour and Scientific Explanation.* Dordrecht: Reidel.

Harsanyi, J. C. 1977a. *Rational Behavior and Bargaining Equilibrium in Games and Social Situations.* Cambridge: Cambridge University Press.

Harsanyi, J. C. 1977b. Morality and the theory of rational behavior. *Social Research* 44:623–56.

Harsanyi, J. C. 1978. Bayesian decision theory and utilitarian ethics. *American Economic Review*, Papers and Proceedings, 68:223–28.

Harsanyi, J. C. 1987. Von Neumann-Morgenstern utilities, risk taking and welfare. In *Arrow and the Ascent of Modern Economic Theory*, ed. by G. R. Feiwel. London: Macmillan.

Harsanyi, J. C. 1992. Game and decision theoretic models in ethics. In *Handbook of Game Theory with Economic Applications*, ed. by R. Auman and S. Hart, vol. 1. Amsterdam: North-Holland, pp. 669–707.

Harsanyi, J. C., and R. Selten. 1972. A generalized Nash solution for two person bargaining games with incomplete information. *Management Science* 18:80–86.

Hart, H. L. A. 1963. *Punishment and Responsibility.* Oxford: Oxford University Press.

Hart, H. L. A. 1982. *Essays on Bentham: Studies in Jurisprudence and Political Theory.* Oxford: Clarendon Press.

Hausman, D. M., and M. S. MacPherson. 1996. *Economic Analysis and Moral Philosophy.* Cambridge: Cambridge University Press.

Havelock, E. A. 1978. *The Greek Concept of Justice: From Its Shadow in Homer to Its Substance in Plato.* Cambridge: Harvard University Press.

Hayek, F. A. 1976a. *The Mirage of Social Justice, Law, Legislation and Liberty.* London: Routledge and Kegan Paul.

Hayek, F. A. 1976b. *Law, Legislation and Liberty*, vol. 2. Chicago: University of Chicago Press.

Heller, A. 1986. *Beyond Justice.* Oxford: Basil Blackwell.

Helvetius. 1953. *De l'Esprit.* Paris.

Hicks, J. 1959. *Essays in World Economy.* Oxford: Basil Blackwell. Preface, reprinted as "A Manifesto." In *Wealth and Welfare.* Oxford: Basil Blackwell, 1981, pp. 135–41.

Hirschman, A. 1973. The changing tolerance for income inequality in the course of economic development. *Quarterly Journal of Economics* 87:544–65.

Hobbes, T. [1668] 1947. *Leviathan*, ed. with intro. by Michael Oakeshot. Oxford: Oxford University Press.

Hochman, H. M., and J. D. Rodgers: 1969. Pareto-optimal redistribution. *American Economic Review* 49, pt. 1:542–57.

Höffe, O. 1985. *Introduction à la philosophie pratique de Kant.* Fribourg: Castella.

Hohfeld, W. N. 1919. *Fundamental Legal Conceptions as Applied in Judicial Reasoning*, ed. by Walter Wheeler Cook. New Haven: Yale University Press.

Hook, S., ed. 1962. *Human Values and Economic Policy.* New York: New York University Press.

Hume, D. [1752] 1966. *Enquiry Concerning the Principle of Morals.* 2d ed. Chicago: Open Court.

Hurwicz, L., D. Schmeidler, and H. Sonnenschein, eds. 1985. *Social Goals and Social Organization*. Cambridge: Cambridge University Press.

Jakobsson, U. 1976. On the measurement of the degree of progression. *Journal of Public Economics* 5:1961–68.

Jeffrey, P. 1981. *Reading Nozick*. Totowa: Rowan and Littlefield.

Johansen, L. 1981. Review and comments. *Journal of Public Economics* 16:123–28.

Jorgenson, D. W., and D. T. Slesnick. 1984a. Inequality in the distribution of individual welfare. *Advances in Econometrics* 3.

Jorgenson, D. W., and D. T. Slesnick. 1984b. Aggregate consumer behaviour and the measurement of inequality. *Review of Economic Studies* 51:369–92.

Jouvenel, B. de. 1957. *Sovereignty*. Chicago: University of Chicago Press.

Kainz, H. P. 1988. *Ethics in Context*. London: Macmillan.

Kalai, E. 1985. Solutions to the bargaining problem. In *Social Goals and Social Organization*, ed. by L. Hurwicz, D. Schmeidler, and H. Sonnenschein. Cambridge: Cambridge University Press.

Kalai, E., and M. Smorodinski. 1975. Other solutions to Nash bargaining problem. *Econometrica* 43:513–18.

Kaldor, N. 1939. Welfare propositions of economics and interpersonal comparisons of utility. *Economic Journal* 49:549–52.

Kamenka, E., and A.E.-S. Tay, eds. 1979. *Justice*. London: Edward Arnold.

Kaneko, M., and K. Nakamura. 1979. The Nash social welfare function. *Econometrica* 47:423–35.

Kant, I. [1785] 1969. *Fundamental Principles of the Metaphysics of Morals*, or *Foundations of the Metaphysics of Morals*, ed. by R. Wolff. Indianapolis: Bobbs-Merrill.

Kant, I. [1797] 1981. *Metaphysics of Morals*, II, trans. by J. W. Ellington. New York: Harper.

Karni, E. 1978. Collective rationality, unanimity and liberal ethics. *Review of Economic Studies* 45:571–74.

Kelly, J. 1978. *Impossibility Theorems*. San Diego: Academic Press.

Kelly, J. 1987. *Social Choice Theory: An Introduction*. Berlin: Springer-Verlag.

Kelly, J. 1994. The free triple assumption. *Social Choice and Welfare* 11:97–101.

Kelsen, H. 1945. *The General Theory of Law and State*. New York: Russell and Russell.

Kelsen, H. 1957. *What Is Justice? Law, and Politics in the Mirror of Science*. Berkeley: University of California Press.

Kelsen, H. 1962. *Théorie pure du droit*. Paris: Sirey.

Kelsen, H. 1963. *Das Naturrecht in der Politischen Theorie*. Salzburg.

Kelsen, H. 1967. *The Pure Theory of Law*. Berkeley: University of California Press.

Kemp, M. C., and A. Asimakopulos. 1952. A note on "social welfare functions" and cardinal utility. *Canadian Journal of Economics and Political Science* 18:195–200.

Kemp, M. C., and Y. K. Ng. 1976. On the existence of social welfare functions, social orderings and social decision functions. *Economica* 43:59–66.

Kinzler, C. 1984. *Condorcet, l'instruction publique et la naissance du citoyen*. Paris: Minerve.

Kleinberg, M. 1980. Fair allocations and equal incomes. *Journal of Economic Theory* 23:189–200.

Kolm, S.-Ch. 1959. *Les Hommes du Fouta-Toro*. Saint-Louis: MAS.

Kolm, S.-Ch. 1964. *Les Fondements de l'économie publique: Introduction à la théorie du rôle économique de l'état*. Paris: IFP.

Kolm, S.-Ch. 1966a. The optimal production of social justice. In International Economic Association Conference on Public Economics, Biarritz. Proceedings ed. by H. Guitton, and J. Margolis. *Economie Publique*, Paris: CNRS, 1968, pp. 109–77. *Public Economics*, London: Macmillan, 1969, pp. 145–200.

Kolm, S.-Ch. 1966b. *Les Choix financiers et monétaires (théorie et technique modernes)*. Paris: Dunod.

Kolm, S.-Ch. 1967. Décisions et concernements collectifs. *Analyse et Prévision* 4.

Kolm, S.-Ch. 1968a. *La Théorie économique générale de l'encombrement*. Paris: Futurible.

Kolm, S.-Ch. 1968b. *Prix publics optimaux*. Paris: CNRS.

Kolm, S.-Ch. 1969a. Théorie démocratique de la justice sociale. *Revue d'Economie Politique* 1:138–41.

Kolm, S.-Ch. 1969b. *L'Etat et le système des prix*. Paris: Dunod-CNRS.

Kolm, S.-Ch. 1969c. *La Théorie des contraintes de valeur et ses applications*. Paris: Dunod-CNRS.

Kolm, S.-Ch. 1970a. *Le Service des masses*. Paris: Dunod-CNRS.

Kolm, S.-Ch. 1970b. *La Valeur publique*. Paris: Dunod-CNRS.

Kolm, S.-Ch. 1970c. L'inégalité des valeurs des vies humaines. *Cahiers du Séminaire d'Économétrie*, ed. by R. Roy, 18:40–62.

Kolm, S.-Ch. 1970d. L'économie normative des services de masse. *Revue d'Economie Politique* 80:61–84.

Kolm, S.-Ch. 1971. *Justice et équité*. Paris: CEPREMAP. Reprinted Paris: CNRS, 1972.

Kolm, S.-Ch. 1972. La taxation de la consommation ostentatoire (Taxing conspicuous consumption). *Revue d'Économie Politique* 1:65–79.

Kolm, S.-Ch. 1973a. Super-équité. *Kyklos* 26:841–43.

Kolm, S.-Ch. 1973b. More equal distribution of bundles of commodities. Paris: CEPREMAP.

Kolm, S.-Ch. 1973c. Laissez-faire quand même. *Revue d'Économie Politique* 2:348–56.

Kolm, S.-Ch. 1974a. Sur les conséquences économiques des principes de justice et de justice pratique. *Revue d'Économie Politique* 1:80–107.

Kolm, S.-Ch. 1974b. Rectifiances et dominances intégrales de tous degrés. Paris: CEPREMAP.

Kolm, S.-Ch. 1975a. La Réciprocité générale. Paris: CEPREMAP.

Kolm, S.-Ch. 1975b. Multidimensional inequality comparisons. Paris: CEPREMAP.

Kolm, S.-Ch. 1976a. Unequal inequalities: I. *Journal of Economic Theory* 12:416–42.

Kolm, S.-Ch. 1976b. Unequal inequalities: II. *Journal of Economic Theory* 13:82–111.

Kolm, S.-Ch. 1976c. Public safety. *American Economic Review* 66:382–87, and in *Essays in Public Economics*, ed. by A. Sandmo, Lexington: Lexington Books, 1978, pp. 1–9.

Kolm, S.-Ch. 1977a. Multidimensional egalitarianism. *Quarterly Journal of Economics* 91:1–13.

Kolm, S.-Ch. 1977b. *La Transition socialiste*. Paris: Editions du Cerf.

Kolm, S.-Ch. 1977c. *Les Élections sont-elles la démocratie?* Paris: Editions du Cerf.

Kolm, S.-Ch., ed. 1978. *Solutions socialistes.* Paris: Editions Ramsay.

Kolm, S.-Ch. 1979a. A general theory of socialist failures. In *Surviving Failures,* ed. by B. Persson. Stockholm: Almquist and Wicksell Int.; and Atlantic Highland, NJ: Humanities Press, pp. 61–70.

Kolm, S.-Ch. 1979b. Systèmes sociaux et choix individuels. Paris: CEPREMAP.

Kolm, S.-Ch. 1980a. Choix social, choix collectif, optimum social. *Revue d'Économie Politique,* no. 4:246–54.

Kolm, S.-Ch. 1980b. La philosophie bouddhiste et les hommes économiques. *Social Science Information* 3:489–588.

Kolm, S.-Ch. 1981a. Psychanalyse et théorie des choix. *Social Science Information* 19:269–340, and proceedings of the 5th Congress of Economic Psychology, *Revue de Psychologie Économique.*

Kolm, S.-Ch. 1981b. Réciprocité et autogestion. In *L'autogestion, un système économique?* ed. by A. Dumas. Paris: Dunod, pp. 45–62.

Kolm, S.-Ch. 1981c. Liberal transition to socialism: Theory and difficulties. *Review* 5:205–18.

Kolm, S.-Ch. 1981d. Efficacité et altruisme: Le sophisme de Mandeville, Smith et Pareto. *Revue économique* 32:5–31.

Kolm, S.-Ch. 1981e. Altruisme et efficacité: Le sophisme de Rousseau. *Social Science Information* 20:293–344.

Kolm, S.-Ch. 1981f. De l'individualisme. *Commentaires.*

Kolm, S.-Ch. 1982a. *Le Bonheur-liberté (bouddhisme profond et modernité).* Paris: Presses Universitaires de France. New edition 1994.

Kolm, S.-Ch. 1982b. La théorie bouddhique de la liberté. *Critique.*

Kolm, S.-Ch. 1982c. Les logiques du libéralisme moderne. *Commentaires.*

Kolm, S.-Ch. 1983a. Altruism and efficiency. *Ethics* 94:18–65.

Kolm, S.-Ch. 1983b. Introduction à la réciprocité générale. *Social Science Information* 22:569–621.

Kolm, S.-Ch. 1983c. Problèmes du libéralisme économique. *Commentaires* 6:49–56.

Kolm, S.-Ch. 1983d. Au deuxième siècle après Marx. *Commentaires* 6:521–25.

Kolm, S.-Ch. 1983e. Le bouddhisme et les "hommes économiques." *Bulletin du MAUSS* 6:52–83.

Kolm, S.-Ch. 1984a. *Le Libéralisme moderne.* Paris: Presses Universitaires de France.

Kolm, S.-Ch. 1984b. *La Bonne économie: La Réciprocité générale.* Paris: Presses Universitaires de France.

Kolm, S.-Ch. 1984c. *Sortir de la crise.* Paris: Hachette.

Kolm, S.-Ch. 1984d. Théorie de la réciprocité et du choix des systèmes économiques. *Revue Economique* 35:871–910.

Kolm, S.-Ch. 1984e. Marxisme et bouddhisme. *Cahiers internationaux de sociologie* 77:339–60.

Kolm, S.-Ch. 1984f. La société bien ordonnée: la justice comme justesse. Paris: CERAS, 31.

Kolm, S.-Ch. 1985a. *Le Contrat social libéral (Théorie et pratique du libéralisme).* Paris: Presses Universitaires de France.

Kolm, S.-Ch. 1985b. Libres, égaux et fraternels: La logique profonde de la morale républicaine. *Revue française de science politique* 35:639–54.

Kolm, S.-Ch. 1985c. Must one be Buddhist to grow? In *Economics and Philosophy*, ed. by P. Koslowski. Tübingen: J.-C. B. Mohr (Paul Siebeck), pp. 221–42.

Kolm, S.-Ch. 1985d. Le raisonnement d'éthique sociale. Paris: CERAS, 41.

Kolm, S.-Ch. 1986a. *Philosophie de l'économie*. Paris: Editions du Seuil.

Kolm, S.-Ch. 1986b. The Buddhist theory of "no-self." In *The Multiple Self*, ed. by J. Elster. Cambridge: Cambridge University Press, pp. 133–263.

Kolm, S.-Ch. 1986c. L'allocation des ressources naturelles et le libéralisme. *Revue économique* 37:207–41.

Kolm, S.-Ch. 1986d. Alternative ethical foundations of fiscal systems. Paris: CERAS, 50.

Kolm, S.-Ch. 1986e. Is only egoism productive? *Development* 3.

Kolm, S.-Ch. 1987a. *L'Homme pluridimensionnel (bouddhisme, marxisme, psychanalyse pour une économie de l'esprit)*. Paris: Albin Michel.

Kolm, S.-Ch. 1987b. Public Economics. In *New Palgrave Dictionary in Economics*, ed. by J. Eatwell et al. London: Macmillan, pp. 1047–55.

Kolm, S.-Ch. 1987c. The freedom and consensus normative theory of the state: The liberal social contract. In *Individual Liberty and Democratic Decision-Making: The Ethics, Economics and Politics of Democracy*, ed. by P. Koslowski. Tübingen: J.C.B. Mohr, pp. 97–127.

Kolm, S.-Ch. 1987d. Libéralismes classiques et renouvelés. In *Nouvelle histoire des idées politiques*, ed. by Pascal Ory. Paris: Hachette, pp. 575–87.

Kolm, S.-Ch. 1987e. Libres, égaux et fraternels: Problèmes et pièges logiques dans la définition et la réalisation des valeurs modernes. *Revue Européenne des Sciences Sociales* 74:195–216.

Kolm, S.-Ch. 1987f. Adequation, equity and fundamental analysis. Paris: CERAS, 59.

Kolm, S.-Ch. 1987g. Liberty-based public economics: Its foundations, principle, method, application and structural results. Paris: CERAS, 60.

Kolm, S.-Ch. 1987h. Free-riding and voluntary contributions in large numbers. Paris: CERAS, 63.

Kolm, S.-Ch. 1987i. Freedoms, cores and public goods. Paris: CERAS, 66.

Kolm, S.-Ch. 1987j. Freedom and the provision of public goods with all degrees of exclusion. Paris: CERAS, 67.

Kolm, S.-Ch. 1987k. Freedom, core, efficiency with public goods in general interdependence. Paris: CERAS, 68.

Kolm, S.-Ch. 1988. *Adequacy, Equity and Fundamental Dominance*. Paris: CERAS, 76.

Kolm, S.-Ch. 1989a. Free and equal in rights: The philosophies of the 1789 Declaration of the Rights of Man and of the Citizen. Bicentennial Conference, Canadian Political Science Association, Québec; *Journal of Regional Policy* 11-1(1991):5–62.

Kolm, S.-Ch. 1989b. Authority and inequality under capitalism and socialism: Review of Barrington Moore. *Annales (Économie, Sociétés, Civilisations)* 5:178–80.

Kolm, S.-Ch. 1989c. The psychology of happiness and of liberty. *The Journal of Oriental Studies*, The Institute of Oriental Philosophy, 2:11–20, and in *Buddhism Today*, Tokyo: The Institute of Oriental Philosophy, 1990, pp. 34–45.

Kolm, S.-Ch. 1989d. Le devoir général de réciprocité. In *Les devoirs de l'homme*, le supplément, *Revue d'Ethique et Théologie Morale* 168:135–46.

Kolm, S.-Ch. 1989e. Cooperative-game properties of international coordination. Paris: CERAS, 77.

Kolm, S.-Ch. 1990a. Employment and fiscal policy with a realistic view of the social role of wages. In *Essays in Honor of Edmond Malinvaud*. Cambridge: MIT Press, pp. 226–86.

Kolm, S.-Ch. 1990b. *The General Theory of Justice*. Paris: CERAS.

Kolm, S.-Ch. 1991a. The normative economics of unanimity and equality: Equity, adequacy and fundamental dominance. In *Markets and Welfare*, ed. by K. J. Arrow. London: Macmillan, pp. 243–86.

Kolm, S.-Ch. 1991b. Philosophical reasons for equity. Paris: CERAS, 99.

Kolm, S.-Ch. 1991c. The ethical economics of envy. German Bernacer Lecture, University of Alicante. Paris: CERAS, 90.

Kolm, S.-Ch. 1991d. Super-Equity. German Bernacer Lecture, University of Alicante. Paris: CERAS, 98.

Kolm, S.-Ch. 1991e. Full process liberalism. IMF working paper (Fiscal Affairs), and Paris: CGPC.

Kolm, S.-Ch. 1991f. Economic development and the theory of social ethics. *Journal of Regional Policy* (March–April):427–32.

Kolm, S.-Ch. 1992a. What sense social choice? Paris: CGPC.

Kolm, S.-Ch. 1992b. The impossibility of utilitarianism. Paris: CGPC.

Kolm, S.-Ch. 1992c. Reciprocity. *Political Economy of the Good Society, Newsletter*, 2:1–6.

Kolm, S.-Ch. 1992d. Fundamental analysis. Paris: CGPC.

Kolm, S.-Ch. 1993a. Free and equal in rights: The philosophies of the 1789 Declaration of the Rights of Man and of the Citizen. *Journal of Political Philosophy* 1:158–83.

Kolm, S.-Ch. 1993b. Distributive justice. In *A Companion to Political Philosophy*, ed. by R. Goodin and P. Pettit. Oxford: Basil Blackwell, pp. 438–61.

Kolm, S.-Ch. 1993c. The impossibility of utilitarianism. In *The Good and the Economical*, ed. by P. Koslowski and Y. Shionoya. Berlin: Springer-Verlag, pp. 30–66.

Kolm, S.-Ch. 1993d. Efficient economic justice. Paris: CGPC.

Kolm, S.-Ch. 1993e. *Equal Liberty*. Paris: CGPC.

Kolm, S.-Ch. 1993f. The economics of envy. Paris: CGPC.

Kolm, S.-Ch. 1993g. *Inequalities and Super-Equity*. Paris: CGPC.

Kolm, S.-Ch. 1994a. L'égalité de la liberté. *Recherches Économiques de Louvain* 1:81–86.

Kolm, S.-Ch. 1994b. Rational normative economics against social choice and social welfare. *European Economic Review* :721–30.

Kolm, S.-Ch. 1994c. The meaning of fundamental preferences. *Social Choice and Welfare* 11:193–98.

Kolm, S.-Ch. 1994d. The theory of reciprocity and of the choice of economic systems. *Investigaciones economicas* 18:67–95.

Kolm, S.-Ch. 1994e. Rational justice and equality. In *Models and Measurement of Welfare and Inequality*, ed. by W. Eichhorn. Berlin: Springer-Verlag, pp. 970–92.

Kolm, S.-Ch. 1994f. Review of J. Roemer's *Egalitarian Perspectives*. *Review of Economics* :210–14.

Kolm, S.-Ch. 1995a. The economics of social sentiments: The case of envy. *Japanese Economic Review* 46:63–87.

Kolm, S.-Ch. 1995b. Meanings and rationalities in Social Choice Theory. In *Facets of Rationality*, ed. by D. Andler, P. Banerjee, M. Chaudhury, and O. Guillaume. New Delhi, London: Sage, pp. 79–103.

Kolm, S.-Ch. 1995c. Economic justice: The central problem. *European Economic Review* 39:661–73.

Kolm, S.-Ch. 1995d. Sens ou nonsens du calcul économique public: Le principe de compensation. *Entreprise ethique* 2:1–9.

Kolm, S.-Ch. 1995e. The modern theory of justice. *L'Année Sociologique* 5:297–315.

Kolm, S.-Ch. 1995f. Income justice: Its reason and optimum policy. Paris: CGPC.

Kolm, S.-Ch. 1995g. Risk and justice: Harsanyi's enigmas and social policy. Paris: CGPC.

Kolm, S.-Ch. 1996a. Moral public choice. *Public Choice* 87:117–48.

Kolm, S.-Ch. 1996b. The theory of justice. *Social Choice and Welfare* 13:151–82.

Kolm, S.-Ch. 1996c. Rational just social choice. In *Social Choice Re-examined*, ed. by K. Arrow, A. Sen, and K. Suzumara. London: Macmillan, vol. 2, pp. 167–95.

Kolm, S.-Ch. 1996d. Risk, justice, and social policy. In *Restructuring the Welfare State: Ethical Issues of Social Policy in an International Perspective*, ed. by P. Koslowski and A. Føllesdal. Berlin: Springer-Verlag, pp. 287–318.

Kolm, S.-Ch. 1996e. Playing fair with fairness. *Journal of Economic Surveys* 10(2).

Kolm, S.-Ch. 1996f. The values of liberty. *Nordic Journal of Political Economy*, forthcoming.

Kolm, S.-Ch. 1996g. The comparison of pairwise preferences and its normative consequences. Paris: CGPC.

Kolm, S.-Ch. 1997a. The values of freedom. In *The Economics and Philosophy of Liberty*, ed. by M. Fleurbaey, J.-F. Laslier, and A. Trannoy. London: Routledge.

Kortian, G. 1980. *Metacritique: The Philosophical Argument of Jürgen Habermas*. Cambridge: Cambridge University Press.

Kranich, L. J. 1988. Altruism and efficiency: Welfare analysis of the Walrasian mechanism with transfers. *Journal of Public Economics* 36:369–86.

Kymlicka, W. 1989. *Liberalism, Community and Culture*. Oxford: Clarendon Press.

Laffont, J.-J., ed. 1979. *Aggregation and Revealed Preferences*. Amsterdam: North-Holland.

Lambert, P. 1993. *The Distribution and Redistribution of Income*. Oxford: Basil Blackwell.

Lange, O. 1942. The foundations of welfare economics. *Econometrica* 10:215–28.

Larmore, C. 1987. *Patterns of Moral Complexity*. Cambridge: Cambridge University Press.

Lebreton, M. 1984. An elementary proof of a theorem on affine functions. Discussion paper 8409. LEME.

Lebreton, M. 1995. Arrovian social choice in economic domains. In *Social Choice Re-examined*, ed. by K. Arrow, A. Sen, and K. Suzumura. London: Macmillan.

Lerner, M. J., and S. C. Lerner, eds. 1981. *The Justice Motive in Social Behavior: Adaptating to Times of Scarcity and Change*. New York: Plenum.

Leventhal, G. S. 1976. The distribution of rewards and resources in groups and organisations. In *Advances in Experimental Social Psychology*, vol. 9, ed. by L. Bertowitz and E. Walster. New York: Academic Press.

Leventhal, G. S. 1980. What should be done with equity theory? New approaches to the study of fairness in social relationships. In *Social Exchange: Advances in Theory and Research*, ed. by K. J. Gergen, M. S. Greenberg, and R. H. Wilis. New York: Plenum Press.

Leventhal, G. S., and D. Anderson. 1970. Self-interest and the maintenance of equity. *Journal of Personality and Social Psychology* 15: 57–62.

Lind, E. A., and T. R. Tyler. 1988. *The Social Phychology of Procedural Justice*. New York: Plenum.

Lindbeck, A. 1985. Redistribution policies and the expansion of the public sector. *Journal of Public Economics* 28:309–28.

Little, I. M. D. 1950. *A Critique of Welfare Economics*. Oxford: Clarendon Press.

Little, I. M. D. 1951. Social choice and individual values. *Journal of Political Economy* 60.

Little, I. M. D. 1952. L'avantage collectif. *Economie appliquée* 5:455–68.

Little, I. M. D. 1957. *A Critique of Welfare Economics*, 2d ed. Oxford: Oxford University Press.

Locke, J. [1690] 1960. *Second Treatise of Government*, ed. by P. Laslett. Cambridge: Cambridge University Press.

Loria, A. 1934. La Sintisi Economica (Politica e economica). *Nuova collana di economisti stranieri e italiani*, no. 12. Torino.

Lucas, J. R. 1980. *On Justice*. Oxford: Oxford University Press.

Luce, R., and H. Raiffa. 1957. *Games and Decisions*. New York: Wiley.

Lukes, S. 1973. *Individualism*. Oxford: Basil Blackwell.

Lukes, S. 1985. *Marxism and Morality*. Oxford: Clarendon Press.

L'Utile et le juste. Collection of essays in *Archives de Philosophie du Droit*, vol. 26 (1981).

Lyons, D. 1965. *Forms and Limits of Utilitarianism*. Oxford: Clarendon Press.

Maasoumi, E. 1986. The measurement and decomposability of multidimensional inequality. *Econometrica* 54:991–98.

MacCormick, D. N. 1981. Natural law reconsidered (A review of Finnis,1980). *Oxford Journal of Legal Studies* 1:99–109.

MacCormick, D. N. 1982. *Legal Right and Social Democracy: Essays in Legal and Political Philosophy*. Oxford: Clarendon Press.

Machan, T. 1982. *The Libertarian Reader*. Totowa, NJ: Rowman and Littlefield.

MacIntyre, A. 1985. *After Virtue: A Study in Moral Theory*. London: Duckworth.

MacIntyre, A. 1988. *Whose Justice? Which Rationality?* London: Duckworth.

Macpherson, C. B. 1985. *The Rise and Fall of Economic Justice*. Oxford: Oxford University Press.

Margolis, H. 1982. *Selfishness, Altruism and Rationality*. Cambridge: Cambridge University Press.

Marx, K. [1843] 1972. On the Jewish question. Reprinted in *The Marx-Engels Reader*, ed. by R. C. Tucker. New York: Norton, pp. 24–51.

Marx, K. [1867] 1976. *Das Kapital*, vol. 1, trans. by B. Fowlkes. Harmondsworth: Penguin Books.

Marx, K. [1875] 1972. Critique of the Gotha programme. Reprinted in *The Marx-Engels Reader*, ed. by R. C. Tucker. New York: Norton, pp. 363–98.

Maskin, E. 1978. A theorem on utilitarianism. *Review of Economic Studies* 45: 93–96.

Maskin, E. 1979a. Implementation and strong Nash equilibrium. In *Aggregation and Revealed Preferences*, ed. by J.-J. Laffont. Amsterdam: North-Holland.

Maskin, E. 1979b. Decision-making under ignorance with implications for social choice. *Theory and Decision* 11:319–37.

Maskin, E. 1980. On first-best taxation. In *Income Distribution: The Limits to Redistribution*, ed. by D. Collard, R. Lecomber, and M. Slater. Dorchester: Wright and Sons.

Maskin, E. 1985. The theory of implementation in Nash equilibrium. In *Social Goals and Social Organization*, ed. by L. Hurwicz and D. Schmeidler. Cambridge: Cambridge University Press.

Maskin, E. 1987. On the fair allocation of divisible goods. In *Arrow and the Ascent of Modern Economic Theory*, ed. by G. R. Feiwel. London: Macmillan.

Masters, J. C., and W. P. Smith, eds. 1987. *Social Comparison, Social Justice, and Relative Deprivation : Theoretical, Empirical and Policy Perspectives*. Hillsdale, NJ: Erlbaum.

Mayston, D. J. 1974. *The Idea of Social Choice*. London: Macmillan.

Mayston, D. 1975. *The Idea of Social Choice*. New York: St. Martin's.

Meade, J. E. 1964. *Efficiency, Equality and the Ownership of Property*. London: Allen and Unwin.

Meade, J. E. 1976. *The Just Economy*. London: Allen and Unwin.

Melden, A. I., ed. 1970. *Human Rights*. Belmont, CA: Wadsworth.

Messick, D. M., and K. S. Cook, eds. 1983. *Equity Theory: Psychological and Sociological Perspectives*. New York: Praeger.

Mikula, G., ed. 1980. *Justice and Social Interaction: Experimental and Theoretical Contributions from Psychological Research*. New York: Springer-Verlag.

Mill, J. S. [1859]. *On Liberty*, ed. by R. B. McCallum. Oxford: Basil Blackwell.

Mill, J. S. [1861] 1957. *Utilitarianism*. New York: Bobbs-Merrill.

Mill, J. S. 1962. *Utilitarianism, On Liberty, Essay on Bentham*, ed. by M. Warnock. London: Fontana Library.

Mill, J. S. 1969. *Essays on Ethics, Religion and Society. Collected Works*, 10 vols., ed. by J. M. Robson. Toronto: University of Toronto Press.

Miller, D. 1976. *Social Justice*. Oxford: Clarendon Press.

Mirrlees, J. 1971. An exploration in the theory of optimum income taxation. *Review of Economic Studies* 38: 175–208.

Mirrlees, J. 1974. Notes on welfare economics, information and uncertainty. In *Essays on Economic Behaviour under Uncertainty*, ed. by M. S. Balch, D. McFadden, and S. Y. Wu. Amsterdam: North-Holland.

Mirrlees, J. 1986. The theory of optimal taxation. In *Handbook of Mathematical Economics*, vol. 3. ed. by K. J. Arrow and M. D. Intriligator. Amsterdam: North-Holland.

Mishan, E. J. 1960. A survey of welfare economics, 1939–1959. *Economic Journal* 70:247.

Mongin, P. 1994. Harsanyi's aggregation theorem: Multi-profile version and unsettled questions. *Social Choice and Welfare* 11:331–55.

Mongin, P. 1995. Consistent Bayesian aggregation. *Journal of Economic Theory* 66: 313–51.

Moore, B., Jr. 1978. *Injustice: The Social Bases of Obedience and Revolt*. London: Macmillan.

Moore, G. E. 1912. *Ethics*. London: Williams and Norgate.

Mosler, K. 1994. Multidimensional welfarism. In *Models and Measurement of Welfare and Inequality*, ed. by W. Eichhorn. Heidelberg: Springer-Verlag.

Moulin, H. 1981. Implementing just and efficient decision making. *Journal of Public Economics* 16: 193–213.

Moulin, H. 1983. *The Strategy of Social Choice*. Advanced Textbooks in Economics, no. 18. Amsterdam: North-Holland.

Moulin, H. 1984. Implementing the Kalai-Smorodinski bargaining solution. *Journal of Economic Theory* 33:32–45.

Moulin, H. 1988. *Axioms of Cooperative Decision Making*. Cambridge: Cambridge University Press.

Moulin, H. 1990a. Fair division under joint ownership: Recent results and open problems. *Social Choice and Welfare* 7:149–70.

Moulin, H. 1990b. Joint ownership of a convex technology: Comparison of three solutions. *Review of Economic Studies* 57: 439–52.

Moulin, H. 1992. Welfare bounds in the cooperative production problem. *Games and Economic Behavior* 4:373–401.

Moulin, H. 1994. Social choice. In *Handbook of Game Theory*, vol. 2, ed. by R. J. Aumann and S. Hart. New York: Elsevier Science.

Moulin, H. 1995. *Cooperative Microeconomics*. Princeton: Princeton University Press.

Moulin, H., and W. Thomson. 1988. Can everyone benefit from growth? *Journal of Mathematical Economics* 17:339–45.

Mueller, D. C. 1979. *Public Choice*. Cambridge: Cam,bridge University Press.

Munzer, S. R. 1990. *A Theory of Property*. Cambridge: Cambridge University Press.

Murakami, Y. 1968. *Logic and Social Choice*. New York: Dover.

Musgrave, R. A. 1959. *The Theory of Public Finance*. New York: McGraw-Hill.

Musgrave, R. A., and A. T. Peacock, eds. 1962. *Classics in the Theory of Public Finance*. London: Macmillan.

Myerson, R. B. 1981. Utilitarianism, egalitarianism, and the timing effect in social choice problems. *Econometrica* 49:883–97.

Nagel, T. 1975. Rawls on justice. In *Reading Rawls*, ed. by N. Daniels. New York: Basic Books.

Nagel, T. 1986. *The View for Nowhere*. Oxford: Clarendon Press.

Nagel, T. 1991. *Equality and Partiality*. Oxford: Oxford University Press.

Narveson, J. 1976. A puzzle about economic justice in Rawls' theory. *Social Theory and Practice* 4:1–27.

Narveson, J. 1983. On Dworkinian equality. *Social Philosophy and Policy* 1:1–23.

Nash. J. F.1950. The bargaining problem. *Econometrica* 18:155–62.

Nash. J. F. 1953. Two-person cooperative games. *Econometrica* 21:128–40.

Newbery, D., and N. Stern. 1987. *The Theory of Taxation for Developing Countries*. Oxford: Oxford University Press.

Ng, Y. K. 1979. *Welfare Economics*. London: Macmillan.

Nielsen, K. 1986. *Equality and Liberty: A Defense of Radical Egalitarianism*. Lanham, MD: Rowman.

Nino, C. S. 1980. *Introduccion al analisis del derecho*. Buenos Aires: Depalma.

Nitzan, S. 1975. Social preferences orderings in a probabilistic model. *Public Choice* 24:93–100.

Nitzan, S., and J. Paroush. 1985. *Collective Decision Making: An Economic Outlook*. Cambridge: Cambridge University Press.

Norman, R. 1987. *Free and Equal: A Philosophical Examination of Political Values*. Oxford: Oxford University Press.

Nozick, R. 1974. *Anarchy, State and Utopia*. New York: Basic Books.

Paley, W. 1785. *The Principles of Moral and Political Philosophy*. London.

Pareto, V. 1916. Il massimo di utilità per una collettività. *Giornale degli economisti*. 3rd serie: 337–41 (also in *Trattatodi sociologica gererale* and *Mind and society*).

Pareto, V. 1916. *A Treatise on General Sociology*. New York: Dover.

Parfit, D. 1984. *Reasons and Persons*. Oxford: Clarendon Press.

Parks, R. P. 1975. An impossibility theorem for fixed preferences: A dictatorial Bergson-Samuelson social welfare function. *Review of Economic Studies* 43:447–50.

Parsons, T. 1977. *Social Systems and the Evolution of Action Theory*. New York: Free Press.

Pattanaik, P. K. 1977. *Voting and Collective Choice*. Cambridge: Cambridge University Press.

Pattanaik, P. K. 1978. *Strategy and Group Choice*. Amsterdam: North-Holland.

Pattanaik, P. K., and M. Salles, eds. 1983. *Social Choice and Welfare*. Amsterdam: North-Holland.

Paul, E. F., F. D. Miller, and J. Paul, eds. 1985. *Ethics and Economics*. Oxford: Basil Blackwell.

Paul, E. F., F. D. Miller, and J. Paul, eds. 1985. *Liberty and Equality*. Oxford: Basil Blackwell.

Paul, E. F., F. D. Miller, J. Paul, and Ahrens, eds. 1988. *The New Social Contract: Essays on Gauthier*. Oxford: Basil Blackwell.

Paul, J., ed. 1982. *Reading Nozick*. Oxford: Basil Blackwell.

Pazner, E., and D. Schmeidler. 1974. A difficulty in the concept of fairness. *Review of Economic Studies* 41:441–43.

Pazner, E., and D. Schmeidler. 1978. Egalitarian-equivalent allocations: A new concept in economic equity. *Quarterly Journal of Economics* 92:671–87.

Peleg, B. 1984. *Game Theoretic Analysis of Voting in Committees*. Cambridge: Cambridge University Press.

Pen, J. 1971a. *Income Distribution*. London: Allen Lane.

Pen, J. 1971b. *Income Distribution: Facts, Theories, Policies*. New York: Praeger.

Perelman, C. 1963. *The Idea of Justice and the Problem of Argument*. London: Routledge and Kegan Paul.

Perelman, C. 1972. *Justice et raison*. 2d ed. Brussels: Bruylant.

Peters, H. J. M. 1992. *Axiomatic Bargaining Game Theory*. Dordrecht: Kluwer.

Peters, R. 1966. *Ethics and Education*. London.

Pettit, P. 1980. *Judging Justice*. London: Routledge and Kegan Paul.

Pettit, P. 1986. Free riding and foul dealing. *Journal of Philosophy* 83:361–79.

Phelps, E. S. 1973a. Wage taxation for economic justice. In *Economic Justice*, ed. by E. S. Phelps. Harmondsworth: Penguin Education.

Phelps, E. S., ed. 1973b. *Economic Justice*. Harmondsworth: Penguin Books.

Phelps, E. S. 1977a. Recent developments in welfare economics: Justice et équité. In *Frontiers of Quantitative Economics*, vol. 3, ed. by M. D. Intriligator. Amsterdam:

North-Holland. Reprinted in E. Phelps, *Studies in Macroeconomic Theory*, vol. 2. New York: Academic Press.

Phelps, E. S. 1977b. Linear "maximin" taxation of wage and property income on a "maximin" growth path. In *Economic Progress, Private Values and Public Policy: Essays in Honor of William Fellner*, ed. by B. Balassa and R. Nelson. Amsterdam: Elsevier North-Holland.

Phillips, D. 1979. *Equality, Justice and Rectification*. San Diego: Academic Press.

Phillips, D. L. 1986. *Toward a Just Social Order*. Princeton: Princeton University Press.

Pigou, A. C. [1920] 1952. *The Economics of Welfare*, 4th ed. London: Macmillan.

Piketty, T. 1993. Existence of fair allocations in economies with production. In Ph.D. dissertation. Paris: Delta.

Piketty, T. 1994. *Introduction à la théorie de la redistribution des richesses*. Paris: Éditions Economica.

Plott, C. R. 1973. Path independence, rationality and social choice. *Econometrica* 41:1075–91.

Plott, C. R. 1976. Axiomatic social choice theory: An overview and interpretation. *American Journal of Political Science* 20:511–96.

Pommerhene, W., and F. Schneider. 1981. Free riding and collective action: An experiment in public microeconomics. *Quarterly Journal of Economics* 96:689–704.

Poole, R. 1991. *Morality and Modernity*. London: Routledge and Kegan Paul.

Posner, R. 1977. *The Economic Analysis of Law*, 2d ed. Boston: Little Brown.

Posner, R. 1981. *The Economics of Justice*. Cambridge: Harvard University Press.

Quinton, A., ed. 1967. *Political Philosophy*. Oxford: Oxford University Press.

Rae, D. 1981. *Equalities*. Cambridge: Harvard University Press.

Raiffa, H. 1953. Arbitration schemes for generalized two-person games. In *Contributions to the Theory of Games II*, ed. by H. W. Kuhn and A. W. Tucker. Princeton: Princeton University Press.

Raphael, D. D. 1976. *Problems of Political Philosophy*, rev. ed. London: Macmillan.

Raphael, D. D. 1980. *Justice and Liberty*. London: Athlone Press.

Raphael, D. D. 1981. *Moral Philosophy*, Oxford: Oxford University Press.

Rawls, J. 1971. *A Theory of Justice*. Cambridge: Harvard University Press.

Rawls, J. 1979. A well-ordered society. In *Philosophy, Politics and Society*, 5th series, ed. by P. Leslett and J. Fishkin. Oxford: Basil Blackwell, pp. 6–20.

Rawls, J. 1982a. Social unity and primary goods: In *Utilitarianism and Beyond*, ed. by A. Sen and B. Williams. Cambridge: Cambridge University Press, pp. 159–85.

Rawls, J. 1982b. The basic liberties and their priority. In *The Tanner Lectures on Human Values*, vol. 3, ed. by S. MacMurrin. Cambridge: Cambridge University Press, pp. 1–89.

Rawls, J. 1985. Justice as fairness: Political not metaphysical. *Philosophy and Public Affairs* 14:223–51.

Rawls, J. 1987. The idea of an overlapping consensus. *Oxford Journal of Legal Studies* 7:1–25.

Rawls, J. 1989. The domain of the political and overlapping consensus. *New York University Law Review* 64:233–55.

Raz, J. 1975. *Practical Reason and Norms*. London: Hutchinson.

Raz, J. 1979. *The Authority of Law: Essays on Law and Morality*. Oxford: Clarendon Press.

Raz, J. 1980. *The Concept of a Legal System: An Introduction to the Theory of Legal System*, 2d ed. Oxford: Clarendon Press.

Raz, J. 1986. *The Morality of Freedom*. Oxford: Oxford University Press.

Rees, J. 1972. *Equality*. London: Macmillan.

Reiman, J. 1990. *Justice and Modern Moral Philosophy*. New Haven: Yale University Press.

Rescher, N. 1966. *Distributive Justice: A Constructive Critique of the Utilitarianism Theory of Distribution*. New York: Bobbs-Merrill.

Rials, S., ed. 1989. *La Déclaration de 1789*. Paris: Presses Universitaires de France.

Riley, J. 1986. *Liberal Utilitarianism: Social Choice Theory and J. S. Mill's Philosophy*. Cambridge: Cambridge University Press.

Roberts, K. 1980. Possibility theorems with interpersonally comparable welfare levels. Interpersonal comparability and social choice theory. *Review of Economic Studies* 47:409–39.

Robinson, J. 1933. *The Economics of Imperfect Competition*. London: Macmillan.

Roemer, J. 1982. *A General Theory of Exploitation and Class*. Cambridge: Harvard University Press.

Roemer, J. 1985. Equality of talent. *Economics and Philosophy* 1:151–88.

Roemer, J. 1986a. Equality of resources implies equality of welfare. *Quarterly Journal of Economics* 101:751–84.

Roemer, J. 1986b. An historical materialist alternative to welfarism. In *Foundations of Social Choice Theory*, ed. by J. Elster and A. Hylland. Cambridge: Cambridge University Press.

Roemer, J. 1986c. The mismarriage of bargaining theory and distributive justice. *Ethics* 97:88–110.

Roemer, J. 1986d. *Value, Exploitation and Class*. Chur: Harwood.

Roemer, J. 1990. Welfarism and axiomatic bargaining theory. *Recherches Economiques de Louvain* 56:287–301.

Roemer, J. 1993. A pragmatic theory of responsibility for the egalitarian planner. *Philosophy and Public Affairs* 22:146–66.

Roemer, J. 1994. *Egalitarian Perspectives*. Cambridge: Cambridge University Press.

Roemer, J. 1996. *Distributive Justice*. Cambridge: Harvard University Press.

Ross, D. 1930. *The Right and the Good*. Oxford: Clarendon Press.

Ross, D. 1939. *Foundations of Ethics*. Oxford: Oxford University Press.

Roth, A. 1979. *Axiomatic Models of Bargaining*. New York: Springer-Verlag.

Rothbart, M. 1973. *For a New Liberty*. New York: Macmillan.

Rousseau, J. J. [1755] 1973. *A Discourse on the Origin of Inequality*. In *The Social Contract and Discourses*. London: Dent and Son.

Rousseau, J. J. [1762] 1913. *Du Contrat Social*, trans. by G. D. H. Cole. London: Dent.

Rubinstein, A., Z. Srafa, and W. Thomson. 1992. On the interpretation of the Nash bargaining solution. *Econometrica* 60:1171–86.

Runciman W. G. 1966. *Relative Deprivation and Social Justice*. London: Routledge.

Salles, M. 1975. A general possibility theorem for group decision rules with Pareto-transitivity. *Journal of Economic Theory* 11:110–18.

Salles, M. 1976. Characterization of transitive individual preferences for quasi-transitive collective preferences under simple games. *International Economic Review* 17:308–18.

Samuelson, P. A. 1967. Arrow's mathematical politics. In *Human Values and Economic Policy*, ed. by S. Hook, pp. 41–51.

Samuelson, P. A. 1981. Bergsonian welfare economics. In *Economic Welfare and the Economics of Soviet Socialism*, ed. by S. Rosefielde. Cambridge: Cambridge University Press.

Sandel, M. 1982. *Liberalism and the Limits of Justice*. Cambridge: Cambridge University Press.

Sartre, J. P. [1943] 1962. *Being and Nothingness*. New York: Harper and Row.

Satterthwaite, M. A. 1975. Strategy-proofness and Arrow's conditions: Existence and correspondence theorems for voting procedures and social welfare functions. *Journal of Economic Theory* 10:187–217.

Savage, L. J. 1954. *The Foundations of Statistics*. New York: Wiley.

Scanlon, T. M. 1986. Equality of resources and equality of welfare: A forced marriage. *Ethics* 97:111–18.

Scanlon, T. M. 1988. *The Significance of Choice*. Tanner Lectures on Human Values, vol. 8. Salt Lake City: University of Utah Press.

Scheffler, S. 1982. *The Rejection of Consequentialism*. Oxford: Clarendon Press.

Scherer, K. 1992. *Justice, Interdisciplinary Perspectives*. Cambridge: Cambridge University Press.

Schoeman, F. D. 1992. *Privacy and Social Freedom*. Cambridge: Cambridge University Press.

Schokkaert, E., and L. Lagrou. 1983. An empirical approach to distributive justice. *Journal of Public Economics* 21:33–52.

Schokkaert, E., and B. Overlaet. 1989. Moral intuitions and economic models of distributive justice. *Social Choice and Welfare* 6:19–31.

Schwartz, T. 1986. *The Logic of Collective Choice*. New York: Columbia University Press.

Schwinger, T. 1980. Just allocations of goods: Decisions among three principles. In *Justice and Social Interaction: Experimental and Theoretical Contribution from Psychological Research*, ed. by G. Mikula. New York: Springer-Verlag.

Schwinger, T., W. Nährer, and E. Kayser. 1982. *Prinzipien der gerechten Vergabe von Zuneigung und Geld in Verschiedenen Sozialbeziehungen*. Bericht aus dem Sonderfor-schungsbereich 24: Universität Mannheim.

Scitovsky, T. 1941. A note on welfare propositions in economics. *Review of Economic Studies* 9:77–88. Reprinted in *Readings in Welfare Economics*, ed. by K. J. Arrow and T. Scitowsky. Homewood, Il: Irwin, pp. 390–401.

Seade, J. 1977. On the shape of optimal tax schedules. *Journal of Public Economics* 7:203–36.

Seidl, C. 1975. On liberal values. *Zeitschrift für Nationalökonomie* 35.

Seidl, C. 1986. The impossibility of nondictatorial tolerance. *Journal of Economics*, suppl. 5:211–25.

Seidl, C. 1988. Poverty measurement: A survey. In *Welfare and Efficiency in Public Economics*, ed. by D. Bos, M. Rose, and C. Seidl. Berlin: Springer-Verlag.

Seidler, V. J. 1986. *Kant, Respect and Injustice: The Limits of Liberal Moral Theory*. London: Routledge.

Sen, A. 1970. The impossibility of a Paretian liberal. *Journal of Political Economy* 78:152–57.

Sen, A. K. 1976. Poverty: An ordinal approach to measurement. *Econometrica* 44:219–31.

Sen, A. K. 1985. *Commodities and Capabilities.* Amsterdam: North-Holland.

Sen, A. K, and B. Williams, eds. 1982. *Utilitarianism and Beyond.* Cambridge: Cambridge University Press.

Sher, G. 1987. *Desert.* Princeton: Princeton University Press.

Shorrocks, A. F. 1983. Ranking income distributions. *Economica* 50:1–17.

Shorrocks, A. F., and J. E. Foster. 1987. Transfer sensitive inequality measures. *Review of Economic Studies* 54: 485–97.

Sidgwick, H. 1874. *The Method of Ethics.* London: Macmillan.

Smart, J., and B. Williams. 1973. *Utilitarianism, For or Against.* Cambridge: Cambridge University Press.

Soltan, K. E. 1982. Empirical studies of distributive justice. *Ethics* 92:673–91.

Steedman, I. 1989. *From Exploitation to Altruism.* Cambridge: Polity Press.

Steiner, H. 1978. Nozick on appropriation. *Man* (January).

Steiner, H. 1982. Justice and entitlement. In *Reading Nozick*, ed. by J. Paul. Oxford: Basil Blackwell.

Steiner, H. 1994. *An Essay on Rights.* Oxford: Blackwell.

Steinhaus, H. 1948. The problem of fair division. *Econometrica* 16:101–104.

Sterba, J. 1980. *The Demands of Justice.* Notre Dame: University of Notre Dame Press.

Sterba, J. 1994. From liberty to welfare. *Ethics* 105:64–98.

Stigler, G., and G. Becker, 1977. De Gustibus non est disputandum. *American Economic Review* 67.

Stoljar, S. J. 1984. *An Analysis of Rights.* London: Macmillan.

Sugden, R. 1981. *The Political Economy of Public Choice.* Oxford: Martin Robertson.

Summer, L. W. 1987. *The Moral Foundation of Rights.* Oxford: Oxford University Press.

Suppes, P. 1957. Two formal models for moral principles. Technical report no. 15. Office of Naval Research Contract. Applied Mathematics and Statistics Laboratory, Stanford University, Stanford, CA.

Suppes, P. 1966. Some formal models of grading principles. *Synthèse* 16:284–306.

Suzumura, K. 1976. Remarks on the theory of collective choice. *Econometrica* 43:381–90.

Suzumura, K. 1980. On distributional value judgments and piecemeal welfare criteria. *Economica* 47:125–39.

Suzumura, K. 1983a. Resolving conflicting views of justice in social choice. In *Social Choice and Welfare*, ed. by P. K. Pattanaik and M. Salles. Amsterdam: North-Holland.

Suzumura, K. 1983b. *Rational Choice, Collective Decisions, and Social Welfare.* Cambridge: Cambridge University Press.

Suzumura, K. 1987. Social welfare function. In *New Palgrave Dictionary in Economics*, ed. by J. Eatwell et al. London: Macmillan, pp. 418–20.

Taussig, F. W. 1939. *Principle of Economics*, 4th ed. New York: Macmillan.

Tawney, R. H. 1964. *Equality*, 4th ed. London.

Taylor, C. 1985. The nature and scope of distributive justice. In *Philosophical Papers*, vol. 2. Cambridge: Cambridge University Press, pp. 289–317.

Taylor, M. 1982. *Community, Anarchy and Liberty*. Cambridge: Cambridge University Press.

Tebaldeschi, I. 1979. *La vocazione filosofica del diritto*. Milan: Giuffré.

Temkin, L. 1993. *Inequality*. New York: Oxford University Press.

Thomson, G. 1987. *Needs*. London: Routledge and Kegan Paul.

Thomson, W. 1982. An informationally efficient equity criterion. *Journal of Public Economics* 18:243–63.

Thomson, W. 1983. The far division of a fixed supply among a growing population. *Mathematics of Operations Research* 8:319–26.

Thomson, W. 1988. A study of choice coorespondences in economics with a variable number of agents. *Journal of Economic Theory* 46: 237–54.

Thomson, W. 1990. The consistency principle. In *Game Theory and Applications*, ed. by T. Ichiishi, A. Neyman, and Y. Tauman. New York: Academic Press.

Thomson, W. 1994a. *Bargaining Theory: The Axiomatic Approach*. San Diego: Academic Press.

Thomson, W. 1994b. Consistent extensions. *Mathematical Social Sciences* 28:35–49.

Thomson, W. 1995. *The Theory of Fair Allocation*. Princeton: Princeton University Press.

Thomson, W., and T. Lensberg. 1989. *Axiomatic Theory of Bargaining with a Variable Number of Agents*. New York: Cambridge University Press.

Thomson, W., and H. Varian. 1985. Theories of justice based on symmetry. In *Social Goals and Social Organization*, ed. by L. Hurwicz, D. Schmeidler, and H. Sonnenschein. Cambridge: Cambridge University Press.

Tillion, G. 1960. *L'Afrique bascule dans l'avenir*. Paris: Editions de Minuit.

Tinbergen, J. 1946. *Redelijke Inkomensverdeling*. Haarlem: De Gulden Pers.

Tinbergen, J. 1957. Welfare economics and income distribution. *American Economic Review* 47:490–503.

Tinbergen, J. 1975. *Income Distribution*. Amsterdam: North-Holland.

Tobin, J. 1970. On limiting the domain of inequality. *Journal of Law and Economics* 13:363–78.

Tocqueville, A. de [1843] 1966. *Democracy in America*, trans. and ed. by G. Lawrence, J. P. Meyer, and M. Lerner. New York: Harper and Row.

Tocqueville, A. de [1856] 1991. *L'Ancien régime et la révolution*. Paris: Laffont.

Törnblom, K. Y. 1977. *The Psycho-Sociological and Behavioral Definitions of Equity and Their Extension to Social Dimensions*. Reports/Studies EQU. 2. Paris: UNESCO.

Törnblom, K. Y., and W. L. Griffith. 1992. *Beyond Equity Theory: Emerging Approaches to the Social Psychological Study of Justice in Resource Allocations*. New York: Plenum.

Townsend, P. 1971. *The Concept of Poverty*. London: Heineman.

Tsui, K.-Y. 1996. Multidimensional generalizations of the relative and absolute inequality indices. *Journal of Economic Theory*, forthcoming.

Tuck, R. 1979. *Natural Rights Theories: Their Origin and Development*. Cambridge: Cambridge University Press.

Vallentyne, P. 1991. *Contractarianism and Rational Choice, Essays on Gauthier's Morals by Agreements*. Cambridge: Cambridge University Press.

Van der Veen, R. 1988. *Social Policy and Social Justice*. Leiden.

Van Parijs, P. 1995. *Real Freedom for All. What (If Anything) Can Justify Capitalism?* Oxford: Oxford University Press.

Varian, H. 1974. Equity, envy and efficiency. *Journal of Economic Theory* 9:63–91.

Varian, H. 1976. Two problems in the theory of fairness. *Journal of Public Economics* 5:249–60.

Varian, H. 1980. Redistributive taxation as social insurance. *Journal of Public Economics* 14:49–68.

Vickrey, W. 1945. Measuring marginal utility by reactions to risk. *Econometrica* 13: 319–33.

Villey, M. 1975. *Philosophie du droit*. Paris: LGDJ.

Vohra, R. 1992. Equity and efficiency in non-convex economics. *Social Choice and Welfare* 9:185–202.

Voigt, L., and W. E. Thornton. 1984. *The Limits of Justice: A Sociological Analysis*. New York: University Presses of America.

Von Neumann, J., and O. Morgenstern. 1944. *Theory of Games and Economic Behavior*. Princeton: Princeton University Press.

Waldron, J., ed. 1984. *Theories of Rights*. Oxford: Oxford University Press.

Waldron, J. 1988. *The Rights to Private Property*. Oxford: Clarendon Press.

Walras, L. [1898] 1936. *Etudes d'économie sociale*. Paris: F. Pichon.

Walzer, M. 1983. *Spheres of Justice*. Oxford: Basil Blackwell.

Weber, M. 1962. *Basic Concepts in Sociology*. New York: Citadel Press.

Weinreb, L. L. 1987. *Natural Law and Justice*. Cambridge: Harvard University Press.

Weizsäcker, C. C. 1973. Modern capital theory and the concept of exploitation. *Kyklos* 26:245–81.

Welch, C. 1987. Utilitarianism. In *New Palgrave Dictionary in Economics*, ed. by J. Eatwell et al. London: Macmillan.

Wellman, K. 1985. *A Theory of Rights: Persons under Laws, Institutions and Morals*. Totowa, NJ: Rowman and Allanheld.

Weymark, J. 1993. Harsanyi's social aggregation theorem and the weak Pareto principle. *Social Choice and Welfare* 10:209–21.

Weymark, J. 1994. Harsanyi's social aggregation theorem with alternative Pareto principle, In *Models and Measurement of Welfare and Inequality*, ed. by W. Eichhorn. Heidelberg: Springer-Verlag.

White, A. R. 1984. *Rights*. Oxford: Clarendon Press.

Wicksteed, P. H. 1933. *The Common Sense of Political Economy*. London: Rabbin.

Williams, B. A. O., and J. J. C. Smart. 1973. *Utilitarianism, For and Against*. Cambridge: Cambridge University Press.

Williams, B. A. O. 1985. *Ethics and the Limits of Philosophy*. Cambridge: Harvard University Press.

Willman, P. 1982. *Fairness, Collective Bargaining and Income Policy*. Oxford.

Wolff, R. P. 1977. *Understanding Rawls*. Princeton: Princeton University Press.

Wriglesworth, J. L. 1985. *Libertarian Conflicts in Social Choice*. Cambridge: Cambridge University.

Yaari, M. E. 1981. Rawls, Edgeworth, Shapley, Nash: Theories of distributive justice re-examined. *Journal of Economic Theory* 24:1–39.

Yaari, M. E., and M. Bar-Hillel. 1984. On dividing justly. *Social Choice and Welfare* 1.

Young, H. P., ed. 1985. *Fair Allocation*. AMS Short Course Lecture Notes, vol. 33. Providence: American Mathematical Society.

Young, H. P. 1987. On dividing an amount according to individual claims or liabilities. *Mathematics of Operations Research* 12:398–414.

Young, H. P. 1990. Equal sacrifice and progressive taxation. *American Economic Review* 80:253–66.

Young, H. P. 1992. *Equity*. Princeton: Princeton University Press.

Zeckhauser, R. 1974. Risk spreading and distribution. In *Redistribution through Public Choice*, ed. by H. M. Hochman and G. E. Peterson. New York: Columbia University Press.

Zeuthen, F. 1930. *Problems of Monopoly and Economic Welfare*. London: Routledge.

Index

Act(s), 87
Act-freedom, 49, 54, 87, 95, 337
  basic liberty as, 176
  full, 64, 87–92, 95, 99, 113
  and practical justice, 185
  redistributions with, 126–35
  and social contract, 96
  universal, 92–93
Action, 39n.15, 38, 41, 48
  liberty as, 44
Adequacy, 158
Agent, 38, 44
  and act-freedom, 93
Aggregate ethics, 51
Agreement failure, 100, 105. *See also*
  Market failures
Aim-freedom, 49, 54, 87
  full, 99
  non-full, 90
  and retributive justice, 232
  and taxes, 95n.9
Akrasia, social, 114
All-moralism, 385
Allocation of resources, 53–63. *See also*
  Human resources
  adequacy of, 158
  and economic justice, 32
  efficient super-equitable, 121–22
  equal, 117
  evaluation functions for, 303
  and free exchange, 212
  and full process liberalism, 104, 136
  and others' tastes or preferences, 142,
    180, 221–22, 244–45, 463
  vs. process-freedom, 216
Altruism, 25, 388, 389n.4, 390, 480. *See
  also* Moral motivations
  and collective gift-giving, 26, 91, 388
  and equality vs. liberty, 26
  and full process liberalism, 106
  and justice, 482
Amoralism, 384–85, 387–88
Anarchism, and Libertarians, 16n.32,
  337, 340n.2, 346, 352, 385
A priori "freedom to," 381–83
Aristotle, 9, 37n.10, 44, 158, 162, 172,
  482
Arrow, K. J., 22, 369, 412, 438, 440, 441,
  443, 465
Arts, and income inequality, 125, 126,
  173
Atkinson's index, 307n.27
Autonomy, 39n.15, 49n.27
  and Kant, 39n.15, 40n.17, 45, 49n.27,
    236, 452

Average preferred state, 372–77
Averaging, 311–12
Axiom of choice, 369, 438, 439, 441, 458

Bargaining
  behavioral, 372
  consequential maximizing, 426
Bargaining capacities or skills, 14, 61,
  116, 119–20, 141, 184, 215, 218, 220,
  222, 243
Bargaining problem, 367
Barry, Brian, 208
Basic liberties or rights, 11, 20–21, 93–
  94, 161, 172, 176, 197
  and basic needs, 322
  as inalienable, 103
  and moral polyarchy, 478
  priority of, 20, 47, 196, 471
  and process- or act-freedom, 337
  for Rawls, 20–21, 21, 64, 87, 97, 170,
    171, 171n.1, 176, 176n.5
  Rights of Man and of Citizen as, 175
Basic needs, 11, 66, 149–50, 161, 185,
  320
  as cultural, 70
  definition of, 322, 323–24
  and equality of opportunity, 236
  and global distribution, 75, 475
  guarantee of, 321
  and other principles, 186–87
  and Practical Justice, 60, 471
  and solidarity, 149
Behavioral bargaining, 372
Benevolence, 274–75, 276–79, 295–99,
  389n.4
  and evaluation functions, 307
  for evaluation functions and measures
    of inequality and justice, 305
  and examples, 292–95
  and P3I, 284
  reasons for, 280–87
  reasons against, 287–91
Bentham, Jeremy, 16–17, 18, 173, 406,
  410, 411–12, 413, 428–29, 432
Bergson, Henri-Louis, 170–71
Berlin, Isaiah, 37n.10, 49n.27, 477n.3
Blanqui, Auguste, 60, 136, 321
Buchanan, James
  and constitution, 98, 343, 353–55, 359,
    381, 382, 385
  and market failures, 382
  and morality, 25, 346
  and Public Choice school, 337
  and Social Contract, 16n.32, 72, 73, 84,
    96, 98, 99